Handbook of Loss Prevention
Prevention

Handbook of Loss Prevention and Crime Prevention

Sixth Edition

Edited by

Lawrence J. Fennelly
Security Consultant

Butterworth-Heinemann is an imprint of Elsevier
The Boulevard, Langford Lane, Kidlington, Oxford OX5 1GB, United Kingdom
50 Hampshire Street, 5th Floor, Cambridge, MA 02139, United States

British Library Cataloguing-in-Publication Data

A catalogue record for this book is available from the British Library

Library of Congress Cataloging-in-Publication Data

A catalog record for this book is available from the Library of Congress

ISBN: 978-0-12-816459-4

For Information on all Butterworth-Heinemann publications
visit our website at https://www.elsevier.com/books-and-journals

Publisher: Joe Hayton
Acquisition Editor: Brian Romer
Editorial Project Manager: Emma Hayes
Production Project Manager: Surya Narayanan Jayachandran
Cover Designer: Mark Rogers

Typeset by MPS Limited, Chennai, India

Dedication

I wish to dedicate this book to a close and a very dear friend, Marianna A. Perry, CPP, CPO, she is the most highly dedicated person I've ever met who knows more about reducing crime than anyone I know. Truly a 100% Professional Practitioner.

Contents

List of contributors

Curtis Baille

Mark Beaudry

Bronson S. Bias

Inge Sebyan Black

Norman R. Bottom

James Broder

Chain-Link Fence Manufacturers Institute

Jason Thomas Destein

Matthew R. Dimmick

Jack F. Dowling

James M. Edgar

Michael J. Fagel

John J. Fay

Lawrence J. Fennelly

Robert Fischer

Mary Lynn Garcia

Charles M. Girard

Gion Green

Edward L. Halibozek

Glen Kitteringham

Russell Kolins

Jay C. McCormick

William D. McInerney

Joseph Nelson

Thomas Norman

Marianna A. Perry

Caroline Ramsey-Hamilton

Charles Chuck Sennewald

Brad Spicer

Introduction

Ten principles of crime Prevention, I have to tell you I was thrilled to see this material on line because my intention for this book is to bring crime prevention into the 21st century. When I started out in Crime Prevention at the Harvard University Police Department, I had a great boss Jack Morse, Assistant Director. He would always ask me....

"What's new in Crime Prevention?" He not only made me find and research what was new, but he also made me a better officer by asking this question.

I was sent to the National Crime Prevention Institute (NCPI) in Louisville, Kentucky, to learn about Crime Prevention, and I was fortunate to have as instructors Tim Crowe, C. Ray Jefferies, Wil Ryker, Bill McInary, and so many others who were like the Gods of the industry. This book is modeled after the NCPI three-hole binder they gave us.

I met Dr. George Kelling one day at the Kennedy School of Government, and we had a heavy discussion about a poster I had designed. Needless to say we did not agree on the poster; I have always admire this man for what he has done and accomplished.

Over the years my best friends were the faculty and past directors of the institute. Marianna Perry, CPP, CPOI, was the last Director of NCPI, with whom and I wrote several books; CPTED and Traditional Security Countermeasures, 150 Things You Should Know is the most recent.

In the 1970s, ASIS and IFPO organizations were growing at an unbelievable rate. So consider these three organizations that established their own brand of security, loss prevention and crime prevention training, through the different styles of education, concepts, and strategies.

In this sixth edition, I plan on make many changes to the books content and design. Chapter 1, Designing security and working with architects part 1, will be a modern day version of crime prevention followed by Chapter 2, Designing security and working with architects part 2, on CPTED. Why? Because we are all practitioners, and these concepts will aid you with solutions to reduce crime and prevent future losses. To do this you have to have a degree of imagination. Now make these concepts work for you.

"Take a Bite out of Crime" and the McGruff dog, was the brain child of B. Mac Gray, former Director of NCPI and a contributor to first edition of this handbook.

He came up with the idea by thinking outside the box; he used his own trench coat and lectured on Crime Prevention Concepts. *His concept later became a USA postage Stamp in September 26, 1984 the McGruff dog symbol became a Crime Fighter.*

Mac Gray said in the paper we published,[1] "The practice of crime prevention is much more than simply applying techniques and countermeasures to a problem once it is discovered. Planning is required since it is an approach that recommends stopping a problem before it occurs, of reducing hazards in given situations and of forecasting rather than reacting to circumstances."

Charles M. Girard, PhD, was in the second edition and wrote about this. Salesmanship: A Critical Element in Crime Prevention is his paper in which he stated, "As with sales in general, selling crime prevention is quite complex since an officer must deal with many facets of human nature."

John Fay, CPP, is another past Director of NCPI whose recent book is Contemporary Security Management Fourth Edition. I have to confess, he is one of my favorite authors. I say this because of the hard work he put into his books, second to none.

Bill McInerney, my lock teacher at NCPI, taught me to pick a lock.

I treasure his visit to my home and the cold beers we had on the porch.

---

1. Fennelly, L.J. (Ed.), 1982. Handbook of Loss Prevention and Crime Prevention. Buttyerworth Publishers. Gray II, B.M. History and Principles of Crime Prevention.

Tim Crowe is a past director to NCPI, and as I said, I was his student at NCPI and I can clearly remember him talking about CPTED and moving from the parking lot in the back of the school to the front of the school. Then, I thought, "He is crazy, no one is going to do that." I told him this story when we were lecturing together in Australia for Rick Draper.

Tim Crowe wrote Chapter 9, Encompassing effective crime prevention solutions in 2020 and beyond: concepts and strategies in the third edition of this book, and its title was Crime Prevention through Environmental Design Strategies and Application, in which he wrote, "What are you trying to do here, and how are can we do it better? .... Crime and loss are the by-product of human functions that are not working."

Robert Hanna was a police officer in Quincy, Massachusetts, and he was their Crime Prevention Officer. Over the years we became great friends, and I had the highest respect for the work he was doing in his town.

He wrote a chapter in the fourth edition and titled it:

Awareness and Knowledge Strategies:

Awareness and Knowledge strategies are basically aimed at informing the public as to what crime prevention is, and what services and resources are available to them.

The 10 basic knowledge areas for crime prevention, in the 21st century[2]:
Description of program:

1. CPTED principles, design, and concepts for colleges and schools
2. Crime risk management and crime displacement
3. Physical security devices, deterrents, and concepts
4. Neighborhood watch concepts and community involvement
5. Situational crime prevention principles and concepts
6. Target hardening, door hardware, alarms, mass notification
7. Dissemination of proactive information to your community
8. Safety awareness programs
9. Development of specific programing and assessments
10. Formulation of critical partnerships

Marianna Perry, CPP, was the last director of NCPI; we became best of friends and met while we both were on the ASIS, Crime Prevention and Loss Prevention Council. We were trying to make a dozen YouTube videos for the council. In the fifth edition of this handbook, she wrote an article on Designing Crime Risk Management Systems, in which she explored the Crime Pattern Analysis as crime prevention officer this is a must read and she wrote the following: "A convenient way to understand crime pressure is the crime rate by opportunity, which compares the number of crimes of a particular type with the number of potential targets of that particular crime over a defined period of time."

According to Rachel Boba, "Crime analysis is a law enforcement function that involves systematic analysis for identifying and analyzing patterns and trends in crime and disorder."[3]

Time have changed, as has the threats to which are too numerous to mention, but we must strive to "Think Prevention and be Proactive."

Lawrence J. Fennelly, CPOI, CSSM

2. Atlas, R.I., 2008. 21st Century Security and CPTED. CRC Press.
3. en.wikipedia.org/wiki/Crime analysis, According to Rachel Boba, https://www.bartleby.com/essay/Crime-Analysis-PKLVZ5YTJ.

Chapter 1

Designing security and working with architects, part 1

Matthew R. Dimmick and Lawrence J. Fennelly
Security Consultant

Security must be supported by designing and managing spaces and buildings to define clearly legitimate boundaries between private, semi-private, community-group and public space.

CPTED Guidelines, Queensland, Australia, 2007

Introduction

Why get involved and work with architect?

We are pondering this question because we want to try to answer this in a noncomplicated way. We have always said "It's like conducting a risk assessment, but the property isn't built yet." As you know, the security assessment is custom tailored for each project but typically includes the tasks, such as risk identification and analysis; threat and vulnerability assessment; review of site and facility security; and analysis of crime data, including loss history, police calls for service, crime statistics, and crime forecast reports. In addition, review of physical security systems, of electronic security systems, and of architectural security plans[1] take place before a hole is in the ground.

Also to reduce the vulnerability of people and property to crime by removing opportunities which may be unwittingly provided by the built environment. It also aims to reduce fear of crime and, in doing so, improve people's quality of life.

Physical security systems

Physical security concerns the physical measures designed to safeguard people; prevent unauthorized access to equipment, installations, material, and documents; and safeguard against terrorist attacks and even detect an active shooter. As such, all security operations face new and complex physical security challenges across the full spectrum of your operations. Challenges relative to physical security include the control of populations, information dominance, multinational and interagency connectivity, antiterrorism, and the use of physical security assets as a versatile force multiplier.

A *physical security systems infrastructure* is a network of electric security systems and devices that is configured, operated, maintained, and enhanced to provide security functions and services (such as operational and emergency communications and notification, intrusion detection, physical access control, video surveillance, visitor management, officer patrol tour management, and security administration) to achieve specific risk mitigation objectives.[2]

My concern was always about the products that would be used, "Am I getting the very latest in technology or something on the shelf." So you need to ask specific question, such as what control panel will be used, manufactured, and modeled, and is this the latest model unit. Addition security concerns are barriers, bollards, and fences, access control, locking devices, intrusion detection systems, fire alarm system, security surveillance system (CCTV), doors and windows hardware, and security lighting.

1. <http://silvaconsultants.com/physical-security-assessments-by-silva-consultants.html> used as a reference, Oct. 2018.
2. Barnard R., 2010. Physical Infrastructure? Security Technology Executive. p. 6.

Handbook of Loss Prevention and Crime Prevention. DOI: https://doi.org/10.1016/B978-0-12-817273-5.00001-6

Designing security into a project need not increase costs and can work out cheaper in the long term. However, it does require some thought and imagination. The best solutions often result from a coordinated approach, bringing together the ideas and experience of the developer, the designer, the local authority, the police, and the community.

Natural surveillance and natural access control

The clarity of the properties and their boundaries: a clear definition of space and real estate provides a basis for identifying the responsibilities and the competences of the stakeholders in charge of surveillance.

The visibility of the spaces: the design of the space impacts on the capacity to "see and be seen" with regard to both the human and technical surveillance modes.

The accessibility of the space for those in charge of surveillance: surveillance capacities are dependent on it. If access to an area is not physically possible, clear sight lines can improve the quality of visual surveillance from outside the site.

How can design reduce crime?

Crime is the product of many factors. However, studies have shown that design is an element that can influence the occurrence of crime—both positively and negatively. The aim of "designing out crime" is to reduce the vulnerability of people and property to crime by removing opportunities that may be unwittingly provided by the built environment. It also aims to reduce the fear of crime and, in doing so, improve people's quality of life.

Designing security into a project need not increase costs and can work out cheaper in the long term. However, it does require some thought and imagination. The best solutions often result from a coordinated approach, bringing together the ideas and experience of the developer, the designer, the local authority, the police, and the community.

Open spaces and landscaping

Open spaces should be designed for maximum surveillance to encourage their use rather than misuse.[3] Pedestrian routes through open spaces should be carefully designed to ensure safety and convenience and have good overall levels of lighting and clear signposting.

Landscaping can be a useful crime prevention and CPTED tool. Careful placing of suitable plant and tree species can reduce opportunities for concealment or vandalism and help define public and private spaces. Good deterrent plants, such as berberis, robinia, and rose varieties, can be employed where suitable. Conversely, poorly designed, ill-maintained landscaping schemes may obscure views and create shadows and places for people to hide, thereby encouraging opportunist criminals and increasing fear of crime.

Designing security and site layout

Designing security into a new complex should begin with interior security, then move out to the exterior of the building(s), and then to the outer perimeter of the property.[4] Keep in mind the following points before you sit down with the architects:

- Eliminate all but essential doors and windows; the idea should be few entrances but many exits.
- Specification of fire-resistant material throughout the interior.
- Install fire, intrusion, and environmental control systems.
- Separate shipping and receiving areas if possible.
- Ensure that the site meets American Disability Act (ADA) requirements.
- Plan for adequate lighting around the perimeter, before, during, and after construction.
- Review architectural design plans and layout.
- Plan a site assessment/site survey.
- Have interior/exterior detection systems.
- Apply natural surveillance and other CPTED principles and strategies.
- Will there be security/protection officers as well as supervision?

---

3. http://www.westminster.gov.uk/planningandlicensing/udp/index.cfm
4. Fennelly, L., Perry, M., 2017. Physical Security, 150 Things You Should Know. Elsevier Publisher.

- Make employees aware of policy and procedures.
- Be educated of the physical security programs.
- Carry out budget planning and have a 5-year plan.
- Audits/assessment/future needs and risks.

Landscape

Landscaping can be a useful crime prevention and CPTED tool. Careful placing of suitable plant and tree species can reduce opportunities for concealment or vandalism and help define public and private spaces. Good deterrent plants, such as berberis, robinia, and rose varieties, can be employed where suitable. Conversely, poorly designed, ill-maintained landscaping schemes may obscure views and create shadows and places for people to hide, thereby encouraging opportunist criminals and increasing fear of crime.

The conclusion of your site layout report should reflect every aspect of the security operation and have measures in place to deny, deter, delay, and detect unauthorized individuals or criminal activity.

Designing for security: a checklist

Some of the most important considerations that must be analyzed before designing a security protection system include the following factors that I have broken down into five categories[5]:

1. *Exterior perimeter protection*
   a. 6- to 8-ft chain-link fence (depending upon the application) with three strands of barbed wire at the top
   b. 8-ft walls and bushes not higher than 3 ft
   c. Security surveillance system and digital consider solar cameras
   d. Security/protection officers (contract or proprietary)
   e. Energy efficient—exterior lighting (such as light-emitting diode)
   f. Leadership in Energy and Environmental Design (LEED) concept and high-performance buildings design
   g. CPTED concepts and strategies
2. *Entrance protection*
   a. Overhead and pedestrian doors (such as strength of door frame)
   b. Windows (locks and grills)
   c. No miscellaneous entry points (roof, basement, subterranean utility access, etc.)
3. *Interior protection*
   a. Security policies and procedures
   b. Lighting
   c. Keys or access card control or biometrics
   d. Security surveillance system
   e. Special situations (hours of operation)
   f. Inventory control (computer safeguards)
   g. Safe, high-value, and security-sensitive areas
   h. Intrusion detection systems and fire alarm (alarm sensors)
   i. Local audible alarm versus central station alarm
4. *Environmental considerations*
   a. Areas of building to be protected
   b. Insurance requirements [Underwriters Laboratory (UL) listed]
   c. History of losses (loss experience)
   d. Type and demographics of employees
   e. Opening and closing procedures
   f. Fire and safety regulations and codes
   g. Delivery and shipping policies/procedures
   h. Situations peculiar to the building or industry

5. Fennelly, L., Perry, M., 2017. Physical Security, 150 Things You Should Know. Elsevier Publisher.

5. *Law enforcement involvement*
    a. Transmission of alarm signal
    b. Central station or direct connection to police station
    c. Municipal ordinances and city codes
    d. Police response time
    e. Neighborhood/business watch programs and community policing
    f. Formulating partnerships

Reduce fear of crime

We believe that the key objective here is to have community partnerships within the community with programs like CPTED, community policing and neighborhood watch because alone, a concept is weak but when combined they are extremely effective and will reduce the fear of crime.

Risks

There are many types of security risk assessments to take under consideration when working with architects including:

- facility physical vulnerability,
- information systems vulnerability,
- physical security for IT,
- insider threat,
- workplace violence threat,
- schools and churches with active shooter,
- proprietary information risk,
- board level risk concerns,
- critical process vulnerabilities,
- brand risk,
- reputation risk, and
- terror and civil unrest related risks.

Chapter 2

Designing security and working with architects part 2

Matthew R. Dimmick and Lawrence J. Fennelly
Security Consultant

The fundamental idea of Crime Prevention Through Environmental Design (CPTED) is that it is possible *to use knowledge and creativity to design those built environments in ways that lessen or prevent the incidence of such crime.*

CPTED Guidelines, Queensland, Australia, 2007

Leadership in energy and environmental design

As with crime prevention through environmental design (CPTED), some of the leadership in energy and environmental design (LEED) concepts complement security concerns, whereas others conflict with physical security principles. The LEED Green Building Rating System represents the US Green Building Council's (USGBC) effort to provide a national standard for what constitutes a "green building." Through its use as a design guideline and third-party certification tool, it aims to improve occupant well-being, environmental performance, and economic returns of buildings using established and innovative practices, standards, and technologies. US Green Building Council (2002) LEED is a voluntary building assessment methodology that is utilized in a variety of applications, including commercial, institutional, and high-rise residential construction. To achieve LEED Certification, owners, architects, and engineers must work together and strike a balance between aesthetic, function, and efficiency objectives for the facility design.

LEED's latest evolution LEED v4 has improved on previous scoring methods to further encourage interdisciplinary project teams to focus on an integrated project delivery process. This current version looks at six basic credit categories: location and transport, sustainable sites, water efficiency, energy and atmosphere, materials and resources, and indoor environmental quality. Within each category, there are minimum requirements referred to as prerequisites for certification. Additionally, credits are awarded for achieving specific goals. A total of 100 points is possible. A score of 40 points achieves LEED certification, 50 points achieves LEED silver, 60 points achieves LEED gold, and 80 points achieve platinum certification. The LEED rating is awarded after the project has been documented by the USGBC.

Another goal in the LEED effort is to encourage more sustainable construction practices. LEED encourages manufacturers to provide materials that:

- contain high recycled content and sustainable use raw materials,
- are manufactured close to the construction site,
- have low volatile organic compound emissions, and
- are designed to minimize energy consumption and packaging.

Twelve elements that influence a person's perception of security in a public space:

1. clear purpose of the area with adequate references;
2. sight-lines with no obstacles;
3. transparency with no obstacles;
4. art and decoration;
5. use of transparent materials;

Handbook of Loss Prevention and Crime Prevention. DOI: https://doi.org/10.1016/B978-0-12-817273-5.00002-8

6. use and color of material;
7. social interaction, not only at platforms or in stations but also outside;
8. natural boundaries (guiding lines on the street, flowerbeds, illuminated routes, etc.);
9. natural illumination, low intensity, and color to avoid dramatic contrast with light and dark;
10. use of music or fragrance (though fragrance can be controversial);
11. natural associations to engender desired behavior (e.g., people in a library usually silent); and
12. mirrors to activate self-image (you do not want to see yourself throwing your litter or trash away).

Crime prevention through environmental design planning and design review

CPTED has been defined as "the proper design and effective use of the built environment that can lead to a reduction in the fear and incidence of crime and an improvement in the quality of life."[1] Typically, the most cost effective time to implement CPTED is during the planning stages of a new project. It is during the planning stages that security professionals, CPTED practitioners, and architects can have the greatest impacts on project outcomes, thus facilitating a safer and secure environment for the facility's or community's users. Further, including considerations for CPTED during planning may alleviate potentially costly omissions and allow for identification of areas that are mutually beneficial for CPTED, design, and environmental stewardship. One such example may include the effective placement of windows to provide natural lighting to interior spaces and allow occupants of a facility or community members to observe activities in the surrounding area (Crowe, 2000).

CPTED can also be beneficial when appropriately applied for retrofitting or renovating existing facilities, organizations, or jurisdiction. School districts, housing authorities, transportation systems, and local governments all have fundamental responsibilities for public safety. It is necessary that a formal relationship between crime prevention and planning be established. Private companies and critical infrastructure operators control extensive properties and huge labor forces and are responsible for providing these assets a level of protection that is commensurate with associated risks to the asset. Prior to protective decisions being made, a methodical review of threats, potential vulnerabilities, and consequences should be undergone. It is this assessment that will determine the mitigation strategies and/or security measures that should be applied at the site.

Applying CPTED principles in the design of new facilities or in the renovation of existing facilities may provide substantial benefits in the reduction of criminal activity and in the comfort level, and psychological well-being of the users of the designed space. Research on the impact of the built environment on human behavior indicates steps that can be taken by designers and owners of facilities to increase the perception of a potential adversary that their activity may be observed, reported on, and/or responded to. The seven design principles of CPTED First Generation are identified and defined as follows:

- Natural surveillance: Increases the threat of apprehension by taking steps to increase the perception that someone's activities will be observed.
- Natural access control: Intended to physically guide people through the site. It is accomplished through the application of strategic design of streets, sidewalks, building entrances, and landscaping.
- Territorial reinforcement: Provides the perception that property is owned and controlled. The use of fences, different paving material, changes in street elevation, signs, and other landscaping can express ownership.
- Maintenance: Allows for the continued use of the space for its intended purpose. Ensuring that lighting, vegetation where applicable, cameras, windows, doors, and other elements contributing to the sense of ownership and activity observation are effectively maintained.
- Target hardening (physical security): Applied in higher risk areas where the threat of terrorism and/or violent criminal activity is expected. Target hardening is the use of physical barriers to entry (bollards, vehicle barriers, boulders, fountains, etc.) and enhanced technological security to mitigate risks. Target hardening will be discussed in greater detail in the through the physical security discussion later in this chapter.

Each organization or community has its own process for making decisions about new development and investment. To be successful the CPTED concept and process must be incorporated into these ongoing processes. Multidisciplinary teams have been found to create greater value when working on projects incorporating CPTED. For communities, in particular, the CPTED process relates to and must be part of the following functions:

1. Crime Prevention through Environment Design—C. Ray Jeffrey.

- *Comprehensive plans.* These determine the future patterns of land use and development. Comprehensive plans present the values of a community and a vision of what it will look like in the future. These plans establish goals and objectives for up to 50-year time periods. Crime prevention elements are clearly necessary in a community's comprehensive plan. Day-to-day decisions about problems and needs are improved by ensuring that they are consistent with comprehensive plans.
- *Zoning ordinances.* These are established to promote the health, safety, and welfare of the people by formally identifying the locations of land uses to ensure that activities are compatible and mutually supportive. Zoning regulations affect land uses, development densities, yard setbacks, open space, building height, location and amount of parking, and maintenance policies. These, in turn, will affect activities and routines that concern exposure to crime, surveillance opportunities, and the definition of space for territorial control.
- *Subdivision regulation.* This includes lot size and dimension, street and right-of-way locations, sidewalks, amenities, and location of utilities. These elements directly influence access to neighborhoods, reduction of pedestrian and vehicle conflict, street lighting, and connections with other parts of the community.
- *Landscape ordinances.* These govern the placement of fences, signs, and plant materials. They may be used to improve spatial definition, surveillance, access control, and way-finding. Hostile landscaping can make unwanted access to parking lots and private property less desirable. Landscape planting materials may also help to reduce graffiti by making large areas of walls inaccessible. Good horticulture improves the quality of life and helps to reduce exposure to crime.
- *Architectural design guidelines.* These guidelines specify goals and objectives for site and building performance. They will affect the location of activities and the definition of public and private space. The site decisions and plans for a building will directly affect opportunities for natural surveillance, pedestrian and vehicle access, way-finding, and links to adjacent neighborhoods or land uses.
- *Accessibility requirements* focused on making private and public properties available to persons with disabilities. These requirements generally improve accessibility and way-finding, especially for persons with disabilities, but rarely consider the risk of victimization that may be created by the use of out-of-the way doors, hallways, or elevators.

Review process

The work of builders, designers, and planners has long been affected by codes that govern nearly every aspect of a structure, except for security. Historically, a few jurisdictions enacted security ordinances, but most of these related to windows, doors, and locking devices. It is now becoming more common to find a local law or procedure calling for a full security or crime prevention review of plans before they are finalized. Nevertheless, it is still generally true that more attention is placed on aesthetics, drainage, fire safety, curb cuts, and parking access than on gaining an understanding of how a building or structure will affect the area in terms of security. A CPTED design review process must be established within communities and organizations to ensure that good planning is being conducted.

The manner in which physical space is designed or used has a direct bearing on crime or security incidents. The clear relationship between the physical environment and crime is now understood to be a cross-cultural phenomenon, as recent international conferences on CPTED have disclosed the universal nature of human/environment relations. That is, despite political and cultural differences, people basically respond the same way to what they see and experience in the environment. Some places make people feel safe and secure, while others make people feel vulnerable. Criminals or other undesirables pick up on the same cues. They look at the environmental setting and at how people are behaving. This tells them whether they can control the situation or run the risk of being controlled.

Someone has to question design, development, and event planning decisions. Do you think that anyone from the police department, or fire department for that matter, asked the builder of a major hotel in Kansas City whether they had extra steel reinforcing rods leftover when they built the cross bridge that fell and resulted in many deaths and injuries? Did anyone ask the planners what effect the downtown pedestrian malls would have when the fad swept the country in early 2000–05? No! Major planning mistakes were made then and now because no one is asking hard questions.

The intersection of security and sustainability

Security and CPTED are not always conducive to sustainable design and LEED principles. This dichotomy is best resolved in the predesign planning stages of the project. At this stage, it must be recognized by both security professionals and architects that, while there are definite areas where principles conflict, the two are not mutually exclusive. Architects must consider the potential liabilities associated with risks that are not effectively addressed in planning.

Likewise, security professionals must understand that sustainability and certification result in substantial financial and reputational benefits for the organizations and communities that achieve them.

With the above in mind, it is important to the overall success of the security team to identify solutions that fit into the sustainable design practices. The examples that follow may support the development of a more secure environment within sustainable design:

- Utilize open, pedestrian accessible, plazas and wide walkways to achieve and harden standoff distances from potential explosive hazards. Features such as mature trees (preferably existing trees that were untouched), fountains and other architectural barriers, natural barriers (boulders, berms, etc.), plinth or retaining walls, reinforced street furniture, and engineered sculptures all can contribute to the security of the space and enhance natural surveillance while also providing park like environments with vegetation and shade to reduce heat island effects.
- Exterior security lighting is very important to effective security design. The goal of security lighting is to provide uniform coverage of the illuminated area utilizes luminaires that provide light with higher color rendition index (CRI). To achieve sustainability in design, light emitting diode (LED) luminaires may be utilized. In addition to excellent CRI, LED lighting draws little energy in relation to other forms of lighting and has virtually no restrike time (the time it takes from power up to full light capacity being reached). The minimal restrike time of LEDs allows them to be easily paired with sensors to turn lights on, when needed, and off when not in use. To reduce glare and light pollution the design team should select full cutoff luminaires. Full cutoff luminaires keep light where it is needed, uniformly spread on the site with less impacts on the night sky and surrounding properties.

The above are only a few examples of how LEED requirements and CPTED principles can be blended into a cohesive strategy that protects assets, enhances safety, and is also environmentally responsible.

Target hardening guidelines

Much of the discussion, at this point, has revolved around the design environments prevalent in sustainability and crime prevention practices. While target hardening is included in CPTED principles, the foundation for target hardening is based upon time-tested best practices in the field of physical security. The remainder of this chapter will be dedicated to the identification of some of these best practices along with the coordination one can expect from the architectural and engineering stakeholders of the project. It should be noted that the guidelines below are not one-size-fits-all. Qualified security specialists should work as part of the multidisciplinary project team to facilitate the inclusion of the appropriate physical security measures given the level of risk, risk appetite, and funding of the project and its stakeholders.

Eight elements of design that make users feel unsafe:

1. dark, hidden places;
2. large obstacles that obstruct sight-lines and transparency;
3. dark, solid materials like concrete;
4. bad or absence illumination;
5. easy accessible walls for graffiti;
6. absence of litter bins without communicating you are not allowed to eat, drink, etc., total deterioration;
7. possibilities for youth to hang around; and
8. nonrepaired acts of vandalism.

Five ways to modify a situation are as follows:

1. increasing the effort the offender must make to carry out the crime;
2. increasing the risks the offender must face in completing the crime;
3. reducing the rewards or benefits the offender expects to obtain from the crime;
4. reducing or avoiding provocations that may tempt or incite offenders into criminal acts; and
5. removing excuses that offenders may use to "rationalize" or justify their actions.

Doors

A door system includes the door, frame, locking hardware, and anchorage to the building; the doors might also be electronically controlled (Bernard, 2010). As part of a balanced design approach, exterior doors in high-risk buildings should be designed to withstand the maximum dynamic pressure and duration of the load from the design threat explosive blast. These threats should be reexamined (more effective explosives, delivery mechanisms, canisters, backpacks, vehicles by size and type) to continue to design and redesign an environment to be responsive to changing threat conditions. Other general door considerations are as follows:

- Provide hollow steel doors or steel-clad doors with steel frames.
- Provide blast-resistant doors for high threats and high levels of protection.
- Limit normal entry/egress through one door, if possible.
- Keep exterior doors to a minimum while accommodating emergency egress. Doors are less attack-resistant than adjacent walls because of functional requirements, construction, and method of attachment.
- Ensure that exterior doors open outward from inhabited areas. In addition to facilitating egress the doors can be seated into the door frames so that they will not enter the buildings as hazardous debris in an explosion.
- Replace externally mounted locks and hasps with internally locking devices, because the weakest part of the door system is the latching component.
- Install doors, where practical, so that they present a blank, flush surface to the outside to reduce their vulnerability to attack.
- Locate hinges on the interior or provide concealed hinges to reduce their vulnerability to tampering.
- Install emergency exit doors so that they facilitate only exiting movement. It is suggested that the handles on exit-only exterior doors be removed to further inhibit reentry into the building through unauthorized openings.
- Equip any outward-opening double door with protective hinges and key-operated mortise-type locks. Consider protecting all electronic and electrical wiring inside the doorjamb or place in protection jacketing to protect against vandalism.
- Provide solid doors or walls as a backup for glass doors in foyers.
- Strengthen and harden the upright surfaces of doorjambs.

General guidelines for windows and glazing

General guidelines for windows and glazing include the following:

- Do not place windows adjacent to doors because, if the windows are broken, the doors can be unlocked.
- Minimize the number and size of windows in a façade. If possible, limit the amount of glazed area in building façades to 15%. The amount of blast entering a space is directly proportional to the amount of openings on the façade. Consider placing fewer windows on the lower floors to reduce the impact of blast on the structure of the building; the notion of reducing all windows on façades above blast vulnerability area seems excessive.
- Consider using burglary- and ballistic-resistant glazing in high-risk buildings.
- Consider using laminated glass in place of conventional glass.
- Consider window safety laminate (such as Mylar) or another fragment retention film over glazing (properly installed) to reduce fragmentation.
- Consider placing guards, such as grilles, screens, or mesh work, across window openings to protect against covert entry. Affix protective window guards firmly to the structure.
- Consider installing blast curtains, blast shades, or spall shields to prevent glass fragments from flying into the occupied space.
- Consider curtains, blinds, and shades to limit entry of incendiary devices.
- Consider narrow recessed windows with sloped sills because they are less vulnerable than conventional windows.
- Consider windows with key-operated locks because they provide a greater level of protection than windows with simple latches. Stationary, nonoperating windows are preferred for security.
- Position the operable section of a sliding window on the inside of the fixed section and secure it with a broomstick, metal rod, or similar device placed at the bottom of the track.

Building design to achieve a desired protection level

The assessment process determines the level of protection sought for the building structure and defines the threat/hazard specific to the facility. Explosive blast threats usually govern building structure design for high-risk buildings. A structural engineer should determine the building design features needed to achieve the desired level of protection against the design blast threat, considering collapse of the building, as well as incipient injuries and fatalities.

Physical security systems

Physical security concerns the physical measures designed to safeguard people; prevent unauthorized access to equipment, installations, material, and documents; and safeguard against terrorist attacks. As such, all security operations face new and complex physical security challenges across the full spectrum of operations. Challenges relative to physical security include the control of populations, information dominance, multinational and interagency connectivity, antiterrorism, and the use of physical security assets as a versatile force multiplier.

A *physical security systems infrastructure* is a network of electric security systems and devices that is configured, operated, maintained, and enhanced to provide security functions and services (such as operational and emergency communications and notification, intrusion detection, physical access control, video surveillance, visitor management, officer patrol tour management, and security administration) to achieve specific risk mitigation objectives Bernard (2010).

Fifty things you should know—checklist is as follows:

- Ensure that exterior doors into inhabited areas open outward. Ensure emergency exit doors only facilitate exiting.
- Secure room access hatches from the interior. Prevent public access to building roofs.
- Restrict access to building operation systems.
- Conduct periodic training of heating, ventilation, and air-conditioning (HVAC) operations and maintenance staff.
- Evaluate HVAC control options.
- Install empty conduits for future security control equipment during initial construction or major renovation.
- Do not mount plumbing, electrical fixtures, or utility lines on the inside of exterior walls.
- Minimize interior glazing near high-risk areas.
- Establish written plans for evacuation and sheltering in place.
- Integrating multiple security systems in a layered effect—including CPTED.
- Illuminate building access points.
- Restrict access to building information.
- Secure HVAC intakes and mechanical rooms.
- Limit the number of doors used for normal entry/egress.
- Lock all utility access openings.
- Provide emergency power for emergency lighting in restrooms, egress routes, and any meeting room without windows.
- Install a modern public address system that will direct individuals where to go in case of an emergency.
- Stagger interior doors and offset interior and exterior doors.
- Eliminate hiding places.
- Install a second and separate telephone service.
- Install radio telemetry distributed antennas throughout the facility.
- Use a badge identification system for building access.
- Install a security surveillance system (CCTV).
- Install fire, intrusion, and environmental control systems.
- Install rapid response and isolation features into HVAC systems.
- Use interior barriers to differentiate levels of security.
- Locate utility systems away from likely areas of potential attack.
- Install call buttons at key public contact areas.
- Install emergency and normal electric equipment at different locations.
- Avoid exposed structural elements.
- Reinforce foyer walls.
- Use architectural features to deny contact with exposed primary vertical load members.
- Isolate lobbies, mail rooms, loading docks, and storage areas.
- Locate stairwells remotely. Do not discharge stairs into lobbies, parking, or loading areas.
- Elevate HVAC fresh-air intakes.
- Create "shelter-in-place" rooms or areas.
- Separate HVAC zones. Eliminate leaks and increase building air tightness.
- Install blast-resistant doors or steel doors with steel frames.
- Physically separate unsecured areas from the main building.
- Install HVAC exhausting and purging systems.
- Connect interior nonload bearing walls to structure with nonrigid connections.

- Use structural design techniques to resist progressive collapse.
- Treat exterior shear walls as primary structures.
- Orient glazing perpendicular to the primary façade facing uncontrolled vehicle approaches.
- Use reinforced concrete wall systems in lieu of masonry or curtain walls.
- Ensure active fire system is protected from single-point failure in case of a blast event.
- Install a backup control center.
- Avoid eaves and overhangs or harden to withstand blast effects.
- Establish group floor elevation 4 ft above grade.
- Secure with greater purpose and hardware all openings to building within 14 ft of ground level or 14 ft of access to roof.

Integrating multiple security systems in a layered effect—including CPTED and environmental security, critical infrastructure protection, building designs, interior/exterior layout, detection systems, structural barriers, access controls, communications, and CCTV assessment—contributes to the protection of assets as well as the control and reduction of losses.

Glossary

Terms and definitions for door and window security

access control a method of providing security by restricting the movement of persons into or within a protected area

accessible window (1) residential, any window located within 3.7 m (14 ft) of grade or a building projection and (2) commercial, any window located within 4.6 m (18 ft) of grade or within 3 m (10 ft) of any fire escape or other structure accessible from public or semipublic areas (check local codes)

ace lock a type of pin tumbler lock in which the pins are installed in a circle around the axis of the cylinder that move perpendicularly to the face of the cylinder. The shear line of the driver and bottom tumblers is a plane parallel to the face of the cylinder. This type of lock is operated with a push key

active door (or leaf) the leaf of a double door that must be opened first. It is used in normal pedestrian traffic. This leaf is usually the one in which a lock is installed

Americans with disabilities act

anchor a device used to secure a building part or component to adjoining construction or to a supporting member. See also floor anchor, jamb anchor, and stud anchor

antifriction latch a latch bolt that incorporates any device which reduces the closing friction between the latch and the strike

applied trim a separately applied molding used as the finishing face trim of a frame

apron the flat member of a window trim placed against the wall immediately beneath the windowsill

architectural hardware see finish builders' hardware

area-way an open subsurface space adjacent to a building that is used to admit light or to provide a means of access to the building

armored front a plate or plates that is secured to the lock front of a mortised lock by machine screws in order to provide protection against tampering with cylinder set screws. Also called armored face plate

auxiliary lock a lock installed on a door or window to supplement a previously installed primary lock. Also called a secondary lock. It can be a mortised, bored, or rim lock

back plate a metal plate on the inside of a door that is used to clamp a pin or disc tumbler rim lock cylinder to the door by means of retaining screws. The tail piece of the cylinder extends through a hole in the back plate

backset, flush bolt a distance from the vertical centerline of the lock edge of a door to the centerline of the bolt

backset, hinge on a door the distance from the stop face to the edge of the hinge cutout. On a frame, the distance from the stop to the edge of the hinge cutout

backset, lock the horizontal distance from the vertical centerline of the face plate to the center of the lock cylinder keyway or knob spindle

backset, strike the distance from the door stop to the edge of the strike cutout

baffle see guard plate

balanced door a door equipped with double-pivoted hardware designed to cause a semicounterbalanced swing action when it is opened

barrel key a key with a bit projecting from a round, hollow key shank that fits on a post in the lock

barricade bolt a massive metal bar that engages large strikes on both sides of a door. Barricade bolts are available with locking devices and are completely removed from the door when not in use

bevel (of a door) the angle of the lock edge of the door in relation to its face. The standard bevel is 0.32 cm in 5.1 cm (1/8″ in 2″)

bevel (of a latch bolt) a term used to indicate the direction in which a latch bolt is inclined: regular bevel for doors opening in, reverse bevel for doors opening out

bevel (of a lock front) the angle of a lock front when not at a right angle to the lock case, allowing the front to be applied flush with the edge of a beveled door

bicentric pin tumbler cylinder a cylinder having two cores and two sets of pins, each having different combinations. This cylinder requires two separate keys, used simultaneously, to operate it. The cam or tail piece is gear operated

bit a blade projecting from a key shank that engages with and actuates the bolt or level tumblers of a lock

bit key a key with a bit projecting from a round shank. Similar to the barrel key but with a solid rather than hollow shank

bitting see cut

biometrics a method of providing a higher level of security to an area by way of solid core doors

blank an uncut key or an unfinished key as it comes from the manufacturer, before any cuts have been made on it

blind stop a rectangular molding, located between the outside trim and the outside sashes, used in the assembly of a window frame. Serves as a stop for storm, screen, or combination windows as well as resisting air infiltration

bolt that part of a lock which, when actuated, is projected (or "thrown") from the lock into a retaining member, such as a strike plate, to prevent a door or window from moving or opening. See also dead bolt, flush bolt, and latch

bolt attack a category of burglary attack in which force, with or without the aid of tools, is directed against the bolt in an attempt to disengage it from the strike or to break it

bolt projection (bolt throw) the distance from the edge of the door, at the bolt centerline, to the furthest point on the bolt in the projected position

bored lock (or latch) a lock or latch whose parts are intended for installation in holes bored in a door. See also key-in-knob lock

bottom pin one of the pin tumblers that determine the combination of a pin tumbler cylinder; it is directly contacted by the key. They are varied in length and usually tapered at one end, enabling them to fit into the "V" cuts made in a key. When the proper key is inserted, the bottom pins level off at the cylinder core shear line, allowing the core to turn and actuate the lock

bottom rail the horizontal rail at the bottom of a door or window connecting the vertical edge members (stiles)

box strike a strike plate that has a metal box or housing to fully enclose the projected bolt and/or latch

builders' hardware all hardware used in building construction, but particularly that used on or in connection with doors, windows, cabinets, and other moving members

bumping a method of opening a pin tumbler lock by means of vibration produced by a wooden or rubber mallet

burglar-resistant glazing a type of hinge with matching rectangular leaves and multiple bearing contacts. It is designed to be mounted in mortises in the door edge and in the frame

butt hinge a type of hinge with matching rectangular leaves and multiple bearing contacts. It is designed to be mounted in mortises in the door edge and in the frame

buttress lock a lock that secures a door by wedging a bar between the door and the floor. Some incorporate a movable steel rod that fits into metal receiving slots on the door and in the floor. Also called police bolt/brace

cabinet jamb a door frame in three or more pieces, usually shipped knocked down for field assembly over a rough buck

cam the part of a lock or cylinder that rotates to actuate the bolt or latch as the key is turned. The cam may also act as a bolt

cam, lazy a cam that moves less than the rotation of the cylinder core

cam lock see crescent sash lock

cane bolt a heavy cane-shaped bolt with the top bent at right angles; used on the bottom of doors

case the housing in which a lock mechanism is mounted and enclosed

casement hinge a hinge for swinging a casement window

casement window a type of window that is hinged on the vertical edge

casing molding of various widths and thicknesses used to trim door and window openings at the jambs

center-hung door a door hung on center pivots

center rail the horizontal rail in a door, usually located at lock height to separate the upper and lower panels of a recessed panel type door

chain bolt a vertical spring-loaded bolt mounted at the top of a door. It is manually actuated by a chain

chain door interviewer an auxiliary locking device that allows a door to be opened slightly but restrains it from being fully opened. It consists of a chain with one end attached to the doorjamb and the other attached to a keyed metal piece that slides in a slotted metal plate attached to the door. Some chain door interviewers incorporate a keyed lock operated from the inside

change key a key that will operate only one lock or a group of keyed-alike locks, as distinguished from a master key. See also keyed-alike cylinders and master key system

changes the number of possible key changes or combination changes to a lock cylinder

checkrails the meeting rails of double-hung windows. They are usually beveled and thick enough to fill the space between the top and bottom sash due to the parting stop in the window frame

clearance a space intentionally provided between components, either to facilitate operation or installation, to ensure proper separation, to accommodate dimensional variations, or for other reasons. See also door clearance

clevis a metal link used to attach a chain to a padlock

code an arrangement of numbers or letters used to specify a combination for the bitting of a key or the pins of a cylinder core

combination doors or windows storm doors or windows permanently installed over the primary doors or windows. They provide insulation and summer ventilation and often have self-storing or removable glass and screen inserts

common entry door (of a multiple dwelling) any door in a multiple dwelling that provides access between the semipublic, interior areas of the building, and the out-of-doors areas surrounding the building

component a subassembly that is combined with other components to make an entire system. Door assembly components include the door, lock, hinges, jam/strike, and jamb/wall

composite door a door constructed of a solid core material with facing and edges of different materials

connecting bar a flat metal bar attached to the core of a cylinder lock to operate the bolt mechanism

construction master keying a keying system used to allow the use of a single key for all locks during the construction of large housing projects. In one such system, the cylinder cores of all locks contain an insert that permits the use of a special master key. When the dwelling unit is completed, the insert is removed and the lock then accepts its own change key and no longer accepts the construction master key

continuous hinge a hinge designed to be the same length as the edge of the moving part to which it is applied. Also called a piano hinge

coordinator a mechanism that controls the order of closing of a pair of swing doors, used with overlapping astragals and certain panic hardware that require that one door close ahead of the other

core see cylinder core

CPTED the design or redesign of a building or place to reduce crime opportunity and fear of crime through the specific application of strategies and tactics to reduce crime opportunity through environmental design; these strategies involve surveillance, access control, territoriality, maintenance, and place management. The tactics of CPTED are further specified into natural, mechanical, and procedural components. CPTED plans are best developed and implemented by multidisciplinary teams

crash bar the crossbar or level of a panic exit device that serves as a push bar to actuate the lock. See also panic hardware

cremone bolt a surface-mounted device that locks a door or sash into the frame at both the top and bottom when a knob or lever is turned

crescent sash lock a simple cam-shaped latch that does not require a key for its operation, usually used to secure double-hung windows. Also called a cam lock

cut an indention made in a key to make it fit a pin tumbler of a lock. Any notch made in a key is known as a cut, whether it is square, round, or V-shaped. Also called bitting

cylinder the cylindrical subassembly of a lock, including the cylinder housing, the cylinder core, the tumbler mechanism, and the keyway

cylinder collar see cylinder guard ring

cylinder core (or plug) the central part of a cylinder, containing the keyway, which rotates to operate the lock bolt

cylinder guard ring a hardened metal ring, surrounding the exposed portion of a lock cylinder, that protects the cylinder from being wrenched, turned, pried, cut, or pulled by attack tools

cylinder housing the external case of a lock cylinder. Also called the cylinder shell

cylinder lock a lock in which the locking mechanism is controlled by a cylinder. A double-cylinder lock has a cylinder on both the interior and exterior of the door

cylinder, mortise type a lock cylinder that has a threaded housing that screws directly into the lock case with a cam or other mechanism engaging the locking mechanism

cylinder, removable core a cylinder whose core may be removed by the use of a special key

cylinder, rim type a lock cylinder that is held in place by tension against its rim applied by screws from the interior face of the door

cylinder ring see guard ring

cylinder screw a set screw that holds a mortise cylinder in place and prevents it from being turned after installation

cylindrical lock (or latch) see bored lock

dead bolt a lock bolt that does not have an automatic spring action and a beveled end as opposed to a latch bolt, which does. The bolt must be actuated to a projected position by a key or thumb turn and when projected is locked against return by end pressure

dead latch a spring-actuated latch bolt having a beveled end and incorporating a feature that automatically locks the projected latch bolt against return by end pressure

disc tumbler a spring-loaded, flat plate that slides in a slot that runs through the diameter of the cylinder. Inserting the proper key lines up the disc tumblers with the lock's shear line and enables the core to be turned

dogging device a mechanism that fastens the crossbar of a panic exit device in the fully depressed position and retains the latch bolt or bolts in the retracted position to permit free operation of the door from either side

dogging key a key-type wrench used to lock down, in the open position, the crossbar of a panic exit device

door assembly a unit composed of parts or components that make up a closure for a passageway through a wall. It consists of the door, hinges, locking device or devices, operational contacts (such as handles, knobs, push plates), miscellaneous hardware and closures, the frame including the head and jambs, the anchorage devices to the surrounding wall, and the surrounding wall

door bolt a rod or bar manually operated without a key, attached to a door to provide a means of securing it

door check (door closer) a device used to control the closing of a door by means of a spring and either hydraulic or air pressure or by electrical means

door clearance the space between a door and either its frame or the finished floor or threshold or between the two doors of a double door. See also clearance

door frame an assembly of members surrounding and supporting a door or doors and perhaps also one or more transom lights and/or sidelights. See also integral frame

doorjambs the two vertical components of a door frame called the hinge jamb and the lock jamb

door light see light

door opening the size of a doorway measured from jamb to jamb and from floor line to sill to head of frame. The opening size is usually the nominal door size and is equal to the actual door size plus clearances and threshold height

door stop the projections along the top and sides of a door frame against which a one-way swinging door closes. See also rabbeted jamb

double-acting door a swinging door equipped with hardware that permits it to open in either direction

double-bitted key a key having cuts on two sides

double-cylinder lock see cylinder lock

double door a pair of doors mounted together in a single opening. See also active door and inactive door

double-egress frame a door frame prepared to receive two single-acting doors swinging in opposite directions, and both doors are of the same hand

double glazing two thicknesses of glass, separated by an air space and framed in an opening, designed to reduce heat transfer. In factory-made double-glazing units, referenced to as insulating glass, the air space between the glass sheets is desiccated and sealed airtight

double-hung window a type of window composed of upper and lower sashes that slide vertically

double-throw lock a bolt that can be projected beyond its first position, into a second, or fully extended one

double-throw lock a lock incorporating a double-throw bolt

driver pin one of the pin tumblers in a pin tumbler cylinder lock, usually flat on both ends, that is in line with and pushes against the flat ends of the bottom pins. They are projected by individual coil springs into the cylinder core until they are forced from the core by the bottom pins when the proper key is inserted into the keyway

drop ring a ring handle attached to the spindle that operates a lock or latch. The ring is pivoted to remain in a dropped position when not in use

dry glazing a method of securing glass in a frame by use of a preformed resilient gasket

drywall frame a knocked down door frame for installation in a wall constructed with studs and gypsum board or other drywall facing material after the wall is erected

dummy cylinder a mock cylinder without an operating mechanism, used for appearance only

dummy trim trim only, without lock; usually used on the inactive door in a double door

Dutch door a door consisting of two separate leaves, one above the other, which may be operated either independently or together. The lower leaf usually has a service shelf

Dutch door bolt a device for locking together the upper and lower leaves of a Dutch door

dwelling unit entry door any door giving access to a private dwelling unit

electric strike an electrically operated device that replaces a conventional strike plate and allows a door to be opened by using electric switches at remote locations

escutcheon plate a surface-mounted cover plate, either protective or ornamental, containing openings for any or all of the controlling members of a lock such as the knob, handle, cylinder, or keyhole

exit device see panic hardware

expanded metal an open mesh formed by slitting and drawing a metal sheet: it is made in various patterns and metal thicknesses, with either a flat or an irregular surface

exterior private area the ground area outside a single family house, or a ground floor apartment in the case of a multiple dwelling, which is fenced off by a real barrier, and is available for the use of one family and is accessible only from the interior of that family's unit

exterior public area the ground area outside a multiple dwelling that is not defined as being associated with the building or building entry in any real or symbolic fashion

exterior semiprivate area the ground area outside a multiple dwelling that is fenced off by a real barrier and is accessible only from the private or semiprivate zones within the building

exterior semipublic area the ground area outside a single family house or multiple dwelling that is accessible from public zones but is defined as belonging to the house or building by symbolic barriers only

face (of a lock) see face plate

face glazing a method of glazing in which the glass is set in an L-shaped or rabbeted frame, the glazing compound is finished off in the form of a triangular bead, and no loose stops are employed

face plate the part of a mortise lock through which the bolt protrudes and by which the lock is fastened to the door

fast pin hinge a hinge in which the pin is fastened permanently in place

fatigue structural failure of a material caused by repeated or fluctuating application of stresses, none of which is individually sufficient to cause failure

fence a metal pin that extends from the bolt of a lever lock and prevents retraction of the bolt unless it is aligned with the gates of the lever tumblers

fidelity loss a property loss resulting from a theft in which the thief leaves no evidence of entry

filler plate a metal plate used to fill unwanted mortise cutouts in a door or frame

finish builders' hardware hardware that has a finished appearance as well as a functional purpose and that may be considered as part of the decorative treatment of a room or building. Also called finish hardware and buildings' finish hardware

fire stair any enclosed stairway that is part of a fire-resistant exitway

fire stair door a door forming part of the fire-resistant fire stair enclosure and providing access from common corridors to fire stair landings within an exitway

floor anchor a metal device attached to the wall side of a jamb at its base to secure the frame to the floor

floor clearance the width of the space between the bottom of a door and the rough or finished floor or threshold

flush bolt a door bolt so designed that when installed, the operating handle is flush with the face or edge of the door. Usually installed at the top and bottom of the inactive door of a double door

flush door a smooth-surfaced door having faces that are plain and conceal its rails and stiles or other structure

foot bolt a type of bolt applied at the bottom of a door and arranged from foot operation. Generally the bolt head is held up by a spring when the door is unbolted

forced entry an unauthorized entry accomplished by the use of force upon the physical components of the premises

frame the component that forms the opening of and provides support for a door, window, skylight, or hatchway. See also door frame

frame gasket resilient material in strip form attached to frame stops to provide tight closure of a door or window

front (of a lock) see face plate

gate a notch in the end of a lever tumbler that when aligned with the fence of the lock bolt allows the bolt to be withdrawn from the strike

general circulation stair an interior stairway in a nonelevator building that provides access to upper floors

glass door a door made from thick glass, usually heat tempered, with no structural metal stiles

glazing any transparent or translucent material used in windows or doors to admit light

glazing bead a strip of trim or a sealant such as calking or glazing compound, which is placed around the perimeter of a pane of glass or other glazing to secure it to a frame

glazing compound a soft, dough-like material used for filling and sealing the spaces between a pane of glass and its surrounding frame and/or stops

grand master key a key designed to operate all locks under several master keys in a system

grating, bar type an open grip assembly of metal bars in which the bearing bars, running in one direction, are spaced by rigid attachment to crossbars running perpendicular to them or by bent connecting bars extending between them

grout mortar of such consistency that it will just flow into the joints and cavities of masonry work and fill them solid

grout frame a frame in which all voids between it and the surrounding wall are completely filled with the cement or plaster used in the wall construction

guard bar a series of two or more crossbars, generally fastened to a common back plate, to protect the glass of screen in a door

guard plate a piece of metal attached to a door frame, door edge, or over the lock cylinder for the purpose of reinforcing the locking system against burglary attacks

hand (of a door) the opening direction of the door. A right-handed door is hinged on the right and swings inward when viewed from the outside. A left-handed door is hinged on the left and swings inward when viewed from the outside. If either of these doors swings outward, it is referred to as a right-hand reverse door or a left-hand reverse door, respectively

handle any grip-type door pull. See also lever handle

hasp a fastening device consisting of a hinged plate with a slot in it that fits over a fixed D-shaped ring, or eye

hatchway an opening in a ceiling, roof, or floor of a building large enough to allow human access

head top horizontal member of a door or window frame

head stiffener a heavy-gauge metal angle or channel section placed inside, and attached to, the head of a wide door frame to maintain its alignment; not a load-carrying member

heel of a padlock that end of the shackle on a padlock that is not removable from the case

hinge a device generally consisting of two metal plates having loops formed along one edge of each to engage and rotate about a common pivot rod or "pin," used to suspend a swinging door or window in its frame

hinge backset the distance from the edge of a hinge to the stop at the side of a door or window

hinge edge or hinge stile the vertical edge or stile of a door or window to which hinges or pivots are attached

hinge pins come in two types: removable pins and nonremovable pins for higher security

hinge reinforcement a metal plate attached to a door or frame to receive a hinge

hold-back feature a mechanism on a latch that serves to hold the latch bolt in the retracted position

hollow core door a door constructed so that the space (core) between the two facing sheets is not completely filled. Various spacing and reinforcing materials are used to separate the facing sheets; some interior hollow core doors have nothing except perimeter stiles and rails separating the facing sheets

hollow metal hollow items such as doors, frames, partitions, and enclosures that are usually fabricated from cold-formed metal sheet, usually carbon steel

horizontal sliding window a type of window, composed of two sections, one or both of which slide horizontally past the other

impression system a technique to produce keys for certain types of locks without taking the lock apart

inactive door (or leaf) the leaf of a double door that is bolted when closed; the strike plate is attached to this leaf to receive the latch and bolt of the active leaf

integral frame a metal door frame in which the jambs and head have stops, trim, and backbends all formed from one piece of material

integral lock (or latch) see preassembled lock

interior common-circulation area an area within a multiple dwelling that is outside the private zones of individual units and is used in common by all residents and the maintenance staff of the building

interior private area the interior of a single family house; the interior of an apartment in a multiple dwelling; or the interior of a separate unite within a commercial, public, or institutional building

interior public area an interior common-circulation area or common resident-use room within a multiple dwelling to which access is unrestricted

interior semipublic area an interior common-circulation area or common resident-use room within a multiple dwelling to which access is possible only with a key or on the approval of a resident via an intercom, buzzer-reply system

invisible hinge a hinge so constructed that no parts are exposed when the door is closed

jalousie window see louvered window

jamb the exposed vertical member of either side of a door or window opening. See also doorjambs

jamb anchor a metal device inserted in or attached to the wall side of a jamb to secure the frame to the wall. A masonry jamb anchor secures a jamb to a masonry wall

jamb depth the width of the jamb, measured perpendicular to the door or wall face at the edge of the opening

jamb extension the section of a jamb that extends below the level of the wash floor for attachment to the rough floor

jamb peeling a technique used in forced entry to deform or remove portions of the jamb to disengage the bolt from the strike. See jimmying

jamb/strike the component of a door assembly that receives and holds the extended lock bolt. The strike and jamb are considered a unit

jamb/wall that component of a door assembly to which a door is attached and secured by means of the hinges. The wall and jamb are considered a unit

jimmying a technique used in forced entry to pry the jamb away from the lock edge of the door a sufficient distance to disengage the bolt from the strike

jimmy-pin a sturdy projecting screw, which is installed in the hinge edge of a door near a hinge, that fits into a hole in the doorjamb and prevents removal of the door if the hinge pins are removed

key an implement used to actuate a lock bolt or latch into the locked or unlocked position

key changes the different combinations that are available or that can be used in a specific cylinder

keyed-alike cylinders cylinders that are designed to be operated by the same key. (Not to be confused with master-keyed cylinders.)

keyed-different cylinders cylinders requiring different keys for their operation

keyhole the opening in a lock designed to receive the key

key-in-knob lock a lock having the key cylinder and the other lock mechanism such as a push or turn button, contained in the knobs

key plate a plate or escutcheon having only a keyhole

keyway the longitudinal cut in the cylinder core. It is an opening or space with millings in the sides identical to those on the proper key, thus allowing the key to enter the full distance of the blade. See also warded lock

knifing see loiding

knob an ornamental or functional round handle on a door; may be designed to actuate a lock or latch

knob latch a securing device having a spring bolt operated by a knob only

knob shank the projecting stem of a knob into which the spindle is fastened

knocked down disassembled; designed for assembly at the point of use

knuckle the enlarged part of a hinge into which the pin is inserted

laminate a product made by bonding together two or more layers of material

laminated glass a type of glass fabricated from two layers of glass with a transparent bonding layer between them. Also called safety glass

laminated padlock a padlock, the body of which consists of a number of flat plates, all or most of which are of the same contour, superimposed and riveted or brazed together. Holes in the plates provide spaces for the lock mechanism and the ends of the shackle

latch (or latch bolt) a beveled, spring-actuated bolt that may or may not include a dead-locking feature

leading edge see lock edge

leaf, door an individual door, used either singly or in multiples

leaf hinge the most common type of hinge, characterized by two flat metal plates or leaves, which pivot about a metal hinge pin. A leaf hinge can be surface mounted or installed in a mortise. See also butt hinge and surface hinge

lever handle a bar-like grip rotated in a vertical plane about a horizontal axis at one of its ends, designed to operate a latch

lever lock a key-operated lock that incorporates one or more lever tumblers, which must be raised to a specific level so that the fence of the bolt is aligned with the gate of the tumbler in order to withdraw the bolt. Lever locks are commonly used in storage lockers and safety deposit boxes

lever tumbler a flat metal arm pivoted on one end with a gate in the opposite end. The top edge is spring loaded. The bitting of the key rotates against the bottom edge, raising the lever tumbler to align the gate with the bolt fence. Both the position of the gate and the curvature of the bottom edge of the lever tumbler can be varied to establish the key code

light a space in a window or door for a single pane of glazing. Also, a pane of glass or other glazing material

lintel a horizontal structural member that supports the load over an opening such as a door or window

lip (of a strike) the curved projecting part of a strike plate that guides the spring bolt to the latch point

lobby that portion of the interior common area of a building that is reached from an entry door and provides access to the general circulation areas, elevators, and fire stairs and from these to other areas of the building

lock a fastener that secures a door or window assembly against unauthorized entry. A door is usually key operated and includes the keyed device (cylinder or combination), bolt, strike plate, knobs or levers, trim items, and so forth. A window lock is usually hand operated rather than key operated

lock clip a flexible metal part attached to the inside of a door face to position a mortise lock

lock edge the vertical edge or stile of a door in which a lock may be installed. Also called the leading edge, the lock stile, and the strike edge

lock edge door (or lock seam door) a door that has its face sheets secured in place by an exposed mechanical interlock seam on each of its two vertical edges. See also lock seam

lock face plate see face plate

locking dog (of a padlock) the part of a padlock mechanism that engages the shackle and holds it in the locked position

lock-in-knob see key-in-knob lock

lock pick a tool or instrument, other than the specifically designed key, made for the purpose of manipulating a lock into a locked or unlocked condition

lock rail the horizontal member of a door intended to receive the lock case

lock reinforcement a reinforcing plate attached inside of the lock stile of a door to receive a lock

lock seam a joint in sheet metal work formed by doubly folding the edges of adjoining sheets in such a manner that they interlock

lock stile see lock edge

locks come in different shapes and styles, for example: pin tumbler, the most widely used; warded lock, was the first developed (see warded lock); level lock, used in cabinets, lockers, desk drawers; dial combination, a dial with combination instead of a key is used to open the lock

loiding a burglary attack method in which a thin, flat, flexible object such as a stiff piece of plastic is inserted between the strike and the latch bolt to depress the latch bolt and release it from the strike. The loiding of windows is accomplished by inserting a thin, stiff object between the meeting rails or stiles to move the latch to the open position, or by inserting a thin stiff wire through openings between the stile or rail and the frame to manipulate the sash operator of pivoting windows. Derived from the work "celluloid." Also called knifing and slip-knifing

loose joint hinge a hinge with two knuckles. The pin is fastened permanently to one and the other contains the pinhole. The two parts of the hinge can be disengaged by lifting

loose pin hinge a hinge having a removable pin to permit the two leaves of the hinge to be separated

louver an opening with a series of horizontal slats so arranged as to permit ventilation but to exclude rain, sunlight, or vision

louvered window a type of window in which the glazing consists of parallel, horizontal, movable glass slats. Also called a jalousie window

main entry door the most important common entry door in a building; provides access to the building's lobby

maison keying a specialized keying system, used in apartment houses and other large complexes, that enables all individual unit keys to operate common-use locks such as main entry, laundry room, and so forth

master disc tumbler a disc tumbler that will operate with a master key in addition to its own change key

master key system a method of keying locks that allows a single key to operate multiple locks, each of which will also operate with an individual change key. Several levels of master keying are possible: a single master key is one that will operate all locks of a group of locks with individual change keys, a grand master key will operate all locks of two or more master key systems, and a great grand master will operate all locks of two or more grand master key systems. Master key systems are used primarily with pin and disc tumbler locks, and to a limited extent with lever or warded locks

master pin a segmented pin, used to enable a pin tumbler to be operated by more than one key cut

meeting stile the vertical edge member of a door or horizontal sliding window, in a pair of doors or windows, which meets with the adjacent edge member when closed. See also checkrails

metal-mesh grille a grille of expanded metal or welded metal wires permanently installed across a window or other opening in order to prevent entry through the opening

mill finish the original surface finish produced on a metal mill product by cold rolling, extruding, or drawing

millwork generally, all building components made of finished wood and manufactured in millwork plants and planning mills. It includes such items as inside and outside doors, window and door frames, cabinets, porch work, mantels, panel work, stairways, moldings, and interior trim. It normally does not include flooring, ceiling, and siding

molding a wood strip used for decorative purposes

mono lock see preassembled lock

mortise a rectangular cavity made to receive a lock or other hardwire; also, the act of making such a cavity

mortise bolt a bolt designed to be installed in a mortise rather than on the surface. The bolt is operated by a knob, lever, or equivalent

mortise cylinder see cylinder, mortise type

mortise lock a lock designed for installation in a mortise, as distinguished from a bored lock and a rim lock

mullion (1) a movable or fixed center post used on double-door openings, usually for locking purposes. (2) A vertical or horizontal bar or divider in a frame between windows, doors, or other openings

multiple dwelling a building or portion of a building designed or used for occupancy by three or more tenants or families living independently of each other (includes hotels or motels)

muntin a small member that divides a glass or openings of sash or doors

mushroom tumbler a type of tumbler used in pin tumbler locks to add security against picking. The diameter of the driver pin behind the end in contact with the bottom pin is reduced so that the mushroom head will catch the edge of the cylinder body at the shear line when it is at a slight angle to its cavity. See also spool tumbler

night latch an auxiliary lock having a spring latch bolt and functioning independently of the regular lock of the door

nonremovable hinge pin a type of hinge pin that has been constructed or modified to make removing it from the hinge difficult or impossible

offset pivot (or hinge) a pin-and-socket hardware device with a single bearing contact, by means of which a door is suspended in its frame and allowed to swing about an axis that normally is located about 1.9 cm (3/4 in.) out from the door face

one-way screw a screw specifically designed to resist being removed, once installed. See also tamper-resistant hardware

opening size see door opening

operator (of a window sash) the mechanism, including a crank handle and gear box, attached to an operating arm or arms for the purpose of opening and closing a window. Usually found on casement and awning type windows

overhead door a door that is stored overhead when in the open position

padlock a detachable and portable lock with a hinged or sliding shackle or bolt, normally used with a hasp and eye or staple system

panel door a door fabricated from one or more panels surrounded by and held in position by rails and stiles

panic bar see crash bar

panic hardware an exterior door-locking mechanism that is always operable from inside the building by pressure on a crash bar or lever

patio-type sliding door a sliding door that is essentially a single, large transparent panel in a frame (a type commonly used to give access to patios or yards of private dwellings); "single" doors have one fixed and one movable panel and "double" doors have two movable panels

pin (of a hinge) the metal rod that serves as the axis of a hinge thereby allowing the hinge (and attached door or window) to rotate between the open and closed positions

pin tumbler one of the essential, distinguishing components of a pin tumbler lock cylinder, more precisely called a bottom pin, master pin, or driver pin. The pin tumblers, used in varying lengths and arrangements, determine the combination of the cylinder. See also bottom pin, driver pin, and master pin

pin tumbler lock cylinder a lock cylinder employing metal pins (tumblers) to prevent the rotation of the core until the correct key is inserted into the keyway. Small coil compression springs hold the pins in the locked position until the key is inserted

pivoted door a door hung on pivots rather than hinges

pivoted window a window that opens by pivoting about a horizontal or vertical axis

plug retainer the part often fixed to the rear of the core in a lock cylinder to retain or hold the core firmly in the cylinder

preassembled lock a lock that has all the parts assembled into a unit at the factory and, when installed in a rectangular section cutout of the lock edge, requires little or no assembly. Also called integral lock, mono lock, and unit lock

pressed padlock a padlock whose outer case is pressed into shape from sheet metal and then riveted together

pressure-locked grating a grating in which the crossbars are mechanically locked to the bearing bars at their intersections by deforming or swaging the metal

privacy lock a lock, usually for an interior door, secured by a button, thumb turn, and so forth, and not designed for key operation

push key a key that operates the Ace type of lock

quadrant see Dutch door bolt

rabbet a cut, slot, or groove made on the edge or surface of a board to receive the end or edge of another piece of wood made to fit it

rabbeted jamb a doorjamb in which the projecting portion of the jamb that forms the door stop is either part of the same piece as the rest of the jamb or securely set into a deep groove in the jamb

rail a horizontal framing member of a door or window sash that extends the full width between the stiles

removable mullion a mullion separating two adjacent door openings that is required for the normal operation of the doors but is designed to permit its temporary removal

restricted keyway a special keyway and key blank for high-security locks with a configuration that is not freely available and must be specifically requested from the manufacturer

reversible lock a lock that may be used for either hand of a door

rim cylinder a pin or disc tumbler cylinder used with a rim lock

rim hardware hardware designed to be installed on the surface of a door or window

rim latch a latch installed on the surface of a door

rim lock a lock designed to be mounted on the surface of a door

rose the part of a lock that functions as an ornament or bearing surface for a knob and is normally placed against the surface of the door

rotary interlocking dead bolt lock a type of rim lock in which the extended dead bolt is rotated to engage with the strike

rough buck a subframe, usually made of wood or steel that is set in a wall opening and to which the frame is attached

rough opening the wall opening into which a frame is to be installed. Usually, the rough opening is measured inside the rough buck

sash a frame containing one or more lights

sash fast a fastener attached to the meeting rails of a window
sash lock a sash fast with a locking device controlled by a key
screwless knob a knob attached to a spindle by means of a special wrench, as distinguished from the more commonly used side-screw knob
screwless rose a rose with a concealed method of attachment
seamless door a door having no visible seams on its faces or edges
secondary lock see auxiliary lock
security glass or glazing see burglar-resistant glazing
setback see backset
shackle the hinged or sliding part of a padlock that does the fastening
shear line the joint between the shell and the core of a lock cylinder; the line at which the pins or discs of a lock cylinder must be aligned in order to permit rotation of the core
sheathing the structural exterior covering, usually wood boards or plywood, used over the framing studs and rafters of a structure
shell a lock cylinder, exclusive of the core. Also called housing
shutter a movable screen or cover used to protect an opening, especially a window
side light a fixed light located adjacent to a door within the same frame assembly
signal sash fastener a sash-fastening device designed to lock windows that are beyond reach from the floor. It has a ring for a sash pole hook. When locked, the ring lever is down; when the ring lever is up, it signals by its upright position that the window is unlocked
sill the lower horizontal member of a door or window opening
single-acting door a door mounted to swing to only one side of the plane of its frame
skylight a glazed opening located in the roof of a building
slide bolt a simple lock that is operated directly by hand without using a key, a turnpiece, or other actuating mechanism. Slide bolts can normally only be operated from the inside
sliding door any door that slides open sideways
sliding metal gate an assembly of metal bars, jointed so that it can be moved to and locked in position across a window or other opening in order to prevent unauthorized entry through the opening
slip-knifing see loiding
solid core door a door constructed so that the space (core) between the two facing sheets is completely filled with wood blocks or other rigid material
spindle the shaft that fits into the shank of a door knob or handle and that serves as its axis of rotation
split astragal a two-piece astragal, one piece of which is surface mounted on each door of a double door and is provided with a means of adjustment to mate with the other piece and provide a seal
spool tumbler a type of tumbler used in pin tumbler locks to add security against picking. Operates on the same principal as the mushroom tumbler
spring bolt see latch
spring bolt with antiloading device see dead latch
stile one of the vertical edge members of a paneled door or window sash
stool a flat molding fitted over the windowsill between the jambs and contacting the bottom rail of the lower sash
stop (of a door or window frame) the projecting part of a door or window frame against which a swinging door or window closes, or in which a sliding door or window moves
stop (of a lock) a button or other device that serves to lock and unlock a latch bolt against actuation by the outside knob or thumb piece. Another type holds the bolt retracted
stop side that face of a door that contacts the door stop
store front sash an assembly of light metal members forming a continuous frame for a fixed glass store front
storm sash, window, or door an extra window or door, usually placed on the outside of an existing one as additional protection against cold or hot weather
strap hinge a surface hinge of which one or both leaves are of considerable length
strike a metal plate attached to or mortised into a doorjamb to receive and hold a projected latch bolt and/or dead bolt in order to secure the door to the jamb
strike, dustproof a strike that is placed in the threshold or sill of an opening, or in the floor, to receive a flush bolt, and is equipped with a spring-loaded follower to cover the recess and keep out dirt
strike, interlocking a strike that receives and holds a vertical, rotary, or hook dead bolt
strike plate see strike
strike reinforcement a metal plate attached to a door or frame to receive a strike
strike, roller a strike for latch bolts, having a roller mounted on the lip to reduce friction
stud a slender wood or metal post used as a supporting element in a wall or partition
stud anchor a device used to secure a stud to the floor
subbuck or subframe see rough buck
surface hinge a hinge having both leaves attached to the surface and thus is fully visible

swing see hand

swinging bolt a bolt that is hinged to a lock front and is projected and retracted with a swinging rather than a sliding action. Also called hinged or pivot bolt

tail piece the unit on the core of a cylinder lock that actuates the bolt or latch

tamper-resistant hardware builders' hardware with screws or nut-and-bolt connections that are hidden or cannot be removed with conven-·tional tools

template a precise detailed pattern used as a guide in the mortising, drilling, and so forth, of a door or frame to receive hardware

template hardware hardware manufactured within template tolerances

tension wrench an instrument used in picking a lock. It is used to apply torsion to the cylinder core

three-point lock a locking device required on "A-label" fire double doors to lock the active door at three points. The normal position plus top and bottom

threshold a wood or metal plate forming the bottom of a doorway

throw see bolt projection

thumb piece (of a door handle) the small pivoted part above the grip of a door handle, which is pressed by the thumb to operate a latch bolt

thumb turn a unit that is gripped between the thumb and forefinger and turned to project or retract a bolt

tolerance the permissible deviation from a nominal or specified dimension or value

transom an opening window immediately above a door

transom bar the horizontal frame member that separates the door opening from the transom

transom catch a latch bolt fastener on a transom that has a ring by which the latch bolt is retracted

transom chain a short chain used to limit the opening of a transom; usually provided with a plate at each end for attachment

transom lift a device attached to a door frame and transom by means of which the transom may be opened or closed

trim hardware see finish builders' hardware

tryout keys a set of keys that includes many commonly used bittings. They are used one at a time in an attempt to unlock a door

tumbler a movable obstruction in a lock that must be adjusted to a particular position, as by a key, before the bolt can be thrown

unit lock see preassembled lock

vertical bolt lock a lock having two deadbolts that move vertically into two circular receivers in the strike portion of the lock attached to the doorjamb

vision panel a fixed transparent panel of glazing material set into an otherwise opaque wall, partition, or door; a nonopening window. See also light

ward an obstruction that prevents the wring key from entering or turning in a lock

warded lock a lock containing internal obstacles that block the entrance or rotation of all but the correct key

weather stripping narrow or jamb-width sections of flexible material that prevent the passage of air and moisture around windows and doors. Compression weather stripping also acts as a frictional counterbalance in double-hung windows

wet glazing the sealing of glass or other transparent material in a frame by the use of a glazing compound or sealant

window frame see frame

window guard a strong metal grid-like assembly which can be installed on a window or other opening

windows designed to provide ventilation, illuminative, visual access, or any combination. They come in different shapes, sizes, strengths, and appearance

wire glass glass manufactured with a layer of wire mesh approximately in the center of the sheet

References

Bernard R., 2010. What is a security infrastructure? Security Technology Executive Publications, 6.

Crowe, T.D., 2000. CPTED.. Butterworth-Heinemann, Boston, MA, pp. 3–54.

US Green Building Council, 2002. LEED green building Z rating system for new construction and major renovation version 2.1. Available from: <http//www.usgbc.org>.

Chapter 3

Designing buildings and site layout

Lawrence J. Fennelly
Security Consultant

Proactive refers to being prepared even before an incident takes place. A proactive person takes the initiative and is prepared, unlike a reactive person.[1]

Introduction

Proactive crime prevention

Awareness allows a person to use more proactive crime prevention measures. Proactive crime prevention increases risks to criminals, who use situational or flexible techniques and tactics not only to stop criminal behavior but also to have them arrested and confined. Proactive crime prevention is approached through four general strategies that are as follows:

1. reducing the reward in the perception of the criminal;
2. removing excuses of a criminal's purpose for approaching you or your property;
3. increasing the effort required to commit the crime; and
4. Increasing the risk to the potential offender that he might be harmed and/or apprehended.

Building design

When designing, building, and installing engineered security controls, security practitioners must consider a variety of factors to ensure optimum results. While not doing so, they can leave access control systems prone to nuisance alarms, which can also lead to limited or no authorization controls at all. *Your objective should be to prevent penetration and provide authorized access through layered levels of security within your complex.*

Layered levels of security

The outer perimeter/outer protective layer can be a man-made barrier controlling both traffic and people flow. The inner layer contains the interior lobby and main entrance, turnstiles, revolving doors, handicap gates, elevators, emergency doors alarmed, and private occupied space. The inner protective layer contains biometrics, mirrors, and security surveillance systems (CCTV applications). The middle layer consists of exterior parts of the building.

Designing security and site layout

Designing security into a new complex should begin with interior security and then move outward to the exterior of the building(s) and then to the outer perimeter of the property.[2] Keep in mind the following points before you sit down with the architects:

---

1. https://www.differencebetween.com/difference-between-reactive-and-vs-proactive/
2. Fennelly, L.J., Perry, M.A., 2017. Physical Security: 150 Things You Should Know. Elsevier Publishers.

Handbook of Loss Prevention and Crime Prevention. DOI: https://doi.org/10.1016/B978-0-12-817273-5.00003-X

- Eliminate all but not the essential doors and windows; the idea should be few entrances, but many exits.
- Specification of fire-resistant material throughout the interior.
- Install fire, intrusion, and environmental control systems.
- Separate shipping and receiving areas, if possible.
- Ensure that the site meets ADA (Americans with Disabilities Act) requirements.
- Plan for adequate lighting around the perimeter, before, during, and after construction.
- Review architectural design plans and layout.
- Plan a site assessment/site survey.
- Have interior/exterior detection systems.
- Apply natural surveillance and other crime prevention through environmental design (CPTED) principles and strategies.
- Will there be security/protection officers as well as on-site supervision?
- Make employees aware of policy and procedures.
- Be educated about the physical security programs.
- Carry out budget planning and have 5-year plan.
- Audits/assessment/future needs.

The conclusion of your site layout report should reflect every aspect of the security operation and should have measures in place to deny, deter, delay, and detect.

Designing for security: a checklist

Some of the most important considerations that must be analyzed before designing a security protection system include the following factors[3]:

1. *Exterior perimeter protection*
   - **a.** a 6- to 8-ft chain-link fence (depending upon the application) with three strands of barbed wire at the top;
   - **b.** 8-ft walls and bushes not higher than 3 ft;
   - **c.** a video surveillance system;
   - **d.** security/protection officers (contract or proprietary);
   - **e.** energy-efficient exterior lighting (type, light-emitting diode);
   - **f.** leadership in energy and environmental design and high-performance building design; and
   - **g.** CPTED concepts and strategies.
2. *Entrance protection*
   - **a.** overhead and pedestrian doors (type, strength of door frame, etc.);
   - **b.** windows (locks, grills, etc.); and
   - **c.** no miscellaneous entry points (roof, basement, subterranean utility access, etc.).
3. *Interior protection*
   - **a.** security policies and procedures;
   - **b.** lighting;
   - **c.** key or access card control;
   - **d.** video surveillance system;
   - **e.** special situations (hours of operation);
   - **f.** inventory control (computer safeguards);
   - **g.** safe for high-value items and security-sensitive areas;
   - **h.** intrusion detection systems (alarm); and
   - **i.** local audible alarm versus central station alarm.
4. *Environmental considerations*
   - **a.** identify areas of building to be protected;
   - **b.** insurance requirements (Underwriters Laboratories listed etc.);
   - **c.** history of losses (loss experience);
   - **d.** type and demographics of employees;
   - **e.** opening and closing procedures;
   - **f.** fire and safety regulations and codes;

3. Fennelly, L.J., Perry, M.A., 2017. Physical Security: 150 Things You Should Know. Elsevier Publishers.

g. delivery and shipping policies/procedures; and
h. situations peculiar to the building or industry.

5. *Law enforcement involvement*
   a. transmission of alarm signal;
   b. central station alarm or direct connection to police station;
   c. municipal ordinances;
   d. police response time;
   e. neighborhood/business watch programs; and
   f. formulating partnerships.

Our crime prevention measures

Typical crime prevention measures[4] incorporated in accommodation for older people could include the following:

The building

Secure entry doors and accessible windows, including windows to apartment balconies, by the following steps:

1. main access control systems;
2. video entry system for residents' guests;
3. proximity key card locks to the residential aspects of the development and to each apartment; and
4. peep-holes on flat entrance doors plus adequate hardware.

The grounds

1. perimeter access controls and restrictions, such as to garages;
2. strategic use of a digital recording system;
3. landscaping, and tree and planting, to ensure natural surveillance and secure boundaries;
4. lighting across the development, such as pole lighting at the front, bollard lighting at the rear or in the garden, and wall lighting to both front and rear of the property;
5. fencing and gating, such as a minimum of 1.8 m high metal railings to secure the perimeter with matching powered access gates;
6. the removal of climbing points/recesses; and
7. covered cycle stands in visible locations.

Lighting/street lighting

Introduction

Appropriate lighting is frequently cited as being a feature, which people associate with enhanced safety.[5] In addition to facilitating surveillance, lighting is often used to beautify a site and make it attractive to people. Street lighting (under old standards) had little regard to pedestrian safety and was merely a tool for marking the position of the road ahead at night.

Intent

The intention is to promote the development of lighting plans and providing pedestrian and street lighting, which enhances the amenity of a site and which further promotes safety, by optimizing opportunities for surveillance and reducing feelings of fear and vulnerability, and to provide security for all road users.

Planning features

1. Lighting to meet minimum established standards.
2. Lighting should be directed onto areas accessed by people using the site and away from neighboring properties.
3. Lights should not be obscured by foliage and does not produce shadows.

---

4. https://www.pbctoday.co.uk/news/planning-construction-news/39271/39271/
5. https://www.kempsey.nsw.gov.au/development/pubs/crime-prevention-environmental-design-guidelines.pdf, modified and updated 2018.

4. Possible entrapment spots, such as loading bays, rubbish containers, and alleys, should be lit with vandal-resistant and energy-saving lighting.
5. Entrances and exits should be clearly identified via lighting. Lighting used in car parks should illuminate continuously in hours of darkness.
6. Lights should be in accordance with established standards and highly mounted on buildings/structures.
7. Street lighting should be evenly placed to ensure that the entire street is sufficiently lit and "black spots" are avoided.
8. Street lighting should be of an appropriate intensity and color of illumination, to ensure that sufficient light is cast to illuminate the streets and to permit visual surveillance of a street.
9. Street lighting should provide sufficient light spill onto footpaths and minimize light spill into residential windows.
10. Street lighting must be planned to permit effective and timely maintenance of nonfunctioning lights.
11. Street lighting should have effective and timely maintenance of nonfunctioning lights.

Chapter 4

The 10 principles of crime prevention*

Lawrence J. Fennelly
Security Consultant

The Crime Prevention Coalition defined crime prevention as "a pattern of attitudes and behaviors directed both at reducing the threat of crime and enhancing the sense of safety and security, to positively influence the quality of life in our society, and to develop environments where crime cannot flourish."

NCPI, 1970

Target hardening

Making your property harder for an offender to access.

- upgrading the locks on your doors, windows, sheds and outbuildings;
- fitting sash yammers to vulnerable doors and windows;
- using secure passwords to prevent criminals hacking your online accounts;
- fitting better doors, windows or shutters, window or door locks, alarms, screens in banks, government buildings, etc.;
- fencing systems;
- repairing damaged and derelict property; and
- fitting a wheel lock to a vehicle, chain to a bicycle/motorcycle, etc.

Target removal

Ensuring that a potential target is out of view.

- not leaving items, such as laptops, phones, keys, and bags, on view through your windows;
- putting your vehicle in the garage if you have one and not leaving valuables on display; and
- being cautious about what you post online as it may be used to identify or locate you offline.

Examples include the following:

1. removing radio and navigation system from parked cars;
2. keeping car keys out of sight, inside a pocket or drawer;
3. placing valuable items in a secure location; and
4. removing jewelry/valuables from shop windows at night.

*https://www.westyorkshire.police.uk/advice/10-principles-crime-prevention/10-principles-crime-prevention/10-principles-crime-prevention

Handbook of Loss Prevention and Crime Prevention. DOI: https://doi.org/10.1016/B978-0-12-817273-5.00004-1

FIGURE 4.1 Leaving a ladder under an open window is clearly an invitation plus an opportunity for the criminal.

Reducing the means

Removing items that may help commit an offense.

- not leaving tools and ladders in the garden and clearing up any rubble/bricks;
- keeping wheelie bins out of reach, as they may be a climbing aid or help transport items; and
- making sure that bricks and rubble are cleared up.

What could be changed to reduce the chance of a crime taking place (Fig. 4.1)?

The ladder provides easy access to the open window. Removing such items after cleaning, painting, or similar work would remove the means to commit crime. Think about how many times you have seen ladders or large *wheelie* bins in the proximity of commercial premises or even residences. These can easily be used as platforms. To remove this threat, they could be chained or locked up so that they cannot be moved.

Other examples of removing the means to commit crime are as follows:

- locking up tools and similar equipment;
- securing building materials, such as scaffolding; and
- using plastic drinking glasses in venues where there is a history or possibility of violence.

Reducing the payoff

Reducing the profit and gain the criminal can make from the offense.

- security marking your property;
- marking your property in such a way that others will not want to buy from the thief (Operation Id.);
- not buying property you believe or suspect to be stolen;
- using a safe to reduce the amount of cash held in a till; and
- using a replica in shop display.

Access control

Restricting access to sites, buildings, or parts of sites and buildings.

- looking at measures that will control access to a location, a person, or object;
- locking your doors and windows to both your house and your vehicle;
- ensuring that fencing, hedges, walls, and other boundary treatments are in a good state of repair, see landscape security concept next; and
- putting a security system in place at a commercial site (entry barriers, security guards, and ID cards).

FIGURE 4.2 Intercoms and door bells today come quipped with security video system.

There are many forms of *access control*. While some can be quite complex, others are relatively simple (Fig. 4.2). Examples include the following:

- door locks and making sure doors are shut;
- identity cards;
- access card systems or push button keypad;
- entry phones (Intercom);
- baggage screening; and
- separate entries and exits.

Surveillance

Making sure that criminals would be visible if they carried out a crime.

Improving surveillance around homes, businesses, or public places to deter criminals.

- removing high hedges/fences at the front of your home that allows an offender to work unseen;
- consider adding security surveillance system (CCTV) to a commercial site or public place; and
- establishing a Neighborhood Watch Scheme in your street.

Unlike any of the other principles, there are three types of surveillance, which are as follows:

- natural,
- formal, and
- informal.

In common with the other principles, there are various methods and techniques that can be applied.

Natural surveillance—involves modifying the existing surroundings to increase visibility.

It can include:

1. pruning or removing shrubbery;
2. improving or installing lighting;
3. changing the height of fences; and
4. placing a playground area so that it overlooks nearby homes and is overlooked by those homes.

Environmental change

Changing the environment of a building, a site, an estate, or a town to reduce opportunities for committing crime.

Ensuring your property and wider community looks cared for:

- ensuring that graffiti and domestic/commercial waste are cleared up, within 24 hours;
- reporting issues with fly-tipping or broken street lights to the relevant authority; and
- working with the police and local authority to close a footpath.

The emphasis is on putting a range of preventive measures in place at the planning stage of a development, irrespective of whether this is of a commercial or residential nature. Crime prevention through environmental design (CPTED) can be used in existing environments as well as in new developments.

It can include a whole range of features:

1. visibility/surveillance;
2. target hardening;
3. street and pathway layout; and
4. lighting.

Incorporating crime prevention measures into a new housing development at the planning stage could ensure the following:

1. All doors and windows have good quality locks.
2. Planting is kept to a minimum to increase surveillance.
3. The estate has an open design which also increases surveillance.

Rule setting

The introduction of legislation and codes of conduct which set out what is acceptable behavior.

- changing our habits by setting rules and positioning signage in appropriate locations;
- introducing a rule that the last person entering/leaving should lock the door and remove the keys;
- informing visitors to commercial sites that they must report to reception on arrival; and
- informing users that a particular site is closed between certain times and should not be accessed.

The following are some examples of rule setting:

1. laws enacted by law enforcement;
2. wearing of ID badges/visitor passes;
3. internal rules within businesses;
4. the limiting of alcohol consumption in public places; and
5. no trespassing signs prohibiting access to buildings or certain areas in buildings.

Increase the chances of being caught

Anything that slows a criminal down or increases their risk of being caught.

- making use of dusk to dawn security lighting is in place and in working order;
- using good quality security surveillance system (CCTV) and/or alarm systems, especially on commercial sites and public places; and
- upgrading security to delay an offender, meaning they have to spend more time to gain access.

Preventive methods are more effective if criminals risk being caught. Anything that slows down a criminal or increases the chance of detection is an effective method of prevention. This means that good "target hardening" increases the time it takes to enter a building and increases the chances of being spotted. The longer it takes to commit an offense, the more vulnerable a criminal will feel.

Increasing the chance of a criminal being caught can be achieved by:

1. proper management of CCTV systems;
2. lighting that makes intruders/criminals more visible;
3. making sure security equipment operates properly;

4. alerting offenders to the fact that CCTV systems and alarms are being used;
5. publicizing successes in detecting criminals;
6. running youth diversionary schemes with partner agencies; and
7. referring offenders to drug rehabilitation programs.

Deflecting offenders

Deterring an offender or deflecting their intention.

- using timer switches to make our homes look occupied if vacant after the hours of darkness.

Diverting the offenders and potential offenders from committing crime.

- This involves agencies working with young people and offenders to influence standards, thinking, and attitudes. The aim is to prevent potential offenders turning to crime.
- This involves agencies working with young people and offenders to influence standards, thinking, and attitudes. The aim is to prevent potential offenders turning to crime.

Examples include the following:

- education and schools programs;
- youth groups and organizations; and
- providing training and work experience.

This method of preventing crime is undertaken by neighborhood policing teams, school liaison officers, and crime prevention officers, working in partnership with Government agencies, tenants' associations, schools, and sporting associations, among others.

Conclusion

Modern Crime Prevention, Home Office, United Kingdom, March 2016 report[1]:

1. *opportunity*—removing or designing out opportunities to offend, offline, and online;
2. *character*—intervening early with those exposed to factors that might lead to a high propensity to commit crime;
3. *effectiveness of the criminal justice system (CJS)*—ensuring that the CJS acts as a powerful deterrent to would-be offenders; and
4. *profit*—making it harder for criminals, particularly organized criminals, to benefit financially from their crimes.

Data and technology are not drivers of crime in themselves. Rather, they are tools that are critical to successfully preventing crime and have valuable applications across all six drivers.

As the preceding chapters have highlighted, sharing the right security information with consumers and working with manufacturers to design crime risks out of products and services are keys to reducing opportunities.

Drugs—publish a new drug strategy, which builds on the approach published in 2010 to restrict the supply of drugs and tackle the organized crime behind the drugs trade, prevent drug misuse in our communities, help people resist getting involved in drugs, and support people dependent on drugs through treatment and recovery.

Alcohol—making the nighttime economy safe so that people can consume alcohol safely without fear of becoming a victim of alcohol-related crime or disorder, enabling local economies to grow.

Reduce property crime:

Remember all of these can be done through the formulation of community partnerships. Partnerships are often formed in response to a rash of crimes that target a particular location. *Crime through CPTED recommendation, focused on the physical environment strategies, such as turning troubled area's around. Partnership holds a great deal of promise and it works. your object is always to reduce criminal opportunity.*

1. Tap into the energy and idealism of youth. Involve young people in all vandalism prevention efforts.
2. Organize a graffiti clean-up project in your neighborhood.
3. Work with Neighborhood Watch and ask the city or a local business for cleaning supplies and paint.

1. Modern Crime Prevention, Home Office UK, March 2016 report.

4. Work with schools or the arts community to paint murals on areas that are vulnerable to graffiti. Make it a contest for teens.
5. Adopt a street or park, perhaps in cooperation with a church or business.
6. Plant trees, bushes, and flowers. Repair equipment and install trash containers. Organize a monthly park patrol to clean up litter and keep an eye on things.
7. Ask police or a city agency to start a hotline for reporting vandalism.
8. Have a community meeting on vandalism to discuss its victims, costs, and solutions.
9. Make certain that city or town officials promptly remove abandoned car.

Chapter 5

International crime prevention

Lawrence J. Fennelly
Security Consultant

Crime is down but it is changing. What we might call "traditional" crimes like burglary, vehicle theft and street violence have more than halved. But in recent years, more and more victims have found the courage to come forward and report crimes that many previously suffered in silence, such as rape, domestic abuse and the sexual exploitation of children.

As with so many of the challenges we face as a society, the prevention of crime is better than the cure. Stopping crime before it happens, and preventing the harm caused to victims, must be preferable to picking up the pieces afterwards.

The Rt. Hon. Theresa May launched the new Strategy at the 2016 International Crime and Policing Conference in London.

Introduction

The prevention of crime is an international activity conducted by many agencies in order to provide safe communities. Within this chapter, we will show what is going on in a variety of counties, and how and what they are doing to reduce crime.

Principles of opportunity reduction

1. Criminal behavior is learned behavior.[1]
2. Reducing criminal opportunity reduces the opportunity to learn criminal behavior.
3. Criminal opportunity can be lessened by improved security measures (target hardening) and by increasing the level of surveillance on the part of the community.
4. Long-range crime prevention will not be achieved unless criminal opportunities are reduced either on a local or national bases.
5. Security is in a pivotal position and as such they should be highly trained in crime prevention and crime prevention through environmental design (CPTED) and becomes involved in the preplanning of any community design or activity, where their services will be later requested.

Basic principles for the prevention of crime

United Nations

- *Government leadership* at all levels is required to create and maintain an institutional framework for effective crime prevention.[2]
- *Socioeconomic development and inclusion* refer to the need to integrate crime prevention into relevant social and economic policies and to focus on the social integration of at-risk communities, children, families, and youth.
- *Cooperation and partnerships* between government ministries and authorities, civil society organizations, the business sector, and private citizens are required given the wide-ranging nature of the causes of crime and the skills and responsibilities required to address them.

---

1. Authored by Wil Rykert, NCPI Director, 1978, University of Louisville.
2. Guidelines for the Prevention of Crime, ECOSOC Resolution 2002/13, Annex.

Handbook of Loss Prevention and Crime Prevention. DOI: https://doi.org/10.1016/B978-0-12-817273-5.00005-3

- *Sustainability and accountability* can only be achieved if adequate resources to establish and sustain programs and evaluation are made available, and clear accountability for funding, implementation, evaluation, and achievement of planned results is established.
- *Knowledge-based* strategies, policies, and programs need to be based on a broad multidisciplinary foundation of knowledge, together with evidence regarding specific crime problems, their causes, and proven practices.
- *Human rights/rule of law/culture of lawfulness*—the rule of law and those human rights—are recognized in international instruments to which Member States are parties must be respected in all aspects of crime prevention, and a culture of lawfulness actively promoted.
- *Interdependency* refers to the need for national crime prevention diagnoses and strategies to take into account, where appropriate, the links between local criminal problems and international organized crime.
- The principle of *differentiation* calls for crime prevention strategies to pay due regard to the different needs of men and women and consider the special needs of vulnerable members of society.

Scotland

We seek to support, develop, and rationalize the current partnerships involving Police Scotland and the various public, private, and third sector organizations.[3]

How we do this:

- Mental health, places of safety, and suicide prevention—we have helped shape the new national suicide prevention strategy and are working with partners to develop effective, efficient, and sustainable approaches to dealing with "people in distress" who impact heavily on critical services including the Police.
- Neighbourhood Watch Scotland—it is currently working with a number of partners including Police Scotland on a web-based message alert system. This is being piloted currently in Rutherglen with a view to facilitating Scotland wide roll out. This system allows messages to be sent to participants giving them updates on crime trends and intelligence in their area allowing them to carryout crime prevention measures or report information to the police.
- Scottish Business Resilience Centre—they are a unique organization comprising contributions and secondments from Police Scotland, Scottish Government, Scottish Fire and Rescue, major banks, industries, investors, and private membership. They provide their members with a one-stop shop for business security services and advice.
- Scottish Community Safety Network—it is the national forum for officers who are responsible for the strategic development of community safety at both local and national levels. We contribute to this shared vision that encourages the effective development of policy, partnership working, and effective practice for community safety in Scotland.

South Africa

Before leaving your location

- Get off your phone while approaching your vehicle.[4]
- Take a stroll around your vehicle to confirm that there is no one lurking around or in your vehicle.
- If your child drives with you, let them sit behind the driver of the vehicle. This will ensure that in the event of an incident, the driver can remove and shield the child.
- Ensure your number plates are both on the vehicle and no papers are stuck to the rear or front windows of your vehicle. This is a trend used by suspects to lure you into stopping while your vehicle is running to either retrieve the number plate or remove the papers.
- Place all valuable items out of sight either under the seat or in the boot of your vehicle. This can also help prevent smash-and-grabs.
- Ensure your windows and doors are closed and locked before leaving.
- Plan your route before departure.

---

3. http://www.scotland.police.uk/assets/pdf/138327/150739/police-scotland-crime-prevention-strategy?view = Standard
4. https://brakpanherald.co.za/162465/crime-prevention-tips-help-stay-safe-road/

National Crime Prevention Strategy (Canada)

Overview of programs[5]:

- Associated subjects
  Aggressiveness in children Alcoholism—Prevention Alternative schools British Columbia Bullying in schools Canada Crime Crime prevention Crime prevention—Evaluation Criminal justice, Administration of—Evaluation Drug abuse—Treatment Evaluation Evidence-based social work High school dropouts Juvenile delinquency—Prevention Juvenile delinquents—Prevention Legislators National Crime Prevention Strategy (NCPS) (Canada) Newfoundland and Labrador—St. John's Problem youth—Services for—Evaluation Schools—Safety measures School violence School violence—Prevention Social planning Substance abuse Substance abuse—Treatment Violence—Prevention Women—Violence against Youth—Alcohol use Youth—Drug use.

Security checklist: Cheshire Police Department in the United Kingdom

Secure your home

Here is a list of some of the things you can do to improve the security around your home[6]:

- If you are replacing or fitting new doors and windows, get ones that are certified to *British Standard BS7950* (windows) or *PAS 24-1* (doors).
- Fit *mortise locks* (Kitemarked BS3621) to all front and back doors and locks to all downstairs windows or windows that are easy to reach.
- Keep your *house and car keys safe* and away from doors and windows.
- Fit a *burglar alarm*, but make sure it is installed properly and works.
- Keep your *garage and garden shed locked* with proper security locks, and keep any tools secure and out of sight.
- Trim back any plants or hedges that a burglar could *hide behind*.
- Make sure you have up-to-date *home insurance*.

Why a National Crime Prevention Strategy in South Africa

High levels of crime pose a serious threat to our emergent democracy.[7] Violent crime often leads to a tragic loss of life and injury, and the loss of possessions and livelihood due to crime is incalculable. Crime results in the deprivation of the rights and dignity of citizens and poses a threat to peaceful resolution of differences and rightful participation of all in the democratic process.

Crime casts fear into the hearts of South Africans from all walks of life and prevents them from taking their rightful place in the development and growth of our country. It inhibits our citizens from communicating with one another freely, from engaging in economic activity and prevents entrepreneurs and investors from taking advantage of the opportunities that our country offers.

The rights and freedoms that the constitution entrenches are threatened every time a citizen becomes a victim of crime.

For these reasons the government regards the prevention of crime as a national priority. This applies not only to the Cabinet, and the departments concerned with security and justice, but also to all other national departments which are able to make a contribution to a reduction in crime levels. Provincial governments will work together with us to implement the NCPS.

We accept that some of the causes of crime are deep rooted and related to the history and socioeconomic realities of our society. For this reason a comprehensive strategy must go beyond providing only effective policing. It must also provide for mobilization and participation of civil society in assisting to address crime.

To effectively reduce crime, it is necessary to transform and reorganize government and facilitate real community participation. We need to weave a new social fabric, robust enough to withstand the stresses of rapid change in a newborn society. To expect this to happen too quickly is to sabotage proper planning and solid construction of new criminal justice machinery.

5. https://novascotia.ca/just/Prevention/
6. https://www.cheshire.police.uk/advice-and-support/home-safety-and-security/
7. https://www.gov.za/documents/national-CRIME-prevention-strategy-summary

Most fundamentally this strategy requires that government moves beyond a mode of crisis management and reaction. Government must ensure that effective planning and sustainable success in reducing crime will reach well into the next century.

What is community policing?

Community policing in Ireland is a partnership based, proactive, community-orientated style of policing.[8] It is focused on crime prevention, problem-solving, and law enforcement, with a view to building trust and enhancing the quality of life of the entire community.

Community Gardaí engage in community partnership building, to enhance delivery of the Garda service within communities. Such engagement is a joint process requiring An Garda Síochána and community groups, to work together, to improve the "quality of life" of people in those areas, and to reflect their needs and priorities. The establishment of partnerships at local level should be seen as a cooperative effort to facilitate problem-solving. The problems presented to and faced by An Garda Síochána cannot be solved by the Gardaí working alone. Crime and the prevention of crime is everybody's business.

Community Gardaí are required to be proactive, in building positive partnerships, through initiatives, such as Neighbourhood Watch, Community Alert, Campus Watch, Hospital Watch, Garda Clinics, Supporting Safer Communities Campaigns, and Garda Schools Programme. Flexible engagement practices are required to cater for individuals, community groups and can ultimately lead to a community being empowered. The establishment of partnerships at local level should be seen as a cooperative effort to facilitate problem-solving.

Our community policing objectives

- To engage in partnership opportunities (e.g., JPC, Neighbourhood Watch, Community Alert, Local Policing Fora, various retail fora, Business Watch).
- To provide an accessible and visible garda service to communities.
- To establish effective engagement processes to meet the needs of local communities and provide feedback to communities.
- To use problem-solving initiatives, devised in partnership with communities and local agencies, to tackle crime, drugs, public disorder, and antisocial behavior, through targeted enforcement, crime prevention, and reduction initiatives.
- To engage in a community-focused approach to provide solutions that reduces the fear of crime.
- To engage meaningfully with young people to develop and foster positive relationships and promote personal and community safety.
- To enhance communication strategies that articulate community policing objectives and outcomes.
- To be accountable to the community we serve.[9]
- To work in partnership with other agencies ensure safety on our streets and roads.

The Queensland Australia Crime Prevention

Strategy outlines six key principles to guide all crime prevention activities in Queensland Australia. These are:

- community involvement and ownership,
- working better and working together,
- a comprehensive approach,
- a focus on people and places,
- value for money, and
- a focus on outcomes and on what works.

The strategy identifies following five key goals:

- strengthening communities,

8. https://www.garda.ie/en/Crime-Prevention/Community-Policing/
9. https://www.yellowpages.com.au/content/if/extract/contentstore/2014/11/28/10/08/1081201115/1/crimepreventionmanual.pdf

- supporting families, children, and young people,
- reducing violence,
- enhancing public safety, and
- dealing with offending.

It is widely acknowledged that the interface—or partnership—between government and local communities in the planning and management of crime prevention activities is integral to the successful implementation of the Queensland Crime Prevention Strategy.

The establishment of community–government crime prevention partnerships recognizes and values:

- the body of knowledge held by the community and its importance in developing local crime prevention plans,
- the existing activities undertaken by communities to address issues of concern, and
- diversity within communities.

Websites: http://www.unodc.org/unodc/en/urban-safety/crime-prevention.html

Scotland

Crime prevention through better design advice to be given at Scotland's Royal Highland Show

Crime prevention advice on how farmers and the rural community in Scotland can make their businesses and properties more secure will be given by officers from Police Scotland attending the Royal Highland Show, at Ingliston Showground, 21–24 June.[10]

The officers specializing in rural crime will be staffing an exhibition stand sponsored by Secured by Design (SBD), the United Kingdom's national police crime prevention initiative. Alongside the stand will be a working farm tractor decked out as a police vehicle, complete with flashing blue lights.

It is the first time that SBD has taken part in the show, which is expected to attract more than 250,000 visitors over the 4 days.

By working alongside Police Forces around the country, SBD seeks to reduce crime by introducing proven crime prevention measures at the planning stage and by encouraging companies that have security-related products to achieve SBD's Police Preferred Specification standard. SBD has more than 650 companies that have achieved this accreditation.

As the Police Service itself is unable to recommend specific products, SBD can act as an effective gatekeeper and signpost people to companies and products that meet SBD's high-security standards for deterring crime, such as being sufficiently robust to resist attack by casual or opportunist housebreakers.

Detective Chief Superintendent John McKenzie, chairman of SPARC—the Scottish Partnership Against Rural Crime—said: "We are grateful to Secured by Design for sponsoring our stand at the show, as it allows us to put across many crime prevention messages to a huge audience. We know that 'one size does not fit all' when it comes to preventing crime, and therefore we will be showing visitors to the stand the many ways they can protect themselves from criminality."

> *"That could be by helping them identify better design of their farm estate and what physical security measures they can take such as using gates, fences, floodlighting or CCTV, or online through the cyber safety clinics we are holding on the stand each day."*

Stuart Ward, National Designing Out Crime Manager, Police Scotland, said the idea behind the stand is to raise awareness of crime reduction measures that can be applied to rural and farming communities, as SBD is the only way for companies to obtain police accreditation for security-related products in the United Kingdom.

He said, "By combining proven crime prevention techniques and SBD-accredited products, we can reduce the risks from criminal activity within these areas, and we will also be raising awareness of tracking devices and equipment security such as fuel theft alarms."

The show is the biggest event in Scotland for farming and rural community. It will have around 1000 exhibitors and 900 competitions to attract visitors.

---

10. http://www.securedbydesign.com/news/crime-prevention-through-better-design-advice-to-be-given-at-scotlands-royal-highland-show/

SBD is self-funding through its Member Companies supplying robust security-related products to the construction industry, businesses, and consumers. SBD seeks to achieve sustainable reductions in crime to enable people to live in a safer society.

Designing out graffiti—Australia

Designing out graffiti is about applying CPTED principles with graffiti reduction and prevention in mind. The WA Police Force Graffiti Team has developed an information resource for community members and asset owners on how to apply these principles to *design out graffiti.* Click here to download the designing out graffiti booklet.

The Graffiti Team has also developed a series of information guides on specific aspects of *Designing out Graffiti.* Click https://www.goodbyegraffiti.wa.gov.au/Prevent%20Graffiti to download the following guides:

- Designing out Graffiti—Lighting and Surveillance
- Designing out Graffiti—Landscaping and Planting
- Designing out Graffiti—Protective Surfaces and Rapid Removal

Conducting a CPTED audit may assist in identifying areas where *Designing out Graffiti* principles can be implemented. Click here to download the CPTED Audit Checklist.

Our crime prevention measures

Typical crime prevention measures incorporated in accommodation for older people could include the ones in the following subsections.[11]

The building

- Secure entry doors and accessible windows, including windows to apartment balconies.
- Main access control systems.
- Video entry system for residents' guests.
- Proximity key card locks to the residential aspects of the development and to each apartment.
- Spyholes on flat entrance doors.

The grounds

- Perimeter access controls and restrictions, such as to car parks.
- Strategic use of CCTV.
- Landscaping, and tree and planting, to ensure natural surveillance and secure boundaries.
- Lighting across the development, such as pole lighting at the front, bollard lighting at the rear or in the garden, and wall lighting to both front and rear of the property.
- Fencing and gating, such as a minimum of 1.8 m high metal railings to secure the perimeter with matching powered access gates.
- The removal of climbing points/recesses.
- Covered cycle stands in visible locations.

Upton village, Northampton

We advised on security at an Extra Care Village built as part of a larger development of 1020 private homes and affordable housing and up to 700 m^2 of retail units at Upton, to the south west of Northampton.

Upton is a partnership between Northampton Borough Council, English Partnerships, and the Prince's Foundation for Building Community, which promotes best practice in sustainable urban growth to ensure strict environmental and building design standards.

11. https://www.pbctoday.co.uk/news/planning-construction-news/39271/39271/

Developed by a number of different developers over the years, it is modeled on Poundbury, an urban extension to Dorchester, which was built from 1993 on the principles of architecture and urban planning as advocated by the Prince of Wales in a Vision of Britain.

The care home achieved full SBD security compliance in 2017, marking the climax of our long association with the whole development, which began prior to outline planning permission in 1997.

How Secured by Design works

SBD-trained police officers and staff, known principally as Designing Out Crime Officers, liaise with architects, developers, and local authority planning officers on new build developments at the outset to incorporate proven crime prevention techniques.

These measures encompass layout and landscaping, such as to increase surveillance and limit through movement, to make criminals feel uncomfortable with a greater likelihood of them being seen and challenged.

We are also working to increase the physical security of the buildings by encouraging the use of a wide range of security products that meet our Police Preferred Specification standards. For example, our accredited doors, windows, and locks, which are sufficiently robust to resist physical attack from casual or opportunistic burglars.

Northern Ireland

Policing with the Community Branch has particular responsibility for the following[12]:

- *Behavioral standards*—Promoting a style of policing which demonstrates collaborative decision-making, accountability and courtesy, fairness and respect on a daily basis in our everyday interactions with colleagues and the public be they a victim, offender, suspect, witness, or bystander. This responsibility is delivered by ensuring new policies and procedures reflect these behavioral standards and by assessing compliance against these standards through quality of service assessment delivered through satisfaction surveys.
- *Reducing vulnerability*—This involves ensuring that the needs of individuals who have particular characteristics as a member of a protected grouping are recognized and attention is paid to addressing these needs when developing new policies and procedures. This particular area of responsibility dovetails with section 75 monitoring and compliance responsibilities which PWC Branch leads on for PSNI.
- *Community planning and engagement*—PWC Branch provides central advice and guidance on community planning and strategic engagement for districts and departments. This advice and direction reflect international best practice and is informed by high level engagement with key individuals and partners in the community and voluntary sector and with statutory representatives.
- *Reflectiveness and representativeness*—PWC Branch provides advice, guidance, and practical support on outreach to districts and departments to try to improve the percentage of persons from underrepresented groups working in and across PSNI in various roles and functions. Particular efforts are focused on increasing the representation of Catholics and women in the uniformed ranks.
- *Crime prevention*—PWC provides central advice and coordination to District Crime Prevention officers on crime prevention campaigns and crime prevention design advice.

Websites: http://www.unodc.org/unodc/en/urban-safety/crime-prevention.html
Video: https://youtu.be/jZ7oeAQcHmc

12. https://www.psni.police.uk/inside-psni/our-departments/district-policing-command/policing-with-the-community/

Chapter 6

Crime prevention glossary of terms

Lawrence J. Fennelly and Marianna A. Perry
Security Consultant

The CPTED Concept is the proper design and effective use of the building environment can lead to a reduction in the fear of crime and the incidence of crime and to an improvement in the quality of life.

Dr. C. Ray Jeffrey

Introduction

The following list of terms are included to assist the reader and to facilitate common terminology usage. It should be noted that the definitions of the terms listed reflect their utilization in the area of community crime prevention.

"Design out crime" is a concept that first appeared in the 1930s in the United States and was developed into theories such as the "defensible space" theory by Oscar Newman in the 1970s and the "broken windows" theory by Wilson and Kelling. Broadened understanding of the design out crime concept led to the establishment of international organizations such as the European Design Out Crime Association.[1] Also in the 1970s we saw the development of crime prevention through environmental design (CPTED) by C. Ray Jefferies and Tim Crowe. This concept has developed during the past 50 years into what it is today.

Security awareness.[2] It is broken down into three parts, education and imparting of knowledge, training to develop security skills. *So what* is *security awareness?* The method through which an individual is made conscious of, and accepts, his or her own role and responsibilities in the protection of the assets of an organization. It should engender protective attitudes and behaviors—both personally and on behalf of the organization.

Awareness and raising consciousness. An effective security awareness program is NOT a process of waving the big stick a series of unplanned and unrelated communications about security issues knowing the name of the security officer, having a copy of the facility security policy manual in the desk drawer not just limited to staff.

Behavior modification. A change in behavior patterns brought about by education or training in crime prevention principles and/or techniques.

Broken windows theory. A policy-oriented explanation of crime, which states that minor signs of disorder in a neighborhood, when left unchecked, can result in more severe disorder and ultimately serious crime. The term comes from a 1982 article in *The Atlantic Monthly* by James Q. Wilson and George L. Kelling.

Burglary. The unlawful entry or trespass within a structure with the intent to commit a crime therein (related terms: breaking and entering. Housebreaking and unlawful entry).

Citizen awareness. A state in which the members of the community are cognizant of a situation (in this case, a crime risk) and possible solutions or methods of dealing with it (related term: citizen education).

Citizen crime reporting. It includes encouraging citizens, either witnesses or victims, to report crimes and assist police in apprehension of the offenders. Should provide procedures for making such reports accurate and useful (related tern: community involvement).

Citizen community patrols. A concept in which residents of a community (residential, business, etc.) organize into a group and provide security patrols of the environs of that community.

1. https://www.uitp.org/design-out-crime-increase-feelings-safety
2. Rick Draper, update of POA Manual on Awareness, 2017.

Handbook of Loss Prevention and Crime Prevention. DOI: https://doi.org/10.1016/B978-0-12-817273-5.00006-5

Community action programs. Programs undertaken by the residents of a community with specific goals in mind (related term: community involvement).

Community crime prevention. Direct involvement of a single sector or a combination of sectors in a community in the planning, funding, implementation, and operation of a crime prevention program, usually stressing cooperation with the local criminal justice system (related term: community involvement).

Community anticrime efforts. Actions taken by the members of a community to prevent crime or to increase the amount of cooperation with the police in reporting crime.

Community policing. Work with the community. The police must establish a partnership with the community, in order to cooperatively address its problems and needs. Community Consultative Groups, with representatives from all communities identified, are an effective and successful way to initiate and carry out communication and cooperation between the police and their community.

Crime analysis

It can be defined as the study of daily reports and crime to determine the location, time of day, special characteristics, and similarities to other crimes as well as any significant data that will or may identify the existence of patterns of criminal behavior.

Crime control program. Various programs dealing with the control of prevention of specific types of crime, based on patterns of occurrences and known officers and victims.

Crime displacement. Theory that states that criminals denied the opportunity to commit crimes in a certain area will move to other areas or to other crimes.

Crime prediction. A system of predicting future crime risk patterns and trends using past patterns as trends as indicators.

Crime prevention. The anticipation, recognition and analysis of a crime risk, and the initiation of some action to remove or reduce it.

Crime prevention training. The training of crime prevention practitioners in the theory and principles of crime prevention.

Crime resistance. A term used by the Federal Bureau of Investigation and other law enforcement and criminal justice agencies, which is synonymous with crime prevention.

Crime-specific countermeasures. Specific strategies that are intended to prevent certain crimes through target hardening (e.g., an antiburglary campaign).

CPTED. The design or redesign of a building or place to reduce crime opportunity and fear of crime through the specific application of strategies and tactics to reduce crime opportunity through environmental design; these strategies involve surveillance, access control, territoriality, maintenance, and place management. The tactics of CPTED are further specified into natural, mechanical, and procedural components. CPTED plans are best developed and implemented by multidisciplinary teams. The three Ds of CPTED are design, designation, and definition.

Defensible space. A term for the range of mechanisms—real and symbolic barriers, strongly defined areas of influence, improved opportunities for surveillance—that combine to bring an environment under the control of its residents (related term: environmental design).

Deterrence. A concept which holds that the threat of punishment or the denial of opportunity will forestall the criminal or delinquent act (related term: punitive crime prevention).

Designing out crime. The aim of "designing out crime" is to reduce the vulnerability of people and property to crime by removing opportunities, which may be unwittingly provided by the built environment. It also aims to reduce fear of crime, and in doing so, improves people's quality of life.

Displacement of crime

Can you move crime from one location to another? Yes, you can. I know criminologist will say show me the data and we cannot. However, talk to veteran officers who have been working the various sectors for years and they will tell you that they have done it. Years ago in a dormitory that had only one entrance and individual was stealing wallets and cash from unlocked rooms. This was going on night after night, so we put a cruiser out front of the dormitory, and every night around 3:00 a.m. the car was back a few spaces then forward. Crime stopped. Was it luck or skill. I know that the cruiser was a deterrent. If the police car is outside then the officer must be inside, and there is a likelihood I will get caught the crook is thinking, so he goes to another location.

We know that drug dealing and prostitution are burning problems, so by closing off the street and preventing traffic from going up and down the street, the individuals will move to another location and be arrested on the new street.

Steven P. Lab states in his book titled Crime Prevention seventh edition "There is little reason to ever expect total displacement of a crime, regardless of the type of displacement considered." He then discusses the various types of displacement, that is, territorial, temporal, tactical, target, and functional; he further states that although it is not 100% at the same time, they show that displacement does occur.

Dynamic risk. A risk situation that carries the potential for both benefit and cost or loss. Normally considered to be the type of risk that is inherent in doing business (related terms: risk management, risk assessment, and pure risk).

Environmental design. Selectively creating variables in the planning, design, and the effective use of physical space to create physical and social conditions, which will promote citizen surveillance, reduce criminal opportunity, and increase the risk of apprehension arrest.

Environmental security

"Environmental security" is an urban planning and design process that integrates crime prevention with neighborhood design and urban development. It is a comprehensive environmental design approach that combines traditional techniques of crime prevention with newly developed theories and techniques. Environmental security is not only concerned with the reduction of crime but also the fear of crime, since it has become recognized that the fear of crime is equally serious and is a major contributor of the urban decay process.

The main idea behind environmental security is that our urban environments can be designed or redesigned to reduce criminal opportunities and the fear of crime. We need not resort to building fortresses that result in the deterioration in the quality of urban life.

Enterprise security risk management (ESRM). Defined by our security partner as ESRM is a strategic security program management approach that ties an organizations security practices to its mission and goals using globally established and accepted risk management principles.

ESRM recognizes that security responsibilities are shared by both security and business leadership, but that all final security decision-making is the responsibility of the business leaders. The role of the security leader in ESRM is to manage security vulnerabilities to enterprise assets in a risk decision-making partnership with the organization leaders in charge of those assets.[3]

Holistic

This concept is not new. It is really what we both have been saying all along about integrating all of the components of the security process so that they all work together for the benefit of the whole organization and not compartmentalizing individual parts of security.

Hot spots

We look at hot spots that have become law enforcement's predominant tool for crime analysis. The use of hot spots is convenient as they show both the density and intensity of crimes in a given location and are ideal to summarize areas of concern and the types of incidents that occur.

Information transfer. A means by which professionals and practitioners exchange ideas, concepts, and programmatical information to facilitate the development and the practice of crime prevention.

Information transfer. A means by which professionals and practitioners exchange ideas, concepts, and programmatical information to facilitate the development and the practice of crime prevention.

Master plan and best practices of crime prevention through environmental design

In a recent security assessment, we did the company wanted a master plan for their property. So we included a current set of best practices that fit the situation.

A master plan should also dovetail the corporation's mission statement. Master planning is a catalyst for defining a vision for all aspects of service.

3. ASIS Website Apr. 29, 2018.

Mechanical crime prevention. Concept development based upon opportunity reduction (emphasis on target hardening).

Media campaigns. The use of mass media (radio, television, social media, newspapers, etc.) as part of a public awareness program.

Neighborhood watch. A community action program administered by the National Sheriff's Association which encourages neighborhood residents to organize with a purpose of neighborhood security and cooperation with the criminal justice system (related terms: block watch, dog watch, and community action programs).

Operation identification. A program in which citizens mark property for identification purposes. Intent of program is to facilitate the recovery and return of stolen property, and to provide a deterrent to potential offenders. It is important of inventory your property as well as taking photos on your camera or iPad (related term: property identification).

Physical crime prevention. Prevention of anticipated crimes or delinquencies by placing obstacles in the way of potential offenders so that it becomes difficult or impossible for them to perpetrate the offense (related term: opportunity reduction).

Private security. Self-employed individuals and privately funded business entities and organizations who provide security-related services to a restricted clientele for a fee, for the individual or entity that retains or employs them, or for themselves in order to protect their persons, private property, or interests from various hazards (related terms: security systems and deterrence).

Property identification. See operation identification.

Pure risk. A risk situation in which there is no possibility for benefit, only cost or loss (e.g., fire and flood) (related terms: risk management, risk assessment, and dynamic risk).

Residential security. Security concepts utilizing mechanical electronic, procedural, and other methods to protect the home from crime and other hazards (related terms: physical crime prevention, operation identification, and security systems).

Risk assessment

It is the process of assessing security-related risks from internal and external threats to an entity, its assets, and its personnel. This is done by:

- getting the facts by conducting a threat, risk, and CPTED assessment;
- analyzing the facts;
- making a decision about what works best for that particular environment;
- implementing the security measures;
- developing a "culture" of security; and
- ensuring there is administration "buy in" and that safety/security policies and procedures are enforced.

Risk management. The anticipation, recognition and appraisal of a risk, and the initiation of some action to remove the risk or reduce the potential loss from it to an acceptable level (NCPI) (related terms: dynamic risk. Pure risk and risk assessment).

Robbery. Unlawful and forcible taking of property in the possession of another, from his person or immediate presence, and against his will by use of violence or threat of violence, and with the intent to steal.

Security codes and ordinances. Laws which require that buildings, recreational facilities, streets, and other public areas meet certain security requirements (related terms: environment design. Defensible space, alarm, and deadbolt laws).

Security surveys. Surveys of residences, businesses, public buildings and other facilities for the purpose of evaluating the degree of security present in order to make recommendations for physical and procedural improvement (related term: vulnerability analysis and risk assessment).

Security systems. Methods and materials employed to ensure the protection of persons and premises against encroachment (related terms: alarm systems, security hardware, lighting, and target hardening).

Street lighting. A concern to the crime prevention practitioner. Street lighting is an important component of environmental security (related terms: defensible space, deterrents, and environmental design).

Situation crime prevention incorporates other crime prevention and law enforcement strategies in an effort to focus on place-specific crime problems. Results and objectives: reduce violent crime, reduce property crime, displacement of crime, and eliminate the threats and risk. Contrary to traditional criminological approaches that have mainly been concerned with explaining why certain individuals are more likely to engage in criminal behavior compared to others, situational crime prevention focuses not upon changing offenders, but on modifying the settings, with its opportunity structures, in which crime occurs (Clarke, 1997; Weisburd, 1997; Welsh and Farrington, 2010).

Target hardening. Concept of opportunity reduction that seeks to deter the criminal act by making a potential target of attack inaccessible or unattractive and by making the attack itself dangerous or unprofitable to the criminal (related terms: opportunity reduction, Security hardware, and security systems). Now a concept in CPTED 2018.

Target-specific measures. Specific strategies intended to protect a certain premise from crime risk or safety hazards.

Urban warfare is combat conducted in urban areas such as towns and cities. Urban combat is very different from combat in the open at both the operational and tactical level. Complicating factors in urban warfare include the presence of civilians and the complexity of the urban terrain.

Vigilante. Those who extralegally assume authority for summary action, to keep order and to punish criminals professedly because of the alleged inadequacy or failure of the usual law enforcement agencies.

Whistle stop. A program designed to provide women with a means of signaling for help in the event of attack. A secondary purpose is to increase public awareness and public participation in crime prevention programs.

Youth service programs. (As applied to crime prevention) Programs that focus on youths and attempt to divert them from criminal activities. Some of these deal with children in schools, others deal with students who have dropped out, and others are based in the community (related term: juvenile delinquency prevention).

Conclusion

We both have strong backgrounds in crime prevention and CPTED. We realize that in the United States we do not have a leading crime prevention organization, which is a part of the federal government like the British Home Office and others. So we have therefore loaded this book up with crime prevention materials with the hope that you find this information helpful.

Chapter 7

Encompassing effective CPTED solutions in 2020 and beyond: concepts and strategies

Lawrence J. Fennelly and Marianna A. Perry
Security Consultant

The theory of Crime Prevention Through Environmental Design is based on one simple idea: that crime results partly from the opportunity presented by physical environment. This being the case, it should be possible to alter the physical environment so that crime is less likely to occur.

Ronald V. Clarke

Introduction

Crime Prevention Through Environmental Design (CPTED) does not require an extensive technical background or understanding. To be effective as a community strategy, basic CPTED concepts have to be understood by as many people as possible (in layperson's terms). Otherwise, true public policy setting will remain in the hands of technocrats and politicians.

The following learning objectives should be considered the absolute minimum for successful completion of this 10-module design.

We feel participants should be able to

1. recognize the CPTED underlying premise and
2. recall the two underlined words in the definition as key CPTED descriptors.

CPTED's premise: "That the proper design and effective use of the built environment can lead to a reduction in the incidence and fear of crime and to an increase in the quality of life."

The seven basic CPTED strategies have been updated, and you should be able to recognize and define (in one-sentence definition or examples) them that are listed and properly footnoted next.

Participants should be able to distinguish (by definitions or examples) between the crime prevention strategies that are classified as organized, mechanical, and natural.

In the sixth module, participants should be able to recall the reference to the CPTED approach to space assessment and list the components of the 3Ds CPTED concept: *designation*, *definition*, and *design*.

Participants should be able to demonstrate new awareness and understanding of CPTED concepts by providing a descriptive example(s) of a good and a bad CPTED setting in at least one of the following types of locations:

- a residential neighborhood that is near a major street intersection
- neighborhood parks
- neighborhood schools
- public parking lots
- public housing area
- industrial/commercial center

Handbook of Loss Prevention and Crime Prevention. DOI: https://doi.org/10.1016/B978-0-12-817273-5.00007-7

The participant should be able to describe the functions and location of the following types of information:

- crime-analysis data and crime patterns
- demographic data
- land use
- observations
- resident or user interviews

The participant should be able to draw a simple map of his/her residential or business neighborhood showing

- street layout;
- land use;
- pedestrian and vehicular usage;
- crime (or fear) problem areas; and
- current boundaries of geographic, ethnic, or neighborhood identities.

Broken windows, community policing, and Neighborhood Watch

Broken windows live

On October 28, 2017, Lawrence Fennelly had the honor of hearing Dr. George Kelling make a presentation about the History of Law Enforcement and Community Policing.

First, we have broken down his first book on the following topics:

1. claim the high moral ground
2. learn to solve problem
3. prepare to win in court
4. involve the community

The points from Dr. Kelling's presentation are as follows:

1. Do not let the neighborhood get out of control, restore order.
2. Model of community policing is a now collaboration.
3. Safe handling of community policing.
4. Law enforcement must be evenly provided to all.
5. We live in a "fear of police."
6. Law enforcement has to listen to the people, and develop *Coffee with a Cop* programs.
7. A key factor is "to know the person's name" you are addressing.
8. Bring line officers to community meetings as well as detectives, prosecutors, and judges. Law enforcement needs to be the role model.
9. Foot patrol has a very positive impact.
10. We have eight categories of homelessness (which made me think about this very important social issue).

When we asked Dr. Kelling, if he was to write his book today, what would he add? He replied, "The Outreach of Authority."

Six points of the broken windows theory are

1. increase in physical deterioration;
2. increased concern for personal safety among residents and proprietors;
3. decreased participation in maintaining order on the street;
4. increased delinquency, rowdiness, vandalism, and disorderly behavior among locals;
5. further increase in deterioration and further withdrawal from the streets by residents and other locals; and
6. potential offenders from outside the neighborhood, attracted by vulnerability, move into the area.

CPTED and the "broken windows theory"[1] suggest that one "broken window" or nuisance, if allowed to exist, will lead to others and ultimately to the decline of an entire neighborhood. Neglected and poorly maintained properties are

1. Ferreira, B.R., 1996. The Use and Effectiveness of Community Policing in a Democracy, Policing in Central and Eastern Europe: Comparing Firsthand Knowledge With Experience From the West. ©1996 College of Police and Security Studies, Slovenia. <https://www.ncjrs.gov/policing/use139.htm>.

breeding grounds for criminal activity. It is important to develop a formal CPTED-based maintenance plan to help preserve the property value and make it a safer place.

Contemporary approaches

Contemporary approaches,[2] including CPTED, emerged out of research on the relationship between crime and place, and theories are known variously as environmental criminology, situational crime prevention, rational choice theory, and routine activity theory, among others. Each theoretical approach focuses on considerations of how a criminal perceives and interacts with the environment in the planning, selection, and decision-making related to committing a crime.

CPTED and associated theoretical research ask the question, "Why here?" Research has revealed the following:

1. Crime is specific and situational.
2. The distribution of crimes is related to land use and transportation networks.
3. Offenders are opportunistic and commit crimes in places they know well.
4. Opportunity arises out of daily routines and activities.
5. Places with crime are usually places without observers or guardians.

CPTED examines crime problems and the ways in which various features of the environment afford opportunities for undesirable and unwanted behaviors. CPTED attempts to remove or reduce these opportunities by changing aspects of the building, site, location, and how the space may be used.

Neighborhood and community policing

Defining community policing

Cox and Fitzgerald (1992:159) claimed that community-oriented policing is in many ways an old idea that can be traced back to Sir Robert Peel.[3] Many authors have referred to the difficult task of defining community policing in one paragraph, let alone one sentence! Friedmann (1992:2) noted "community policing became a 'buzz word' that is taken for granted by professionals and scholars who used the term to replace other terms such as foot patrol, crime prevention, problem-oriented policing, community-oriented policing, police-community relations and more." Trojanowicz and Bucqueroux (1994:2–3) suggested that, with the trend of short sound-bite media coverage of events, we must attempt to create a simple and concise definition of community policing. If we do not define community policing ourselves, then others, who do not understand the concept, will do so. They suggested the following definition and called it the "Nine Ps" of community policing: "Community policing is a philosophy of full-service personalized policing, where the same officer patrols and works in the same area on a permanent basis, from a decentralized place, working in a proactive partnership with citizens to identify and solve problems."[4]

Community policing can appear to be a difficult concept to understand, because community policing is geographically specific—no two communities or areas are exactly alike, and as a result, no two communities will require exactly the same method of community policing service delivery. Investigation and enforcement are essential elements of community policing, but the way in which these and other services are delivered to the community will depend upon several factors such as the nature of crime and social problems found in the community, the resources (both human and financial) available to the community to solve these problems, the needs expressed by community members, the community's cultural makeup and diversity, and its size.

It is really not hard to identify community policing. There are a few essential factors of community policing, which can serve as a guideline to those responsible for its implementation in any individual community. If these elements are present, community policing takes place.

2. https://protus3.com/what-is-crime-prevention-through-environmental-design/.

3. Community Policing. Retrieved on November 11, 2018 from: <https://www.bjs.gov/index.cfm?ty = tp&tid = 81>.

4. The Use and Effectiveness of Community Policing in a Democracy. Retrieved on November 11, 2018 from: <https://www.ncjrs.gov/policing/use139.htm>.

Direct service delivery

- *Identify the community, or communities, present in an area.* A community consists of a group of people who share certain elements: geographical location, cultural or racial background, socioeconomic status, common interests or goals, or concern with the same crime or social issues. People may belong to more than one community group (e.g., a person may consider themselves a member of an Aboriginal community and a specific residential community area), and there may be more than one community of people within a detachment or city boundary. Each group must be clearly identified by the police, so that the needs of the community members can be met.
- *Work with the community.* The police must establish a partnership with the community, in order to cooperatively address its problems and needs. Community consultative groups, with representatives from all communities identified, are an effective and successful way to initiate and carry out communication and cooperation between the police and their community.
- *Identify common problems and concerns.* The police who are providing policing service to the community must be aware of its concerns, needs, and expectations, so that their efforts are community-oriented and community-driven. The community must be aware of the concerns, abilities, and limitations of the police, so that their demands are appropriate and able to be met by the police. Once each group understands the other, compromises and agreements on which problems are most important can be reached.
- *Resolve the identified problems.* A problem is defined as a group of incidents, which are similar and are of concern to both the police and the community. Problem incidents may be similar in the crime, victim or time of day or year. The responsibility for resolving problems must be shared by both the police and the citizens, and all abilities and resources found within the community must be directed toward finding and carrying out effective and innovative solutions that must attack and remove the root cause of the problem, so that the problem itself, not just its symptoms, is removed.
- *Empower police officers to make decisions and take action.* Community policing often involves innovative approaches to problem-solving, which have, in the past, not been considered part of "traditional policing." Empowerment involves delegating a certain level of authority and enabling factors (proper training, guidance and information). Managers must trust their employees and take the risk to allow general duty officers, in daily personal contact with the community, to be able to make necessary appropriate and innovative decisions and take the initiative to act to address the concerns of the public.
- *Support the general duty officer.* The general duty officer has the most direct contact with the community and must be regarded as the most important member of the policing service. The efforts of all other specialized members of the force must be directed toward supporting this community service position.
- *Make patrol, enforcement, and investigation work effective and directed.* There should be no such thing as a random or preventive patrol. When a member leaves the detachment, it should be with a purpose of monitoring traffic in a problem area; liaising with local farmers, business owners, or people on the street; or attending a complaint. Law enforcement and investigation (often the focus of contemporary, reactive policing) are still a necessary part of police work, but they are only one part. The police need to get back to crime reduction, not just crime control. Through community consultation, police services can determine the amount of time to spend on these efforts, and the problems, of concern both to the community and the police, which should be concentrated on.

Administrative organization

- *Decentralize.* The police cannot meet the needs of a community effectively if their actions and decisions are dictated to them from the higher authority. The members working in a community are the most qualified people to decide how best to serve that community. Authority and decision-making on issues, such as programs, resource deployment, and budgeting, must be delegated down to the detachment level.
- *Use modern management concepts.* Problem resolution, innovative resource deployment, risk management, downward delegation of authority, flattening organization hierarchy, participate management, and client consultation can be used to ensure that the service provided to the client community is efficient, effective, and responsive to its needs. Each detachment should provide a custom-designed service directed to the needs, concerns, and problems of its community.
- *Create an enhanced generalist career path.* In community policing the general duty officer, in direct daily contact with the client community, is the most important position within the police service. The existing generalist position

may be augmented to allow and encourage experienced and tenured members to remain there and continue to direct their expertise toward serving the community, while still being rewarded for their service and initiative.

- *Reduce paper burden.* A large amount of time police presently spend in administrative "paperwork" tasks. The statistical and paperwork demands, both from the internal and external sources, must be reduced to allow more time for direct community service.
- *Evaluate effectiveness through citizen satisfaction surveys.* The satisfaction of the community is the best indicator of the success of its policing service; if the client is happy, the job is done well. Some statistical data such as crime rates will still be required but should be balanced against the concerns of the community in deciding how to direct police resources.

Take a stand against crime

Join a Neighborhood Watch

Neighborhood Watch, Block Watch, Town Watch, Building Watch, Crime Watch, whatever the name, it is one of the most effective and least costly ways to prevent crime and reduce fear.[5] Neighborhood Watch fights the isolation that crime both creates and feeds upon. It forges bonds among area residents, helps reduce burglaries and robberies, and improves relations between police and the communities they serve.

Why Neighborhood Watch?

It works throughout the country, dramatic decreases in burglary and related offenses are reported by the law enforcement professionals in communities with active Watch Programs.

Today's transient society produces communities that are less personal. Many families have two working parents and children involved in many activities that keep them away from home. An empty house in a neighborhood where none of the neighbors know the owner is a primary target for burglary.

Neighborhood Watch also helps build pride and serves as a springboard for efforts that address other community concerns, such as recreation for youth, child care, and affordable housing.

How does a Neighborhood Watch start?

A motivated individual, a few concerned residents, a community organization, or a law enforcement agency can spearhead the efforts to establish a Watch. Together they can do the following:

- Organize a small planning committee of neighbors to discuss needs, the level of interest, and the possible community problems.
- Contact the local police or sheriff's department, or local crime prevention organization, for help in training members in home security and reporting skills, and for information on local crime patterns.
- Hold an initial meeting to gauge neighbors' interest, establish the purpose of the program, and begin to identify issues that need to be addressed.

Select a coordinator

- Ask for block captain volunteers who are responsible for relaying information to the members.
- Recruit members, keeping up-to-date information on new residents and making special efforts to involve the elderly, working parents, and young people.
- Work with local government or law enforcement to put up Neighborhood Watch signs, usually after at least 50% of all households are enrolled.

Who can be involved?

Any community resident can join—young or old, single or married, and renter or homeowner. Even the busiest of people can belong to a Neighborhood Watch—they too can keep an eye out for neighbors as they come and go.

5. https://troopers.ny.gov/Crime_Prevention/General_Safety/Neighborhood_Watch/.

I live in an apartment building. Can I start a Neighborhood Watch?

Yes. Watch Groups can be formed around any geographical unit: a block, apartment building, townhouse complex, park, business area, public housing complex, office building, or marina.

What does a Neighborhood Watch do?

A Neighborhood Watch is neighbors helping neighbors. They are extra eyes and ears for reporting crime and helping neighbors. Members meet their neighbors, learn how to make their homes more secure, watch out for each other and the neighborhood, and report activity that raises their suspicions to the police or sheriff's office.

What are the major components of a Watch Program?

1. *Community meetings*. These should be set up on a regular basis such as bimonthly, monthly, or six times a year.
2. *Citizens' or community patrol*. A citizens' patrol is made up of volunteers who walk or drive through the community and alert police to crime and questionable activities. Not all Neighborhood Watches need a citizens' patrol.
3. *Communications*. These can be as simple as a weekly flier posted on community announcement boards to a newsletter that updates neighbors on the progress of the program to a neighborhood electronic bulletin board.
4. *Special events*. These are crucial to keep the program going and growing. Host talks or seminars that focus on current issues, such as hate or bias-motivated violence, crime in schools, teenage alcohol and other drug abuse or domestic violence. Adopt a park or school playground and paint over graffiti. Sponsor a block party, holiday dinner, or volleyball or softball game that will provide neighbors a chance to get to know each other.
5. *Other aspects of community safety*. For instance, start a Block Parent Program to help children in emergency situations.

What are my responsibilities as a watch member?

1. Be alert!
2. Know your neighbors and watch out for each other.
3. Report suspicious activities and crimes to the police or sheriffs' department.
4. Learn how you can make yourself and your community safer.

What kind of activities should I be on the lookout for as a watch member?

1. Someone screaming or shouting for help.
2. Someone looking in windows of houses and parked cars.
3. Property being taken out of houses where no one is at home or from closed businesses.
4. Cars, van, or trucks moving slowly with no apparent destination or without lights.
5. A stranger sitting in a car or stopping to talk to a child.
6. Report these incidents to the police or sheriffs' department. Talk about concerns and problems with your neighbors.

How should I report these incidents?

Call 911 or your local emergency number and give your name and address; explain what happened; briefly describe the suspect: sex and race, age, height, weight, hair color, clothing, distinctive characteristics, such as a beard, mustache, scars, or accent and also describe the vehicle if one was involved: color, make, model, year, license plate, and special features such as stickers.

Crime prevention through environmental design and security awareness

Security awareness is broken down into three parts, education and imparting of knowledge and training to develop security skills.[6]

6. Draper, R., 2017. Update of POA Manual on Awareness. Not Published.

So, what is security awareness?

The method through which an individual is made conscious of and accepts his or her own role and responsibilities in the protection of the assets of an organization. It should engender protective attitudes and behaviors—both personally and on behalf of the organization.

Awareness, raising consciousness

An effective security awareness program is NOT a process of waving the big stick a series of unplanned and unrelated communications about security issues knowing the name of the security officer, having a copy of the facility security policy manual in the desk drawer not just limited to staff.

Displacement of crime

Can you move crime from one location to another? Yes, you can. I know criminologists will say show me the data and we cannot. However, talk to veteran officers who have been working the various sectors for years and they will tell you that they have done it. Years ago, in a dormitory that had only one entrance and individual was stealing wallets and cash from unlocked rooms. This was going on night after night, so a police cruiser was put out in front of the dormitory, and every night around 3:00 a.m. the car was back a few spaces then forward. Crime stopped. Was it luck or skill? The cruiser was a deterrent. It is logical for a would-be criminal to assume that if a police car is outside then the officer must be inside and there is a likelihood that I will get caught, so he goes to another location.

We know that when drug dealing and prostitution are problems, and the street is closed off to prevent traffic from driving up and down the street, the drug dealers and prostitutes will move to another location.

Steven P. Lab states in his book titled Crime Prevention, seventh edition "There is little reason to ever expect total displacement of a crime, regardless of the type of displacement considered."[7] He then discusses the various types of displacement, that is, territorial, temporal, tactical, target, and functional, he further states that although it is not 100% at the same time, they show that displacement does occur.

What is suspicious activity?

An example of suspicious activity is a total stranger in your neighborhood or in your neighbor's home while your neighbor is away. Or possibly, someone crossing through your neighbor's yard for no apparent lawful reason and then you observe him/her trying to open your neighbor's door. Or you see a moving truck pull into your neighbor's driveway, while they are on vacation. Keep in mind that burglaries can happen in daylight, in full view of observers.

Let us take the case of a suspicious person who enters your workplace is stopped at the front desk and asks to you to use the bathroom. The goal here is to get past the front desk and inside the facility.

Door-to-door solicitors without proper identification

You have to use your senses in many of these cases. Breaking glass, for example, could be a signal of a possible burglary, vandalism, or a larceny in progress. Screams, yelling, loud noise, or a fight may be an indication of an armed robbery or life-threatening event; again, your senses are telling you, *we have a problem.*

An improperly parked car, an abandoned vehicle, a stolen car with the dashboard taken apart, combined with screaming may indicate that someone is being forced into a vehicle.

Call the police, 911

Successful efforts to combat crime require a community working closely with law enforcement. Today just about everyone has a cell phone attached to their hip, so call. The police cannot be everywhere, for this reason success against crime is dependent on the community involved with a safe and secure environment. Crime can be reduced when the community is alert to suspicious activity and law enforcement is notified.

7. Lab, S.P., 2010. Crime Prevention, seventh ed. Routledge Publishers, London.

Crime reduction

Examples of how we can help you and how we have helped others in the past include the following[8]:

- analyzing crime data and linking it to the environment and the community to identify answers;
- implementing community safety into everything from major new town regeneration projects to home zones;
- designing and managing crime out of housing estates, shopping centers, or even supermarkets;
- surveying existing environments of all types and identifying crime generators and how to change them;
- evaluating, managing, and improving existing security such as security surveillance systems (CCTV);
- making your facilities, such as housing, hospitals or schools, fit for purpose;
- consulting with ALL relevant stakeholder to ensure everyone's views are noted;
- ensuring crime and fear of crime is managed within both urban and rural environments, to deliver inclusive and sustainable communities;
- making certain solutions are cost commensurate and are ranked in order of priority; and
- testing your security, for example, by "mystery shopping" your facilities and giving you a report on the weaknesses.

Environment and design

The conceptual thrust of a CPTED program is that the physical environment can be manipulated to produce behavioral effects that will reduce the incidence and fear of crime, thereby improving the quality of life. These behavioral effects can be achieved by reducing the propensity of the physical environment to support criminal behavior. Environmental design, as used in a CPTED program, is rooted in the design of the human/environment relationship. It embodies several concepts.

The term *environment* includes the people and their physical and social surroundings. However, as a matter of practical necessity, the environment defined for demonstration purposes is that which has recognizable territorial and system limits.

The term *design* includes physical, social, management, and law enforcement directives that seek to affect positively human behavior as people interact with their environment.

So, a CPTED program seeks to prevent certain specified crimes (and the fear of crime) within a specifically defined environment by manipulating variables that are closely related to the environment itself.

A CPTED program does not purport to develop crime prevention solutions in a broad universe of human behavior but rather solutions limited to variables that can be manipulated and evaluated in the specified human/environment relationship. CPTED involves the design of physical space in the context of the needs of legitimate users of the space (physical, social, and psychological needs), the normal and expected (or intended) use of the space (the activity or absence of activity planned for the space), and the predictable behavior of both legitimate users and offenders. Therefore in the CPTED approach, a design is proper if it recognizes the designated use of the space, defines the crime problem incidental to and the solution compatible with the designated use, and incorporates the crime prevention strategies that enhance (or at least do not impair) the effective use of the space. CPTED draws not only on physical and urban design but also on contemporary thinking in behavioral and social science, law enforcement, and community organization.

Space

The continuum of space within a residential complex (i.e., a property consisting of one or more buildings containing dwelling units and associated grounds or, more broadly, a neighborhood consisting primarily of residential uses) may be divided into four categories[9]:

Public space

Space that, whatever its legal status, is perceived by all members of a residential area or neighborhood as belonging to the public as a whole, which a stranger has as much perceived right to use as a resident.

Semipublic space

Semipublic space is accessible to all members of the public without passing through a locked or guarded barrier. There is thought to be an implied license for use by the public and strangers will rarely be challenged. This is generally associated with multifamily housing.

8. http://www.griffinrc.co.uk/prevention.htm.
9. Tyska, L.A., Fennelly, L.J., 1998. Physical Security—150 Things You Should Know. Elsevier Publishers, Boston, MA.

Semiprivate space

This space is restricted for use by residents, guests, and service people on legitimate assignments. In multifamily housing, semiprivate space is usually secured by protection officers (or doormen), locks, or other forms of physical barriers. Strangers can be expected to be challenged as potential trespassers.

Private space

Private space is restricted for use by residents of a single-dwelling unit, their invited guests, and service people, with access generally controlled by locks and other physical barriers. Unauthorized use is always challenged when the opportunity for challenge presents itself.

Target hardening

The emphasis on design and use deviates from the traditional target hardening approach to crime prevention. Traditional target hardening focuses predominantly on denying access to a crime target through physical or artificial barrier techniques (such as locks, alarms, fences, and gates). Target hardening often leads to constraints on use, access, and enjoyment of the hardened environment. Moreover, the traditional approach tends to overlook opportunities for natural access control and surveillance. The term *natural* refers to deriving access control and surveillance results as a by-product of the normal and routine use of the environment. It is possible to adapt normal and natural uses of the environment to accomplish the effects of artificial or mechanical hardening and surveillance. Nevertheless, CPTED employs pure target hardening strategies, either to test their effectiveness as compared to natural strategies or when they appear to be justified as not unduly impairing the effective use of the environment.

As an example, a design strategy of improved street lighting must be planned, efficient, and evaluated in terms of the behavior it promotes or deters, and the use impact of the lighted (and related) areas in terms of all users of the area (offenders, victims, other permanent or casual users). Any strategies related to the lighting strategy (e.g., Block Watch or Neighborhood Watch, and 911 emergency service, police patrol) must be evaluated in the same regard. This reflects the comprehensiveness of the CPTED design approach in focusing on both the proper design and effective use of the physical environment. In addition, the concept of proper design and effective use emphasizes the designed relationship among strategies to ensure that the desired results are achieved. It has been observed that improved street lighting alone (a design strategy) is ineffective against crime without the conscious and active support of citizens (in reporting what they see) and of police (in responding and conducting surveillance). CPTED involves the effort to integrate design, citizen and community action, and law enforcement strategies to accomplish surveillance consistent with the design and use of the environment.

Crime prevention through environmental design strategies

There are the following seven overlapping strategies in CPTED (as shown in Fig. 7.1):

1. natural access control
2. natural surveillance
3. territorial reinforcement
4. image and/or maintenance[10]
5. activity program support[11]
6. target hardening[12]
7. geographical juxtaposition (wider environment)[13]

10. Lawrence J. Fennelly and Marianna Perry, CPTED and Traditional Security Countermeasures, CRC Press, 2018.

11. Cozens, P.M., Saville, G., Hillier, D., 2005. Crime prevention through environmental design (CPTED): a review and modern bibliography. Property Manage. 23 (5), 328–356.

12. Cozens, P.M., Saville, G., Hillier, D., 2005. Crime prevention through environmental design (CPTED): a review and modern bibliography. Property Manage. 23 (5), 328–356.

13. Cozens, P.M., Saville, G., Hillier, D., 2005. Crime prevention through environmental design (CPTED): a review and modern bibliography. Property Manage. 23 (5), 328–356.

FIGURE 7.1 Seven concept of CPTED. Designed by Marianna Perry.

Natural access control

Access control and surveillance have been the primary design concepts of physical design programs. At the outset of the CPTED program, access control and surveillance systems—preexisting as conspicuous concepts in the field of CPTED—received major attention. Access control and surveillance are not mutually exclusive classifications since certain strategies achieve both, and strategies in one classification typically are mutually supportive of the other. However, the operational thrust of each is distinctly different, and the differences must be recognized in performing analysis, research, design, implementation, and evaluation.

Access control is a design concept directed primarily at decreasing crime opportunity. Access control strategies are typically classified as organized (e.g., security officers), mechanical (e.g., locks, lighting, and alarms), and natural (e.g., spatial definition). The primary thrust of an access control strategy is to deny access to a crime target and to create a perception of risk in offenders.

Natural surveillance

Surveillance is a design concept directed primarily at keeping intruders under observation. Therefore the primary thrust of a surveillance strategy is to facilitate observation, although it may have the effect of an access control strategy by effectively keeping intruders out because of an increased perception of risk. Surveillance strategies are typically classified as organized (e.g., police patrol), mechanical (e.g., lighting, locks, and alarms), and natural (e.g., windows) (Fig. 7.2).

Photos 7.1–7.3 reflect good natural surveillance (photos taken by Marianna Perry).

Traditionally, access control and surveillance, as design concepts, have emphasized mechanical or organized crime prevention techniques while overlooking, minimizing, or ignoring attitudes, motivation, and use of the physical environment. More recent approaches to physical design of environments have shifted the emphasis to natural crime prevention techniques, attempting to use natural opportunities presented by the environment for crime prevention. This shift in emphasis led to the concept of territoriality.

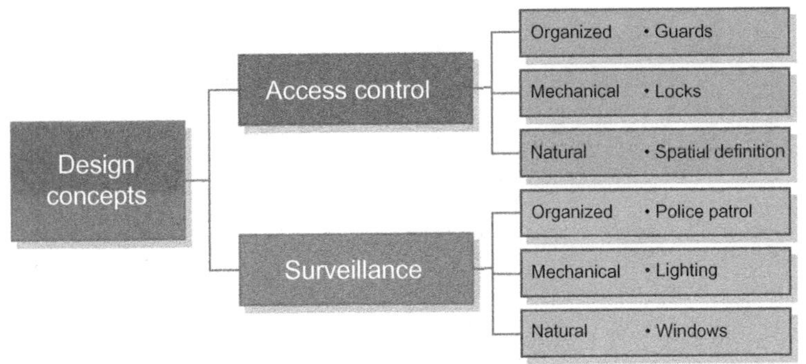

FIGURE 7.2 Typical access control surveillance concepts as well as classifications of strategies.

PHOTO 7.1

PHOTO 7.2

Territorial reinforcement

The concept of territoriality (elaborated most fully to date in the public housing environment) suggests that physical design can contribute to a sense of territoriality. That is, physical design can create or extend a sphere of influence so that users develop a sense of proprietorship—a sense of territorial influence—and potential offenders perceive that territorial influence.

PHOTO 7.3

PHOTO 7.4

Photo 7.4 reflects physical design based on territoriality (photo taken by Marianna Perry).

At the same time, it was recognized that natural access control and surveillance contributed to a sense of territoriality, making it effective for crime prevention. Natural access control and surveillance will promote more responsiveness by users in protecting their territory (e.g., more security awareness, reporting, and reacting) and also greater perception of risk by offenders.

Image and/or maintenance

Finally, care and maintenance allow for the continued use of a space for its intended purpose, as well as contributing to territorial reinforcement. Deterioration and blight indicate less concern and control by the intended users of a site and also a greater tolerance of disorder. Proper maintenance protects the public health, safety, and welfare in all existing structures, residential and nonresidential and on all existing premises by establishing minimum standards, best practices as well as a master plan. Maintenance is the responsibility of the facilities manager, owners, and occupants.

We recently conducted a physical security assessment of several housing and urban development (HUD) properties in the Northeast area. Some of the properties were in fairly good condition and some in simply deplorable. We will discuss the worst of the properties that are listed next:

- We estimated that there were over 2000 pieces of paper and/or litter on the ground.
- This complex had 250 units and supplied only two small dumpsters on each side of the complex for trash. Trash was literally everywhere.

PHOTO 7.5

- Four sets of old mattresses and box springs were leaning against the fence in the dumpster area and appeared as if they had been there for some time.
- We counted six broken down, damaged vehicles with flat tires in the parking area. Two of these cars appeared to be having work done to them and were on car jacks in precarious positions.
- Drug dealers were openly selling drugs at 3:30 p.m. and individuals who appeared "high" and/or under the influence were sitting on steps at building entrances.
- Homeless individuals who congregated at the far end of the street from the complex were given cell phones and would call the drug dealers and warn them if they saw law enforcement approaching the complex.

Here is a question for you ... "what you think about the *Image and maintenance* of the complex we have described?" You cannot get to the next level of security until you fix this mess.

The effort to achieve a balance between design for crime prevention and design for effective use of environments contributed to the shift in focus from organized and mechanical strategies per se to natural strategies. This was because natural strategies exploited the opportunities of the given environment both to naturally and routinely facilitate access control and surveillance, and to reinforce positive behavior in the use of the environment. The concept reflects a preference, where feasible, to reinforce existing or new activities, or to otherwise reinforce the behavior of environment users so that crime prevention flows naturally and routinely from the activity being promoted.

The conceptual shift from organized and mechanical to natural strategies has oriented the CPTED program to develop plans that emphasize natural access control and surveillance and territorial reinforcement.

Photo 7.5 reflects mechanical layout of mounted camera with street/parking lot lighting (photo taken by Marianna Perry).

Although conceptually distinct, it is important to realize that these categories of strategy tend to overlap in practice. It is perhaps most useful to think of territorial reinforcement as the umbrella concept, comprising all-natural surveillance principles, which in turn comprises all access control principles. It is not practical to think of territorial reinforcement, natural surveillance, and access control as independent strategies because access control operates to denote transitional zones, not necessarily impenetrable barriers. If these symbolic or psychological barriers are to succeed in controlling access by demarcating specific spaces for specific individuals, potential offenders must perceive that unwarranted intrusion will elicit protective territorial responses from those who have legitimate access. Similarly, natural surveillance operates to increase the likelihood that intrusion will be observed by individuals who care but are not officially responsible for regulating the use and treatment of spaces. If people observe inappropriate behavior but do nothing about it, then the most carefully planned natural surveillance tactics are useless in terms of stopping crime and vandalism.

In Photo 7.6 (taken by Marianna Perry), can you see the man hiding behind the bushes?

Landscaping and architectural design uses simple, inexpensive CPTED guidelines to improve security for property

- Ensure shrubs and trees do not create blind spots or hiding places.
- Trim bushes and hedges to a maximum height of 3 ft.

PHOTO 7.6

- Use walkways and landscaping to direct visitors to the proper entrance and away from private areas.
- Sidewalks, parking lots, doorways, and all areas of the property should be well lit.
- Remove objects that may provide informal seating for loiterers.
- Recessed doorways can provide cover for criminal behavior or loitering. Change these to be flush with the walls, or install gates.
- Prevent easy access to the roof or fire escape from the ground.

Crime prevention through environmental design and landscape security

An important element of CPTED that defines semiprivate and private spaces within a complex is your landscape design. It is recommended that the height of bushes be no higher than 3 ft. We have recently read that FEMA recommends the height of bushes to be 18 in. And that tree branches are between 7 and 8 ft[14] off the ground as a means for Natural Surveillance and Safety. You want to be able to detect intruders and not allow them a hiding spot. Your landscape if properly laid out can also be a deterrent and prevent criminal opportunity.

Landscape furniture should be vandal-resistant, and if benches are installed, they need to be designed so that individuals cannot sleep on them.

Also, into consideration, exterior lighting, video surveillance, vegetation, maintenance, barriers, the entrances and exits on your property, and signage and the surface structure.

Holistic approach

We recommend applying the frameworks, principles, and concepts from many including[15]

- situational crime prevention
- designing out crime
- CPTED and management
- crime opportunity profiling
- secured by design principles
- target hardening
- SARA

Activity program support

The concept of activity support is to deliberately design formal and informal support for increasing the levels of human activity in particular spaces as a crime prevention strategy.

14. The 8 ft clearance is also recommended by ASIS Physical Security Principle Book, 2015, p. 214.
15. http://www.griffinrc.co.uk/prevention.htm.

How do we accomplish this strategy? First, review how the complex is being used. Then, if necessary, add bus stops, a community garden, food trucks, children's playgrounds, and a concrete table and two seats (immovable—fastened to the ground) for playing chess or checkers. The designed use of the grounds will bring community members together to interact—and for a positive purpose.

Target hardening

Dr. Jennifer Hesterman wrote *Soft Target Hardening: Protecting People from Attack*, the 2014 ASIS International Security Book of the Year. Dr. Hesterman put a tremendous amount of research into this book exploring case studies, presenting best practices and discussing methodologies for identifying soft target vulnerabilities and reducing risk in the United States. It is a must-read for every security practitioner.

Target hardening is not a fortress mentality concept, but instead a "good security practice". We both live in gated communities where access to the neighborhood is limited to two entrances. Neighbors are aware of who lives in their communities and what types of vehicles they drive.

On Cape Cod, MA, in Larry Fennelly's neighborhood, there are homes that have rolling window shutters for protection against storms, especially when the home owners are away, but they also work well as effective security devices. Everyone in the neighborhood has good locks on their doors and windows, follow good landscape principles, and have fences that comply with local ordinances. The residents are constantly walking to and from the beach with cell phones in their hands.

There is very little crime in the community because of the image and perception of the property as well as the maintenance that is done to all townhouses and houses. In addition, there are several retired law enforcement officers who actually patrol the neighborhood first, when they leave their home to run errands. Yes, the cell phone is a *crime prevention device* because it can be used to call for help.

Geographical juxtaposition

By definition, geographical juxtaposition is "assessing the potential influence on crime levels, of proximal land-users that may generate crime."[16]

We suggest that you read closely about Tim Crowe's CPTED Strategies and 3Ds concept. This material has been updated based on the past writings and newly discovered material of Crowe's work which was found in 2016.

We see CPTED as a process of a series of concepts and strategies, that address risk, reduce crime and the fear of crime, and improve the quality of life for our communities.

The 3D approach

For CPTED to be a success, it must be understandable and practical for the normal users of the space, that is, the normal residents of a neighborhood and the people who work in buildings or commercial areas must be able to use these concepts.[17] Why? Because these people know more about what is going on in that environment and they have a vested interest (their own well-being) in ensuring that their immediate environment operates properly. The technologist or specialist, who may be a traffic engineer, city planner, architect, or security specialist, should not be allowed to shoulder the responsibility alone for safety and security. A specialist needs to follow the dictates of the users of the space, because he or she can often be swayed by misperceptions or by the conflicting demands of his professional competition.

To determine which CPTED strategies are needed for a particular environment, you have to first assess the space you are evaluating. To do this the 3Ds approach is normally used. This approach is based upon the following functions:

- All human space has some DESIGNATED purpose.
- All human space has social, cultural, legal, or physical DEFINITIONS that prescribe the desired and acceptable behaviors.
- All human space is DESIGNED to support and control the desired behavior.

16. Creating Defensible Space. Retrieved on November 11, 2018 from: <https://www.huduser.gov/publications/pdf/def.pdf>.
17. Crowe, T.D., Fennelly, L.J., 2013. Crime Prevention Through Environmental Design, third ed. Elsevier Publishers, Boston, MA.

The 3Ds approach to space assessment provides a simple guide for the layperson to use in determining the appropriateness of how her space is designed and used. The 3Ds concept is based on the following three functions or dimensions of human space:

1. All human space has some designated purpose.
2. All human space has social, cultural, legal, or physical definitions that prescribe the desired and acceptable behaviors.
3. All human space is designed to support and control the desired behaviors.

By using the 3Ds as a guide, space may be evaluated by asking the following types of questions:

Designation

- What is the designated purpose of this space?
- What was it originally intended to be used for?
- How well does the space support its current use? Its intended use? Is there conflict?

Definition

- How is the space defined?
- Is it clear who owns it?
- Where are its borders?
- Are there social or cultural definitions that affect how that space is used?
- Are the legal or administrative rules clearly set out and reinforced in policy?
- Are there signs?
- Is there conflict or confusion between the designated purpose and definition?
- Define the rules and how they are or will be enforced?

Design

- How well does the physical design support the intended function?
- How well does the physical design support the definition of the desired or accepted behaviors?
- Does the physical design conflict with or impede the productive use of the space or the proper functioning of the intended human activity? Is there confusion or conflict in the manner in which the physical design is intended to control behavior?
- How well does the space support its current or intended use?
- Is there physiological support for the intended function?
- Is there physiological control of the property, especially problem areas?
- Design space to increase the perception of natural surveillance?

The seven CPTED strategies of territorial reinforcement, natural access control, natural surveillance, image and/or maintenance, activity program support, target hardening, and geographical juxtaposition (wider environment)[18] are inherent in the 3Ds concept. Does the space clearly belong to someone or some group? Is the intended use clearly defined? Does the physical design match the intended use? Does the design provide the means for normal users to naturally control the activities, to control access, and to provide surveillance? Once a basic self-assessment has been conducted, the 3Ds may then be turned around as a simple means of guiding decisions about what to do with human space. The proper functions have to be matched with space that can support them—with space that can effectively support territorial identity, natural access control and surveillance and intended behaviors have to be indisputable and be reinforced in social, cultural, legal, and administrative terms or norms. The design has to ensure that the intended activity can function well, and it has to directly support the control of behavior.

18. Cozens, P.M., Saville, G., Hillier, D., 2005. Crime prevention through environmental design (CPTED): a review and modern bibliography. Property Manage. 23 (5), 328–356.

Examples of strategies in action

There are hundreds of examples of CPTED strategies in practice today. In each example, there is a mixture of the seven CPTED strategies that are appropriate for the setting and to the particular security or crime problem. Some of the examples were created with the direct application of CPTED concepts. Others were borrowed from real-life situations. The common thread is the primary emphasis on naturalness—simply doing things that you already do, but doing them just a little better.

Some examples of CPTED strategy activities are as follows[19]:

- providing clear border definition of controlled space;
- providing clearly marked transitional zones that indicate movement from public to semipublic to private space;
- relocating gathering areas to locations with natural surveillance and access control, or to locations away from the view of would-be offenders;
- placing safe activities in unsafe locations to bring along the natural surveillance of these activities to increase the perception of safety for normal users and risk for offenders;
- placing unsafe activities in safe spots to overcome the vulnerability of these activities with the natural surveillance and access control of the safe area;
- redesignating the use of space to provide natural barriers to conflicting activities;
- improving scheduling of space to allow for effective use and appropriate critical intensity;
- redesigning space to increase the perception or reality of natural surveillance; and
- overcoming distance and isolation through improved communications and design efficiency.

Use of information

It goes without saying that all informed decisions should be based on good, reliable information. This is especially true when the design and use of the physical environment is at stake. It is imperative that at least five basic types of information be collected and used. Unless a rational basis is used to make an informed decision, the same mistakes that caused the original problem to develop will continue to be made.

The five basic types of information needed for good CPTED planning are crime-analysis information, demographic information, land-use information, observations, and resident or user interviews. This information does not have to be sophisticated. It exists in a fundamental form in every community or location. Moreover, unless it can be presented in its most basic form, it is of little value. For instance, very little can be done with a statistical measure that says burglaries are up by 5%. Much more can be done with a crime map that shows a clustering of burglaries in a specific block.

Even more can be done when one finds that the burglar used an alleyway as his/her approach to a series of related offenses because it afforded good cover for his vehicle in order to not be observed.

The other bits of information that are needed should be available in simple, usable formats. Following is a simple guide to each type of information:

Crime analysis

This type of information is available in every police department; it is obtained by plotting offenses on a wall map and organizing the information on crime reports for the major purpose of identifying patterns of criminal activity. There are two basic types of patterns: geographic and similar offense.

Demographic

This information describes the nature of the population for a given city, district, or neighborhood. It is available through city planning departments or the city manager's or mayor's office. Another source of this type of information is the Census Bureau and the city and county data books that may be found in most public libraries.

19. Crowe, T.D., Fennelly, L.J., 2013. Crime Prevention Through Environmental Design, third ed. Elsevier Publishers, Boston, MA.

Land use

City planning departments, zoning boards, traffic engineering councils, and local councils of government have information and maps that describe and depict the physical allocations and uses of land. Simple wall maps with colored sections showing residential areas, commercial areas, industrial areas, parks, schools, and traffic flows can be of immeasurable assistance in understanding the physical setting. Natural boundaries and neighborhoods are easier to visualize on such maps, especially in relation to land use and pedestrian and traffic flows.

Observations

It is very helpful to conduct either formal or informal visual reviews of physical space to get firsthand knowledge of how, when, and by whom that space is used, and where problems may arise. Environmental cues are the key to normal user and offender behavior. Observations may include pedestrian/vehicle counts, on- and off-street parking, maintenance of yards and fences, the degree of proprietary behaviors prohibited by residents and/or users, the presence of either controlling or avoidance behaviors, and other potential indicators of territorial concern such as the percentage of window blinds drawn in homes and businesses overlooking parks or schools.

Resident or user interviews

This source of information is needed to balance the other data sources. People's perceptions of where they feel safe and where they feel endangered often vary from the locations on crime maps where the most offenses occur. It is vital to determine the residents' or users' perceptions and extent of identity with the surrounding space, what affects their behavior or reactions as they move about, and what they think the needs are. Any attempt to skip the basics in favor of more complex forms of information gathering or analysis often obscures the picture. Professionals often suppress the active participation of residents or space users by relying on complex modes of analysis. This is dangerous because it can cause some very basic ideas or explanations to be overlooked. It is axiomatic that very little good will be accomplished without the full and active involvement of the users of space.

Some benefits of crime prevention through environmental design planning activities

In addition to dealing with the reduction of crime and fear problems, other benefits of CPTED planning include the following:

Treatment of crime problems at various environmental scales

The CPTED process for identifying crime/environment problems, selecting CPTED strategies, and initiating, implementing, and evaluating anticrime projects can be applied to entire neighborhoods or types of institutional settings within a city, such as secondary schools, or the process can be applied equally well to a small geographic area or to one particular institution.

Integration of prevention approaches

CPTED principles are derived from an opportunity model of criminal behavior that assumes that the offender's behavior can be accounted for by understanding how, and under what circumstances, variables in the environment interact to induce crime. Once an assessment of the opportunity structure is made, then appropriate strategies can be designed and integrated into a coordinated, consistent program.

Identification of short-and long-term goals

Comprehensive broad-based programs such as CPTED have ultimate goals that may take years to accomplish. Unlike CPTED, however, many programs fail to develop short-term or proximate goals and adequate ways to measure their success. The CPTED approach includes an evaluation framework that details proximate goals relating to increased access control, surveillance, and territorial reinforcement. The rationale is that the ultimate program success is directly related to its success in achieving the proximate goals.

Encouragement of collective responses to problems

The CPTED emphasis is on increasing the capacity of residents to act in concert rather than individually. Strategies are aimed at fostering citizen participation and strengthening social cohesion.

Interdisciplinary approach to urban problems

An explicit policy of interdisciplinary teaming ensures effective cooperation among diverse city departments such as public works, social services, economic development, and police. Each participant benefits from exposure to the responsibilities, jurisdiction, and skills of the others.

Encouragement of better police/community relations

A key strategy is to coordinate law enforcement and community service activities with the result of improving police/community relations and developing an anticrime program that is not solely dependent on enforcement agencies.

Development of security guidelines and standards

CPTED program can lead to the creation of security criteria for newly constructed or modified environments to avoid planning and design decisions that inadvertently provide opportunities for crime.

Assistance in urban revitalization

Through its impact on physical, social, and economic conditions, CPTED can be instrumental in revitalizing communities, including downtown areas. Once business leaders, investors, and other citizens perceive that a comprehensive effort is underway to reduce crime and fear, there will be an improvement in community identity and cohesiveness.

Acquisition of development funds

The incorporation of CPTED into existing programs can provide additional jurisdiction for awarding grants, loans, and community development funds.

Institutionalization of crime prevention policies and practices

CPTED projects can create a local management capability and expertise to maintain ongoing projects. This capability can be incorporated into existing citizen organizations or municipal agencies.

An ounce of prevention: A new role for law enforcement support of community development

Public/private sector partnerships enhance public safety by sharing information, making the community more aware of threats and involving them in the problem-solving process. Collaboration is a key word for partnerships because all partners must recognize that their goals or missions overlap and they work together to share resources and achieve common goals. The added value of public–private sector partnerships is the cross transfer of skills, knowledge, and expertise between the public and the private sector.[20] In order for a partnership to be successful, each partner has to understand the value they will gain from participating. Successful partnerships involve partners that are committed to working together to achieve common goals—building the community. There are a number of compelling reasons for law enforcement to be involved in CPTED aside from the formulation of partnerships:

1. CPTED concepts have been proven to enhance community activities while reducing crime problems.
2. CPTED concepts are fundamental to traditional law enforcement values, in terms of helping the community to function properly.

20. Fusion Center Guidelines Developing and Sharing Information and Intelligence in a New Era. Retrieved on November 11, 2018 from: <http://it.ojp.gov/documents/d/fusion_center_guidelines.pdf>.

3. CPTED requires the unique information sources and inherent knowledge of the community that is endemic to the law enforcement profession.
4. CPTED problems and issues bear a direct relationship to repeat calls or service and to crime-producing situations.
5. CPTED methods and techniques can directly improve property values, business profitability, and industrial productivity, thereby enhancing local tax bases.

Law enforcement agencies, regardless of size, must be involved formally in the review and approval process of community and business projects. Their participation must be active and creative, rather than passive and reactive. Moreover, any such involvement should not be understood to expose the agencies to possible litigation, since it is the role of law enforcement in CPTED concepts to provide additional information and concerns that may not have occurred to the persons who are responsible (and qualified) for making changes to the environment. The expression, "pay me now or pay me later," conveys the idea that the early involvement of a knowledgeable law enforcement agency in the conceptualization and planning of community projects can lead to improvements in the quality of life and to reductions in the fear and incidence of crime. This early involvement is one of the most cost-effective methods of crime prevention.[21]

Crime prevention through environmental design assessments

While conducting a CPTED assessment, focus on the CPTED's principles of[22]

1. natural surveillance
2. natural access control
3. territoriality reinforcement
4. image and/or maintenance
5. activity program support
6. target hardening
7. geographical juxtaposition (wider environment).[23]

Be sure that you notice positive attributes of the area while identifying needed changes or improvements. Logically organize your observations and recommendations.

Questions to be answered during an assessment

- Are there casual *surveillance* opportunities? If not, can they be added?
- Is there sufficient *lighting* for all vehicular and pedestrian pathways and activity areas used during hours of darkness?
- Is there sufficient activity *lighting* indoors and is it supplemented by sources of natural light? Is there emergency lighting?
- Is *access* managed? If not, what combination of strategies could be used to better manage access?
- Are all *spaces designated and delineated* for specific use? If not, can they be?
- Are there *conflicts* between uses?
- Is there sufficient *capacity*? Is *crowding* creating tension, fear, or potential dangers?
- Are there expressions of pride and ownership (territoriality)? Can they be increased?
- Are all areas well *maintained*, kept clean, and functional with no needed repairs or replacements? If not, when were they last maintained?
- Are *rules of conduct* communicated? Enforced?
- Are there *supporting activities* that enhance surveillance, access management and social order? If not, can they be added?

21. Crowe, T.D., Fennelly, L.J., 2013. Crime Prevention Through Environmental Design, third ed. Elsevier Publishers, Boston, MA.

22. Using Crime Prevention Through Environment Design in Problem-Solving. Retrieved on November 11, 2018 from: <www.popcenter.org/tools/cpted/>.

23. Cozens, P.M., Saville, G., Hillier, D., 2005. Crime prevention through environmental design (CPTED): a review and modern bibliography. Property Manage. 23 (5), 328–356.

PHOTO 7.7

- Are the grounds *legible*? Is it easy to understand where you are at any given point? Is it obvious which path or direction you need to take to arrive at a desired location?
- Does the *landscaping* enhance the ability to read the site? Does it provide shade and buffering where needed? Does it provide an esthetic quality? Is it accessible? Is it healthy and well maintained? Is it a problem?
- How do the site users *behave*? Is there respect for the environment? Are there areas where tensions and disorder are common?
- Is there *graffiti* or other signs of vandalism?
- Is there *CCTV or video surveillance*? If so, are they placed in prime locations? Are there other means of surveillance?
- Are there successful *CPTED applications* already in place? If so, take note and use them as positive examples.[24]

Photo 7.7 shows vegetation obstructing casual surveillance and lighting. Yes, there is a light pole in the middle of this photo, taken by Marianna Perry.

Surrounding neighborhood observations

- adjacent land uses
- condition of adjacent streets and properties
- traffic patterns and volumes on adjacent streets
- pedestrian crossing safeguards (marked crossings and traffic lights)
- recommendations for improvements

Perimeter and points of entry

- first impressions on approaching the site/location
- walls and/or fencing
- type, location, hours of operation and users
- special staff and/or visitor access points
- sign(s) that identify the site/location, welcome visitors, and info about special visitor parking and entry
- signs and/or maps to guide visitors to special parking and entry
- signs and/or pavement markings to guide vehicles
- surveillance opportunities from interior spaces
- landscaping and cleanliness
- lighting
- recommendations for improvements

24. Crime Prevention Through Environmental Design. Retrieved on November 11, 2018 from: <http://cptedsecurity.com/cpted_design_guidelines.htm>.

PHOTO 7.8

PHOTO 7.9

Photo 7.8 shows an environment in need of landscaping and cleanliness.

Vehicular travel routes and parking facilities

- motor vehicle traffic patterns, including bus and student drop-off/pick-up loops in school applications
- signs and/or maps to guide visitors to appropriate parking and entry locations
- sign(s) to identify visitor parking
- surveillance of parking lots from interior spaces
- lighting
- recommendations for improvements

Photo 7.9 shows clearly identified vehicle traffic patterns and pedestrian crosswalks.

Pedestrian travel paths and gathering areas

- pedestrian routes to and from building(s)
- pedestrian crosswalk markings or designated pedestrian routes
- signage, landscaping, and/or landmarks to guide pedestrians
- surveillance of walkways and exterior corridors
- formal and informal gathering areas
- lighting
- recommendations for improvements

Building exteriors and grounds

- esthetics, building design, location, and security of windows and doors
- surveillance capability both natural and mechanical
- hidden nooks and alcoves
- use of mirrors and/or security surveillance systems, CCTV.
- cleanliness and landscaping
- lighting
- recommendations for improvements

Building interiors

- external and/or internal surveillance capability
- access management (observed versus policy and procedure)
- hidden nooks and alcoves in corridors, stairwells, and special use areas
- use of mirrors and/or CCTV/security surveillance system
- restrooms
- alarmed areas
- cleanliness, maintenance other territorial reinforcement
- natural, artificial, and emergency lighting
- recommendations for improvements

Maintenance and delivery areas

- access doors, location, and surveillance opportunities
- security and access management during delivery/maintenance
- dumpster/trash location(s)
- storage of fuels and chemicals
- after-hours use
- recommendations for improvements

Crime prevention through environmental design survey for colleges and universities

30 Vulnerabilities based on crime prevention through environmental design assessments are as follows:

1. poor visibility at entry to campus
2. easy vehicular access onto campus
3. no clear boundary separating the campus from public property
4. inadequate distance between campus buildings and neighbors
5. exterior doors to buildings unlocked 24/7
6. areas and buildings on campus hidden by landscaping or vegetation
7. school adjacent to traffic hazard
8. portions of buildings or campus inaccessible to emergency vehicles
9. secluded hangout areas on campus
10. no safety/security awareness program for students, faculty, and staff
11. perimeter of campus not visible from streets
12. no barriers between parking and lawn
13. gravel in parking area
14. dangerous traffic routes or patterns on campus
15. enclosed courtyard that offers concealment to criminals
16. high parapets on buildings that hide criminals
17. no security officers on site for access control or patrol duties
18. no "escort-to-vehicle" program during darkness
19. inadequate lighting on campus
20. no lighting maintenance plan to repair or replace nonoperational lights

21. crime magnet or hangout located close to campus
22. no vegetation/landscape planting and maintenance program
23. benches on campus that can be used for sleeping by homeless individuals
24. faculty, staff, and students not displaying ID badges
25. bollards not used to prevent vehicles from driving on sidewalks
26. no cameras or video surveillance program
27. exterior doors in dorms propped open
28. courtesy desk at entrance to dorms not staffed 24/7
29. parking areas that are not clearly visible from buildings
30. proper signage on campus

CPTED recommendations:

The following are some environmental problems and issues (as well as recommendations), which may be documented in part of a CPTED assessment:

- One-way street systems have been found not only to improve traffic flow but also to create dead zones for business, with resulting crime or fear of crime that deters development efforts.
- Through traffic in neighborhoods has been found to be detrimental to residential housing values, stability and crime rates.
- Downtown projects continue to fail by making fundamental errors that reduce natural surveillance and natural access control, resulting in the loss of desired users and domination by unwanted users.
- Fortress effects are produced by designers of convention centers, hotels, banks, senior citizen housing, and parking lot structures. These destroy the surrounding land uses and create a "no-man's land."
- Bleed-off parking enhances conflict between commercial and residential and uses, both lose.
- Design and management can actually reduce business and increase victimization of employees and customers.
- Mall and major event facility parking areas with poorly planned access control and layout can produce traffic congestion and become magnets for undesirable activity.
- School and institutional designs can inadvertently create dysfunctional areas where surveillance is impossible, resulting in increased behavioral and crime problems and overall impediments to successful operations (e.g., students' achievement in schools).
- Public housing and affordable housing can become projects that serve as magnets for transients, as opposed to local poor, with further detrimental effects on existing neighborhoods.

Nearly every environmental situation or location is amenable to the application of CPTED concepts. The law enforcement agency can assist in asking the right questions and in supplying the right kind of information to help the community to make more informed decisions.

CPTED adds a new dimension by incorporating these elements into space design and management[25]:

Natural access control

Your space should give some natural indication of where people are allowed and are not allowed. Do not depend just on locks, alarms, surveillance systems, and security officers, but make security part of the layout (see landscape security later).

Natural surveillance

Again, traditional factors such as good lighting are important, but do not overlook a natural factor such as a strategically placed window or the placement of an employee work station.

Territorial reinforcement

This is an umbrella concept, embodying all-natural surveillance and access control principles. It emphasizes the enhancement of ownership and proprietary behaviors.

CPTED proposes that the proper design and effective use of the built environment can lead to a reduction in the opportunity, fear and incidence of predatory stranger-to-stranger type crime, as well as result in an improvement of the quality of life. Crime prevention design solutions should be integrated into the design and function of the buildings, or at least the location where they are being implemented.

25. Crowe, T.D., Fennelly, L.J., 2013. Crime Prevention Through Environmental Design, third ed. Elsevier Publishers, Boston, MA.

In his writings on CPTED, Tim Crowe stated, "It is clear that light affects human behavior and too much or too little light will have different effects. It is now generally accepted that performance improves and fatigue levels drop in direct proportion to increased levels of light, but it also relates to the work or play environment."[26]

The ancient field of chronotherapy, or photobiology as it is now called, is making a comeback because through research many scientists have discovered that color and light can affect health and behavior. Richard J. Wurtman, a nutritionist at the Massachusetts Institute of Technology, states that light is the most important environmental input, after food in controlling bodily function.[27]

Many psychologists believe that light has a tremendous influence on human behavior. There is a level of light that people experience as the most pleasant. Brightly lit rooms are more arousing than dimly lit rooms. Light also influences the image of a retail store as shoppers look at and scrutinize merchandise to purchase.

CPTED principles were not only founded upon social interactions, criminology, and architecture but also on the psychological impact of the principles. Colors have a physical aspect in security, such as assisting in finding way and moving people to safer locations, proper entrances, etc., but there is also a psychological impact. Security practitioners do well in applying the physical aspect of color such as using lighter colors to reflect more light, but not very well at considering the emotions evoked from a particular color. Many security practitioners believe that the use of color may be one aspect to consider for preventing crime and may have a positive impact on workplace violence, school safety, and a number of other applications. Any designer or interior decorator can tell you how important color is for setting the mood for an environment. Research has shown that different colors affect blood pressure, pulse, respiration rates as well as brain activity and biorhythms.[28]

Psychological properties of colors

Red—Red is a powerful color. Its effect is physical, strong, and basic. Red is stimulating and lively as well as friendly.[29] A person wearing a red tie does so because it is called a power tie.

Positives: Physical, courage, strength, warmth, energy, basic survival, fight or flight, stimulation, masculinity, and excitement.

Negatives: Defiance, aggressive and aggression, visual impact, and strain.

Blue—Blue is the color of the mind and is essentially soothing. It affects us mentally, rather than the physical reaction we have to red. Strong blues will stimulate clear thoughts and lighter while soft blues will calm the mind and aid concentration. The world's favorite color is blue, but it can be perceived as cold, unemotional, and unfriendly.

Positives: Intellectual, communication, trust, efficiency, serenity, duty, logic, coolness, reflection, and calm.

Negatives: Coldness, aloofness, lack of emotion, and unfriendliness.

Yellow—The yellow wavelength is relatively long and essentially stimulating. The wrong color scheme with yellow can cause fear and anxiety.

Positives: Emotional, optimism, confidence, self-esteem, extraversion, emotional strength, friendliness, and creativity.

Negatives: Irrationality, fear, emotional fragility, depression, anxiety, and suicide.

Green—If a green color scheme is used incorrectly, it can indicate stagnation.

Positives: Harmony, balance, refreshment, universal love, rest, restoration, reassurance, environmental awareness, equilibrium, and peace.

Negatives: Boredom, stagnation, blandness, and enervation.

Violet—The excessive use of purple can bring about too much of the wrong tone faster than any other color of it communicates something cheap and nasty.

Positives: Spiritual awareness, containment, vision, luxury, authenticity, truth, and quality.

Negatives: Introversion, suppression, and inferiority.

26. Crowe, T.D., Fennelly, L.J., 2013. Crime Prevention Through Environmental Design, third ed. Elsevier Publishers, Boston, MA.

27. Color Has a Powerful Effect on Behavior, Researchers ASSERT. Retrieved on November 11, 2018 from: <http://www.nytimes.com/1982/10/19/science/color-has-a-powerful-effect-on-behavior-researchers-assert.html>.

28. Color Has a Powerful Effect on Behavior, Researchers ASSERT. Retrieved on November 11, 2018 from: <http://www.nytimes.com/1982/10/19/science/color-has-a-powerful-effect-on-behavior-researchers-assert.html>.

29. Psychological Properties of Colours. Retrieved on November 11, 2018 from: <http://www.colour-affects.co.uk/psychological-properties-of-colours>.

Orange—Orange let our minds focus on issues of physical comfort—food, warmth, shelter, and sensuality. It is a fun color. Too much orange suggests a lack of serious intellectual values.

Positives: Physical comfort, food, warmth, security, sensuality, passion, abundance, and fun.

Negatives: Introversion, decadence, suppression, and inferiority.

Black—Black totally absorbs all colors and creates barriers, as it absorbs all the energy coming toward you. BLACK IS THE ABSENCE OF LIGHT. Many people are afraid of the dark. In cowboy movies ... the good guys wear what color hats? The bad guys where what color hats? We wear a black tie to a funeral. We wear black to look thinner; however, in 2016 a fashion designer stated multicolor clothing was the way to go. Black race horses look faster.

Positives: Sophistication, glamour, security, emotional safety, efficiency, and substance.

Negatives: Oppression, coldness, menace, and heaviness.

Gray—The heavy use of gray usually indicates a lack of confidence and fear of exposure.

Positives: Psychological neutrality.

Negatives: Lack of confidence, dampness, lack of energy, depression, and hibernation.

Pink—Being a tint of red, pink also affects us physically, but it soothes rather than stimulates. Pink is a powerful color, psychologically.

Positives: Physical comfort, food, warmth, security, sensuality, passion, abundance, and fun.

Negatives: Inhibition, emotional claustrophobia, emasculation, and physical weakness.

White—White is total reflection. It reflects the full force of the spectrum to the eyes. White is purity, the negative effect of white on warm colors is to make them look and feel garish.

Positives: Hygiene, sterility, clarity, purity, cleanness, simplicity, sophistication, and efficiency.

Negatives: Sterility, coldness, barriers, unfriendliness, elitism.

Brown—Brown usually consists of red and yellow with a large percentage of black.

Positives: Seriousness, warmth, nature, earthiness, reliability, and support.

Negatives: Lack of humor, heaviness, and lack of sophistication.

Purple—Throughout her 2016 presidential campaign, Hilary Clinton's outfits have been symbolic. A popular color for her has been white, the color of the suffragette movement.[30] She wore it when she accepted the nomination at the Democratic National Convention, at the final presidential debate and on election day itself.

While making her concession speech to president-elect Donald Trump and the nation on Wednesday however, Clinton went with another color: Purple.[31] This color too holds a tremendous amount of symbolism.

Purple along with white and gold are the colors of the National Women's Party[32] according to the New York Times. An early statement by the party said that purple symbolizes "loyalty, constancy to purpose, and unswerving steadfastness to a cause."[33]

Example: A local bank

At a local bank, we noticed the warm color scheme of the bank interior and the lighting levels were designed to help customers feel safe and comfortable. We could tell that someone had certainly done their homework. In addition, the bank manager was in the lobby greeting customers. The comfort zone they were hoping for definitely worked. They earned an A + ! Many hospitals and other medical facilities use green as an interior color to project calmness and relaxation to help patients feel less nervous and anxious.

When discussing the psychology of color, remember that blue and green have a relaxing effect, while red and orange are stimulating, Warm colors are perceived as being protective and clear and saturated colors are experienced as more pleasant. Dark colors are perceived as more dominant and more strongly suggest hostility and aggression.

30. On Election Day, the Hillary Clinton White Suit Effect. Retrieved on November 11, 2018 from: <http://www.nytimes.com/2016/11/07/fashion/hillary-clinton-suffragists-white-clothing.html>.

31. What Does Hillary Clinton's Purple Suit Mean? Her Concession Speech Outfit Was Symbolic. Retrieved on November 11, 2018 from: <https://www.romper.com/p/what-does-hillary-clintons-purple-suit-mean-her-concession-speech-outfit-was-symbolic-22329>.

32. Why Hillary Wore White. Retrieved on November 11, 2018 from: <http://www.nytimes.com/2016/07/30/fashion/hillary-clinton-democratic-national-convention.html>.

33. History and Collection. Retrieved on November 11, 2018 from: <http://nationalwomansparty.org/the-national-womans-party-and-the-meaning-behind-their-purple-white-and-gold-textiles/>.

The psychology of color is complex. There are differing opinions about color as well as scientific research on colors and the combinations of colors.

Colors and lighting for parking garages

The ceiling of parking garages should be painted white to get the best reflection possible from lighting. In addition, consider LED lighting because it is the most cost effective. Also, painting the walls white will enhance the effect and strength not only the CPTED principle of surveillance but also that of access control (due to visual sense of place) and maintenance, as related in the "broken windows theory"[34] of crime and disorder. Remember that the placement of lighting must be carefully considered in conjunction with video surveillance to avoid conflicting uses, obscuring or making images undetectable due to glare and possible "hot spots" when using warm lighting sources.

Street lighting

Recent studies proved that an increase in light provides safety and reduces the fear of becoming victimized in a particular environment as well as a reduction in crime. Street lighting is generally seen as the most important physical feature of an environment to affect *perceived* personal safety. The general consensus is that adequate street lighting can help reduce not only crime rates but also the fear of crime. Consideration again must be given to the environment that is addressed and its intended use. Overlighting or too much light in a neighborhood may have a negative consequence on the surveillance principle of CPTED because residents may close their blinds or curtains to block out the offending, trespassing light which will limit natural surveillance.

Crime prevention through environmental design landscape security recommendations

Adequate lighting, in conjunction with clear access to walkways and entryways to buildings, should be clearly visible for members of the community utilizing the space. Landscape should be maintained to minimize obstacles to clear observability and places of concealment for potential assailants. This is achieved by trimming bushes so they are no higher than 36 in. in height and trimming tree branches to 8 ft from the ground.

Sidewalks, streets, and parking lots must be clean (power washed) and free of graffiti. Ensure that there is proper signage and adequate lighting.

Parks should have a 360-degree view of the area, and park benches should be designed to not allow someone to sleep on the bench. Create a venue for after school activities that encourage youth to take ownership of the space for socializing, such as small shelter areas with cell phone chargers and Wi-Fi access.

Signage plays an important role in park security. There should be signs indicating the hours the park is open and rules for those utilizing the space. Proper signage removes the excuses for unacceptable behavior, draws attention to the illegitimate activity, and legitimizes police involvement, thus making the violation of the information on the posted signs an excellent crime prevention tool.

There is a vast array of traffic-calming devices, such as speed bumps and raised crosswalks. These areas should be painted yellow and proper signage posted. At the entrance to neighborhoods or communities, post *Neighborhood Watch* or *Block Watch* signs.

Eliminate "hot spots" by planting thorny bushes (Barberry, Holly, etc.) in problem areas. Use boulders or bollards to control vehicular access. Consider adding community art or sculptures which not only control access but also reinforce the purpose by giving implied ownership to the artists.

Photo 7.10 shows an effective use for bollards to control vehicular access (photos taken by Marianna Perry).

For security purposes, perimeter fencing should be 7 ft in height, with three strands of barb wire on the top, spaced 6 in. apart, for a total fence height of 8 ft. We would not make this recommendation unless it was a large property and the perimeter was a significant distance from the buildings on the property. Careful consideration must be given to the type of fencing, the desired impact (boundary definition vs security) and the location of the facility (rural vs urban) must be taken into account, and there should be at least 10 ft of clear space on both sides of the fence.

Photo 7.11 shows an 8-ft security fence with clear space on both sides of the fence.

LED lighting is cost effective and should meet lighting standards and guidelines for illumination but may not be appropriate for all applications.

34. Broken Windows Theory. Retrieved on November 11, 2018 from: <http://www.britannica.com/topic/broken-windows-theory>.

PHOTO 7.10

PHOTO 7.11

PHOTO 7.12

Bus stops should be located in areas where at least one open business can clearly observe the area. Alternatively, this problem may be addressed by contacting the school or bus company to monitor the space via video surveillance.

Do not allow tagging or graffiti in public spaces. Consider the use of paint or coatings that will allow for easy removal of graffiti. All graffiti or tagging should be removed within 24 hours.

Photo 7.12 shows graffiti/tagging that should be removed.

Hot spots

"Hot spots" should be eliminated. If they cannot be completely eliminated, develop a program to keep unauthorized users or unwanted individuals out of the area.

Community policing programs, including the formulation of public–private sector partnerships,[35] can be used to fight disorder and crime.

Vacant lots are best monitored by citizens that we give "ownership" of them. One example is a place in Richmond, VA where a community flower garden was placed. People that worked in the garden monitored the space. Another option is for the city to share the property via giving the lot to Habitat for Humanity to build a structure on within a given time frame, thus resulting in tax revenue. Inspections from local government agencies can also result in the owners of vacant property being held responsible for the upkeep of the property or pay fines for noncompliance.

Redesign properties using CPTED principles to make them more crime resistant by reducing the criminal opportunity within the community.

There are some properties, such as HUD properties that may need a higher level of protection, such as additional lighting and video surveillance systems. Law enforcement support is also needed as to address specific issues and to support a safe community.

Locate open spaces and recreational areas in neighborhoods so they are visible (natural surveillance) from nearby homes as well as the street. Avoid landscaping that might create blind spots or hiding places. Make sure there is effective lighting. Design streets to discourage cut through or high-speed traffic using "traffic-calming" measures. Join or start a Neighborhood Watch in your neighborhood.[36]

In apartment buildings, ensure that interior hallways are well lit with a secure front door. Install good quality, deadbolts locks and provide door viewers (peepholes) on individual apartment exterior doors. Provide a secondary locking device to any sliding glass doors, windows on ground floor and fire escapes. Provide a common space in central locations to encourage tenant interaction. Join or start an Apartment Watch or Neighborhood Watch in your building.

For retail businesses, locate checkout counters near the front of the store, clearly visible from outside. Window signs should cover no more than 15% of the windows to provide clear visibility into and out of the store. Use shelving and displays no higher than 4 ft to see who is in the store.[37] Avoid creating outdoor spaces that encourage loitering. Install mirrors at strategic locations as well as a security surveillance system.

Measuring and evaluation of crime prevention through environmental design

Very little has been written on how to measure the effectiveness of CPTED programs. Some work was done in 2005—see references for this material.

An example

Let us call the site in question "the complex" since CPTED concepts will cover the full spectrum. First, obtain 3 years of crime data from the local police department for the area around the property and compare year over year changes in crime. Second, obtain internal incident reports (whether or not they were reported to law enforcement) to identify issues that have occurred on the property. Conduct a full security assessment and be sure to pay close attention to natural surveillance, (landscape security) natural access control, and territoriality, to help determine how to best "harden" the target.

The job of security is becoming more proactive. Security awareness programs and *Neighborhood Watch* or similar programs can be implemented in neighborhoods with monthly law enforcement follow-up, by analyzing crime and incident data to determine the effectiveness of physical security measures currently in place and where changes need to be made.

35. http://www.policechiefmagazine.org/magazine/index.cfm?fuseaction = display_arch&article_id = 902&issue_id = 52006.

36. Neighborhood Watch. Retrieve on November 11, 2018 from: <http://www.ncpc.org/topics/home-and-neighborhood-safety/neighborhood-watch>.

37. Working Safely at Home. Retrieved on November 11, 2018 from: <http://www.ncpc.org/topics/workplace-safety>.

Awareness

- Become aware of your community and who the strangers are. The guy walking down the street with the black dog—who is he?
- Look for signs of behavior that does not fit the normal pattern. Ask, "Can I help you?" Then evaluate the response.
- Have you ever gone for a walk and see four newspapers on the lawn? What does that tell you? Thieves also do assessments and evaluate your house.

Fear of crime

- We have seen fear many times, such as on television, when a school is in lock-down mode and anxious parents are waiting outside to see their child and seeking reassurance that their child has not been harmed. This is not a pretty sight.
- It is interesting to note that research has shown that the fear of crime is actually much higher that actual crime victimization rates.[38]

Crime prevention through environmental design strategies

- The previous discussion suggests a series of general design strategies that can be applied in any situation to improve natural access control, natural surveillance, and territorial behavior.
- Provide a clear border definition of controlled space.
- Provide a clearly marked transition from public to semipublic to private space.
- Locate gathering areas in places with natural surveillance and access control and away from the view of potential offenders.
- Place safe activities in unsafe locations and unsafe activities in safe locations.
- Provide natural barriers to conflicting activities.
- Improve the scheduling of space to provide the effective and critical intensity of uses.
- Design spaces to increase the perception of natural surveillance.
- Overcome distance and isolation through improved communications and design efficiencies, for example, emergency telephones and pedestrian paths.
- Turn soft targets into hard targets.

Obtaining results

After all of the abovementioned items have been completed and security is maintained at the highest level, you should have a reduction in crime risks and crime as well as a reduction in fear of crime. Then, after 3 years, compare the data with the previous 3 years to see your results.

Conclusion

CPTED involves the design of physical space in the context of the needs of legitimate users of the space (physical, social, and psychological needs), the normal and expected (or intended) use of the space (the activity or absence of activity planned for the space), and the predictable behavior of both intended users and offenders. Therefore in the CPTED approach, a design is proper if it recognizes the designated use of the space, defines the crime problem incidental to and the solution compatible with the designated use and incorporates the crime prevention strategies that enhance (or at least do not impair) the effective use of the space.

CPTED addresses the potential victim and the potential criminal's mindset in preventing crime through manipulating the built environment and better planning for its intended use.

A security assessment is the process of evaluating a site for security vulnerabilities, and making recommendations to address said vulnerabilities. The goal is to either remove or reduce the potential vulnerability.

---

38. Fear of Crime in the United States: Avenues for Research and Policy. Retrieved on November 11, 2018 from: <https://www.ncjrs.gov/criminal_justice2000/vol_4/04i.pdf>.

- Reduce opportunities for crime and fear of crime by making open areas more easily observable, and by increasing activity in the neighborhood.
- Provide ways in which neighborhood residents, business people, and law enforcement can work together in partnership to more effectively to reduce opportunities and incentives for crime.
- Increase neighborhood identity, investor confidence, and social cohesion.
- Provide public information programs that help schools, businesses, and residents protect themselves from crime.
- Make the area more accessible by improving transportation services.
- Improve the effectiveness and efficiency of governmental operations.
- Encourage citizens to report crimes so they can be a part of the problem-solving process.

The steps taken to achieve these objectives include the following:

- improved, cost-effective outdoor lighting
- sidewalk and landscaping improvements
- partnerships with law enforcement and other local officials
- Neighborhood Watch, Business Watch, and School Watch Programs
- neighborhood cleanups
- a campaign to educate businesses about safe cash handling procedures and how to discourage robberies
- improve and expand public transportation

Basic improvements in neighborhoods and communities can enhance the "quality of life" and provide an atmosphere of cohesiveness. The application of CPTED concepts has been used successfully throughout the world to reduce not only the incidence of crime but also the fear of crime as well. This leads to an improvement in the quality of life for everyone who lives, works, or visits the neighborhood or community.

Second-generation crime prevention through environmental design

"Second-generation CPTED is a new form of ecological, sustainable development."[39] It includes a focus on building neighborhoods on a small, local scale and then incorporating community building and the social aspects of the environment. To a large extent, this goes back to C. Ray Jeffery's CPTED model, which included engineering the social environment and the built environment as well as recognizing the importance of rewards and disincentives for behavior. This model also includes the role of enforcement.

The second-generation of CPTED consists of four strategies referred to as the four Cs[40]:

1. social cohesion
2. community connectivity
3. community culture
4. threshold capacity

Social cohesion is the core of second-generation CPTED. A safe community is the goal, which incorporates a wide range of strategies in order to reach this goal. These include emotional intelligence training, which develops self-esteem and personal confidence. Cohesion strategies will enhance relationships between residents.

Community connectivity is when the neighborhood has a positive relations and influence with outside agencies such as local law enforcement, fire department and emergency medical technician (EMTs), moreover access to grant-writing services, regular activities with outside groups, social media, shared pathways and facilities for bike paths and walking to the beach or other locations within the community.

A *community culture* is formed when residents come together to share a sense of cohesion to display territorially. Together, residents participate in community events, such as festivals and flea markets.

Threshold capacity is a strategy intended to keep the neighborhood ecosystems within suggested levels and also promoting human-scale and pedestrian-oriented neighborhood functioning through effective management. If neighborhood ecosystems exceed their carrying capacity, the result will be increased levels of crime.

39. Saville, G., Cleveland, G., 1998. Second generation CPTED: an antidote to the social Y2K Virus of urban design. In: Paper presented to the third International CPTED Association Conference, Washington, DC, December 14–16, 1998.

40. Atlas, R., 2008. 21st Century Security and CPTED: Designing for Critical Infrastructure, Protection and Crime Prevention. Florida.

The second-generation of CPTED focuses on strategies to eliminate the reasons for criminal behavioral and create a sustainable, livable environment.

Third-generation crime prevention through environmental design

The basic premise of third-generation CPTED is that a sustainable, green urban environment is perceived by community members (as well as outsiders) to be safe. The focus is on building a sustainable green environment that is safe from not only crime, but the fear of crime also.[41]

Third-generation CPTED suggests that a sustainable environment utilizes strategies that use green technologies. This strategy focuses on reducing the fear of crime and increasing the perception of security in the community.[42]

What is green technology?

- harvesting of natural energy
- incorporating zero-carbon and clean energy such as nuclear energy
- reduce carbon footprint
- hybrid vehicles
- wireless services and wireless networks
- target energy consumption
- harvested energy as a power source for street lighting
- use of energy efficient light sources such as LED bulbs and fixtures
- enhancing a citizen sense of belonging through lectures and training
- Digital Water Pavilion
- the cloud
- urban furniture

Kerry Kirpatrick, the Social Media Director for Buildings Magazine, stated that research has revealed that increased productivity is a benefit of green buildings through a study that was designed to reflect indoor environments encountered by large numbers of people every day. "These findings have far ranging implications for worker productivity, student learning, and safety."[43]

It is efficient and economical to use "green environment designs," but keep in mind that when you use these strategies, they must also lead to safer and more secure environment. Applications for "green" answers to crime and fear of crime are still evolving, but it appears as though this strategy is a viable approach.

Below is a QR code with material prepared by Diane Zahm, entitled, *Using CPTED in Problem Solving Tool Guide No. 8* (2007) POP Guide. A special thanks to Rick Draper for designing this QR code.

Emerging Trends 2019

International Design Out Crime Conferences, iDOC 2019 What is New DOC? New Directions in CPTED Overview

Overview

The iDOC 2019 International Design Out Crime and CPTED Conference focuses on *New Directions in CPTED* and *Night-Time Economy CPTED*.

There are many new changes to *CPTED* and *Design Out Crime*. These are driven by a large number of factors changing in the world at large, which are as follows:

- increased use of evidence on what works and what does not, where, when, and why;
- the extention of CPTED into new areas such as antiterrorism, crowded places, and event management;
- new technologies transforming CPTED (e.g., face recognition, virtual following, 360 degree 24/7 surveillance, biometric access control, and drones);

41. Green Answers for Crime: 3rd Generation CPYED. Retrieved on November 11, 2018 from: <http://safe-growth.blogspot.com/2015/12/green-answers-for-crime-3rd-gen-cpted.html>.

42. Cozen, P.M., 2002. Sustainable urban development and CPTED for the British City towards an effective urban environment for the 21st Century Cities. Int. J. Urban Policy Plan. 19 (2) 129–132.

43. Event Highlights Sustainability and Economic Development. Retrieved on November 11, 2018 from: <http://energyalliancegroup.org/author/kerry/>.

- new thinking about CPTED in relation to health, gender, equity, control, economic development, legal liabilities, etc.;
- professionalization of CPTED practices;
- new forms of CPTED training and certification; and
- CPTED standards.

The conference presentations will include academic papers (peer-reviewed), "Tales from the Field," and "specialist topic" presentations. Presentations will be grouped under two tracks: "New Directions in CPTED" and "Night-Time Economy CPTED." Before the conference, during the day on the 13th February, there will be a program of workshops and desktop team exercises.

Conference themes:

- Use of evidence in CPTED
- Night time economy CPTED (a major theme of this conference)
- New technology CPTED (e.g. face recognition, virtual following, 360 degree 24/7 surveillance, biometric access control, drones. . .)
- Risk vs threat vs vulnerabilities vs guidelines in CPTED
- Counter-terrorism and Crowded Places CPTED
- Event CPTED
- CPTED and gender
- Social equity issues and CPTED
- CPTED and health
- CPTED and social control
- CPTED and privacy
- CPTED, young people, and public space
- Legal and financial liabilities from CPTED
- CPTED and economic development
- CPTED across the life of developments
- Dark sides of CPTED (adverse consequences)
- Occupational Health and Safety and CPTED
- Professional CPTED practices
- Training, certification and standards in CPTED

Conclusion

I totally agree, times change and we also must change by staying ahead of the curve or we will fall behind. When Marianna Perry and I did the book "CPTED and Traditional Security Countermeasures—150 Things You Should know." I cannot tell you how many people say you cannot list seven concepts to First Generation well the first six were around since 1983 and Paul Cozen listed item seven. Yes, we need to change and update and evaluate what we have said and done or fall behind.

Lawrence J. Fennelly (2018)

Suggested reference materials

Risk analysis and security countermeasure selection

Norman, T.L., 2016. CPP, PSP, CSC. CRC Press, p. 281.

Fennelly, L.J., 2017. Effective Physical Security, fifth ed. Elsevier Publishers.

Fennelly, L.J., Perry, M., 2018. CPTED and Traditional Security Countermeasures: 150 Things You Should Know. CRC Press.

Chapter 8

Mental health issues and Crime Prevention Through Environmental Design

Lawrence J. Fennelly and Marianna A. Perry
Security Consultant

Research as shown that green spaces reduce depression

Design Council, United Kingdom, 2017

Introduction

We all know someone who is affected by some form of a mental health condition. Should it be a close friend or relative, then the concern becomes much greater for their safety and security. When it comes to living environments and mental health, most security practitioners do not have a clue.

Can CPTED and urban design create a safer and healthier community? Yes, it can . . .

Mental health and living environments even senior citizens housing need to be a priority and address urban living conditions because those living in our cities are at an increased in risk of depression and a double risk of developing schizophrenia compared to those living in the country. Some causes are density, overcrowding, noise, smell, sight, disarray, pollution, feeling overloaded, lack of brain stimulation, and fear of crime.

As early as 1986, The Ottawa Charter of the World Health Organization stated that the living environment of people is where most of health is created. The Ottawa Charter states, "Health promotion works through concrete and effective community action in setting priorities, making decisions, planning strategies and implementing them to achieve better health. At the heart of this process is the empowerment of communities – their ownership and control of their own endeavors and destinies. Community development draws on existing human and material resources in the community to enhance self-help and social support, and to develop flexible systems for strengthening public participation in and direction of health matters."[1]

With the growth of mental health issues, especially among adolescents and senior citizens, these concerns must be met with changes in the environments where people live. This can be accomplished with the development of local communities that are more inclusive and socially supportive, so people can live a higher quality of life.[2] The primary focus needs to be on favorable living environments and good neighborhoods. The planning and designing communities that are socially supportive are critical in order to achieve a higher quality of life.

Symptoms of dementia

Dementia symptoms vary depending on the cause, but common signs and symptoms include the two of the following changes:

1. Living Environments. From: <https://www.ntnu.edu/chpr/living-environments> (retrieved 09.04.18.).

2. The Coordination Reform. From: <https://www.regjeringen.no/contentassets/d4f0e16ad32e4bbd8d8ab5c21445a5dc/en-gb/pdfs/stm200820090047000en_pdfs.pdf> (retrieved 06.03.18.).

Handbook of Loss Prevention and Crime Prevention. DOI: https://doi.org/10.1016/B978-0-12-817273-5.00008-9

Cognitive changes:

- memory loss, which is usually noticed by a spouse or someone else as well as a degree of lying, because the individual cannot answer the question;
- difficulty in communicating or finding words;
- difficulty in reasoning or problem-solving and problems in managing money;
- difficulty in handling complex tasks;
- difficulty with planning and organizing;
- difficulty with coordination and motor functions and getting lost, driving; and
- confusion and disorientation.

Psychological changes:

- personality changes;
- depression;
- anxiety;
- inappropriate behavior;
- paranoia;
- agitation; and
- hallucinations.

According to the Mayo Clinic,[3] dementia develops in adults with damaged nerve cells in their brains. Many people with Alzheimer's disease display buildup of plaque in certain areas of brain, which affects memory and damage blood vessels, which impacts the brain's blood supply.

Dementia solutions—aside from medical

Regular physical exercise may help lower the risk of some types of dementia. Research has shown that exercise may directly benefit brain cells by increasing blood and oxygen flow to the brain. There are some solutions that may help someone who is suffering from dementia or other mental health issues, including the development of green space to help reduce depression.

The following list is based on research from the Design Council in the United Kingdom: www.designcouncil.org.uk/news-opinion/designing-good-mental-health[4] and www.webmd.com.[5]

1. Areas for regular exercise, walking, or swimming. Exercise can be just as effective as antidepressant medication for mild and moderate depression. It can also reduce stress and anxiety and help alleviate some of the symptoms associated with ADHD, dementia, and even schizophrenia.
2. Reduce dark corners or hidden spot and create natural surveillance or sight lines.
3. Reduce feeling unsafe or the fear of crime.
4. Maintain this area and create a positive image.
5. Community activity is an important part for mental health, refer the section on *The Villages* and the variety of activities they have.
6. Good street lighting increases the perception of safety.
7. In landscape architecture the built environment is understood to mean a human-made landscape, as distinguished from the natural environment; for example, a city park is a built environment.[6]
8. One study in Denmark found health benefits for bicycle commuting far beyond calories burned. Bike commuters also ate healthier diets and felt less stress at work, among other positive effects. If we could make biking transportation fully safe and accessible in our cities, the health impacts would be immense.[7]
9. Eat healthy foods such as, fruits and whole grain, take vitamin D, and limit caffeine.
10. Listen to soft music, get a pet, have therapeutic massages, and get exercise.

---

3. Dementia. From: <https://www.mayoclinic.org/diseases-conditions/dementia/symptoms-causes/syc-20352013> (retrieved 06.01.18.).
4. Designing good mental health into cities: the next frontier for urban design, Design Council, 2017, *Rachel Toms, Insight & Standards Manager, Cities Programme (Secondment)*.
5. What Are the Treatments for Dementia?. From: <https://www.webmd.com/alzheimers/dementia-treatments-overview#1> (retrieved 13.03.18.).
6. Urban Design. From: <https://en.wikipedia.org/wiki/Urban_design> (retrieved 15.02.18.).
7. Cycling Is Healthier Than You Think. From: <http://www.cycling-embassy.dk/2015/04/30/cycling-is-healthier-than-you-think/> (retrieved 18.02.18.).

11. Utilize urban design using Crime Prevention Through Environmental Design (CPTED) concepts.
12. Assisted living, for the individual hard to accept, but your neurologist can help in this matter.

It is our intention with the items abovementioned to pass on information needed to aid in the improvement of the quality of life of those affected by these mental health issues.

Current trends

The goal of effective urban design is to create sustainable urban environments with long-lasting structures, buildings, and overall livability for legitimate users of the environment. Walkable urbanism is another idea that is defined as the *Charter of New Urbanism.* It aims to reduce environmental impacts by altering the built environment to create smart cities that support sustainable transport.[8] Compact urban neighborhoods encourage residents to drive less. This encourages residents to go outside, walk, and connect with others. In addition, these neighborhoods have significantly lower environmental impacts when compared to sprawling suburbs.[9]

As a result of the recent New Classical Architecture movement, sustainable construction aims to develop smart growth, walkability, architectural tradition, and classical design.[10] When we look at great architecture of 100, 500, or 2000 years ago, it is noted that their power is still undiminished. It contrasts from modernist and globally uniform architecture.[11] In the 1980s urban design began to oppose this increasing solitary housing estates and suburban sprawl that we had become accustomed to.[12]

Urban designers

Urban designers[13] are similar to urban planners when preparing design guidelines, regulatory frameworks, legislation, advertising, etc. Urban planners also overlap with architects, landscape architects, transportation engineers, and industrial designers. They must also deal with "place management" to guide and assist the use and maintenance of urban areas and public spaces.

There are professionals who identify themselves specifically as urban designers and through architecture, landscape, and planning programs incorporate urban design theory into their projects. There is hope for the future because there are an increasing number of university programs offering degrees in urban design.

Following are the consideration of the urban design:

- pedestrian zones—to encourage walkability and connectivity;
- incorporation of nature within a city—to reduce mental issues, such as depression;
- aesthetics—to increase territorial reinforcement by residents;
- urban structure—arrangement and relation of business and people;
- urban typology, density, and sustainability—spatial types and changes related to intensity of use, consumption of resources, and production and maintenance of viable communities;
- accessibility—safe and easy transportation;
- legibility and wayfinding—accessible information about travel and destinations;
- animation—designing places to stimulate public activity;
- function and fit—places support their varied intended uses;
- complementary mixed uses—locating activities to allow constructive interaction between them;
- character and meaning—recognizing differences between places;
- order and incident—balancing consistency and variety in the urban environment;

8. Boeing, G., et al., 2014. LEED-ND and livability revisited. Berkeley Plann. J. 27, 31–55. From: <https://escholarship.org/uc/item/49f234rd> (retrieved 15.04.18.).

9. Ewing, R. Growing Cooler—The Evidence on Urban Development and Climate Change. From <http://smartgrowthamerica.org> (retrieved 16.03.18.).

10. The Charter of the New Urbanism. From: <https://www.cnu.org/who-we-are/charter-new-urbanism> (retrieved 08.03.18.).

11. Beauty, Humanism, Continuity Between Past and Future. Traditional Architecture Group. From: <http://www.traditionalarchitecture.co.uk/aims.html> (retrieved 23.03.18.).

12. Issue Brief: Smart-Growth: Building Livable Communities. American Institute of Architects. From: <https://www.aia.org/SiteObjects/files/smart-growth05.pdf> (retrieved 14.03.18.).

13. Urban Design. From: <https://en.wikipedia.org/wiki/Urban_design> (retrieved 24.02.18.).

- continuity and change—locating people in time and place, respecting heritage and contemporary culture; and
- civil society—people are free to interact as civic equals.

The Villages calls itself the healthiest hometown in America

Alice Grimes, a good friend of ours, told us about the community she lives in and the activities they have. We asked her to take a minute and tell us in detail about all the activities, she replied:

> *The Villages now has over 300 activities, such as heated swimming pools and recreation centers – all within one or two miles. There are 38 executive golf courses with nine holes, and 12 championship courses, most with 27 holes. The executive courses are included in our dues of $148 a month along with all the activities, pools, and common maintenance. Classes are taught by volunteers who are retired people, experienced in that field. What's great is that there should be something for everyone. If they don't like to exercise, there are social activities, like card games, groups making things for charities, clubs for train enthusiasts, etc. Most streets have frequent get togethers with their neighbors, whether it's monthly Flamingo parties in the street (a Flamingo is placed in the front yard when that person is hosting), groups meals out, or parties for events such as Super Bowl, etc. If anyone has surgery, loses a partner, etc., the neighbors all rally around and take food and give support. This is a great place for widows and widowers because there's so much going on and it's easy to make friends and keep busy. The other thing is that if there isn't an activity or club someone is interested in, they can start one! We even have support groups for those with diseases like Parkinson's, so they can learn from each other. Oh, and I forgot the three town squares with restaurants and shops, and free, live entertainment every night except Thanksgiving and Christmas Day, where people can go to watch or dance.*

See the following links for more information on *The Villages:*

- https://www.thevillages.com/lifestyle/marketSquare.asp
- https://www.thevillages.com/Calendar/index.html

First-generation Crime Prevention Through Environmental Design

The basic idea when developing a CPTED program is that the physical environment can be manipulated to produce behavioral effects that will reduce the incidence as well as the fear of crime, so that quality of life will be improved. These behavioral effects can be accomplished by reducing the inclination of the physical environment to support criminal behavior. In a CPTED program, there is a strong relationship between humans and their environment. The term *environment* includes the people and their physical and social surroundings. The term *design* includes physical, social, management, and law enforcement directives that seek to affect positively human behavior as people interact with their environment. The desired result of a CPTED program is to prevent crime and fear of crime within a specific environment by manipulating variables.

CPTED relies not only on physical and urban design but also on contemporary thinking about behavioral and social science, law enforcement, and community organization. The concepts of CPTED continue to evolve, but traditionally (first-generation CPTED) it involves the following concepts: natural surveillance, territoriality, access control, activity support, and image/maintenance[14] Jane Jacobs's idea of "eyes on the street" influenced the concept of natural surveillance and believed that the safest urban place is one that is continuously watched by human beings.[15] Research was later done by Oscar Newman on "defensible space," and he found that crimes more likely occurred in spaces where there was no natural surveillance by residents. Both Jacobs and Newman used urban planning and design to help develop places with close-knit social networks to develop voluntary community guardianship.[16]

There are some problems if high levels of the fear of crime keep residents from going outside and spending time in public spaces. This in turn decreases physical activity levels, which can lead to physical and mental health issues. When CPTED concepts are used to reduce fear of crime and in turn increase outdoor activities and active living, this will help improve the quality of life. There is a relationship between neighborhood conditions and health, and there are direct and indirect effects on individual and public health. Direct effects include violence, homicide, dangerous driving,

14. Moffatt, R.E., 1983. Crime prevention through environmental design—a management perspective. Can. J. Criminal. 25, 19–31.
15. Jacobs, J., 1961. The Death and Life of Great American Cities. Vintage Books, New York.
16. Marzbali, M.H., Abdullah, A., Tilaki, M.J.M., 2016. The effectiveness of interventions in the built environment for improving health by addressing fear of crime. Int. J. Law Crim. Justice.

and substance abuse. Indirect effects include stress, fear of crime, repeat victimization, and social isolation. Research shows that residents' fear of crime negatively influences their active lifestyles, particularly by minimizing their time spent in walking outdoors and eventually affecting their physical and psychological health.[17]

Target hardening

The emphasis on design and use deviates from the traditional target hardening approach to crime prevention. Traditional target hardening focuses predominantly on denying access to a crime target through physical or artificial barrier techniques (such as locks, alarms, fences, and gates). Target hardening often leads to constraints on use, access, and enjoyment of the "hardened" environment. Moreover, the traditional approach tends to overlook opportunities for natural access control and surveillance. The term *natural* refers to deriving access control and surveillance as a secondary result of the normal and routine use of the environment.

These three original concepts of first-generation CPTED—natural surveillance, natural access control, and territorial reinforcement—are reinforced by the activity support of legitimate users of the space to increase eyes on the street[18] and target hardening, such as locks and alarms. CPTED emphasizes "natural" strategies as the preferred approach, which can be supplemented (as needed) by organized and mechanical strategies.[19]

Second-generation Crime Prevention Through Environmental Design

Second-generation CPTED "seeks to cultivate while building or rebuilding our Urban Areas" (Saville and Cleveland, 2008).

There are few opportunities for positive and social interactions between people and groups within the community (Green et al., 1998; Saville and Clear, 2000).

What are the concepts of second-generation CPTED?

1. Social cohesion
2. Connectivity
3. Community culture
4. Threshold capacity

Second-generation CPTED reduces crime motives by dealing with the cultural social and emotional needs of people at the specific locales where crime is or maybe most acute.

Social cohesion

A few of the characteristics that define social cohesion include:

- participation in local events and organizations;
- presence of self-directed community problem-solving;
- extent to which conflicts are positively resolved within the community, for example, restorative justice programs;
- prevalence of friendship networks within the community; and
- extensive positive relations between friendships networks.

Connectivity

Connectivity means the neighborhood has positive relations and influence with external agencies such as government funding sources.

Some characteristics of connectivity include:

- existence of networks with outside agencies, for example, shared websites;

17. Hallal, P.C., Reis, R.S., Parra, D.C., Hoehner, C., Brownson, R.C., Simões, E.J., 2010. Association between perceived environmental attributes and physical activity among adults in Recife, Brazil. J. Phys. Act. Health.

18. Eyes on the Street. From: <https://www.npr.org/2016/09/28/495615064/eyes-on-the-street-details-jane-jacobs-efforts-to-put-cities-first> (retrieved 18.02.18.).

19. Zahm, D. Using Crime Prevention Through Environmental Design in Problem Solving. From: <http://www.popcenter.org> (retrieved 23.02.18.).

- grant writer or access to a grant writing service;
- formal activities with outside groups, organizations, and neighborhood; and
- adequate transport facilities. (ride-sharing, bicycle paths, and public transit) linking to outside areas.

Community culture

CPTED practitioners sometimes forget what is significant about Jane Jacob's "eyes on the street,"[20] not the sight lines of the streets—but the eyes. We do not need neighborhoods of watchers but a sense of community where people care about who they are watching. Community culture brings people together in a common purpose. This is how local residents begin to share a sense of place and why they bother to exert territorial control in the first place (Adams and Goldbard, 2001).

A few characteristics that define culture within a community include:

- the presence and effectiveness of gender and minority equality strategies;
- gender-based programs, for example, violence against women;
- extent of social and cultural diversity within a neighborhood;
- prevalence of special places, festivals and events;
- extent of community traditions and cultural activities, for example, art fairs, sports role models; and
- a unique sense of pride or distinctiveness based on the attributes or characteristic of the residents, occupants, or users of the space involved.

Conclusion

Research indicates that there is a relationship between mental health and the physical living environment. These issues can be partially addressed through proper urban design and planning utilizing CPTED concepts. Certain environments increase the fear of crime and are associated with negative health and well-being issues. Changes in the physical environment may discourage criminal behavior but, at the same time, encourage human interaction and social connectivity. When individuals are isolated, afraid, prevent interaction and outside activity with others, mental health may deteriorate.

Six issues of emerging trends

There are six issues related to emerging trends, which are as follows: (1) there is a strong link between neighborhood conditions and health; (2) the objective is to promote healthy behaviors and reduce mental stress; (3) plus responses to homelessness as well; (4) alcohol counseling and programs dealing with mental illness; (5) although there is much environmental psychological research on; and (6) crime compared to social, cultural, economic, or mental health factors.

We raised these issues as a means of added information, should you have someone or even know of someone with mental issues, we want you to be aware of this very complex problem. It is also very stressful for the caregiver, so you should seek support and educate yourself to the many issues at hand.

20. Eyes on the Street. From: <https://www.npr.org/2016/09/28/495615064/eyes-on-the-street-details-jane-jacobs-efforts-to-put-cities-first> (retrieved 18.02.18.).

Chapter 9

Encompassing effective crime prevention solutions in 2020 and beyond: concepts and strategies

Lawrence J. Fennelly, Marianna A. Perry and Michael J. Fagel
Security Consultant

Where Government, law enforcement, businesses and the public work together on prevention we can deliver significant and sustained cuts in certain crimes

British Home Office, United Kingdom, 2016

Introduction

Crime Prevention has been around since the early 1970s, and with the growth of various crime prevention organizations, the growth of ASIS and IFPO, Loss Prevention and Crime Prevention have come a long way. We have seen over half-a-dozen books come out on new crime prevention through environmental design (CPTED) concepts. The 10 principles of crime prevention from the West Yorkshire Police Department and Modern Crime Prevention Strategy (2016) from the British Home Office.

Independent crime survey

According to the independent Crime Survey for England and Wales,[1] it is still far too high. Our new approach is based on targeting six key drivers of crime:

1. Opportunity—removing or designing out opportunities to offend, offline and online.
2. Character—intervening early with those exposed to factors that might lead to a high propensity to commit crime.
3. Effectiveness of the Criminal Justice System (CJS)—ensuring that the CJS acts as a powerful deterrent to would-be offenders.
4. Profit—making it harder for criminals, particularly organized criminals, to benefit financially from their crimes.
5. Drugs—publish a new drug strategy, which builds on the approach published in 2010 to restrict the supply of drugs and tackle the organized crime behind the drugs trade, prevent drug misuse in our communities, help people resist getting involved in drugs, and support people dependent on drugs through treatment and recovery.
6. Alcohol—making the nighttime economy safe so that people can consume alcohol safely without fear of becoming a victim of alcohol-related crime or disorder, enabling local economies to grow.

Deterrents

It is defined as—"Serving to Deter Relating to deterrence."

Category A

1. Modern Crime Prevention Strategy March 2016, British Home Office UK.

Handbook of Loss Prevention and Crime Prevention. DOI: https://doi.org/10.1016/B978-0-12-817273-5.00009-0

- Security surveillance system used to prevent crime in private and public locations
- CPTED principles and concepts
- Defensible space principles and concepts
- Situational crime prevention principles and concepts
- Neighborhood watch
- Lighting that meets standards and design by increased visibility
- Biometrics and access control to specific areas
- CPTED design
- CPTED landscape principles
- Signage or visible security signs
- Padlocks and door locks and peep-holes
- Intrusion alarms and signage of alarm
- Security surveillance systems (CCTV)
- Security awareness programs
- Planters and thorny bushes
- Bollards or barricades closing down streets.
- Barking dog, inside or outside
- Vehicle in driveway
- Area traffic and escape route available
- Policy and procedures
- Training programs
- Metal detectors (Fig. 9.1)

Category B

- Security officers armed and unarmed in private function, that is, hotel doorman, bus drivers, tickets sellers or ticket takers, conductors.
- Police officers in uniform and armed security who may deduce that a crime is about to be committed and deter the incident in their presence.
- Security officer patrolling the parking lots of hotels, hospitals, and retail locations, protecting corporate assets and customer protection.

FIGURE 9.1 Photo taken by Marianna Perry, reflects to many signs.

- Guardian Angels patrolling streets, neighborhoods, and subways.
- People in the area.
- Crime displacement theory by target hardening and soft target moving to another location.
- Guard shacks if occupied are a deterrent.

Category C

- Plus, security awareness programs, Planters and thorny bushes, Bollards or barricades closing down streets, Barking dog—inside or outside, Vehicle in driveway, Area traffic and escape routes available, Policies and Procedures, Training programs, Unarmed security officers in private functions, that is, hotel doorman, bus drivers, tickets sellers or ticket takers, public transportation monitors. Police officers in uniform and armed security officers who may deter a crime that is about to be committed by their presence. Security officers patrolling the parking lots of hotels, hospitals and retail locations, protecting corporate assets and customer protection. Guardian Angels patrolling streets, neighborhoods, and subways. People in the area walking a dog and neighborhood watchers.

Neighborhood watch

Want to know the best crime prevention tool ever invented?

A good neighbor! In fact, neighbors working together in cooperation with law enforcement can make one of the best crime-fighting teams around.[2]

We call it . . . neighborhood watch

What is it?

Neighborhood watch is a crime prevention program that enlists the active participation of citizens in cooperation with law enforcement to reduce crime in their communities.

It involves the following:

- neighbors getting to know each other and working together in a program of mutual assistance;
- citizens being trained to recognize and report suspicious activities in their neighborhoods; and
- implementation of crime prevention techniques such as home security, Operation Identification.

You may hear it called neighborhood watch, home alert, citizen crime watch, or block watch. The idea is the same: Neighbors looking out for each other!

Who can participate?

City people, country people, suburban residents, apartment dwellers, mobile home residents, young people, senior citizens, men, women, families, couples and singles.

Models of crime prevention: their application

Situational crime prevention. The situational theory of crime prevention suggests that the best way to stop criminals is to design physical space and environment in a manner that will make the commission of crime harder and increase the likelihood of apprehending criminals.[3] The idea is to change criminals' perceptions of the rewards of crime by making the situation harder and much riskier for them. The situational concept of crime prevention was developed initially in the 1980s by criminologist Ronald Clarke. Clarke (1992) suggested that the most effective way to prevent crime is to implement strategies that create conditions that make it harder for criminals to commit crime. Thus as an intervention model, situational crime prevention requires the proper identification of routines, factors, and patterns associated with criminal activity. Clarke and Cornish (2003) presented five types of techniques that criminology practitioners should consider when using the situational model: "1) increasing effort required to commit crimes; 2) increasing risks of

2. http://www.ascensionsheriff.com/documents/Crime%20Prevention/Neighborhood%20Watch.pdf

3. https://www.ukessays.com/essays/criminology/examining-models-of-crime-prevention-and-their-application-criminology-essay.php> Latest edition May 2 ed., 2017 UK Essays.

committing crimes; 3) reducing rewards out of crimes; 4) reducing conditions that provoke crime; and 5) removing excuses for committing crimes" (as cited in Homel, 2005, p. 132).

Crime impacts overall quality of life, because it influences one's actions, where one lives, how one travels, people one associates with, and others. The major conceptual models of crime prevention are the situational, social, and developmental crime prevention strategies. However, there has been increasing acceptance that crime is more complex in nature, so not one single strategy is effective in deterring crime. The emergence of hybrid approaches toward crime addresses both situational and social factors and is considered to be more appropriate for the complexity of the 21st century.

Future care and maintenance

Effective management is key to maintaining safe, sustainable, and attractive places over the long term. Crime is more likely to occur where places become untidy, unattractive, and show ongoing evidence of neglect, such as broken windows, abandoned vehicles, or persistent graffiti. While high standards of maintenance will encourage active use and enjoyment of the area by local residents, poor maintenance leads to a vicious circle of neglect, environmental degradation, and reduced usage. Developers should consider management and maintenance issues following best practice guidelines from the earliest stages of project planning. Where appropriate, developers should demonstrate to the council, at the earliest stages of project planning, that adequate provision has been made to ensure the long-term maintenance of buildings, car parks, footpaths, cycle ways, public spaces, landscaped areas, and lighting to ensure that crime reduction measures, environmental quality, and amenity benefits are safeguarded for future generations.[4]

Situational crime prevention

Situational crime prevention incorporates other crime prevention and law enforcement strategies in an effort to focus on place-specific crime problems.

Results and objectives are as follows:

1. Reduce violent crime.
2. Reduce property crime.
3. Displacement of crime.
4. Eliminate the threats and risk.
5. Reduce the likelihood of more incidents.

Situational crime prevention focuses on the following:

- crime theories;
- crime, not criminality;
- events, not dispositions;
- near, not distant causes of crime;
- how crime occurs, not why it happens; and
- situational and opportunity factors.

Property crimes and internal theft

Property protection—line of defense:

- Perimeter is your first line of defense. It is either man made or natural.
- The building complex is your second line of defense.
- Inner defenses are alarmed areas and secured safes or secured and locked containers.

Protected by:

4. https://www.suffolk.police.uk/sites/suffolk/files/design_guide_new_format.pdf.
Designing Out Crime Residential Design Guide.

- Security, safety audits.
- Covered by insurance. Supervised by other devices.

External theft:

- Robbery—armed or unarmed
- Shoplifting
- The professional theft to the unprofessional
- Burglary
- Checks and credit/debit cards

Controlled by:

- Digital surveillance
- Sales personnel
- Security personnel

Internal theft

By definition, internal theft is the theft of property committed by individuals who are employed in some way by a corporation/client, etc. The best defense for this is background checks, preemployment screening, internal controls, and auditing. Some other techniques for preventing internal theft are as follows:

- Background checks to identify and eliminate future internal problems.
- Internal controls, ID badges, sign-in sheets, separation of common space from internal space.
- Audits and accountability for detecting and uncovering loses and problems, a common method of internal controls to defect fraud through financial transactions.
- A story policy signed off by all employees. If you steal anything, prosecution to the full extent of the law and termination.

It should be noted that internal theft is the hardest of all crimes to deal with, solve, and to obtain a conviction.

You need to have strong security controls, processes, and procedures in place that minimize opportunity for unethical business conduct.

In a retail environment the number 1, most desirable, items are cash and/or theft from a safe followed by the following:

- fraudulent refunds,
- fraudulent voids,
- fraudulent suspension,
- sweet-hearting, and
- merchandise.

Internal theft is a crime committed by person or persons known within your community, for example, employees, executives, vendors, contractors, janitors, and security personnel. Over the years, unusual crimes occur within a variety of security disciplines and security managers are called to address the issue. Our advice to you is NEVER, NEVER say "I'm stuck and don't know what to do" (unless you plan on getting another job).

Consider these six objectives:

1. Formulate a committee to address this problem.
2. Perform an overall crime analysis study.
3. Contact associates who may have had similar problems.
4. Bring in a consultant.
5. Improve your physical security.
6. Conduct a security survey of your complex.

Consider these six controls:

1. Conduct background checks of all personnel.
2. Establish adequate policy and procedures.
3. Conduct audits.
4. Reduce risk factors.

5. Conduct proper investigations.
6. Sue parties for recover of losses.

Apprehension of the thief can be obtained by the following:

1. Undercover investigators
2. Covert security surveillance system (CCTV) setup
3. Employee awareness and orientation

a. Fact No. 1: A total of 25% of all employees will steal from their employer of opportunity presents itself.
b. Fact No. 2: A total of 30% all businesses fail due to internal theft.
c. Fact No. 3: Employee deviance leads to more dishonesty, deterioration of productivity, and customer dissatisfaction.
d. Fact No. 4: Employee awareness programs are vital to reducing loss in any type of company.
e. Fact No. 5: There are several ways of detecting employee dishonesty.
    i. Coworker tip-off
    ii. Security audit
    iii. Shopping services
    iv. Electronic surveillance

Crime prevention through environmental design

Lighting/street lighting

Appropriate lighting is frequently cited as being a feature that people associate with enhanced safety. In addition to facilitating surveillance, lighting is often used to beautify a site and to attract people to a site. Street lighting (under old standards) had little regard to pedestrian safety and was merely a tool for marking the position of the road ahead at night.[5]

Intent

To promote the development of lighting plans and providing pedestrian and street lighting, which enhance the amenity of a site and which further promote safety, by optimizing opportunities for surveillance and reducing feelings of fear and vulnerability, and to provide security for all road users.

Planning features

- Lighting to meet minimum established standards.
- Lighting should be directed onto areas accessed by people using the site and away from neighboring properties.
- Lights not to be obscured by foliage and should not produce shadows.
- Possible entrapment spots such as loading bays, rubbish containers, and alleys should be lit with vandal-resistant and energy-saving lighting.
- Entrances and exits should be clearly identified via lighting. Lighting used in car parks should illuminate continuously in hours of darkness
- Lights should be in accordance with established standards and highly mounted on buildings/structures.
- Street lighting should be evenly placed to ensure that the entire street is sufficiently lit and "black spots" are avoided.
- Street lighting should be of an appropriate intensity and color of illumination, to ensure that sufficient light is cast to illuminate the streets and to permit visual surveillance of a street.
- Street lighting should provide sufficient light spill onto footpaths and minimize light spill into residential windows.
- Street lighting must be planned to permit effective and timely maintenance of nonfunctioning lights.
- Street lighting should have effective and timely maintenance of nonfunctioning lights

5. https://www.kempsey.nsw.gov.au/development/pubs/crime-prevention-environmental-design-guidelines.pdf modified and updated 2018.

Security lighting

The purpose of security lighting is to discourage unauthorized entry, protect employees, owner operators, and visitors on the site, and detect intruders.[6] Lighting will also help distinguish public from private space, which may help to reduce liability. Security lighting should complement other security measures such as physical barriers, intrusion detection systems, video surveillance systems, and security officer activities.

Protective lighting

Research shows that there is a significant relationship between crime/the fear of crime and illumination. Lighting is a powerful tool for crime prevention by enhancing safety and may possibly reduce potential liability.

Perimeter or boundary lighting should allow detection of those who loiter outside the site and those who or entering or exiting the site. Lighting should allow safe movement and easy detection of hazards and threats out to a distance of at least 30 ft.

Primary lighting sources

Security lighting and protective lighting

Lighting is the single most cost-effective deterrent to crime. An illuminated area acts as a psychological and physical deterrent, and it can reduce criminal opportunity. Research shows that there is a close relationship between crime/the fear of crime and illumination. Lighting is a powerful tool for crime prevention by enhancing safety and may possibly reduce potential liability.

Industry standards for lighting

- Occupational Safety and Health Administration Code of Federal Regulation
- Illuminating Engineering Society of North America, G-1-03 Guide of Security Lighting for People, Property and Public Spaces
- American National Standards Institute
- Department of the Army

Goals of security lighting

Objective illumination—will allow observation of the protected item.

Physical deterrence—uses a sufficient light level to cause psychological responses such as pain and temporary blindness. The light source can be continuous or event-responsive, 100,000 fc will cause temporary blindness for 2–3 minutes.

Glare projection—achieved by projecting light away from the protected property so that an approaching intruder cannot see onto the premises, but they are highly visible from the inside.

Psychological deterrence—results when lighting leaves a potential intruder fearful that they will be detected identified and apprehended.

Illumination

Illumination intensity—As light bulbs age, the light that they put out decreases. Some objects and colors reflect light better than others and this affects intensity.

Illumination distribution—Lighting fixture have to be spaced so that there is no area without proper illumination.

Illumination quality—Color perception may or may not be important.

Illumination reliability may be problem if the lights are vulnerable to physical attack or vandalism.

Lighting and the intensity of illumination falling on a surface are measured in foot candles (fc) which are English units for lux, which are metric units.

1 fc equals 1 lm of light per one square foot of space.

1 lm is the measure of light at its source and the amount of light need to light an area of 1 ft^2 to 1 cp.

6. 150 Things You Need To Know About Physical Security, Elsevier, 2016.

FIGURE 9.2 Photo taken by Marianna Perry.

Illumination levels

Horizontal illuminance—measured at grade level with the light meter placed on horizontal surface, such as the pavement.[7]

Vertical illuminance—measured 5 ft above grade with the light meter at 5 ft above grade. Vertical illuminance should be provided where there is a need to identify people—face and body—at a distance of 30 ft. There should be a uniformity ratio of no more than 4:1. The higher the background illuminance, the higher the vertical illuminance to maintain the 4:1 ratio to prevent silhouetting ().

Outdoors

In Fig. 9.2, you good natural surveillance and a safe environment, with new LED lighting. Two points here are as follows:

1. Eliminate vulnerabilities and protect assets.
2. Building away crime or designing out crime.

Risk

Risk management is defined[8] as the process by which an entity identifies its potential losses and then decides what is the best way to manage these potential losses.

- Risk: exposure to possible loss (i.e., fire, natural disasters, product obsolescence, shrinkage, work stoppages).
- Security managers are primarily interested in crime, shrinkage, accidents, crises.
- Risk managers generally are more focused on fire and safety issues.
- Pure risk: risk in which there are no potential benefits to be derived (i.e., earthquake, flood).
- Dynamic risk: Risk that can produce gain or profit (i.e., theft, embezzlement).
- Possible maximum loss: maximum loss sustained if a target is totally destroyed.
- Probable maximum loss: Amount of loss a target is likely to sustain.

7. Source: US Dept. of Labor, CFR 1926.56.

8. Broder, J.F., 2006. CPP Risk Analysis and the Security Survey, third ed. Elsevier.

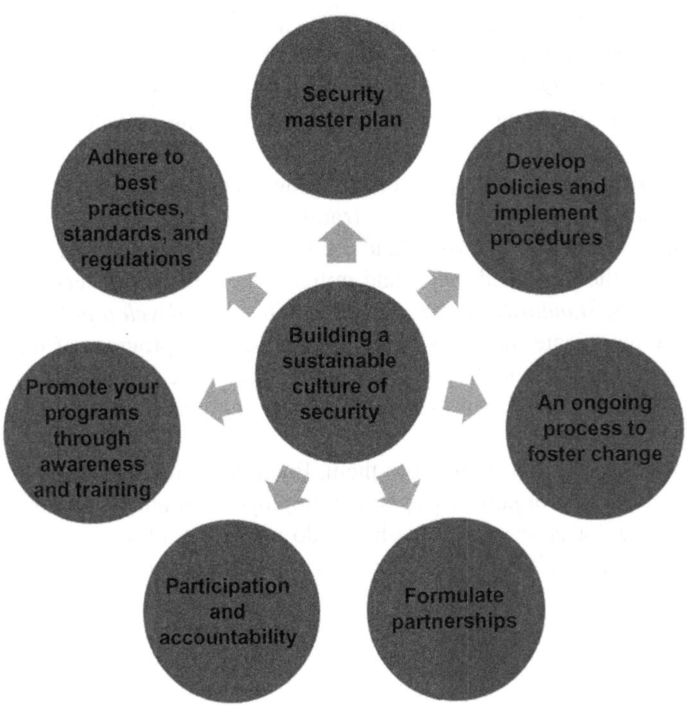

FIGURE 9.3 Prepared by Marianna Perry.

Mass notification procedures

- Develop a mass notification program, which includes e-mails, text messages, social media, and public address system announcements, as well as audible and visual alarms.
- Ensure your mass notification program complies with ADA (Americans with Disabilities Act) standards (physically handicapped, visually impaired, hearing-impaired, or special needs students, faculty, staff and visitors, etc.). Have designated individuals trained to assist.
- Ensure that your procedures meet NFPA Standards and Guidelines, which include a communication program, an incident management system, and individuals trained in ICS.

Building a sustainable culture of security

Introduction

What is a *sustainable culture of security*?[9] If asked, the majority of organizations will say that they have one, but when asked to define it, they have difficulty. A culture of security is initially driven vertically from the top of the organization down. From there, it is driven from the bottom of the organization up and also across horizontally by all levels of employees. A *sustainable culture of security* has to be a part of every operation within the organization and is ingrained into the *Policies and Procedures*. It cannot be separated from the mission of the organization and should be a part of the overall *Security Master Plan*. We raised this question in a recent presentation at ASIS in Las Vegas in 2018 (Fig. 9.3).

Will it be easy to develop a culture of security in your organization? The answer to this question is ..."it depends." To have a *sustainable culture of security* in your organization depends upon whether or not you have total support from upper management. In the security industry, this is frequently called "buy-in," but it is really much more than that. You have to have management participation as well as buy-in. Buy-in and participation are *not* the same thing. Employees of the organization need to see management actively participating and engaged in the security program. For a security program to be successful, no one is exempt from following security procedures, regardless of their title or role in the organization. Ensure that your organization does not have the "us and them" mentality or that management is "allowed"

9. The Professional Protection Officers Handbook Ninth Edition, Elsevier Publishers, 2019 Sandi Davies and Lawrence J. Fennelly, paper on Culture of Security by Fennelly and Perry.

to disregard security procedures out of a sense of entitlement. When there is a *sustainable culture of security*, security belongs to everyone in the organization and everyone in the organization is an active participant.

In the article, *The Importance of a Security Culture Across the Organization*, Kevin Beaver states, "A strong security culture is both a mindset and mode of operation. One that's integrated into day-to-day thinking and decision-making can make for a near-impenetrable operation."[10]

In order to develop a *sustainable culture of security* in an organization, you first have to develop security awareness to ensure employees understand what security is and how important it is to the organization. What is the organization securing against? A vulnerability or threat assessment will help identify the assets and the risks of the organization and then security countermeasures are put in place to help secure the identified assets and mitigate the risks. Your security program is seen as professional if you *adhere to best practices, standards, and regulations*. When you *develop policies and implement procedures*, they will define and clearly communicate the goals of the overall security program of the organization. Remember that organizational policies change less often than organizational procedures. Ensure that emergency procedures are a part of the *policies and procedures* of the organization and review and update them every 5 years or more often if necessary.

Employees are a critical component of any security program. Make it personal to them. Encourage employee *participation and accountability*. One of the largest security issues facing organizations is that employees do not understand *what* to report. Help them to understand what suspicious behavior is or what they should do when they observe something that does not seem quite right. Employees need to describe specifically what they observed, including:

- *who* or *what* you saw;
- *when* you saw it;
- *where* it occurred; and
- *why* it's suspicious.[11]

Ensure that the organization has a visitor management program in place and that security officers and employees are trained to identify suspicious behavior and activity. This emphasizes the need to greet visitors or customers and have someone available to answer questions and direct them to the proper location. Think about the national campaign, *If You See Something, Say Something* licensed through the Department of Homeland Security, that advises "if you see something you know shouldn't be there—or someone's behavior that doesn't seem quite right—say something. Because only you know what's supposed to be in your everyday."[12] Many times, it's as simple as approaching someone who is not wearing a company badge (employee, visitor, contractor, or vendor) and asking if you can be of help or, depending on the situation, contacting security and/or law enforcement, and reporting the individual using as much detail as possible. Security officers and/or trained employees are ideal for detecting suspicious behavior and activity.

Another critical component of developing a positive security culture is using metrics to measure the effectiveness of employee *security awareness training*. When effectiveness is measured, successes can be celebrated and areas that need improvement can be identified. How will you know if an employee recognized a suspicious person or incident, reduced risk or prevented a loss? Measuring your successes will help management justify the cost of the *security awareness and training programs*.

Everyone in the organization needs to understand how crime or security breaches can be prevented or they will assume that security incidents will not really impact the organization as a whole or affect them personally. Identify the risks of the organization for employees and help them understand their role in helping the organization achieve its security goals to ensure profitability and also safety. Define specific incremental goals and celebrate successes when they are achieved. Each employee in the organization must act individually and directly to support the security plan in order to keep the workplace safe.

Many times, when a security breach is discovered, it is not the technology or the security policies or procedures that failed, but the action or inaction of *people*. To put it another way, it is the *people* operating the system or the *people* that are trying to circumvent the policies or procedures that are the problem. It is true that people are an organization's most valuable asset, but they are also an organization's greatest vulnerability and/or liability. A *Culture of Sustainable*

10. The Importance of a Security Culture. United States, 2015. From: <https://securityintelligence.com/the-importance-of-a-security-culture-across-the-organization/> (retrieved 24.10.16.).

11. "If You See Something, Say Something" campaign. From: <https://www.dhs.gov/see-something-say-something/about-campaign> (retrieved 24.10.16.).

12. "If You See Something, Say Something" campaign. From: <https://www.dhs.gov/see-something-say-something/about-campaign> (retrieved 24.10.16.).

Security is not for the technology within the organization. It is for the people who *develop the policies, implement/ enforce procedures*, and follow the procedures every day. *Promote your programs through awareness and training* through incentives such as *Security Is Everyone's Business.*[13] This means preventing crime and instilling *security awareness* are not just the responsibility of security officers or designated staff members. *Security Is Everyone's Business* is a great idea but be sure it is happening in reality and not just a concept.

A *sustainable culture of security* is part of an overall *Security Master Plan*. Timothy Giles defines a *Security Master Plan* as, "a document that delineates the organization's security philosophies, strategies, goals, programs, and processes. It is used to guide the organization's development and direction in these areas in a manner that is consistent with the company's overall business plan. It also provides a detailed outline of the risks and the mitigation plans for them in a way that creates a five-year business plan."[14]

Your security program is *an ongoing process to foster change* and will define and set the climate for how the plan will be implemented, so the organization will reach its security goals. The first step is to have a vulnerability or risk assessment conducted by a trained security professional, so the organization will know what assets they need to protect and what risks to retain, transfer or mitigate. When the appropriate countermeasures are put into place, the emphasis will be on layers of security along with security *policies and procedures*. It also may be helpful to have a safety and security committee.

The *formulation of partnerships* is not a new idea. *Partnerships* have just become more visible in recent years. Decide the goal of the partnership—is it to reduce crime and the fear of crime, for emergency response or for a different reason? Develop relationships with all resources that are available in the local area. Next, identify the stakeholders in your partnership. The goal of your partnership will determine the stakeholders. Discuss security concerns and daily operations of the organization with first responders and involve them in training and drills. The basic idea is plan, practice, and prepare. Regardless of the goal of the partnership, remember it is a proactive approach, not a reactive approach where members of different groups work together. These may be law enforcement, local government officials, fire department, emergency medical services, local emergency management personnel, community leaders, owners of commercial and residential property, area residents, area housing management, community members, local schools, neighborhood business owners, faith-based organizations, and houses of worship. The key to successful *partnerships* is to understand the roles, responsibilities, and resources of each partner to prepare, plan, and train together. The idea is a total coordination of efforts. In order for a partnership to be successful, planning needs to be done and the lines of communication have to stay open. Through training and practice, each partner develops a better understanding of each other's capabilities, roles, responsibilities, and available resources. It is important to remember that *partnerships* will require ongoing maintenance to keep them engaged.

At the completion of the vulnerability or risk assessment, a discussion with the security professional about recommended countermeasures will help to design a blueprint of effective security measures. The foundation for an effective physical security program that is a part of the overall *security master plan* is the four D's (deter, detect, delay, and deny) and layered security (defense-in-depth).[15] All countermeasures implemented should be "best practices" for the specific industry of the organization.

To ensure the success of your *security master plan* and security program, you will need to *promote your programs through education and training*. This means that employees need to understand their roles and responsibilities. Each individual should know what part they play in the overall *security master plan*. This is not a one-time or annual training. Instead, in order to have a *sustainable culture of security*, the job of security must belong to everyone in the organization from the lowest paid job in the organization to the top management position. Everyone has to feel like they are an important part of the security program. To develop *security awareness*, security has to become a part of the daily routine or a part of every job that is performed in the organization and also a part of every decision the organization makes. In order to hold employees accountable, first you must help them to learn *security awareness*. A *security awareness program* helps to create a security-conscious culture within an organization, where employees are subconsciously considering risks and threats in their daily routines. As security professionals, we put security countermeasures in place to mitigate these risks and threats.[16]

---

13. Security is Everyone's Business. From: <https://blog.detectify.com/2015/09/21/security-is-everyones-business/> (retrieved 23.08.17.).

14. Giles, T.D., 2009. How to Develop and Implement a Security Master Plan. Auerbach Publications, Florida.

15. Knoke, M.E. (Managing Editor), 2015. Physical Security Principles. ASIS International, United States.

16. Creating a Security Culture by Tom Andreas Mannerud. From: <http://www.mannerud.org/2014/09/27/creating-a-security-culture/> (retrieved 24.10.16.).

Research has shown that the fear of crime or perception of crime is much higher than the actual crime rate, but fear is real and should be addressed. To reduce fear of crime, you have to identify and understand what people are afraid of and then address that specific fear. One of the purposes of a security program is to not only implement security policies, procedures, training, and countermeasures but to also direct efforts that reduce fear of crime. For example, if a source of fear in the organization is that a stranger could walk into the building at any time, organizing a company softball team is not going to fix that particular problem. A company softball team may reinforce the concept of teamwork, but it is not going to help the access control problem. To address the problem, consider access control measures such as installing a card access system at all entry locations and monitor other doors with video surveillance. Another solution may be to have security or courtesy officers in the front lobby of the building providing customer service to each individual that enters the building. The response to employee fear has to be tailored to that specific issue. It is important that people "feel" safe at work. Since people are the weakest link in any security program, a *culture of security* must be developed to help the people in the organization see "where they fit" into the big picture of security and what they can do personally to ensure the success and the security of the organization.

Many may not want to admit it, but every organization has a security culture, whether it is good or bad. It is important to understand that a negative (bad) security culture can be changed into a positive (good) and *sustainable culture of security* if the organization makes a conscious decision about the *ongoing process to foster change* and then invests in security. To promote your security program, be specific about the objectives and how these objectives will be achieved. Good communication within the organization to clearly identify security responsibilities and expectations will help ensure success.

Developing a good (positive) and *sustainable culture of security* is an ongoing process that will deliver a return on investment for the entire organization, but an investment of time and resources must be a priority. It doesn't matter what product or service an organization makes, sells, or provides; security has to be a part of it. Security should be a part of the mission statement or vision of the organization and simply be "just the way things are done around here."

Appendix Emerging trends

By Dr. Michael Fagel, CEM

What's in a word?

Today, more than ever we must prepare our schools and universities for the inevitable. It is not IF an event will occur, but when, or when again. We have talked about the "Culture" at your organization that needs to be improved, and that is the culture of planning, preparation, and practice as key elements that must be interwoven into your organization at each and every level. Many organizations say that there plan is over there, on the shelf. It was updated just a couple of years ago. Remember, a plan is not as important as the planning process. The process is a key.

Recently, a school planning seminar failed to follow a basic training protocol when simulating an active shooter event. The even went "outside" of the training participants; an errant text was misdirected and sent to a civilian 40 miles away. The civilian that got the horrific text then called 911 to relay the information. 911 then researched to determine where the building mentioned in the text actually was. The alert operator then called the appropriate 911 public safety answering point in the community. The operator asked the caller on the phone that originally sent the text, and said it was confirmed, thinking it was a part of the exercise. At that point, the 911 operator then did a regional emergency dispatch to all law enforcement within 60 miles. Nearly 60 squad cars, SWAT officers, and heavy response vehicles came to the scene, which one police chief stated reminded him of the scene from the "Blues Brothers."

One key lesson to learn here is that we must always practice, but, practice safely. Always mention during any drill or Exercise: THIS IS AN EXERCISE-EXERCISE MESSAGE TO FOLLOW. Any written data must also carry the HEADER AND FOOTER that states—THIS IS AN EXERCISE-THIS IS AN EXERCISE. All radio or telephone traffic begin with THIS IS AN EXERCISE, or EXERCISE EXERCISE EXERCISE. You must make every effort to make the training realistic, BUT, must make the authorities aware of an event.

For example, our team will always call the dispatch center, speak to the supervisor, and deliver a code word, for example, "Purple Snow Cone" to dispatch as them knowing via your code word that this is part of the planned event. When you call 911 as the exercise team, you use the CODE WORD handshake and also use the word when all clear, exercise is over, and the normal dispatch protocols will follow.

That way, the training event will have a beginning and end, while engaging your public safety authorities at all times. Also, it never hurts to have a conversation with the expected public safety responders and their respective dispatch centers IN ADVANCE of the event. You can go quite a long way in helping to cement relationships as well as sharing information that may be lifesaving. Your organizations can all share critical information and can help be better prepared for the event as they occur.

Culture of training, planning, and preparing must be a continuous process. Dialing 911 and hoping for the best is not an answer. Engage with emergency planning process as soon as you can and adjust, train, and educate all on the needs for this ongoing process. Remember, words DO matter! Start the planning, training, and education process today!

Chapter 10

What is crime prevention in 2020?

Lawrence J. Fennelly
Security Consultant

Crime Prevention is the anticipation, recognition, and appraisal of a crime risk, and the initiation of action to remove or reduce it. Crime Prevention is an active approach utilizing public awareness and preventive measures to reduce crime.

Definition originally from the British Home Office in the UK and defined further by the National Crime Prevention Institute, in Louisville Ky.

Crime Prevention—New York State Police, https://www.troopers.ny.gov/Crime_Prevention, 2018

Introduction

Problem-oriented policing

This enhances traditional policing strategies[1] because it

- emphasizes the ends of policing as well as the means;
- seeks out the long-term results of a response as well as the immediate customer service–driven response;
- addresses the cause of the problem in addition to its symptoms; and
- addresses the factors, situations, and conditions of the problem.

Community policing

A philosophy that promotes organizational strategies, which supports the systematic use of partnerships and problem-solving techniques, to proactively address the immediate conditions that give rise to public safety issues, such as crime, social disorder and dear or crime.[2]

Routine activity theory states that when a crime occurs, three things happen at the same time and in the same space as follows:

1. A suitable target is available.
2. There is the lack of a suitable guardian to prevent the crime from happening.
3. A likely and motivated offender is present.

A suitable target can either be
a person
an object
a place

---

1. www.cops.usdoj.gov, June 12, 2018.
2. USDOJ, 2007.

Handbook of Loss Prevention and Crime Prevention. DOI: https://doi.org/10.1016/B978-0-12-817273-5.00010-7

Reactive policing versus proactive policing

Reactive policing

Police respond to citizens' calls for assistance
Patrol is routine and unstructured
911 calls drive police activity
Dispatch section dictates police activity
Emphasis on solving crimes

Proactive policing

Police seek crime solutions before the crimes occur
Patrol is targeted
Crime patterns drive police activity
Records management/research dictates police activity
Emphasis on preventing crimes

Situational crime prevention

The art and science of reducing opportunities for crime, which is based on the crime theories of rational choice and routine activity.

Situational crime prevention focuses on the following:

- crime theories
- crime, not criminality
- events, not dispositions
- near, not distant causes of crime
- how crime occurs, not why it happens
- situational and opportunity factors

Loss control/loss prevention/crime prevention is primarily about increasing the efforts or hardening the target.

Protection of assets

Assets are as follows:

- money
- accounts receivable
- physical property
- intellectual property
- proprietary information
- people
- reputation

Hazards faced by organizations are human—caused by insiders or outsiders or catastrophic—fires, earthquakes, floods, tornadoes, etc.

Systems approach

A comprehensive approach to a total problem using

- a vulnerability assessment—determines the excesses and deficiencies in existing security;
- countermeasures—may be hardware, software, or people; and
- testing of the system—audit the system to see what changes need to be made.

Key factors in an asset protection plan

1. an adequate plan to prevent losses from occurring
2. adequate countermeasures to limit the losses
3. management support of the plan

Four Ds of physical security:

- *Deny* the criminal access to targets.
- *Delay* the criminal so an apprehension can be made.
- *Deter* the criminal from attacking.
- *Detect* the criminal if there is an attack.

Displacement of crime

Can you move crime from one location to another? Yes, you can. I know criminologists will ask to show them the data and we cannot. However, talk to veteran officers who have been working in the various sectors for years and they will tell you that they have done it. Years ago in a dormitory that had only one entrance, an individual was stealing wallets and cash from unlocked rooms. This was going on night after night, so we put a cruiser out front of the dormitory, and the car was back a few spaces then forward every night around 3:00 a.m. Crime stop. Was it luck or skill. The cruiser was a deterrent, I know that. The crook must be thinking that if the police car is outside then the officer must be inside and there is a likelihood that he/she will get caught, so he goes to another location.

We know that drug dealing and prostitution are serious problems, so by closing off the street and prevent traffic from going up and down, the individuals will move to another location and be arrested on the new street.

Steven P. Lab states in his book titled Crime Prevention seventh edition that "There is little reason to ever expect total displacement of a crime, regardless of the type of displacement considered." He then discusses the various types of displacement, that is, territorial, temporal, tactical, target, and functional; he further states that although it is not 100%, at the same time, they show that displacement does occur.

SARA process

"SARA" stands for *S*canning, *A*nalysis, *R*esponse, and *A*ssessment.

Scanning—the initial identification (ID) of the problem, where problems are defined as a group of related or recurring incidents or a particular concern of the community.
Analysis—an in-depth exploration of the problem and its underlying cause.
Response—implements an analysis-driven strategy to address the problem, focusing on the factors identified in the analysis phase.
Assessment—consists of ongoing review and monitoring of the progress of the response by achieving its objectives.

What is necessary for a crime to occur?

1. the *desire* or motivation on the part of the criminal to commit the crime
2. the skills, tools, and *ability* needed to commit the crime
3. the *opportunity* to commit the crime

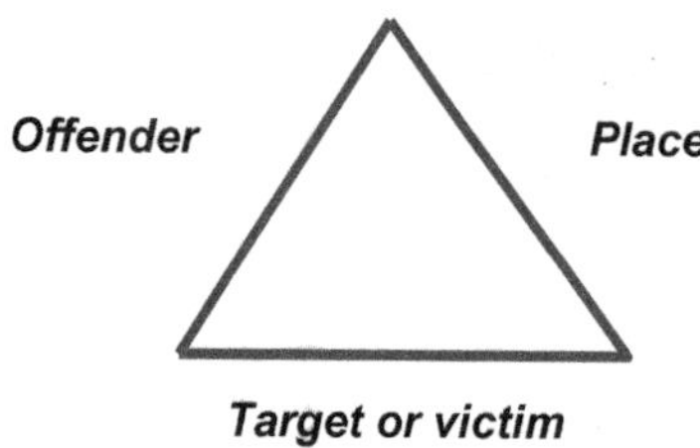

Crime prevention can be as follows:
victim-focused prevention
offender-focused prevention
community-focused prevention
situation- or environment-focused prevention

Ten principles of opportunity and crime

1. Opportunities play a role in causing all crime.
2. Crime opportunities are highly specific.
3. Crime opportunities are concentrated in time and space.
4. Crime opportunities depend on everyday movements.
5. One crime produces opportunities for another.
6. Some products offer more tempting crime opportunities.
7. Social and technological changes produce new crime opportunities.
8. Opportunities for crime can be reduced.
9. Reducing opportunities does not usually displace crime.
10. Focused opportunity reduction can produce wider declines in crime.[3]

Operation Identification

A nationally recognized theft prevention program that involves marking and/or engraving property with traceable ownership information, recording serial numbers, model numbers, and other pertinent information about the item. We mention this program because it works, realizing that it is an older concept and not that much active now. The four final points are as follows[4]:

1. Engrave property or mark with an indelible pen with personal property—state abbreviation in front of your driver's license number.
2. Engrave property or mark with an indelible pen with business property—state abbreviation in front of your state sales tax number.
3. Create an inventory sheet of your property listing model and serial along with the marking you made.
4. Also take photos of all property and model and serial numbers.

3. Clarke, R.V., 2004. 25 Techniques of Situational Crime Prevention. In: Presented at the Problem-Oriented Policing Conference, Charlotte, NC.
4. www.opid.org.

About the Operation Identification program

Operation ID is nationally recognized by the law enforcement as a citizen's burglary-prevention program for use in homes or businesses. This program has existed for over 30 years.

The Operation ID program allows law enforcement to detect, identify, and return stolen or lost property to its rightful owner.

The Operation ID program involves marking or engraving property with an identifying number and displaying a window decal to discourage burglary and theft. The ideal identifying number is your state-issued driver's license number that is easily recognized and traced by law enforcement. Avoid using your social security number. Businesses should mark property using their state-issued sales tax number.

1. Mark property or valuables with an identifying mark, preferably your driver's license with state abbreviation followed by a number: for example, KY-A12-345-678.
2. Inventory your marked property on a form with descriptions, including item, location of home or office, serial number, model number, where marked, photo and the value of the item. Keep your inventory list in a safe place.
3. Display the Operation ID decal on windows *only after* items 1 and 2 has been completed to show your participation in the program and to discourage burglary.
4. At least inventory all property, list model, and serial numbers, then using the iPhone or iPad take pictures of the property.

Crime prevention

- Crime prevention is proactive, rather than reactive.
- Proactive policing attempts to prevent the crime from occurring in the first place.
- Reactive policing responds to crime after it has occurred.

In 1971 the National Crime Prevention Institute defined crime prevention as the "anticipation, recognition, and appraisal of a crime risk and initiation of some action to remove or reduce it."

In 1990 the Crime Prevention Coalition defined crime prevention as "a pattern of attitudes and behaviors directed both at reducing the threat of crime and enhancing the sense of safety and security, to positively influence the quality of life in our society, and to develop environments where crime cannot flourish."

Recipe for an effective crime prevention office on the college campus:

1. aware of and implements CPTED principles,
2. aware of mass notification program,
3. develops proactive programs,
4. weekly notification to college community of crime data for past week and steps to prevent situational crime events,
5. is active in community policing,
6. conducts security assessments of college property,
7. understands the principles and concepts of physical security devices, and
8. manages the college's physical security program.

Chapter 11

What is risk?*

James Broder, Charles Chuck Sennewald and Curtis Baille
Security Consultant

Security managers are primarily interested in crime, shrinkage, accidents, crises. Risk managers generally are more focused on fire and safety issues

James F. Broder, CPP

Risk defined

Risk is a subjective concept that needs to be viewed and quantified on an individual basis. What risks do you, your company, or your client face? What is your tolerance for risk? The answers to these questions will shape your definition of and approach to risk.

Definitions need to be business specific; for example, financial businesses will define risk related to possible loss of funds or investments, while the medical sector will define risk related to loss of life or possibility of infection. The definition of risk used should reflect the perspective you take in your particular context—the core is the same but perspective causes subtle changes in the approach.

For many security professionals, an all hazards approach, which includes the possibility of harm to or loss of people, property, reputation, and/or assets caused by an event, offers a good starting point in defining risk for their organization.

Risk management programs and the security professional's role

A risk management program is the formal process utilized to quantify, qualify, and mitigate specific concerns an organization may discover or define. Many companies have some forms of risk management program. These programs may be very mature and well defined or may appear to have developed without planning or foresight. It is important for the security professional to identify the program in place and understand the approach accepted in a particular company. The specific model utilized by the company will give the security professional an understanding of the role he or she has in the program. This is critical whether the security professional is an employee or a consultant for a company. Questions that aid in defining the program include what the assessment process involves and who manages the overall risk management program. Answers to these questions illustrate the formality of the program and the level of management oversight and support of the program.

Risk programs may apply to the enterprise or to a specific business line, depending on the perspective the company takes when defining risk. An enterprise approach is a concerted effort by various divisions within a company to measure risk across the company. This may allow for a broad application of mitigation techniques that produce efficiencies as well as effective spans of control by a smaller number of risk managers. Other programs may focus on key business divisions that have regulatory mandates for reviewing specific risks or have been identified as businesses that operate within a risk culture. These programs tend to address well-defined and known risks with singularly focused mitigation strategies. For example, documents containing sensitive information need to be transported

*James Broder CFE, CPP, FACFE. Risk Analysis and the Security Survey 2016; Chuck Sennewald and Curtis Baillie, Effective Security Management, sixth ed. 2016. Permission obtained from author to reproduce.

Handbook of Loss Prevention and Crime Prevention. DOI: https://doi.org/10.1016/B978-0-12-817273-5.00011-9

according to regulations issued by a government agency to protect the individuals listed on these documents. The regulating agency has produced standards for protecting these documents. The security professional's role in this scenario may be to compare the protection in place for these documents to the regulatory requirements and identify gaps that may exist. Once gaps are identified, the security professional may present mitigating steps in a report to a senior manager.

The security professional's approach could be different if he or she was asked to perform an assessment of life safety and traditional security concerns at the direction of a staff member within a company's corporate security division. This request may require the security professional to review fire systems and their adequacy given the size of a facility and/or the items stored in the facility. In addition, he or she may have to review local fire department response times and capabilities. The reporting and mitigation plan in this example would be centered on preserving life and mitigating fire damage but would not necessarily adhere to a regulatory mandate.

The security professional should understand the requirement behind the program and the overall process so that he or she can fulfill the objectives of the overall risk review. Although these examples show the security professional as the one completing reviews and reporting, it does not preclude the security professional from acting as the lead or senior-most manager in the program.

Many programs are conducted at the direction of and managed by the security professional. Security directors may also be responsible for the risk management program and/or may have converged areas reporting to them, such as corporate security, IT security, business continuity, and life safety, which are critical components of the risk mitigation program for many organizations. Further, the security professional may be asked to relate these security functions and their inherent risks to one another. This allows for a streamlined approach and reporting of an overall mitigation strategy. For example, a traditional security hazard, such as a fire in an office building, may cause the activation of a business continuity plan for a particular business unit within a company. In addition, the risk (i.e., the fire) represents concern for life safety. If both areas report to the same manager and have built close cooperative relationships, the manager may be able to direct a response to the immediate need, preservation of life, while activating a plan to meet the secondary need—resumption of business operations.

Risk program components

Although the roles and programs will differ, risk programs have the following several common components:

- risk analysis,
- risk assessment and risk rating,
- risk mitigation, and
- risk reporting.

Each component is necessary for a successful program. Organizations such as ASIS International, standards organizations, and government agencies offer many standards and documents to help manage a risk program. The goal of this chapter is to provide an understanding of the methodology for risk programs and examples of the application of risk concepts. The security professional must then apply this understanding to the unique situations he or she will encounter. The outline of a program and its components, included here, represents an attempt to define as many general areas found in security risk programs as possible and is by no means meant to capture every example and nuance of risk review and/or mitigation strategy.

Risk analysis

Risk analysis includes identification of the assets to be protected and the risks to those assets. These assets can be intellectual property or physical items; however, security traditionally views these assets as:

- people (employees/customers, etc.);
- facilities (owned/leased properties);
- property (sensitive documents/financial instruments/vehicles); and
- reputation (public perception/client perception).

The formulation of the assets that are of value sets the framework for assessing the associated risks. The risks must be identified and described before they can be analyzed. They should be viewed from both the internal (company employees/policies, etc.) and external (natural disasters/competitors, etc.) perspectives. The typical risks to the assets listed previously include the following:

- natural disasters (hurricane/flood/earthquake);
- man-made disasters (fire/workplace violence);
- criminal behavior (fraud/embezzlement); and
- terrorism (international/domestic).

To accurately evaluate risk, a correlation of assets and threats described must be made. The risks should be described in a formal manner and related directly to the asset. For example, consider a fire at a clothing manufacturer's facility. The manufacturer may have a warehouse that holds inventory while waiting for distribution. The assets in this example are the facility, all of the equipment in the facility, the employees, and the merchandise stored within the facility. Focusing on fire as the risk, this phase of the program must include naming the risk (fire) and describing what danger the risk poses to the asset, which in this case could be loss of the facility (partial or complete), life, and merchandise. Each asset should be addressed in context of the risk; in the case of the merchandise, the risk to the asset includes total loss due to fire. In addition, loss of access to the merchandise may have financial impact as orders cannot be filled, or the merchandise may lose value due to smoke imbedded in the clothes. Potential damage to the asset is linked directly to the specific risk factor we have analyzed.

Risk assessment and risk rating

Once the risk analysis is complete, a measurement of the risk must take place. The risk assessment validates the risk and measures the likelihood of occurrence and the extent of the impact the risk could have. During the assessment, additional risks may be identified as gaps in protection, or other process flaws are discovered. Normally, the assessment is conducted using a checklist or template and, at times, may be part of the security survey process. Depending upon the role, the security professional has in the risk management program, the risk assessment and the security survey process may be one and the same.

The assessment will vary in length, depth of research, and total staff required. To be properly completed the assessment process must be flexible enough to allow for these variables.

The risk assessment will measure the following:

- qualification of the risk (whether the risk actually exists);
- probability (is likely to occur, very likely, not likely at all);
- other risks/vulnerabilities to the asset;
- knock-on effect (fire in the facility also damages trucks in loading bays); and
- total effect of risk (probable loss/total maximum loss).

The risk identified during the analysis needs to be validated in the field. For the most part, this is academic; however, field-validating the risk may expose other vulnerabilities. Also, the risk may become better defined, and the extent of the risk may become more clearly understood. After the risk has been validated the assessment must then measure the probability of an event occurring.

Measuring the probability requires balancing craft and the facts that are readily available. The craft portion is based on personal experiences, intuition, and insight into a situation. This is only part of assigning probability; the other part—applying fact—is more scientific. This requires a review of all facts related to the risk and asset to assign a high, medium, or low rating of probability (other rating scales, such as numerical assignments, can also be used). To properly rate probability the following indicators should be reviewed:

- previous occurrences (whether the facility has been prone to fires in the past);
- occurrences in the area or business sector (burglaries in the neighborhood/protests against like businesses);
- activities in the business sector (whether the business is a target based on its product; e.g., animal rights);
- company profile (whether the company is well known and thus more of a symbolic target); and
- geography (whether the plant is next to a terrorist target or likely to be collateral damage to an attack on a neighbor).

The abovementioned list illustrates some common concerns to be reviewed when assessing probability. Taking the same areas to be considered, let us illustrate a method of assigning probability.

Previous occurrences: The plant has had two fires in the last year; the operation and materials on site are unchanged since these events. Given these facts, the probability of a fire at this location would be high.

Occurrences in area/sector: The adjoining office building has suffered from laptop thefts at a high rate over the past month. It is likely that the burglaries will spread to the adjoining buildings as well.

Activities in business sector: Other similar businesses have had protests at their laboratories. Protests have occurred frequently regardless of the company size or the laboratory location. It is very likely that protests will occur at the laboratory of this business as well.

Company profile: The company is very prominent and has a well-recognized brand. This company has higher visibility and, therefore, is a more attractive target than lesser known companies in the same industry.

Geography: The company's headquarters building is over a major transportation hub. There has been information that terrorist groups have been targeting transportation hubs. This places the facility at risk of being a secondary target.

While reviewing these facts, other vulnerabilities may come to light, which need to be considered. For example, while reviewing the possibility of an attack on the transportation hub and its collateral effects on the headquarters building, other risks from the transportation hub should be considered. What risk does fire in the hub or crowds from the hub pose to the facility and employee base when there are major transportation issues? How likely are these scenarios and how does their probability affect the overall likelihood that an event in the hub will put the asset at risk?

Risks should be named and probability assigned to those risks. The assessment should record additional risks and/or vulnerabilities discovered while completing the assessment. The assessment results should be documented and the risk rated. The risk rating can be a score, such as a point value or a rating of high, medium, or low. This allows the report to be filtered to show risk criticality. Further assessments may need to be completed based on the rating. The risk rating is the end result of the assessment, the probability of an incident occurring, and the results of an asset being lost to the event.

Risk mitigation

Mitigation of risk is a broad field. An array of options is available to minimize losses, avoid risk, or insure against the results of a risk event. The security professional is an integral part of the risk mitigation plan for most risk programs. The security professional may have a role in every component of the risk program or may play only a limited role, but he or she will always have a role in the mitigation portion of all plans. The mitigation role could be preventive in nature, such as designing a physical security plan, to include alarms and security surveillance systems (CCTV) to prevent robbery. Traditionally, in addition to the security planning, the security professional may be called upon to investigate the robbery. The hope is to recover the funds taken and thus eliminate the loss, mitigating the effect of the risk event.

So far, we have identified the assets, qualified the risk, and measured and assigned a rating to the risk. The mitigation phase is where we review and plan to minimize the probability and effects of the identified risk to our assets. Mitigation tools should not be limited to device installation or the adding of personnel/guard staff. These are legitimate and appropriate security mitigants; however, other options, such as training, a robust security plan, and implementing policy changes, are also valid and strong mitigation tools to be considered. Through a strong security plan that includes training and security-minded policies, many risks (particularly, employee-driven risk) can be minimized.

The application of risk mitigants should be goal oriented and designed to mitigate the specific risk identified. The better defined the goals the better the results. This is particularly true regarding the security professional's role in risk and risk mitigation. To better understand this point, consider training as an example of risk mitigation.

Security guards receive training as part of their jobs. In many cases, minimum training requirements are mandated by local laws for guards to become licensed prior to becoming a security guard. This mandatory training normally offers very general rules to be followed and covers laws that are applicable to situations guards have historically confronted. The security guard is then assigned to a post in the company to perform certain tasks. Typically, the guard receives some on-the-job training, usually supervised by another security guard familiar with the duties. In addition, the guard may be given an operating manual with procedures and post orders to enhance the understanding of the tasks and actions required. This level of training is adequate for the guard to begin working; however, more focused training is needed to truly mitigate risk. This training will not address specific access-control guidelines to be followed by the guard. If access control is a mitigating strategy managed by the security guard, more in-depth training must occur for the strategy to be effective. Let us take this example and look deeper into training as a mitigation tool.

During the assessment phase, unauthorized access to the facility is identified as a risk at the company. One of the conclusions from the security survey is that the main entry to the facility is an area in need of additional security and

TABLE 11.1 Layering.

Tool	Implementation
Policy change	Add or alter employee practices to address a specific risk
Preventive measures	Conduct device installation/training sessions
Minimize effects	Perform business continuity planning/evacuation planning
Insurance	Purchase a policy that will defray associated event costs

monitoring, since it is the most frequently utilized entry for employees and visitors. To mitigate the risk of unauthorized entry, the company installs access control devices and a reception desk staffed with a security guard. The reception desk duties include typical access control and verification, as well as visitor management tasks.

One evening, a recently terminated employee arrives attempting to gain access to the facility through the entry previously described. What level of training does the guard need to truly mitigate this risk? Is an acceptable level of mandatory licensing training enough? Is the on-the-job training conducted by another security guard adequate? Specific facility access control training in combination with the previously listed training, situational drills, and escalation procedures may place the guard in a better position to properly mitigate this risk. The goal is to highlight that a guard at the entry is not the proper mitigant to the assessed risk; the correct mitigation tool is a properly trained security guard at the entry.

The goal of risk mitigation is to minimize the potential impact of the identified risk to the point, where the concern of the risk is minimal. However, often the risk cannot be mitigated to the minimum, and some level of risk must be accepted. For example, everyone has a heating or cooling system in their homes. The possibility of an electrical fire, gas line explosion, or oil tank leak exists, yet nearly every home utilizes one or more of these to heat, cool, or cook every day. We generally accept the risk but have mitigation strategies in place, such as circuit breakers and shut-off valves. We accept the risk we cannot completely eliminate and potentially insure against the outcome of the risk event. This is another example of a risk mitigation strategy—layering mitigation tools to minimize the risks.

After the strategy has been put in place to mitigate the risk, and other risks that cannot be eliminated have been accepted (or possibly insured against), the security professional should begin to understand the company's willingness to accept risk. This means that if the culture tends to accept the risk early on and lessen the mitigation tools, then this is a high risk-acceptance culture. However, if a strategy and layering of mitigation tools is called for prior to accepting any risk, perhaps this represents a culture of low risk tolerance. Table 11.1 is an example of layering that can serve as a guide to a mitigation strategy.

Risk reporting

The security professional will be called upon to present the findings of the risk review, regardless of the extent of the review. If the security professional is retained as a consulting subject matter expert, he or she will be asked to formally report all findings to the client. The security professional, who is acting on behalf of his or her employer to review risk, will also be required to articulate the findings at some point. In either case, when reporting risk, the security professional should keep the following things in mind:

- The written presentation will "live" longer than the oral presentation.
- Understand the stakeholders to whom you will be reporting.
- Where will this report go? The client may share it with the insurance company; a supervisor may pass it to another supervisor, and so forth.
- Present the facts without exemption; there are many reasons for accepting or ignoring risk. Present the findings and proposed plan, and then allow the decision process to begin.
- Include the security survey and other supporting products utilized to identify the facts.
- There is always a measure of risk acceptance—no plan is absolute.

The previous list represents themes the security professional should consider, when framing the report. Remembering to whom you ultimately report and the scope of your role will help create a true summation of the process. The report and the presentation must be fact driven. It becomes difficult, at times, to keep personal opinion or the desires of a particular stakeholder out of a report. The security professional's role in this process should be impartial but as practical as possible.

The report should emphasize the threat, the risk (in real terms) the threat poses to the organization, the suggested steps to reduce the risk, and a summary that relays the frequency of reevaluation. This will allow the decision makers to analyze how much risk they are willing to accept based on the analysis presented and the frequency with which the risk will be reviewed.

Summary

A common idea presented throughout this chapter has been that risk is subjective. Security professionals that excel are the ones that are most flexible and adaptable. Although the approach to risk or the methodology is similar from one program to the next, each risk is different and the security professional should be applying his or her craft to the facts appropriately. The basic methodology outlined in this chapter should be used as the basis for risk review. A fully implemented program will have these components at its core with subtle differences depending on the company's culture, the security professional's role in the process, and/or the specific requirements of the program.

Creation of a risk profile that clearly describes the risk, the probability, and the significance of an event, including potential loss, is important to the long-term success of the program. In describing the risk in this manner, through analysis and assessment, a full view of the risk and the knock-on effects can be reported. A major role of the risk program is to use the mitigation techniques in response to the risk profile. The goal of the mitigation plan is to avoid and/or minimize the occurrences and effects of an event. The mitigation plan should include education, policy/procedure changes, physical design, and insurance to name a few of the tools available.

It is important to understand the company's approach to risk management as this defines roles and responsibilities. Understanding the company's approach helps the security professional understand his or her role in the process. Risk assessment and risk vulnerability assessment are roles the security professional can fill; however, risk mitigation is historically a role the security professional plays in most risk management programs. The emphasis of the mitigation plan is on avoidance planning and minimizing the negative impact through tools, such as training and device installation. The security professional will be called upon for risk mitigation after an event as well, for such things as investigation, to help minimize the effects. The more successful the proactive mitigation tools are, the more successful the program will be.

Review

1. Name the components of a risk program.
2. List common assets that may be at risk at a company and some risks that can cause loss to these assets. Are there other tangent risks to these assets?
3. What factors would raise the probability of any of the risks identified in this chapter? What factors may lower the probability of any of these risks?
4. What is risk acceptance?
5. Describe a layering mitigation strategy that you could put in place for any of the risks identified in exercise 2.

Chapter 12

Vulnerability assessment process inputs—establish protection objectives*

Mary Lynn Garcia
Retired

Risk Assessment – (Short) a process to identify, report and evaluate risk-related items and issues. The Risk Assessment is key to making decisions before an operation, monitoring risk to active operations and creating Risk Management Programs.

Ric Peregrino

Introduction

Before starting a vulnerability assessment (VA), it is critical to understand protection system objectives. These objectives include threat definition, asset identification, and facility characterization. Each enterprise defines VA and risk assessment differently. Rather than focusing on the semantics of what is included in each of these evaluations, suffice it to say that because a VA concentrates on determining physical protection system (PPS) effectiveness, defined threats and prioritized assets are required inputs to the process. This chapter provides an overview of determining protection objectives before performing a VA. In addition, there are some basic facility functions, operations, and other characteristics that must be considered during the VA. The key concepts discussed in this chapter include

- defining the threat;
- identifying assets and prioritizing them by consequence of loss;
- creating a matrix relating threats and assets; and
- characterizing a facility to perform a VA.

At sites where the threat and assets have not already been defined, this task must be included as part of the VA project. This will likely add cost and time to the project; therefore it is critical to know if this information exists before finalizing these details in the project plan.

Defining the threat

Threat definition establishes the performance required from the PPS. We would not evaluate a PPS protecting an asset from vandals the same way as a system protecting an asset from armed criminals. By describing the threat, the assumptions that were made to perform the assessment are documented and used to show how they influence required upgrades. As such, threat definition is a tool, which helps site managers understand the impact of successful attacks by defined adversaries, and helps PPS designers understand the requirements of the PPS.

*Originally from Garcia, M.L., 2006. Vulnerability Assessment of Physical Protection Systems. Butterworth-Heinemann, Boston, MA. Updated by the editor, Elsevier, 2011.

Handbook of Loss Prevention and Crime Prevention. DOI: https://doi.org/10.1016/B978-0-12-817273-5.00012-0

The following is a brief summary of the threat definition process described in the *Design* textbook. After this review of the overall process, some of the methods that are used to define threats are discussed. The process for threat definition consists of three basic activities:

1. listing the information needed to define the threat;
2. collecting information on the potential threat; and
3. organizing the information to make it usable.

Listing information needed

Before the threat can be defined, information that would be most useful to know about the adversary must be understood. Typically, this information includes the adversary class (insider, outsider, collusion between insiders and outsiders), and their goals, motivation, and capabilities. Adversary goals include theft, sabotage, or other goals such as workplace violence, sale of illegal drugs on-site, and creating negative publicity about activities or ownership at the facility. Theft can include removing physical items or information. Sabotage may involve damaging critical equipment, release of hazardous material, or modification of data or proprietary information. The goal of some adversaries is to draw attention to a site because of philosophical objections. The key concept is that by defining this information about the expected adversary, the PPS can be designed to assist in the protection of the appropriate assets. For example, a protestor may want to climb the fence at a company, which raises and supplies laboratory animals for scientific research, to express their concern about animal cruelty. This is a much lower threat than an employee who brings a gun to work to shoot a manager or coworker. If a gun is one of the expected tools of the adversary, there are ways to design a PPS for detecting entry of weapons. A threat definition often includes a spectrum of threats that reflects the presence of a variety of assets at the facility.

Collecting information

The collection of threat information is accomplished by reviewing available documentation and by contacting agencies that may have useful threat information. These organizations could include local, state, federal, or military law-enforcement agencies and related intelligence agencies. The following types of information may be reviewed for their use in defining threats:

- Incident reports at the site. This could include criminal reports, intelligence reports, and other historical data.
- A list of contacts for law-enforcement activities.
- The number of personnel at the facility and types of positions. Employee numbers versus the number of contractors, visitors, and vendors. Any problems that may have occurred with any of these groups and incidents, such as domestic violence, union disputes, downsizing, and other problems, should be identified.
- Reports of criminal or terrorist activities in the area.
- Review publicly available information from sources such as the Internet, local newspapers, professional associations, and government sources. U.S. Department of State (2005a,b) compiles lists of terrorist activities each year, which are available to the public. The Department of Homeland Security is also a source of threat information for many critical infrastructure segments. In the US Department of Justice, Office of Justice programs also provide crime statistics online at http://www.ojp.usdoj.gov/bjs/.

Organizing information

After potential threat information has been gathered, it should be organized to make it usable, and to facilitate decisions concerning which threats will be included in the threat spectrum used to assess the effectiveness of the existing PPS. A table to assist in the organization of the data was provided in the *Design* textbook.

Since the threat definition will likely consider both insiders and outsiders, characteristics of both types of adversary should be part of the threat definition. A determination is also made concerning an insider's desire and ability to collude with an outsider to accomplish their theft or other goal. At a minimum, a single insider should be considered in collusion with an outsider. An insider's actions depend on a number of factors, including their access to the asset, position in the organization, ability to carry weapons onto the site, and their knowledge of security at the site. Insiders generally include groups such as contractors, vendors, and visitors.

Threat definition methods

We have seen four methods used to define threats, and each is useful in specific applications.

1. Develop threat from historical or intelligence data.
2. Use a policy-based threat issued by an appropriate agency or organization.
3. Create a range of potential threats (threat spectrum).
4. Use defined scenarios of adversary attack.

In some cases, there is sufficient historical data for developing an accurate profile of the likely threats facing a site or enterprise. An example of this might be vandals or criminals who damage or steal lower value assets. There are usually crime statistics available for these types of attacks, and this information can be used to help define these threats, in addition to the site's own internal incident data. This is common practice at medium to large US corporations.

In other cases, there is little historical data, but intelligence data indicate the likelihood of a specific threat. An example is the terrorist threat to many critical US facilities. The intelligence community makes every effort possible to gather current and relevant information for providing early warning of a malevolent act at a specific location. This information often forms the basis for the PPS design at critical government facilities and some private industry sites, particularly those identified as critical infrastructures.

Some organizations, including the US Department of Energy and Department of Defense, as well as large multinational US corporations, use a policy-based threat as their threat definition. In these cases, a specific group within the organization creates the threat definition that is used by all other groups within the organization. The group defining the threat generally has access to intelligence information and has studied various attacks on their sites or other sites that are similar in some aspect, and use this information to create a credible threat definition. For some organizations, this threat is a single threat statement, and for others, it includes a threat spectrum. In either case, the threat that is created is called the design basis threat (DBT) and is used in all VAs conducted across the organization. In addition, local attributes are commonly used to modify the threat as needed. It is important to emphasize that the DBT may not represent the real threat; it is an assessment by informed and qualified people, which represents credible threat capabilities. The real threat may be higher or lower than the DBT; thus the DBT is used as a management and design tool to document one assumption of the PPS design or evaluation.

In some cases, there is little historical or intelligence data available to assist an analyst in the development of a threat profile. In this case the organization might just select and define a range of threats and capabilities, for example, vandals, criminals, and competitors, and use these as benchmarks for the VA of their PPS.

In addition to the methods listed previously, some organizations take a slightly different approach to threat, which is to use certain defined scenarios. This method can achieve the same goal as threat definition as long as the scenario provides enough detail about adversary tools, capabilities, and tactics so that the VA team has enough information to be able to complete their analysis. For example, one scenario at a facility located along a waterfront might be that adversaries use a boat to access the site, enter a building, damage a hazardous chemical control valve so that the chemical will slowly drain from a tank, and then run back to the boat and escape. While this seems like a fairly detailed scenario, it would be much more effective for the VA team to know how many people are part of the attack, whether they are carrying weapons, what tools they are carrying, and whether they would actually use their weapons. In addition, this adversary group could have insider assistance in the form of information so that the adversaries would know where to find the tools on-site needed to damage the valve. Although the threat is generally defined first and then used to create credible attack scenarios, the use of scenarios in place of a threat definition can be useful as long as the scenario description is detailed enough to allow the VA team to analyze the PPS and determine vulnerabilities. A range of scenarios is often created, and each site is left to select those that are applicable; this leaves open the possibility that some sites will only select one scenario, whereas others may select several, often occurring simultaneously. This variation can cause different sites with similar assets to implement different protection schemes, which could be counterproductive to the protection objectives of the larger enterprise. In this case an asset that is similarly valued by an organization could actually have different levels of protection, which could create attack opportunities for an adversary.

It is worth pointing out that recent malevolent attacks, such as the sarin gas attack in the Tokyo subway, 9/11, the anthrax attacks in Florida and New York, and the Madrid train bombings, demonstrate that some adversary groups are developing new capabilities in chemical, biological, and explosives weapons of mass destruction. As a result, a number of recent US laws have established new expectations with respect to security at some facilities. These include the USA Patriot Act, the Bioterrorism Preparedness Act, and the Maritime Transportation Security Act of 2002. These laws are having some effect on threat definition at certain facilities, and there is a corresponding expectation that security at these sites will be appropriate for these threats. One example is the requirement to improve security at ports, rail stations, airports, and other transportation systems.

Insider threat

One category of threat, which causes considerable problems when designing a security system, is insiders. Reports consistently show that insiders are responsible for the many security events that occur at all sites overall (Hoffman et al., 1990; Federal Bureau of Investigation/Computer Security Institute, 2005). Since insiders already have authorized access to a site, many PPS elements cannot be used to detect insider intrusions. For example, exterior perimeters will not be effective against insiders, because they will enter the site through entry control points using legitimate photo badges or electronic credentials, and detection will not be possible. As a group, insiders can exploit their knowledge of the facility and its operations, including security elements; can choose the best time and strategies for a successful attack; may have access to the most critical areas of a site; and may have access to the PPS, which can be used to conceal an attack.

Depending on the particular site and their policies and procedures, it can be difficult to collect all the pertinent information required to define insiders. Examples of issues include the disparity in reporting and categorizing insider crimes and the lack of prosecutor feedback after case disposition. Insider attacks can include theft of equipment, money, proprietary or classified information, high-value products, such as precious metals, or embezzlement. Acts of sabotage include such things as vandalism, arson, bomb threats or actual bombings, and equipment tampering. One study showed that insider criminals are among the most difficult adversaries to protect against and that financial gain was their primary motivation, although other factors such as family ties, intimate relationships, dissatisfaction, and ideological beliefs also played a role. This study also showed that guard forces present a special and troublesome problem. Insider acts can be accomplished by individuals, in cooperation with other insiders, or as allies of outsiders. A more recent study, although focused on computer security, provides additional insights into insider capabilities and motivation.

Just as with outsiders, insiders may be willing to kill or be killed, may abort an attack to avoid capture if they suspect they have been detected, and may use covert or overt actions as tactics. The insider can be divided into four categories, as shown in Fig. 12.1. Insiders may be passive or active, with active insiders further broken down into rational and irrational groups. The rational group can then be subdivided into violent or nonviolent types.

Passive insiders provide information to other insiders or outsiders; active adversaries actually participate in the attack in some way. An irrational insider may not follow a clear decision process and can use violence indiscriminately. This group could include employees who are mentally unstable or under the influence of illegal substances or alcohol. Rational nonviolent insiders may tamper with, and use limited covert force against, PPS elements and are likely to try to avoid identification; rational violent insiders use force, weapons, and possibly explosives against PPS hardware, barriers, or personnel to ensure success. Characteristics of each insider threat category are shown in Fig. 12.2.

Insiders complicate the evaluation (and thus the design of upgrades) of a PPS for a number of reasons. In some cases the insider threat is not even considered because of cultural values. For example, the Japanese, until recently, would not include insiders as part of their threat spectrum at critical sites. In other cases, it can be hard to convince senior management that insiders are a threat to critical assets. This view is often accompanied by the belief that some levels of employees are more trusted than others; for example, senior managers versus production personnel. Protection is needed against all insiders, regardless of their level of access, authority, or knowledge. In addition, PPS measures to detect insiders often have an adverse operational impact such as the use of two-person rules or requiring security clearances.

In general, insider threats are addressed by removing them from the employee population, reducing their opportunities for theft, preventing any actual attempted thefts, recovering stolen material, and by material controls to verify that thefts have not occurred. These techniques are incorporated into the PPS through the use of background

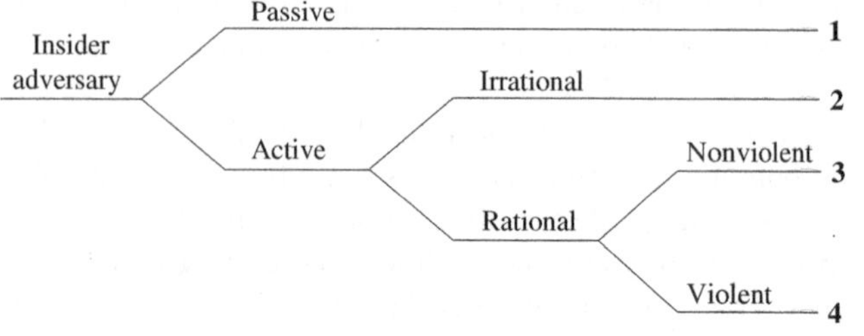

FIGURE 12.1 Insider threat categories.
All categories may not exist at a site, but each group has special characteristics that are important to consider when evaluating the PPS. *PPS*, Physical protection system.

Insider category	Characteristic
1. Passive	Provides information to a colluding adversary or an outside group
2. Irrational	Does not follow a clear decision rule; uses violence indiscriminately
3. Rational nonviolent	May tamper with and use limited covert force against protection elements; is not willing to be identified
4. Rational violent	Uses overt force, weapons, and explosives against hardware, barriers, or personnel to increase chances of success

FIGURE 12.2 Characteristics of insiders.
Note that passive insiders only provide information; the other categories are all subsets of an active insider threat. Irrational threats may be a result of mental illness or drug or alcohol abuse.

investigations, varying access controls across a site, inventories of critical assets, reduction and consolidation of some critical assets at a site, and periodic drug testing at some sites. All aspects of insider protection are required to be integrated into the overall PPS to be effective, which is one reason why this is such a complex problem. When conducting a VA, it is important to note the PPS elements in place to prevent insider attacks, assuming insiders are part of the threat spectrum. This choice can be made by individual clients and customers, but we have yet to visit a site where insiders were not an actual threat, so we recommend including them in any VA.

Other notes on threat definition

Many companies and agencies have a DBT that describes the threat applied at a facility. Although these may exist, they often do not contain sufficient detail, or they may need to be modified for some locations. For instance, the use of explosives by some threats is a concern since the attacks on 9/11. When considering the use of explosives, it is important to specify the quantity that will be used. The amount of explosives in a backpack will have a different effect than the amount that can be carried in a large vehicle such as a dump truck. The use of a vehicle bomb should specify the amount of explosives and the vehicle type and weight. In the past, vehicle attacks were limited to vehicles that weighed 4000 lb; however, this has recently been increased to 15,000 lb by some government agencies. This is why threat definition should be as specific as possible—the vulnerability of the PPS depends on the adversary and their tools. By thoroughly defining the threat, we are establishing the required performance of the final PPS.

If a large company or a government agency is planning to do VAs at their facilities, it should agree on the threat before the evaluations begin. One of the biggest benefits of using a defined threat in a VA is that multiple sites can be compared to each other based on the same set of assumptions. In this way, senior management can see an "apples to apples" comparison of all sites, and a more accurate view of the current vulnerabilities can be presented. This controlled comparison will assist senior managers in making informed decisions about which sites need the most attention, and help them prioritize the application of their limited resources. Constant changing of the threat at different sites will make it difficult to make meaningful comparisons of the results of all the VAs and use the results to optimum advantage.

Whichever process is used to define threats, it is critical that customers concur with the threat definition that will be used. Occasionally, at sites that have no existing threat definition, this concurrence does not occur until the end of the on-site part of the VA, because the threat is developed in parallel with the VA. To mitigate the difficulty created by this arrangement, a variety of threats should be analyzed to cover a threat spectrum that will include all credible threats under consideration. It should be noted that time to develop the DBT on-site will delay the start of site evaluation activities and may delay delivery of the final report.

Estimating likelihood of attack

Another aspect of threat definition, which has proven to be difficult to accomplish at times, is determining the probability of attack by the defined threat. As noted previously, historical data can be used to define the adversary; it can also be used to predict the probability of attack. Criminal statistics exist for different crimes in different geographic locations, so this is a ready source of data. Probability of attack is really a part of risk assessment, but many organizations

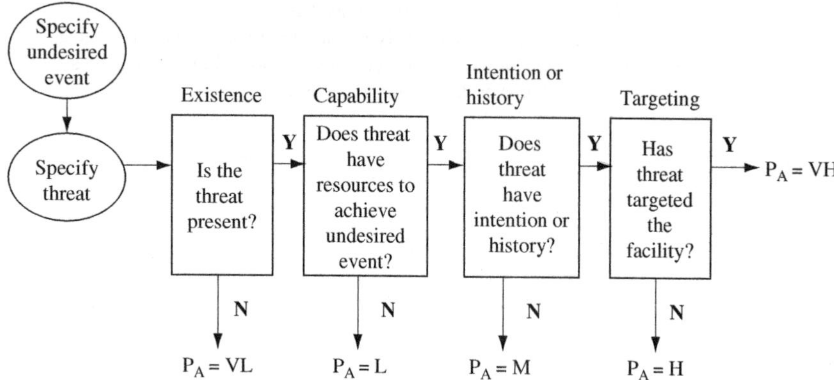

FIGURE 12.3 Simple method to estimate probability of attack.
By following the flow of criteria, a crude determination of the probability of attack can be made. If desired, a conversion from a qualitative to quantitative estimate can be made by selecting a numerical value to represent the qualitative level, although this is not a mathematically rigorous approach.

want to know this as part of the VA. Fig. 12.3 shows a crude but simple method of estimating the probability of attack in a qualitative manner.

The probability of attack may also be expressed as a frequency or likelihood. These terms are often used interchangeably, although there are some differences. Probability is the likelihood that a specific event will occur, expressed as the ratio of the number of actual occurrences to the number of possible occurrences. Frequency is the number of times a specified periodic phenomenon occurs within a specified interval. A probability provides a quantitative description of the likely occurrence of a particular event; frequency includes a time element. Either term can be useful in threat definition. At some point, the likelihood of attack may be less important than the value of a highly critical asset. In the largest sense, this is a function of the asset owner's risk tolerance, but all businesses have some critical assets, and they must be protected. In these cases, it can be more useful to consider how well protected the asset is, assuming an adversary attacks.

This concept is captured through the use of conditional risk, where the condition is that there is an attack. The use of conditional risk allows the organization to focus on the protection around the asset, rather than spend a lot of time debating the likelihood of attack. This is most useful for highly valued or unique assets, which probably require protection irrespective of the likelihood that an adversary will attack. Customers occasionally misinterpret conditional risk to mean that the likelihood of attack is 1.0 (i.e., it is a certainty that the asset will be attacked). This is not the case at all; more accurately, this means that we do not know the likelihood of attack and that the consequence of loss of the asset is high enough so that the estimate is not required. No matter what the likelihood of attack is, loss of the asset is an unacceptably high consequence, and it will be protected. This is a subtle but important point.

Asset identification

In addition to threat definition the VA team must have an understanding of the assets to be protected at the site. As with threat definition, some customers do not have their assets identified and prioritized before performing a VA. In this case, this step must be accomplished before performing the VA. The following discussion is a brief overview of the asset identification process. Once assets have been identified, this information must be shared with the VA team. Occasionally, local management at a site will add assets to the already prioritized list, which can complicate the VA. In this case, we recommend including the new assets, while still focusing on the agreed list.

Asset identification methods

Asset identification is an evaluation of what to protect by considering the value of the asset to the facility or enterprise. There are three steps for identification of assets: (1) specify undesirable consequences; (2) select asset identification technique; and (3) identify areas, components, or material to be protected.

Three methods for asset identification are reviewed in this section. They include manual listing, logic diagrams to identify vital areas for sabotage attacks, and the use of consequence analysis to screen and prioritize assets. The first two techniques were covered in the *Design* textbook, so they will only be summarized here, whereas the use of consequence analysis is described in more detail later. Other methods of asset identification can also be found in Fisher and Green and Hess and Wrobleski.

Other aspects of asset identification include consideration of the form of the asset and adversary tactics. The form of the asset cannot be ignored—once a particular asset is identified as valuable enough to protect, it must be protected in all forms. For example, if the asset is a trade secret that is stored on paper in a safe and also in an electronic file on a network, the protection must be equal. This is another example of balanced protection—all paths to the asset must be equally difficult for the adversary. At a high level, this implies that network and physical protection must be roughly equal. If they are not, the asset may still be vulnerable, even if the PPS is very effective. In addition, there are several adversary tactics that can be used to steal information. Insiders can memorize details over a period of time, fax the information off-site, or carry it out on small electronic media such as USB drives. Some of these attacks are difficult to detect and prevent, but are worth considering in the overall protection scheme. Another insider tactic is protracted theft. In this case, a knowledgeable insider may steal low quantities of tangible assets, such as computer chips, drugs, or other valuable items, and accumulate larger quantities over time. This can be difficult to detect, even in cases where process controls are used, and it is another example of why the form of the asset is important. While it is a given that there can never be absolute security, the form of the asset should be considered when defining threats, identifying assets, and evaluating the effectiveness of a PPS.

Manual listing

For theft of localized items, such as computers, tools, proprietary information, or work-in-process, the manual listing of assets is an appropriate technique. Since these are theft targets, the undesirable consequence to be avoided is loss of the asset. This technique consists of listing the assets of concern and their locations. The list provides the assets to be protected. The manual technique can also be applied to theft of product-in-process (such as semiconductors or drugs) or sabotage of critical components if the facility is small or processing is very simple. Product-in-process may also include individual pills before packaging or filled bottles waiting to be loaded into cases. Intermediate process steps may be good theft targets, particularly for insiders. If a production line is very complex or if multiple production lines are at work, the opportunities for theft of these assets may be broadly distributed throughout the plant, not limited to the end of the production line. In addition, storage and shipping areas are also locations of interest. Consider a large petrochemical plant with sabotage as a concern. Many complex systems, each with hundreds of components, interact to produce, route, and store the finished products. Furthermore, many support systems, such as electrical power, ventilation, and instrumentation, are interconnected to primary components, such as pump motors, in a complex manner. Asset identification must consider which systems and components to protect, as well as their interaction with other support systems.

Logic diagrams

The logic diagram is a useful tool for determining potential theft and sabotage targets for a complex facility. Due to the complex nature of this process, experienced experts in the use of logic diagrams should be consulted before initiating this activity. Since logic diagrams are used to ensure there is a thorough understanding of where theft or sabotage can occur, the undesirable consequences may vary. Theft assets may have loss of revenue or competitive advantage as undesired consequences, whereas sabotage targets may use loss of life or environmental damage as the undesired consequence. Excellent resources on the use and construction of logic diagrams are provided in Kumamoto and Henley and by the Nuclear Regulatory Commission.

Consequence analysis

For some large organizations or facilities, there may be too many targets of attack to use manual listing or logic diagrams to identify assets. In these cases, it may be more appropriate to use a screening methodology to help reduce the number of assets to a more manageable number. Over time, all assets can be evaluated using a VA, but by using a screening methodology, assets can be prioritized, with the highest ranked assets receiving the most immediate attention. Asset screening using consequence analysis is described in this section.

Consequence of loss

It is not possible or practical to protect everything at a site at the same level. Effective security protects what needs to be protected to prevent undesirable consequences. Much of this determination will be a function of the risk tolerance of the enterprise that owns the assets, but some assets have an unacceptably high consequence of loss and must be protected. Some examples of undesirable consequences are

- damage to national security,
- successful terrorist attacks,
- loss of control of nuclear material or weapons,
- loss of life as a result of hazardous material release, and
- loss of market position.

Note that the undesired consequence is the final result of a successful adversary attack and not just the completion of the attack tasks. For example, in a boat attack on a chemical valve, the adversary completes the attack when the valve is damaged; the undesired consequence is leakage of enough hazardous chemical to cause environmental damage, injuries to people, or loss of life.

Depending on the undesired consequences that the site is trying to avoid, different adversary tactics need to be considered, and an analysis of the potential harm that will occur is required. For example, if the undesired consequence is loss of life because of release of a toxic gas by a saboteur, a consequence analysis is conducted to determine the potential effect of this malevolent event. Some sites may have multiple undesirable consequences and, therefore, may need to capture all of these states in a single overarching statement of undesirable consequence, such as loss of facility, and then list under this all the consequences that could cause this outcome. In some government agencies the assets to be protected range from low-value items, such as laptop computers, to unique national resources such as the Statue of Liberty or the Brooklyn Bridge. Due to this diversity of assets and their corresponding diversity of value, a screening methodology is used to help identify the most critical assets that need protection. This screening approach is accomplished through the use of consequence analysis. A good example of this is the problem faced by the US Department of Homeland Security—with so many potential targets available across the nation, a screening process must be developed that will identify a prioritized list of assets. This allows the application of limited resources to the most critical assets first, then attention to other assets over time. The key to a good consequence analysis is development of a set of criteria.

Criteria

The most critical part of screening is to develop a small set of criteria that can be used to judge which assets have the highest potential of causing the undesirable consequences if they get lost. Screening identifies undesired events, evaluates the consequences of these events, and uses the results to decide whether a particular facility or asset should be included in the assessment. The outcome of the screening methodology is a list of assets that are designated as high, medium, or low consequence.

The VA project leader is responsible for facilitating the screening process with appropriate personnel, which will include facility safety, operations, management, and security staff, and may also include local, state, or federal government agencies, depending on the site to be evaluated. It is worth noting that some industrial sites are now designated as part of the national critical infrastructure, and as such they are receiving greater scrutiny by various elements of the government. As a result, there is a greater need for these sites to perform VAs that are accepted by these agencies. It is likely that future VAs at these sites will use common threats and asset criteria so that the results can be compiled and compared. The asset-screening process is composed of five steps:

1. *Identify undesired events*. Indicate which undesired events are most important to the site owner or which will have the greatest potential impact on their continuing operation.
2. *Determine consequence criteria*. For each undesired event, determine one or more measures of consequence. We recommend making these quantifiable, not subjective, criteria. The use of quantifiable criteria will be easier to defend under external scrutiny and will prevent manipulation of the criteria to achieve a desired answer.
3. *Determine measures for consequence criteria*. For each criterion, determine what values would constitute a high, medium, or low measure of consequence. This establishes the screening matrix.
4. *Consequence analysis*. Evaluate each asset that can produce the undesired consequence if attacked, using the criteria and measures.
5. *Prioritize assets*. Using the completed consequence analysis, rank assets, in order, from highest to lowest and determine what level will be used to identify assets for the VA.

The screening process flow is summarized in Fig. 12.4.

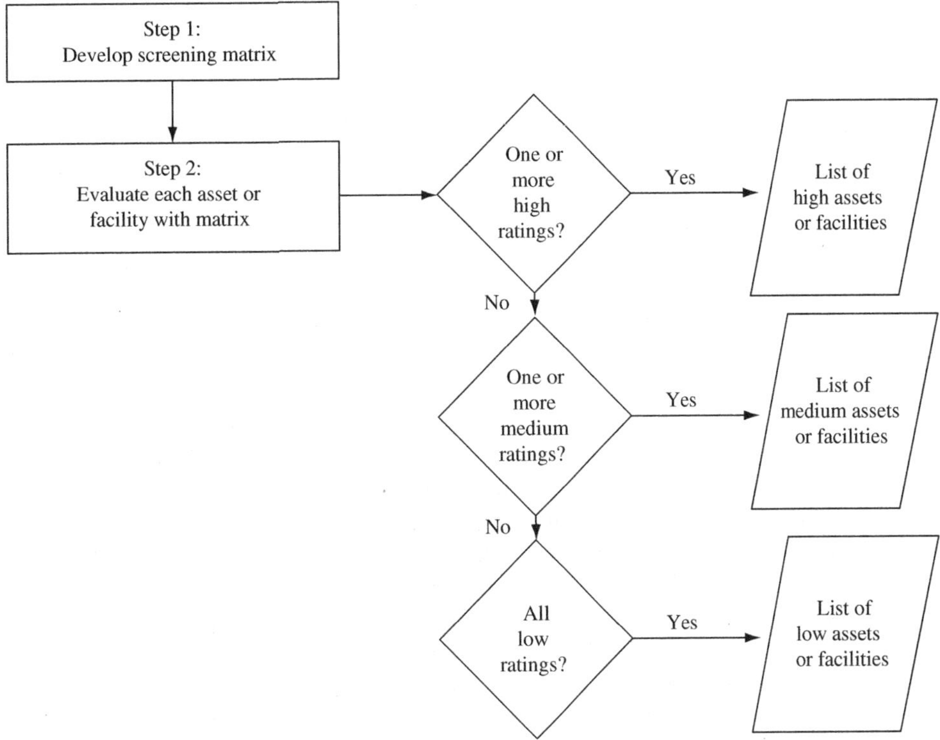

FIGURE 12.4 Asset-screening flowchart.
This is a summary of the asset identification screening process. First, the criteria for screening are developed and then assets are rated using the criteria. Assets are prioritized based on the overall rating of the asset.

TABLE 12.1 Sample screening matrix for asset identification.

Undesired event	Criteria	High	Medium	Low
Damage to national security	Loss of classified information	Loss of top secret	Loss of secret	Loss of unclassified
Terrorist attack	Loss of life	>3000	100–3000	<100
	Number of injured	>5000	1000–5000	<1000
	Property damage	>$1 billion	$100 million to $1 billion	<$100 million
Hazardous material release	Loss of life	>1000	10–1000	<10
	Environmental damage	>$20 million	$1–$20 million	<$1 million
Loss of customer confidence	Customers lost	>50	10–50	<10
Loss of major function	Revenue loss	>$10 million	$1–$10 million	<$1 million

Note: By specifying the undesired event, criteria, and a range of consequences, critical assets can be identified and prioritized for protection.

An example of the screening matrix that includes undesirable consequences, criteria, and measures is shown in Table 12.1. Note that this is not a table from an actual site, but shows a variety of undesirable consequences and criteria and what measures define high, medium, and low effects. Once the matrix is constructed, different site assets are compared and judged using the matrix. The more "highs" the asset scores, the higher its priority is. Once this exercise is completed, decisions can be made about how far down the list the VA team will go for its site evaluation.

High consequence	Terrorist (sabotage)		Insider (theft)
Medium consequence		Insider (sabotage)	
Low consequence	Vandal (graffiti)		Hacker (web deface)
	Low probability	**Medium probability**	**High probability**

FIGURE 12.5 Threat and asset matrix.
This is a useful presentation tool that summarizes much of the information collected when establishing protection system objectives. Note that it relates threat level, tactics, and probability of attack to consequence of loss of assets.

Threat/asset matrix

After threats have been defined and assets have been prioritized, a considerable amount of information will be generated, which can be used to establish protection system objectives. The volume of information can be combined into a matrix that relates probability of attack, threat level and tactic, and consequence of loss of assets. Fig. 12.5 shows an example of how this chart is constructed. Presentation of data to senior managers of the enterprise using this technique will quickly summarize and relate these details to each other. This is a good way to reduce information to an understandable matrix and focus management attention on the highest risk events.

The different shading is used to emphasize the areas of highest risk (i.e., where the probability of attack and consequence of loss are both high) and lowest risk. The highest risks must be addressed to protect assets; lower risk assets may be addressed through procedural changes or other risk-management alternatives. The decisions about which combinations of probability of attack and consequence of loss represent the highest risk are a reflection of the enterprise's risk tolerance.

Facility characterization

The major part of a VA is facility characterization, which primarily consists of evaluating the PPS at the site. Considerable detail about how this is done will be provided in the following chapters, but an overview of the process is described here. The goal of a VA is to identify PPS components in the functional areas of detection, delay, and response and gather sufficient data for estimating their performance against specific threats. The PPS is characterized at the component and system levels, and vulnerabilities to defeat by the defined threat are documented.

Data collection is the core of PPS characterization; accurate data are the basis for conducting a true analysis of the ability of the PPS to meet its defined objectives. Accuracy, however, is only one of several factors to consider. The data gathered must be appropriate to the purpose and scope of the VA, and the quantity and form of the data must be sufficient to support analysis based on available resources and desired confidence in the results.

An ideal assessment uses statistically significant data derived from a series of tests that evaluate the system and individual components under all expected conditions. In almost all cases, this is not practical because of time or resource constraints and the desire to minimize the disruption caused by the VA team. To address this issue, historical performance test data are used in lieu of actual performance tests, although specific installation and maintenance of components, along with many other factors at a site, influence the actual performance of those components. For example, a specific type of sensor installed at a site may have a significantly different actual detection probability than the detection probability developed by a testing organization under controlled conditions. The historical performance data are then modified by security system experts based on conditions at the facility that cause degradation in performance of the installed component.

Methods used to collect PPS characterization data for a VA include site tours and observations, document reviews, and interviews. Evaluation testing is another valuable data-collection method for determining the effectiveness of the installed PPS. A detailed discussion of these activities is provided next.

Characterization tools

A site tour is usually conducted early in a VA. During the initial site tour, the VA team begins to gather information regarding the general layout of the facility, the locations of key assets, information about facility operations and production capabilities, and locations and types of PPS components. Subsequent tours and observations of facility operations are conducted by VA team members to

- become familiar with specific facility layouts,
- examine the locations of PPS components,
- verify that documentation accurately reflects the current condition and configuration of the site,
- identify anomalies or deficiencies that require further investigation, and
- select specific areas or components as candidates for evaluation testing.

Group and individual tours allow the VA team to observe the actual operating environment at the site and note details that affect system performance. This is often one of the most productive activities of the VA team because of the nature of the information that can be obtained. To quickly gather information and obtain maximum benefit from these tours, the following should be considered:

- Observe procedures during normal operations whenever possible. For example, observe vehicle search procedures while interviewing entry control personnel.
- Observe actual operations. For example, ask the people who normally conduct operations to demonstrate procedures rather than having other staff describe or demonstrate how they think a procedure is performed.
- Note areas that require further review.

The review of key documents and selected records are two important PPS characterization activities. These are useful in the evaluation of the effectiveness of a PPS and may begin during the planning phase of a VA. PPS documentation reflects the site's philosophy and approach to implementation and maintenance of the system. Information obtained from document reviews will verify information received from briefings, site tours, and interviews; gather information about the existence and performance of PPS components; support PPS analysis; and give an overall view of the PPS at a facility.

The PPS characterization step of a VA includes interviews with key site personnel. Interviews are critical for clarifying impressions or contents of document reviews and to gain greater insight into specific facility-operating procedures. Interviews with personnel at all organizational levels are recommended. Frequently, interviews with key personnel will reveal whether policies and directives are effectively communicated and implemented, and whether systems actually function as described in documentation. Interviews are not necessarily formal and will frequently take the form of discussions that occur during site tours and evaluation testing.

The VA team should ensure that the personnel being interviewed understand the question and answer accordingly, and that the right questions are asked of the right people. One useful technique is to ask personnel in one group how other groups perform. For example, ask alarm operators how long it takes to get equipment repaired. Another useful technique is to ask questions while observing personnel perform routine activities. These are some questions to consider when using this technique:

- Is this a normal procedure?
- How long has it been this way?
- Are there alternatives to this procedure and when are they used?
- Is there training on this procedure?

Testing is the most valuable data-collection method for evaluating the effectiveness of a PPS. Evaluation testing can determine whether personnel have the skills and abilities to perform their duties, whether procedures work, and whether equipment is functional and appropriate. Evaluation tests include functional, operability, and performance tests. Functional tests verify that a device is on, and that it is performing as expected (i.e., a sensor still has a probability of detection of 0.9). Operability tests verify that a device is on and working (i.e., a sensor is on and detects, but has moved because of vibration, so it is aimed at the wrong location). Performance testing is the characterization of a device by repeating the same test enough times to establish a measure of device capability against different threats. (A sensor is tested many times using crawling, walking, and running tactics, and under day, night, and varying weather conditions to fully characterize the probability of detection and nuisance alarm rate.) Performance tests may be conducted on individual PPS components or on the overall PPS. Since performance testing is fairly rigorous and requires many repetitions over time, they are generally impractical during a VA. Performance testing is typically performed in a lab or nonoperational facility.

Evaluation tests may vary in complexity from a simple test of a sensor through an attempt to carry a contraband item into a facility, and up to a tactical response exercise involving adversaries and large numbers of security response personnel. Some tests can be conducted under normal conditions, in which the component, system, or person is not affected or alerted. Other tests must be conducted under artificial conditions, although realism is always a primary planning consideration. The project leader works with team members and on-site staff to coordinate the planning and conduct of tests. This process can be informal for simple technical-evaluation tests, or very structured for more complex tests requiring more coordination such as response force exercises.

Facility states

One of the goals of the VA team before any system analysis is performed is to identify the various facility states that can exist at the site. A VA is used to establish vulnerabilities at a site at all times of the day and at all times of the year. As such, the team must understand the various facility states so that they can determine whether the PPS is more or less vulnerable at these times. If the team does not identify these states and determine system effectiveness during all of these different states, the VA will be incomplete and may lead to a false sense of protection. Examples of facility states include normal operating hours, nonoperational hours, a strike at the site, emergencies, such as fire or bomb threats, and shift changes. For example, it is common practice to turn off interior intrusion alarms in work areas during operational hours. This eliminates constant alarms as personnel carry out their work, and is called access. Other facility states that address the status of intrusion sensors include secure (all sensors are operating) and alarm (sensors are activated by something). The status of other PPS elements should also be considered. If vaults, safes, gates, or doors are open and unlocked at different times of the day, they will have different performance against malevolent threats than if they are closed and locked. In addition, performance of all PPS elements must be considered under daylight or nighttime, and the expected weather conditions at the site. Exterior sensors and cameras are affected by fog, rain, snow, and wind; interior cameras may not work well if the lights are turned off in rooms. It should be clear that these facility states and combinations must be considered to truly determine how vulnerable the site is to an attack.

Security checklists

Most, if not all, security textbooks use a security survey to support the evaluation of a site when establishing vulnerabilities (Fisher and Green, 1998; Hess and Wrobleski, 1996). These can be useful starting points, but should not be relied on for a thorough evaluation. One problem is that these surveys do not document the effects of the observed state of equipment. Asking if there are fences or cameras or access controls present is not sufficient to determine if they are working properly. Another problem is that these lists are somewhat vague in their criteria. For example, almost every checklist asks if lighting is adequate, but it is unclear what adequate means. Is it adequate if lights are present? What if lights are present, but they do not light areas where cameras are located? Or, what if lights are present with cameras, but the light-to-dark ratio is too high or too low? The general point is that checklists are only a starting point. The VA is used to establish what PPS components are installed at a site, and how vulnerable they are to an adversary attack. Checklists may document presence, but not effectiveness, of installed components. Documenting the presence of components is not the recommended approach to evaluating a PPS, particularly when protecting critical assets.

Summary

This chapter discussed the protection objectives of a VA, especially the importance of defining the threat, identifying assets, and characterizing the PPS at the site. Threat definition was reviewed, along with some resources to help define threats in preparation for a VA. Asset identification methods were also reviewed, and additional details were given about how to screen many assets and reduce them to a prioritized list. This is useful when dealing with very large enterprises with a variety of assets. This chapter ended with an introduction to facility characterization, particularly focusing on the PPS at the site. This section introduced some of the activities and techniques used by the VA team when performing their evaluation. Considerable additional detail on this aspect of a VA is described in the following chapters.

References

Federal Bureau of Investigation/Computer Security Institute, 2005. Annual computer security survey. Available from: <www.goCSI.com>.

Fisher, R.J., Green, G., 1998. Introduction to Security, sixth ed. Butterworth-Heinemann, Boston, MA, pp. 168–171.

Hess, K., Wrobleski, H., 1996. Introduction to Private Security, fourth ed. West Publishing, Minneapolis, MN/St. Paul, MN, pp. 423–429.

Hoffman, B., Meyer, C., Schwarz, B., Duncan, J., 1990. Insider crime: The threat to nuclear facilities and programs. In: RAND Report to U.S. Department of Energy.

U.S. Department of State, 2005a. Significant terrorist incidents, 1961–2003: a brief chronology. Available from: <http://www.state.gov/r/pa/ho/pubs/fs/5902.htm>.

U.S. Department of State, 2005b. Country reports on terrorism 2004. Available from: <http://www.state.gov/documents/organization/45313.pdf>.

Further reading

Southwest Emergency Response Network (SWERN), 2005. Available from: <www.SWERN.gov>.

Transportation Research Board, 2005. Available from: <http://www4.trb.org/trb/homepage.nsf/web/security>.

U.S. Secret Service, 2005. Insider Threat Study: Illicit Cyber Activity in the Banking and Finance Sector. National Threat Assessment Center (NTAC). Available from: <http://www.secretservice.gov/ntac_its.shtml>.

National Law Enforcement and Corrections Technology Center (NLECTC), 2005. Criminal justice links. Available from: <http://www.nlectc.org/links/justnet.html>.

Kumamoto, H., Henley, E.J., 1996. Probabilistic Risk Assessment and Management for Engineers and Scientists, second ed. IEEE Press, Piscataway, NJ, pp. 165–26.

Vesely, W.E., Goldberg, F.F., Roberts, N.H., Haasl, D.F., 1981. Fault Tree Handbook (NUREG-0492). Nuclear Regulatory Commission (NRC). Available from: <http://www.nrc.gov/reading-rm/doccollections/nuregs/staff/sr0492/> (accessed 20.04.05.).

Chapter 13

Security surveys and auditing

Lawrence J. Fennelly and Matthew R. Dimmick
Security Consultant

Introduction

This chapter will discuss security surveys and security audits and the difference between these two terms, how each of them might be used, when they will occur, how to prepare for them, and how to upgrade your facility's physical security after based on the findings of the survey or audit. As with other physical security program components, security surveys and/or audits are contributory to the overall continuous improvement process that has become a central premise of the modern security program.

For the purposes of this chapter, we will utilize the following definitions for security survey and security audits:

- Security surveys are an on-site assessment of the physical security measures in place at a given location. Security surveys provide a snapshot of the security mitigation strategies that have been implemented at the assessed site to identify potential gaps in the protective elements and/or vulnerabilities in the implemented strategies.
- Security audits are conducted through the lens of compliance and or conformity to an agreed upon standard or standards. Security audits will, in most cases, be checklist based and be utilized to determine the presence or absence of a required or expected security mitigation strategy or technology.

These methods of security assessment may be applied to a variety of locations and types of facilities including, but not limited to, industrial plant, business, residential locations, and whether part of public or private institutions, to ascertain the current level of protection and develop considerations for improvements to the site's security. A security survey should include a review of each potential protective layer including, but not limited to, site boundaries and perimeter, owned space, the facility exterior, and internal spaces requiring additional protection.

The security survey may serve as part of the broader risk assessment, which includes the identification of threats, controls, level of risk, and your completed risk assessment, which should include risk analysis, risk identification, and risk evaluation.

It is interesting to note that a definition of *crime prevention* as outlined by the British Home Office Crime Prevention Program—"the anticipation, recognition and appraisal of a crime risk and the initiation of action to remove or reduce it"—could, in fact, be an excellent description of a security survey. The only difference, of course, is that a survey generally does not become the "action" as such but rather a basis for considerations to improve the security mitigation strategies that are in place.

This definition can be divided into five components and utilized as a working foundation for the security surveyor:

1. *Anticipation*. How does the anticipation of a crime risk become important to the security or crime prevention surveyor? A primary requirement for the security or crime prevention survey is to anticipate and prevent aspects of given acts or threats. Keeping the anticipation of threats in perspective helps the surveyor to maintain a proper balance when developing the survey results and considerations for improvement. In other words the anticipatory stage could be considered a prognosis for further action. A security survey may be conducted to contribute to the vulnerability assessment portion of a broader risk assessment.
2. *Recognition*. What does an individual need to conduct a survey of the relationships between anticipation and appraisal? The ability to recognize and interpret potential crime risks is an important skill for the security surveyor. Understanding how adversaries act and the potential pathways they may take into a protected area or facility contributes to the ability of the surveyor to observe and recognize vulnerabilities.

Handbook of Loss Prevention and Crime Prevention. DOI: https://doi.org/10.1016/B978-0-12-817273-5.00013-2

3. *Appraisal.* The responsibility to develop, suggest, and communicate considerations for improvement to reduce risk is certainly a hallmark of any security survey.
4. *Crime risk.* As defined in this text, a crime risk is the opportunity gained from crime. The total elimination of opportunity or risk is not possible. Therefore the cost of protection is measured in (1) protection of depth and (2) delay time. The implementation of the considerations should not exceed the total (original or replacement) cost of the item(s) to be protected. There may be exceptions to this rule, for example, where life or significant injury may result from the risk.
5. *The initiation of action to remove or reduce a crime risk.* This section indicates the phase of a survey in which the recipient of the recommendations decides whether to act, based on the suggestions (recommendations) set forth by the surveyor. In some cases the identification of security risk is made early in a survey and it is advisable to act on the recommendation prior to completing the survey.

The initiation of corrective actions based on the findings and considerations in the survey is the sole responsibility if the individual(s) who receive the survey report. It is assumed that the individual(s) who receive the security survey report have the commensurate responsibility and authority to act. Ultimately it is also up to the property owner how the risk is treated. In addition to mitigation strategies being implemented, there are also the options that a risk may be avoided (i.e., eliminate the activity or asset), transferred (insurance vehicles, bonds, etc.), or accepted (a risk is noted but no further action is taken).

Remember a threat and *risk assessment* is a more in-depth study, including risk management, analysis of risk factors, environmental and physical security measures, and analysis of crime patterns, fraud, and internal theft. It is a process of assessing threats and risk and the formulation of strategies to minimize the risk and enhance security.

What is risk analysis

Risk analysis[1] is a management tool, the standards for which are determined by whatever management decides it wants to accept in terms of actual loss. To proceed to a logical manner to perform a risk analysis, it is first necessary to accomplish some basic tasks (Broder, 2006).

What are assets

Simply put—people, property, and reputation/image

How is risk determined

Three dimensions of essential elements—likelihood, consequences, and perception

Crime risk

An illegal or socially undesirable event, described in terms of the event and the consequences, for example, the risk of injury to community members through assault in the alley.[2] To be effectively assessed, it must be clearly defined that risk does not have to be quantified to be understood, but the level of risk must be able to be interpreted context that is critical to identify and understand risk.

Risk management includes the application of logical and systematic methods for communicating and consulting throughout the process establishing the context for identifying, analyzing, evaluating, treating and monitoring risks and reviewing risks reporting and recording the results.

Risk assessment is a part of risk management—it attempts to answer the following fundamental questions:

1. What can happen and why (risk identification)?
2. What are the consequences (various contexts)?
3. What is the probability of occurrence?
4. What factors mitigate the consequences or reduce the likelihood that a risk will be realized?

1. Broder, J.F., 2006. Risk Analysis and the Security Survey. Elsevier.
2. ISO 31010.

Alignment with CPTED and situational crime prevention

Specific outcomes that need to achieve are

1. improved quality of life, and enhanced use of space, lower crime risk;
2. need to understand factors that run contrary to required outcomes;
3. need to identify and implement appropriate strategies;
4. need to be able to describe risks accurately in order to analyze/assess, but not every possible risks; and
5. useful to draw up a matrix with key stakeholder issues/possible risk events associated with those issues/consequence considerations

The best time to conduct the survey

The most effective time to conduct a threat and risk assessment is prior to or as part of the initial planning stages of the facility or in support of major renovations. This is primarily because these are the most cost-effective points in the process to develop and implement new security measures. Unfortunately, more often than not, they are much more likely to be approved by management and conducted after a crisis within the corporation, a breaking and entering or major larceny, after major changes in physical infrastructure and/or operational process, or upon request from auditors.

Crime prevention officers and others should be aware that there are times when a merchant may call their office and request that they conduct a survey. Prior to engaging, it may be prudent for the officer to attain some degree of assurance that, to the greatest extent possible, the merchant will implement mitigation strategies to reduce the risks posed to their facility. When these assurances are not made nor met by the facility, the value of the officer's time and of the survey, and the potential benefits from conducting the survey are not realized. The following example shows how the implementation of considerations for improvement plays a key role in the management of risk:

> *A security professional conducted a security survey of a factory warehouse and an office building. The security professional developed a well thought out list of considerations for improvement. Despite the comprehensive report which was submitted to the facility owner's representative the owner did not implement corrective actions. In fact, the recipient of the survey results followed only one of the considerations for improvement submitted. The implemented consideration was to leave a light on over the safe in the back room of his warehouse. Other considerations including hardware improvements on doors, windows, and skylight received little to no support. Unfortunately, the business was, again, targeted by criminals and it suffered losses potentially due to the failure of management to take the actions needed to reduce risk.*

Why conduct a security review?

There are several reasons to conduct a security review:

1. to identify what needs to be protected;
2. to ascertain current risk/security management needs;
3. to determine the vulnerability of an organization's assets; and
4. to validate that the security management plan combats identified threats in a cost-effective and proactive manner.

Classification of survey recommendations

The classifications we will use are very high, high, medium, and low security. There are common elements that may be found in each of these levels of security. Depending upon the program you refer, the most common terminology found will follow the vein of deter, detect, delay, assess, communicate, and respond.[3] For the very high and occasionally high security classifications, the addition of defend and/or deny may be used to bolster the response portion of the system implemented.

The various classifications of mitigation strategies can be best explained through an example. The example selected is a museum that contains $25 million in various art treasures; the complex has no security.

Very high security is intentionally not considered an option for our museum. Despite the value of the items and the need for a strong security posture, the museum's business can only thrive by allowing people to view its assets. Very

3. NERC CIP-014 Guidelines and Technical Basis Requirement 5.

high security might be applied to a nuclear power generation plant, some government facilities, or a secure military installation. Very high security may involve many elements including heavily armed security and/or law enforcement personnel, multiple perimeter barriers with layered security technologies, structurally reinforced buildings and entryways, and entry control and screening programs. One of the potential differentiators with very high security is the capability and equipment of the response force and its ability to defend and/or deny access to assets against aggressors. To help visualize very high security, one must only think of the security for the gold bullion stored in Fort Knox or the vault or enemy lair in any number of movies in the espionage and action category.

High security

When looking at our museum example, it is reasonable to break the facility down into layers and apply security countermeasures at each layer. High security in relation to a museum is most likely focused on protecting the assets and artifacts themselves from theft. The assets being protected are contained within the innermost layer of protection and thus have the benefit of all previous levels of security as additional protection. The easiest way to think of this layered protection is to look at sliced Swiss cheese. Hold up one piece and you can easily see through the layer. As you stack on each additional slice, each of the holes becomes filled until ultimately you cannot see what is on the other side of the cheese. Alternatively, to adding more cheese slices, the survey may identify ways to fill in holes in the existing slices to increase protection. To achieve a layered approach to high security, the survey may provide considerations that discuss how security mitigation is applied at each layer or approaching each asset. Given the nature of the assets being protected in our museum, we can assume that an alarm system is needed; hence, our consideration for a high security alarm system or intrusion detection system (IDS) may read,

> *Museum management should consider implementing a layered Intrusion Detection System (IDS) to protect the museum and its assets. This system should include all potential entry points into the facility including, but not limited to: exterior and interior doors, windows and skylights, and mechanical points of entry large enough for entry by an adversary. High value assets should be protected by additional tamper and breakage resistance containers that are equipped with tamper, capacitance, and/or proximity alarm systems as an added layer of IDS. In addition to the systems identified above management should consider training of personnel on the identification and reporting of suspicious activities and the function and operation of the IDS system.*
>
> *These, of course, are not all-inclusive considerations. Instead, it is provided as an illustration of the level of detail which should be provided by the security surveyor.*

Medium security

Each time when we move down a level regarding security (i.e., from high to medium), there are elements of the security program, which may not implemented or will be implemented differently. It is not that for each level of security, you essentially peel back a slice of Swiss cheese. Instead, the vulnerabilities are addressed; but, the level of detail in the planning, or procedures or the application of a technology may be handled in a way that is more cost effective and, more importantly, more suited to the potential losses. The reason why it is so important to be able to scale your considerations for improvement is that the cost of protection should not outweigh the cost of the item protected. To use the Fort Knox analogy from earlier, would it make sense to have the level of security the facility does if they were protecting bricks made of clay instead of gold? Given the nature of the assets being protected in our museum, we can assume that an alarm system is needed; hence, our consideration for a medium security alarm system or IDS may read,

> *Museum management should consider implementing an Intrusion Detection System (IDS) to protect the museum and its assets. This system should include all ground level and subgrade entry points into the facility including, but not limited to: exterior and interior doors, windows, and mechanical points of entry large enough for entry by an adversary. High value assets should be protected by additional tamper and breakage resistance containers that are equipped with tamper, capacitance, and/or proximity alarm systems as an added layer of IDS. In addition to the systems identified above management should consider training of personnel on the identification and reporting of suspicious activities and the function and operation of the IDS system.*

Low security

A low security classification will most often be utilized to protect facilities where there are not high value assets at risk. For example, if our museum was more of a novelty museum where the artifacts, artwork, etc. are not of historical significance, priceless, or otherwise valuable, low security may be in order. It is important to note that, as this chapter is primarily focused on crimes against property, the security classification consideration examples do not reflect the importance of life safety. To continue with our museum example, considerations for IDS, which are intended to provide a low security level, might read,

> *Based upon a review of this facilities assets it was determined that a Low level of security should be adequate to secure the items identified as assets. Museum management should consider implementing an Intrusion Detection System (IDS) only as needed to protect the most valuable of the assets in the museum. In addition to the systems identified above management should consider training of personnel on the identification and reporting of suspicious activities and the function and operation of the IDS system.*

First step

The classifications of security levels provided are intended to provide structure examples, which clearly show the varying degrees of security that can be obtained when developing a security program. When conducting a security survey, the first step you should take is to interview the individual(s) to whom you will be submitting the report. During this interview, you should utilize these levels and descriptions of the classifications to assist the recipient of the report with determining the degree of protection desired for their assets.

There may be instances where it is beneficial to include considerations for high, medium, and low levels of security in the same report. This approach is particularly beneficial when a facility development project is in the early planning stages and the assets to be stored or used at the facility have not been identified or their exact location has not been determined.

The tools of the trade

Like most professionals, security surveyors need tools to do an effective job. The following are suggested to assist you when conducting your surveys: tape measure or laser ruler, floor plans, light meter, flashlight, camera with flash, small tape recorder, screwdriver, pen and pencil, pad of paper, and surveyor's wheel. Many surveyors now utilize their smartphones in place of carrying a separate flashlight, and camera voice recorder. These phones have applications that may eventually be able to take the place of light meters and other equipment. As technology continues to evolve, the amount of computing power and capability that fits into a surveyor's pocket will only increase. Apps continue to emerge, which allow for geolocation and labeling of images, completion of checklists and forms, and population of report data and findings directly on the device.

The survey process

Your survey should be conducted systematically, and the findings and considerations should be presented in a manner that allows the recipient to visualize and process them. You may find it effective to review the security of the site based on the security layers discussed earlier (site boundaries and perimeter, owned space, the facility exterior, and internal spaces requiring additional protection). Truthfulness is one of the security surveyor's greatest assets. Report recipients expect that the surveyor may identify gaps or flaws in their security programs. It is likely that you have been engaged for or tasked with this very purpose. How else is the recipient going to make improvements without honest input on the status of the program? When you are conducting your surveys, you should consider taking photos of the various buildings you are surveying. You may find that taking an introductory picture (a wide view from across the street or a facility identification sign) as your first picture of each site will make it easier to keep track of your images when conducting surveys of multiple sites. Taking pictures throughout your survey will not only help memorialize gaps and site conditions, but also it will also aid with your report and inspection. After you have done several surveys you will develop your own style for putting them together and they become easier to conduct.

Dos and don'ts in developing a report

Dos

1. Familiarize yourself with industry standards and guidance as they relate to security surveys. ISO 17799, ISO 27001, and ISO 27002 are examples of standards that may be beneficial to the security professional. Other valuable guidance may be found in publications by ASIS International or in government standards and publications.

2. Be confident and honest in your recommendations.
3. Consider the use of simple language; short sentences are best.
4. Be critical—visualize the facility and gaps in its security in your mind as part of the process.
5. Keep it as simple as possible, but not simpler.

Don'ts

1. Don't exaggerate your reports. Truthfulness and accuracy are important.
2. Don't inflate the reports with filler materials including unnecessary maps and floor plans. Only include these items if they effectively illustrate vulnerabilities.
3. Don't repeat your statements.
4. Don't make statements beyond your core capability, certifications, and training. It is acceptable to report observations outside of your purview; but, providing considerations for improvement outside of your domain experience is risky, and not a best practice.

The written report is the primary form of communicating your findings to its recipient. It is imperative that the report is clear, concise, and easy to use. The written report should include the following:

1. Cover letter—introduce the report to the recipient.
2. Executive summary—provide a short summary of the scope, assessment, and major items for consideration.
3. Introduction—discuss the facility's size, layout, use, occupancy, and other similar factors.
4. How to use this report—provide guidance for the recipient on the benefit and use of the sections that follow.
5. Methodology—describe your approach to the survey, assessment, or audit and indicate any standards, guidelines, or approved methodologies that were used as the basis for the review.
6. Observations and findings—provide detailed descriptions and images of the items you noted during your survey or audit. This section should include positive items about the program and/or site's security in addition to the vulnerabilities, gaps, or deficiencies you identify.
7. Considerations for improvement—provide thoughtful mitigation strategies for the deficiencies noted. Your mitigation strategies should be rooted in accepted industry practices and take advantage of the technologies, processes, and personnel improvements available to today's modern security professionals.
8. Implementation priority matrix—The implementation priority matrix should guide the recipient through the considerations for improvement from "low-hanging fruit" to capital projects, which require significant investment. Priority may be weighed on by a variety of factors including risk reduction, cost, and potential return on investment.
9. Appendices—information beneficial to the recipient, including glossary of terms, references, and checklists, may be included as an appendix to the report. The recipient's needs or requests for information should be the driving factor for any appendices to the report.

The following general statements can be included in the report:

1. Physically inventory of all property at least once a year. Your inventory should list the name of the item, manufacturer, model, serial number, value, color, and purchased date.
2. Engrave all property in accordance with the established operation identification program.
3. All computers should be bolted down and all files, cabinets, and rooms containing valuable information or equipment should be locked when not in use.

Other keys to being an effective surveyor

Being able to visualize the potential for criminal activity is a skill that can be refined through practice. Only when you have developed this ability sufficiently will you become an effective security surveyor.

It is important that, when you arrive on a survey site, you are prepared to give a property owner sound advice on the type of security precautions to consider. Consider environmental criminology and how crimes occur at specific places, times, and settings, and where offenders, victims, and targets of opportunity coincide. Merely identifying these variables can provide value and greater clarity for the survey.

To be a good crime prevention practitioner, you must be a good investigator. You must understand criminal methods of operation and the limitations of standard security devices. In addition, you must be knowledgeable about the type of security systems and hardware necessary to provide varying degrees of protection.

Nine points of security concern are as follows:

1. *General purpose of the building* (i.e., residence, classroom, and office). Consider the hours of use, people who use the building, people who have access, key control, and the maintenance schedule. Who is responsible for maintenance? Is the building used for public events? If so, what type and how often? Is the building normally opened to the public? Identify the significant factors and make recommendations. Who is the facility manager and who has overall responsibility for crime prevention and security?
2. *Hazards involving the building or its occupants.* List and assign priorities (e.g., theft of office equipment, wallet theft, and theft from stockrooms). Identify potential hazards that might exist in the future. Conducting a threat assessment prior to a survey may enhance the surveyor effectiveness and ability to visualize potential activities.
3. *Police or security officer applications.* What can these officers do to improve the response to the building and occupants from a patrol, investigation, or crime prevention standpoint? Would the application of security officers be operationally effective or cost effective?
4. *Physical recommendations.* Inspect doors, windows, lighting, and access points. Recommend physical changes that would make the building more secure, such as pinning hinges on doors and fences.
5. *Locks, equipment to be bolted down, potential application of access control systems, and key control.* Make specific recommendations.
6. *IDS or alarms.* Would an alarm system be cost effective? Would the use of the building preclude the use of an alarm? Are the potential benefits of an alarm such that the building use should be changed to facilitate it? Consider all types of alarms, building-wide or in specific offices. Consider closed circuit television and portable or temporary alarm devices.
7. *Storage.* Does the building have specific storage problems, such as expensive items that should be given special attention, petty cash, stamps, calculators, or microscopes? Make specific recommendations.
8. *Trespassing.* Are "No Trespassing" signs posted? Are the penalties for trespass noted? Are other signs needed, such as: "No Solicitation" or "No Skateboarding"?
9. *Facilities personnel.* Can facilities personnel be used in a manner that would be better from a security standpoint?

Personality of the complex

Each complex that you survey has a distinctive personality. Let us take an average building, which is open from 9:00 a.m. to 5:00 p.m. The traffic flow is heaviest during this period. During the span from 5:00 p.m. to 12:00 a.m., the building is closed to the public. Some staff members may work late. Who secures the building? At 12:00 a.m. the cleaning crew arrives and prepares the building for another day. The whole personality of the complex must be taken into consideration before your report is completed.

Let us take a further look at building personality through some examples. You are given a facility that is 100′ × 100′ and it has two solid-core doors, one large window at the front of the building and is air conditioned. How might the security for the facility be different given the personalities described next:

Case 1. The complex is a credit union on the main street next door to the local police department versus the same credit union on the edge of town.
Case 2. This is a large doctor's office. The doctor is an art buff and has half a million dollars in art in the office versus a doctor who has no art but has a small safe with about $200 worth of Class A narcotics inside.
Case 3. This building houses a variety store that closes at 6:00 p.m. versus a liquor store that is open until 2:00 a.m.

In these cases, I give six examples of the personality of a complex. As stated previously, the considerations for improvement provided must be tailored to fit the lifestyle and vulnerabilities of these buildings.

Positive and negative impacts of mitigation strategies

Considerations for improvement may have both positive and negative impacts on the site, operations, and the property owner. Take, for example, a housing complex that has a high crime rate from outsiders and within. Your recommendation is "Build a 10-foot high fence around the complex."

Positive aspects

Criminals may be deterred—Physical barriers, such as the 10′ fence, provide for very clear territorial boundaries and may seem challenging to overcome to low-level criminal elements. Crimes of opportunity may be reduced and the potential that an individual attempting to cross site boundaries unauthorized is increased.

Access control is improved—This ensures the property of the residents, adding to their secure environment. Limiting the number of points of entry and establishing access control primarily decreases crime opportunity and keeps out unauthorized persons.

Negative aspects

Fortress-type environment— Fortress environment may create more of a psychological barrier than a physical one. It is socially undesirable and yet is replicated throughout our country at an increasing rate.

Community buy-in and reaction—The importance of the community's reaction to the implementation of security measures cannot be disregarded. To improve the chances of a successful implementation, get the residents, occupants, employees, etc., involved in the early planning process.

Consciousness of fear may develop by those tenants whose apartments face the fence; but as the tenants come and go, it will eventually be accepted.

All fences are subject to graffiti. Consider using cyclone fencing or other see-through fencing to discourage visible graffiti from being applied to the fence. Antigraffiti coatings may allow for easier cleanup, and your maintenance program should address graffiti as soon as practical. An eye-pleasing architectural crime prevention through environmental design (CPTED) feature might be to recommend stones, gardens, terraces, etc., to improve the physical appearance and avoid the stigma of a fortress environment.

Crime analysis

It is not necessary for you to be a statistician, but the more you know about and understand the local crime problems, the better equipped you are to analyze the potential for loss when surveying a business or a home.

Collection, in crime analysis, is the gathering of raw data concerning reported crimes and known offenders. Generally, such information comes from crime reports, arrest reports, and police contact cards. This is not to say that these are the only sources available for collecting crime data. Police reports, security officers' reports, reports from the fire department, web-based searches of the location on the Internet, and reviewing local newspapers are all sources available to obtain valuable data.

The analysis process as applied to criminal activity is a specific step-by-step sequence of five interconnected functions: crime data collection, crime data collation, data analysis, dissemination of analysis reports, and feedback and evaluation of crime data.

Crime analysis of the site you survey supplies you with specific information to enable you to further harden the target in specific areas where losses have occurred. It is a means of responding "after the fact," when a crime has been committed.

Key control

Whether a place has physical keys or electronic keys, key control is an extremely important inclusion in a crime prevention or security survey. Check whether the clients are in the habit of picking up physical and electronic keys from employees at their termination and if they have an accurate record of who has which keys. Within a few short minutes, you should realize whether the organization has a problem.

Almost every company has some sort of master key system, because many people must have access to the building without the inconvenience of carrying two dozen keys around every day. The use of grand master, master, and to a lesser extent, submaster keys should be very limited. The broader the use of master keying the less secure the locking system may be. The issuance of master keys of any type should be limited to those person(s) with the greatest need. Some examples may include company executives, senior managers, the security department, and the facilities or maintenance department.

Guidelines for key control

1. Purchase a key cabinet that is adequate for your facility size and scope to store and control any keys to your facility.
2. Conduct a thorough inventory of locks and their associated keys to determine which keys still have a valid use. Properly dispose of keys that are no longer in use.
3. There are quite a few electronic key control boxes available on the market today. These boxes provide significant capabilities regarding the issuance and management of keys to personnel in the operations of the facility. For organizations that cannot afford or do not desire to implement electronic key boxes, an alternative strategy for key control should be implemented. One traditional method of key control that has been found to work well in the past follows:
   a. Two sets of key tags should be furnished or obtained with the new key cabinet: One tag should read "file-key, must not be loaned out," and the second tag should read "Duplicate." The key cabinet should be equipped with *loan tags*, which identify the person to whom a key is loaned. This tag is to be hung on the numbered peg corresponding to the key that was used.
4. Establish accurate records and files listing the key codes, the date the key was issued, and who received it.
5. Ensure that the electronic card keys are used properly and that data are captured and recorded.
6. Have each employee sign a receipt when he or she receives a key.
7. All alarm keys should be marked and coded.
8. A check should be made of what keys are in the possession of guards and staff.
9. Do not issue keys to any employee unless access to areas secured by the locks is required for the performance of their duties.
10. Establish a designated key control custodian and an alternate to manage the program and be the single point of contact for issuance of keys.
11. Change the key cylinder when an authorized key holder is discharged for cause. Furthermore, discharged or retired employees should produce keys previously issued at the time of termination.
12. Periodic inspections should be made to ensure that possession of keys conforms to the record of issuance. These periodic inspections should be utilized to remind key holders that they should immediately notify you of any key loss.
13. The original issue of keys and subsequent fabrication and reissuance of keys should ensure that their identity is coded on the keys so the lock for which they were manufactured cannot be identified in plain language.

Electronic access control systems have many benefits regarding key control. Management of access cards (credentials) is very important. It is suggested that your program includes procedures for issuance of new credentials, handling of lost or stolen badges, and removal of access from all credentials upon termination of an employee.

Digital video imaging systems and digital video management systems

Digital video imaging systems, still referred to by many professionals as CCTV, are an asset to any security package and an even more valuable tool if a digital video management system (DVMS) is utilized. digital video recorders are still in wide use, and even analog video recorders are still used in some applications. The capabilities of DVMS or IP video management systems far outweigh analog video system components and the benefits of their use are many. CCTV is a surveillance tool that provides an added set of eyes. Whether the video system is actively monitored or only recorded for follow-on investigations depends on the application for use and the required level of security. If this equipment is on the site, it is an important aspect of your security survey to evaluate its operation and validate its effectiveness. The outward appearance of the system's components (imagers or cameras, wiring, installation and mounts, housings and domes, etc.) is usually good indicators of the system's health. Additional questions for consideration by the surveyor are included as follows:

1. Is the system working properly? How is the video quality? Do the cameras successfully address their intended purpose (i.e., provide sufficient image clarity to identify individuals entering an area and reveal activity in the field of view)? Are all the cameras working? Is the system set up for triggered events (e.g., on motion, door opening, or another dry-contact prompt)? Are there issues with frame rates or network bandwidth, which make the video images choppy, slow, or worse yet still? Are the pan-tilt-zoom cameras commissioned for a purpose (e.g., with preset camera view positions at critical areas)? Are privacy zones set up where appropriate?

2. Is the system being actively monitored? What is the recording media (analogue, digital)? What is the average retention time for the recorded video? Thirty days of storage was the standard for many analog video recorder applications. Due to new regulations, in some industries, and the greater capability of systems to compress and retain data; 90 days of retention has become the norm for most digital video storage applications. DVMS have the capability to save video events on the digital storage media indefinitely, if required. Given these advancements, it is not uncommon for auditors of security programs to expect 90 days as a minimum to be available.
3. Do camera fields of views provide coverage of areas where they will be most beneficial?
4. Are the lighting levels in the areas being video monitored sufficient for the setting, place, and activity to be detected? Modern imagers have a greater capacity to adjust for poor lighting conditions than previous analogue cameras. That said, lighting color, warmth, brightness, glare, etc. are all still factors to consider. In addition, understanding how the lighting in a space changes throughout the day is an important factor for the surveyor.
5. Is the security recording hardware system secured in a locked cabinet or enclosure? The systems installation should be "clean" with wires managed well and labeled clearly.

Intrusion alarms

If the site you are surveying already has an alarm system, check it out completely. Physically walk through every motion detector unit. Evaluate the quality of the existing alarm products versus what is available to meet the needs of the client.

I surveyed a 5-year-old warehouse recently. It was interesting to note that the warehouse had a two-zone alarm system. The control panel was to the right of the front door, which was about 15 ft from the receptionist. Both alarm keys were in the key cylinders, and according to the president of the company, "The keys have been there since the system was installed." My point is, for a dollar, another key could be duplicated, and then the area is vulnerable to attack.

Another time, while doing a survey of an art gallery in New York, the security director stated that he had not had a service call on his alarm system in 2 years. We then proceeded to physically check every motion detection unit and magnetic contact. You can imagine his reaction when he found out that two-thirds of the gallery's motion detection units were not working.

In conclusion, intrusion alarms come in all shapes and sizes. They may be line of site or volumetric, utilizing passive or active sensor technologies and a wide variety of other operational variables. It is advisable for surveyors to be familiar with the various types of sensors available, there vulnerabilities, and how to effectively operationalize them in order to produce an effective report.

Lighting and security

What might happen if we shut off all the lights at night? Think about it. Such a foolish act may create an unsafe environment. Regular citizens might be too frightened to go out, and communities may experience a rapid increase in criminal activity including, but not limited to, theft and vandalism. Commercial areas might experience a much higher rate of burglaries, unauthorized entries, or looting. When we consider this illustration of the importance of lighting, you can clearly see that lighting and security go hand in hand. This example may seem a little excessive; particularly considering that the 2003 North East Blackout resulted in very minimal impacts on crime in cities plunged into darkness, except for Ottawa, which witnessed serious issues of looting. It is believed, based on the authors experience and research, that improving lighting in several cities may have contributed to a decrease in vandalism, street crime, suspicious persons, and commercial burglaries. It is a comfortable position to take that stating that effective lighting will generally coincide with a reduction in criminal activity.

Streetlights

Streetlights have received widespread notoriety for their value in reducing crime. Generally, streetlights are rated by the size of the lamp and the characteristics of the light dispersed.

There are several factors that go into street lighting. The Illuminating Engineers Society of North America (IESNA) is one of the premiere resources for information about lighting. They describe luminaires as "full cutoff, cutoff, semi-cutoff, and noncutoff."[4] Full cutoff luminaires provide the highest degree of lighting efficiency for the security

4. https://www.lrc.rpi.edu/programs/nlpip/lightinganswers/lightpollution/cutoffclassifications.asp

practitioner by keeping the light on the ground where it is directed. These luminaires produce less "sky glow" effects and often less glare, which can impact natural and technological surveillance, than other fixtures. The type of light utilized is the second item to consider with regards to street lighting. Following are a few types of lights that may be utilized in street lighting:

- Low-pressure sodium—Among the most efficient types of lamps available. Low-pressure sodium lamps produce monochromatic yellow light that may significantly complicate observations of activities with the naked eye and especially when utilizes color cameras.
- High-pressure sodium—High-pressure sodium lamps maintain much of the efficiency of the low-pressure sodium lamps while also providing a broader range of the light spectrum improving upon the color rendition of the lamps.
- Mercury vapor—Mercury vapor lights have long life but are slow to fully illuminate and are generally dim lighting fixtures with little spread of the illumination beyond the light source. These are typically recommended for single structure locations such as a garage or back alley or access point to an infrequently used walkway.
- Metal halide—However, when high use of the property is expected, or it is imperative to observe who or what is using a property, one lighting source that is frequently recommended is the metal halide. Metal-halide lamps produce a bright white light and provide excellent color rendition for video recording and human eye observation. This type of light is typically seen at new car lots and gas stations. There is a complication with metal-halide lighting that the fixtures must cool completely (usually for 15–20 minutes) before being restarted in the event of a power outage or similar issue. This restrike time may result in periods of extended darkness if alternative or supportive fixtures and lamps are not utilized.
- Light-emitting diode (LED)—The newest entrant to the street light market is the LED light. This is the preferred lighting for all security applications for several reasons. LED lighting is extremely energy efficient, has the greatest color rendition index and lighting warmth of the available fixtures, and is not inhibited by warm up or restrike times, which impact other lighting types.

The surveyor should rely heavily on guidance from IESNA when reviewing lighting on a property and/or when providing considerations for improvement.

Other security aspects

Depending on the type of facility you are surveying, the following should be reviewed:

1. communications networks, utility closets, IP data networks, walkie-talkies or cell phones with walkie-talkie features, and locations of interior and exterior phones
2. guard force and security personnel and their training, police powers, uniforms, use of badges, and methods of operation (typically called standard operating procedures and post orders)

Your objectives are to identify vulnerabilities, evaluate the site, and provide critical assessment. Each surveyor may apply their own style and/or methodology to the survey. That said, all your findings and your methodology must be defensible, and the documents and deliverables provided must be an effective representation of you, your company, and your department.

Security survey follow-up

How one conducts security survey follow-up depends upon the type of engagement and/or relationship the surveyor has with the organization receiving the survey. In consultant arrangements, it is often the responsibility of the surveyor to follow up on the assessment results not specifically on the implementation of the considerations for improvement. In most proprietary relationships or supportive relationships, as seen from the local crime prevention officer, follow-up on the implementation becomes a key part of the process. This follow-up may take many forms. The most effective for follow-up involves tracking implementations and monitoring metrics, such as incident reporting, which may provide insight into the effectiveness of the measures implemented. This type of follow-up is resource intensive and may be time-consuming. It will yield the best results for continuous improvement of the organization or facility's security program.

Some police departments produce five to seven surveys a day. They do not evaluate their performance because of the time and personnel involved. In this way, they fail to examine their own effectiveness. The reason for the follow-up is to encourage increased compliance with your recommendations and to improve the overall security of the facility.

Without follow-up, you will not know if the recipient has taken any action or if your survey has provided the community with the expected benefits.

The basic security survey framework consists of five steps:

1. generating the survey request
2. conducting the physical inspection
3. delivering survey recommendations
4. following up after the report is completed
5. evaluating the program

For every crime committed, there is a crime prevention or loss reduction defense or procedure that, if followed, could potentially deter the criminal or mitigate the impacts of the act.

Physical security involves implementing those measures that could mitigate the risks, threats, vulnerabilities, and crimes determined during the survey. Acts that may potentially be mitigated through physical security measures may include but are not necessarily be limited to unauthorized entry, larceny, fraud, sabotage, fire, and vandalism. This chapter on security surveys was geared to assist both private security and public law enforcement to harden a target and assist the community to further reduce losses.

To further assist you with developing and completing your security survey, the following sample checklists are provided in support of this chapter. Each of these survey checklists should serve only to guide the surveyor in the development and implementation of a survey process and tools that are fitting to your unique situation.

Residential security

It is difficult to balance protection of residential structures. There are weak spots including the windows and doors which are frequently utilized by burglars to enter the structure. In many cases, the front, back, garage, or windows were left unsecured and accessible. Alternatively, the locking mechanisms or level of security of the window or door is lacking. The items mentioned later may help enhance the security of residential structures, if implemented.

Defensive measures

1. *Doors (front, rear, basement, and garage).* The first important item is to install dead bolts on all entry doors. A cylinder dead bolt with a 1-in. projecting bolt, made of hardened steel, should be utilized. This lock should be used in conjunction with a standard entry knob lock. Viewing devices with a wide-angle lens on entry doors are also recommended. These devices allow the user to potentially identify persons seeking access without removing or opening locking devices.
2. *Doors with glass in them.* Due to the concealment available when utilizing a back door, they are frequently among a burglar's favorite entryways. Glass in doors or adjoining panels makes the door more vulnerable to force entry. One measure that should be taken with this type of door is to use a double-cylinder dead bolt for protection. This type of lock requires a key to open it from the inside as well as the outside, because most burglars break the glass and try to gain entry by opening the locked door from inside.
3. *Sliding glass doors.* These entries should be secured so they cannot be pried out of their track. Also, you can prevent jimmying of your door by putting a "Charley bar" made from wood or metal and cut to size and placed in the track when the door is closed (Fig. 13.1).

Bulkheads should also be included as part of your overall security package and secured with square bolt or dead bolt locks.

Windows

Windows come in a variety of shapes, sizes, and types, each of which presents a different type of security problem. Windows provide an inviting entryway for a burglar who does not like to break glass because the noise may alert someone. You can improve the security of double-hung sash-type windows by drilling a hole through the top corner of the bottom window into the bottom of the top window. Once drilled you can place a solid pin into the hole to make it more difficult for a criminal to open the window (Fig. 13.2).

Keyed window latches may also be installed to prevent the window from being opened. In addition, grilles and grates may be installed over extremely vulnerable accesses.

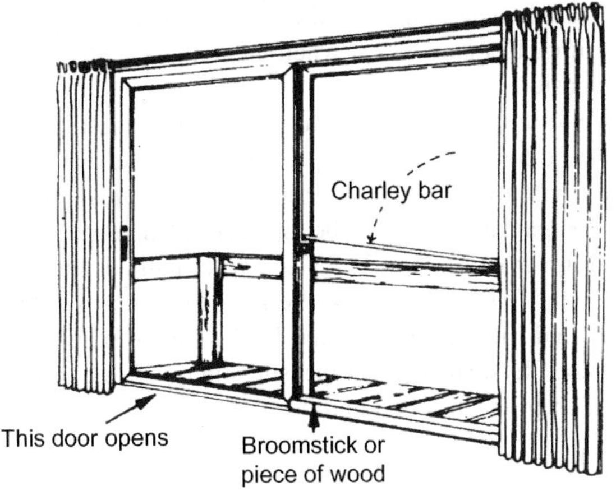

FIGURE 13.1 Preventing force sliding of aluminum doors. Mount a Charley bar that folds down from the side.

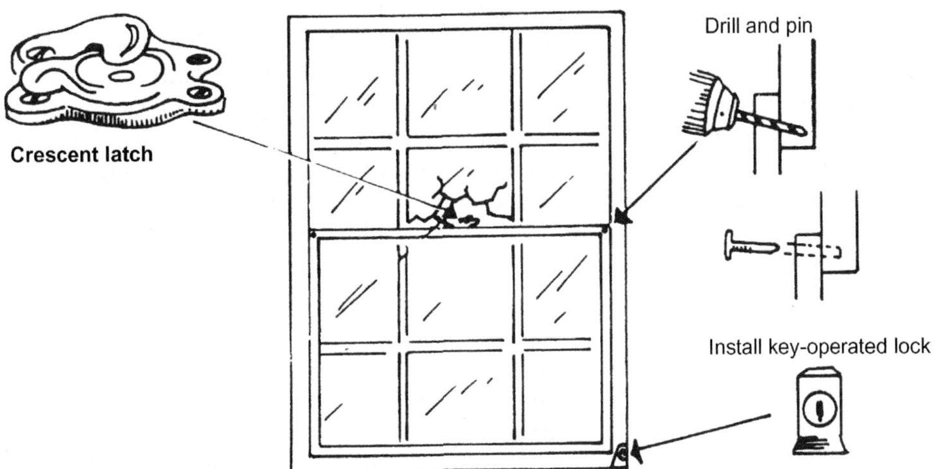

FIGURE 13.2 A double-hung window can be easily jimmied open with a screwdriver. Glass can be broken adjacent to the crescent latch or by prying against hardware, and the screws can be popped out. To prevent this, drill a hole through the top corner of the bottom window and place a solid pin in the hole. You can also install a key-operated lock.

Window films and/or anticut screens available on the market today may slow adversary entry for a higher degree of security around these potential entries.

Entrances

Any opening through which a human body can pass is an entrance. Front doors, basements, patio doors, and garages that have access to the house, and windows on the second floor are all entryways to burglars. No one way is more important to protect than another.

Setting up inner defenses

Even with the precautions already mentioned, a burglar may still get into the home. An effective security design will delay the intruder from accessing the assets of in the home. Delay is effective, as time is the one element working against the criminal. One way to add delay features is to convert a closet into a "vault." This can be done by reinforcing the walls, frame, and closet door and installing a dead bolt lock on the door. You have now considerably strengthened the inner layer defenses. Restricting access from one part of the home to another via dead bolts and the like gives the burglar yet another obstacle to overcome.

Having a burglar alarm is like purchasing an insurance policy. The homeowner may never need it, but it is comfortable to know it is there. The very best system is a perimeter system that detects an intruder before entering the dwelling, but it is costly. Less expensive methods involve using door contacts, motion detectors, and cameras. There are a variety of newer systems available for residential applications. These systems are wireless and very easy to install mostly working off cellular and/or home Wi-Fi systems. The systems can notify homeowners directly to their mobile devices or through a central monitoring station, similar to other alarms.

Remember, no home can be made 100% burglar proof. The goal of implementing residential security measures is to make it difficult for the burglar to enter the home, thus discouraging crime. In many cases, when challenged with security measures, burglars will move on to a home where the pickings are easier.

Residential security is more important than we realize. Just ask the victim of a home that has been burglarized. The mother and wife responds, "I felt personally threatened and upset over the losses but more upset over the fact that our home was violated." The father and husband responds, "I'm happy my wife and daughter weren't home or they could have been hurt. Now I've got to call the police, my insurance agent, the repairman, and maybe an alarm company."

Too often people say, "It won't happen to me," "Our neighborhood never had a theft," "I sleep with a small gun by my bed," "I have a dog for protection," or "I don't need an alarm system." These are before-the-incident excuses. The cause of residential crime can be found in the individual's environment and lifestyle. Crime and losses can be managed through the application of measure to correct or improve human behavior. Physical security measures play an important role in preventing many crimes, but these measures are effective only if they are installed and used properly.

Alarms

Residential intrusion alarms are popular and installed frequently. The control panel, look for Underwriters Laboratories (UL) listed units, may also handle the fire alarm system. An audible horn distinguishes which system has gone off. The control panel should have an entrance/exit delay feature, which aids in the overall reduction of false alarms. Depending on the style of the home, any number of components can be used. However, keep in mind that only a total coverage system should be recommended and installed. Recent advances in IP technology allow homeowners, property owners and place managers to operate their home intrusion detection systems remotely, giving added value to the security system's components installed on the property because they have become part of the property management function of the home.

Lighting

Improved lighting provides another residential security measure. Although some studies documented crime reduction after improved lighting systems were installed, these studies typically have not accounted for displacement effects. Even if individuals living in a residence reduce the likelihood of a burglary by better lighting, they may only be displacing the burglary to another, less lit area. For the individual homeowner, this is a win. For the broader community, it may be ineffective at crime reduction.

Home security checklist

Massachusetts Crime Watch puts together the following home security checklist, which deals with 35 security checkpoints:

Entrances

1. Are the doors of metal or solid wood construction?
2. Are door hinges protected from removal from outside?
3. Are there windows in the door or within 40 in. of the lock?
4. Are there auxiliary locks on the doors?
5. Are strikes and strike plates securely fastened?
6. If there are no windows in the door, is there a wide-angle viewer or voice intercommunications device?
7. Can the lock mechanism be reached through a mail slot, delivery port, or pet entrance at the doorway?
8. Is there a screen or storm door with an adequate lock?
9. Are all exterior entrances lighted?
10. Can entrances be observed from the street or public areas?
11. Does the porch or landscaping offer concealment from view from the street or public area?
12. If the door is a sliding glass door, is the sliding panel secured from being lifted out of the track?
13. Is a Charley bar or key-operated auxiliary lock used on the sliding glass door?
14. Is the sliding door mounted on the inside of the stationary panel?

Entrances from garage and basement

1. Are all entrances to living quarters from garage and basement of metal or solid wood construction?
2. Does the door from garage to living quarters have auxiliary locks for exterior entrance?
3. Does the door from basement to living quarters have an auxiliary lock operated from the living quarters' side?

Ground floor windows

1. Do all windows have key-operated locks or a method of pinning in addition to the regular lock?
2. Do all windows have screens or storm windows that lock from inside?
3. Do any windows open onto areas that may be hazardous or offer special risk of burglary?
4. Are exterior areas of windows free from concealing structure or landscaping?

Upper floor and windows

1. Do any upper floor windows open onto porch or garage roofs or roofs of adjoining buildings?
2. If so, are they secured as adequately as if they were at ground level?
3. Are trees and shrubbery kept trimmed back from upper floor windows?
4. Are ladders kept outside the house where they are accessible?

Basement doors and windows

1. Is there a door from the outside to the basement?
2. If so, is that door adequately secure for an exterior door?
3. Is the outside basement entrance lighted by exterior light?
4. Is the basement door concealed from the street or neighbors?
5. Are all basement windows secured against entry?

Garage doors and windows

1. Is the automobile entrance door to the garage equipped with a locking device?
2. Is the garage door kept closed and locked at all times?
3. Are garage windows secured adequately for ground-floor windows?
4. Is the outside utility entrance to the garage as secure as required for any ground-floor entrance?
5. Are all garage doors lighted on the outside?

Protecting personal property

Several programs have been developed throughout the country, which are geared to aid the citizens in the reduction of losses in the community. A sampling of these programs is included below:

1. *Operation identification* is a program started in 1963 in Monterey Park, California.. This program encourages citizens to engrave their personal property with a state driver's license number.
2. *Bicycle registration and antitheft program.* Some communities have started a mandatory registration of bicycles as well as an educational program. The educational program identifies poor quality locks used to secure bikes and provides instructions for properly securing a bike.
3. *Auto theft prevention* is another educational program, which is generally implemented by the distribution of printed material and covered at community meetings. How many times have you seen a person keep the engine running while going into the store to buy milk? This is an example of giving the criminal an opportunity to commit a crime.
4. *Neighborhood Watch.* This program, initiated in 1971; encourages people to report suspicious circumstances in their neighborhoods to the police and familiarizes the citizens with crime prevention techniques to reduce criminal opportunity (see Chapter 10: What is crime prevention in 2019?). Be alert for these suspicious signs:
   a. a stranger entering a neighbor's house when the neighbor is not home
   b. unusual noises, such as a scream, breaking glass, or an explosion;
   c. people, male or female, in your neighborhood who do not live there;
   d. someone going door-to-door in your neighborhood, if he or she tries to open the doors or goes into the backyard, especially if a companion waits out front or a car follows close behind;
   e. someone trying to force entry into a home, even if wearing a uniform; and
   f. a person running, especially if carrying something of value.

In Neighborhood Watch, a person who sees anything suspicious should call the police immediately. Give the responding officers a physical description of the person and license plate number of the car. Even if nothing is wrong, such alertness is appreciated. Remember, research has shown that the value of these citizen participation programs tends to wane over time without some periodic booster activities and part-time paid coordination to keep the program operating effectively and consistently.

1. *Security surveys.* Many police departments today have trained crime prevention officers who can provide security survey assistance to residents, enabling the citizen to better protect the family, home, and environment. Security professionals are also available as well as some auditors.
2. *Citizen patrols.* The citizen patrol can be viewed as part of the long historical tradition of neighbor helping neighbor. As far back as has been recorded, human beings have formed communities, tribes, groups, etc. for the protection this style of living offers. While some people may be sleeping, or away from home, other members of the community may be watchful of suspicious activities, fires, or other threats to the community. While community bonds may be lessening over the years with factors, such as supercommuting, urbanization, and even globalization, playing a role, the development of Neighborhood Watches and/or citizen patrols is reported to be increasing in several suburban communities and cities across the country. These citizen patrols perform a relatively simple and narrowly defined role deterring criminal activity by their presence. Their function should remain that of a passive guard watchful for criminal or suspicious activity. Their primary recourse is to alert the police when they see it. Drawing on information that exists about current citizen groups, the advantages of patrols over other protective measures include that they

   a. are relatively inexpensive,
   b. perform a surveillance function effectively,
   c. take advantage of existing behavior patterns,
   d. can improve an individual's ability to deal with crime, and
   e. contribute to other desirable social goals related to neighborhood cohesiveness and the provision of a desirable alternative to less acceptable activity.

   In practice, however, patrols exhibit some of the following serious shortcomings:

- The typical patrol is formed in response to a serious incident or heightened level of fear about crime. The ensuing pattern is cyclic: increased membership, success in reducing criminal activity at least in a specific area, boredom, decreasing membership, dissolution. As a result, patrols tend to be short-lived.
- The passive role of a patrol is difficult to maintain without at least a paid part-time coordinator.
- The police are reluctant to cooperate with a patrol and may even oppose it.
- The patrol may aggravate community tensions. The principal problems of patrols relate to their inability to sustain the narrow, anticrime role they initially stress. They may be an effective temporary measure to deal with criminal contagion in an area. Over the longer term, however, the inherent risks may outweigh the continued benefits. The proliferation of patrols in recent years is evidence that they fill a need, but it should be recognized that patrols are no substitute for adequate police protection.

Residential security can best be obtained by getting the facts on what you can do to secure the home, analyzing these facts, and arriving at a decision and implementing security measures.

Top ten security threats

The top ten security threats to most communities are listed (in no order of priority), followed by some questions that companies may use to assess their vulnerability to each threat.

1. *Staff members and staffing agencies.* How confident are we that we are hiring bona fide people; do we carry out preemployment screening? Do our suppliers and agencies carry out screening too? Who has access to our facilities?
2. *Loss of data or information.* How much of a concern are data breaches? Are we confident that our data, including those held by third parties, are secure? Are our systems secure, and who has access to them?
3. *Extremism and terrorism.* How concerned are we by terrorist or extremist threats? Are we complacent, or have we carried out a reasonable assessment of the threats?

4. *Lack of contingency or business-continuity planning*. Have we put contingency plans in place? Have we considered business continuity scenarios and communicated the plans to our employees?
5. *Physical security*. How confident are we that our access controls and physical security measures are robust? Do they prevent social engineering and break-ins?
6. *Theft and fraud*. Are we confident that we have preventative measures in place and processes to deal with events that may arise?
7. *Lack of security awareness*. Are employees aware of security? Do they change passwords, lock doors, and report issues?
8. *Storage and disposal of data and information*. Are we confident that access to sensitive data is controlled? Is secure storage available and used? Do we destroy confidential waste in accordance with relevant standards, such as the BS8470: 2006 Secure Destruction of Confidential Materials guidelines?
9. *Lack of training or competency*. Do our staff members know what to do? Have they been trained in emergency procedures? Do they protect information?
10. *Regulatory compliance*. Do we employ illegal workers? How do we investigate any infiltrations or allegations of noncompliance? Is a site compliant with required reporting and controls from Sarbanes–Oxley, HIPPA, ISO, UL, or other mandatory or voluntary standards?

The audit

Introduction

Compared to 20 years ago audits have become more popular and more demanding. They have become a very useful way to have an independent pair of eyes and ears reviewing your operation.

An actual audit review checklist, currently used by a very familiar Fortune 500 corporation, is discussed.

Exterior access controls

Objective: To determine whether sufficient controls are in place at this facility to deter and detect unauthorized access to

1. external utility areas
2. parking facilities
3. building entrances

Approach: Review the latest version of the security manual related to exterior security.

1. Verify that facilities management has posted signs indicating property boundaries and entry restrictions.
2. Validate that critical utilities have been identified (generators, water systems, electrical stations, etc.), documented, and revalidated within the last 12 months. Determine if any required controls are implemented.
3. Verify that the minimum lighting requirements have been met and that no lights are burned out.
4. Verify that access from the parking structure is limited and secure. Determine if the area is well lit with concealment areas minimized using CPTED principles.
5. If it is a company-controlled site, determine if access to the parking structure is restricted to vehicles or drivers that are authorized and that there is an adequate number of handicap parking spaces.
6. If it is a company-controlled site, verify that there are physical deterrents (such as barriers or landscape techniques), which impede vehicular access to lobbies or other glassed areas of buildings where there is a concentration of people.
7. Verify that building access points below the third floor (grills, grates, manhole covers, utility tunnels, skylights, and roof vents, etc.) are secured to prevent entry into the building or damage to critical utilities, unless prohibited by local ordinances, codes, laws or regulations.
8. Verify that there is a clear line of sight maintained around the perimeter of the building.
9. All renovation and construction of any site security control centers must be reviewed and approved by the Director of Corporate Security.

Interior access controls

Objective: To determine whether appropriate access controls are in place within the facilities.

Approach: Review the latest version of the security manual related to building perimeters and interior security. Test for specific controls related to the various types of designated spaces that are as follows:

- perimeter doors
- windows and exterior glass walls
- internal space
- restricted space
- internal shared space
- tenant restricted space
- loading docks
- lobbies and sensitive areas

1. Verify that all perimeter doors designed as entrances are constructed of heavy-duty material and are alarmed or monitored. Verify that all emergency exit doors are constructed of heavy-duty material and are alarmed. Determine if the door jambs, hinges, and locks are designed to resist forced entry.
2. Validate that windows on the ground floor cannot be opened more than 10 in. (25 cm).
3. Verify that all general use areas, such as lobbies, elevators, and loading docks, have a system to control access into interior space.
4. Validate that there are inconspicuous panic alarm devices in staffed lobbies that are monitored by security or another constantly staffed workstation. Validate that staffed loading docks are equipped with panic alarm devices that are monitored by security or another constantly staffed workstation. Verify that there is a documented response procedure and that the alarm devices are tested as required. In unstaffed lobbies and loading docks that are controlled by remote access doors, verify that there are monitoring devices to allow identification of an individual prior to allowing access to the building.
5. Validate that alarms (e.g., for doors, emergency exits, and panic buttons) are tested to ensure they are operational and that the results are documented within the required time frame. Determine if corrective actions were taken and any deficiencies were documented.
6. Determine if the interior space is isolated from the public space (such as lobbies and public restrooms) with slab-to-slab construction techniques.
7. Determine if the restricted space has a supervised control access system with an audit trail, and that the audit trail is reviewed by management every 90 days. If cipher locks with audit function are used, validate that the combinations are changed every 90–95 days (or when employees change assignments).
8. Validate that no unauthorized individuals have access to terminals and printers. Determine if the contracts with tenants prohibit such access.
9. In locations where banking facilities (such as automated teller machines) exist, validate that there is a process for third-party monitoring for response to robberies and burglaries.
10. When a company shares space with a noncompany function, company employee offices and proprietary information must be secured when unattended.
11. CCTV digital recordings are saved for an appropriate period; refer to industry benchmarks for the appropriate recording retention length for your application (a 6-month period or longer; auditors want recorded data be available for at least 90 days).
12. Have e-mails been saved from managers that give his/her approval for specific employees to enter his specific space and has the approval been sought and given for specific employees to have access to a specific space?

Mail services security

Objective: To determine whether appropriate access controls are in place for the mail services area.

Approach: Review the latest version of the security manual related to mail services security.

1. Validate that access to the mailroom is restricted to authorized individuals only and a controlled access system is used.
2. Verify that doors and windows are equipped to protect against forced entry.
3. Verify that registered, certified, and confidential mail that is not delivered by the end of the workday is secured. This is not required if intrusion detection is installed that covers the entire mailroom area.
4. Verify that mailrooms that are multipurpose rooms (e.g., copier and fax), which serve as a mail delivery location or allow after-hours access, are equipped with lockable cabinets or lockable doors.

5. Verify that there are printed instructions regarding package identification posted in the mailrooms.
6. Learn whether there have been any past incidents at this site, or in this particular industry, where harm or risk has come to the place through the mail operation (e.g., bomb and threatening packages), and determine whether an off-site collection and mail screening facility is recommended.

Badges, locks, and key control

Objective: To determine whether badges, lock, and key program controls are adequate to deter and detect misuse. These requirements are only applicable to facilities where there is exclusive control of all keys providing access to space.

Approach: Review the latest version of the security manual related to lock and key controls.

1. Validate that master level keys (e.g., grand master keys, building master keys, and floor master keys as defined in the security manual) are adequately controlled and only specific authorized people have MASTER access on their badges.
   a. Daily and/or shift accountability is maintained.
   b. Keys are restricted and controlled.
   c. If more than six access keys are available, site security manager documents approval every twelve months.
   d. Process to control access to master keys kept outside of security to allow landlords or fire/emergency response personnel access.
2. If Fireman Access Boxes, Knox Lock Boxes, or a Morse Watchmen Key Control or Badge Process is used, then do the following:
   a. Verify that these boxes are alarmed to a security control center or constantly staffed workstation.
   b. Determine if duplicating hardware is secured when not in use.
   c. Validate that all duplicate, blank, and unissued keys are properly secured when not in use.
   d. Determine if key codes and pinning combinations are secured and available on a need-to-know basis.
   e. If key operations are contracted, verify they are audited against requirements every 12 months.

Access controls and badge designs

Objective: To determine whether the processes and technology in support of physical access are operating effectively.

Approach: Review the latest version of the security manual related to access controls and badge designs.

1. Determine if badges are issued per requirements, for example,
   a. Documentation of management authorization for noncompany personnel was obtained prior the badge being issued.
   b. Proof of identity was obtained prior to a badge being issued to noncompany personnel.
   c. Temporary contractor badges are authorized by a manager, purchasing buyer, coordinator, or authorized predesignated contract company supervisor. Visitor identity (those requiring escort) must be validated by the person authorizing the visit.
   d. Badges are in compliance with the security manual design requirements (e.g., sealed, white photo background with a postage-guaranteed post office box return address on the reverse).
2. Validate that all badges have an expiration date in the database.
   a. Determine whether badges that are not returned on the due date (e.g., temporary or visitor badges) are deactivated.
   b. Determine whether badges reported as lost have immediate action taken to place the badge in lost status and whether the profiles are kept in the database for 6 months.
3. Validate that all hardware, badge stock, and other components of the badge process are secured when not in use.
4. Validate that user IDs are assigned to all operating personnel in compliance and authorization reviews are performed every 6 months.
5. Verify that an effective process is in place to remove employee access in a timely manner:
   a. Category manager reports are distributed to category managers every 90–95 days.
   b. Every 30 days security must match database to the HR database.
   c. Process must be in place to deactivate lost badges or termed individuals within 24 hours.

Search policy

Objective: Verify that the processes and technology in support of physical searches are operating effectively.

Approach: Review the latest version of the security manual related to search policy.

1. Validate that searches of personal effects, made without the employee's knowledge, are approved by management.
2. Validate that the policy for electronic searches (such as metal detectors, X-ray machines, and handheld wands) has the approval of the senior site/location manager or senior location executive and the security manager. Determine if local laws have been followed.

Emergency planning

Objective: To determine whether emergency plans have been established by senior location management that adequately address anticipated emergencies and catastrophes.

Approach: Review the latest version of the security manual related to emergency planning.

1. Verify that the senior location management emergency plan contains procedures for immediate response to emergencies.
2. Validate that the emergency plan addresses various types of emergencies (i.e., natural or human-made disasters, threats or acts of violence against people or property, political/civil disturbances, and catastrophic events in close proximity to the site).
3. Validate that the security department, on behalf of the senior location manager, has reviewed the emergency plan within the last 6 months and updated the plan as needed.
4. Verify that a crisis management team (CMT) has been designated, which has met as a group once per year to conduct an exercise and training.
5. Validate that emergencies are promptly reported to corporate security.
6. Validate that the emergency plan is filed and that the senior location executive certifies that the plan is up to date.
7. Verify that requirements for the CMT are met: members have equipment such as a mobile phone, emergency plan, and aerial or site photo, and a room for the CMT is designated meeting the necessary requirements (emergency power, capability to receive national news, two telephones, and workstation connectivity).

Reporting of incidents

Objective: To determine whether there is an implemented process for the reporting of incidents to security.

Approach: Review the latest version of the security manual related to reporting significant incidents and responses.

1. Verify that a process exists to report all significant incidents (e.g., threats of violence, natural disasters, espionage, sabotage, thefts, and chemical spills) to corporate security.
2. Verify that referrals to law enforcement agencies are made when appropriate with the director of security notified.
3. Validate that the location has implemented the security incident management system for reporting and classifying types of incidents and that relevant incidents are reported.

Investigations

Objective: To determine whether incidents are investigated, reported, and closed appropriately.

Approach: Review the latest version of the security manual related to investigations.

1. Validate that incidents have been reported to corporate security as appropriate and that knowledge of the investigation is limited to persons with a need to know.
2. Investigations involving government officials or law enforcement authorities must be referred to the vice president of corporate security.
3. Validate that the use of covert monitoring (e.g., cameras and audio recorders) have required approvals.
4. Verify that any actions involving the sale or purchase of stolen property have the required approvals.

Emergency response

Reference: Company security manual

Objective: In the event of an emergency, it is essential that employees know what to do in order to avoid danger and secure their safety. Proactive involvement in security emergency planning and emergency response will enhance employee well-being programs.

Approach:

1. Are emergency procedures developed for fire, first aid, pandemics, terrorist attacks, and any locally foreseeable disasters/emergencies? Does coordination exist between concerned parties, for example, local fire departments, law

enforcement, security, and location management? Was consideration given to the timeliness of response from community response services?
2. Were employees and site visitors made aware of emergency procedures?
3. Were emergency procedures developed and tested periodically to check effectiveness? Were practice evacuation fire drills conducted at least annually?
4. Did provisions exist for maintenance of adequate supplies and equipment?
5. Did a postincident review process exist?
6. Did the designated emergency response organization have the appropriate training, have the capability to respond in a timely manner, and have the appropriate resources to handle emergencies? If emergency response teams are used, are all emergency response team members trained? Were emergency response equipment and vehicles maintained?

Fire and life safety

Objective: To determine if the location had implemented an effective process to detect, annunciate, and suppress fires to ensure life safety, and to comply with insurance company and regulatory requirements.

Approach: Review the fire/life safety program and related documentation.

1. *Building design*. Do all new buildings and modifications to existing buildings meet local/national codes and the requirements of NFPA 101 or equivalent standard?
2. *Maintenance*. Are fire alarm systems, emergency lighting, fire dampers, automatic door closers, sprinkler and fire suppressant systems, fire extinguishers, and other similar safety features subject to inspection and maintenance as specified in local/national codes and insurance schedules?
3. *Contingency measures*. Where there is a necessity to temporarily disable any building feature designed to protect users, the risks should be assessed and, where necessary, contingency measures introduced. Were there controls established to prevent unauthorized impairment of essential fire safety equipment?
4. *Life safety and fire prevention*. Was there a fire prevention program implemented to address work practices that minimize the likelihood and consequences of fire?
5. *Testing the effectiveness of arrangements*. Were buildings subjected to a required periodic practice fire evacuation to assess the effectiveness of arrangements, familiarize occupants with requirements, and identify improvements?
6. *Fire prevention*. Are fire wardens in place and are fire evacuation drills conducted annually?

Further reading

Kingsbury, A., 1973. Introduction to Security and Crime Prevention Surveys. Charles C Thomas, Springfield, IL.

LaFaver, D., 2010. The Home Security Book: Agenda Security Services. Shell Oil Company, p. 6. Permission obtained from Norman Mortell, BA, Director of Operations.

Massachusetts Crime Watch, 1980. Home Security Test Booklet. LEAA, Waltham, MA.

Momboisse, R.M., 1968. Industrial Security for Strikes, Riots and Disasters. Charles C Thomas, Springfield, IL.

Washington Crime Watch. Crime Prevention Training Manual. Security Survey Section. p. 8. https://www.theiacp.org/sites/default/files/all/s/Spokane-NeighborhoodWatch.pdf.

<www.tssbulletproof.com>.

<www.pacificbulletproof.com>.

Appendix 3.A Site survey and risk assessment

Victor Harold and John O'Rourke, CPP

Crime prevention, or lessening the potential for crime, begins with a major in-depth security analysis of the business or facility. A survey of the interior and exterior will point out security deficiencies and potential for intrusion or the probability that a crime will occur at that spot.

After the survey, an appraisal and recommendation for action should be immediately undertaken. A timetable for implementing the recommendations should be originated and strictly followed.

It is possible the site survey is beyond the ability of most business managements. If it is, you are advised to obtain the services of a qualified security professional.

You are also urged to have this service performed immediately. Consider the vulnerability of your business to imminent criminal intrusion. Many burglarized companies as well as those that were victimized by white collar crime have suffered irreversible losses, slowdown, and even shutdown.

This appendix broadly points out the external and internal geographical areas that may require immediate and long-term consideration to help prevent criminal breach of the premises.

1. Can you obtain a neighborhood crime statistics report from the local police?
2. Can you determine if there has been any labor unrest in the area?
3. Can you obtain a report that details the extent of damage a labor unrest may have had on a firm in the area?
4. What is the prevalent type of damage done to companies during a labor unrest in the area?
5. Has your company ever been victimized by the labor unrests of other companies in the area?
6. Have prior tenants or owners of your facility ever reported a criminal incident?
7. What types of crimes are the most prevalent in the area? List by percentage and frequency.
8. Is your facility very visible from the local roads?
9. Is there easy access by emergency vehicles to your building from the local roads?
10. Do you have a chart showing the frequency of police patrols in the area?
11. Do you know how long it would take an emergency or police vehicle to reach your facility?
12. Do you have an evaluation of your building's roof and doors that details the length of time it will take for a break-in to be successful?
13. Do you have an evaluation of the safes, locks, and other devices to ascertain how long they can delay being opened?
14. If you require separate storage of high-risk or valuable items, are they placed in a high security area that may discourage intrusion?
15. Is personnel movement into and within the building controlled?
16. Have the door and window hardware been evaluated for ease of entry?
17. Have window openings been secured? (Check with local fire department codes.)
18. Are important files and computer operations secured in an area that prohibits unauthorized entry?
19. Is the lighting sufficient throughout all work areas?
20. Are vent and roof access panels and doors wired and latched to prevent intrusion?
21. Have you prevented external access to the locker rooms and vending and lounge areas?
22. Are the financial handling areas separate and secure?
23. Do you keep your safe's contents and the combinations and the controls needed to maintain security confidential?
24. Are the removable panels and grates in which a person or inventory may be concealed periodically removed and checked?
25. Can these panels and grates be more securely fastened without compromising the item to which they are installed?
26. Will you require police, fire department, or building department approval to more securely fasten those panels and grates?
27. Are the incoming electrical lines well secured and vandal free?
28. Are the panels on all electrical items fastened?
29. Are the electrical power grids, panels, backup, power supplies, etc., kept in a separate locked area?
30. Have you conducted a walk around the property to see if trees, hedges, walls, and fences can hide a person or goods?
31. Have you considered immediate action to correct?
32. If some visibility obstructions exist, are you taking steps to correct?
33. To prevent inventory from going out with the trash, are you keeping a secure trash collection area?
34. To prevent roof access, are trees and their branches next to buildings removed?
35. Are ladders kept secure?
36. Are you aware that noisy equipment can mask unauthorized entry?
37. Are all exterior building entry points alarmed?
38. Are you aware that certain internal and external conditions may affect the alarm?
39. Is there a log of alarm malfunctions and their causes?
40. Have all the causes of alarm malfunction been remedied?
41. Is there an alarm listing and maintenance schedule?
42. Has the police or security company's response to an alarm been tested?
43. Are key management personnel frequently tested on alarm use?
44. Have key personnel been given specific alarm control assignments, including alarm opening, closing, checkout procedures, and accountability?

45. Are there clearly established money handling procedures to follow for safeguarding cash deposits, etc.?
46. Do you have a policy for reporting thefts other than security breaches? (Anonymously, if you think it is best.)
47. Are office machines, shop equipment, and other easily movable items marked for identification purposes?
48. Are vendors, salespeople, and repair persons logged in and out and, when necessary, given visitor's passes?
49. Are the employees frequently updated on security procedures?
50. Are you keeping a file of security deficiencies and a schedule for correction?

Appendix 3.B Physical security survey*

Victor Harold and John O'Rourke, CPP

Exterior physical characteristics: perimeter grounds

1. Is the fence strong and in good repair?
2. Is the fence height (a minimum of 8 feet excluding a 1 foot top guard of 3 strands of barbed wire) designed so that an intruder cannot climb over it?
3. Is the design of the fence from the building designed so that an intruder cannot climb over it?
4. Are boxes or other materials placed at a safe distance from the fence?
5. Are there weeds or trash adjoining the building that should be removed?
6. Are stock, crates, or merchandise allowed to be piled near the building?
7. Is there a clear area on both sides of the fence?
8. Are unsecured overpasses or subterranean passageways near the fence?
9. Are the fence gates solid and in good condition?
10. Are the fence gates properly locked?
11. Are the fence gate hinges secure and nonremovable?
12. What types of locks and chains are used to secure the gates?
13. Have unnecessary gates been eliminated?
14. Do you regularly check those gates that are locked?
15. Are blind alleys near buildings protected?
16. Are fire escapes and exits designed for quick exit but difficult entry?
17. Is the perimeter reinforced by protective lighting?
18. Has shrubbery near windows, doors, gates, garages, and access roads been kept to a minimum?
19. What are the physical boundaries of the residence's grounds?
20. Does lighting illuminate all roads?
21. Is there a procedure to identify vendors, subcontractors, and visitors before entrance to the gate?
22. Is proper signage in place?

Exterior doors

1. Are all doors strong and formidable?
2. Are all door hinge pins located on the inside?
3. Are all door hinges installed so that it would be impossible to remove the closed door(s) without seriously damaging the door or jam?
4. Are all door frames well constructed and in good condition?
5. Are the exterior locks double cylinder, dead bolts, or jimmy proof?
6. Can the breaking of glass or a door panel allow the person to open the door?
7. Are all locks working properly?
8. Are all doors properly secured or reinforced?
9. Are all unused doors secured and alarmed?
10. Are the keys in possession of authorized personnel?
11. Are keys issued only to personnel who actually need them?
12. Are the padlocks, chains, and hasps case hardened?
13. Are the hasps installed so that the screws cannot be removed?

Exterior windows

1. Are nonessential windows bricked up or protected with steel mesh or iron bars?
2. Are all windows within 14 feet of the ground equipped with protective coverings?
3. Are the bars or screens mounted securely?
4. Do those windows with locks have locks designed and located so they cannot be reached or opened by breaking the glass?
5. Are small or expensive items left in windows overnight?
6. Is security glass used in any of these windows?
7. Are windows located under loading docks or similar structures protected?
8. Can windows be removed without breaking them?
9. Do all vents and similar openings have a gross area of 1 square foot or more secured with protective coverings?
10. Are windows connected to an alarm system adequately protected?
11. Are windows not secured by bars or alarms kept locked or otherwise protected?
12. Have windows (doors) been reinforced with Lexan?
13. Are all windows properly equipped with locks, reinforced glass, or decorative protective bars or sturdy shutters?
14. Are unused windows permanently closed?

Other openings

1. Do you have a lock on manholes that give direct access to your building or to a door that a burglar could easily open?
2. Have you permanently closed manholes or similar openings that are no longer used?
3. Are your sidewalk doors or grates locked properly and secured?
4. Are your sidewalk doors or grates securely in place so that the entire frame cannot be pried open?
5. Are your accessible skylights protected with bars and/or an intrusion alarm?
6. Did you eliminate unused skylights, which are an invitation to burglary?
7. Are exposed roof hatches properly secured?
8. Are fan openings or ventilator shafts protected?
9. Does a service tunnel or sewer connect to the building?
10. Do fire escapes comply with city and state fire regulations?
11. Are your fire exits or escapes designed so that a person can leave easily but would have difficulty entering?
12. Do fire exit doors have a portable alarm mounted, to communicate if the door is opened, or is it hooked up to the intrusion alarm?
13. Can entrance be gained from an adjoining building?

Exterior lighting

1. Is the lighting adequate to illuminate critical areas (alleys, fire escapes, ground level windows)?
2. How many foot-candles is the lighting on horizontal at ground level?
3. Is there sufficient illumination over entrances?
4. Are the perimeter areas lighted to assist police surveillance of the area?
5. Are the protective lighting system and the working lighting system on the same line?
6. Is there an auxiliary system that has been tested?
7. Is there an auxiliary power source for protective lighting?
8. Is the auxiliary system designed to go into operation automatically when needed?
9. Are the protective lights controlled automatically by a timer or photocells or is it manually operated?
10. What hours is this lighting used?
11. Does it use a switch box(es) or is it automatically time secured?
12. Can protective lights be compromised easily (e.g., unscrewing of bulbs)?
13. What type of lights are installed around the property?
14. Are they cost effective?
15. Are the fixtures vandal proof?
16. Is there a glare factor?
17. Is there an even distribution of light?

Interior physical characteristics

1. Name of the site.
2. Address.
3. Full name and exact title of the administrative officer.
4. Telephone number.
5. Name of the surveying officer.
6. Full name and exact title of the security liaison.
7. Describe the security problem at this site.
8. What is the general purpose of the site?
9. What is the range of hours in use?
10. Which hours and days represent high-activity use?
11. How many people have access to the site?
12. Is the site normally open to the public?
13. List the number of rooms occupied by the various departments and offices.
14. Who does maintenance?
15. On what schedule does maintenance operate?
16. List the estimated dollar value of equipment and property in each department or office.
17. What area has the highest dollar value?
18. What area contains the most sensitive material?

Interior lighting

1. Is there a backup system for emergency lights?
2. Is the lighting provided during the day adequate for security purposes?
3. Is the lighting at night adequate for security purposes?
4. Is the night lighting sufficient for surveillance by the local police department?

Doors

1. Are doors constructed of a sturdy and solid material?
2. Are doors limited to the essential minimum?
3. Are outside door hinge pins spot welded or bradded to prevent removal?
4. Are those hinges installed on the inward side of the door?
5. Is there at least one lock on each outer door?
6. Is each door equipped with a locking device?

Offices

1. Can entrances be reduced without loss of efficiency?
2. Are office doors locked when unattended for long periods?
3. Does the receptionist desk have a clear view of the entrance, stairs, and elevators?
4. Are maintenance people and visitors required to show identification to the receptionist?
5. Are desks and files locked when the office is left unattended?
6. Are items of value left on desks or in an unsecured manner?
7. Are all computers bolted down?
8. Are floors free of projections, cracks, and debris?
9. During normal working hours, is the storage facility kept locked when not in use?
10. How many people have keys to this door?

Keys

1. How many keys are issued? How many master keys?
2. Is there a key control system?
3. What is the basis of issuance of keys?

4. Is an adequate log maintained of all keys issued?
5. Are key holders ever allowed to duplicate keys?
6. Are keys marked “Do Not Duplicate”?
7. If master key(s) are used, are they devoid of markings identifying them as such?
8. Are losses or thefts of key(s) promptly reported to security?
9. Who (name and title) is responsible for issuing and replacing keys?
10. When was the last visual key audit made (to ensure they had not been loaned, lost, or stolen)?
11. Were all the keys accounted for? (If not, how many were missing? How often do you conduct visual audits?)
12. Are duplicate keys stored in a secure place? Where?
13. Are keys returned when an employee resigns, is discharged, or is suspended? (If not, why not?)

Locks

1. Are all entrances equipped with secure locking devices?
2. Are they always locked when not in active use? (If not, why not?)
3. Is the lock designed or the frame built so that the door cannot be forced by spreading the frame?
4. Are all locks in working order?
5. Are the screws holding the locks firmly in place?
6. Is the bolt protected or constructed so that it cannot be cut?
7. Are locks’ combinations changed or rotated immediately on resignation, discharge, or suspension of an employee having possession of a master key(s)? If not, why not?
8. Are locks changed once a year regardless of transfers or known violations of security? If not, why not?
9. When was the last time the locks were changed?

Petty cash

1. How much petty cash is kept?
2. Are funds kept to a minimum?
3. Where is petty cash secured?
4. Are blank checks also stored there?
5. Are checks presigned?
6. Is the accounting system adequate to prevent loss or pilferage of funds accessible to unauthorized persons at any time?
7. Are funds kept overnight in a safe, locked desk, or file cabinet?
8. Is this storage area secure?
9. Are locks in the storage area replaced when keys are lost, missing, or stolen?
10. How many people handle petty cash?

Safes

1. What methods are used to protect the safe combination?
2. Are combinations changed or rotated immediately on resignation, discharge, or suspension of an employee having possession of the combination? If not, why not?
3. Is your safe approved by UL?
4. Is your safe designed for burglary protection as well as fire protection?
5. Where is (are) the safe(s) located?
6. Is it well lit at night?
7. Can it be seen from outside?
8. Do you keep money in your safe?
9. Do you keep cash at a minimum by banking regularly?
10. Do you use care in working the combination so that it is not observed?
11. Do you spin the dial rather than leaving it on “day lock”?
12. Do you have a policy of making certain that the safe is properly secured and the room, door(s), and windows are locked; night-light(s) is on; and no one is hidden inside?

13. Is your safe secured to the floor or wall?
14. Are combinations changed at least every 6 months? If not, when was the last time?
15. Do you have a protective theft alarm? If yes, is it local or central?
16. When was the system tested last?

Inventory control

1. When was the last time an inventory of business equipment was made, listing serial numbers and descriptions?
2. Were any items missing or unaccounted for?
3. Are all computers and similar equipment bolted down or otherwise secured?
4. Has the firm marked all its business equipment?
5. Is all expensive business equipment stored in a security cabinet or room?

Appendix 3.C Plant security checklist*

Victor Harold and John O'Rourke, CPP

1. Have you obtained a list of certified protection professionals (CPP) from the American Society for Industrial Security International (Arlington, Virginia)?
2. Have you assigned a senior executive (CSO) to act as liaison with the security consultant?
3. Have you assessed overall plant vulnerability to a variety of risks?
4. Have you checked with local police agencies about the incidence of vandalism, damage, reported internal losses, burglaries, and other crimes in the vicinity?
5. Have you checked with fire officials about the local incidence and type of fires and extent of losses?
6. Do you do periodic reviews of the plant security system, especially with a view toward effectiveness?
7. Do you periodically review the efficiency and willingness of the assigned security executive to carry out the function?
8. In many situations, the cost of security is far greater than the actual or expected loss. Have your circumstances been analyzed for cost-effectiveness?
9. Do you maintain a list of security regulations? Is it properly posted? Is it periodically reviewed?
10. Are you certain there has been no negligence in the guard force?
11. How often do you review the methods used to screen new employees, and are you certain screening is done?
12. Is there a policy to prevent laxity and indiscriminate use of badges and passes?
13. On termination of employment of a senior executive, are locks, codes, and passwords changed and badges deleted?
14. Have you trained line supervisors to daily check the plant's interior and exterior physical condition?
15. Do you tell your plant engineers to daily check critical utility areas, such as sewers, telephone, water, and electricity, for damage?
16. If security equipment is to be installed, has the installation plan been approved by a qualified group, such as the fire department, architect, police department, or engineer?
17. Has there been a recent security evaluation of hardware, containers, fire control equipment, safety items, locks, and bars?
18. Do you have a daily inspection of interior and exterior intrusion detection systems, fire systems, and sprinkler systems?
19. Do you daily test and examine your alarm system for proper operation?
20. Is your alarm system of the divided type; that is, can small segments be disconnected from the still operational main system?
21. Do you have a security communication network? Are all parts operating?
22. If you use CCTV and cameras, are all stations functioning well?
23. When purchasing new equipment, is the suitability and reliability of the items checked out by a dependable group?
24. Do you have a study showing that your security measures can generate a return on investment because losses are avoided and assets are recovered?
25. Has a thorough security survey identified various probable events, such as pilferage or white collar crime, to which the company is vulnerable?
26. Can an approximate dollar amount be placed on each factor?

27. Will the survey estimate the cost versus benefit ratio of attempting to correct any security infringement?
28. Does the security survey or audit answer the following:
    a. What is the possibility of a specific occurrence?
    b. What is the probability of a specific occurrence?
    c. What set of circumstances has to be in place for a situation to happen?
    d. If a problem occurs, how much will it cost to correct and restore?
    e. Is there any personal risk to people?
    f. If we do not install a security system, can we handle most situations on our own?
    g. What is the correct security level required to accomplish the mission?
29. Do you minimize contact between employees and nonemployees (as much as possible)?
30. Do you keep a record of which employees have keys to specific areas?
31. Are locks changed regularly?
32. Are doors double or triple locked?
33. Are external signs posted stating that alarm systems are in operation?
34. Because the roof is a weak spot, has it been properly protected from intrusion, such as with sensitive sonic alarms or microwave?
35. Have perimeter entrances been minimized to prevent accessibility by key?
36. Have you determined whether you need a badge or employee pass identification system?
37. Are your employees trained to challenge an unrecognized visitor or nonpass-wearing person?
38. Are outside service vendors escorted to the job site? Periodically checked or stayed with? Escorted out?
39. Do you retain a security consultant to annually review physical security needs and update security devices?
40. Do your employees know you will prosecute theft offenders?
41. Have you requested that your alarm agency notify you if the premises have been visited during unusual hours by an employee with a key?
42. Are office keys given only to those who need access?
43. Do you have a record of which key was given to whom?
44. Do you collect keys immediately from discharged employees?
45. Do you change the locks of areas in which discharged employees had access?
46. Are keys marked with "Do Not Duplicate" logos?
47. Are serial numbers ground off keys to prevent duplication by number?
48. Is a responsible executive in charge of key distribution?
49. Are spare keys kept in a secure cabinet?
50. Are duplicate records kept, indicating key distribution and date and time issued?
51. Can your telephones be locked to prevent unauthorized after-hours use?
52. Do you have a locksmith who periodically checks all lock operations?
53. Can personal items be secured in a locked desk drawer?
54. Are important papers kept in a double-locked and fireproof file?
55. When filing cabinets are unlocked for use, are keys removed and secured?
56. Are office machines bolted down and locked?
57. Are your office machines and plant equipment marked for identification?
58. Are the serial numbers of office and plant equipment recorded, duplicated, and secured?
59. Are briefcases with important documents left in a locked cabinet?
60. Are important papers removed from desks and locked when the area is not staffed?
61. When the building shuts down for the evening or weekend, are doors and windows checked by a manager?
62. Do service personnel from outside vendors have proper identification?
63. When shutting down for the evening, are potential hiding places checked?
64. Are the police and fire department numbers posted near each telephone?
65. Are safe combinations changed very frequently?
66. Are security officers' rounds checked every day?
67. Have you determined if a shredder is necessary?
68. Do you avoid keeping large sums of cash overnight?
69. Do visitors sign in?
70. If the employees wear passes, do your security people check them even if the wearers are familiar?
71. If you have a facility that requires constant security, do you escort your visitors?

72. Is a vigil kept on outside maintenance people?
73. If you have a sensitive security area, is access to it kept limited?
74. Is the security area marked with signs and color coded?
75. Do you need an area where sensitive talks take place?
76. Do you periodically check offices for signs of tampering, such as moved desks, paint marks, putty and other fillers used to seal holes, dust and scratch marks, and more?
77. Do you avoid discussing on the phone what you are going to do about your security situation?
78. Do you avoid ordering security sweeps and changes in security structure over the phone?
79. Do you test the integrity of the security service by ascertaining if they will plant a device?
80. Do your security officers observe the counter-surveillance people at work?
81. Are the items prone to tapping or targets for security intrusion sealed? Are the seals checked regularly?
82. If a bug is found, do you continue to search for more?
83. Are all entry places alarmed?
84. Do you have a locker area for employees' personal use? Is the facility kept secure?
85. Are your security officers routinely given polygraphs, fingerprinted, and vetted?

Appendix 3.D Security officers checklist*

Victor Harold and John O'Rourke, CPP

1. Have you determined whether or not you have limited security requirements?
2. If you have determined that your security needs are complex, have you talked about your needs to a select group of trustworthy agencies?
3. If your security needs are simple, are you aware that it is time consuming and a waste of productivity to obtain a wide variety of competitive bids?
4. Have you checked with a local law enforcement official for recommendations?
5. Have you checked with colleagues who use security services for recommendations?
6. If you are analyzing a security agency, have you requested information on the amount, type, and stipulations of their insurance coverage?
7. Have you requested information on the security agency's clients, the names of current customers, and the length of time the account has been with the agency?
8. Have you requested information on the agency's financial status?
9. Is the agency willing to reveal security officer training techniques?
10. Does the agency have security officer incentive programs?
11. Does the agency have a career program for its security officers?
12. Do the guards meet educational and criminal background checks?
13. Has the agency a set of standards to which security officers are held? What are they?
14. Have you reviewed the credentials of the senior executives of the guard service company?
15. Will your account have a representative assigned who is from the highest level of management?
16. Will the agency you select have the capabilities to offer other services, such as investigations, disaster planning, executive protection, employee screening, and polygraph testing?
17. Have you determined if the agency you are selecting has a union affiliation? Which one?
18. Will there be a union conflict if your employees go on strike?
19. Have you visited the agency's local office?
20. Have you discussed prior clients and why they no longer are clients?
21. Have you visited current accounts and talked to management?
22. In the contractual arrangement with the guard company, have you avoided too much control over their employees?
23. Have you double-checked the insurance liability of the agency?
24. Does the contract with the guard company assure that it is an independent contractor, relieving your firm of joint employer liability?
25. Have you reviewed the contract's provisions for replacing unsatisfactory guards and terminating the contract?
26. Does the contract guarantee costs?
27. Does the contract contain penalties for nonperformance or poor performance?
28. Is there an agreement by the guard company to refrain from doing business with a competitive company?

29. Have you assigned a senior person to monitor security services to determine that standards are being met and the agency's contractual obligations are being fulfilled?
30. If your plant is paying for guard services, have you discussed wages and job-related expenses, such as travel, holidays, and supervisors?
31. Have you discussed any special training required to accomplish the assignment, such as firearms, cardio pulmonary resuscitation (CPR), fire safety, and first aid?
32. If your situation requires a formal presentation and contract, have the documents been reviewed by your legal counsel and insurance company?
33. Have you reviewed provisions for contract terminations?

Appendix 3.E Office security checklist

Victor Harold and John O'Rourke, CPP

The UCLA Campus Police Department put together the following office security checklist, which deals with 30 security points pertaining to operational procedures as well as physical characteristics.

1. Do you restrict office keys to those who actually need them?
2. Do you keep complete, up-to-date records of the disposition of all office keys?
3. Do you have adequate procedures for collecting keys from former employees?
4. Do you secure all computers and similar equipment with maximum security locks?
5. Do you restrict duplication of office keys, except for those specifically ordered by you in writing?
6. Do you require that all keys be marked "Do Not Duplicate" to prevent legitimate locksmiths from making copies without your knowledge?
7. Have you established a rule that keys must not be left unguarded on desks or cabinets; and do you enforce that rule?
8. Do you require that filing cabinet keys be removed from locks and placed in a secure location after opening cabinets in the morning?
9. Do you have procedures that prevent unauthorized personnel from reporting a "lost key" and receiving a "replacement"?
10. Is a responsible person in charge of issuing all keys?
11. Are all keys systematically stored in a secured wall cabinet either of your own design or from a commercial key control system?
12. Do you keep a record showing issuance and return of every key, including name of person, date, and time?
13. Do you use telephone locks to prevent unauthorized calls when the office is unattended?
14. Do you provide at least one lockable drawer in every secretary's desk to protect purses and other personal effects?
15. Do you have at least one filing cabinet secured with an auxiliary locking bar so that you can keep business secrets under better protection?
16. Do you record all equipment serial numbers and file them in a safe place to maintain correct identification in the event of theft or destruction by fire?
17. Do you shred all important papers or place them in a recycle bin for shredding?
18. Do you lock briefcases containing important papers in closets or lockers when not in use?
19. Do you insist on identification from repair personnel who come to do work in your office?
20. Do you deposit incoming checks and cash each day so that you do not keep large sums in the office overnight?
21. Do you clear all desks of important papers every night and place them in locked, fireproof safes or cabinets?
22. Do you frequently change the combination of your safe to prevent anyone from memorizing it or passing it on to a confederate?
23. When working alone in the office at night, do you set the front door lock to prevent anyone else from getting in?
24. Do you have the police and fire department telephone numbers posted and handy?
25. Do you check to see that no one remains behind hiding at night if you are the last to leave the office?
26. Are all windows, transoms, and ventilators properly protected?
27. Do you double-check to see that all windows and doors are securely locked before you leave?
28. Are all doors leading to the office secured by heavy-duty, double-cylinder dead bolt locks?
29. If your office is equipped with a burglar alarm system or protected by a guard service, do you make sure the alarm equipment is set properly each night?
30. Do you have a periodic security review made by a qualified security expert or locksmith?

Appendix 3.F Home security checklist*

Victor Harold and John O'Rourke, CPP

Exterior

1. Do you have a burglar alarm?
2. Are there stickers on your windows and doors, stating that the property is alarmed?
3. Are bicycles, garden equipment, and other items kept indoors and locked?
4. Is your mailbox locked?
5. Are front and back doors kept lighted in the evening?
6. Are shrubs and trees trimmed low, below window level?
7. Do you arrange for mail and newspaper pickup or stop deliveries if you are not at home?
8. Is your grass kept mowed while you are away?
9. Is there a neighborhood watch program?
10. Do you place lights on timers or photocells if you go away?
11. Are police notified of your extended absence?

Doors

1. Do all doors, especially to the garage and basement, close tightly?
2. Are all doors double locked?
3. Are overhead doors locked when not in use? Is there a track lock?
4. If padlocks are used, are they of high quality?
5. If hinges and hasps show, are the screws and hinge pins of the type that cannot easily be removed?
6. If your car is in the garage, are the doors locked and the keys removed?
7. Are the entrance doors solid core?
8. Is there a security plate in the lock area to prevent jimmying?
9. Are there peepholes or viewing windows in the entrance doors?
10. If the entry doors have glass, is the glass 40 or more inches from the lock?
11. Are sliding doors locked and has an anti-slide bar on the lower track, as well as bars on top of the doors, been installed to prevent lifting the door off the track?

Windows

1. Are the window air conditioners bolted to prevent removal from the outside?
2. Can the basement windows be locked?
3. Do you use auxiliary pins and other locks on all windows?
4. If windows are kept open for ventilation, can they be locked in the open position?

General home security

1. Can all exterior doors be locked from the inside?
2. Are the locks on all exterior doors of the dead bolt type?
3. If a door or window is opened while you are home, will there be a warning sound or light?
4. When you retire or leave, do you check doors and windows to be certain they are locked?
5. When repair people and utility company representatives come to your door, do you request identification?
6. Can your basement door be locked to prevent entry into the house?
7. Are extra house keys kept isolated or hidden?
8. Do you avoid indiscriminate handing out of duplicate keys?
9. If you park your car in a public lot, do you separate the car keys from the house keys?
10. Do you have an outside light that remains on all night?
11. Are all low-level windows that are easily accessible kept doubly secure with latches and bolts?

12. Have you installed window and door devices that audibly and visually indicate that a break-in is in progress or has occurred?
13. Are your skylights well secured, that is, not easily removed from the roof?
14. Are window air conditioners well installed and not removable from the outside?
15. Are your portable fire extinguishers kept in good condition?
16. Are they kept in easily accessible areas?
17. Are smoke and heat detectors installed near sleeping areas and on every level of the house?
18. Are the detectors tested frequently?
19. Are fire drills a regular routine with your family?
20. Do you have an emergency notification system to enable other households to know that a situation (medical, panic, robbery) is occurring?
21. If a suspicious vehicle is in the area, is a description and the license number noted?
22. If you go away, can you get a neighbor to park a spare car in your driveway?
23. Do you have a home safe for valuable items?
24. Should you have an alarm system survey to help determine your security and safety needs?

Miscellaneous

1. Is valuable property inventoried, and is the list periodically updated and secured?
2. Is the list of serial numbers of those items that have been recorded kept off the premises?
3. Are valuable items marked with a scriber and an identifying number?
4. Are emergency telephone numbers memorized and prominently displayed near the telephone?
5. Do you avoid keeping cash in the house?
6. If you have weapons, are they secured?

Appendix 3.G Fire safety inspection

Michael A. Stroberger, CPP

The following inspection is designed to be the basis of a revised and property-specific inspection program. Some of the entries refer to functions performed with a "reasonable frequency." In reviewing your specific property or location, care should be taken to consider the nature of the structure, geographic location, intended use, and actual use. In many cases, functions that are best performed on a daily basis in one environment can be reasonably performed on a weekly or possibly monthly basis in a different environment.

In addition, note that every application is unique in some manner. As such, what might be prudent for one location, however seemingly similar, might be insufficient at another location. Although benchmarking of a similar program is highly recommended, this also should be seen as simply a basic guideline in the creation of a customized, location-specific program.

Some sections pose inspection inquiries that reference a large number of possible locations or items to be reviewed. One example would be the inspection of sprinkler heads. In designing the actual checklist for such an inspection, it is often desirable to break down the physical layout of the facility into reasonable and manageable zones. Identifying sets of sprinkler heads by the room in which they are installed allows the person performing the inspection to review them as a set and make comments in reference to that area of coverage. In cases such as fire doors, it might be reasonable to identify them with a location number, which could be included not only on the inspection form, but a numbered tag, on the hinge-side edge of the door, for later identification.

Administrative and planning phase

1. Are copies of all locally enforced codes maintained on site for reference?
2. Does the facility meet requirements of locally enforced Building Code?
3. Does the facility meet requirements of locally enforced Fire Prevention Code?
4. Does the facility meet requirements of locally enforced Life Safety Code?
5. Does the facility have a written and appropriately distributed Fire Prevention and Response Plan? Is this plan known to all employees? Is training provided to those with defined responsibilities? Is all training documented and securely filed? Is the plan reviewed annually, updated as required, and redistributed?

6. Does the facility maintain a fire brigade? Is the fire brigade training documented and securely filed? Is the fire brigade training conducted in conjunction with the local fire department? Is the fire brigade composed of persons, or positions, that are present or represented at all times?
7. Are all inspection reports retained for a reasonable number of years, as defined by local codes, insurance requirements, or industry standards? Are inspection reports filed in a secure location?
8. Are all employees trained in basic fire prevention concepts and fire event response procedures? Is the content of this training consistent and reasonably inclusive? Is this training documented and securely filed? Is annual refresher training conducted? Is annual refresher training documented and securely filed?

General physical inspection phase

1. Are all fire exit routes clearly marked? Are all exit routes unobstructed at all times? Are all exit routes and egress hardware items in compliance with the Americans with Disabilities Act requirements?
2. Are all fire doors and egress hardware items in proper working order?
3. Are service areas secured against unauthorized entry when not in use?
4. Are all areas free of loose or disorganized combustible items (such as rags or empty boxes)?
5. Are all storage areas well organized to allow ease of access in emergency situations?
6. Are flammable or combustible items properly stored to protect against accidental ignition?
7. Are flammable or combustible items properly stored to protect against unauthorized usage or tampering?
8. Are all fire lanes clearly marked? Are fire lanes maintained in an unobstructed condition at all times?
9. Are master keys available at all times for Fire Department use?
10. Are all electrical panels accessible at all times? Are all panels clearly marked to facilitate emergency power disconnection?
11. Are gas line shutoff valves accessible at all times?
12. Are all gas-operated pieces of equipment inspected for wear and damage with reasonable frequency? Are inspections documented and filed in a secure location?
13. Are all heat-generating devices (such as boilers, furnaces, and dryers) provided a reasonable clear zone, based on levels of heat output, where storage of any kind is prohibited?
14. Are all ducts inspected regularly and cleaned as required?
15. Is the use of extension cords discouraged in all areas?
16. Are all electrical cords and electrically operated items inspected for wear or damage with reasonable frequency? Are such inspections documented?
17. Are designated smoking areas clearly defined and at a proper minimum safe distance from any common or identified ignition threats? Are appropriate ash and cigarette receptacles available for use in these areas?

Extinguisher inspection phase

1. Have all extinguishers been inspected and serviced as required by a licensed vendor or trained technician within the past 12 months?
2. Are all extinguishers of a type appropriate for most probable types of fires in the immediate area?
3. Are specialty extinguishers available in those areas that would require them?
4. Are persons trained in the use of the extinguishers available in the areas where they are typically present? Is this training documented and filed in a secure location?
5. Are extinguishers inspected with reasonable frequency (daily, in most cases) to ensure that they are present and have not been tampered with or discharged? Is each extinguisher inspection fully documented and securely filed?

Stand pipe, fire hose, and control valve inspection phase

1. Do tamper switches, linked to an alarm system, monitor all control valves?
2. Are all control valves inspected and tested annually by a licensed vendor or trained technician?
3. Are all stand pipes, control valves, and fire hoses accessible at all times?
4. Are fire hoses inspected, per manufacturer recommendations, for wear and decay?

Sprinkler system inspection phase

1. Are all flow switches inspected and tested annually by a licensed vendor or trained technician?
2. Are all sprinkler heads of a type appropriate for the location in which they are installed?
3. Are all sprinkler heads installed and maintained within the manufacturers' recommendations?
4. Are all sprinkler heads provided with a clear area of operation in compliance with the local Fire Code?
5. Does the sprinkler system have a pressure maintenance pump? If so, is this pump inspected and tested with reasonable frequency (weekly, in most cases) by a licensed vendor or trained technician?
6. Are all areas requiring sprinkler system coverage, per the local Fire Code, provided with such coverage?

Hazardous materials inspection phase

1. Are proper warning placards utilized in areas of chemical storage and usage?
2. Is proper personal protective equipment (PPE) provided for initial response to fire and emergency situations related to any hazardous materials maintained or utilized on site? Is training provided in the use of this PPE? Is such training documented and filed in a secure location?
3. Is the Fire Department made aware of storage areas, use areas, and large arriving or departing shipments of hazardous materials?
4. Are all appropriate containment, standoff distance, and warning signs utilized in storage areas?
5. Is the MSDS on file and accessible 24/7?

Alarm system inspection phase

1. Is the system monitored by a licensed, off-site monitoring service?
2. Is the system inspected and tested annually by a licensed vendor or trained technician?
3. Is this inspection documented and filed in a secure location?
4. Is the area of coverage broken down into identified zones?
5. When activated, does the alarm system clearly identify the location of the potential fire?
6. Are audible alarms heard in all areas of a zone when activated? Is the system designed to warn adjacent zones, inclusive of floors above or below?
7. Are strobes visible in all areas of a zone when activated? Is the system designed to warn adjacent zones, inclusive of floors above or below?
8. Does the alarm system record activation and use history? For what length of time is this history retained?
9. Does the system's audible signal include a prerecorded advisory message? If so, does this message recommend a route or method of egress? If so, does this message advise against the use of elevators, if any are present?
10. Does the system automatically recall or drop elevators on activation? Are override keys available for Fire Department use?
11. Are detector types installed, as appropriate for the specific location of installation? If the intended use of a given area is altered, is the type of detector also reviewed and changed to match the updated intended use of that area?

Summary

This is added for informational use only as it is not typically considered in the domain of the security professional.

In January 2003 the American Society for Industrial Security International came out with a set of General Security Risk Assessment Guidelines, which recommended that, when conducting a security survey or risk assessment of a complex, a company should consider the following seven points from their report:

1. Assets are people, property, intangible property, and information; identify the risks attached to each.
2. Conduct a cost/benefit analysis and explore the value of all benefits to be accrued. Are the recommendations made affordable, feasible, available, practical, and state of the art?
3. Consider the risk, risk analysis, risk assessment, probability, and vulnerability to incidences.
4. Gather statistical data: material obtained from in house, material obtained from local and state police agencies, material from the FBI Uniform Crime Report database, and the type of incidents in similar complexes as well as the rating of the current Homeland Security color code.
5. Examine the frequency of events and what can be done to reduce and remove the overall threat.

6. Identify the assets; for example, a warehouse with a million-dollar inventory, 30 people have access and maybe more, alarm system control panel is a dialer non-UL that is 22 years old; or a museum with a 52-million-dollar inventory, four people have total access, and the 5-year-old fire and intrusion alarm at all points is tested monthly.
7. Reassess your complex annually.

Finally, we realize not all security personnel deal with fire safety and life safety issues, but some do.

Appendix 3.H Bullet-resistant glazing for a secure workplace

Michael A. Stroberger

Total Security Solutions offers a full line of bullet-resistant glass in acrylic, polycarbonate, and glass-clad polycarbonate. These products are available at UL protection Levels 1–8, providing protection ranging from 9 mm to a 12 gage. These products are typically used in banks, credit unions, gas stations, and convenience stores but are appropriate for any business with cash on hand that wants to provide their employees with a secure work environment.

In addition to providing bullet-resistant products to glaziers and mill shops, Total Security Solutions provides custom milling and installation of secure barrier systems. We take pride in our ability to develop and install bullet-resistant architecture that fits the design of a customer-friendly workplace.

Typical materials used in construction or sold directly include

- Interior/exterior transaction windows
- Bulletproof doors
- Ballistic counters
- Package passers
- Bullet-resistant barriers and framing
- Bullet-resistant transparencies and fiberglass

Bullet-resistant fiberglass wall panels

These are used to provide bullet-resistant protection to the walls of corporate executive offices, boardrooms, conference rooms, lobbies, reception area counters, customer service counters, and safe rooms. This bullet-resistant fiberglass can be installed by the manufacturer or even by your general contractor. Once installed, this product will never be seen but will provide high-quality ballistic protection and peace of mind for years and years to come.

Bullet-resistant doors

Along with protection for the walls and lobbies of your offices, there are a wide variety of doors to meet your needs, such as solid executive-style veneered doors to match existing doors; the only difference is that they will also offer bullet-resistant protection. Again, these doors provide invisible bullet-resistant protection, and nobody will know it is there. Aside from custom-made, executive-style office doors, normally there are full vision clear doors, half vision clear doors, plastic laminate no-vision doors, and bullet-resistant steel doors. All of these doors are prehung, so any contractor can install them within minutes.

Bullet-resistant windows

Bullet-resistant windows come in a full range of windows that are custom built for the needs of each individual client. You can replace your office windows with bullet-resistant windows ranging from levels 1–5, or you can leave your existing windows in place and add a second bullet-resistant window behind the existing window in such a way that it will be virtually invisible to the general public and still add protection.

Bullet-resistant executive office products

- High-quality executive-style bullet-resistant doors
- Bullet-resistant wall armor to line all the walls of the office
- Bullet-resistant, custom-made windows to protect all existing window locations
- High-security electronic mag-locks to lock doors in the event of an attack

Bullet-resistant board rooms or conference rooms

- High-quality, executive-style bullet-resistant doors
- Bullet-resistant wall armor to line all the walls of the conference room or board room
- Bullet-resistant, custom-made windows to protect all existing window locations
- High-security electronic mag-locks to lock door in the event of an attack
- Bullet-resistant transaction or reception area
- Bullet-resistant transaction window systems
- Package exchange units
- Bullet-resistant reception door with electric strike
- Bullet-resistant fiberglass for reception counter die wall
- Stainless steel deal trays for small transactions

Residential high-level security for corporate executives

- Provide bullet-resistant protection to point of entry (garage, front doors, front windows, etc.)
- Build safe room including walls, doors, windows, and high-security locksets
- Convert closet into a high-level safe room
- Convert master bedroom into a high-level safe room (add invisible bullet-resistant protection to all walls, doors, and windows)

Finally, be advised that there are standards that apply to these installations and the products.

Appendix 3.1 Window film

Michael A. Stroberger

Window film is not bulletproof and there is *no* film product out there that is. However, window film can be resistant to small arms and shotguns, and Lumar window film products have a bomb blast proof film product.

Window film comes in four categories:

1. Security or safety film
2. Decorative or safety film
3. Anti-graffiti film
4. Solar film

One benefit of security or safety film is that when an outer pane of glass breaks, the inner pane will remain intact. It is used to protect retail, commercial, and residential buildings as well as other types of window structures from flying glass due to earthquakes, windstorms, attacks, vandalism, theft, and accidents.

Decorative film makes glass surfaces clear and visible, enhances safety in public spaces, and allows you to customize your space with a corporate logo.

Antigraffiti window film is a protective film that helps prevent scribing on or defacing of your base surface. The film is easily peeled off and replaced, eliminating graffiti and the replacement cost of glass.

Solar film has many benefits: it reflects and absorbs heat and light, increases energy efficiency, reduces HVAC cost, protects furniture and carpets, and provides greater temperature stability. Below are a list of websites in the event you seek additional information.

- www.iwfa.com
- www.extremewindowsolutions.ca
- www.acelaminate.com
- www.securityfilm.biz/index.htm

Chapter 14

Unmanned aerial vehicle (drone) usage in the 21st century

Lawrence J. Fennelly and Marianna A. Perry

Security Consultant

Drones are an open architecture, advanced intelligent software platform that enables Drone-Sentry and Drone-Home to provide coordinated autonomous missions. It is a cloud-based machine learning A.I. that ingests data from individual drones, teams of drones and external IoT devices. Drone-IQ is the universal Command, Control and Communication software that processes drone payload and telemetry data.

www.dronecore.us

Introduction

Drones can be remotely controlled or be guided through software-controlled flight plans working with a GPS. DJI, a Chinese technology company, is one of the business making consumer drones that executive Randy Braun describes as "flying robots with high-quality cameras attached."[1]

According to the Federal Aviation Administration (FAA)[2]

- There are no "traditional" pilot requirements for unmanned aerial vehicles, but if used for commercial purposes, the operator must have remote pilot airman certificate, be 16 years old, and must pass Transportation Security Administration (TSA) vetting.
- Cannot fly within 5 miles of an airport without prior notification to airport and air traffic control.
- Must *always* yield right of way to manned aircraft.
- The operator must keep the aircraft in sight (visual line of sight).
- Must undergo preflight check to ensure the UAS is in condition for safe operation.
- Must fly under 400 ft.
- Must fly during the day.
- Must fly at or below 100 mph.
- Must be under 55 lbs and must be registered if over 0.55 lbs.
- Must yield right of way to manned aircraft.
- Must *not* fly over people.
- Must *not* fly from a moving vehicle.
- Never fly over groups of people.
- Never fly over stadiums or sports events.
- Never fly near emergency response efforts such as fires.
- Never fly under the influence of drugs or alcohol.
- Understand airspace restrictions and requirements.
- Must follow any community-based safety guidelines.

1. www.theguardian.com/technology/2015/nov/08/dublin-web-summit-things-learned-tinder-drones-apps.
2. www.faa.gov/uas/.

Handbook of Loss Prevention and Crime Prevention. DOI: https://doi.org/10.1016/B978-0-12-817273-5.00014-4

Features and benefits[3]

- camera drone
- connects to smartphones and tablets via Wi-Fi
- includes VR headset and VR viewer mode
- headset fits most smartphones (suction cup attachment)
- you see what the drone sees
- remote includes smartphone holder for non-VR mode
- records video and photos right onto your phone
- one key return (flies back in the direction of its take-off point)
- 6 axis gyro (omnidirectional)
- 4 channel/2.4 GHz
- 10″ × 10″ × 2.5″ (with blades and landing gear)

Legal or regulatory basis[4]

- Public Law 112-95, Section 336—special rule for model aircraft
- FAA interpretation of the special rule for model aircraft
- Title 14 of the Code of Federal Regulations (14 CFR) Part 107
- many jurisdiction now have passed laws, so it's important to check what you can and cannot do

The use of drones or UAS is a challenging issue for both the FAA and the entire aviation community because the United States has the busiest, most complex airspace in the world.[5] Both manned and unmanned aircraft systems are required to operate safely. It does appear that technology is moving faster than laws because drones are commonly used by businesses and commercial ventures for

- aerial views of virtually anywhere
- collection of data
- hobbyists
- recreational use that has become more popular
- roof inspections
- filmmakers
- US military
- survey of property lines
- geo-mapping
- search and rescue
- missing persons
- public safety at disaster scenes or gauging where first responders need to be
- firefighting
- perimeter patrols during large forest fires
- monitoring crops and livestock
- inspecting critical infrastructure such as pipelines and utility lines for repairing
- package delivery
- real estate photography
- on a ranch or farm, make owners aware of predators approaching their livestock
- as a teaching tool in education
- protection against illegal excavations or mining
- monitor weather
- monitor flooding, storms and hurricanes, landslides, tsunamis, and earthquakes
- measuring and monitoring nuclear accidents (too dangerous for humans)
- volcanic eruptions to analyze and track ash clouds

3. www.gophercentral.com (November 16, 2018).
4. www.gophercentral.com (November 16, 2018).
5. www.gophercentral.com (November 16, 2018).

Security applications for drones

Security professionals are constantly discussing how the drone industry will change the security industry. New ways to maximize the use of drones will continue to revolutionize the security industry. Some possible uses of drones in the law enforcement and security industry are as follows:

- Civil security—operations against looters.
- Antipiracy when deployed by the coast guard or water patrols.
- Surveillance by law enforcement of high-crime areas or "hot spots."
- Assist police officers in a foot or vehicle pursuit. Helicopters have been used to support teams on the ground but are expensive and require time to deploy. A drone could be immediate air support, more cost effective, and just as successful alternative.
- For surveillance or apprehension, drones can enter narrow and confined spaces, produce minimal noise, and can be equipped with night vision cameras and thermal sensors, allowing them to provide images that the human eye is unable to detect.
- Crime scene photography to aid in the investigation of crimes and the location of evidence.
- Surveillance of evidence in criminal cases.
- Monitor serious vehicle, train, or airplane crash scenes and ship collisions.
- Monitor traffic for flow to determine alternate routes, vehicle accidents, stranded motorists, inoperable traffic signals, etc.
- Private property and city-owned streets could be monitored for inoperable lighting that needs repair or replacement.
- Drone security teams protecting large areas of property can patrol the perimeter of a property with an infrared camera on a drone instead of having a human security team walk the perimeter. This may be a security/protection officer on private property or used by local, state, or federal law enforcement.
- Ground security cameras in a fixed position can lead to blind spots, but since a drone has the ability to move, security teams can search around corners and get a closer look to avoid blind spots.
- If a security team does find an intruder on the property and the intruder runs, the drone can easily continue monitoring the location of the intruder and the drone operator can relay information to the security team.
- In the Corrections Industry, prison guards can monitor the prison yard more efficiently and safely with the assistance of a drone. A monitor could send a drone to an area if a fight breaks out to assess the situation before correctional officers respond.
- Help identify trespassers who hope to vandalize property. The presence of a drone security camera may also serve as a deterrent for trespassers.
- If security or protection officers patrol an area with vehicles at night, the headlights easily let intruders know the security team is arriving and give them a chance to hide. Utilizing a drone will help apprehend the criminal or intruder.
- The water industry (which includes water engineering, operations, and water and wastewater plant construction), wind farms, and oil pipelines could use drones to protect large infrastructure against acts of terrorism or vandalism.
- Help security or protection officers monitor and protect people and exhibits at open-air museums and help guard historic artifacts and cultural heritage.
- Currently, the FAA does not allow drones to be flown over stadiums when they are in use. At some point, there may be potential to apply for a waiver to operate the drone during the event, but they could still be used for security when the stadium is not being used.
- Drone security teams can patrol the parking lots of large commercial industries and large venues (such as concerts) during and after events.
- On large college or university campuses, drones can be deployed to areas that have become trouble spots, giving staff more eyes, without the expense of hiring more security or protection officers. Drones can more than likely to be able to reach destinations quicker than a security or protection officer can.
- Patrol a dockyard for loss prevention and movement and also monitor incoming and outgoing shipments.
- Stop poachers by helping guide animals out of danger or recording and monitoring poachers' actions and location for apprehension and prosecution.
- Monitor activity at borders and be used by the US Customs and Border Protection to deter drug smuggling.
- Monitor borders along waterways to detect people coming in on small water craft.
- Patrol large land areas that are not bordered by walls and fences, which can lower a company's need for manpower for patrols.

- Help secure foreign embassies and consulates by monitoring the surroundings better that fixed video surveillance.
- For maximum security applications, a team of drones could be deployed instead of just one drone.
- When equipped with cameras, a powerful strobe light, and audio speakers, drones can be used to engage an intruder.
- The presence of a drone flying overhead may be a deterrent for potential offenders.
- Routine patrols could be done more efficiently by a drone with video and an infrared camera rather than a security or protection officer. Drones can cover a much wider area in a short amount of time than a human, although for a limited amount of time. Consider a drone doing a perimeter check around a secure facility. Even a drone is used to patrol in Neighborhood Watch Programs.
- With the appropriate learning software, drones could recognize threats and identify who an intruder is and follow the thermal image until human backup personnel can arrive.

A few things to consider are as follows:

- Technology and regulations have not yet created the space for automated drone security solution, either, so an operator would have to fly a drone and relay data to those on the ground. This may negate a portion of the potential labor savings in security and limits the opportunity.
- For any law enforcement or protection application, thermal imaging cameras can be used for "night vision" and anyone who will be operating a drone at night will need to apply for a night waiver from the FAA.
- Drones usually have fairly short battery lives, which means they are not a 24/7 security solution. When a drone's battery gets low, another drone could take its place.
- About half a dozen drones were to be used in Time Square to aid police, in January 1, 2019, but it rained. Point is a new trend to use them in a positive manner.

Accident reporting under the small UAS rule (Part 107) to the FAA[6]

The remote pilot in command of the small UAS is required to report an accident to the FAA within 10 days if it results in at least serious injury to any person or any loss of consciousness, or if it causes damage to any property (other than the UAS) in excess of $500 to repair or replace the property (whichever is lower).

An online portal is available through www.faa.gov/uas for the remote pilot to report accidents in accordance with reporting requirements in the Part 107 rule. Accident reports may also be made by contacting your nearest FAA Flight Standards District Office.

A new use of drones

As at the 2018 Super Bowl, the Pyeongchang games in 2018 drone show comes compliments of Intel's Shooting Star platform, which enables a legion of foot-long, 8 oz, plastic, and foam quadcopters to fly in sync, swooping, and swirling along an animator's prescribed path.

"It's in essence technology meeting art," says Anil Nanduri, general manager of Intel's drone group.

Intel's Shooting Star drones are about a foot-long, weigh 8 oz and can fly in formation for up to 20 minutes.

Further reading

Davies, S., Fennelly, L.J., 2019. The Professional Protection Officer Handbook, ninth ed. Elsevier.

6. www.gophercentral.com (November 16, 2018).

Chapter 15

The legalization of marijuana and the security industry

Lawrence J. Fennelly and Marianna A. Perry
Security Consultant

Chapter Objectives

- Pros and cons
- Medical or recreational
- FDA and ALA
- Long-term effects
- Facilities security plan

Introduction

Marijuana—the pros and cons

Marijuana is the dried leaves, flowers, stems, and seeds from the hemp plant, *Cannabis sativa*. The plant contains the mind-altering chemical, *delta-9-tetrahydrocannabinol* (THC). Extracts with high amounts of THC can also be made from the cannabis plant. The THC in marijuana is the chemical responsible for most of marijuana's psychological effects, because it acts much like the cannabinoid chemicals made naturally by the human body. The cannabinoid receptors are concentrated in the areas of the brain associated with thinking, pleasure, coordination, and time perception. The THC in marijuana attaches to these receptors and activates them and affects a person's memory, pleasure, movements, thinking, concentration, coordination, and sensory and time perception.

Marijuana is the third most popular recreational drug in the United States, behind alcohol and tobacco, according to the marijuana reform group NORML, and they state that marijuana is less dangerous than alcohol or tobacco because approximately 50,000 people die each year from alcohol poisoning and more than 400,000 deaths each year are attributed to tobacco use. By comparison, marijuana is nontoxic and cannot cause death by overdose. The organization supports a legally controlled market for marijuana, where consumers can buy marijuana for recreational use from a safe legal source.

The legalization of marijuana—whether it is for medical use or recreational use is a controversial subject. There are pros and cons on both sides of the argument and each side cites research data supporting their stance on the subject that the other calls "low quality." Proponents say that marijuana helps the economy and the job market and others say that it causes more crime and puts people at risk. The bottom line is that marijuana use can be good or bad, depending upon who you ask. For these reasons the debate over marijuana continues.

Should marijuana be legal for medicinal and/or recreational purposes?

Voters in several states across the nation have been asked to decide whether marijuana should be legal for use as a medicine, but the National Cancer Institute states that marijuana has been used for medicinal purposes for over 3000 years. Voters made their decisions about the legalization of marijuana for medicinal purposes on the basis of medical anecdotes, beliefs about the dangers of illicit drugs, and a smattering of inconclusive science. In order to help policymakers and the public make better informed decisions, the White House Office of National Drug Control Policy asked the Institute of Medicine (IOM) to review the scientific evidence and assess the potential health benefits and risks of marijuana.

Handbook of Loss Prevention and Crime Prevention. DOI: https://doi.org/10.1016/B978-0-12-817273-5.00015-6

The IOM report, Marijuana and Medicine: Assessing the Science Base, *released in March 1999, found that the THC in marijuana is potentially effective in treating pain, nausea and vomiting and AIDS-related loss of appetite. They add that additional research involving clinical trials need to be conducted. The report also states that the therapeutic effects of smoked marijuana are modest and there may be medicines that are more effective. The report acknowledges that there are some patients that do not respond well to other medications they may "have no effective alternative to smoking marijuana."*

The IOM report stated the following findings:

The profile of cannabinoid drug effects suggests that they are promising for treating wasting syndrome in AIDS patients. Nausea, appetite loss, pain, and anxiety are all afflictions of wasting, and all can be mitigated by marijuana. Although some medications are more effective than marijuana for these problems, they are not equally effective in all patients. A rapid-onset (that is, acting within minutes) delivery system should be developed and tested in such patients. Smoking marijuana is not recommended. The long-term harm caused by smoking marijuana makes it a poor drug delivery system, particularly for patients with chronic illnesses. Terminal cancer patients pose different issues. For those patients the medical harm associated with smoking is of little consequence. For terminal patients suffering debilitating pain or nausea and for whom all indicated medications have failed to provide relief, the medical benefits of smoked marijuana might outweigh the harm.

Most research studies on both sides of the issue do agree that smoked marijuana is not a completely safe substance. It is a drug that when used can produce a variety of effects. However, except for the harm associated with smoking, the adverse effects of marijuana use are within the range tolerated for other medications. The Original Equipment Manufacturer (OEM) has cautiously endorsed the medical use of marijuana, but smoked marijuana is a crude way to deliver THC because it also delivers harmful substances. Based on this information, it does appear as though marijuana does have medical value, but its therapeutic components must be used in conjunction with conventional therapy to be safe and useful.

The Food and Drug Administration (FDA) has not approved smoked marijuana as a safe and effective drug but recognizes that patients are looking for treatment options for some conditions, such as nausea and vomiting, caused by chemotherapy. Even, though the FDA has not approved *botanical* marijuana because they have not found it safe and effective, they do, however, recognize the interest in using marijuana for medicinal purposes. The FDA has approved the drug, Dronabinol, which is a medicine made from THC, a light yellow resinous oil that is extracted from the marijuana plant. It is used to treat or prevent the nausea and vomiting associated with chemotherapy to increase the appetites of patients with AIDS.

The American Lung Association does encourage continued research into the benefits, risks, and safety of marijuana use for medicinal purposes. They recommend that any patients who are considering marijuana for medicinal purposes make an informed decision by consulting with their doctor and also consider other methods of administration other than smoking.

In 2014 Colorado was the first state to allow the sale of marijuana for recreational use to anyone aged 21 or older. Marijuana sold at retail stores carries a 25% state tax, plus the Colorado state sales tax of 2.9%, which makes recreational marijuana one of the most heavily taxed consumer products in Colorado.

As of June 19, 2015, 23 states and the District of Columbia currently had laws legalizing marijuana use in some forms. Four states and the District of Columbia have legalized marijuana for recreational use. Many states have decriminalized the possession of small amounts of marijuana for recreational use, while others have passed medical marijuana laws allowing for limited use. Some medical marijuana laws are broader than others and list specific medical conditions that allow for treatment, but this varies from state to state. There are some states that have passed laws allowing residents to possess cannabis oil if they suffer from certain medical illnesses. For example, Virginia has laws that allow the possession of marijuana as long as the individual has a prescription from a doctor. Federal law prohibits doctors from prescribing marijuana, so basically the state laws are not valid. This means that doctors can write a recommendation for medical marijuana but not a prescription. While possession, sale, and consumption of marijuana remain illegal at the federal level, it is permitted for recreational use in four US states: Alaska, Colorado, Oregon, and Washington, plus the US capital, Washington.

It is common knowledge that smoke is harmful to lung health. It does not matter whether the smoke is from burning wood, tobacco, or marijuana because toxins and carcinogens are released from combustion. Smoke from marijuana combustion has been shown to contain many of the same toxins, irritants, and carcinogens as tobacco smoke. Because marijuana smokers tend to inhale more deeply and hold their breath longer than cigarette smokers, there is greater exposure. Marijuana smoke injures the cell lining of the large airways and many marijuana smokers have symptoms, such as a chronic cough, phlegm production, wheezing, and acute bronchitis.

Smoking marijuana affects the immune system and the body's ability to fight against disease, especially for individuals with weakened immune systems or those taking immunosuppressive drugs. Smoking marijuana also kills the cells in the lungs that help remove dust and germs, which may lead to an increased risk of lower respiratory tract infections.

The short-term effects of marijuana

The THC in marijuana passes from the lungs into the bloodstream and stimulates the receptors in the parts of the brain. This causes the "high" that users feel. Other effects include

- altered senses (e.g., seeing brighter colors),
- altered sense of time,
- changes in mood,
- impaired body movement,
- difficulty with thinking and problem-solving, and
- impaired memory.

The long-term effects of marijuana

Marijuana also affects brain development. When teenagers use marijuana, it may permanently affect their thinking, memory, and learning functions.

Long-term marijuana use has also been linked to mental illnesses and mental health problems, which are as follows:

- temporary *hallucinations*—sensations and images that seem real though they are not;
- temporary *paranoia*—extreme and unreasonable distrust of others;
- worsening symptoms in patients with *schizophrenia* (a severe mental disorder with symptoms, such as hallucinations, paranoia, and disorganized thinking);
- depression and schizophrenia;
- anxiety and psychosis; and
- suicidal thoughts among teens.

Is marijuana addictive?

Marijuana can be addictive. Research suggests that about 1 in 11 users becomes addicted to marijuana (Anthony, 1994; Lopez-Quintero, 2011). This number increases among those who start as teens (to about 17%, or one in six) (Anthony, 2006) and among people who use marijuana daily (25%–50%) (Hall and Pacula, 2003).

Security for marijuana farms and dispensaries

For those who either cultivate or sell marijuana, it is important that they should know how to protect their investment—equipment, inventory, products, and above all, their employees. The marijuana industry certainly comes with its own security challenges.

The legalization of recreational marijuana in Colorado and Washington introduced a new element for the cannabis industry in the United States—effective security that "fits" with this industry. Medicinal marijuana is legal in 23 states but is still considered a Schedule 1 controlled substance by the US government, which makes growing and selling marijuana illegal under federal law. This elevates the security situation for marijuana farms and dispensaries to a new level, because many banks are reluctant to accept money that is generated from the sale of marijuana, so this has forced the industry to be an all-cash business. This has led to the development of "specialty" security companies for a niche market. Not only do these "specialty" security companies protect product and cash on hand, they are also responsible for securing the perimeter of the property, access control in and out of areas and buildings, monitoring video surveillance and response, monitoring the intrusion-detection systems, and providing on-going consulting services, they have to constantly monitor the temperature and lighting within the growing facilities. It is important that marijuana farms and dispensaries consider all possible threats, they have the state-of-the-art technology as a part of their security master plans and that the security operation is efficient and either minimizes or eliminates any security vulnerability.

CNN reports that there are now big-box stores, named "weGrow," that offer marijuana growing equipment, supplies, and services (including recommendations for security) and they are being called, the "Walmart of Weed." None of the "weGrow" stores actually sell marijuana, but they advertise that their services and products are designed especially for cultivating marijuana. This is a perfect example of the premise, supply, and demand.

"weGrow" also offers a "dispensary security plan" that covers facility as well as operational security that is touted as something that "... every dispensary or cultivation owner must have! Essential document for anyone that plans to own a marijuana dispensary." It includes a sample security plan and advertises that custom plans are also available. The security plans are designed to "minimize security exposure and prevent breaches before they even occur. However, in the event that preventative measures fail, the Operational Security Plan is designed to quickly observe, monitor, protect, counter and report any situations that do occur."

The facility security plan, after a risk assessment, includes the following:

- location and site security
- secured employee parking
- around the clock coverage
- security surveillance systems (CCTV)
- maintenance of security systems
- access control/ingress and egress and biometrics
- perimeter security
- product security
- fire alarm system
- intrusion alarm system

The operational security plan includes the following:

- security threats and countermeasures
- transactional security
- delivery security
- hazardous weather
- human resource policies and protocols
- employee security training
- inventory control
- guest, media, and visitor procedures
- neighborhood involvement
- emergency response
- contingency planning

The "specialty" security companies are meeting the needs of the marijuana industry, because some dispensary owners have stated that ADT, the largest security provider in the nation, has dropped or is refusing to accept customers in the marijuana industry. ADT told CNN money it will not "sell security services to businesses engaged in the marijuana industry because it is still illegal under federal law."

So, what is currently being done to address the fire hazards at marijuana grow and extraction facilities?[1]

The topic of fire safety at marijuana processing and extraction facilities was introduced to the full NFPA 1 Technical Committee during its first draft meeting in October 2015. As a result of the committee's interest, a task group was formed to develop the language further and proposed a new chapter for NFPA 1, Fire Code, to the committee at the second draft meeting. The marijuana chapter passed ballot easily, but it will still need to get through the NITMAM process. See the second draft of NFPA 1.

Two education sessions to be presented at NFPA's Conference & Expo

NFPA's Conference & Expo will be held in Boston, June 4–7, and there will be two education sessions dedicated to fire safety in marijuana grow and extraction facilities. Check back soon to NFPA's C&E site to get more details about the following sessions:

- *Marijuana grow facilities—an Authority having jurisdiction (AHJ) perspective*

1. https://www.nfpa.org/Public-Education/By-topic/Property-type-and-vehicles/Marijuana-grow-and-extraction-facilities

This presentation will focus on an AHJ perspective with respect to marijuana grow facilities and the common issues faced during the plan review and approval process. Case studies of functioning marijuana grow facilities will be reviewed and discussed with topics, including NFPA 72 notification appliance coverage, NFPA 30 flammable gas-extraction processes, and NFPA 101 egress concerns.

- *Marijuana facilities—evaluating the fire and explosion hazards*

With the increase in legalization of marijuana use, there has been a follow-on increase in explosions and ensuing fires. The ability to recognize the inherent fire hazards in this cutting edge of America's societal evolution will enhance the fire protection community's efforts to contain and control these hazards, because not all aspects of the legal marijuana community are hazardous.

From NFPA Journal

In the cover story of the September/October 2016 issue of NFPA Journal, Associate Editor Jesse Roman talks about a host of lessons learned in the industry, including safety practices at commercial grow and extraction facilities, inspection protocols, and more.

NFPA Journal's Jesse Roman takes a trip to Colorado to report on the burgeoning commercial marijuana industry and how public agencies are battling to ensure that marijuana grow and extraction facilities are safe for employees, firefighters, and the public.

Canada

San Diego in a rare move, the US government has approved the importation of marijuana extracts from Canada[2] for a clinical trial, highlighting a new avenue for American researchers who have had trouble obtaining the drug for medical studies.

Researchers at the University of California, San Diego announced Tuesday the Drug Enforcement Administration has OK'd their plan to import capsules containing two key cannabis compounds from Tilray Inc. They want to study the drug's effectiveness in treating tremors that afflict millions of people.

Marijuana is illegal under federal law, but the United States has a program for supplying it for research. Scientists have long complained about its quality and lack of variety.

Additional information

- Denver, CO marijuana extraction facility fire code.
- Colorado Fire Marshals' Special Task Group Marijuana Facility Guidance.
- List of marijuana facility hazards.
- Take our poll—how prepared is your public safety agency for this emerging industry? *Note: You must be logged in to NFPA Xchange to take the poll.*

  https://www.nfpa.org/Public-Education/By-topic/Property-type-and-vehicles/Marijuana-grow-and-extraction-facilities

Emerging trend

Owners in the marijuana cultivation and dispensary business state that they are concerned not only with thieves but also with federal authorities who are eager to see them put out of business.

With demand for security services to protect the marijuana industry, there is certainly not a shortage of opportunities for security professionals; however, keep in mind that you may or could have a conflict with federal law. Clearly this is a current emerging trend, with local towns actually voting to allow the sale of marijuana in their specific community.

On the positive side, doctors are recommending medical marijuana for a variety of issues, such as, cancer. Marijuana is not harmless, reports of higher chance of motor vehicle accidents and chronic bronchitis from long-term use, and is considered an illegal drug by Federal officials.

---

2. <https://www.kdlt.com/2018/09/18/dea-approves-marijuana-import-from-canada-for-clinical-trial/> Sept. 2018.

Notes

https://www.drugabuse.gov/publications/drugfacts/marijuana
http://www.livescience.com/24553-what-is-thc.html
http://norml.org
http://www.livescience.com/24553-what-is-thc.html
http://medicalmarijuana.procon.org/view.answers.php?questionID = 255
http://www.fda.gov/NewsEvents/PublicHealthFocus/ucm421163.htm
http://www.livescience.com/24553-what-is-thc.html
http://www.lung.org/stop-smoking/smoking-facts/marijuana-and-lung-health.html
http://www.cnn.com/2013/12/28/us/10-things-colorado-recreational-marijuana/
http://www.governing.com/gov-data/state-marijuana-laws-map-medical-recreational.html
http://www.taipeitimes.com/News/biz/archives/2016/03/06/2003640899
http://www.lung.org
https://www.drugabuse.gov/publications/drugfacts/marijuana
http://www.securityinfowatch.com/article/11601437/booming-cannabis-industry-presents-wealth-of-opportunities-to-security-system-installers-manufacturers
http://www.cnn.com/2011/US/05/31/arizona.marijuana.superstore/index.html?iref = allsearch
http://wegrowstore.com/index.php?page = shop.product_details&flypage = flypage.tpl&product_id = 35&vmcchk = 1&option = com_virtuemart&Itemid = 262
http://money.cnn.com/2013/04/29/smallbusiness/marijuana-security/
http://www.who.int/entity/substance_abuse/publications/cannabis_report/en/index4.html
http://churchillcoalition.weebly.com/marijuana-and-the-brain.html

Chapter 16

Active shooter: common-sense thinking, common-sense planning or in other words . . . thinking outside the box

Lawrence J. Fennelly, Marianna A. Perry and Caroline Ramsey-Hamilton
Security Consultant

October 1, 2017 will be remembered by the nation, especially within the communities of Las Vegas and Southern Nevada, as a day of inordinate loss.

FEMA . . .. October After Action Report 2018.

Introduction

The recent shooting, at Marjory Stoneman Douglas High School in Parkland, Florida,[1] has rekindled the hot debate about gun control in the United States. Sen. Chris Murphy (D-CT), a proponent of more restrictions on firearms, argued, "This happens nowhere else, other than the United States of America. It only happens here not because of coincidence, not because of bad luck, but as a consequence of our inaction. We are responsible for a level of mass atrocity that happens in this country with zero parallel anywhere else."[2]

Unfortunately, this has become the routine in the United States. After every mass shooting the debate over guns and gun violence begins again.

In response to Senator Murphy's (and others) attacks on Second Amendment rights, the National Rifle Association (NRA) "officially spends about $3 million per year" lobbying to influence gun policy. Since its founding in 1871 the NRA has continued to promote gun safety programs and is the primary firearms educational organization in the United States.[3]

Here's something to think about . . . Is it guns that kill people or people who kill people? Because, a mentally ill person commits a mass shooting, is it fair to say that because of that, no one else can own a gun? Opponents of gun control argue that the Bill of Rights gives us, as American citizens, the right to own a gun for protection. What would happen if only people who acquired them illegally had guns? Would more people die because others were unable to protect themselves? Using that same logic, if we say that guns are not allowed for anyone because someone with a mental illness kills someone, it is like saying, "nobody can eat sugar just because there are people with diabetes."[4]

In order for someone to purchase a firearm, it is only common sense to require a rigorous background check; restrict gun sales to only those individuals over 21 years of age; and to prevent the purchase of, or take guns away from those individuals, who are mentally ill, but as the old adage goes, "Common sense ain't too common." If only it were this easy . . ..

1. https://www.miamiherald.com/news/local/community/broward/article223839585.html.
2. America's gun problem explained. From: <https://getpocket.com/explore/item/america-s-gun-problem-explained-1060655345> (Retrieved 04.03.18.).
3. NRA. From: <https://home.nra.org/about-the-nra/> (Retrieved 04.03.18.).
4. Is gun control a violation of the Bill of Rights? From: <http://www.debate.org/opinions/is-gun-control-a-violation-of-the-bill-of-rights> (Retrieved 04.03.18.).

Handbook of Loss Prevention and Crime Prevention. DOI: https://doi.org/10.1016/B978-0-12-817273-5.00016-8

Fortune magazine has identified a group of "gun super-owners," who love guns more than the average gun-lover and it should come as no surprise that these "super-owners" drive the firearms market in the United States. To illustrate this point with the numbers, approximately 2% of Americans (1 in 50) own half of the guns (50%) in the United States.[5]

In 2015 *The Washington Post's* Wonkblog site revealed that the average number of firearms owned by a "typical gun-owning household in the United States" has roughly doubled between 1994 and 2013 to 8.1 guns per household, *and* the trend has only gone up since. A recent Harvard/Northwestern University joint study estimates that America's 319 million citizens own about 265 million guns. From 1994 to 2016 the number of Americans who owned guns decreased from 25% to 22%. In the last 18 months (May 2016 through November 2017), the FBI National Instant Criminal Background Check System data indicates that gun sales set new records in the United States. This means that there are fewer households who own guns, but there are more gun sales, so there is an increase in the number of guns owned per gun-owning household.[6]

The following six items are being proposed to help with what is commonly called the "gun problem," in the United States:

1. Universal background checks
2. "No fly—no buy" barring people on the no-fly list from purchasing guns
3. Creating a federal database for gun purchases
4. Banning assault-style weapons
5. Prohibiting the sale of bump stocks
6. Installation of metal detectors, security surveillance systems, and locks on classroom doors, thereby obtaining detection at front door

The question is whether or not the "problem" is really a mental health problem that is partially fueled by the breakdown of the family structure and support system in the United States. Is it possible to detect a mental health issue with a background check before a gun can be purchased? The answer is "maybe yes" and "maybe no."

Are people in the United States so accustomed to violence that it has become a way-of-life and we have become desensitized to it?

Consider the following statistics:

- Number of murders seen on TV by the time an average child finishes elementary school: 8000
- Number of violent acts seen on TV by age 18: 200,000
- Percentage of Americans who believe TV violence helps precipitate real life mayhem: 79

According to the A.C. Nielsen Co., an average American watches more than 4 hours of TV each day (or 28 hours/week, or 2 months of nonstop TV-watching per year). This means a 65-year life, that person will have spent 9 years watching TV, so how many murders and violent acts have they seen?[7]

Some things to think about

Should the chief of police in every city or town be assigned the task of issuing gun permits so law enforcement in that city or town will know who in their area has a weapon? What if individuals had to be certified by law enforcement to carry (and possibly use) their weapon of choice? Would this have an effect on gun crimes in the United States?

Everyone agrees that someone with a mental health condition should not be able to purchase a gun or obtain a gun permit. What if a doctor had to certify that the person was of sound mind? Would this help the problem?

We also agree that there should be signage posted that no guns should be allowed within 1000 ft of any school and area to be posted. Again, will this help the problem? What if it is a mentally ill person with an illegally obtained firearm in the area of a school? Will they obey the law and stay back 1000 ft if they have a gun?

5. You'll never guess how many guns the average gun owner has. From: <https://www.fool.com/investing/2017/01/09/youll-never-guess-how-many-guns-the-average-gun-ow.aspx> (Retrieved 03.03.18.).

6. You'll never guess how many guns the average gun owner has. From: <https://www.fool.com/investing/2017/01/09/youll-never-guess-how-many-guns-the-average-gun-ow.aspx> (Retrieved 03.03.18.).

7. Television and health. From: <https://www.csun.edu/science/health/docs/tv&health.html> (Retrieved 04.03.18.).

Video games and porn

The Huffington reported in May 29, 2018 that a GOP Congresswoman stated that porn is a big part of what's driving the spike in school shootings. Rep. Diane Black also sighted the deterioration of families' poor economic and cultural conditions. About a year ago a shooter was deeply involved into the video game DOOM as were several others. We mention these two factors to add to the already very complicated issue:

- *Active shooter* the *video game* pulled from platform shelves after outcry—NBC News. https://www.nbcnews.com/news/us-news/active-shooter-video-game-prompts-outrage-amid-spate-school-shootings-n8781561 day ago ... A *video game* that simulated school shootings has been pulled before its release date after facing a colossal backlash.
- There is no need to comment on this video, we mention it only, to give you an idea of the various issues connected with this problem.

Frustration

Every mass-shooting incident (especially at a school) creates frustration—for law enforcement, politicians, school administrators, teachers, parents, and even the students. Why? On Wednesday, February 27, a Broward County School Board member said that the security measures that were in place and the active shooter training that was conducted at Marjory Stoneman Douglas High School in Florida were not enough to stop a gunman from killing 17 people. So, what is "enough" security? Consider the fact that you may have too many entrances and exits and, therefore, no control over who enters your property. Control is the main entrance, a metal detector and an SRO.

Does this need to be a very complicated issue?

This may not have to be such a complicated issue. We need to use a common sense, proactive approach. There are two approaches ... we need to reduce the risk of mentally ill individuals obtaining guns and causing mass casualties or give everyone a gun and then active shooter will be the "new normal." We are supposed to be a civil society but at times that does not appear to be the case. Regardless of the reasons—mental illness, gun availability, desensitivity to violence and death, overexposure to violence through television or video games, anger issues, etc., it does appear as though some individuals think only with their trigger finger.

What about "smart" guns?

A "smart" gun[8] is a firearm that uses technology to prevent anyone except the owner from firing the weapon. This is achieved in different ways depending on the design, including through fingerprint sensors, radio-frequency identification, magnets and biometric sensors that unlock the weapon based on a combination of grip style, and the strength and size of the person's hand. Since technology is used in order for the weapon to fire, there is some concern that if "smart" guns become more readily available, they may run the risk of being hacked.

One of the major issues holding up "smart" gun technology is the question of reliability. Some proponents of "smart" guns believe that law enforcement agencies should take the lead on testing this technology, because that would help with further development and consumer acceptance. There are law enforcement-friendly models, in spite of the lack of firepower currently available in "smart" guns, but the question is whether or not this untested technology should be put in the hands of first responders. Gun grab safety issue for plain clothes detectives (who do not have a safety holster) is one of the most common arguments for why "smart" guns could make a huge difference in officer safety.

Gun control supporters support laws to prohibit the sale of firearms that do not possess "smart" technology and would also prohibit the manufacture of traditional handguns. The NRA does not oppose the development of "smart" guns, but they do oppose any law prohibiting Americans from acquiring or possessing firearms that do not possess "smart" gun tech.

8. Five things to know about smart guns. From: <https://www.policeone.com/police-products/firearms/articles/391099006-5-things-to-know-about-smart-guns/> (Retrieved 15.03.18.).

Texas Governor's school safety plan: more armed guards, no big gun controls

Two weeks after a student shot and killed 10 people at a high school outside Houston, Gov. Greg Abbott of Texas on Wednesday proposed spending more than $100 million to put more police and armed guards on school campuses and expand programs to identify students at risk of engaging in mass violence. Abbott also proposed stepping up security at schools by limiting the number of entrances and exits, and installing alarms specifically designated to warn of active shooters. His school safety plan[9] contained only modest changes to gun laws: he proposed requiring parents to keep firearms locked away from children under the age of 18, a tightening of current law which requires such controls for families with children younger than 17. He also proposed improvements to the system for reporting felony convictions and adjudications of mental illness, both of which trigger prohibitions on gun possession under federal law. Abbott also asked state legislators to "consider the merits" of passing a so-called red flag law that would allow the police, family members, or a school employee to petition a judge to temporarily take guns away from someone deemed a threat to themselves or others. Texas would become 1 of only about 10 states with red flag laws, if legislators were to pass such a law, though proposals for similar legislation are pending in more than a dozen other states.

How safe are school buildings? Recent shootings prompt schools to assess security concerns

As officials at all levels of government grapple with how to prevent school shootings and keep children safe in school buildings, security experts say that fortifying entrances can be a good start.[10] In addition, a sequence of locked doors with an intercom system and security cameras is a top priority for schools looking to bolster security. From 1999 to 2015 the percentage of students who said their school's entrance was locked during the school day rose from 38 to 78, according to the National Bureau of Justice Statistics. Many schools are embracing the "mantrap" design, which allows a guard, staff member, or digital driver's license scanner to scrutinize visitors in a confined area prior to entry. The majority of school shooters are current or former students, meaning that swipe tags or colored lanyards may be easy to copy, steal, or borrow. Teachers should be locking their classroom doors whenever class is in session, according to Christopher Wagner, Denville, New Jersey police chief.

SEVENTEEN-YEAR-OLD ACTIVE SHOOTER AT SANTA FE, TEXAS HIGH SCHOOL KILLS 10, INJURES 13, AFTER STUDYING MASS SHOOTING TECHNIQUES FROM NEWS REPORTS

At 7:25 am on a Friday morning in Santa Fe, Texas, a 17-year-old student walked into his classroom, wearing a trench coat and armed with his dad's Remington 970 shotgun and 38 caliber pistol that he used to shoot 23 people inside his school. Ten were killed and 13 were injured in the planned shooting. Armed officers responded within four minutes and a gun battle ensued with the subject.

Although a romantic failure may have triggered the attack, the shooter had long been a fan of active shooters and studied previous shootings, like pulling of the fire alarms in the recent Parkland shooting. He wore a trench coat, mirroring the horrific Columbine High School shooting in April, 1999, in which two teenage boys with weapons hidden under trench coats killed 12 students and one teacher.

According to a witness, the shooter yelled "WOO HOO," as he shot up the classroom. Multiple media accounts say the gunman taunted some of his victims, asking some hiding in a closet if they wanted to answer their ringing cell phones. "You want to get that?" the attacker said.

According to The Wall Street Journal.

He spared others saying he wanted his story told. Police also found five homemade pipe bombs that did not detonate.

The shooter had pursued a romantic interest, Shana Fisher, for the past 4 months, according to her mother, but she refused to date him. Shana was shot and killed in the incident. Her mother said that the previous week, her daughter, Shana, has said in media accounts that her 16-year-old daughter had rejected four months of aggressive advances from Pagourtzis.

9. From Oppel, R., via Security Management, May 31, 2018. Texas Governor's school safety plan: more armed guards, no big gun controls. New York Times. From: <asis.online.com>.

10. From Zimmer, D.M., Scanning the Schoolyard, May 27, 2018. How safe are school buildings? Recent shootings prompt schools to assess security concerns. Security Management Magazine (June 2018). From: <Azcentral.com>.

Fisher finally stood up to him in front of the entire class and proclaimed that she would never go out with him, embarrassing him in class, her mother told the Los Angeles Times.

According to the Texas Lt. Governor, Dan Patrick, "The video games issue, we have got to address in this country. Based on all the research we have done, 97%, according to psychologists and psychiatrists . . . of teenagers view video games, and 85% of those video games are violent."

Lessons learned

1. Even with a relatively quick 4-minute response time, there were still 10 killed and 13 injured, demonstrating that even a well-armed police officer cannot quickly stop the killing, once shooting starts!!
2. Texas State officials blamed the attack on video games, on abortions, and on too many entrances and exits to the high school buildings, even though the school lacked any access control, no metal detection, and no screening of any kind.
3. Underage students should not have ready access to firearms. The shooter's parents apparently missed the fact that he assembled pipe bombs in his bedroom, access to guns, and avidly recounted mass shootings.
4. Why are parents fined if their child is late in returning a library book, but not if their child shoots and kills people with daddy's guns?

PARKLAND UPDATE: OF COURSE IT HAPPENED HERE! June 11, 2018

Parkland, Florida

SAYS EX-SECRET SERVICE AGENT WHO REPORTED TO AUTHORITIES THAT MSD HIGH SCHOOL WAS VULNERABLE!

According to a retired Secret Service agent, Parkland's Marjorie Stoneman Douglass staff was well aware of the lack of security as much as 60 days before the fatal shooting took place.

The former agent, Steve Wexler, was invited to review the high school for security and he reported numerous weaknesses to the MSD staff including: "Gates were unlocked. Students did not wear identification badges. A fire alarm could send students streaming into the halls. Active-shooter drills were inadequate," *he said.*

In addition, he noted, "This stuff is blatantly obvious. You've got to fix this," Wexler said.

He never heard from the school again. His recommendations included the following:

1. School gates should be locked, and students should wear ID badges showing they belong on campus. The schools' policy requires gates to be locked during the day, but Wexler said that he found they were not. The shooter on February 14 was able to get on campus, because the gates were opened at the end of the school day.
2. Active-shooter drills should be routine. After the shooting, some students said that they had not been involved in drills this year.
3. Any adult should be able to declare a Code Red to lock down the school. Clark, the school district spokeswoman, said that is the current protocol, but Wexler said he was told an assistant principal notifies the principal, who then makes the call. "That's a problem," he said he told the staff. "This stuff happens fast. This playing telephone is no good. By that time we could sit down and have breakfast."
4. Schools should not immediately evacuate students for a fire alarm without first confirming that there is a fire. During the shooting the gunfire set off the smoke alarm, and students fled into the halls, where the shooter could take aim.

Lessons learned

1. Do not lose track of psychiatric patients! They are *at risk* of violence and should be in an isolation room where they cannot hurt themselves or injure hospital staff.
2. Police delivering psychiatric patients to hospitals should make sure that they have left the patients with a responsible party who will make sure about their proper care.

Emergency management

Emergency management practitioner Michael Fagel, Ph.D., said recently, "Always after an incident you should conduct an assessment, make improvements, improve training, check all physical security devices to make sure their working, and to review your emergency management response plan."

How can crime prevention through environmental design help?

Crime prevention through environmental design (CPTED) concepts may help reduce the likelihood of crime or violence and many times helps people "feel" safer in their environment.

Lobby

All visitors must sign in and show identification before being granted access to the building. Consider a visitor and volunteer-management system, such as the systems by Raptor Technologies.[11] The technology has the capability of tracking who is inside school buildings and uses facial recognition software to help keep pedophiles out. Your video-surveillance system should not have any "blind spots" with no camera coverage. Why? To be effective, your security-surveillance system needs to have a 360 degree of coverage of the perimeter of the building.

Windows

Numerous windows in the front of building (especially school buildings) should have line-of-sight visibility through natural surveillance. In other words, there should be a clear view of the outside property from inside the building.

Natural surveillance

Surveillance is a design concept directed primarily at keeping intruders under observation. Therefore, the primary goal of a surveillance strategy is to facilitate observation, although it may have the effect of an access-control strategy by effectively keeping intruders out because of an increased perception of risk. Surveillance strategies are typically classified as organized (e.g., police patrol), mechanical (e.g., lighting, locks, and alarms), and natural (e.g., windows).

Traditionally, access control and surveillance, as design concepts, have emphasized mechanical or organized crime-prevention techniques while overlooking, minimizing, or ignoring attitudes, motivation, and the use of the physical environment. More recent approaches to physical design of environments have shifted the emphasis to natural crime-prevention techniques, attempting to use natural opportunities presented by the environment for crime prevention. This shift in emphasis led to the concept of territoriality.

Crime prevention through environmental design landscape security

An important element of CPTED, which defines semiprivate and private space on a campus, is your landscape design. It should be clear when someone is passing from public to semiprivate to private space. This can be achieved in different ways. If bushes are used, it is recommended that the height of bushes be no higher than 3 ft. We have recently read that FEMA recommends the height of bushes to be 18 in. and that tree branches should be between 7 and 8 ft off the ground as a means for Natural Surveillance and Safety. You want to be able to easily detect intruders and not allow for any hiding spots. Your landscape, if properly laid out, can also be a deterrent for crime and prevent criminal opportunity.

Landscape furniture should be vandal resistant and if benches are installed, they need to be designed so that individuals cannot sleep on them.

Also, take into consideration, exterior lighting, video surveillance, vegetation, maintenance, barriers, the entrance and exit of your property, signage, and the surface structure.

11. Raptor technologies. From: <https://raptortech.com/protect-your-school/> (Retrieved 16.03.18.).

Controlling access

The perimeter of the property should be fenced. Although fencing does not deter a determined trespasser, it does make individuals approaching the building from an unauthorized are more obvious.

To effectively control access to the property and the building(s), the number of entrances should be limited. The general idea is few entrances and many exits. Monitored video surveillance and intrusion detection (such as door prop alarms) can monitor secondary points of entry or those emergency exits not used for entry into the building. Police officers or security officers can respond to unauthorized entry at these locations. Effective access control requires that entry to and from the building be actively monitored.

Mass-notification system

The following recommendations will strengthen mass-notification practices at your k to 12 or college and universities.

1. *Prerecorded messages*: Prerecorded messages need to be developed to address most likely and most catastrophic emergency situations that will require utilization of mass-notification systems. Furthermore, prerecorded messages will allow security officers to initiate mass notification, significantly reducing the time delay.
2. *Protocol*: Your college management must establish a clear protocol to address the following:
   a. Activation guidelines: Description of situations/criteria that require utilizing the CCC Alert system.
   b. Authority: Authority to activate CCC Alert must be given to security operators/dispatchers tasked with monitoring all of college's security systems. This will allow for quick and efficient mass notification in the case of an emergency situation.
3. *Practice*: It is recommended that mass notification be included as part of any emergency drills conducted at college. This will prepare security operators to utilize mass notification in times of crisis. Furthermore, such ongoing practices will significantly reduce the amount of time it takes to send a message through the mass-notification system.

Immediate steps to shore up school security (Caroline Ramsey-Hamilton, 2018)

1. *Access control is the starting point.* If you cannot control access, anyone can bring any kind of gun into our schools. Stand-alone metal detectors are relatively inexpensive and easy to install. Wand scanners could be deployed asap. Backpacks and cases need to be scanned or opened.
2. *Limit and alarm entrances to the schools.* No school is secure if there are multiple entrances, and if anyone can enter the school undetected. All exterior doors should be locked 100% of the time, not propped open, and doors should be checked weekly to make sure they close effectively.
3. *Actively monitor security cameras.* Cameras should be set up for active monitoring on every egress door, so that if a shooter somehow gets in, they can be discovered at the first shot and then isolated so that students are removed from the immediate area. Students could have been prevented from putting themselves in harm's way, or even rescued.
4. *Leverage gunshot detection solutions.* Gunshot detection software can alert at the sound of the first round fired.
5. *Color photo ID badges should be issued to every student and worn at all times.* They cost almost nothing and instantly help to keep people out who should not be in the facility, such as the shooter who carried out this massacre.
6. *Use bullet-resistant backpacks and white boards.* Though they cannot stop a gunman, these products can help children and staff protect themselves when all else fails.

Florida schools are required to "lockdown" if an active shooter code is called. This is not an effective procedure and the number of victims in the Parkland massacre shows that it is ineffective. It does not limit the shooter once they are inside the facility, and it prevents students from being able to exit quickly.

Bulletproof Back Packs

Guard Dog Security Top Products, including Guard Dog Security Bags & Backpacks, Guard Dog Security Backpacks, Guard Dog Security Flashlights

https://shop.opticsplanet.com/guard-dog-security-brand.html?gclid = EAIaIQobChMIz8Wipefs3AIVwWSGCh2pDAiCEAAYASAAEgJuvPD_BwE

Long-term solutions

Long-term solutions should always be pursued but they must include a national discussion on access to lethal and automatic weapons. More stringent background checks need to be implemented, as we have seen with every active shooter incident, including the 2013 shooting at Los Angeles International Airport, the aforementioned massacre at the Pulse nightclub, and even the 2016 New York bombing, in which the suspect's father called the FBI.

These are long-term political solutions, but the conversation today and tomorrow and the day after that needs to be about preventing school shootings and mass casualty events, which require the implementation of mandatory controls/solutions that can be deployed tomorrow, not in 3 years.

Back in Parkland, this close-knit community has been terrorized and there is no resolution. The most aggravating thing about the Parkland massacre is: one more time, it is too late. No matter how many drills and training were done, it did not help.

The Pulse nightclub

Once again, as was the case in the Pulse nightclub shooting in Orlando, we saw law enforcement holding back instead of entering the school sooner and finding and eliminating the shooter before he kills more students.

The importance of a security assessment

A full site security assessment or safety audit conducted by a security professional is the most effective way to identify security-related strengths and weaknesses on your campus. The assessment can then be used to address immediate areas of vulnerability and budget for more long-term security enhancements.

Long-term solutions

Long-term solutions should always be pursued but they must include a national discussion about access to lethal and automatic weapons. We all agree that before a gun can be purchased, a more stringent background check should to be conducted. Think about the events leading up to the 2013 shooting at Los Angeles International Airport, the Pulse nightclub shooting, and even the 2016, New York bombing where the suspect's father called the FBI to report that his child was planning to kill people and nothing was done. Long-term solutions need to be developed, but in the meantime, the discussion today, tomorrow, and the next day needs to be about how we can prevent or lessen the likelihood that a mass casualty, violent event can occur. This will require the implementation of mandatory controls/solutions that can be deployed today and tomorrow, not in 3 years.

The close-knit community of Parkland, FL has been terrorized and forever changed. There is no resolution for those families who lost loved ones or those students and teachers who survived the shooting. The most aggravating thing about the Parkland, FL massacre is that for one more time, again it is too late. It did not matter how much training was done or how many drills were conducted, in this instance, it did not help.

In January 23, 2018, in Kentucky at Marshall County High School, the shooter Gabe Parker, age 16, considered his active shooter incident as an experiment to see how the police and students would react. He brought a gun and knife into the school, killed 2 and injured about 14. We need to prevent guns from getting into the schools.

Conclusion

Long-term solutions are a partial answer and we say this because this is not a single-answer issue. It is a multi-answer and multisolution issue that cannot be fixed overnight. The safety of the students, faculty, and staff in our schools is of paramount importance. We need to keep everyone safe and learn how to prevent these senseless acts of violence from occurring. We are at a point maybe social workers and clinical psychologist maybe needed in all school districts.

Let us look at this issue like we are playing a football game. There is offense and defense and both sides make changes and adjust their strategies as their opponent does. We need to not only think one play ahead but several plays ahead by being proactive. If an active shooter changes his/her offense tactics, we must change our defense tactics. We are not trying to make light of the seriousness of active shooters but instead use this sports analogy to initiate a common-sense discussion about solutions. The strategy is plan ahead, have security policies and procedures in places that are consistently followed, implement target-hardening security measures, conduct training and drills, and consistently work not only to reduce the likelihood of an active shooter incident but to reduce fear and improve quality of life. Safety is our touchdown.

Run, hide, and fight

The following 10 points were put together by Dr. Michael Fagel on what to do in the event of an active shooter incident in your schools. Dr. Fagel strongly believes all school now to have risk assessments, natural surveillance and tight access controls in place. “Don’t make it easy for individuals to access on to your property,” he said.

1. Be aware of your surroundings at all times
2. Silence your cell phone
3. Listen for commands, information
4. Be prepared to take action based on information received
5. Inform others and communicate safely
6. Secure your area, block doors, tie door handles with belts, category 5 cable anything to keep door from opening, use the desks and chairs. Do something to block entrance.
7. If assailant enters, interfere with their concentration, counter by having something to throw or drop, dropping or tossing a books, tossing a water bottle, cell phone, throwing a stapler or something to make assailant duck or break concentration
8. Rush the attacker as a group
9. Do not do nothing at all
10. Take the earbuds out and pay attention

Emerging trends

Active shooter/hostile event preparedness and response

By the numbers:

- Active shooter events in the United States: 2000–13
- 160 Incidents
- Combined 1043 killed and wounded, not including shooter(s)
- 486 Killed
- 557 Wounded
- Active shooter events in the United States: 2014 and 2015
- 40 Incidents
- Combined 231 killed and wounded, not including shooter(s)
- 92 Killed
- 139 Wounded
- Shooter events occurring with greater frequency and loss
- Three active shooter events, over the course of less than 17 months, produced more than 50% of the casualties reported from 2000 to 2013.
- 49 Dead, 58 wounded
- Las Vegas, Nevada (October 1, 2017): 59 dead, 441 wounded
- Sutherland Springs, Texas (November 5, 2017): 27 dead, 20 wounded
- Two of the deadliest tragedies on record happened within 5 weeks of each other.

It is not stopping nor is it slowing down 2018 will be a record year.

Appendix 1: A look at solutions to active shooter part two

Lawrence J. Fennelly, Marianna Perry, Thomas Norman

Introduction

It doesn't matter if you're in a coffee shop, a nightclub, a place of worship, a school or corporate America, ninety-nine percent of the concepts discussed here will apply to your situation. As a means of introduction, this is a topic we have researched for several years. An important part of our research included a review of past response procedures and post-incident recovery from active shooter incidents. We realize your organization *wants* to ensure the safety of employees and property and everything you need to change or purchase to accomplish this cannot be done immediately. The reality is that we all have to operate within budget constraints and follow bureaucratic procedures. For these reasons, we suggest you consider developing a Five-Year Security Plan and create a list of needed changes and prioritize those changes. Your list of needed changes will be taken from the Security Assessment that a qualified security professional completes of your property. Discuss the recommendations with the security professional and get their input about the hierarchy of security procedures or components to put in place. In other words, what you will do, when. We recommend that you begin your Plan with the installation of LED lighting which is "green" and also energy efficient. With the electrical energy savings, you will have additional money in the budget for more security enhancements. Of course, if you already have LED lighting, you will move to the next item on your Five-Year Security Plan.

Twelve no-cost or low-cost security improvements that you can make fairly quickly are:

1. Develop natural access control and open lines- of-sight to ensure natural surveillance around the perimeter of your property and also around all structures.
2. A vestibule entrance makes an excellent second layer for your security plan when access to building entry doors are controlled by authorized staff.
3. Reduce the number of doors being used by following the philosophy of "few entrances, many exits" and install prop or local audible alarms if a door is opened or propped open.
4. Develop common sense security policies and procedures that include a training and awareness program. All aspects of the security policies and procedures require not just management approval, but also management participation. This program needs to be reviewed regularly and evaluated for updates annually.
5. Set up a Mass Notification Program that can be integrated/interfaced with your existing telephone and communications systems. Ensure there is communication with all buildings and outside areas. Conduct routine tests of your system to ensure operability and make sure to include employee training. Assign rally points for evacuations and procedures for sheltering in place. Building wardens should be assigned to account for all employees, staff, visitors and contractors.
6. Implement a Maintenance/Image Program and do not allow for or provides for immediate correction of any form of vandalism, inadequate maintenance, defacement of property or deterioration on or about your property. Do your homework and educate yourself about the Broken Windows Theory.[12] The Broken Windows model was first discussed in an article written by George L. Wilson and James Q. Kelling in 1982. Basically, the Model focuses on the importance of disorder (or broken windows) in generating and leading to more serious crime. Even though disorder is not directly linked to serious crime, it leads to increased fear and withdrawal from the legitimate users of the property which may allow more serious crime problems in the area because there is less informal social control.
7. In May of 2018, the National Fire Protection Association (NFPA) released NFPA 3000™ (PS), Standard for an Active Shooter / Hostile Event Response (ASHER) Program to help communities holistically deal with the increasing number of mass casualty incidents that continue to occur throughout the world.[13] NFPA 3000 provides unified planning, response and recovery guidance, as well as civilian and responder safety considerations. Educate yourself about NFPA 3000 and incorporate it into your emergency procedures and training your employees as a part of your response plan.

12. What is broken windows policing? From: <https://cebcp.org/evidence-based-policing/what-works-in-policing/research-evidence-review/broken-windows-policing/> (Retrieved 12.05.18.).

13. NFPA releases the world's first active shooter/hostile event standard with guidance on whole community planning, response, and recovery. From: <https://www.nfpa.org/News-and-Research/News-and-media/Press-Room/News-releases/2018/NFPA-releases-the-worlds-first-active-shooter-hostile-event-standard> (Retrieved 12.05.18.).

8. Invite local law enforcement, the local fire department and local emergency medical services to your property for a walk-through and get their input about response and recovery for your emergency response plan. Give them paper and electronic blue prints/diagram of your property and all building. Consider letting local law enforcement use your property (during non-working hours) for training exercises. Not only will you will be a good community partner by supporting law enforcement, but they will also be familiar with your property if there is an incident.
9. Conduct fire drills, severe weather drills, evacuation exercises and shelter-in-place exercises so everyone will know the proper procedures - practice and practice.
10. Educate yourself about the concept of layered security and develop a strong focus on deterrents and traditional security countermeasures, such as electronic & mechanical locking devices, fencing, video surveillance and intrusion detection systems.
11. A current architectural trend is for more high-performance glass which will allow more natural light into buildings. This will reduce your energy consumption and save on lighting costs. When replacing traditional glass with high-performance glass, consider installing "unbreakable" glass which may be either glass or polycarbonate. Many types are also bullet-resistant and may be considered one layer in your security program.
12. Remember the old saying "If You See Something - Say Something?"™[14] Make this mantra an important educational and awareness building component of your security program. Dr. Jennifer Hesterman wrote, *Soft Target Hardening: Protecting People from Attack* (CRC Press, second edition 2019) and in her book, Dr. Hesterman asks the question, "What is the cost of doing nothing?" Answer this same question about your organization as you make a pitch to the C-Suite for more money to enhance security measures. We suggest you also look for ways to obtain a return on your investment (ROI.) For example, think about the ROI for installing cost-effective LED lighting.

We have prepared a list of ROI ideas for your consideration:

- Reduce energy consumption
- Replacement of old boilers
- Replacement of old air conditioner units
- Switch to using LED bulbs, re-lamp every unit
- Reduce use of cooling systems
- Replace old appliances and computer monitors with energy-efficient units
- Control swimming pool operation
- Replace old pumps
- Reduce 80-ton HVAC with a 40-ton unit
- Add another 40-ton for HVAC upgrade
- Solar windows transformed into sun-powered heaters
- More natural sunlight
- Daylight sensors that adjust to all levels
- Recycle paper, cans, bottles, cardboard, plastic and wooden pallets
- Upgrade existing chillers and cooling towers with a new heat recovery chiller
- Pump and hydroponics systems modification
- Insulation of all steam valves and fittings
- Modernize power plant and infrastructure upgrades
- Install solar energy systems
- Sensors can be effective to control temperature
- Install indoor environmental-quality low-glare ambient lighting
- Solar powered systems provide electricity is a growing concept
- Use solar-powered cameras and lighting
- Consider an audit of your waste management output
- In residential and commercial settings, consider a use of low-flow shower heads
- Implement an effective and efficient maintenance program
- Consider geothermal-hybrid heat pumps
- Consider utilizing wind energy and wind power

14. If you see something say something. From: <https://www.dhs.gov/see-something-say-something> (Retrieved 12.05.18.).

- Use smart plug electrical outlet strips
- Install outdoor, LED wall-pack lighting with built-in with motion detectors
- A reflective roof will cool down a building by 20%
- Restrooms can save water four ways: faucets, urinals, toilets and leaky units
- Install fans for cooling

Coverage for Events

We recently attended a high school graduation event in Boston, MA. The day before the graduation ceremony, a person was stopped as they attempted to enter the building with two, concealed 38 caliber handguns. His explanation was that he had the guns to protect a family member. He was arrested. During the ceremony, we saw a maintenance man frantically working on the PA system, but there was no sense of security – no security officers and no teachers or parents at the doors – nothing. In light of the recent shooting incidents, this is amazing.

We must help people become proactive and get away from the, "it won't happen" here mentality.

There could have been a very simple, common-sense solution to this ... parents could have been asked or volunteered to be a presence at the entry doors. We MUST learn to harden our soft targets by layered security and a visible security presence.

The following 12-point plan has some suggestions for you to consider:

1. Develop a plan and train your people about good security principles and how to identify suspicious individuals and behavior.
2. Increase your situational awareness program.
3. Work with your internal community and your external community (those inside your organization and those outside).
4. Develop an open, but secured complex.
5. Reduce the opportunity and reduce the likelihood of being a potential target. The key word here is very simple. It's OPPORTUNITY. None of live in a house with unlocked doors when no one is home and the windows are not left open wide when we're gone. Retail stores don't keep their rear doors unlocked and left wide open. The only think you can control is opportunity, so think like a criminal and harden your targets.
6. Conduct table-top exercises with your community partner and develop a strong set of security policies and procedures.
7. Have a Risk Assessment and Risk Analysis conducted of your complex. We challenge you to visit your complex some Sunday when it is closed. Think like a thief who wants to break into your facility. How would you get in?
8. Have a complete background check completed on of all your employees and staff. The results may surprise you.
9. Prioritize your developed plan, which consists of training, and the installation of physical security devices.
10. Be aware of the person who says "It won't happen to us" or "We are safe and secured already" or "We don't have the money." We have listed things that need to be done that are low-cost or no-cost, plus we've given you tips on how to save money.
11. Check with your local Homeland Security Officer and ask for assistance and training material. Establish a community connection for training and planning table top excises.
12. Develop an Emergency Management Plan. Implement it and test it. Creative coping is the trend, not creative panic.

NFPA 3000

What You Need to Know About NFPA 3000:

As more hostile events continue to occur around the world, it is critical for first responders, emergency personnel, facility managers, hospital officials, community members, and others to have the information they need to be prepared when attacks occur. NFPA® has developed a new standard – NFPA 3000, which is the Standard for Preparedness and Response to Active Shooter and/or Hostile Events – to address that need.

The purpose of NFPA 3000 is to identify the minimum program elements necessary for organizing, managing, and sustaining an active shooter and/or hostile event response program and to reduce or eliminate the risks, effect, and impact on an organization or community affected by these events.

NFPA addresses areas:

- Risk assessment
- Planning
- Resource management
- Organizational deployment
- Incident management
- Facility readiness
- Finance
- Communications
- Competencies for law enforcement
- Competencies for fire and EMS
- Personal protective equipment
- Training
- Community education
- Information sharing
- Readiness of receiving hospitals
- Recovery

Appendix 2: Saving a life, it's in your hands

Michael J. Fagel, Greg Benson

First aid training for everyone can save lives. The Protection officers must learn how to render lifesaving immediate first aid measures in a crisis.

The rules of engagement have changed, and, we Must train AND Educate our protection officers for an increasingly important role in today's era of mass casualty incidents. Training for "Stopping the Bleeding" is a critical first step in this effort.

There are numerous campaigns about stopping the immediate bleeding before trained technical EMT's responders arrive. During an emergent crisis, the victims need our help and, sadly may not survive without it.

Just look at this sobering event: TSA Officer Gerardo Hernandez bled to death, while waiting 33 minutes to be wheeled into an ambulance. Reports indicate that Paramedics were kept away from the scene by law enforcement due to the scene being unsafe or "hot" (November 2013).

It is our role to be prepared and have the necessary lifesaving equipment at our fingertips. When I was in uniform, I carried a small pack commonly called an IPOK (Individual Patrol Officer Kit) along with 2 CAT tourniquets.

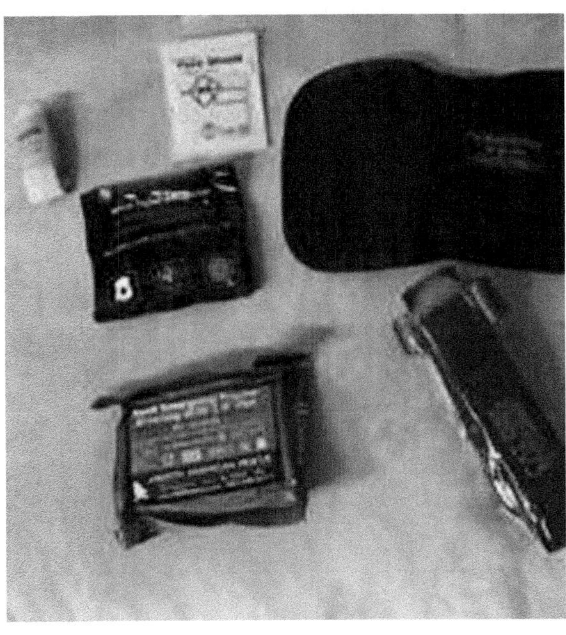

IPOK KIT (Photo by Mike Fagel) (Available from numerous vendors)

I had 3 devices I could apply to myself or have one to throw to another individual to apply. I have trained hundreds of public safety personnel in this life saving skill set you can carry with you at all times. You can learn how to utilize these critical tools by partaking in a "Stop the Bleed" campaign training, your local Trauma Hospital team, or Fire-Rescue-EMS may be able to assist you.

It is not "someone else's job, it's YOUR job to learn this lifesaving skill. The life you save may be your own. As an instructor for several of the coalitions listed below:

1. Add these critical lifesaving skills to your tool belt, at work, at home, everywhere you go.
2. Be prepared.
3. Safety is in YOUR hands.

GET THE FACTS

How Much Do You Know about Tourniquets?

Think you know all there is to know about tourniquets? Take this quick quiz and see just how much you know. Be sure to challenge your friends' knowledge while you are at it, and share this quiz on social media.

First,[15] Apply pressure! Remember, pressure stops the bleeding. Here is how it works, Just apply continuous pressure until bleeding stops. Q. How Long? A. There is no definite amount of time. Use your hands to apply a firm but steady amount of pressure until the bleed stops. As a rule you should hold pressure for at least 5 minutes before looking at the wound. If the bleeding does not stop, call 911 and continuing applying pressure until medical help arrives.

If you can, try to ensure the injured person is on a firm surface. That way, when you apply force to the bleeding, you are pressing into something. Using ? If you have gauze available, use that. If not, use whatever we you have available, such as a shirt, newspaper or your hand.

Then continue applying pressure until medical help arrives.

Finally

So far approx 275 City of Victorville CA, employees have been trained in Stop the Bleed. Community groups are next. Our goal is 1000 by year end (2018).

For additional information, visit the following websites:

www.Aurorasafety.com

https://www.dhs.gov/stopthebleed

http://stopthebleedingcoalition.org/

https://www.dhs.gov/stb-learn-how-stop-bleed

https://www.bleedingcontrol.org/

https://www.nsc.org/safety-training/first-aid/courses/emergency-medical-response

15. https://www.bleedingcontrol.org/.

Chapter 17

Neighborhood Watch guidelines for the 21st century

Marianna A. Perry
Security Consultant

Scottish Government's Building Safer Communities Programme (BSC) is a collaborative partnership with local and national partners and communities, including Neighbourhood Watch Scotland, to drive forward and Champion Community Safety.

Scottish Government's Building Safer Communities Programme June 1, 2018.[1]

Introduction

At National Crime Prevention Institute (NCPI) one of the things we are doing is going back to basics in promoting Neighborhood Watch and Operation Identification by working with neighborhood and community leaders. We have conducted training and assessment programs and are involving as many people as possible from a particular neighborhood such as business owners, the church community, police department community resource officers, planning and zoning committees, code enforcement, change makers, public housing residents, city council members, and, of course, the residents. We actually worked under grant funds secured by the local health department to help provide a healthy community with a higher quality of life as it relates to crime, fear of crime, violence prevention, outdoor physical activity, and access to services. As a part of this process, we are gathering crime stats, calls for service, census data, and other demographic information for the neighborhood. Our goal is to educate the community with an on-site training program on crime prevention, physical security, and crime prevention through environmental design and then follow up with a neighborhood assessment that is completed by the instructor(s). A formal written report with recommendations is then prepared and incorporated into the current initiatives for the neighborhood. This plan incorporates well into community policing concepts in terms of the community coming together for problem-solving results.[2]

Ten secrets of Neighborhood Watch are as follows:

1. *Awareness and knowledge strategies are number one.* Inform your community as to what crime prevention is, how it works, how to be proactive. What is Neighborhood Watch? What can citizens/employees do and what is available to them?
2. *Communication.* We are living in the electronic era: e-mails, tweeters, LinkedIn, Facebook, YouTube, cell phones, texting, radio public services spots, posters, chain calling, brochures and community newspapers, etc. just to name a few. Verbal communication is also very important. The facilitator or practitioner should completely explain the program and objectives to his/her community.
3. *Knowledge.* The awareness campaign, although important, opens the door to private citizen participation. A public awareness campaign results in widespread recognition of crime prevention. This will trigger awareness in target

1. https://www.neighbourhoodwatchscotland.co.uk/news
2. Awareness and knowledge strategies are reprinted with permission from National Crime Prevention Institute. Understanding Crime Prevention, second ed. Butterworth-Heinemann, Boston, MA. Available from: www.bh.com, copyright 2001. In addition, sections of the material were originally compiled by Crime Prevention Officer Robert Hanna, Quincy Police Dept. (retired). In 2010 sections of this material were used in a YouTube presentation for ASIS International for the Crime Prevention Council by Marianne Perry CPP and Lawrence J. Fennelly.

Handbook of Loss Prevention and Crime Prevention. DOI: https://doi.org/10.1016/B978-0-12-817273-5.00017-X

hardening, security surveys of a complex, and the turning on of lights and added patrol. Some police departments offer training resulting into a 40-hour program. So look into this. Contact your chief of police as a neighborhood group.

4. *Neighborhood Watch guidelines.* Citizens should call the police immediately about any and all suspicious activity. They should not have to worry about "bothering" the police because this is what they are for, even if the suspicious activity was unfounded. So, what is suspicious activity?
   a. a stranger entering a neighbor's house or property
   b. you hear a scream for help
   c. strangers selling merchandise out of their trunk
   d. the sound of breaking glass
   e. seeing the same car driving around the neighborhood in circles
   f. individuals lecturing or hanging around serving as lookouts
5. *Watchers can reduce crime.* How? By reducing the opportunity to commit a crime and acting as extra eyes and ears for law enforcement.
6. *Avoiding injuries.* Watchers must be told in their training to keep alert for the unexpected. Yell and scream to attract attention. Even blow a whistle.
7. *The community.* Whether it is called Neighborhood Watch, Office Watch, Business Watch, or Laboratory Watch, the concepts and methods are all the same. Know what your community is.
8. *Involvement.* Getting involved in your community is the first step. Partner with police and vendors in the community and everyone involved will reduce crime and even move it to another location.
9. *Education of your watchers.* Consider the following:
   a. residential burglar alarms;
   b. educate small business owners in how they should confront a robber or shoplifter;
   c. lights, locks, cameras, and alarms; and
   d. how to become "street smart."
10. *Crime characteristics.* Every neighborhood has its own characteristics. Learn what those characteristics are. The practitioner must be prepared to help those ready and willing to start taking action. For the individual, this means providing crime risk management guidance and security surveys. For the citizen group or civic group, it means providing accurate information on subjects of interest to members. A business group, for example, might be primarily interested in commercial burglary or robbery prevention and asset protection. A neighborhood group might be interested in preventing street crime. Women's and senior citizens' groups may be interested in reducing crime risk from assault, purse snatching, fraud, and so on. Each special group has a special need.

The practitioner

The practitioner must be prepared to respond quickly and skillfully to all public requests for assistance, because this is how he or she establishes a record of accomplishment or high-quality client service. Such service delivery may mean working overtime; citizen groups seldom meet during the normal business days. Nevertheless, the dedicated practitioner will be prepared to sacrifice his or her own convenience, because the ultimate success of citizen participation strategies depends on a high-quality response by the practitioner at this stage.

The primary focus of the practitioner at this citizen knowledge-developing stage is to further educate those who have expressed preliminary interest and further attract those who, by virtue of position with the community, need to be involved.

The practitioner, in meeting these knowledge needs, sets the stage for additional knowledge delivery services, because "satisfied customers" create other clients. If one women's group hears an interesting talk on rape prevention, the word will spread and other groups will want to follow suit. This natural process builds demand for additional services.

Thus the practitioner builds a wider clientele through delivery of quality services and "word-of-mouth" promotion of those services. This domino effect of the knowledge-building strategy is to be both desired and expected. The practitioner should not hesitate to use volunteers to share and extend the workload. Interested persons can and should be trained to help in the knowledge-spreading process. Citizen-volunteer spokespeople, although their total knowledge of crime prevention is more limited than that of the practitioner, are sometimes more effective in educating colleagues and social peers than the practitioner.

It is also essential at this stage that the practitioner reaches out to provide knowledge to a variety of community officials, starting with members of law enforcement agencies and extending to elected and appointed officials throughout government. These are the people who will later provide the political, economic, and direct service support of the comprehensive crime prevention program; they must become involved at the knowledge stage if they are to support the program in the action stages.

How to report

The police need accurate information as quickly as possible about a suspicious activity or crime in progress. The caller should

- give his or her name and identify himself or herself as a member of a watch group;
- describe the event in as brief a manner as possible: where, when, how, and who did it;
- tell if the crime is in progress or has occurred;
- describe the suspect—sex, race, age, height, weight, hair color, clothing, accent, beard or moustache, and distinctive characteristics or clothing; and
- describe the vehicle if one was involved—color, make, model, year, license plate, special markings, dents, and which way it went.

How to avoid becoming the victim of an attacker

The following recommendations help citizens avoid becoming victims:

1. Keep alert for the unexpected. While walking, pay attention to what is going on.
2. Take no unnecessary chances.
   a. Walk confidently, know where you are going.
   b. Be extra alert, know who and what are around you at all times.
   c. Whenever possible, walk with another person.
   d. Stay near people. Walking in deserted areas invites trouble.
   e. Stay in well-lit areas.
   f. Avoid shortcuts.
3. If you are followed, you should do the following:
   a. Cross the street.
   b. Reverse direction.
   c. Go to a business that is open and ask for help.
   d. In a residential area, go to a home and ask for help.
   e. Attract attention: yell, scream, and flag down a passing car. You may also carry a whistle and blow it to attract attention.
   f. Act suspicious. Keep looking back at the persons following you to let that person know you cannot be taken by surprise.
4. If you are attacked, you should do the following:
   a. Yell and scream to attract attention and scare your attacker off.
   b. Swing an umbrella, briefcase, or anything you have in your hand at the attacker's head.
   c. Make a scene. Take your attacker by surprise.
   d. Jab the attacker with your elbow.
   e. Twist your body to break free from the attacker's hold.
   f. Bite the attacker hard.
   g. Scratch the attacker's face with your fingernails.
   h. Bend the attacker's finger back.
   i. Kick the attacker with the toe of your shoe.
   j. Punch the attacker in unprotected areas.
   k. Get away from the attacker.
5. Get a description of your attacker. Try to remember
   a. height;
   b. weight;
   c. age;
   d. skin tone;

e. hair color;
f. eye color;
g. color and type of clothes;
h. any jewelry the attacker may be wearing;
i. any scars, tattoos, or disabilities the attacker may have;
j. any odor you may detect about the attacker's person, such as alcohol, drugs, and/or cologne;
k. anything of which you were suspicious of prior to the attack, such as a motor vehicle that may have passed you several times or someone who may have been watching you;
l. anything the attacker may say to you and whether the attacker had an accent; and
m. a description of any weapon used.

6. Carrying a weapon is discouraged unless you are thoroughly trained in its use and licensed to carry it. Two things to remember:
   a. Anything you use as a weapon can also be taken from you and used against you.
   b. You would be better off using the time that it would take getting a weapon out to get out of the situation or attract attention. An umbrella is a good weapon to have in your hand and be ready to use in case of attack.
7. What about self-defense? Karate, judo, and other martial arts can improve your self-defense skills, but you must remember that it takes years of practice to become good at these skills.

Above all, the victim should report anything suspicious to the police department immediately. Following these suggestions diminishes the chance of becoming the victim of an attacker.

Safety checklist for apartments

Look at the building

- Is there some kind of control over who enters and leaves the building?
- Are entrances, parking areas, hallways, stairways, and laundry rooms well lighted?
- Are fire stairs locked from the stairwell side?
- Are laundry rooms and storage areas kept locked?
- Are there mailboxes in a well-traveled area? Do they have good locks?
- Have any apartments been burglarized recently? If so, how did the thieves get in?

Look at the apartment

- Does the entry door have a dead bolt lock and a peephole?
- Are sliding glass doors leading to balconies secured by pins in the frame or a wooden rod in the track?
- Does the manager permit tenants to change locks when they move in?
- Does the tenant leave a radio playing and a light on while out?
- Does the tenant alert neighbors or their building manager when on a trip or vacation?

Securing the apartment or condominium

The following tips can make a home more burglary resistant:

- All exterior doors should be checked for adequate security.
- After moving in, ask the management to have a licensed locksmith rekey all exterior door locks.
- Dead bolt locks should be installed on exterior doors. Do not give master keys to these locks to management, because that defeats their purpose. If necessary, keys in sealed envelopes should be given to managers for emergency use only.
- Secure all sliding glass doors and windows regardless of which floor the apartment is on.
- Doors and windows should always be locked when the tenant leaves, even if just for a few minutes.
- Demand adequate lighting for stairwells, laundry rooms, parking lots, and the building's exterior.
- Have shrubs trimmed so they cannot conceal burglars or attackers.
- When taking vacations or trips, tenants should tell trusted neighbors of plans and where to reach them. Have newspapers and mail picked up. Stop other deliveries.

- Be cautious of door-to-door solicitors who want to give something for nothing. Never let a stranger into the home.
- Women living alone should not use their first initial and last name on mailboxes and telephone listings. Using a listing such as "The Smith Family" gives a potential thief the idea that more than one person lives at this address.
- Elevators are potential places for assault. If the building has an elevator, make sure the ground floor elevator is well lighted and visible from the street or manager's office. Before entering an elevator, see who is already onboard. Do not get on if a person already on looks suspicious.

Residential burglar alarms

Residential burglar alarms are not universal solutions to home burglary. They are no substitute for locked doors and windows or for precautions the police department can suggest.

It may be appropriate to obtain alarm protection if the person lives in an isolated area, is absent from home for considerable periods of time, or keeps many valuables in the home (a practice that is not recommended).

The purpose of an alarm system is to deter potential intruders (most burglars would reconsider forced entry if they knew an alarm system was in operation) and alert police to apprehend the burglar.

To accomplish these objectives, alarms must complete an operation cycle consisting of sensing, signaling, and response. Sensing and signaling are mechanical aspects of the alarm system, whereas response involves human interaction with the system.

The sensing cycle involves a series of electronic components designed to establish a secure perimeter, space, or point. The alarm emits a signal if an intruder enters the space. The signal can either sound at the site (local alarm), at some remote location, or both. Who receives the alarm signal and the expected response are important design considerations. Alarms must have an on-site signal if they are to alert occupants.

If a house is in an isolated area, it makes little sense to depend solely on a local alarm to alert neighbors or scare off the intruder. In this case a remote signal is also needed. The remote signal alarm is constantly monitored. Any time the alarm is activated, the police respond.

The most dependable alarm system is operated on household power with emergency battery power. It is a good idea to have at least one smoke detector built into an alarm system. Smoke is the primary killer in a fire, and smoke detectors placed in hallways between bedrooms can save lives. Check to see whether the community *requires* smoke detectors in homes and apartments.

Get to know your neighbors and work together

- Think about organizing an apartment watch so that neighbors can look out for each other.
- In large complexes and buildings, consider volunteer tenant patrols to watch for crime in and around the building, provide escort services for the elderly and people who may be out at night, or sit in the lobby to monitor people who may be out at night and people entering the building. Teenagers can be great resource for these efforts.
- Work to ensure that management provides adequate building security.
- If someone has been the victim of a crime, be a good neighbor. Lend an ear and lead the victim to others who can help.

Robbery prevention—tips for small business

Businesses are robbed 10 times more often than individuals, but common sense can reduce the chance of becoming a victim as well as the amount of money lost if robbed. The following are some simple tips to prevent robbery at a business.

Cash

- Keep small amounts on hand and advertise that fact.
- Make frequent bank deposits.
- Have a drop safe or time delay safe.
- Vary your deposit times and route.
- Count your cash in a private area.

Lights, locks, and alarms

- Have exterior and interior lighting that allows visibility into the store from the street.
- Have an emergency alarm system and test it occasionally to make sure it works.
- Encourage a buddy system signal with a neighboring store in case a suspicious person enters.
- Keep rarely used doors and windows locked at all times.
- Use mirrors, cameras, or one-way glass to observe all areas of store.
- Employees
  - have more than one person who can open and close the store;
  - carefully screen employees before hiring. Instruct employees to call the police about any suspicious person who may be hanging around the store; and
  - train your employees how to effectively handle and report a robbery situation.
- Also
  - Arrange the stock to allow clear visibility in the store.
  - Set up a signal with the police patrol officer in case of problems.
  - Arrange for a security survey with the local police department or security consultant.

If confronted by a robber

Following are some tips for the small business owner confronted by a robber:

- Stay as calm as possible. Try not to panic or show any sign of anger or confusion.
- Consider your well-being and that of your employees as the highest priority.
- Do not escalate the incident into a violent confrontation in which someone may be injured or killed.
- Make a conscious effort to get an accurate description of the robber(s)—approximate age, height, weight, type, and color of clothing. After the robber leaves, call the police immediately.

Following these tips reduces the chances of robbery and the chance of injury during a robbery.

Burglary prevention—tips for small business

Burglary is a property crime that occurs when the business is closed. The burglar may enter through any opening (door, window, air-conditioning duct, and skylight) or even create one through an interior shared wall or outside wall. The risk should be reduced as much as possible. Burglary is a crime of opportunity that can be prevented.

Surveillance and security are critical

- Install bright interior and exterior lighting to make all openings visible from both the outside and inside of the store.
- Purchase high-quality door locks and use them. Grilles and storefront gates delay entry. Use an Underwriters Laboratories listed money safe, bolted to the floor, and visible from the street.
- Know who has a key and restrict access to the front door. Rekey the lock if a once-trusted employee is discharged for cause. Rekey locks annually if you have a high turnover of employees. Consider an access control system rather than keys.
- Install a good quality alarm system to detect unauthorized entry. Check with the Chamber of Commerce and law enforcement people before making this investment.
- Consider burglar-resistant glass in accessible areas. Unbreakable polycarbonate may work even better, particularly if you have high-value items in window displays.
- Keep areas around the store clean to aid visibility. Display the most valuable articles near the center of the store to force a burglar to take the longest possible escape route. Keep merchandise displays organized to allow maximum visibility throughout the store. Check closets and restrooms before locking up—no "visitor" should be able to stay inside the store after closing hours. These techniques certainly diminish the chance of becoming a victim of burglary.
- Security surveillance system (closed-circuit television), which basically consists of a specific type of camera, monitor, time-lapse record, and high-grade tape, has frequently been a tool for security and law enforcement when the equipment has recorded criminal in the act of or about to commit a crime.

Businesses can reduce their vulnerability to crime in many ways. Measures such as locks, alarms, and good lighting make any establishment a less attractive target for criminals. A major ally is the local police department; its officers can conduct a free security survey and give advice on alarm systems and other security devices. Community service and involvement are important safeguards against crime. Customers and neighbors who view a business as a valued resource to the community watch out for its property and employees.

Employees and crime

Employees can help a business be profitable or hurt it through waste, inattention to customers, or stealing. The business owner sets the example for honesty and develops clear policies regarding security and theft.

- Develop and advise all employees of inventory control procedures. All merchandise entering and exiting the premises should be accounted for.
- Screen employees carefully before hiring them. Check their backgrounds to be sure they have not been fired for behavior you find dangerous or unacceptable. A Polaroid photo helps police in any investigation that involves a dishonest employee.
- Train employees in proper cash handing and security measures. Set policy regarding cash on hand and stick to it.
- Research shows that employees steal from businesses that are impersonal and lack clear policies. Show employees you care about them and their property.
- Provide a clean orderly work environment with secure places for employees' personal property. A satisfied employee can be the first line of defense against crime in a business.

How to put burglars out of business, the rest of the story

How to make a business uninviting to a burglar and hard to enter was just discussed. We now discuss other methods of discouraging burglars.

- *Make it hard to find or remove valuable items.* Safes and cash registers should be clearly visible from the street. Leave the cash drawer open and empty after business hours. The safe should be of good quality and firmly anchored. Lock the firm's check protector and blank checks in the safe. Avoid having large amounts of cash on the premises. Make bank deposits at varying times during the day. If good lighting does not scare a burglar, it will make it harder to go unnoticed while working inside or outside the building. If possible, hide or lock in the safe high-value items (such as expensive rings or watches), which would be especially attractive to a thief.
- *Make it likely the thief will get caught.* Consider installing a burglar alarm system. They range from the simple, inexpensive type that merely makes a noise in the building to the complex, expensive, silent type tied into a police station or security agency. What kind you need depends on several factors: how likely it is that a thief would be detected without one, how far the business is from a police station, how the system's cost compares with the cost of the goods to be protected.
- *Get a system that either monitors itself or can be easily checked to make sure it is in good operating condition.* Shop carefully and buy from a reputable company. A good alarm system will probably get the owner a discount on business insurance.
- *In lieu of (or in addition to) an alarm system, hire a security guard or security service to patrol the business at night.* If not, make sure someone (either the owner or an employee) is responsible for checking security of the business before closing time.
- *Record all serial numbers of large-denomination bills.* Also, a small amount of marked "bait" money may help police trace a thief. Try to keep a good inventory of the stock, including serial numbers of valuable goods and theft-prone items and equipment. This helps police trace stolen goods and helps the owner in filing an insurance claim.
- If the business becomes a burglary victim, the owner should cooperate with the police, including pressing charges if they catch a suspect and have evidence to convict.

The first initials of the following items sum up its message—lock it up.

*L*ocks for doors should be the dead bolt type. Doors should be heavy and solid. Protect windows with grillwork or heavy-duty screen.

*O*penings other than doors and windows, such as skylights and ventilators, should be protected. Fences should be high, sturdy, and topped with barbwire.

*C*over is something burglars must not have. Adequate lighting—inside and outside—is a must. Do not stack boxes or leave a vehicle parked next to the building.

*K*eep valuable items out of display windows at night. Hide them or lock them in a safe.

*I*nsurance on the business is something the owner must not be without. How good security is has a bearing on the premium.

*T*rip up a thief by installing an effective alarm system, leaving the cash register drawer open and empty, anchoring safes firmly, and recording serial numbers of large bills.

*U*nderstand the importance of checking out potential employees before hiring. Make one person responsible for checking security before closing.

*P*rotect this business and others by working to improve the effectiveness of crime prevention in the community.

Suspicious situations to report

Suspicious vehicles

The following situations involving vehicles should be reported to the police:

1. Any vehicle moving slowly and without lights or following a course that appears aimless or repetitive should be considered suspicious. Occupants might be "casing" the area for places to rob or burglarize. Vehicles acting like this around schools, parks, or playgrounds should be considered suspicious and reported to police. These individuals could be drug dealers or sex offenders.
2. Parked vehicles with one or more persons inside should be considered suspicious, particularly if they are observed at an unusual hour. These individuals could be waiting for other burglars.
3. Vehicles being loaded with valuables are suspicious if parked in front of a closed business or unoccupied residence. A burglar may go to the trouble of placing signs on the vehicle to make it appear legitimate.
4. Apparent business transactions conducted from a vehicle should be considered suspicious, more so if the vehicle is parked around schools or parks. The occupants could be drug dealers.
5. Anyone being forced into a vehicle could be a victim of kidnaping, rape, or hijacking; call police immediately.
6. Abandoned vehicles parked on a block could be stolen cars.
7. While most, if not all, of these suspicious situations could have innocent explanations, the police would rather investigate a suspicious situation than be called when it is too late. The call could save a life, prevent an injury, or stop a criminal act.

What to report

- *Description of persons*: Clothing, age, race, sex, height and weight (approximately), any unique characteristics such as scars, tattoos, jewelry.
- *Description of vehicle*: Make, model, body style (two doors, four doors, station wagon, and truck), license plate number, and direction of travel.
- *Get as much information as possible and report it to the police immediately*: Call 911 or the local police number. The caller is not required to identify himself or herself. The sooner the call is placed, the sooner the police catch the offender.

Additional suspicious situations to report

The following are some examples of situations involving people to report to the police:

1. Someone going door-to-door in a neighborhood. If, after a few houses are visited, one or more of the persons tries a door to see if it is locked or enters a backyard, it could be a burglar. Such action is even more suspicious if one person remains in the front when this occurs or a car follows a few houses away.
2. Someone waiting in front of a house that is unoccupied or parked in front of a business that is closed.
3. Anyone using force to gain entrance to or tamper with a residence, business, or vehicle.
4. A person running, especially if carrying something of value. This could be a burglar leaving the scene of a crime.
5. Carrying of property could be suspicious too, if it is at an unusual place or the property is not packed as if just purchased.

6. A person exhibiting unusual mental or physical symptoms. The person may be injured or under the influence of drugs or alcohol and need medical or psychiatric help.
7. Many people coming and going from a particular residence. This is not necessarily a suspicious circumstance unless it occurs on a daily or regular basis, particularly at unusual hours. It could be the scene of drug activity or a fencing operation to move stolen property.

Vehicle theft—a big problem

Over 1 million vehicles (cars, trucks, buses, motorcycles, and trailers) are stolen every year. In 2010 2.2 million thefts of contents and almost 1.9 million thefts of accessories were taken from motor vehicles. The recovery rate for stolen motor vehicles in 2010 was about 70%.

In the time it takes to read this section, nine cars will be stolen. The following steps can be taken to protect a vehicle:

- Lock the vehicle and pocket the key whether it is left untended for a minute or several hours. Close the windows all the way and make sure the trunk is locked.
- Control the keys. Never leave an identification tag on a key ring. If keys are lost or stolen, this could help a thief locate the car and burglarize the owner's home.
- Do not leave the registration inside the vehicle. Important identification papers or credit cards should never be left in a glove compartment.
- Keep everything of value in the trunk if possible. If packages, clothing, or other articles are left in the car, they should be out of sight or covered.
- Park in well-lighted and busy areas. Avoid leaving a vehicle in unattended parking lots for long periods of time. If parked in a lot where the key must be left, leave the ignition key only.
- When buying a car, ask about antitheft options, such as steering column locks, alarms, switches that interrupt the fuel or electronic systems, and locks for tape decks, batteries, and gas tanks. Many insurance companies offer reduced rates to owners who install security devices.
- Keep your car's vehicle identification number (VIN) and a complete description in a safe place at home. Since 1969 the federal government has required manufacturers to engrave a unique number, the VIN, on all passenger cars in one visible and several hidden locations. One VIN is engraved on a metal plate on the dashboard near the windshield. VINs are registered with the FBI's computerized National Crime Information Center.

Tips for protecting special vehicles

Follow these steps to protect bicycles, motorcycles, and trail bikes:

- Park the vehicle out of sight in a garage or basement or use a cover.
- Mark it with an operational identification number recommended by local law enforcement.
- Lock the bicycle with a case-hardened chain or cable and lock, winding the cable through the frame and both wheels, then around a fixed object.
- Use the fork lock found on most street motorcycles. For extra protection, invest in a heavy U-shaped lock with sleeve adapter made of extremely hard steel that cannot be hack-sawed or a case-hardened chain and sturdy padlock.
- Watch out for key numbers. Some motorcycle manufacturers stamp the key number on the lock. With this number, anyone can have a key cut that will fit perfectly. Many key makers ask for identification, but it is better to write down the key number and then file it off the lock.
- Many specialized vehicles (such as trucks and recreational vehicles) have no VIN and should be marked with an identification number, such as a driver's license.
- Lock up all easy-to-carry items such as motors and camping gear before leaving a vehicle.
- Use secured "toppers" and tool boxes. Do not assume a thief cannot lift a box because it is heavy.

Do not make it easy for thieves to steal a vehicle

Jack's father finally let him take the family's new car to school on a beautiful spring day. Jack showed off to all his friends—and anyone who would listen—until classes started. The keys were uncomfortable in his jeans, so he left them in his locker. When he went back after lunch, the keys were gone and so was the car.

Because her mother knew Lisa was a good driver, she let her pick up some friends and drive to the mall for a day of shopping. Lisa was so busy talking about last night's dance that she forgot to lock all the car doors. When she came back, several hours later, the car's tape deck and her friends' jackets (they did not want to drag them around the mall) were gone.

Charlie usually hopped on his new motorcycle when school was out and rode to his part-time job at a fast-food restaurant. One evening after work, some friends stopped by and asked him to go out with them. So he left the bike at the restaurant, figuring he would pick it up first thing in the morning. His bike was gone the next day.

Jack, Lisa, and Charlie all became victims of a crime that gets to be a bigger problem every year—vehicle theft.

What to do if it happens

If a vehicle is stolen or tampered with, report it to the police immediately. Stolen vehicles are often used in other crimes. Quick action not only helps recover the vehicle but may also prevent its use for illegal purposes.

Safety skills for children

While most children pass through childhood without experiencing physical harm, some are frightened or hurt by crime. A parental responsibility is to teach children how to protect themselves and respond to threatening situations. Parents should always take the time to listen carefully to children's fears and feelings about people or places that scare them or make them feel uncomfortable. The following are some of the basics children must know:

- Rehearse with children their full name, address, and phone number (including area code) and how to make emergency phone calls from home and public phones.
- Walk the neighborhood with the children. Show them safe places they can go to in an emergency, such as a neighbor's house or an open store.
- Tell children never to accept gifts or rides from someone they do not know very well.
- Check the neighborhood for areas that threaten children's safety, such as brush in wooded areas, overgrown shrubbery, bad lighting, vacant lots littered with debris, absence of sidewalks, or bike paths next to busy streets.
- Teach children to go to a store clerk or security guard and ask for help if you become separated in a store or shopping mall. Tell them never to go into the parking lot alone.
- Accompany children to public restrooms.
- Teach children that no one, not even someone they know, has the right to touch them in a way that makes them feel uncomfortable. Tell them they have the right to say "No" to an adult in this situation.

Talking with kids about violence

No one wants to see kids victimized by violence. No one wants to see kids perpetuate it. But peer pressure, community lifestyles and values, the media, and even the behavior of adults learned when they were children are among a few of the things that can give kids the message that being violent or being a victim of violence is okay.

Talking with children about violence, disagreement, frustration, anger, and conflict can start in a child's earlier years and continue through the teen years. Respect for oneself and others, using examples of conflicts or arguments settled without violence and learning not to use hurtful words are each a positive skill that can last a lifetime.

Child development experts tell us that, for very young children, some physical acts, such as hitting, kicking, and biting, may be just part of early development. But by the age of 3 years, most children are able to understand nonviolent ways to deal with the world, even if they are not perfect at practicing those skills. Here are some ideals to help in talking with children, of whatever age, about preventing violence:

- Be clear with other adults in a child's life about values with respect to violence. It does not help to have a grandparent, cousin, and a parent sending contradictory messages.
- Do not wait until the issue comes up because of a specific incident; talk about family values and violence in advance and in as calm and neutral a setting as possible.
- Be clear that you do not approve of violent behavior by the child or violence done to the child. Explain the difference between feelings of anger and frustration and acting on those feelings.
- Do not cram everything into one short discussion. Make the discussion an ongoing affair that occurs in natural installments.

- Know the child's friends and their views on violence. Know the child's whereabouts and companions at all times.
- Set a good example. Even in tense or difficult personal situations, refuse to resort to violence to settle disputes or relieve frustrations.
- Ask about the child's ideas on violence. Listen and encourage expression of worries, questions, and fears. Show that you respect the youngster's concerns and value a willingness to think about a tough issue.
- Take advantage of teachable moments. When a violent scene appears in the media, talk about what happened and how it might have been prevented. When something happens at school or in the community, talk about what choices—other than violence—might have been available.
- Find out about conflict management and mediation training for adults and children. Conflict management training provides skills in settling disputes peacefully. Mediation training teaches how to assist others to settle disputes peacefully.
- Help develop enjoyable, attractive activities in the community for all young people, so they have better things to do, with an adult mentoring and supervising them.
- Help children get involved in helping the community. If they see how they can play an important role in building the community, they will resist violence that would tear it down.
- To reduce the risk of being involved in violence, children can do the following:
  - Play, walk, or skate with a friend rather than alone. Always let a responsible adult know where they are and with whom.
  - Never go anywhere with someone the child or his or her parents do not know and trust.
  - Do not hang around known trouble spots or with kids who think violence is cool.
  - Do not use alcohol or other drugs; they attract violent types of people and encourage violence as part of their mind-altering properties.
  - Learn how to be a conflict solver for friends and schoolmates. Get training in mediation skills to help others work out problems without force.
  - Do not carry a weapon. It could be lost or used against the child.

What is a stranger?

Explain to children that a stranger is anyone they do not know very well. A stranger can be a man or a woman, well-dressed or shabby, kind or threatening, and pretty or ugly. If a stranger tries to follow them or grab them, they should scream and make lots of noise. Tell children to run to the nearest place where there are people and shout "This person is trying to hurt me!" or "Stay away from me" instead of "Help."

Safety skills at school and play

- Make sure children take the safest route to school and friends' houses, one that avoids danger spots such as alleys, new construction, and wooded areas. Test it by walking together.
- Encourage children to talk and play with friends, not alone, and stay in well-lit, open areas where others can see them.
- Do not hang a house key around a child's neck. It is a telltale sign that parents are not at home when they return from school. Put the key inside a pocket or sock.
- Teach children to walk confidently and stay alert to what is going on around them.
- Tell children to stay away from strangers who hang around playgrounds, public restrooms, and empty buildings.
- Teach children to write down and report to you the license numbers of people who offer rides, loiter around playgrounds, or appear to follow them.

Safety skills at home

- Make sure children can reach their parents at work by phone. Post a work number, along with numbers for a neighbor, the police and fire departments, and poison control center near all home phones.
- Have children check in with a parent at work or a neighbor when they get home. Agree on rules for having friends over and going to someone else's house when no adult is present.
- Work out an escape plan in case of fire.

- Tell children never to open the door to a stranger when they are alone in the house or apartment. Caution them about answering the phone and accidentally letting a stranger know they are alone. Kids can always say their parents are busy and take a message.
- Make sure that children know how to work the door and window locks and that they keep them locked when home alone.

Street smarts—how to protect yourself

- Every day, over 2000 violent crimes are committed against teenagers by strangers.
- Young people are victims of theft more frequently than adults.
- Older teenagers and young adults are physically assaulted at a higher rate than any other age group.
- Two-thirds of violent crimes against teens are committed by other teens. Half of those teens are strangers to their victims.

So, knowing how to protect yourself and your friends makes good sense. No one needs to be a walking statistic.

Be streetwise and safe

- Stand tall and walk confidently. Watch what is happening around you.
- Stick to well-lit, busy streets. Walk with friends. Avoid shortcuts through dark alleys, deserted streets, and wooded areas.
- If harassed from a car, walk quickly or run in the opposite direction to safety. If really scared, scream.
- Never hitchhike. Accept rides only from people you know and trust.
- Do not flash your cash. Just carry enough money for the day. Always carry "emergency" change needed for a phone call.
- Know the neighborhood. What time do stores and restaurants open? Where are police and fire stations, libraries, and schools? You might need them in an emergency.
- If you go out late at night, take a friend. Do not go alone. Most assaults happen to lone victims.
- Let someone know where you are going and when you will be back. Call if you are going to be late.
- If driving, park the car in a well-lit area and lock it. Check for uninvited passengers in the backseat or on the floor before getting back in.

Jogging or biking

- Go with a friend and take familiar, well-traveled routes.
- Do not jog or bike at night.
- Try jogging without stereo headphones. It is safer to remain alert to what happens around and behind you.

On the bus or subway

- Use stops that are well-lit and popular. If your stop is isolated, have someone meet you there.
- Make sure you know which stop is closest to your destination. Check a map or ask the driver.
- Do not fall asleep. Stay alert.
- If you are harassed by anyone, attract attention by talking loudly or screaming.

What to do if you are a victim of a crime

- Try not to panic. Look at the attacker carefully so you can give a good description to the police. Try to remember key things such as age, race, complexion, build, clothing, height, weight, hair, eyes, or unusual features.
- If the attacker has a weapon and only wants your money or possessions, do not fight back. Life and safety are more important.
- If harassed by a gang, go to an open store, gas station, firehouse, or anywhere people are present. Ask for help.

Following these suggestions greatly diminishes the chance of becoming a crime statistic.

The con artist

The clever con artist is a good actor who disarms the victim with an affable "nice guy" approach. Behind this friendly exterior is a shrewd psychologist who can isolate potential victims and break down their resistance to his or her proposals. Each conquest is part of a game in which the con artist must "best" others. The typical con artist is amoral, but seldom violent, and mobile, with an excellent sense of timing. He or she sincerely believes victims deserve their fate. And, if caught, the con artist will probably strike again later. Con artists are seldom rehabilitated.

The victim

Anyone can be a victim, even one who is too intelligent or sophisticated to be "conned." During the 1920s, "Yellow Kid" Weil routinely swindled bankers, saying "That's where the money is." Many victims share certain characteristics. Often, but not always, they are older women living alone. They are trusting of others, even strangers, and may need or desire supplemental income. Loneliness, willingness to help, and a sense of charity are characteristics a con artist exploits to gain a victim's cooperation.

The con artist ultimately exploits the victim's assets, including life insurance benefits, pensions or annuities, "nest eggs," home equity, or other tangible property. The con artist usually obtains the willing cooperation of the victim to complete the scheme.

Keywords

A con artist is difficult to detect by looks alone, but can often be spotted by words or expressions, including the following:

Cash only. Why is cash necessary for a proposed transaction? Why not checks?
Get rich quick. Any scheme should be carefully investigated.
Something for nothing. A "retired" swindler once said that any time you are promised something for nothing, you usually get nothing.
Contests. Make sure these are not a "come-on" to draw you into a money-losing scheme.
Haste. Be wary of any pressure that you must act immediately or lose out.
Today only. If something is worthwhile and available today, it is likely to be available tomorrow.
Too good to be true. Such a scheme is probably not good or true.
Last chance. If it is a chance worth taking, why is it offered on such short notice?
Leftover material. Leftover material might also be stolen or defective.

The following is a list of schemes of "con games" that the con artist is likely to try:

Home improvement. Home repair or improvement artists may pose as a city inspector or termite or pest control inspector.
Bank-related schemes. The con artist may pose as a bank examiner or be part of a pigeon drop.
Investments. These include franchise or vending, land frauds, inventions, security investments, and work-at-home schemes.
Postal frauds. Some examples are chain letters, magazine subscriptions, unordered merchandise, and correspondence courses.

Other cons include bait and switch, charity rackets, computer dating, debt consolidation, contracts, dance lessons, freezer plans, acting as psychics or fortune tellers, health clubs, job-placement services, lonely hearts clubs, medical quackery, missing heirs, referral sales, pyramid schemes, or acting as talent scouts or officials.

Some rules

- Always investigate before investing money or signing a contract.
- Be suspicious of extraordinary promises of high or unusual monetary returns or a "bargain" no one else can match.
- Do not discuss personal finances or give cash to strangers.
- Do not be too embarrassed to report being victimized or swindled.
- Testify in court, if asked to help stop this kind of crime.

The con game

Most successful con games are old schemes for today's circumstances. The old "salting a gold mine" scheme is still being practiced, for example, but today's "salting" occurs in living rooms, not abandoned mines. In the old ruse, unscrupulous mine owners would place a few gold nuggets in exhausted mines so they could sell them for inflated profits.

In one recent scheme a con artist bought six color television sets at the regular price from a retail store and then sold them, still in their cartons, to six prominent persons for one-fifth their original price. Later, he hired several high school students as telephone solicitors to sell "carloads" of TV sets purchased new from a bankrupt retail chain. When potential customers balked, the con artist used as references the original six customers who had been "salted." Before the police were alerted, he had collected almost $60,000.

Victims are not alone

Have you ever done the following:

- Given your credit card number to a phone solicitor?
- Purchased land you have not seen?
- Agreed to home repairs that were quick, cheap, and paid for up front?
- Bought stock on a stranger's suggestion?
- Sent money as part of a chain letter?
- Invested in a promising new company that quickly went out of business?

In 2010 swindlers used scams to cheat consumers out of about $40 million. Be skeptical of anything that sounds too good to be true or promises easy money. Victims of a con artist should report the crime to the police immediately and get the word out to help protect friends and neighbors.

Think smart, avoid cons

1. If it sounds too good to be true, it probably is.
2. Do not trust strangers who offer instant cash.
3. Get more information before buying "the sure thing."
4. Check out charities before contributing.
5. Do not give your credit card number to anyone over the phone.
6. Whenever you are asked to turn over a sizable amount of cash, be cautious. Why is cash necessary? Why not a check? Avoid a large cash transfer. Consult with trusted friends or family before making such a decision.
7. It is unfortunate, but homes have been lost as a result of signing a simple TV repair contract. Signing a contract is not a frivolous matter. The contract may be secured by a deed of trust on your home. It may include a provision that failure to pay on time will permit a judgment to be entered against you. Contracts can be sold to a bank or finance company for collection, although these institutions have no responsibility for the quality of the product delivered or work performed.
8. Be wary of any pressure that you must act immediately or lose out. There is no better insurance than dealing with reputable business or people.
9. Report scams to the police, and if asked, testify in court to help stop this type of crime.
10. If you have any questions about the reliability or legitimacy of a firm, contact the Attorney General's Office of Consumer Affairs.

Crime prevention tips for senior citizens

Senior citizens can help make their community a safer place to live and not let the fear of crime restrict their activities. Being alert to their surroundings, installing good locks on doors and windows, and taking common sense precautions while inside and outside the home can reduce opportunities for crime. For that extra margin of security, they should do the following:

- Use direct deposit for pension and social security checks.
- Not display large amounts of cash in public.

- Be wary of talkative strangers when the conversation turns to money. Read every newspaper report on con games and be ready to say no to a get-rich scheme.
- Travel with friends to go shopping, to the bank, or to a doctor.
- Get to know neighbors and keep their phone numbers handy for emergencies.
- Work out a "buddy" system with a friend to check on each other's welfare daily.
- If living alone, do not advertise it. Use only a first initial in phone books, directories, and apartment lobbies.
- Carry a purse close to the body. Leave no wallet or purse on a counter or in a shopping cart unattended.
- If threatened by physical force, do not resist. Remain calm and observe the assailant to give an accurate description to the police.
- Organize or join a Neighborhood Watch Program or a window watch program to keep an eye out for unusual activity in the neighborhood or complex. A neighborhood where people are active and involved is always a safer, better place to live.

Take action—stop the violence

At home

- Teach children, from preschoolers to teenagers, that guns and other weapons hurt and kill.
- Show children how to settle arguments without resorting to words or actions that hurt. Parents, relatives, older brothers and sisters, teachers, and babysitters should set a positive example.
- Consider removing guns, especially handguns, from homes with children or teens.
- Look at ways other than firearms to protect yourself. Invest in top-grade locks, jamming devices for doors and windows, a dog, or a security system. Ask the police to recommend a self-defense class.
- When owning firearms, handguns, rifles, or shotguns, make sure they are unloaded and securely stored. Invest in trigger locks, gun cabinets with locks, or pistol lock boxes. Lock up ammunition separately.

At school

- Support school staff in their efforts to keep guns, knives, and other weapons out of school.
- Encourage students to report any weapons they know about on school grounds to the police or school authorities.
- Involve students in the issue. Young people can and do organize against handgun violence.
- Show students how to settle arguments without resorting to violence. Teach them to deal with conflict by calming down, identifying the problem, compromising, and asking someone else to listen to both sides.

In the community

- Launch a public education campaign to raise awareness of the danger of firearms and the risks of keeping a gun in the home.
- Report stolen weapons to the police immediately.
- Work with a Neighborhood Watch or other group to hold a forum on how guns and violence affect the community. Include police, school, youth, local government, youth agencies, and religious organizations.

Each year, guns end the lives of thousands of young people. Their families and friends are left to cope with the loss of a life barely lived and to face a future overshadowed by violence.

Protection from telemarketing fraud

The best protection is to just hang up the phone. It is not rude to tell unsolicited callers politely that you are not interested, do not want to waste their time, and please do not call back—then hang up. If caught up in a sales pitch, remember the federal government's telemarketing rules which are as follows:

- You have to be told the name of the company, the fact that it is a sales call, and what is being sold. If a prize is offered, you have to be told immediately that no purchase is necessary to win.
- If the caller says you have won a prize, you cannot be asked to pay anything for it. You cannot be required to pay even shipping charges. If it is a sweepstakes, the caller must tell you how to enter without making a purchase.

- You cannot be asked to pay in advance for services such as cleansing your credit card, finding you a loan, or acquiring a prize already won. You pay for services only if they are actually delivered.
- You should not be called before 8:00 a.m. or after 9:00 p.m. If you tell telemarketers not to call again, they cannot. If they do, they have broken the law.
- If you are guaranteed a refund, the caller has to tell you all the limitations.

Remember, those called should not give telemarketers a credit card number, bank account number, Social Security number, or authorize bank drafts—ever. If fraud is suspected, call the National Fraud Information Center at 1-800-876-7060, or check www.fraud.org for additional information.

Crime prevention tips at ATMs

Using common sense and trusting intuition can prevent people from being a victim at an ATM.

Drive-up ATMs

- Keep your car engine running, the doors locked, and the windows up at all times when waiting in line at a drive-up ATM.
- When possible, leave enough room between cars to allow for a quick exit should it become necessary.
- If an ATM is obstructed from view or poorly lit, go to another ATM. Report the problem to the financial institution that operates the ATM.
- Before rolling down the window, observe the entire area around the ATM. If you see anyone or anything that appears to be suspicious, drive away from the area at once and call the police.
- Minimize the time spent at the ATM by having your card out and ready to use. Once you have completed the transaction, take the money, card, and receipt and immediately drive away from the terminal.
- If you see anyone or anything suspicious while conducting the transaction, cancel the transaction and leave immediately.
- If anyone follows after making a transaction, go immediately to a crowded, well-lit area and call the police.

Walk-up ATMs

- Always observe the surroundings before conducting an ATM transaction. If driving to an ATM, park as close as possible to the terminal. Observe the entire area from the safety of the car before getting out. If anyone or anything appears suspicious, leave the area at once.
- If an ATM is obstructed from view or poorly lit, go to another ATM. Report the problem to the financial institution that operates the ATM.
- When possible, take a companion along when using an ATM, especially at night.
- Minimize the time spent at the ATM by having the card out and ready to use. If the ATM is in use, give the person using the terminal privacy. Allow the person to move away from the ATM before approaching the terminal.
- Stand between the ATM and anyone waiting to use the terminal, so that others cannot see the secret code or transaction amount. Once the transaction is completed, take the money, card, and receipt and immediately move away from the terminal.
- If anyone or anything appears suspicious while conducting a transaction, cancel the transaction and leave immediately.
- If anyone follows after making the ATM transaction, go immediately to a crowded, well-lit area and call the police.

Chapter 18

Crime analysis

Lawrence J. Fennelly
Security Consultant

Crime analysis can be defined as the study of daily reports and crime to determine the location, time of day, special characteristics, and similarities to other crimes as well as any significant data that will or may identify the existence of patterns of criminal behavior.

Introduction

This is done through the collection, collation, analysis of reports, and evaluation of crime data. Crimes are random and nonrandom foreseeable and unforeseeable and take place in high-crime areas as well as low crime areas. Crime analysis becomes an essential tool for short- and/or long-term planning of personnel, budgets, facilities, and equipment. Have your numbers gone up or have they gone down? Your data are key to measurement. Data do not necessarily have to reflect public service needs, phone calls, or unlocking specific doors or cabinets. Even if crime is down, the calls for noncriminal services could be going up and up.

Crime analysis is a critical first step in determining the need for crime/loss prevention programs as well as identifying problems on the site. Crime analysis comes into play again in the evaluation of programs. Is crime up or is it down? Compared to whom and what? Is the city crime rate up and yours down? You can have a low crime rate in a high-crime area. So how do you get such information? Police departments break their crime down into areas or zones. Each zone may be given a number, for example, 1–8 and you are located in zone 6. So how does zone 6 compare to the other 7 areas? Effective programing begins with results of relevant and reliable data/information.

Crime analysis

Crime analysis information should provide the basis for developing crime prevention programs, strategies, and tactics. Yet crime analysis is generally overlooked during the program planning process in favor of traditional crime prevention activities, such as neighborhood watch or community policing. While traditional programs are of value, crime prevention programs should be designed to provide a number of crime prevention services that meet specific and address specific community crime problems. Better results could be achieved by using crime analysis products to focus crime prevention activities on clearly defined problems.

Crime analysis—defined

Crime analysis is a systematic process of collecting data, collating, analyzing it, and disseminating the information timely and usefully, which describes crime patterns, trends, and information on possible suspects as well.

The keywords here are collecting data, collating, analyzing, patterns, suspects, and timely. A systematic process of collecting, by way of spreadsheets or computer program. What do we collect? Based on the crime reports, tactical data on the location and information in all reports. Failure to do so could well skew the results. This in turn might provide the wrong tactical and flawed information and be of no use.

Handbook of Loss Prevention and Crime Prevention. DOI: https://doi.org/10.1016/B978-0-12-817273-5.00018-1

Crime analysis

Crime analysis provides a process, which incorporates crime into site analysis.[1] The analysis is sometimes called a *safety audit or risk assessment.* This process has been developed based on a variety of neighborhoods and sites and in particular areas ranging from neighborhood developments, transit stations, mega-block developments, park designs, public realm plazas, and corporate/business operations. An outline of the analysis process includes:

1. demographic analysis,
2. crime analysis,
3. site analysis,
4. use analysis,
5. neighborhood/user consultation, and
6. pathway analysis.

Situational crime prevention incorporates other crime prevention and law enforcement strategies in an effort to focus on place-specific crime problems.

Crime analysis data needed

Time of day—day of the week—month.

Detailed target description, that is, corner lot, middle of the street, back office, and fourth file cabinet on the right—point of entry and exit—method of attach—tools used—degree of force—targets secured or lack of security.

Item or items taken, physical evidence if any, suspect, suspect vehicles, method of operation (MO), and crime history of the area.

Data collection

The crime analysis process begins with the collection of a wide variety of information. The goal of data collection is to gather crime-specific elements that help to distinguish one criminal incident from another.

Incident reports alone do not provide enough information for analysis purposes. For example, in many crimes against property, an actual time or means of entry are not available from the actual report. Supplemental data sources, such as the time the alarm was tripped, actual time of 911 call, and results from field interviews; all these could be used to narrow the time frame within which a burglary may have occurred.

A valuable point we would like to make based on our experience is visiting the sight. Why? Your instincts are invaluable and you may pick up on something that was not in a report. In addition to this follow-up, you may be able to pass on crime prevention information that will prevent a second loss.

Times have changed

The Los Angeles Police Department, like many urban police forces today, is both heavily armed and thoroughly computerized.[2] The Real-Time Analysis and Critical Response Division in downtown LA is its central processor. Rows of crime analysts and technologists sit before a wall covered in video screens stretching more than 10 m wide. Multiple news broadcasts are playing simultaneously, and a real-time earthquake map is tracking the region's seismic activity. Half-a-dozen security cameras are focused on the Hollywood sign, the city's icon. In the center of this video menagerie, there is an oversized satellite map showing some of the most recent arrests made across the city—a couple of burglaries, a few assaults, and a shooting.

Predictive policing is just one tool in this new, tech-enhanced, and data-fortified era of fighting and preventing crime. As the ability to collect, store, and analyze data becomes cheaper and easier, law enforcement agencies all over the world are adopting techniques that harness the potential of technology to provide more and better information. But while these new tools have been welcomed by law enforcement agencies, they are raising concerns about privacy, surveillance, and how much power should be given over to computer algorithms.

---

1. http://www.designcentreforcpted.org/#Origins, CPTED in Vancouver Canada Aug. 30, 2017.
2. https://www.theguardian.com/cities/2014/jun/25/predicting-crime-lapd-los-angeles-police-data-analysis-algorithm-minority-report website Nov. 2018.

Crime pattern analysis: Crime pattern analysis seeks to determine what crimes are likely to impact particular targets, the criminals likely to commit the crimes, how the crimes are likely to occur, and when they are likely to occur. The process of analysis typically includes the collection and processing of data related to specific areas of study.

Four points I would like to make about current trends[3]:

1. different sets of statistics, (in house and out of house);
2. tools for data analysis such as PPM 2000 and I2 Analyst Notebook;
3. technology tools, such as Microsoft Excel pivot tables or Microsoft business intelligence tools to portray data, by facility, campus, or enterprise; and
4. merging of data and data analytics, correlating crime statistics with access control, camera alarms, and visitor management systems to gain richer information on crime, which is occurring.

Do not be discouraged by the displacement doomsters

Problem-oriented policing often tries to reduce opportunities for crime; for example, window locks may be fitted to prevent burglary in an apartment complex, or CCTV cameras installed to prevent thefts in parking lots.[4] These examples of reducing opportunities for crime often meet the same objection: all they do is move crime around but not prevent it.

This theory of displacement sees crime as being shifted around in five main ways:

1. Crime is moved from one place to another (geographical).
2. Crime is moved from one time to another (temporal).
3. Crime is directed away from one target to another (target).
4. One method of committing crime replaces another (tactical).
5. One kind of crime is substituted for another (crime type).

In each case the theory assumes that offenders are compelled to commit crime, whatever impediments they face. The basis for the assumption is either that the propensity to commit crime builds up and must be discharged in the same way that sexual release is sought, or that "professional" criminals or drug addicts must obtain a certain income from crime to maintain their lifestyles. There is no evidence that offenders must satiate some deep physiological appetite to commit crimes. In fact, there is plenty of evidence that people make choices about whether, where, and when to offend. Whatever its basis, the displacement assumption neglects the important role of temptation and opportunity in crime.

Even in the case of more committed offenders, the displacement theory fails to give enough importance to opportunity. Thus research on drug addicts has shown that they adapt to variations in the supply of drugs and there is no simple progression in drug use. Rather, addicts might be forced to use smaller amounts or less agreeable drugs because the supply of drugs has been cut. As for professional criminals such as bank robbers, there is no reason to assume that they must obtain a fixed amount of money from crime. They would surely commit fewer robberies if these became difficult and risky, just as they would commit more robberies if these became easy. Bank robbers, like everyone else, may sometimes have to adjust to reduced circumstances and be content with lower levels of income.

This does not mean that we can ignore displacement. Indeed, rational choice theory predicts that offenders will displace when the benefits for doing so outweigh the costs. For example, in the early 1990s the New York City Police deployed its Tactical Narcotics Teams to several high-crime, drug-dealing neighborhoods. Dealers responded by shifting their sales locations from curbside to inside the foyers of apartment buildings. But numerous other studies have found that displacement did not occur at all, or only to a limited extent. Following are some examples:

- Intensive gun patrols reduced firearms crimes in a Kansas City, Missouri, high gun-crime neighborhood without displacing these or other crimes to nearby communities.
- New identification procedures greatly reduced check frauds in Sweden, with no evidence of displacement to a range of "conceivable" alternative crimes.
- Extensive target hardening undertaken in banks in Australia lowered robbery rates, but there was no sign that corner stores, gas stations, betting shops, motels, or people in the street began to experience more robberies.
- Burglary was not displaced to nearby apartment complexes when a problem-solving approach drove down burglary in a high-crime apartment complex in Newport News, Virginia.

3. CPP, 2018. Comments from Jeff Slotnick. CPP.
4. Clarke, R.V., Eck, J.E., 2005. Crime Analysis for Problem Solvers in 60 Steps. U.S. Department of Justice. <www.cops.usdoj.gov>.

- When streets were closed in the London neighborhood of Finsbury Park and policing was intensified, there was little evidence that prostitutes simply moved to other nearby locations. According to the researchers, many of the women working on the streets in Finsbury Park were not deeply committed to prostitution but saw it as a relatively easy way to make a living. When conditions changed so did their involvement and many seem to have given up "the game."
- Redesign of a trolley stop to curb robberies and assaults resulted in a reduction in violent crime in San Diego, California, without shifting these crimes to other trolley stops.
- In these examples and numerous others, offenders' costs of displacing seemed to have outweighed the benefits, and the examples bear out the argument that displacement occurs much less than previously believed.

Pay attention to daily and weekly rhythms

Cycles of activities have tremendous influences on problems. The ebb and flow of vehicles caused by commuting and shopping rhythms, for example, changes the number of targets and guardians in parking facilities. This, in turn, influences when vehicle thefts and break-ins are most frequent. Robberies of drunken revelers may be more likely around bar closing time on Fridays and Saturdays, because the number of targets is higher. In this example, two important rhythms concentrate problem activities. The first is the workday/weekend cycle that makes Friday and Saturday nights so popular for entertainment and recreation. The second involves the daily cycle of opening and closing of bars. In this step, we will discuss short-term fluctuations occurring over hours and days. We look at longer time periods covering months and years.

Different facilities have different cycles of activities that can contribute to their associated problems. School rhythms are similar although distinct from job rhythms. Bus stops are influenced not only by the rhythm of commuting and shopping, but also by the more frequent coming and going of buses. Charting the rhythm of crime or disorder events helps identify important activity cycles that may contribute to a problem.

Rachel Boba recommends charting days and hours together. The result shows hot time periods throughout the week. Such charts are easy to produce; all three of these charts were created on a spreadsheet using standard graphing routines.

Temporal analysis is easiest when problem events are frequent. It is more useful for common minor events, such as noise complaints and minor traffic accidents, than for uncommon serious events, such as murder. If there are few events, then you can look at a longer period to collect more events. But if the problem changes in the longer period, the picture that emerges may be distorted or out of date.

Having reasonably exact times of occurrence helps temporal analysis. Contact crimes, such as robbery, rape, and assault, can be accurately pinpointed as victims can often describe when these crimes took place. Property crimes, such as vehicle crimes, burglary, and vandalism, are much harder to pin down because victims usually provide only a time range during which such crimes could have occurred. Although it is common to use the midpoints in these ranges to estimate the times crimes occurred, this can lead to distortion and should be avoided for long periods (e.g., more than 8 hours).

Jerry Ratcliffe also has identified three forms of temporal clustering. First, events may be relatively evenly spread over the entire day. He calls this a diffused pattern. Second, focused patterns show clustering within distinct time ranges. Events clustered around rush hours follow focused patterns. Third, acute patterns are tightly packed within small periods. Disturbances immediately following bar closing time might be an example. Focused and acute patterns immediately suggest temporal cycles that should be investigated. Although Ratcliffe developed his typology for daily patterns, the basic idea can be applied to weekly cycles. If no particular day of the week is routinely troublesome, this indicates a diffused weekly pattern. A cluster of days showing a marked increase in troublesome events indicates a focused pattern. Finally, if 1 or 2 days have a marked concentration of events, this indicates an acute pattern.

Identify risky facilities

Facilities are environments with special functions. Educational facilities involve teaching and study. Industrial facilities produce and process materials. Office facilities process information. Retail facilities involve sales and monetary transactions. Some facilities are frequent sites for crime and incivilities. These include taverns, parks, railway stations, pay phone booths, convenience stores, and public housing projects. These facilities make a disproportionately large contribution to crime and disorder—they are "risky facilities."

But the term also has a more precise meaning. It refers to the fact that within each type of facility a few of them are especially risky. When we described the 80–20 rule, we mentioned that 5% of the stores in Danvers, Massachusetts, accounted for 50% of the reported shopliftings. Here are some other documented examples of risky facilities:

- *Convenience stores*. A national survey found that 6.5% of convenience stores experience 65% of all robberies.
- *Gas stations*. Ten percent of Austin and Texas gas stations accounted for more than 50% of calls for drive offs and drug crimes between 1998 and 1999.
- *Banks*. Four percent of the banks in the United Kingdom have rates of robbery four to six times higher than other banks.
- *Schools*. Eight percent of Stockholm schools suffered 50% of the violent crimes reported in the 1993–94 school year.
- *Bus stops*. Andrew Newton's recent doctoral dissertation reported that 9% of the shelters at bus stops in the British city of Liverpool experienced more than 40% of the vandalism incidents.
- *Parking facilities*. In another British city, Nottingham, just one parking deck (The Royal Moat House) accounted for about 25% (103) of the 415 crimes reported for all 19 downtown lots in 2016.

There are at least eight reasons why facilities are "risky," and different analysis procedures can help determine which reasons are operating in particular circumstances:

1. *Random variation*. It is possible to get concentrations of crime in a few places through some fluke of randomness. This is more likely to occur when you are looking at only a few facilities with few incidents. Try checking the same facilities for a different time period. If the rank order of incidents is roughly the same in both periods, then the variation is not random.
2. *Reporting practices*. Some facilities might always report crimes to the police, while others experiencing the same number of incidents might report fewer of them. This can be difficult to check, but you should ask officers who are familiar with the facilities whether the recorded crime rates match their own perceptions of the crime problems in the facilities.
3. *Many targets*. Some facilities contain many targets. The store with the most shopliftings in Danvers was one of the largest in the city. But this was not the whole story. When its size is taken into account by calculating shopliftings per 100 ft^2, it is still one of the riskiest stores for shoplifting.
4. *Hot products*. A risky facility may not have a large number of targets, but it might have targets that are particularly "hot." Store 15 in the Danvers' list had the highest rate of shoplifting in the city per 1000 ft^2. This store specializes in selling small, high-value electronic items that meet the CRAVED criteria.
5. *Location*. Facilities located in high-crime areas, perhaps where many habitual offenders live, are more likely to be crime risks. This is because offenders prefer not to travel far to commit crime.
6. *Repeat victimization*. Some places attract people who are particularly vulnerable to crime. Compare the people being victimized in risky and nonrisky facilities. If the revictimization rates are different, then repeat victimization may be the cause of the elevated risk.
7. *Crime attractors*. Facilities that draw large numbers of offenders are crime attractors, which have high numbers of offenses and high offense rates. Additional diagnostic checks involve analysis of arrest records and other information containing offender names.
8. *Poor management*. When owners or managers do not exercise proper control or management, a risky facility can develop. A slumlord's negligent management can turn the properties he acquired into risky facilities.

Finally, we offer a plea on behalf of crime analysis as a profession and crime science as a discipline. However much you want to make yourself clearly understood, never give in to the temptation to exaggerate your evidence. Nothing is more likely to damage your reputation, and that of your colleagues, than being seen to stretch the facts. Other people may cut corners or leap to conclusions. Crime analysis lends diligence and integrity to what is sometimes a haphazard process. If you do not know the answer or only partly understand the problem, say so. That way, when you do know the answer, people will be more willing to trust your professional judgment.

The 21st century is becoming the century of analysis in policing, and you can make a large contribution. A 100 years from now, analysis will be firmly established in policing, and much will have changed. The technology will certainly be different. But more important, our successors will know a great deal more about crime and its prevention than we do. And they will know this because you and people like you asked important questions, collected and analyzed data, and reported your results with honesty and clarity.

Chapter 19

Environmental crime control

Glen Kitteringham and Lawrence J. Fennelly
Security Consultant

That the proper design and effective use of the built environment can lead to a reduction in the incidence and fear of crime — and to an increase in the quality of life.

Dr. C. Ray Jeffery (1971)

Introduction

The private security industry has come a long way from when Allan Pinkerton created his world famous Pinkerton's Detective Agency in the middle of the 19th century. In the intervening 17 decades, there has been a great deal of activity. Significant steps have been taken in lock and key systems, access control hardware, the increasing ingenuity of vaults and safes, fencing systems, security surveillance systems, increasing professionalism and training of security officers, and a host of other physical security enhancements. However, proper attention has not been paid to the environmental crime control theories and subsequent practical applications behind the deployment of these human, hardware, and documentation innovations.

While the reader is likely familiar with crime prevention through environmental design (CPTED), there are several other theories that offer insight into crime control opportunities. But the question remains: why should security practitioners know the reasons for applying particular security applications, as well as the theories behind them? Because if you are going to implement a new security application, you should understand why! Learning and applying these theories will allow you to make informed crime control decisions as to why certain security measures should or should not be carried out. Once you understand why an offender carried out unwanted activity in a particular area, you can implement security measures with a far better chance of success. As security measures cost money to implement, the wise security practitioner will not want to waste time, effort, or money. Following criminal activity, an officer may wonder: was there an absence of a capable guardian as Felson and Cohen (1979) theorize? Does the offender make a rational choice either for or against carrying out a criminal act as Cornish and Clarke (2008) believe takes place? A deeper understanding of the offense allows the responding security practitioner, to make keener and more analytical choices about how to respond to the situation. Will it require a simple or a complicated fix? In some cases, simple is usually cheaper and can be just as successful as more expensive security measures.

There is a danger in thinking that once security measures have been implemented, there will never be a crime or unwanted activity again in the same area. Crime may or may not occur. Other factors may be at work, including the effects of displacement and diffusion of benefits (to be explained). This forces the security practitioner to continually review the area from many different perspectives. Has new technology made the old security solutions moot? Will an attack come from a different direction, during a different time of day? Will the attacker be forced to try new methods or bigger or better tools, or will there be a different attacker? Continual awareness and review are necessary.

Environmental crime prevention versus social crime prevention

A simple explanation of environmental crime prevention is that environmental crime practitioners focus their attention and energies on locations of potential criminal activity. These practitioners "look for crime patterns and seek to explain them in terms of environmental influences. From these explanations they derive rules that enable predictions to be made about emerging crime problems, and that ultimately inform the development of strategies that might be employed to prevent crime" (Wortley and Mazerolle, 2008, p. 1). Locks, doors, and other barriers; surveillance equipment; and

Handbook of Loss Prevention and Crime Prevention. DOI: https://doi.org/10.1016/B978-0-12-817273-5.00019-3

TABLE 19.1 Twenty-five techniques of situational prevention.

Increase the effort	Increase the risks	Reduce the rewards	Reduce provocations	Remove excuses
1. *Harden target (both premise and laptop itself)* • steering column locks and immobilizers • antirobbery screens • tamperproof packaging	6. *Extend guardianship* • take routine precautions: go out in groups at night leave signs of occupancy carry phone • "cocoon" neighborhood watch	11. *Conceal targets* • off-street parking • Gender-neutral phone directors • unmarked bullion trucks	16. *Reduce frustrations and stress* • efficient queues and polite service • expanded seating • soothing music/muted lights	21. *Set rules* • rental agreements • harassment codes • hotel registration
2. *Control access to facilities* • entry phones • electronic card access • baggage screening	7. *Assist natural surveillance* • improved street lighting • defensible space design • support whistle-blowers	12. *Remove targets* • removable car radio • women's refuges • prepaid cards for payphones	17. *Avoid disputes* • separate enclosures for rival soccer fans • reduce crowding in pubs • fixed cab fares	22. *Post instructions* • "no parking" • "private property" • "extinguish camp fires"
3. *Screen exits* • ticket needed for exit • export documents • *electronic* merchandise tags	8. *Reduce anonymity* • taxi driver IDs • "how's my driving?" decals • school uniforms	13. *Identify property* • property marking • vehicle licensing and parts marking • cattle branding	18. *Reduce temptation* • controls on violent pornography • enforce good behavior on soccer field • prohibit racial slurs	23. *Alert conscience* • roadside speed display boards • signatures for customs declarations • "shoplifting is stealing"
4. *Deflect offenders* • street closures • separate bathrooms for women • disperse pubs	9. *Use place managers* • CCTV for double-deck buses • two clerks for convenience stores • reward vigilance	14. *Disrupt markets* • monitor pawn shops • control classified ads • license street vendors	19. *Neutralize peer pressure* • "idiots drink and drive" • "it's *okok* to say *no*" • disperse troublemakers at school	24. *Assist compliance* • easy library checkout • public lavatories • litter bins
5. *Control tools/weapons* • "smart" guns • disable stolen cell phones • restrict spray paint sales to juveniles	10. *Strengthen formal surveillance* • red light cameras • burglar alarms • security guards	15. *Deny benefits* • ink merchandise tags • graffiti cleaning • speed bumps	20. *Discourage imitation* • rapid repair of vandalism • V-chips in TVs • censor details of modus operandi	25. *Control drugs and alcohol* • breathalyzers in pubs • server intervention • alcohol-free events

Source: Clarke, R.V. <http://popcenter.org/library/25%20techniques%20grid.pdf> (accessed 07.06.09.).

patrolling security officers are all examples of environmental crime control measures. On the other side of the coin, there is social crime prevention. This area focuses upon social programs, education, employment creation, welfare, unemployment insurance, police, corrections, and other after-the-fact follow-up measures and programs. While the intent of this chapter is not to argue the pros and cons of one theory over the other, one comment will be made. While all the programs and money spent upon social crime control can be considered laudable, it would be a foolish security manager who donated his or her security budget to a social crime control program regardless of how noble it may seem. Government and big businesses have spent billions of dollars on this issue for many years, but physical security forces are required more than ever.

Environmental crime control has not been relegated the same attention and respect as the social crime control model. Social crime control has been practiced in one form or another for hundreds of years. In contrast, environmental crime control grew from work completed at the University of Chicago in the 1920s. It was there that more attention was paid to the area in which the crime was being committed than to the people who committed the criminal acts. The theory lay dormant for several decades but was given a rebirth by the influential writer and social commentator, Jane Jacobs, when she wrote *The Death and Life of Great American Cities* in 1961. Her work inspired both C. Ray Jeffery and Oscar Newman, both of whom took off in new directions: Jeffery, with his book, *Crime Prevention through Environmental Design*, and Newman, with his theory of *Defensible Space*. In turn, both researchers inspired others, such as Paul and Patricia Brantingham, Tim Crowe, Ronald V. Clarke, and Marcus Felson. What follows is an overview of the various environmental crime control theories.

Theories

Rational choice theory

Rational choice theory was first presented by Ronald V. Clarke and Derek B. Cornish in 1986 in *The Reasoning Criminal: Rational Choice Perspectives on Offending*. As Tayler (1997, p. 293) states, the rationale behind the theory is that people will commit a crime if it is in their own best interests. Basically, the offender uses a decision-making process whereby the positive and negative aspects of committing a particular act are weighed. If the perception is that there are more reasons for proceeding, regardless of the existing security countermeasures, then, at the very least, an attempt will be made. If an opportunity presents itself, there is a benefit, and there is little likelihood of being apprehended, then they will commit the crime. Further, Pease (1997, p. 967) quotes Clarke and Cornish (1985), who claim "the underlying assumption is that offenders seek to benefit themselves by their criminal behavior. This entails making decisions and choices, however rudimentary their rationality might be, being constrained by limits of time, ability, and the availability of relevant information."

Following this rationalization, it is up to the security practitioner to convince the potential offender that it is not in the offender's best interests to carry out the act. The application of situational crime prevention techniques is the result of this theory. As rational choice is the theoretical element, what follows are situational crime prevention techniques that are the practical efforts used to reduce criminal opportunities. These techniques involve increasing the effort and the risk, reducing rewards and provocations, and removing excuses. These five techniques are further subdivided into five subcategories to help eliminate opportunities for criminals. They can range from physical access control devices to the use of psychology to deter people's criminal tendencies. Finally, one should remember that criminal decision-making is crime specific. This means that "specific offenses bring particular benefits to offenders and are committed with specific motives in mind" (Cornish and Clarke, 2008, p. 26). The weighed actions, risks, and rewards will be different for the laptop thief than for the arsonist, vandal, or industrial spy. In addition to these issues, even within the narrow confines of a single crime, such as laptop theft, what motivates one offender (e.g., financial desire) will be different from another (e.g., a drug addict who steals to trade for crack cocaine). These situational crime prevention techniques are laid out in Table 19.1.

Rational choice theory also includes the principle that criminals are opportunistic. These opportunistic criminals are not professionals, but average people. If the reward is high enough, deterrents will not work. People will weigh the pros and cons of committing the crime, and these are centered on the specifics of the target. Finally, situational crime prevention works best with the amateur criminal and least with the professional criminal. Bearing in mind that there are different classifications of criminals, primarily amateur criminal and professional, the more security precautions are taken, the more likely all but the most determined attacker will be stopped. Other factors come into play as well; two that will be discussed are displacement and diffusion of benefits.

Displacement of crime

The basis for displacement is that a determined attacker, if stopped at or by one method, location, etc., will try other ways of committing a crime until successful. There are six elements to displacement as laid out in Table 19.2. Displacement claims that, regardless of whether a specific crime is committed at a particular location, the criminal will simply move to a more "criminal user-friendly" location until the crime can be completed. One way to remember the six elements is to consider who, what, when, where, why, and how. Coincidentally, these are also the six elements of a properly written incident report.

Research indicates that displacement is not nearly as strong a factor as many people assume. Common sense indicates that displacement increases the effort on the offender's part, which is exactly why security measures are implemented in the first place. Increasing the effort makes it more costly for the criminal (Clarke, 2008, p. 188). Displacement can also be viewed positively if the security practitioner gives thought from a planning perspective, considers how the criminal may react to existing security measures, and then creates additional security measures. This is why multiple levels of physical, IT, and procedural security measures should be implemented.

TABLE 19.2 Methods of displacement.

		Type	Reason	Issues to consider
1	Who	The offender changes	Quits, moves, goes to jail, retires, dies, is replaced, etc.	The next offender may have different motivations, skill sets, tools, patience, knowledge, etc. Existing security measures may no longer be adequate
2	What	The type of offense carried out	If security measures prove to be adequate, consideration should be given to the offender changing offenses	An addict, failing to gain access to an office to steal laptops to trade for drugs, may conduct a street robbery instead. An offender may switch from robbing banks to writing bad checks. An offender may switch from crimes of violence to Internet-based scams
3	When	The time in which the crime was committed	Daytime, nighttime, morning, afternoon, evening, weekdays, weekends, summer, winter, etc.	The offender may change the time of their offense. If they cannot tunnel into a bank vault at night, they may rob the bank during the day. A laptop thief, if unable to defeat physical security after hours, may decide to talk their way past a receptionist to gain access
4	Where	The location of the criminal act	Moves on to another house, store, neighborhood, city, state/province, country, etc.	If an offender cannot gain access to one building, they may attempt to go next door to gain access. Regardless, the expectation is that they will go elsewhere. They may change locations because they have become too well known in their present area
5	Why	The type of target, which is attacked	Weaker, younger, older, less security, female, male, inability to overcome current security measures, etc.	There are a variety of reasons why the offender may switch targets. If a location is attacked and the target turns out to be removed, the offender may take other items. Retail thieves may enter a pharmacy intending to steal drugs, but if narcotics are not available and cash is, they will switch targets
6	How	The method used to complete the crime	Gun, knife, pen, computer, vehicle, etc.	The offender may change their modus operandi. For example, the terrorists who brought down the World Trade Center towers originally used a vehicle bomb in the underground parking garage. When that failed, they used airplanes as cruise missiles

Displacement of crime part two

Can you move crime from one location to another? Yes, you can. I know criminologists will say show me the data and we cannot. However, talk to veteran officers who have been working the various sectors for years and they will tell you that they have done it. Years ago, in a dormitory that had only one entrance and individual was stealing wallets and cash from unlocked rooms. This was going on night after night, so a police cruiser was put out in front of the dormitory, and every night around 3:00 a.m., the car was back a few spaces then forward. Crime stopped. Was it luck or skill? The cruiser was a deterrent. It is logical for a would-be criminal to assume that if a police car is outside then the officer must be inside and there is a likelihood I will get caught, so he goes to another location.

We know that drug dealing and prostitution are burning problems, so by closing off the street to prevent traffic from driving up and down the street, the drug dealers and prostitutes will move to another location.

Steven P. Lab states in his book titled Crime Prevention, seventh edition, "There is little reason to ever expect total displacement of a crime, regardless of the type of displacement considered."[1] He then discusses the various types of displacement, that is, territorial, temporal, tactical, target, and functional; he further states that although it is not 100% at the same time, they show that displacement does occur.

Diffusion of benefits

Diffusion of benefits is the opposite of displacement. Just as it is assumed by critics of rationalism that crime is simply moved to another location, there is also a belief that the benefits of situational crime prevention techniques are also moved to other locations, thereby resulting in a decrease in crime. As Pease states in reference to both issues:

> *The fact that displacement has been long debated, and that diffusion of benefits has been neglected suggests that displacement is dominant not because it reflects a real attempt to understand crime flux, but because it serves as a convenient excuse for doing nothing* ***('Why bother? It will only get displaced')*** *(1997, p. 978).*

A further, somewhat controversial point to displacement is that there may be a benefit to displacing certain kinds of crimes. For example, drug and prostitution control may be made easier or more tolerable when it is away from residential neighborhoods or concentrated in one locale (Pease, 1997, p. 979).

Routine activity theory

Routine activity theory, developed by Cohen and Felson, revolves around three things: a "potential offender, a suitable target, and the absence of a capable guardian" (Bottoms and Wiles, 1997, p. 320). All three must come together in order for criminal activity to be realized. Routine activity theory relies on the same rational choice methodology as situational crime prevention techniques. As in any theory, routine activity theory has its criticisms. One of the primary criticisms is the assumption that criminals are rational in their decision-making. They may not use the same rationale as the person implementing the security measures. They may not even be aware of the situational crime prevention techniques put into effect. They may be under the influence of drugs or alcohol or, for whatever reason, they may simply not care about the security measures.

Crime pattern theory

Crime pattern theory, developed by Paul and Patricia Brantingham, is a rather complex amalgamation of both rational choice and routine activity theories, as well as a further introduction of sociocultural, economic, legal, and physical environmental cues. The premise is that crime does not occur randomly in time, place, social group cohesiveness, or a host of other aspects. Acknowledging the complexity of the theory, a crime prevention response cannot come from one area alone. Instead, a multidisciplinary approach must be taken in which responses are tailored to the situation. One must consider the criminal opportunity, the individual offender, his or her readiness and willingness to commit crime, and the combination of the previous three aspects as they impact the sociocultural, economic, legal, and environmental cues. Granted, this is not an easy theory to employ from a theoretical or a practical perspective. Some of the components of this theory are certainly beyond the security practitioner's reach to address, but knowing that a detailed examination of the environment is required may enable practitioners to view the environment from a broader perspective.

---

1. Lab, S.P., 2010. Crime Prevention, seventh ed. Routledge Publishers, London.

Knowing that decisions to conduct criminal activity are often carried out for entirely different reasons than previously suspected gives the security officer the opportunity to view criminal activity in a new light.

Crime prevention through environmental design

CPTED[2] (*pronounced Sep-Ted*) is a crime prevention strategy, which outlines how physical environments can be designed in order to lessen the opportunity for crime.

This is achieved by creating environmental and social conditions that

- maximize risk to offenders (increasing the likelihood of detection, challenge, and apprehension);
- maximize the effort required to commit crime (increasing the time, energy, and resources required to commit crime);
- minimize the actual and perceived benefits of crime (removing, minimizing, or concealing crime attractors and rewards); and
- minimize excuse making opportunities (removing conditions that encourage/facilitate rationalization of inappropriate behavior).

The CPTED guidelines consider design and use, identify which aspects of the physical environment affect the behavior of people, and then use these factors to allow for the most productive use of space while reducing the opportunity of crime. This might include changes to poor environmental design, such as street lighting and landscaping.

CPTED concepts and principles are ideally incorporated at the design stage of a development but can also be applied to existing developments and areas where crime and safety are a concern.

CPTED, probably the most well known of the environmental crime control theories, was first discussed by Dr. C. Ray Jeffery in 1971. To quote Tim Crowe, a proponent, CPTED "expands upon the assumption that the proper design and effective use of the built environment can lead to a reduction in the fear of crime and the incidence of crime, and to an improvement in the quality of life" (Crowe, 2013, p. 1).

There are three key concepts specific to CPTED:

The use of natural surveillance. Natural surveillance refers to increasing the ability of legitimate place users to see farther and wider, while decreasing the ability of illegitimate place users to hide when waiting for the right time to carry out their activity. An example of using natural surveillance could be in an underground parking lot. As users leave their cars and head toward either an elevator lobby or staircase, it is often difficult to see what lies inside. By replacing cinder block with a glass partition, the property manager increases the natural surveillance whereby legitimate users can see directly into the vestibule area instead of guessing what lies ahead. Also, it is difficult for an illegitimate user to stay in this area for long, as they are subject to increased visual scrutiny.

The use of natural access control. This concept falls under the umbrella of spatial definition. An example of natural access control is when normal place users are encouraged to use an area for legitimate purposes, and illegitimate users are discouraged from remaining in the area. How this is accomplished is determined by the particular location and imagination of the property manager. For example, if unwanted visitors remain in an area because of a design feature, such as a wall or barrier, the feature should be removed (unless required) or changed to make it less attractive, thereby reducing the overall attractiveness of the area. Another example is skateboarders who use a particular plaza because of the many attractive, flat wooden benches. Pop-up seats could be installed on the benches, making it difficult, if not impossible, for skateboarders to use them.

Territorial behavior. This concept is a key for reclaiming an area if it has been taken over by illegitimate users. If design features have created a haven for illegitimate users and frightened off legitimate users, then one of the most important required actions is for the space to be reclaimed. Initially, this may take the form of enhanced security patrols to keep illegitimate users away until the area is once again seen as desirable for legitimate users. The return of high numbers of normal space users will deter the presence of illegitimate space users. A prime example is based upon the previous example of skateboarders. In one instance an area had practically been taken over by illegitimate users, making it a dangerous area to visit. Several CPTED strategies were employed, including design changes and enhanced security officer's presence. Eventually, a large number of legitimate users returned to the area, which, in turn, further deterred the skateboarders from coming back in large numbers. Although the problem has not completely gone away, it has decreased noticeably.

2. https://www.police.qld.gov.au/programs/cscp/safetyPublic/.

Further, CPTED planners should classify security strategies into three categories. The first category is the use of organized strategies, which includes the use of human resources to increase security, such as security or police officers or some other type of official guardian. The second strategy is to incorporate mechanical methods into enhanced security, which is achieved through the use of hardware, such as video surveillance, locking mechanisms, access control systems, fences, and other barriers. Finally, the third and probably most important strategy is to use natural enhancements to enhance security awareness. This may take the form of increased the presence of legitimate place users, proper use of windows to increase surveillance, or making all users responsible for security, and so on. It is important to start with the natural methods of enhancing security and then augment them through organized and mechanical methods.

Maintenance and image

These are the characteristics of an environment, which express ownership of the property.[3] Deterioration of a property indicates less ownership involvement, which can result in more vandalism, also known as the broken window theory.[4] If a window is broken and remains unfixed for a length of time, vandals will break more windows. Crime is more prevalent in areas that are not maintained; as a result, law-abiding persons do not feel safe and do not want to frequent those areas.

Milieu

This feature is generally associated with environmental land use and reflects adjoining land uses and the ways in which a site can be protected by specific design styles.[5] For example, a diverse housing mix is more likely to have people present at all times of the day, and bedroom communities are more likely to be vacant during various times of the day. Because criminals know their neighborhoods and potential targets of crime, they are more likely to strike at times when they will not be discovered, and possibly apprehended. Another concept that can be implemented, as required, in addition to the three other CPTED principles is described next:

Maintenance and image example

We recently conducted an assessment of several Housing & Urban Development (HUD) properties in the Northeast area. Some properties were in fairly good shape, and some were in deplorable conditions.

The following is information on the worst HUD properties we assessed:

- Roughly over 2000 pieces of litter were on the ground.
- This complex had 250 units with only two small dumpsters on each side of the complex.
- Four sets of old mattresses and box springs were resting up against a fence in the dumpster area.
- Drug dealers were openly selling drugs at 3:30 p.m. and individuals who appeared to be under the influence were outside of buildings and sitting on the steps.
- The homeless were at the top of the street and had been given cell phones and would call the drug dealers if they saw law enforcement coming down the street.

We have a question. Tell us what you think about the *image and maintenance* of this complex? You cannot get to the next security level until you fix this mess.

- Keep trees and shrubs trimmed back from windows, doors, and walkways. Keep shrubs trimmed to 3 ft and prune lower branches of trees up to 8 ft to maintain clear visibility.
- Use exterior lighting at night and keep it in working order.
- Enforce deed restrictions and covenants, in addition to all county codes. Disregard of these issues makes a site appear uncared for and less secure.
- Maintain signs and fencing and remove graffiti promptly.
- Maintain parking areas to high standards without potholes or trash.

Milieu/environmental management

3. CPTED Design Guidelines. www.cptedsecurity.com/cpted_design_guidelines.html.
4. https://www.cptedsecurity.com/broken_windows_theory.htm.
5. Saville, G, Cleveland, G, 2008. 2nd Generation CPTED: An Antidote to the Social Y2K Virus of Urban Design.

- Interaction between neighbors is vital to the awareness of persons and activities in the area. Management may need to create opportunities for neighbors to get to know one another.
- If security systems are utilized, ensure all employees and other authorized persons who are familiar with the security system to avoid false alarms.
- Set operating hours to coincide with those of neighboring businesses.
- Avoid shifts and situations where only one employee is present.
- Fully illuminate interior spaces.
- Business associations should work together to promote shopper and business safety and the appearance of safety.

An environment with CPTED design principles does not guarantee an absence of crime and vandalism. To be effective and truly implement the CPTED principles, the design (industrial) factors must be blended with the social (human) factors of the environment.

We have a question? Tell me what you think about the *maintenance and image* of this complex? You cannot get to the next security level until you fix this mess.

Target hardening

The use of mechanical devices (locks, security systems, alarms, and monitoring equipment) and organized crime prevention strategies (security patrols and law enforcement) make an area harder to access but may have a tendency to make the inhabitants "feel" unsafe.[6] This technique is the opposite of "natural" that reflects crime prevention as a by-product from normal and routine use of an environment. Target hardening often happens after crime has been committed. The integration of similar but customer service–oriented CTPED strategies in the initial environmental design may be as effective, but less threatening.

This is the last resort to resist crime by increasing physical security and is a more recognizable, traditional way to discourage crime. Target hardening is accomplished by features that prohibit entry or access, such as window locks, dead bolts for doors, and interior door hinges. This method of crime prevention is most effective when combined with the strategies identified earlier, so as to achieve a balanced approach.

Opportunities to implement CPTED strategies come with any proposal that involves new construction; revitalization, particularly in a downtown area or existing residential neighborhood; renovation of individual buildings; and repairs to buildings and structures. At the proposal stage, or when reviewing development plans, the application of CPTED can incrementally help to generate a greater level of safety in our communities. The best opportunities for safety, however, come with the establishment of good communities, where neighbors interact effectively and are committed to ensure that their environments are positive. The rest of this document gives examples and provides guidelines on how to apply these CPTED strategies in different urban areas.

Target hardening is not a fortress mentality

In 2015 Dr. Jennifer Hesterman wrote, *Soft Target Hardening: Protecting People from Attack*. The amount of research she did far surpassed other books in the security field and is a must read for practitioners.

> *Target Hardening is not a fortress mentality concept; it's good security practices (M. Perry, NCPI 2012). I live in Gated Communities, where the access is limited by two entrances. Families are aware of our who the neighbors are and who drives what vehicles. The residents are constantly walking back and forth from their homes to the beach and most carry cell phones.*
>
> *The community has zero to very little crime because of the property image and the maintenance provided to all townhouses and homes. Additionally, there are several law enforcement retirees who actually patrol the neighborhood before and after running errands. Nearly everyone now has a cell phones and YES, it is a Crime Prevention device to call for help and assistance, and we have a very good Neighborhood Watch program in our communities.*

6. Cozens, P.M., 2002. Sustainable urban development and crime prevention through environmental design for the British City. Towards an effective urban environmentalism for the 21st Century. Cities 19 (2), 129–137.

Activity support

The concept of activity support is to deliberately design formal and informal support for increasing the levels of human activity in particular spaces as a crime prevention strategy.[7]

How do we accomplish this strategy? First review how the complex is being used then add if necessary, bus stops, community garden, food trucks, children's play grounds, and cement table and two seats for playing chess or checkers. The use of the grounds will bring community together and for a positive purpose.

Geographical juxtaposition

By definition, *geographical juxtaposition is assessing the potential influence on crime levels, of proximal land-users that may generate crime.*[8]

We suggest that you read closely in this book Tim Crowe's CPTED Strategy and 3-D Concept. This material has been updated based on the past writings and newly discovered material of Crowe's found in 2016 (Newman, 1972).

We see CPTED as a process of a series of concepts and strategies that address risk, reduce crime and the fear of crime, and improve the quality of life for our communities.

Second-generation crime prevention through environmental design

Developed in 1998 by Saville and Cleveland (2008, p. 80), second-generation CPTED includes the original emphasis on physical location and adds the newer concept of including the following social factors:

1. *Social cohesion:* It involves the local community in events, associations, and positive problem-solving without resorting to violence and builds positive community relationships.
2. *Connectivity:* the neighborhood has positive relations and influence with external agencies (Saville and Cleveland, 2008, p. 82).
3. *Community culture:* positive social and cultural activities.
4. *Threshold capacity:* positive community resources that do not overwhelm the area, proper land density use and zoning, and a lack of crime generators.

Second-generation CPTED focuses on the physical and social aspects of communities to minimize both criminals and criminal opportunities.

Defensible Space: crime prevention through urban design

This theory revolves around the public housing environment and seeks to reduce crime through the use of natural surveillance, natural access control, and territorial concern.

History of Defensible Space. While Oscar Newman has written many influential pieces on this important concept over the past 30-plus years, two of his most important works are *Architectural Design for Crime Prevention*, published in 1971 through the US Department of Justice, and *Defensible Space*, published in 1972. Additional books, such as *Creating Defensible Space* from 1996, published through the US Department of Housing and Urban Development, add to his significant body of work.

Concept and strategies. While there will not be a detailed analysis of all the concepts that encompass the theory of Defensible Space, a general overview will be made. The writer encourages interested parties who seek a deeper understanding to access the aforementioned books for an in-depth analysis. Basically, Defensible Space calls for proprietors and legitimate users of residential space to act as guardians of their living areas. To quote from *Architectural Design* (p. 2):

Physical mechanisms for achieving Defensible Space are as follows:

7. Cozens, P.M., 2016. Think Crime! Using Evidence, Theory, and CPTED for Planning Safer Cities.
8. Cozens, P.M., 2016. Think Crime! Using Evidence, Theory, and CPTED for Planning Safer Cities.

1. Those which serve to define spheres of influence of territorial influence which occupants can easily adopt proprietary attitudes;
2. Those which improve the natural capability of residents to survey both the interior and exterior of the residential space;
3. Those which enhance the safety of adjoining areas such as communal facilities;
4. Finally, through the judicious building materials to reduce the perception of peculiarity such as vulnerability, isolation and stigma of housing projects and their residents (Newman, 1971).

Third-generation crime prevention through environmental design

The third-generation of CPTED envisions a green sustainable approach to enhance the living standards of urbanites and improve the image of the city as user-friendly, safe, and secure.[9] It also aims to create a sense of belonging and membership to a greater community of soliciting citizen engagement and participation in improving the conditions of urban living.

Third-generation CPTED focuses on three main methodological branches, they suggest to the urban policy-makers an approach to be adopted when planning the security policies of the respective cities:

1. anticipate the dynamics of the city
2. collaborate on improving standards of living

The green environment design must lead to more secure and safer environment. The city's budget has to be managed in a way to achieve multiple results through more intelligent and efficient policies.

The third-generation CPTED that is the subject of investigation and contemplation in this report adds another dimension to the discourse, which is that of the synergies among CPTED, urban sustainability, technology, and the potential of networks.[9]

The premise of third-generation crime prevention through environmental design

The premise of third-generation CPTED is that a sustainable green urbanity is perceived by its members and outsiders as safe. With focus on sustainable green environmental design strategies, perception of urban space as safe:

(1) addresses energy crisis, urban pollution, recycling, and minimizing waste; and (2) reprograming the physical space and material, based on consumption, online services, and cyber functionality.

- green.
- natural energy as a power source.

The third-generation crime prevention through environmental design strategies

1. reprograming urban space
2. urban-scale green urbanism and green space
3. design strategies
4. portal of digital information
5. smart signs
6. perception of safety and security
7. recycle of waste

Practical applications

As one can see, there are some similarities between *Defensible Space* and CPTED applications. The important concept of legitimate users versus illegitimate users, the proper and effective utilization of surveillance, both natural and

9. UNICRI. Improving Security Through Green Environment Design, MIT. <http://www.unicri.it/news/files/2011-04-01_110414_CRA_Urban_Security_sm.pdf> (retrieved 10.07.17.).

man-made, and creating safe havens for normal users are common to both. Knowing and understanding who belongs in an area and who does not (legitimate users versus illegitimate users of space), the importance of various types of surveillance, and encouraging legitimate users of space to use or reclaim areas for activities are recommendations that security practitioners can understand and appreciate.

Crime prevention through environmental design landscape security

An important element of CPTED, which defines semiprivate and private space within a complex, is your landscape design. It is recommended that the height of bushes be no higher than 3 ft. We have recently read that FEMA recommends the height of bushes to be 18 in. and that tree branches are between 7 and 8 ft[10] off the ground as a means for natural surveillance and safety. You want to be able to detect intruders and not allow them a hiding spot. Your landscape if properly laid out can also be a deterrent and prevent criminal opportunity.

Landscape furniture should be vandal resistant, and if benches are installed they need to be designed so that individuals cannot be sleeping on them.

Also, take under consideration exterior lighting, video surveillance, vegetation, maintenance, barriers, the entrance and exit of your property, signage, and the surface structure.

Principles of opportunity reduction

- Criminal behavior is a learned behavior.
- Reducing criminal opportunity reduces the opportunity to learn criminal behavior.
- Criminal opportunity can be lessened by improved security measures (target hardening) and by increasing the level of surveillance on the part of the community.
- Long-term crime prevention will not be achieved unless criminal opportunities are reduced either on a local or national bases.
- Security is in a pivotal position and as such they should be highly trained in crime prevention and CPTED and become involved in the preplanning of any community design or activity, where their services will be later requested.

Partnerships to reduce crime

Much has been said and written about the topic of partnerships.[11] Neighborhoods shift from a dead zone to a livable space, whether you live in New York, New Haven, Connecticut, Kansas City, St. Louis, Detroit, or Chicago. All have been referred to (and some still are) as "crime hot spots."

Why should communities formulate police—community partnerships[12] for problem-solving issues? The primary reason is in order to obtain results that will benefit the community through the partnership of public and private sectors, which will include a team of dedicated individuals who have the will and energy for this task.

Community leaders look toward crime prevention programs, CPTED principles, and neighborhood watch to help with the development of a crime-free zone.

Common goals:

- reduction to removal of drug dealers
- reduction to removal of crime and police calls
- create safe housing
- encourage addressing problem-solving issues
- encourage upgrade of neighborhoods with planning of trees and flowers
- development of neighborhood pride
- development of crime prevention workshops
- building and designing away crime
- develop a checklist for direction

10. Eight feet clearance is also recommended by ASIS Physical Security Principle Book, 2015, p. 214.
11. Geller B and Belsky L, 2012. Building Our Way Out of Crime. <http://wwolneyville/Geller-Belsky-case-study.pdf>.
12. http://www.policylink.org/sites/default/files/pl.police_commun%20engage_121714.c.pdf.

Environment and design

The conceptual thrust of a CPTED program is that the physical environment can be manipulated to produce behavioral effects that will reduce the incidence and fear of crime, thereby improving the quality of life. These behavioral effects can be achieved by reducing the propensity of the physical environment to support criminal behavior. Environmental design, as used in a CPTED program, is rooted in the design of the human/environment relationship. It embodies several concepts.

The term *environment* includes the people and their physical and social surroundings. However, as a matter of practical necessity, the environment defined for demonstration purposes is that which has recognizable territorial and system limits.

The term *design* includes physical, social, management, and law enforcement directives that seek to affect positively human behavior as people interact with their environment.

So, a CPTED program seeks to prevent certain specified crimes (and the fear of crime) within a specifically defined environment by manipulating variables that are closely related to the environment itself.

A CPTED program does not purport to develop crime prevention solutions in a broad universe of human behavior but rather solutions limited to variables that can be manipulated and evaluated in the specified human/environment relationship. CPTED involves the design of physical space in the context of the needs of legitimate users of the space (physical, social, and psychological needs), the normal and expected (or intended) use of the space (the activity or absence of activity planned for the space), and the predictable behavior of both legitimate users and offenders. Therefore in the CPTED approach, a design is proper if it recognizes the designated use of the space, defines the crime problem incidental to and the solution compatible with the designated use, and incorporates the crime prevention strategies that enhance (or at least do not impair) the effective use of the space. CPTED draws not only on physical and urban design but also on contemporary thinking in behavioral and social science, law enforcement, and community organization.

Space

The continuum of space within a residential complex (i.e., a property consisting of one or more buildings containing dwelling units and associated grounds or, more broadly, a neighborhood consisting primarily of residential uses) may be divided into four categories[13]:

Public space

Space that, whatever its legal status, is perceived by all members of a residential area or neighborhood as belonging to the public as a whole, which a stranger has as much perceived right to use as a resident.

Semipublic space

Semipublic space is accessible to all members of the public without passing through a locked or guarded barrier. There is thought to be an implied license for use by the public, and strangers will rarely be challenged. This is generally associated with multifamily housing.

Semiprivate space

This space is restricted for use by residents, guests, and service people on legitimate assignments. In multifamily housing, semiprivate space is usually secured by protection officers (or doormen), locks, or other forms of physical barriers. Strangers can be expected to be challenged as potential trespassers.

Private space

Private space is restricted for use by residents of a single dwelling unit, their invited guests, and service people, with access generally controlled by locks and other physical barriers. Unauthorized use is always challenged when the opportunity for challenge presents itself.

13. Tyska, L.A., Fennelly, L.J., 1998. Physical Security – 150 Things You Should Know. Elsevier Publishers, Boston, MA.

Holistic approach

We recommend applying the frameworks, principles, and concepts from many, including[14]

- situational crime prevention
- designing out crime
- crime prevention through environmental design and management
- crime opportunity profiling
- secured by design principles
- target hardening
- SARA

Some benefits of crime prevention through environmental design planning activities

In addition to dealing with the reduction of crime and fear problems, other benefits of CPTED planning include the following:

Treatment of crime problems at various environmental scales

The CPTED process for identifying crime/environment problems, selecting CPTED strategies, and initiating, implementing, and evaluating anticrime projects can be applied to entire neighborhoods or types of institutional settings within a city, such as secondary schools, or the process can be applied equally well to a small geographic area or to one particular institution.

Integration of prevention approaches

CPTED principles are derived from an opportunity model of criminal behavior that assumes that the offender's behavior can be accounted for by understanding how, and under what circumstances, variables in the environment interact to induce crime. Once an assessment of the opportunity structure is made, then appropriate strategies can be designed and integrated into a coordinated, consistent program.

Identification of short- and long-term goals

Comprehensive broad-based programs such as CPTED have ultimate goals that may take years to accomplish. Unlike CPTED, however, many programs fail to develop short-term or proximate goals and adequate ways to measure their success. The CPTED approach includes an evaluation framework that details proximate goals relating to increased access control, surveillance, and territorial reinforcement. The rationale is that the ultimate program success is directly related to its success in achieving the proximate goals.

Encouragement of collective responses to problems

The CPTED emphasis is on increasing the capacity of residents to act in concert rather than individually. Strategies are aimed at fostering citizen participation and strengthening social cohesion.

Interdisciplinary approach to urban problems

An explicit policy of interdisciplinary teaming ensures effective cooperation among diverse city departments, such as public works, social services, economic development, and police. Each participant benefits from exposure to the responsibilities, jurisdiction, and skills of the others.

Encouragement of better police/community relations

A key strategy is to coordinate law enforcement and community service activities with the result of improving police/community relations and developing an anticrime program that is not solely dependent on enforcement agencies.

---

14. http://www.griffinrc.co.uk/prevention.htm.

Development of security guidelines and standards

CPTED programing can lead to the creation of security criteria for newly constructed or modified environments to avoid planning and design decisions that inadvertently provide opportunities for crime.

Assistance in urban revitalization

Through its impact on physical, social, and economic conditions, CPTED can be instrumental in revitalizing communities, including downtown areas. Once business leaders, investors, and other citizens perceive that a comprehensive effort is underway to reduce crime and fear, there will be an improvement in community identity and cohesiveness.

Acquisition of development funds

The incorporation of CPTED in to existing programs can provide additional jurisdiction for awarding grants, loans, and community development funds.

Institutionalization of crime prevention policies and practices

CPTED projects can create a local management capability and expertise to maintain ongoing projects. This capability can be incorporated in to existing citizen organizations or municipal agencies.

An ounce of prevention: a new role for law enforcement support of community development

Public/private sector partnerships enhance public safety by sharing information, making the community more aware of threats, and involving them in the problem-solving process. Collaboration is a key word for partnerships because all partners must recognize that their goals or missions overlap and they work together to share resources and achieve common goals. The added value of public–private sector partnerships is the cross transfer of skills, knowledge, and expertise between the public and the private sector.[15] In order for a partnership to be successful, each partner has to understand the value they will gain from participating. Successful partnerships involve partners that are committed to working together to achieve common goals—building the community. There are a number of compelling reasons for law enforcement to be involved in CPTED aside from the formulation of partnerships:

1. CPTED concepts have been proven to enhance community activities while reducing crime problems.
2. CPTED concepts are fundamental to traditional law enforcement values, in terms of helping the community to function properly.
3. CPTED requires the unique information sources and inherent knowledge of the community that is endemic to the law enforcement profession.
4. CPTED problems and issues bear a direct relationship to repeat calls or service and to crime-producing situations.
5. CPTED methods and techniques can directly improve property values, business profitability, and industrial productivity, thereby enhancing local tax bases.

Law enforcement agencies, regardless of size, must be involved formally in the review and approval process of community and business projects. Their participation must be active and creative rather than passive and reactive. Moreover, any such involvement should not be understood to expose the agencies to possible litigation, since it is the role of law enforcement in CPTED concepts to provide additional information and concerns that may not have occurred to the persons who are responsible (and qualified) for making changes to the environment. The expression, "pay me now or pay me later," conveys the idea that the early involvement of a knowledgeable law enforcement agency in the conceptualization and planning of community projects can lead to improvements in the quality of life and to reductions in the fear and incidence of crime. This early involvement is one of the most cost-effective methods of crime prevention.[16]

15. Fusion Center Guidelines Developing and Sharing Information and Intelligence in a New Era. From: <http://it.ojp.gov/documents/d/fusion_center_guidelines.pdf> (retrieved 11.11.18.).

16. Crowe, T.D., Fennelly, L.J., 2013. Crime Prevention Through Environmental Design, third ed. Elsevier Publishers, Boston, MA.

Appendix 1 crime prevention through environmental design checklist

Crime prevention through environmental design

CPTED (pronounced sep-ted) is a proven crime prevention approach to reduce opportunities for crime. The concept is to design or modify your home in ways that reduce or prevent the incidence of crime and improve the quality of life for residents.

The police alone cannot provide all the solutions to property crime, therefore homeowners and communities are encouraged to learn basic principles to help themselves secure their properties and neighborhoods.

How can I apply CPTED to my home or business?

A checklist is provided for you to complete, with every "yes" you have your home becomes more secure.

Checklist

1. Are trees and shrubs on your property trimmed to allow a clear view of your house from the street? For natural surveillance.
2. Are your front boundary fences low enough to allow unobstructed views of your house or not solid and able to see through? For natural access control.
3. Do you have working sensor lights on the exterior of your home?
4. Do you always lock your doors and windows?
5. Do you lock entry and exit points while you are present at your property? That is, front door should be locked while you are in the backyard in the garden.
6. Are gates kept locked when not in use?
7. Are bins secured to prevent them being used as a climbing aid?
8. Do you have locks that meet established standards on all your doors and windows, including garage and shed doors?
9. Do you have security screens on doors and windows?
10. Do you have a dog? And are trees and shrubs surrounding your property managed and maintained?
11. Do you report all graffiti to the removal promptly?
12. Is your yard kept litter free and neat at all times?
13. Is the property well maintained?
14. Have hidden space been eliminated?
15. Does the overall location have a propensity to generate crime in the surrounding area?
16. Would you consider the location to be a soft target or a hard target?

Summary

While this chapter has not detailed each and every theory or practice of crime prevention, it has provided an overview of the main existing environmental crime theories. Readers are encouraged to further examine the theories outlined here, as they are an important aspect of crime control. While certainly not the only theories, rational choice, routine activities, CPTED, Defensible Space, crime pattern theory, and situational crime prevention techniques comprise an important basis for explaining some of the root causes of why certain crimes may occur repeatedly in specific locations. Not all the answers are contained here, and while every situation is unique, the security practitioner should understand that there are some basic explanations and rationales behind every criminal activity. Implementing security enhancements should be an educated decision. Hence, a detailed study of the criminal area with the accompanying rationale should reduce criminal opportunity.

References

Bottoms, A., Wiles, P., 1997. Environmental criminology. In: Maguire, M., Morgan, R., Reiner, R. (Eds.), The Oxford Handbook of Criminology, second ed. Clarendon Press, Oxford, pp. 305–359.

Clarke, R.V., 2008. Situational crime prevention. In: Wortley, R., Mazerolle, L. (Eds.), Environmental Criminology and Crime Analysis. Willan Publishing, Portland, pp. 178–194.

Cornish, D.B., Clarke, R.V., 2008. The rational choice perspective. In: Wortley, R., Mazerolle, L. (Eds.), Environmental Criminology and Crime Analysis. Willan Publishing, Portland, pp. 21–47.

Crowe, T.D., 2013. Crime Prevention Through Environmental Design. Butterworth-Heinemann, Boston, MA.

Newman, O., 1971. Architectural Design for Crime Prevention. National Institute of Law Enforcement and Criminal Justice.

Newman, O., 1972. Defensible Space: Crime Prevention Through Urban Design. The Macmillan Company.

Pease, K., 1997. Crime prevention. In: Maguire, M., Morgan, R., Reiner, R. (Eds.), The Oxford Handbook of Criminology, second ed. Clarendon Press, Oxford, pp. 963–995.

Saville, G., Cleveland, G., 2008. Second generation CPTED: The rise and fall of opportunity theory. In: Atlas, R. (Ed.), 21st Century Security and CPTED. CRC Press, Boca Raton, FL, pp. 79–90.

Tayler, I., 1997. The political economy of crime. In: Maguire, M., Morgan, R., Reiner, R. (Eds.), The Oxford Handbook of Criminology, second ed. Clarendon Press, Oxford, pp. 265–303.

Wortley, R., Mazerolle, L., 2008. Environmental Criminology and Crime Analysis. Willan Publishing, Portland.

Resources

Fennelly, L.J., Lombardi, J.H., 1997. Spotlight on Security for Real Estate Managers. Institute for Real Estate Management.

Jacobs, J., 1992. The Death and Life of Great American Cities. Vintage.

National Crime Prevention Institute (NCPI), 2001. Understanding Crime Prevention, second ed. Butterworth-Heinemann.

Newman, O., 1996. Creating Defensible Space. U.S. Department of Housing and Urban Development.

Vellani, K., Nahoun, J., 2001. Applied Crime Analysis. Butterworth-Heinemann.

Further reading

Clarke, R.V., 1997. Situational Crime Prevention: Successful Case Studies, second ed. Harrow and Heston, Albany, NY.

Fennelly, L.J., Perry, M.A., 2018. CPTED and Traditional Security Countermeasure, 150 Things You Should Know. CRC Press.

Module 1, 1999a. Criminological Theory 2: Rational Choice Theory: 277–304, The Scarman Centre for Public Order: University of Leicester.

Module 1, 1999b. Crime Prevention 2: The Situational Approach: 305–344, The Scarman Centre for Public Order: University of Leicester.

Module 5, 2000. Applied Crime Management: Unit 3: Crime Pattern Analysis: 113–168, The Scarman Centre for Public Order: University of Leicester.

Tyska, L.A., Fennelly, L.J., 1998. 150 Things That You Should Know About Security. Butterworth-Heinemann, Boston, MA.

Wortley, R., 2001. A classification of techniques for controlling situational precipitators of crime. In: Fisher, B., Gill, M. (Eds.), Security Journal, vol. 14. Perpetuity Press, pp. 63–82. , No. 4.

Chapter 20

Alarms intrusion detection systems*

Jack F. Dowling
Security Consultant

Building automation systems may integrate with, or share the same software and hardware as, an access control system. Building automation systems share several industry stand protocols such as BACnet, which allows systems or components from different manufacturers to communicate with each other.

The Protection Officers Handbook Ninth Edition 2019.

Introduction

Three points I would like to make: first, a word about integrated systems and the fundamental use of integrated systems to create system redundancy and improved reporting; second, alarms now can be communicated via mobile devices and mobile technology; and third, network video is the new terminology for closed-circuit television.[1]

Although on the decline in the United States, burglary is a big business, and both private homes and businesses are the targets of burglary. Many homeowners and business owners install electronic alarm protection. However, the customer, either homeowner or business owner, needs to be careful in selecting the installation company and the type of system.

The selection of a proper alarm system is not a simple matter, because the needs of each homeowner or business owner are different, like a set of fingerprints. Following are some of the factors that determine the requirements of an individual alarm system and the questions that must be answered when selecting a system:

- The threat and risk. What is the system to protect against?
- The type of sensors needed. What will be protected?
- What methods are available to provide the level of protection needed?
- The method of alarm signal transmission. How is the signal to be sent and who will respond?

Most of the confusion regarding intrusion detection systems is a result of the variety of methods available to provide the protection needed. The combinations of detection methods are in the thousands. An intrusion detection system may deter a would-be intruder. However, the primary function of the alarm system is to signal the presence of an intruder and detect an unauthorized entry. An intrusion detection system can be just a portion of the overall protection needed and may be a part of a larger and comprehensive security and fire alarm system. Many large businesses supplement these systems with security officers and other security personnel. The successful operation of any type of an alarm system depends on its proper installation and maintenance by the alarm installing company and the proper use of the system by the customer. Today, wireless intrusion alarm systems are available, which are easier and less expensive to install. Some are presented as do it yourself (DIY) projects but may lack professional monitoring capabilities, an essential element of an intrusion alarm system. Caution should be exercised in selecting a DIY system for such a vital protection role.

*This material was originally complied by Lawrence J. Fennelly, Mike Rolf, and James Culley.

1. Jeff Slotnick reviewed the chapter September 2018.

Handbook of Loss Prevention and Crime Prevention. DOI: https://doi.org/10.1016/B978-0-12-817273-5.00020-X

Components of alarm systems

Sensing devices are used in the actual detection of an intruder (see Figs. 20.1 and 20.2). Each has a specific purpose and can be divided into three categories: perimeter protection, area/space protection, and object/spot protection.

Perimeter protection

Perimeter protection is the first line in the defense to detect an intruder. The most common points equipped with sensing devices for premise perimeter protection are doors, windows, vents, skylights, or any opening to a business or home. Since most of the burglaries occur through these openings, most alarm systems provide this type of protection. The major advantage of perimeter protection is its simple design. The major disadvantage is that it protects only the openings. If the burglar bursts through a wall, comes through the ventilation system, or stays behind after closing, perimeter protection is useless.

Today, technology has extended the perimeter of a business or home beyond the actual physical property line or structure through the utilization of video motion detection, video analytics, and radar. This early warning capability allows the business or home to detect a potential intruder well before reaching the physical structure.

1. *Door switches*. These are installed on a door or window in such a way that opening the door or window causes a magnet to move away a contact switch, which activates the alarm. They can be surface mounted or recessed into the door and frame. A variety of types of switches are manufactured for all types of doors or windows. The switches are both wide gap type and magnetic standard type.
2. *Glass break detectors*. These detectors are attached to the glass and sense the breakage of the glass by shock or sound. Glass breakage sensors use microphone transducers to detect the glass breakage. A ceiling sensor over a window covers a 30 degree radius.

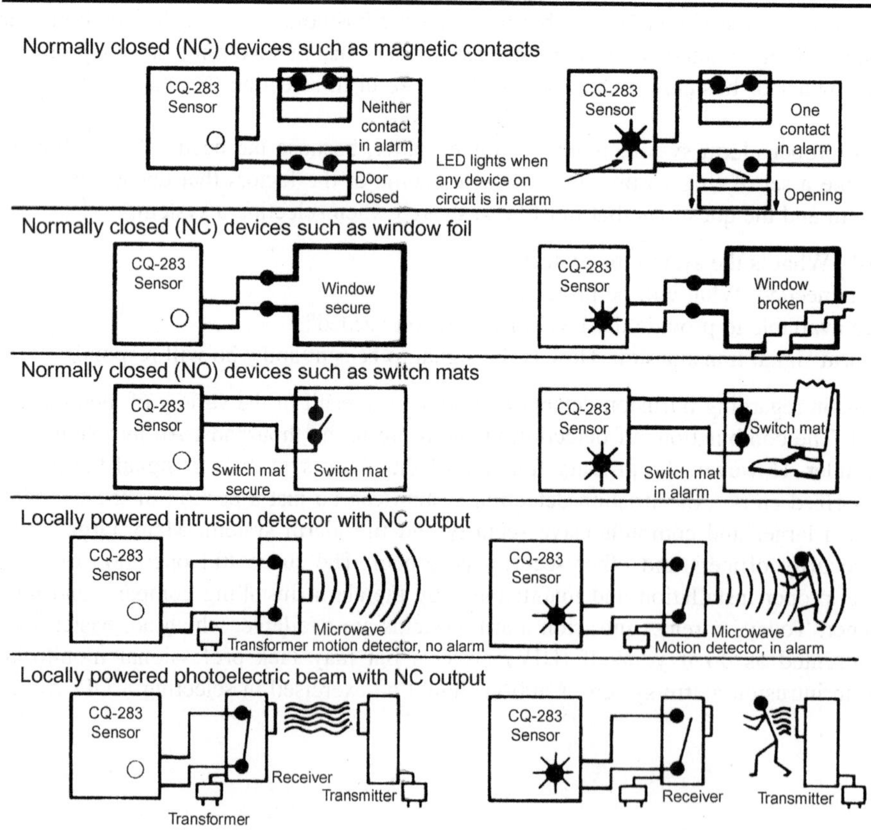

FIGURE 20.1 Typical application of the use of magnetic contacts, window foil, switch mats, motion detection, and photoelectric beam. *Courtesy of Aritech Corporation.*

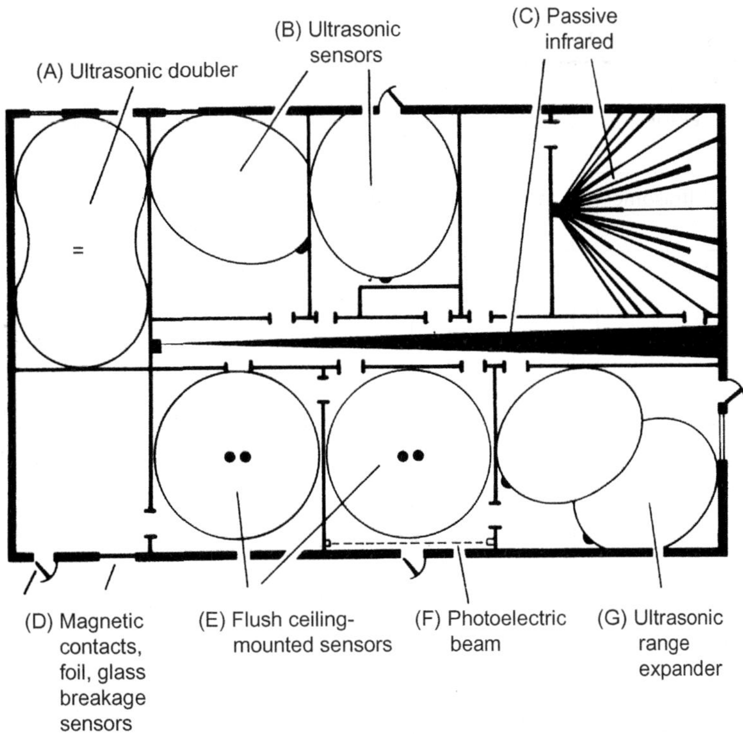

FIGURE 20.2 Sensors.
(A) Ultrasonic doubler: back-to-back ultrasonic transceivers provide virtually double the coverage of single detectors at almost the same wiring and equipment cost. With more than 50 ft × 25 ft of coverage, the doubler is the best value in space protection. (B) Ultrasonic sensors: easy to install, no brackets are needed. Can be mounted horizontally, vertically, or in a corner; surface, flush, or with mounting feet on a shelf. Each UL-listed sensor protects a three-dimensional volume up to 30 ft wide and high. (C) Passive infrared: for those zones where the lower cost ultrasonic sensor is inappropriate, there is no need to buy a complete passive infrared system as both ultrasonic and passive infrared can be used in the same system. (D) Magnetic contacts, foil, and glass breakage sensors: the building's perimeter protection detectors can be wired into the system via universal interface sensor. There is no need for running a separate perimeter loop. (E) Flush ceiling-mounted sensors: only the two small 2-in. diameter transducer caps are visible below the ceiling tiles. Designed for where minimum visibility is needed for esthetic or security purposes. (F) Photoelectric beam: the universal interface sensor allows the connection of any NO or NC alarm device into the system for zoned annunciation. It can be used with photoelectric beams, switch matting, microwave motion detectors, and many other intrusion detectors. (G) Ultrasonic range expander: adding an ultrasonic range expander can increase the coverage of an ultrasonic sensor by 50%–90%, depending on where it is positioned and the surrounding environment. *UL*, Underwriters Laboratories. *Courtesy of Aritech Corporation.*

3. *Wooden screens.* These devices are made of wooden dowel sticks assembled in a cage-like fashion no more than 4 in. from each other. A very fine, brittle wire runs in the wooden dowels and frame. The burglar must break the doweling to gain entry and thus break the low-voltage electrical circuit, causing the alarm. These devices are used primarily in commercial applications.
4. *Window screens.* These devices are similar to regular wire window screens in a home except that a fine, coated wire is a part of the screen. When the burglar cuts the screen to gain entry, the flow of low-voltage electricity is interrupted, which causes the alarm. These devices are used primarily in residential applications.
5. *Lace and panels.* The surfaces of door panels and safes are protected against entry by installing a close lace-like pattern of metallic foil or a fine brittle wire on the surface. Entry cannot be made without first breaking the foil or wire, thus activating the alarm. A panel of wood is placed over the lacing to protect it.
6. *Interior sensors.* They come in many shapes and sizes depending upon the application, for example, interior motion detector units and proximity and boundary penetration.

Area/space protection

Area/space-protection devices (Table 20.1) protect the interior spaces in a business or home. They protect against intrusion whether or not the perimeter protection was violated. It is particularly effective against a stay-behind intruder or the burglar who cuts through the roof or breaks through a block wall. Space-protection devices are only a part of the complete alarm system.

TABLE 20.1 Motion sensor survey checklist.

Environmental and other factors affecting sensor usage	Effect on sensor				
Circle one	**Ultrasonics**	**Microwave**	**PIR**	**Recommendation and notes**	
If the areas to be protected are enclosed by thin walls or contain windows, will there be movement close to the outside of this area?	Yes No	None	Major	None	Avoid using a microwave sensor unless it can be aimed away from thin walls, glass, etc., which can pass an amount of microwave energy
Will protection pattern see sun, moving headlamps, or other sources of infrared energy passing through windows?	Yes No	None	None	Major	Avoid using a PIR sensor unless the pattern can be positioned to avoid rapidly changing levels of infrared energy
Does area to be protected contain HVAC ducts?	Yes No	None	Moderate	None	Ducts can channel microwave energy to other areas; if using a microwave sensor, aim it away from duct openings
Will two or more sensors of the same type be used to protect a common area?	Yes No	None	None (see note)	None	*Note:* Adjacent units must operate on different frequencies
Does area to be protected contain fluorescent or neon lights that are on during protection-on period?	Yes No	None	Major	None	Microwave sensor, if used, must be aimed away from any fluorescent or neon light within 20 ft
Are incandescent lamps cycled on and off during protection-on period included in the protection pattern?	Yes No	None	None	Major	If considering the use of PIR sensor, make a trial installation and, if necessary, redirect protection pattern away from lighting units
Must protection pattern be projected from a ceiling?	Yes No	None, but only for ceiling heights up to 15 ft.	Major	Major	Only ultrasonic sensors can be used on a ceiling, but height is limited to 15 ft; at greater ceiling heights, use rigid ceiling brackets to suspend sensor to maintain 15 ft limitation or, in large open areas, try a microwave sensor mounted high on a wall and aimed downward
Is the overall structure of flimsy construction (corrugated metal, thin plywood, etc.)?	Yes No	Minor	Major	Minor	Do not use a microwave sensor; where considerable structural movement can be expected, use a rigid mounting surface for ultrasonic or PIR sensor

(*Continued*)

TABLE 20.1 (Continued)

Environmental and other factors affecting sensor usage	Effect on sensor				
Circle one	Ultrasonics	Microwave	PIR	Recommendation and notes	
Will protection pattern include large metal objects or wall surfaces?	Yes No	Minor	Major	Minor (major if metal is highly polished)	Use ultrasonic or PIR sensor
Are any radar installations nearby?	Yes No	Minor	Major when radar is close and sensor is aimed at it	Minor	Avoid using a microwave sensor
Will protection pattern include heaters, radiators, air conditioners, or the like?	Yes No	Moderate	None	Major when rapid changes in air temperature are involved	Use ultrasonic sensor, but aim it away from sources of air turbulence (desirable to have heaters, etc., turned off during protection-on period) or use microwave sensor
Will area to be protected be subjected to ultrasonic noise (bells and hissing sounds)?	Yes No	Moderate, can cause problems in severe cases	None	None	Try muffling noise source and use an ultrasonic, microwave, or PIR sensor
Will protection pattern include drapes, carpet, racks of clothing, or the like?	Yes No	Moderate, reduction in range	None	Minor	Use ultrasonic sensor if some reduction in range can be tolerated or use microwave sensor
Is the area to be protected subject to changes in temperature and humidity?	Yes No	Moderate	None	Major	Use an ultrasonic sensor unless changes in temperature and humidity are severe or use a microwave sensor
Is there water noise from faulty valves in the area to be protected?	Yes No	Moderate, can be a problem	None	None	If noise is substantial, try correcting faulty valves and use an ultrasonic sensor; use a microwave or PIR sensor
Will protection pattern see moving machinery, fan blades, or the like?	Yes No	Major	Major	Minor	Have machinery, fans and the like turned off during protection-on period, carefully place ultrasonic sensor, or use PIR sensor
Will drafts or other air movement pass through protection pattern?	Yes No	Major	None	None, unless rapid temperature changes are involved	If protection pattern can be aimed away from air movement or air movement can be stopped during protection-on period, use an ultrasonic, microwave, or PIR sensor

(Continued)

TABLE 20.1 (Continued)

Environmental and other factors affecting sensor usage	Effect on sensor				
Circle one	**Ultrasonics**	**Microwave**	**PIR**	**Recommendation and notes**	
Will protection pattern see overhead doors that can be rattled by wind?	Yes No	Major	Major	Minor	If protection pattern can be aimed away from such doors, use an ultrasonic or a PIR sensor
Are there hanging signs, calendar pages, or the like that can be moved by air currents during protection-on period?	Yes No	Major	Major	Moderate, can be a problem	Use ultrasonic sensor, but aim pattern away from objects that can move or remove such objects, or use PIR sensor
Are adjacent railroad tracks used during protection-on period?	Yes No	Major	Minor	Minor	A trial installation is required if using an ultrasonic sensor
Can small animals (or birds) enter protection pattern?	Yes No	Major	Major	Major (particularly rodents)	Install a physical barrier to prevent intrusion by animals or birds
Does area to be protected contain a corrosive atmosphere?	Yes No	Major	Major	Major	None of these sensors can be used

HVAC, High Vacuum AC; *PIR*, Passive infrared.

They should always be supplemented with perimeter protection. The major advantage of space-protection devices is that they provide a highly sensitive, invisible means of detection. The major disadvantage is that improper application and installation by the alarm company can result in frequent false alarms.

Types of area/space protection:

1. *Video motion detectors*. These cameras detect motion in a wide field of view and transmit an alert.
2. *Video analytics*. These cameras detect specific changes in a narrow field of view and transmit an alert.
3. *Photoelectric eyes (beams)*. These devices transmit a beam across a protected area. When an intruder interrupts the beam, the beam circuit is disrupted and the alarm is initiated. Photoelectric devices use a pulsed infrared beam that is invisible to the naked eye. Some units have a range of over 1000 ft and can be used outdoors, although they are rarely used today.
4. *Ultrasonic*. They (although rarely used today) work on a low-frequency sound wave projected from the unit. The frequency is in kilohertz (23–26), and its area of coverage can be anywhere from 5 to 40 ft in length. The pattern is volumetric and cannot be aimed, although the pattern may be directed by the use of deflectors. Deflectors come in 90 or 45 degree angles. A doubler type uses two 45 degree angles back to back. Ultrasonic work on a change in frequency, called the *Doppler effect*. A motion detector has two transducers; the transmitter sends out a signal that is bounced back to the receiver by immobile objects in the protected area. If an intruder moves toward or away from the unit, the change in its reflected frequency signals an alarm. Ultrasonic may be found as stand-alone units or part of what is called a *master system*. The stand-alone units compare the reflected signal within the unit and trip the control panel by opening or closing a relay contact. Master systems work by sending the signal back to a main processing unit that compares the signal and trips the relay contacts of the processor. False alarms result from three types of sources:
   a. *Motion*. Objects that move in the path of protection and air turbulence are seen as motion because of the frequency of the unit.
   b. *Noise*. Ultrasonic noise is present when audible noises are heard; hissing (such as from high-pressure air leaking or steam radiators) or bells ringing can be a source of these noises.
   c. *Radio or electrical interference*. Induced electrical signals or radio frequency (RF) interference from radio transmitters can cause false alarms.

5. Both grounding and shielding are very important in a master system. If an earth ground is required, it should be a cold water pipe. The length of the ground wire should be as short as possible and with a minimum number of bends. Potential problems include
   a. turbulence and draft, hanging displays, moving draperies, and small pets
   b. noise caused by air hissing, bells, and telephones
   c. temperature or humidity can affect range of the ultrasonic unit
6. Carpets, furniture, and draperies may absorb some of the signal, decreasing the unit's sensitivity. Ultrasonic energy does not penetrate most objects. The signal may be reflected off some smooth surfaces.
7. *Microwave*. Microwave detectors are a volumetric type of space protection and are based on a Doppler shift. They detect intruders by the use of a radiated RF electromagnetic field. The unit operates by sensing a disturbance in the generated RF field, called the Doppler effect. The frequency range is between 0.3 and 300 GHz (1 GHz = 1 billion cps). Any type of motion in the protected area creates a change in frequency, causing an alarm condition. Because the power output from the unit is relatively low, the field radiated is harmless. Microwave energy penetrates most objects and reflects off of metal. One of the most important considerations in placement of these units is vibration. The microwave must be mounted on a firm surface: cinder block, brick, or main support beams are ideal mounting locations. Never mount two microwave units with identical frequencies in the same room or area where the patterns may overlap. This could cause cross talk between the units, causing false alarms. Microwave units draw excessive current, so the proper gauge of wire should be used and the length of the wire run should also be taken into consideration. Current readings should be taken at the end of an installation or while troubleshooting units to ensure that the maximum current of the control panel has not been exceeded. Fluorescent lights may be a problem because the radiated ionization from the lights may be seen as motion by the detector. Potential problems include the following:
   a. Vibrations or movement of mounting surface, mounts on a wall, sense change in electrical current.
   b. Reflection of pattern or movement of metal objects in protected area, such as moving fan blades or movement of overhead doors.
   c. Penetration of thin walls or glass is a potential problem if motion or large metal objects, such as trains or cars, are present.
   d. RF interference, radar, or AC line transients in severe cases can be a problem.
   e. Water movement in plastic or PVC storm drains is a potential interference if located close to the unit. Most microwave units provide a test point, where the amplifier output voltage can be read. By following the manufacturer's recommended voltage settings, the microwave can be set up properly and the unit environment examined.
8. *Passive infrared (PIR) motion detectors*. These detectors are passive sensors, because they do not transmit a signal for an intruder to disturb. Rather, a source of moving infrared radiation (the intruder) is detected against the normal radiation/temperature environment of the room. PIR detects a change in the thermal energy pattern caused by a moving intruder in the field of view of the detector. The field of view of an infrared unit must terminate on an object to ensure its proper operation and stability. An infrared unit should never be set up to look out into midair. Following are the potential problems:
   a. Turbulence and drafts are a problem if the air is blowing directly on the unit or causes a rapid change in temperature of objects in the path of protection.
   b. Stray motion (i.e., drapes blowing, hanging objects or displays, and small animals).
   c. Changing temperatures (i.e., hot spots in machinery and sunlight) may cause false alarms. The temperature of the background infrared level may also affect the unit's sensitivity: PIRs become less sensitive as the temperature increases.
   d. Lightning or bright lights, such as halogen headlights. The infrared radiation pattern is blocked by solid objects as it is unable to penetrate most objects. The pattern of protection may also be affected by reflection off smooth surfaces.
9. *Pressure mats*. These mats are basically mechanical switches. Pressure mats are most frequently used as a backup system to perimeter protection. When used as traps they can be hidden under the carpet in front of a likely target or in hallways where an intruder would travel.
10. *Sound sensors*. These sensors detect intrusion by picking up the noise created by a burglar during an attempt to break into a protected area. These sensors consist of a microphone and an electronic amplifier/processor. When the sound level increases beyond the limit normally encountered, the unit signals an alarm. Some units have pulse-counting and time-interval features. Other types can actually listen to the protected premises from a central monitoring station.

11. *Dual-techs.* Dual-technology sensors, commonly referred to as *dual-techs,* are a combination of two types of space-protection devices. The principle of the unit is that both sections of the detectors must be tripped at the same time to cause an alarm. A dual-tech unit could be a combination passive/microwave or a combination passive/ultrasonic. By using a dual-technology device, an installer can provide space protection in areas that may have presented potential false alarm problems when a single-technology unit was used. A repairer can replace units sending false signals because of environment or placement. Dual-techs are not the solution to all false alarm problems, and unless careful consideration is used in installing or replacing a device, the false alarm problems may persist. Since these contain two different types of devices, there is much more to consider. Dual-techs draw much more current than conventional detectors. Current readings are essential and additional power supplies may be necessary to provide enough operating current and standby power. Until recently, if one section of the unit stopped working or was blocked off in some way by the end user, the unit was rendered inoperable. Manufacturers are working on supervising the microwave section of these units. If the unit is located or adjusted so that one section of the unit is continuously in an alarm condition, the dual-technology principle is worthless.
12. *Interior sensors.* These sensors are generally active or passive, covert or visible, or volumetric or line applications.

Application

For all practical purposes the reason we use space protection is as a backup to the perimeter system. It is not necessary to cover every inch of the premises being protected. The best placement is as a trap in a high-traffic area or spot protection for high-value areas. The worst thing an installer can do is overextend the area being protected by an individual unit (e.g., trying to cover more than one room with a detector or trying to compensate for placement or environment by overadjusting the sensitivity). By using a little common sense and checking for all possible hazards, you can ensure a trouble-free installation. Make sure that the units have adequate power going to each head and the standby batteries are working and charging properly. Be sure to adjust for pets and brief customers and any problems they may create, such as leaving fans or machinery on, and not to open windows in the path of protection. Before leaving an installation, make sure that all units have been walk-tested and the areas in question have been masked out. One of the most important considerations in setting up a number of space-protection devices is *zoning.* Never put more than two interior devices in one zone if at all possible. The majority of false alarms are caused by interior devices. Breaking up the interior protective circuits as much as possible gives the service person a better chance of solving a false alarm problem (even with two heads in one zone you have a 50/50 chance of finding the trouble unit). Zoning a system correctly helps with troubleshooting, makes the police department feel better about the company and the company feel better about the installer, and ensures good relations with the customer.

Object/spot detection

Object/spot detection is used to detect the activity or presence of an intruder at a single location. It provides direct security for objects. Such a detection method is the final stage of an in-depth system for protection. The objects most frequently protected include safes, filing cabinets, desks, art objects, models, statues, and expensive equipment. The types of object/spot protection are as follows:

1. *Video motion detectors.* These cameras detect motion in a wide field of view and transmit an alert.
2. *Video analytics.* These cameras detect specific changes in a narrow field of view and transmit an alert.
3. *Capacitance/proximity detectors.* The object being protected becomes an antenna, electronically linked to the alarm control. When an intruder approaches or touches the object/antenna, an electrostatic field is unbalanced and the alarm is initiated. Only metal objects can be protected in this manner.
4. *Vibration detectors.* These devices utilize a highly sensitive, specialized microphone called an *electronic vibration detector* (EVD). The EVD is attached directly to the object to be protected. It can be adjusted to detect a sledge hammer attack on a concrete wall or a delicate penetration of a glass surface. It sends an alarm only when the object is moved, whereas capacitance devices detect when the intruder is close to the protected object. Other types of vibration detectors are similar to tilt switches used in pinball machines.

Alarm control

All sensing devices transmit a signal, either wired or wireless, to the alarm control panel that receives their signals and processes them. Wireless systems utilize RF, Wi-Fi, Z-Wave, and ZigBee for signal transmission and communication. Some of the most severe burglary losses are caused not by a failure in equipment but simply by someone turning off the alarm system. The type of control panel needed depends on the sophistication of the overall intrusion alarm system. Some control panels provide zoning capabilities for separate annunciation of the sensing devices. Others provide the low-voltage electrical power for the sensing devices.

Included in the control panel is the backup or standby power in the event of an electrical power failure. Batteries are used for standby power. Some equipment uses rechargeable batteries; the control has a low-power charging unit (a trickle charger) and maintains the batteries in a fully charged condition.

Modern control panels use one or more microprocessors, which allows the control panel to send and receive digital information to the alarm station. An alphanumeric pad can display zone information as well as supervisory conditions. Each user can also have a unique code, allowing restriction during specified times or limiting access into certain areas. By using individual code numbers, the alarm control panel can track activity as well as transmit this information off-site.

If the alarm control panel is connected to a central monitoring station, the times that the system is turned on and off are recorded and logged. When the owner enters the building in the morning, a signal is sent. If this happens at a time prearranged with the central station, it is considered a normal opening. If it happens at any other time, the police are dispatched.

The owner or other authorized persons can enter the building during the closed times. The person entering must first call the central station company and identify himself or herself by a special coding procedure. Records are kept at the central station company for these irregular openings and closings.

Tamper protection is a feature that generates an alarm signal when the system is compromised in any way. Tamper protection can be designed into any or all portions of the alarm system (control panel, sensing devices, loop wiring, and alarm transmission facilities).

Alarm transmission/signaling

The type of alarm transmission/signaling system used in a particular application depends on the location of the business or residence, the frequency of police patrols, and the ability of the customer to afford the cost. Remember, after deterrence, the purpose of an alarm is to summon the proper authorities to stop a crime during its commission or lead to the apprehension of the intruder. It is very important that the response by proper authorities to the alarm comes in the shortest possible time. Two types of alarm signaling systems are in general use:

- *Local alarm.* A bell, siren, and/or strobe light signal that an attempted or successful intrusion has taken place. The success of the system relies on someone hearing or seeing the signal and calling the responsible authorities. The local alarm also notifies burglars that they have been detected. This may be advantageous in frightening off the less experienced intruder.
- *Central station system.* The alarm signal is transmitted over telephone lines, the internet through the Internet Protocol (IP) rules, cellular phone, or RF to a specially constructed building called the central station. Here, trained operators are on duty 24 hours a day to supervise, record, and maintain alarms. On receipt of an alarm, the police are dispatched and, in some cases, the alarm company officer or runner. The record-keeping function and officer response ensure thorough documentation of any alarm signal. There are 10 types of alarm transmissions to the central station. Each type of transmission has certain advantages and disadvantages that must be considered in determining the risk. Transmission of an alarm signal to the Underwriters Laboratories (UL)–listed central station is generally regarded as the most reliable method for reducing the burglary losses.
    - *Direct wire systems.* High-risk locations (banks, jewelers, and furriers) are generally protected with a direct wire system. A single dedicated telephone line is run from the protected premises to the central station or police station, where a separate receiver supervises only that alarm. A fixed DC current is sent from the central station to the protected premises and read on a meter at the central station. The advantage of a direct wire system is that problems can be traced very quickly to a specific alarm system. This makes compromising the alarm signal by a professional burglar more difficult. The disadvantage of such a system is the higher cost of leased telephone lines. This becomes a more serious economic factor as the distance from the central station to the protected premises increases. Proper transmission of the alarm signal to the central station is essential. Problems can result on these telephone lines from shorts and broken wires. Most central stations expect these problems and are well equipped to rapidly make repairs. However, some of today's burglars are more sophisticated. They know they can prevent the transmission of the alarm signal to the central system by shunting or jumpering out the leased telephone line. Special methods are used by the alarm company to protect against jumpering of the alarm signal. Alarm systems having this special line security are classified by UL.

- *Multiplex systems.* The multiplex system is designed to reduce leased telephone line charges while providing a higher degree of line security. Multiplex systems introduced data processing (computer-based techniques) to the alarm industry.
- *Digital communicators.* This computer-based type of alarm transmission equipment sends its signal through the regular switch line telephone network. The alarm signal transmitted is a series of coded electronic pulses that can be received only on a computer terminal at the central station.
- *Alarm dialer.* The dialer delivers a prerecorded verbal message to a central station, answering service, or police department when an alarm is activated. Many of the earlier tape dialers were a source of constant problems to police departments, because of their lack of sophistication. Basically, they were relabeled tape recorders. It was not uncommon for the tape dialer to play most of the message before the police could answer the phone. The police knew that an alarm signal had been sent but did not know its location. The newer, modern tape dialers have solved these problems.
- *Radio or cellular signal transmission.* This method takes the alarm signal from the protected premises and sends it via radio or cellular phone to either a central station or police dispatch center. In addition, the alarm signal can be received in a police patrol car.
- *Internet protocol (IP).* This method takes the alarm signal from the protected premises and transmits it over the internet according to current IP rules.
- *Video/audio verification.* Along with standard alarm transmissions, video images are sent to the central station and/or audio monitoring of the property is conducted by the central station. This provides for a higher level of protection while helping to eliminate false alarms by allowing central station operators to see and/or hear what is happening inside the protected area. With the increase of the false police dispatches, video and audio verification is playing a major role in the battle against false alarms. Some police departments will give a priority response to the verified alarm.
- *Enhanced call verification (ECV).* Another method to reduce false alarms is ECV that requires two calls by the central station when an intrusion alarm is received. One call is to the protected premises, and the other call is to the designated contact person for the premises prior to notifying the police dispatch.

Alarms deter crime

False/nuisance alarms waste police resources and alarm company resources. The police and alarm industry are acutely aware of this, and both have initiated efforts across the country to relieve the dilemma that will be fully discussed later.

The National Crime Prevention Institute has long endorsed alarm systems as the best available crime deterrent, and this deterrent value is increased when warning sign(s) are placed at the protected premises indicating the presence of an intrusion alarm system. This education institution realizes that most criminals fear alarm systems; they much prefer to break into an unprotected building rather than risk capture by a hidden sensor.

Problem deterrence is the alarm business, a field that, in fact, extends far beyond protecting premises from burglary. The crisis prevention duties of alarm firms range from monitoring sprinkler systems and fire sensors and watching temperature levels in buildings to supervising industrial processes, such as nuclear fission and the manufacturing of dangerous chemicals.

To alarm companies, deterrence is a sophisticated, specialized art. In the area of crime prevention, companies take pride in spotting potential weaknesses in a building and designing an alarm system that confounds the most intelligent criminals.

Crime prevention is the area where police need the most help.

False/nuisance alarms

The full crime prevention potential in alarm systems has yet to be realized. However, the number of premises protected by alarms is growing and those businesses and residences holding the most valuable goods are thoroughly guarded by the most sophisticated sensor systems.

Yet the main drag on the potential of alarms, as industry leaders and police are aware, remains the false/nuisance alarm problem. A modern instance of the boy who cried "wolf," false alarms erode the effectiveness of alarm systems. They are costly to alarm companies and police agencies.

False alarms are caused by a malfunction of the system and nuisance alarms are caused by nonintruder-related conditions. There are four hard-core reasons for false/nuisance alarms and the secret to reduce them is to clearly identify the cause and make proactive corrections.

- lack of proper education on how to enter and exit the complex, such as improper arming and disarming of the keypad
- weather
- equipment failure (dead batteries) and installation problems
- pets

It is a fact that alarm systems prevent crime. These electronic and electrical systems deter burglars, arsonists, vandals, and other criminals. They are both the most effective and most economical crime prevention tool available.

Police budgets have been reduced in most locales and frozen in others, while private investment in alarm security is growing yearly.

At first, some police departments initiated a written letter program from the police chief to those who have an excessive number of alarm runs. Others have the crime prevention officer make a follow-up visit to the business or residence. However, since many of these steps have failed, most police departments are assessing false alarm fines.

By protecting places, such as hospitals, office buildings, and schools, alarm systems free up police resources and enable patrol officers to spend more time in areas with high crime rates and fewer premises protected by alarm systems. Police may also dedicate more officers to apprehending criminals. In this manner, police and alarm companies work together, complementing one another and waging a mutual war on crime.

To combat the false/nuisance alarm problem, the alarm company industry national associations have initiated training programs for their members, have supported research in this area of concern, and have worked on legislation and with police departments to reduce the false/nuisance alarm occurrences.

In addition to technological improvements for verifying alarms, companies have instituted training programs for their sales, installation, and service personnel. Also, subscribers are educated on the operation of their systems three times: by salespeople, by installers, and by supervisors when they inspect newly installed systems.

Police chiefs and crime prevention officers working in areas troubled by false/nuisance alarms should meet with the heads of the firms in their areas and discuss reduction programs like these.

Today, many police departments will provide a priority response to an intrusion alarm that has been confirmed through video verification, audio verification, or enhanced call verification.

Standard—Criteria used by UL as the primary basis for determining the eligibility of a product to use the UL's Listing, Classification, or Recognition Mark and other markings or certificates that may be required.

Underwriters Laboratories

UL 681—Installation and Classification of Burglar and Holdup Alarm Systems
UL 827—Central Station Alarm Services
UL 1023—Household Burglar-Alarm System Units
UL 1076—Proprietary Burglar-Alarm Units and Systems
UL 1641—Installation and Classification of Residential Burglar-Alarm Systems
UL 1981—Central Station Automation Systems
UL 2050—National Industrial Security Systems for the protection of Classified Materials
National Fire Protection Association (NFPA)
NFPA 71—Standard for the Installation, Maintenance, and Use of Signaling Systems for Central Station Service
NFPA 730—Guide for Premises Security
NFPA 731—Standard for the Integration of Electronic Premises Security Systems

In addition to the UL and NFPA requirements for intrusion alarm systems, the residence and business will be guided and regulated by any applicable federal, state and/or local laws, and nationally accepted industry standards and best practices. Most importantly, the authority having jurisdiction, local regulatory agency, will most likely have the ultimate final approval for any intrusion alarm system.

Conclusion

As we enter the first quarter of 21st century and look back, we have seen a lot of changes occur, with many changes for the better. PIR units are widely used, and ultrasonic motion detectors are rarely used. Foil is no longer placed on glass windows and replaced by a properly placed PIR. Home and commercial applications of PIR units come in all shapes and sizes as well as all necessary patterns for proper coverage. Systems are wireless, keypads replace keys, two-way voice modules are used for communication, and control panels (UL listed) are in single- and multizone panels. Fobs and cell phones are available for remote arming and disarming along with viewing the alarmed premises by means of a smart phone, tablet, or computer.

The growth in technology will continue as will the need for updated technology.

Glossary for alarm systems

absorption the property of materials, such as carpeting, drapes, and acoustic ceilings, which causes them to soak up or deaden sound. The materials also deaden ultrasonics, so a higher than normal range setting may be required[2]

AC abbreviation for alternating current

access control (1) any means of limiting entry into a building or area to those who are authorized. (2) A system that does this by use of coded cards, push button sequence, fingerprint comparison, hand geometry, retinal (eye) scans, or other means

account a subscriber to an alarm company's services

acoustic glass break sensors can be installed on walls or ceilings. Detection is best when installed on a wall *opposite* protected glass, since sound waves need not then reflect off an opposing wall before reaching the detector

active detector one that sends out or transmits energy in order to perform its detection function. Examples are ultrasonic, microwave, photoelectric beams, E-field fence detectors, and capacitance alarms

air turbulence air disturbance or churning caused by a breeze or draft from a fan, furnace, air conditioner, or other source. Air turbulence in the vicinity of an ultrasonic transducer can produce false alarms

alarm condition the presence of a dangerous or undesired situation, such as fire, intrusion, and holdup, sensed and signaled by an alarm system

alarm line a wire or telephone line used to report an alarm condition to a remote location, such as a guard station or an alarm central office

alarm signal an indication that some dangerous or unwanted condition is occurring, such as an intrusion, fire, and holdup

alarm system a collection of detection devices, control unit, annunciation/reporting equipment, control station(s), wiring, phone lines, radio channels, power supply, and other associated equipment connected together to detect and report the existence of an undesirable condition, such as an intrusion, a fire, an unsafe condition in an industrial manufacturing process

annunciator a device, typically a small horn or light, used to attract the attention of someone close by

area protection (1) a detector that is sensitive over a two-dimensional space, such as a strain gauge sensor or a seismic detector. (2) A misnomer for *volumetric protection* (which is three-dimensional)

armed The condition of an alarm system when it is on, ready to be tripped when an intrusion is detected

armed light a light or light-emitting diode, usually red, or other device that indicates the alarm system is armed or set

audible alarm an alarm that makes noise (as opposed to a silent alarm) using a bell or horn

audio alarm a detection device that is triggered upon detecting noises, such as the sounds of breaking and entering. See audio discriminator, vault alarm, sonic detector

audio discriminator In radio, a detector is a device or circuit that extracts information from a modulated radio frequency current or voltage. The term dates from the first three decades of radio (1888–1918). Unlike modern radio stations which transmit sound (an audiosignal) on an.... The ratio detector has the advantage over the Foster-Seeley discriminator

balanced magnetic contact see high security magnetic contact

battery an assembly of two or more cells used to obtain higher voltages than that available from a single cell

capacitance detector a device that detects an intruder's touching of or close approach to a protected metal object. Often used to protect safes and file cabinets. Protected objects must be metal, well insulated from the ground, and not too large. It is also called safe alarm or proximity alarm. See E-field detector

casement window a type of window that hinges outward and is usually opened with a crank. It is often difficult to mount contacts on casement windows. Tamper switches are sometimes used successfully

central station (1) a central location where an alarm company monitors a large number of its own accounts. (2) A company that specializes in monitoring the alarm signals for many alarm companies for a fee

certificated alarm system an alarm system that is installed by a UL-certified alarm company and that meets certain requirements for installation, service, and extent of coverage

circuit breaker an electrical safety valve; a device designed to interrupt dangerously high currents. Unlike a fuse, a circuit breaker can be reset to be used again, thus no replacements are needed. Some circuit breakers can also be used as switches

closed-circuit television (CCTV) an on premises TV system used to enable a guard to "watch" one or more critical areas, such as entrances and high-value areas. The TV signal is used transmitted by coaxial cable or fiber optic cable and is usually limited to distances of a few hundred to a few thousand feet

closing signal a signal transmitted by an alarm system to the central station when the proprietor (user) secures and leaves the premises at the close of business. Usually done on a prearranged time schedule

2. Trimmer, H.W. Understanding and Servicing Alarm Systems, third ed. Butterworth-Heinemann.

coaxial cable a special kind of shielded cable that has one center conductor surrounded by relatively thick insulation, which in turn has a shield (usually braided wires or sometimes spirally laid wires) over it. An outer plastic jacket is usually included. Used primarily for RF work, such as antenna lead-in and for CCTV cameras

commercial alarm an alarm installed in a commercial or business location, as opposed to a residential alarm

day–night switch a switch located at the subscriber's premises used by the subscriber to signal the central station of opening and closing of the premises. Used only on direct wire, supervised accounts (the milliamp signal method), and multiplex systems

dedicated line or circuit a phone line or circuit that is dedicated solely to transmission of alarm signals. Examples are direct wire, McCulloh, multiplex, and derived channel

door switch see magnetic contact

Doppler shift the apparent frequency shift due to motion of an intruder in ultrasonic and microwave detection

double-hung window a type of window popular in older construction. The lower sash (window) can be raised and the upper sash can be lowered. Two contacts are usually used to protect both sashes

dry cell a type of battery that is not rechargeable. Dry cells are occasionally used in alarm work, but because of the required periodic replacement, rechargeable batteries are usually favored. (Rechargeable batteries also have to be replaced periodically, but not as often as dry cells)

dual alarm service protection of one premise by two separate alarm systems, usually serviced by different alarm companies. Thus protected, there is less likelihood that both systems could be successfully compromised and less chance of collusion among dishonest employees of the two alarm companies. Use is limited to high-risk applications because of the cost

duress switch a special type of key switch that can be turned in either of two directions or can be operated with two different keys. One direction (or key) operates the alarm systems in a normal manner. The other direction (or key) signals the central station that the owner of the protected premises is under duress (i.e., has a gun in his back). By comparison a holdup switch is activated secretly, whereas a duress switch is activated openly, and the burglar is unaware of its duress signaling function. (The burglar thinks it is a regular control switch)

E-field detector low-cost, compact, wideband probes for handheld magnetic field testing, custom designs

electronic siren an electronic device with speaker used to simulate the sound of a motor-driven siren

environmental considerations factors that must be considered in the proper application of alarm detectors to reduce false alarms, particularly with motion sensors. Such factors include rain, fog, snow, wind, hail, humidity, temperature, corrosion, moving or swaying objects, vegetation growth, animals, and many others. They depend on the type(s) of detectors that is considered and where they are to be located

exit–entry delay a feature of some alarm systems, particularly in residential applications, that permits locating the on/off station inside the protected premises. When exiting, the user turns the system on, which starts the exit time delay cycle (typically 30–120 seconds). He can then exit through a specific, protected door without tripping the alarm during this delay. Later, when the user returns, the system is tripped when the specific door is opened. This action starts an entry delay cycle but does not cause an immediate alarm (although a small per-alert alarm may sound as a reminder). The user then has, typically, 15–60 seconds to turn the system off. An intruder would not have a key or would not know the secret code to turn the system off, therefore, the alarm would ring or a silent signal be transmitted after the entry delay expired

high security magnetic contact new magnetic switch sensors for low-power smart flow meters

holdup alarm a means of notifying a remote location, such as an alarm central station or police station, that a holdup is in progress. Holdup alarms are always silent and are actuated secretly, otherwise the noise of a local alarm or the obvious pushing of an alarm button could prompt the holdup man to acts of violence. A holdup alarm should not be confused with a panic alarm or with a duress alarm

indicator light any light, either incandescent or LED, which indicates the status of an alarm system, such as the "ready" light

infrared detector (1) passive type is one that detects an intruder by his body heat (which is infrared energy). This type does not emit any infrared energy, it only detects it. (2) Active type is a photoelectric beam that uses infrared instead of visible light. This kind does emit infrared energy

intrusion alarm an arrangement of electrical and/or electronic devices designed to detect the presence of an intruder or an attempt to break into a protected location and to provide notification by making a loud noise locally (bell, siren, etc.) or by transmitting an alarm signal to some remote monitoring location or both

key pad a collection of push buttons mounted on a plate, used to enter a secret code used to arm and disarm alarm systems. Often resembles a touchtone phone pad. Used to replace key-operated switches. Decoding of the correct combination is done by electronics mounted behind the pad. Also called a stand-alone key pad. Compare *system pad*

line security the degree of protection of the alarm transmission path against compromise. Usually implies the application of additional measures to improve that security. See line supervision

line supervision an arrangement where a known current, AC or DC, pulses, or a combination, is present on the line to the central station. Cutting or shorting the line will change this current, signaling an alarm. In high-security systems, complex line supervision systems are used to detect attempts to defeat the system

line voltage (1) 120 V AC "house power." (2) The voltage on a telephone line used for alarm service

magnetic contact a magnetically operated switch that is typically used on doors and windows to detect opening. The switch is mounted on the frame or fixed part, while the magnet is mounted on the movable door or window. Generally much easier to use than *earlier*, mechanically actuated switches. Available in NO, NC, or SPST contact forms

mat switch a very thin, pressure-sensing switch placed under carpets (and carpet padding) to trip an alarm when an intruder steps on it. Typical size is 30 in × 36 in. Sizes vary from 7 in. A prefix meaning × 24 in. Typical thickness is 3/32–1/8 in. Runner mat is 30 in. wide × 25 ft long and is cut to the desired length with scissors. With one exception, all mat switches are normally open. Supervised mats have two sets of leads. For damp or wet locations, sealed type mats should be used

medical alert an alarm system by which an invalid, elderly, or sick person can push a button *to* alert someone that a doctor, ambulance, or other medical assistance is required. These devices are known as personal emergency response systems (PERS) and can be utilized both inside and outside the home

microprocessor a computer on a microchip is the heart of all personal computers. Now it is used as the heart of alarm control panels. With a microprocessor designed into a control, it is possible to obtain features that would be prohibitively expensive otherwise. Some examples are dozens of zones, information displays in English (or other language), and zone parameters (e.g., speed of response and perimeter/interior/entry–exit/instant response) assignable for each zone. Most importantly, these features can be changed, often without requiring a service call to the premises. First introduced by Ron Gottsegen of Radionics in 1977

microwave detector a device that senses the motion of an intruder (and of other things) in a protected area by a Doppler shift in the transmitted RF energy. Microwave detectors generally operate at 10.525 GHz. Older units operated at 915 MHz. Both have been replaced largely by PIR detectors that are less susceptible to false alarms

money trap a special switch placed in the bottom of a cash drawer. It is activated during a holdup by pulling out the bottom bill of the stack, which has been previously inserted into a trap. To prevent a false alarm, care must be taken not to remove that bottom bill at any other time

motion detector any of several devices that detects an intruder by his motion within a protected area or protected volume. See ultrasonic detector, microwave detector, passive infrared detector, area protection, and volumetric protection

multiplex (1) in general, any method of sending many signals over one communications channel. (2) Specifically, any method of sending alarm signals from many subscribers over one pair of wires to a monitoring location. (Technically, a McCulloh circuit does this, but the term "multiplex" is generally used to refer to the newer electronic techniques using polling computers and similar methods)

open and closed loop a combination of an open loop and a closed loop, used on some controls. Note that, unlike the double closed loop, the open loop conductor in this system is not supervised. That is, cutting this wire will disable part of the system without causing an alarm condition

opening (1) any possible point of entry for an intruder, such as windows, doors, ventilators, and roof hatches. (2) Any such point that is protected by an alarm detection device. (3) See opening signal. (4) See scheduled opening and unscheduled opening

opening signal opening signal from the alarm system as valid authorization and will not be required. If an alarm signal is received in connection with a scheduled opening or closing

panic alarm a local alarm or remote silent alarm, either wired or wireless, triggered manually usually by pushing a button (as opposed to being tripped by some kind of detection *device*). The panic button permits the owner/subscriber to trigger the alarm manually in case of intrusion or other emergency. (This definition was added)

power supply any source of electrical energy. More specifically, power supply usually refers to an electronic device that converts AC to DC for use by *alarm* equipment. It may also reduce the voltage from 120 V to the voltage needed by the alarm equipment. Some power supplies have provision for connecting a standby battery. Others will accommodate a rechargeable battery and will provide the necessary charging current for that battery

preventive maintenance testing and checking out *alarm* systems on a regularly scheduled basis to locate and repair potential problems before false alarms or system failures result. Unfortunately, preventive maintenance is usually forgotten until trouble occurs

reversing relay (1) a method of transmitting an alarm signal over a telephone wire by reversing the DC polarity. In the secure mode a voltage is sent over the phone line from the protected premises to the monitoring location to provide line supervision. An alarm signal is transmitted by reversing the polarity, usually by operating a DPDT relay in the subscriber's control. (2) The relay used to reverse the polarity

scheduled opening opening signal from the alarm system as valid authorization and will not be required. If an alarm signal is received in connection with a scheduled opening or closing

shunt switch a key-operated switch located outside the protected premises, which allows the subscriber to bypass usually just one door to permit entry without tripping the alarm system. He will normally proceed to the control or transmitter to turn off the entire system with the on/off switch, usually using the same key. Upon closing the premises the procedure is reversed

silent alarm an alarm system that does not ring a bell or give any other indication of an alarm condition at the protected premises, instead it transmits an alarm'signal to an alarm central station or other monitoring location

siren (1) traditionally, a motor-driven noisemaker used on police cars, fire trucks, ambulances, and so on. (2) An electronic replacement for (1) that produces a very similar sound

sonic detector (1) a Doppler-principle detection device much like ultrasonic except that uses an audible frequency, not very common. (2) A misnomer for ultrasonic

subscriber error a false or loss of alarm protection caused by the subscriber not following the correct procedures in the use of the alarm system

switch a mechanically or magnetically operated device used to open and close electrical circuits

tamperproof box this term is somewhat of a misnomer because few things are "proof" against attack. The term is usually used to indicate that a control, bell, or equipment box is equipped with a tamper switch to signal an alarm when the door is opened. Tamper switches are preferably connected to a 24-hour protective circuit. Bell boxes or other boxes outside the protected area should also be equipped with a double door. Opening the outer door triggers the tamper switch, while the inner door denies the attacker immediate access to the bell or its wiring

transmitter (1) a device that sends an alarm signal to a remote point, such as a McCulloh transmitter. (2) The unit at the end of a photoelectric beam that sends out the light or invisible infrared energy. (3) The ultrasonic transducer that sends out the ultrasonic energy

UL-listed alarm company an alarm company that meets the requirements of Underwriters Laboratories and is so designated by appearing on UL's published list

UL standard for alarms Underwriters Laboratories publishes many standards outlining the requirements that must be met by alarm equipment/alarm companies in order to obtain UL listing. The most important of these is UL 681, which outlines alarm system installation requirements. Many others cover various kinds of equipment. It is important to bear in mind that there are many UL listings for many UL standards, many of which are unrelated to security (e.g., electrical safety). Therefore the term that UL listed is meaningless unless the exact nature of the "list" is detailed. UL 639 outlines transient protection requirements. UL 611 outlines central station units and systems

ultrasonic detector a device that senses motion of an intruder (and of other things) in a protected area by a Doppler shift in the transmitted ultrasonic energy (sound is too high a frequency to be heard by humans). Rarely used anymore

unscheduled opening opening of a protected premise at an unscheduled time, that is, not a scheduled opening time. For a silent alarm, supervised account subscribers notify the monitoring alarm company in advance of their standard opening (and closing) times. If the owner or authorized person wishes to enter at any other time, he has to make special arrangements with the alarm company by phone and prearranged secret code word or, preferably, by letter

vault alarm an alarm system used to protect a vault, such as a bank vault or storage vault. This is a special type of audio alarm and usually has a test feature via the ring-back circuit, which can be actuated from the alarm central station

volumetric protection volumetric-motion sensors are designed to detect intruder motion within the interior of a protected space. Volumetric sensors may be active or inactive

walk test a procedure of actually walking through the area protected by a motion detector to determine the actual limits of its coverage. Indication is usually provided by an LED mounted on the detection unit. This indicator should be disabled or covered when not used for walk-testing. This will prevent a would-be burglar from doing his own walk-testing during open-for-business hours to determine holes in the coverage

zone large protected premises are divided into areas or zones, each having its own indicator or annunciator. This helps pinpoint the specific area of intrusion and is a great aid in narrowing down a problem when troubleshooting. Today's control units may have 16, 30, 48, or more zones.

zone light a light, LED, or other device used to indicate the status of each zone in a multiple zone system. One or more indicators can be provided per zone to indicate any of the following: ready, armed, alarmed, and zoned-out

Chapter 21

Access control and biometrics

Joseph Nelson
Security Consultant

Access control systems are designed to limit exposure and reduce threats. Sophisticated access control systems can be defeated when someone props open a door. Door prop alarms are low cost, desirable solutions to propped open doors. Helping keep energy costs down by ensuring the doors are closed, they also serve a vital security need. Sounding when a door is left open too long, door prop alarms, help ensure access control systems are used as intended.

Security management newsletter August 17, 2018

Introduction

Access control is defined as the means to control privileges or rights to an asset but can also mean to a resource or to an individual. Having access provides one with the opportunity or means to use or benefit from something having value. Most often in security, it is the access to property, services, events, or information, but access can also be to people, such as the right or opportunity to approach or see someone like a public celebrity.

Security of assets is often best achieved by organizing a means to balance the desired use of assets with protection from potential risks associated with their loss. Access control provides a means for asset owners to achieve both their desired use and control over their assets by allowing privileges to only agreed individuals.

The function and practice of access control are fundamental to the protection officer in his or her duties. The security officer will not only be expected to perform a duty relative to access control but will likely dedicate significant security resource time to access control during the course of their employment.

Current day access control is usually achieved with a combination of elements, including administrative and engineered controls. The elements often include technical access control systems and security personnel to monitor the controls, record keeping, policy conformance, and if needed any improvements. In some cases, access to a given area may be by staff only through a security patrol identifying any people in the area being patrolled.

Most typically in larger organizations, access control involves the control and monitoring of physical security systems, such as key systems, large-scale access control, alarms, and network video [closed-circuit TV (CCTV)] systems. For these organizations the familiar example of access control is a uniformed security officer with or without additional access elements behind a desk at the front entrance of an office building, industrial facility, or other property. Typically at a building's perimeter, these access areas can be called different things, such as a checkpoint, security or guard station, and main lobby. These checkpoints are often a fixed post, that is, the officer is posted permanently until relieved or when policy and/or post orders dictate. The presence of the officer in this key location of common access serves many purposes. One is to provide a deterrent to those who may be unauthorized to enter the protected area or structure. In addition to the deterrent function an officer familiar with the protected property and its frequent occupants will recognize those who are common to the property and can challenge those who are unauthorized. Also, security personnel stationed at access points can observe and assist with any service needs, such as requests such as lost badges, visitor processing, or policy exceptions.

Handbook of Loss Prevention and Crime Prevention. DOI: https://doi.org/10.1016/B978-0-12-817273-5.00021-1

Key control

The following procedure will be used by the security officer when you have custody of the client's keys.

- All client keys will be kept on a key ring in the security officer's possession while on duty.
- The key ring will be designed and constructed large enough so it cannot be easily lost, misplaced, or mistakenly removed from the post at the end of each shift.
- The key ring will be secured on a key ring holder. The security officer will securely fasten his or her belt through the key holder. The key ring will remain on the key holder unless keys are being used for locking or unlocking doors.
- Keys and key ring holder will be passed to each shift and indicated as such on shift report.
- The security officer will periodically check the keys, key ring, and key holder to insure key control.
- Keys that are lost or mistakenly removed from the post, contact the branch office immediately.
- Never loan the site's keys to the client, client employee(s), or any unauthorized person.
- The security officer will follow the following provisions in controlling and protecting keys on this facility.

Emerging trends—access control

Access control

This describes how you require people to enter, exit, and access certain areas of your facility. These requirements will be different for staff, students, visitors, emergency responders, and the public. You may identify other groups of people who require special access. These requirements may change based on time of day, on site events, and other conditions. You can use these requirements to define traffic and life patterns to enhance your security programs. Access control measures may also be used to create life patterns that discourage or make unwanted activity stand out against the baseline of normal, which will enhance your monitoring activities.

Request for proposal

Armed with a security program that breaks down your expectations of any technologies, your security consultant can help design a request for proposal (RFP) that will be very informative to potential vendors and facilitate conversations throughout the process. This also turns into a functionality checklist that you should use during the design, build, and commissioning phases.

Residential environment

While many residential environments have physical keys or electronic systems, some large apartment complexes maintain just security staff at their main access checkpoints. This method, serving by recognition of regular occupants by the security officer, can provide an acceptable form of controlling access, along with providing a desired human service level. While less formal, this is a more traditional method of access control, which becomes less effective as the volume of traffic increases. It also lacks formal record keeping of activity that technical security systems provide by creating logs with access activity times, dates, and names of all those accessing a space.

Successfully achieving the objective of controlling access is often dependent on physical controls. For example the task to control access to a property consists of acres of land with no fences or physical boundaries would be much more difficult than a building with one entrance, although continued advances in electronics continue to make the difficulty less so.

Access control could only be achieved by frequent patrols of the protected area, challenging those unfamiliar persons caught on the property. In this example, those challenges may be the accepted form of access control, with no further control necessary. However, most facilities require additional forms of controlling access, such as waste sites, storage yards, and other facilities.

Defensible zone

In some circumstances, large properties or defensible spaces may require a softer form of physical barrier. This may be achieved through dense foliage or even through designated walkways with paint around the area of protection or defensible zone. This form of control merely implies that a certain area is off limits and offers a convenient path around the area.

Many properties and assets cannot depend on a "soft" form of physical security. It is for this reason that it usually becomes necessary to add forms of physical security to achieve suitable access control. Fences may be erected around a property to control access and to "force" or "funnel" visitors or employees to a common entrance or "checkpoint" manned by a protection officer. Appropriate signage indicating a no trespassing order will aid in controlling access through the message that anyone trying to breach security and access the forbidden area risks arrest and trespassing charges. In situations where it is expected that the protection officer will arrest anyone caught trespassing, it is crucial that signage is in accordance with the laws concerning local trespass acts. It is also extremely important that it is within the legal rights of the protection officer to perform the arrest. The addition of locks to alternate entrances to the facility or property will also control access. Other forms of additional physical security, such as monitoring with network video (CCTV), and the use of integrated systems to create system redundancy and improved reporting, such as alarm systems, will further assist in the prevention of unauthorized access.

Antipass back

Modern electronic access systems have many features to increase the level of access control to a facility, area, or room. Integrated systems and the use of integrated systems to create system redundancy and improved reporting are combined with access readers and software rule to prevent what is called "pass back." The main purpose of these "antipass back" arrangements is to prevent a card or token holder from passing their card or token back to a second person to gain entry into the same controlled area. These arrangements are also designed to limit what is called access "piggybacking" similar to tailgating; "piggybacking" refers to when an unauthorized person tags along behind another person who is authorized to gain entry into a restricted area or pass a certain checkpoint.

Some systems have enhancements, such as the addition of "mobility impaired" access, to allow the extended opening time of a door. In the event of a stolen card the card can be "tagged" with an alarm upon use, alerting the operator at the monitoring station to dispatch security personnel to the location of the cardholder. Meanwhile, the card remains active and permits access, so as not to alert the holder of the card.

Systems can be interfaced or integrated with other systems, such as building automation, fire systems, and human resources computer databases. This allows the access holder to gain access and turn on lights or air-conditioning to his or her work area with the use of the access system. With the activation of a fire alarm an access card could be automatically validated for use by the fire department.

Emergency access control

All access control programs must consider how safe emergency exits can be accomplished. It is important that physical security is harmonized with the safety of people by not interrupting safe egress from the property or site in the event of an emergency. Whenever controlling access, it must be assured that emergency egress is not sacrificed. Naturally local and national fire codes can present challenges to controlling access to many facilities; however, it is imperative that there is no sacrifice to the safety of the building occupants in order to achieve better security. In most instances, policies are drastically altered for access in an emergency. Where policy dictates, a fixed post may become a roaming position for the officer to facilitate an escort for emergency medical services or the fire department. The opposite may be true when a roaming officer will be called from a roaming patrol to a fixed position at the entrance of the protected facility to provide speedy access for dispatched emergency services.

Generally, an emergency, such as fire, medical concern, hazardous spill, or gas release, should result in the halt of all work in the facility to help facilitate access. Elevators and other conveyances should be programed to ensure they restrict normal use and are available for potential use by the emergency service personnel. Parking control at a facility entrance or loading dock can be considered an access control duty where entrances are kept clear to make way for emergency personnel.

Example of access control

With a facility or property that has been equipped with fences, locks, and other barriers, access can be controlled at one or more checkpoints as needed. Visitors and workers can be directed to desired points of access. However, since even strong physical controls can be circumvented, a key question must be answered: what prevents unauthorized persons from circumventing these controls and gaining access through the access check points? The answer to this risk is often placing a protection officer at the access point to monitor and assure compliance with a formal organizational access control policy and reduce the unauthorized access concerns.

Access policies should outline a clear definition of the requirements for access to the property; for instance, a facility, such as a bar or nightclub, may only permit access to those of a consenting age; therefore patrons may be required to present a valid operator's license to gain access. In addition, some facilities may require presentation of an invitation or ticket to enter a public venue or private function, such as concerts, large weddings, or other events.

Sometimes, the organization will seek to add to the access monitoring work and have a security guard handle additional duties. For example a protection officer assigned access control to a parking garage might be considered to also collect fees and handling cash. These arrangements should be avoided in almost all cases to maintain the integrity of access control work, which can become much less effective when nonsecurity work becomes part of the assignment. That is not to say a protection officer should avoid related access control work, such as monitoring access to other services. For example, the officer may control access to a conveyance, such as managing elevator bookings or to a loading area or entrance. The issuing of visitor and contractor badges may accomplish control of access in regard to temporary contractors. Office and industrial facilities may require contractors to present company identification. Policies and procedures regarding access control may apply only to certain people in certain areas at certain times.

The identification industry is becoming more and more advanced, and many large corporations are implementing identification systems as corporate standards for all employees. At the same time, those individual looking to circumvent security have unfortunately more tools to copy or replicate access cards and credential. To stay ahead of this criminal capability, organization must take proactive steps with modern security features to their corporate IDs. The use of holograms and watermarking makes replication of a well-designed identification card difficult by unauthorized persons. Company identification can be combined or integrated with an access card for the facility.

A trusted means to validate identify is key to the above example (for regular occupants of a facility) but also for the authorized contractor or temporary staff. In these situations a protection officer may be able to provide additional factors to confirm identity against an access or visitor list or permit. The goal is to have those appearing on permits or lists to be the only persons permitted access and those without the validating elements to be challenged by security or by staff in secure areas of a facility.

Audits and record keeping

Maintaining a security access log, register, or muster list by electronic or paper means has become a common function within access control programs. Linking an individual to an access event even in the most basic form, such as signing a security register, can help deter unauthorized individuals, especially if they are asked for more than one validation action, such as the need to present a credential. The security register has a primary functions as it can be used as an audit trail of who accessed the facilities at any given time, allowing its use to confirm policy conformance. Where access controls are the most assured, access logs can also be used with other means to obtain a sense of "who is in" a space or building during a specific time. Some are able to use such records to assist facility emergency responders gain awareness of how is in a space to assist them in responding to an event such as a fire.

While a register can contain as much information as one might choose, generally it carries the individuals name, organization they are affiliated with, and perhaps an ID number, work location, phone number, as well as the time in and time out of the space. Sometimes it is appropriate to add additional personal data, such as the signature or initials of the individual requiring access. Given the increasing need to protect personal data collected, the officer assigned to building and maintaining the security register should limit the data involved to only the information that is required to accomplish the desired access task. They should also ensure training and assistance to those unfamiliar with the process in order to maintain governance with appropriate, complete, and consistent files. Records of this nature should be archived for retrieval according to local statue and the policies outlined by the employer or the client. Once the agreed retention limit for the records is reached confidential, it should be destroyed prior to disposal. Maintaining confidentiality of these files should be considered part of the duty of officers involved in the access control program.

Access authorization

During the course of performing access control, it may become necessary to deny (block) access to those without proper credentials. Given the variety of reasons access may need to be blocked, protection officers must be aware that a situation where the person wishing to gain access may have legitimate business on the protected property. Therefore some means to validate requests unless an outright denial is agreed should be in place. This could simply be a supervisor or other is consulted before turning someone indicating they are a new employee, client, etc. would help avoid a negative concern, such as the loss of business or goodwill. For this and other related reasons, organizations need a clear policy for the denial of access to individuals without proper credentials.

There are some facilities that may employ a strict "no authorization, no access" policy that can be supported by the organization and will dictate that the person requesting access without proper credentials be denied, while many other facilities will have a procedure to obtain the proper authorization for access. It is often the best practice to escalate these matters consistently to a supervisor who can assist in confirming authority for access. Another example may be to require a visitor requesting access to call an authorized occupant in the facility to provide an escort.

When the security officer is left with the decision of whether or not to allow access, it is usually best that the officer act on the side of caution explain organizational policy that access requires prior approval or other requirements. Advising the person that he or she has to be denied access is an act best accomplished with diplomacy and respect. The event of the denial should also be documented on a report suitable for the employer or client. Policies for clear criteria for granting and/or denying access should be part of the protection officer's post orders or standard operating procedures.

Applying physical security in access control

For many facilities, control of access within the building at any one point would not require a dedicated protection officer, particularly in large facilities with many areas, such as industrial and office buildings. While posting officers at these various checkpoints to control access might be an effective form of access control, in these circumstances the risk may not warrant the cost. These areas could be executive offices, chemical rooms, file rooms, and other areas that may require limiting or curtailing access. In these cases an analysis of the costs and benefits of posting officers should be completed. Where posting an officer is not appropriate, access can be controlled with physical security barriers, such as doors, locks, security surveillance systems (CCTV), alarms, and electronic access control and monitored either actively or passively by the security officer. The effectiveness of physical security is further enhanced by strict key control, effective monitoring of CCTV and alarm systems by the security officer, and accurate database management in electronic access control systems. Other important tools used to aid access control are intercom, telephone, and other voice communications systems. Requests for access can be made from remote points within the facility, allowing an officer to be dispatched or to grant access remotely from an electronic access system, given proper authorization.

Locks and key control

Locks and keys have been around for thousands of years and remain fundamental for controlling access in many situations for many areas. Since their invention, the durability and security of locks and keys have greatly increased along with their use. Today, they help control access to almost every structure imaginable. Locks exist in many forms, but, generally speaking, locks are mechanical devices consist of a cylinder, springs, and several pins or "tumblers" that prevent rotation of the lock cylinder or plug without the insertion of a correctly cut key. Since keys can be duplicated, the high security locks manufactured today make unauthorized replication quite difficult. These specialized "proprietary" systems with unique and controlled key blanks restrict duplication, since they are only available for authorized users in agreement from authorized distributors. So within locks and keys, the restricted proprietary keyway, combined with strict key control, is one of the most effective solutions to controlling access.

The management of keys should include a signature or receipt for issued keys. Keys should each have unique control numbers permanently stamped on the key to record and track its identity from date of issue. The temporary issue of keys should be accompanied by signature on a register or key sign-out form indicating a return time. All codes and control numbers appearing on the keys should be documented for key sign-out. All key control documentation should be considered confidential and should be subject to similar record-keeping procedures as the security register. When the need to revoke access privileges is necessary, keys should be retrieved or, if necessary, locks should be changed. Some newer generation locks can suspend or revoke access to certain keys electronically, similar to an electronic access control system. This can eliminate the costs of lock changes, as well as administrative costs of reissuing new keys to authorized people.

Electronic access control

With the addition of electronic access control to a facility the officer can gain control of many individuals in different areas of the facility at different times, regardless of traffic volume. Most access systems installed today provide ease of access for authorized parties to come and go to their authorized destinations. Access is gained by presentation of a card, badge, token, or software token stored on a mobile device to an access control "reader." The reader may be connected electronically to an "interface" or "controller" or networked directly to a host computer system or to the Internet for cloud based services. Often systems with distributed panel controller are configured so that the remote controller or intelligent reader can make a local decision for access and retain transaction history locally especially in the event of a host computer failure or scheduled maintenance. This feature is known in the industry as "distributed" or "field" intelligence, and the activation of this feature is often referred to as "degraded" or "offline" mode. When access is granted to a given area, the access transaction is stored electronically on disk, tape, or printed media for future retrieval as part of a "history." A person attempting to gain access where not permitted can usually be reported as an alarm on a computer screen, directing the security officer to take a predetermined action. Log records, often including the individuals name, ID number, time of transaction, and type of denial, are also kept electronically to histories, as well as other alarms. Histories and other system reports can be customized in various ways and can be a valuable aid in the investigation of various incidents, as well as in controlling and monitoring time and attendance. Increasingly in the age of data analytics, companies utilize the access control systems data to trend occupancy levels for building space utilization and building service level decisions. This data can also be used as a consideration with energy loads in efforts to save on rising energy prices.

The industry of electronic access systems is continually expanding in terms of technologies, manufacturers, and installations. The majority of these systems are becoming more affordable and easier to use, whereas the technology that makes the systems work is becoming more advanced. Compiling modern, easy-to-use, and graphical user interface software has made the management of "enterprise" scale systems a much easier task than it was just a few years ago. Older enterprise scale systems use operating systems and software that consist mostly of typed command line interfaces that are less user-friendly than the more recent graphical user interface–based technology. Front-end computers on these earlier systems usually require more frequent maintenance and are more costly to repair than the modern systems being installed today. Installation of an electronic access control system will also contribute to the control of keys. Master keys need only to be issued in certain circumstances and may be signed out only when necessary. A daily sign-out control policy can ensure that master keys never need to leave the property. Most installed access systems use a card or similar medium to provide access in place of the key. If lost, the card can easily be voided by the operator of the system. This is a simple solution compared to the loss of a master key, which results in changing many locks and reissuing keys to all key holders. The access card will usually have a numeric or binary code that is verified by a computer host, ensuring validity.

Wireless and radio frequency communication

Most often today access control systems utilize wireless means to transmit card or token information to a card reader, which is read by the system to either permit or deny access. Recent innovations in access control technology have led to the use of contact less "smart" cards. In addition to providing the required data for traditional electronic access control, other information can be stored on the card, such as personal identification numbers to allow access, or even a biometric template, matching the cardholder's thumbprint or retina information to the content of the card. Other uses for the card may involve building automation or cashless vending. This trend is expected to continue with the advent of software tokens on mobile devices, which provides even greater possibilities.

Card/badge specifications

Security cards/badges should be designed and constructed to meet the necessary requirements. Upon issuing a card/badge, security personnel must explain to the bearer the attire required and the authorizations allowed with the card/badge. This includes the followings:

- designation of the areas where an ID card/badge is required;
- a description of the type of card/badge in use and the authorizations and limitations placed on the bearer;
- the required presentation of the card/badge when entering or leaving each area during all hours of the day;

- details of when, where, and how the card/badge should be worn, displayed, or carried;
- procedures to follow in case of loss or damage of the card;
- the disposition of the card/badge upon termination of employment, investigations, or personnel actions; and
- prerequisites for reissuing the card/badge.

Access cards

1. *Proximity cards*. Proximity access cards are most often used for EA systems. They work via the use of passively tuned circuits that have been embedded in a high-grade fiberglass epoxy card. One can gain access when the cardholder holds the card within 2–4 in. from a card reader. The reader's sensor detects the pattern of the frequencies programed in the card, and it communicates with the sensor by electromagnetic, ultrasound, or optical transmission. This pattern is then transmitted to the system's computer. If the pattern matches that of the reader, the reader unlocks the door and records the transaction. If the pattern does not match, no access is granted and this transaction is recorded.
2. *Magnetic stripe cards*. Magnetic cards use various kinds of materials and mediums to magnetically encode digital data onto cards. To gain access, the card user inserts or "swipes" (passes the badge through) the card reader. As the card is withdrawn from the reader, it moves across a magnetic head, similar to that in a tape recorder head, that reads the data programed in the card. The information read from the card is sent to the system's computer for verification. If verification is made, the computer sends a signal to the card reader to grant or deny access, and if access is granted, the door is unlocked. Magnetic cards look like regular credit cards. The most popular medium for this type of access card is a magnetic stripe on which a pattern of digital data is encoded. This type of card is relatively inexpensive and a large amount of data can be stored magnetically compared to other kinds of magnetic media. These cards tend to chip and break, however, through excessive use.
3. *Weigand cards*. Weigand-based access control cards use a coded pattern on magnetized wire embedded within the card. When this card is inserted into a reader, the reader's internal sensors are activated by the coded wire. This type of card is moderately priced and will handle a large amount of traffic. It is less vulnerable to vandalism and weather effects than other types of cards, but it does stand up to a considerable amount of wear and tear.
4. *Biometrics access control*. Biometrics is most accurate when using one or more fingerprints, palm prints or palm scan, hand geometry, or retina and iris scan. Remember deterrent controls delay unauthorized access. Think *proactive management*.
5. *Biometric ID systems operate locks to doors*. Used in high-security areas where limited access is maintained, this system checks physical characteristics that verify and allow access/entry.
6. *Smart cards*. These contain an integrated chip embedded in them. They have coded memories and microprocessors; hence, they are like computers. The technology in these cards offers many possibilities, particularly with proximity card–based card access systems. Optical cards have a pattern of light spots that can be read by a specific light source, usually infrared. Capacitance cards use coded capacitor-sensitive material that is enclosed in the card. A current is induced when the card activates a reader that checks the capacitance of the card to determine the proper access code. Some access devices come in the shape of keys, disks, or other convenient formats that provide users with access tools that look attractive and subdued but at the same time are functional.
7. *Dual-technology card*. Some cards have dual technology, such as magnetic stripe/proximity card and an RFID/proximity card.
8. *Card readers*. Card readers are devices used for reading access cards. Readers come in various shapes, sizes, and configurations. The most common reader is the type where the card user inserts the card in a slot or runs or "swipes" the card through a slot. The other type of reader uses proximity technology where the card user presents or places the card on or near the reader. Some insertion-type card readers use keypads; after the user inserts the card, the user enters a unique code number on the keypad. This action then grants access.
9. *Electronic access control (EAC) systems applications*. Ideally used as part of a fully integrated facility management system. In such a system, electronic access control is interfaced and integrated with fire safety/life safety systems, CCTV systems, communication systems, and nonsecurity systems, such as heating, ventilation, and air-conditioning. In an integrated system, EAC systems allow users to be accessed into various areas or limited areas. They can track access and provide attendance records. As a safety feature and for emergency response situations, they can determine where persons are located in facilities. In general, EAC systems are very flexible, and strides in technology have made them even more so.

Access system database management

Granting and controlling access privileges must also have similar strict procedures to those of the key systems. Access privileges should be formally requested, approved, and controlled by consistent and appropriate documentation. Typically, information is kept in a cardholder's file, along with a history of changes and authorizations. These files should remain easily accessible by authorized personnel until a set time has elapsed since termination of the cardholder's access. Event minor details, such as spelling and field record consistency, are vital to good access system database management. This not only assists in audits but can also control costs, as a card with picture identification can be kept on file in the event that the cardholder returns to work in the near future. Returned damaged or defective cards should be destroyed and documented in the system database, so identical cards can be reissued in the future.

Equal attention should be paid to the overall security and management of electronic access systems and these databases. Best practices for IT security should be the norm with proper continuity elements and procedures in place. Frequent software backups may one day payoff in the event of host server failure.

Access control

This describes how you require people to enter, exit, and access certain areas of your facility. These requirements will be different for staff, students, visitors, emergency responders, and the public. You may identify other groups of people who require special access. These requirements may change based on time of day, on site events, and other conditions. You can use these requirements to define traffic and life patterns to enhance your security programs. Access control measures may also be used to create life patterns that discourage or make unwanted activity stand out against the baseline of normal, which will enhance your monitoring activities.

Request for proposal

Armed with a security program that breaks down your expectations of any technologies, your security consultant can help design an RFP that will be very informative to potential vendors and facilitate conversations throughout the process. This also turns into a functionality checklist that you should use during the design, build, and commissioning phases.

Multiple factors—biometrics technologies

Biometrics technology is becoming more commonly included with access cards and token to increase the level of assurance that only authorized individuals are using access privileges. Requiring more than one factor is very common in higher security environments, such as in airports and other immigration checkpoints. Increasingly biometric technologies are being added to access control system to provide a second access factor. These biometric systems can include hand, eye, and even full facial recognition. The use of facial technology integrated into CCTV systems can be used without access systems to identify individuals who are either wanted by law enforcement or may not be permitted to travel to a given country. Facial recognition technology is expected to be an important tool in the prevention of international terrorism, smuggling of contraband, and child abduction at points of entry in countries around the world.

Types of biometrics device

Fingerprints and palm prints

Formed when the friction ridges of the skin come in contact with a surface that is receptive to a print by using an agent to form the print, such as perspiration, oil, ink, grease, and so forth. The agent is transferred to the surface and leaves an impression that forms the fingerprint.

Hand scanner and finger reader recognition systems

These measure and analyze the overall structure, shape, and proportions of the hand, such as length, width, and thickness of the hand, fingers, and joints, and characteristics of the skin surface such as creases and ridges.

Iris cameras

They perform recognition detection of a person's identity by mathematical analysis of the random patterns that are visible within the iris of an eye from some distance. It combines computer vision, pattern recognition, statistical inference, and optics.

Iris recognition

This is rarely impeded by glasses or contact lenses and can be scanned from 10 cm to a few meters away. The iris remains stable over time as long as there are no injuries, and a single enrollment scan can last a lifetime.

Facial recognition device

This views an image or video of a person and compares it to one in the database. It does this by comparing structure, shape, and proportions of the face; distance between the eyes, nose, mouth, and jaw; upper outlines of the eye sockets; the sides of the mouth; the location of the nose and eyes; and the area surrounding the cheek bones.

The main facial recognition methods are feature analysis, neural network, eigenfaces, and automatic face processing.

Voice recognition voiceprint

This is a spectrogram that is a graph showing a sound's frequency on the vertical axis and time on the horizontal axis. Different speech creates different shapes on the graph. Spectrograms also use color or shades of gray to represent the acoustical qualities of sound.

Digital biometrics signature

This is equivalent to a traditional handwritten signature in many respects since if the signature is properly implemented, it is more difficult to forge than the traditional type. Digital signature schemes are cryptographically based and must be implemented properly to be effective. Digital signatures can be used for e-mail, contracts, or any message sent via some other cryptographic protocol.

Vein recognition

Vein recognition is a type of biometrics that can be used to identify individuals based on the vein patterns in the human finger.

DNA: DNA is perhaps one of the most important biometrics today as it has been used to solve thousands of crimes around the globe. The technology surrounding DNA is always evolving and new enhancements are being applied to the law enforcement community. One of the most recent improvements has been the development of the *Rapid DNA Program Office* established in 2010 by the FBI/(hands free) process of developing a CODIS Core STR profile from a reference sample buccal swab. The "swab in—profile out" process consists of automated extraction, amplification, separation, detection, and allele calling without human intervention.[1] The FBI's imitative is to improve the process and the time that it takes to complete DNA testing by integrating technologies into CODIS and other DNA-related systems. In sum the benefit of using DNA as a biometric identifier is the level of accuracy offered. Similar to fingerprint data, it is nearly impossible for two human subjects to share the same DNA structure.

Writer recognition: There are typically two types of handwriting and writer biometric recognition to include static and dynamic. In the static method, individuals write directly on paper and it is then scanned into a computer system for analysis.[2] Dynamic biometrics record handwriting records in real time through the use of digitizers, tablets, and other devices. The handwriting examples can then be scanned through an automated system or independently.

1. Federal Bureau of Investigations—Biometrics (DNA), 2016. Retrieved from: <https://www.fbi.gov/about-us/lab/biometric-analysis/codis/rapid-dna-analysis>.
2. Chapran, J., 2006. Biometric writer identification: feature analysis and classification. Int. J. Pattern Recognit. Artif. Intell. 483–503.

There are four important things to consider about the use of biometrics for security access control[3]:

1. cost
2. overall convenience
3. secure application
4. identity assurance

Access control in the information age

Today businesses are moving to cloud technologies and replacing the traditional on premises data centers with IT services provided through networked arrangements. We now use these arrangements from everything to Salesforce management to human resource management, finance, sales, and other core business functions. Likely, security access control will follow and with it some additional benefits and challenges.

Years ago, someone would need to be on site in order to circumvent access controls. Today, that risk also includes a computer hacker anywhere in the world as access control systems are connected to larger networks and the Internet. This threat has led to an increase in the IT security field, and further work needed to assure access privileges and their management remain assurance and in control.

Paying extra attention to potential weaknesses in physical security elements, facility design, access systems, components, as well as the organizational policy must be the norm. As with many processes, the policies and procedures for controlling access in facilities are sometimes subject to flaws or have "room for improvement" and should therefore be scrutinized by management. Consideration for control measurements or metrics should be made. Continuous improvement and feedback so that ideas for change and improvement can be made by the protection officers and others through observations, discussions, and control measurements should be encouraged. Tightening security should not be the only criterion for continuous improvement. In many instances the need for faster authentication of authorized personnel may be considered essential, as losses may occur due to an unauthorized person being "held up" by security.

Access control—administrative measures

- Designating alert and tactful security personnel at entry control points.
- Ensuring that personnel possess quick perception and good judgment.
- Requiring entry-control personnel to conduct frequent irregular checks of their assigned areas.
- Formalizing standard procedures for conducting guard mounts and posting and relieving security personnel. These measures will prevent posting of unqualified personnel and a routine performance of duty.
- Prescribing a uniform method of handling or wearing security ID cards/badges. If carried on the person, the card must be removed from the wallet (or other holder) and handed to security personnel. When worn, the badge will be worn in a conspicuous position to expedite inspection and recognition from a distance.
- Designing entry and exit control points of restricted areas to force personnel to pass in a single file in front of security personnel. In some instances the use of turnstiles may be advisable to assist in maintaining positive control.
- Providing lighting at control points. The lighting must illuminate the area to enable security personnel to compare the bearer with the ID card/badge.
- Enforcing access control measures by educating security forces and employees. Enforcement of access control systems rests primarily with the security forces; however, it is essential that they have the full cooperation of the employees. Employees must be instructed to consider each unidentified or improperly identified individual as a trespasser. In restricted areas where access is limited to a particular zone, employees must report unauthorized individuals to the security force.
- Positioning ID card/badge racks or containers at entry control points so they are accessible only to guard-force personnel.
- Appointing a responsible custodian to accomplish control procedures of cards/badges according to policy manual. The custodian is responsible for the issue, turn in, recovery, and renewal of security ID cards/badges as well as monthly verification of individuals in various areas and the deletion of terminated employee badges.

3. Rzemyk, T.J., 2017. Biometrics in the criminal justice system and society today. In: Effective Physical Security Book, fifth ed. DNA & Writer Recognition.

The degree of compromise tolerable in the ID system is in direct proportion to the degree of security required. The following control procedures are recommended for preserving the integrity of a card/badge system:

- Maintenance of an accurate written record or log listing (by serial number) all cards and badges and showing those on hand, to whom they are issued, and their disposition (lost, mutilated, or destroyed).
- Authentication of records and logs by the custodian.
- A periodic inventory of records by a manager or auditors.
- The prompt invalidation of lost cards/badges and the conspicuous posting at security control points of current lists of lost or invalidated cards/badges.
- The establishment of controls within restricted areas to enable security personnel to determine the number of persons within the area.
- The establishment of the two-person rule (when required).
- The establishment of procedures to control the movement of visitors. A visitor-control record will be maintained and located at entry control points.

Building design

When designing, building, and installing engineered security controls, security practitioners must consider a variety of factors to ensure optimum results. While not doing so can leave access control systems prone to nuisance alarms, it can also lead to limited or no authorization controls at all. Your objective should be to prevent penetration and provide authorized access through layered levels of security within your complex.

Layered levels of security

The outer perimeter/outer protective layer can be a man-made barrier controlling both traffic and people flow. The inner layer contains the interior lobby and main entrance, turnstiles, revolving doors, handicap gates, elevators, emergency doors alarmed, and private occupied space. The inner protective layer contains biometrics, mirrors, and security surveillance systems/network video (CCTV) applications. The middle layer consists of exterior parts of the building.

High-security areas are laid within the inner layer with limited access to a select few. Reducing opportunity within your complex's design must be tailored to the specific area's environment.

When designing administrative controls for access control, one must consider the tolerance for process errors. This means we should consider the percentage of unauthorized transactions we can allow with minimal consequence. While engineered controls make a significant difference controlling access capabilities, our tolerance for mistakes or errors in access control often equally relate to the administrative controls that rule the measurement of results and prove our access control levels are operating at the desired levels.

Emerging trends

In addition to those trends in information security, there are many new and emerging trends and tools that relate to the function of access control. These include, but are not limited to, optical high-speed turnstiles, hand-held explosive and biohazard detection, and, most recently, millimeter wave scanning. Millimeter wave scanning is the latest trend in preboard screening at airport facilities. While it is an effective replacement for manually searching passengers, there are concerns to be managed including privacy as some of these new technologies do create additional privacy issues.

As technology and data analytics provide more potential for increased access control assurance, there is no doubt the role of the protection officer performing and facilitating access control will continue to evolve and with it even more dependent on it as a vital first line of defense in the protection of people, assets, and information.[4]

4. Rzemyk, T.J., 2017. Biometrics in the criminal justice system and society today. In: Effective Physical Security Book, fifth ed. DNA & Writer Recognition.

Chapter 22

Security lighting*

Jay C. McCormick
Security Consultant

Adequate light not only helps people recognize and avoid danger, but also in many cases deters criminals by creating in them the fear of detection, identification and apprehension.

Randy Atlas, CPP, 1993.

Introduction

From a business perspective, lighting can be justified because it improves sales by making a business and merchandise more attractive, promotes safety and prevents lawsuits, improves employee morale and productivity, and enhances the value of real estate. From a security perspective, two major purposes of lighting are *to create a psychological deterrent to intrusion* and *to enable detection.* Good lighting is considered such an effective crime control method that the law, in many locales, requires buildings to maintain adequate lighting.

One way to analyze lighting deficiencies is to go to the building at night and study the possible methods of entry and areas where inadequate lighting aids a burglar. Before the visit, contact local police as a precaution against mistaken identity and recruit their assistance in spotting weak points in lighting.

What lighting level aids an intruder? Most people believe that, under conditions of darkness, a criminal can safely commit a crime. But this view may be faulty as one generally cannot work in the dark. Three possible levels of light are bright light, darkness, and dim light. *Bright light* affords an offender plenty of light to work but enables easy observation by others; it deters crime. Without light, in *darkness*, a burglar finds that he or she cannot see to jimmy a good lock, release a latch, or do whatever work is necessary to gain access. However, *dim light* provides just enough light to break and enter while hindering observation by authorities. Support for this view was shown in a study of crimes during full-moon phases when dim light was produced.

This study examined the records of 972 police shifts at three police agencies over a 2-year period to compare nine different crimes during full-moon and nonfull-moon phases. Only one crime, breaking and entering, was greater during full-moon phases. Although much case law supports lighting as an indicator of efforts to provide a safe environment, security specialists are questioning conventional wisdom about lighting. Because so much nighttime lighting goes unused, should it be reduced or turned off? Does an offender look more suspicious under a light or in the dark with a flashlight? Should greater use be made of motion-activated lighting? How would these approaches affect safety and cost-effectiveness? These questions are ripe for research.

Illumination

Lumens (of light output) per watt (of power input) is a measure of lamp efficiency (National Lighting Bureau, n.d.; Kunze and Schiefer, 1995; Smith, 1996; Bowers, 1995). Initial lumens per watt data are based on the light output of lamps when new; however, light output declines with use. *Illuminance* is the intensity of light falling on a surface, which is measured in foot-candles (English units) or lux (metric units). The *foot-candle* is a measure of how bright the

*Portions of the chapter were prepared be Philip P. Purpura, CPP, Lawrence J. Fennelly, CPOI, CSSM, Gerard Honey, and James F. Broder over the years.

Handbook of Loss Prevention and Crime Prevention. DOI: https://doi.org/10.1016/B978-0-12-817273-5.00022-3

light is when it reaches 1 ft from the source. One lux equals to 0.0929 fc. The light provided by direct sunlight on a clear day is about 10,000 fc, an overcast day would yield about 100 fc, and a full moon gives off about 0.01 fc. A number of sample of outdoor lighting illuminances recommended by the Illuminating Engineering Society of North America are as follows: self-parking area, 1 fc; attendant parking area, 0.20–0.90 fc; covered parking area, 5 fc; active pedestrian entrance, 5 fc; and building surroundings, 1 fc. It is generally recommended that gates and doors, where identification of persons and things takes place, should have at least 2 fc, while an office should have a light level of about 50 fc.

Care should be exercised when studying foot-candles. Are they horizontal or vertical? Horizontal illumination may not aid in the visibility of vertical objects, such as signs and keyholes (the preceding foot-candles are horizontal). The foot-candle varies depending on the distance from the lamp and the angle. If you hold a light meter horizontally, it often gives a different reading from holding it vertically. Jay "Chuck" McCormick, PSP, notes that a good understanding of the photometrics can assist with understanding what levels of light are needed in order for natural and/or technical surveillance is needed (4:1). Cameras are a light-averaging device and ratios greater than 4:1 start to diminish the ability of a camera to see as well as place a strain on our eyes to take in visual data.

Maintenance and bulb replacement ensure high-quality lighting.

Types of lamps

The following lamps are applied outdoors (National Lighting Bureau, n.d.; Kunze and Schiefer, 1995; Smith, 1996; Bowers, 1995).

The following options for inclusion are information gleaned from the various books used in the PSP certification process available from ASIS International.

- *Incandescent.* These are commonly found at residences. Passing electrical current through a tungsten wire that becomes white and hot produces light. These lamps, which produce 10–20 lm/W, are the least efficient and most expensive to operate and have a short lifetime of 9000 hours. They have an instant restrike with a good color rendering index.
- *Halogen and quartz halogen lamps.* Incandescent bulbs filled with halogen gas (such as sealed beam–auto headlights) provide about 25% better efficiency and life than ordinary incandescent bulbs.
- *Fluorescent lamps.* Passing electricity through a gas enclosed in a glass tube to produce light, yielding 40–80 lm/W. They create twice the light and less than half the heat of an incandescent bulb of equal wattage and cost 5–10 times as much. Fluorescent lamps do not provide high levels of light output. The lifetime is 9000–20,000 hours. They are not used extensively outdoors, except for signs. Fluorescent lamps use one-fifth to one-third as much electricity as incandescent with a comparable lumen rating and last up to 20 times longer. They are cost effective with yearly saving per bulb of $9.00–25.00. They have an instant restrike with a good color rendering index.
- *Mercury vapor lamps.* They also pass electricity through a gas. The yield is 30–60 lm/W and the life is about 20,000 hours. Checking with state laws maybe illegal to use in some states.
- *Metal halide lamps.* They are also of the gaseous type. The yield is 80–100 lm/W, and the life is about 10,000 hours. They are often used at sports stadiums because they imitate daylight conditions and colors appear natural. Consequently, these lamps complement closed-circuit TV (CCTV) systems, but they are the most expensive light to install and maintain. Slow restrike time (10–15 minutes) with a color rendering index that can range from 60–90 out of 100.
- *High-pressure sodium lamps.* These are gaseous, yield about 100 lm/W, have a life of about 20,000 hours, and are energy efficient. These lamps are often applied on streets and parking lots and are designed to allow the eyes to see more detail at greater distances through the fog. They also cause less light pollution than mercury vapor lamps. Slow restrike time (1–2 minutes) with a color rendering index that is around 21 out of 100.
- *Low-pressure sodium lamps.* They are gaseous, produce 150 lm/W, have a life of about 15,000 hours, and are even more efficient than high-pressure sodium lamps. These lamps are expensive to maintain. Slow restrike time (7–15 minutes) with a color rendering index that is around 0 out of 100.
- *LED (light emitting diodes).* This type of lighting is becoming more and more popular. They use very low energy consumption and are long lasting up to 50,000–80,000 hours. Currently, they are used in many applications, such as in garages, street lighting, and rear taillights in motor vehicles. There is an instant restrike time and an excellent color rendering index. These lights are *the bulb of the future.*

- *Quartz lamps.* These lamps emit a very bright light and snap on almost as rapidly as incandescent bulbs. They are frequently used at very high wattage—1500–2000 W is not uncommon in protective systems—and they are excellent for use along the perimeter barrier and in troublesome areas.
- *Electroluminescent lights.* These lights are similar to their fluorescent cousins; however, they do not contain mercury and are more compact.

Each type of lamp has a different *color rendition index* (CRI), which is the way a lamp's output affects human perception of color. Incandescent, fluorescent, and halogen lamps provide an excellent CRI of 100%. Based on its high CRI and efficiency, the preferred outdoor lamp for CCTV systems is metal halide. Mercury vapor lamps provide good color rendition but are heavy on the blue. Low-pressure sodium lamps, which are used extensively outdoors, provide poor color rendition, making things look yellow. Low-pressure sodium lamps make color unrecognizable and produce a yellow-gray color on objects. People find that they produce a strange yellow haze. Claims are made that this lighting conflicts with esthetic values and affects sleeping habits. In many instances, when people park their vehicles in a parking lot during the day and return to find their vehicle at night, they are often unable to locate it because of poor color rendition from sodium lamps; some even report their vehicles as stolen. Another problem is the inability of witnesses to describe offenders accurately.

Mercury vapor, metal halide, and high-pressure sodium take several minutes to produce full light output. If they are turned off, even more time is required to reach full output because they have to cool down first. This may not be acceptable for certain security applications. Incandescent, halogen, and quartz halogen have the advantage of instant light once the electricity is turned on. Manufacturers can provide information on a host of lamp characteristics, including the "strike" and "restrike" time.

The following sources provide additional information on lighting:

- National Lighting Bureau (http://www.nlb.org): publications.
- Illuminating Engineering Society of North America (http://www.iesna.org): technical materials and services; recommended practices and standards; and many members are engineers.
- International Association of Lighting Management Companies (http://www.nalmco.org): seminars, training, and certification programs.

Seven basic types of protective lighting and illumination and glare

Protective lighting

Lighting is the single most cost-effective deterrent to crime. An illuminated area acts as a psychological and physical deterrent and it can reduce criminal opportunity. Research shows that there is a close relationship between crime/the fear of crime and illumination. Lighting is a powerful tool for crime prevention by enhancing safety and may possibly reduce potential liability.

Lighting systems

The basic systems of security lighting, which may be used either singly or in combination, are perimeter lighting, area lighting, and floodlighting. Other forms of lighting may also be required, such as gatehouse lighting and topping-up lighting.

The seven basic types of protective lighting include the following:

- *Continuous lighting*—fixed and the most common type of lighting where lights are installed in a series to maintain uniform lighting during hours of darkness. These lights frequently set on timers or controlled by sensors.
- *Standby lighting*—turns on with alarm activation or when suspicious activity is suspected.
- *Moveable lighting*—manually operated search lights.
- *Emergency lighting*—can duplicate other lighting systems in the event of an emergency. Use is limited to times of power failure and other emergencies. Emergency lights usually depend on an alternative power source.
- *Controlled lighting*—used outside a perimeter to illuminate a limited space.
- *Area lighting*—used in open areas and parking lots.
- *Surface lighting*—used on the surface of structures and buildings.

Perimeter lighting

Perimeter lighting is used to illuminate the property line or fence itself and an area beyond (i.e., the detection zone). When used with chain-link fencing, a narrow strip inside the fence is also illuminated. When double fences are used, the detection zone lies wholly or mainly between the two fences.

The objective is to reveal an intruder's approach and produce glare toward him, thus reducing visibility into the site. It may therefore be suitable for use with patrolling guards. However, it can be difficult to apply because it may create nuisance or hazard or because of a lack of sufficient open flat ground outside the perimeter.

Illumination and glare

- *Illumination intensity*—as light bulbs age, the light that they emit out decreases. Some objects and colors reflect light better than others and this affects intensity and its time to replace them.
- *Illumination distribution*—lighting fixtures have to be spaced correctly so that there is no area without proper illumination.
- *Illumination quality*—color perception may or may not be important. This may affect the quality of video surveillance.
- *Illumination reliability*—may be problem if the lights are vulnerable to physical attack or vandalism.
- *Lighting and the intensity*
  - Lighting and the intensity of illumination falling on a surface is measured in foot-candles (English units) or lux (metric units) and a general rule, "at night, outside of a building or at a parking lot, one should be able to read a driver's license or newspaper with some eyestrain" (Purpura, 1979).
  - One foot-candle equals to one lumen of light per one square foot of space. One lumen is the measure of light at its source and the amount of light needed to light an area of 1 ft^2 to 1 cp.

Glare

Glare is difficulty in seeing in the presence of bright light, such as direct or reflected sunlight, or artificial light, such as car headlamps at night. Because of this, some cars include mirrors with automatic antiglare functions.

Cost and return on investment

Cost is broken down into three categories: (1) 88% energy cost, (2) 8% capital cost, and (3) maintenance cost. Return on investment is also broken down into three categories: (1) efficiency and energy savings payback, (2) reduce costs by shutting off unnecessary units, and (3) the concept of going green.

Lighting equipment

Incandescent or gaseous discharge lamps are used in streetlights. Fresnel lights have a wide flat beam that is directed outward to protect a perimeter and glare in the faces of those approaching. A floodlight "floods" an area with a beam of light, resulting in considerable glare. Glare can be an effective tool for locations with a response force. It can conceal the location of those on the interior while illuminating those approaching the perimeter. Glare can be an effective strategy for concealment and blinding to those approaching a fence line or a gate as a few examples. Floodlights are stationary, although the light beams can be aimed to select positions. The following strategies reinforce good lighting:

1. Locate perimeter lighting to allow illumination of both sides of the barrier.
2. Direct lights down and away from a facility to create glare for an intruder. Make sure the directed lighting does not hinder observation by the patrolling officer.
3. Do not leave dark spaces between lighted areas for burglars to move in. Design lighting to permit overlapping illumination.
4. Protect the lighting system. Locate lighting inside the barrier, install protective covers over lamps, mount lamps on high poles, bury power lines, and protect switch boxes.
5. Photoelectric cells enable light to go on and off automatically in response to natural light. Manual operation is helpful as a backup.

6. Consider motion-activated lighting for external and internal areas.
7. If lighting is required in the vicinity of navigable waters, contact the US Coast Guard.
8. Try not to disturb neighbors by intense lighting. Some local laws govern light pollution or support a "dark sky initiative."
9. Maintain a supply of portable, emergency lights, and auxiliary power in the event of a power failure.
10. Good interior lighting also deters burglars. Locating lights over safes, expensive merchandise, and other valuables and having large clear windows (especially in retail establishments) let passing patrol officers see in.
11. If necessary, join other business owners to petition local government to install improved street lighting.

Creating your own photometric

If a better understanding of your lighting conditions is needed, photometric data may be available from the design of your facility. If you do not have photometric data, one can be created that is specific to your facility. There are a few concepts that will help with this effort:

1. Bulb life will impact readings.
2. Bulb intensity will decay until catastrophic failure.
3. Creating a photometric is a living document and must be revisited periodically.
4. There are different thoughts on the following, so adapt to what you feel meets your needs—I create a tactical grid to perform a lighting evaluation based on each type of light fixture. Remember 1–3 as mentioned previously.
5. The tactical grid starts at the base of the light fixture and based on the light fixture type, it can be observed with the following tactical grids:

   Cobra hood parking lot fixtures can come in various types. They can be single, double, triple, quadruple, or more. Start at the base of the fixture and move in a tactical grid marking where the lines intersect. A 5-ft by 5-ft tactical grid can be drawn using chalk marking the intersections. This is granular enough to get good data back and larger grid intersections could be used but may be difficult to know where that 4:1 boundary occurs. The grid pattern is easily done during daylight hours, if the parking lot can be free of vehicles. Depending on the direction of the light fixtures, you may need to create a grid in all of the direction of the light fixtures. The data collection can be kept in an excel document by noting where "0" is (the light pole) and then each cell represents your tactical grid measurements. From the brightest reading, you can divide by 4 giving you the 4:1 ratio to see where it may be more difficult for technical surveillance.
6. This same philosophy can be utilized with can lights, wall packs, and any other type. Document the type and location on a site drawing and keep the data as a historical marker to check the next time a survey is performed.

This empirical data can be collected using an inexpensive light meter. Be sure for your report to document the type of meter and any settings so that it can be duplicated at the next assessment.

Look at the lunar cycle and attempt the survey during a waning crescent, new moon (best), or waxing crescent phase of the moon. Know when moonset occurs for the particular night of your survey and use the type of light fixture and restrike time documenting when the survey was performed. Let us use moonset at 9:45 p.m. as an example, and you have low-pressure sodium light, it may take up to 15 minutes before the fixture is at full illumination. Document if the fixture utilizes a photocell or if manually turned on by timer or person. This can vary when you start, but if it is by timer that turns the lights on at 9:45 p.m. then you could not start the survey until 10:00 p.m. If it is by photocell, you will need to be onsite watching for the light fixture to turn on, then delay based on light type. Document everything about the assessment so that the data can be recorded to provide some context of the survey conditions; the darkest night, with light at maximum illumination. I have also created a tool to help provide visual context to the readings being recorded. Again for illustration purposes, let us say that the brightest reading of a light fixture is 4 fc. Using our 4:1 ratio, at the point of our tactical grid that reads 1 fc, I set a 2-ft by 2-ft board painted white with 4-in. by 6-in. blocks painted in primary colors at the 1 fc location and take a photo standing at the 4 fc location—no flash photography. This helps bring the color rendering index to life when discussing where lighting changes may be needed. When writing up the report, include the excel table, lunar data (time/date) of survey, and any photos for historical purposes. Proper documentation of the assessment can qualify the assessment and quantify the findings.

Sample grid layout.

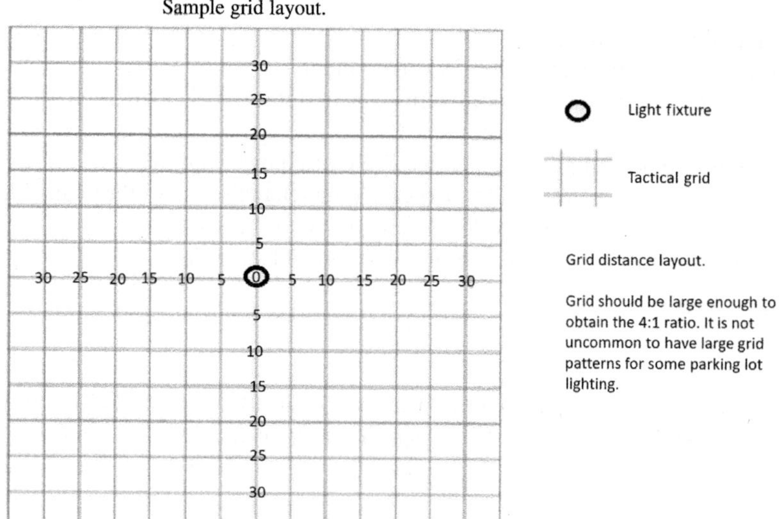

Those numbers can be entered into an excel document as shown, this light fixture was illuminating in one direction, so only half of a tactical grid was required.

Sample from a field survey.

50	45	40	35	30	25	20	15	10	5	0	5	10	15	20	25	30	35	40	45	50
0						1.2	2.4	4.1	6	7.9	6	4.1	2.4	1.2						
5						0.5	1	1.9	3.6	7.1	3.6	1.9	1	0.5						
10						0.4	0.8	1.6	2.9	4.8	2.9	1.6	0.8	0.4						
15						0.5	0.8	1.4	2.2	3.1	2.2	1.4	0.8	0.5						
20						0.3	0.7	1.1	1.2	1.9	1.2	1.1	0.7	0.3						
25						0.2	0.5	0.7	0.7	1.5	0.7	0.7	0.5	0.2						
30																				
35																				
40																				
45																				
50																				

4:1 ratio from brightest to darkest would be 1.97.

From this example, the brightest reading is 7.9. Divide 7.9 by four and the 4:1 ratio is exceeded when the light level reaches 1.97. The grid can show the light pattern produced and within the area 4:1 (left and right of the light fixture) ends about 15 (±) ft away from the fixture and then out from the light fixture at about 20 ft.

Twenty-five things you need to know about lighting

1. *Watts*: Measures the amount of electrical energy used (Tyska and Fennelly, 2000).
2. *Foot-candle*: Measure of light on a surface 1 ft^2 in area on which one unit of light (lumen) is distributed uniformly.
3. *Lumen*: Unit of light output from a lamp.
4. *Lamp*: Term that refers to light sources that are called *bulbs*.
5. *Lux*: Measurement of illumination.
6. *Illuminare*: Intensity of light that falls on an object.
7. *Brightness*: Intensity of the sensation from light as seen by the eye.
8. *Foot-lambert*: Measure of brightness.
9. *Glare*: Excessive brightness.

10. *Luminaire*: Complete lighting unit; consists of one or more lamps joined with other parts that distribute light, protect the lamp, position or direct it, and connect it to a power source.
11. *Ballast*: Device used with fluorescent and high-intensity discharge (HID) lamps to obtain voltage and current to operate the lamps.
12. *HID*: Term used to identify four types of lamps—mercury vapor, metal halide, and high- and low-pressure sodium.
13. *Coefficient of utilization*: Ratio of the light delivered from a luminaire to a surface compared to the total light output from a lamp.
14. *Contrast*: Relationship between the brightness of an object and its immediate background.
15. *Diffuser*: Device on the bottom or sides of a luminaire to redirect or spread light from a source.
16. *Fixture*: A luminaire.
17. *Lens*: Glass or plastic shield that covers the bottom of a luminaire to control the direction and brightness of the light as it comes out of the fixture or luminaire.
18. *Louvers*: Series of baffles arranged in a geometric pattern. They shield a lamp from direct view to avoid glare.
19. *Uniform lighting*: Refers to a system of lighting that directs the light specifically on the work or job rather than on the surrounding areas.
20. *Reflector*: Device used to redirect light from a lamp.
21. *Task or work lighting*: The amount of light that falls on an object of work.
22. *Veiling reflection*: Reflection of light from an object that obscures the detail to be observed by reducing the contrast between the object and its background.
23. *Incandescent lamps*: Produce light by passing an electric current through a tungsten filament in a glass bulb. They are the least efficient type of bulb.
24. *Fluorescent lamps*: Second most common source of light. They draw an electric arc along the length of a tube. The ultraviolet light produced by the arc activates a phosphor coating on the walls of the tube, which causes light.
25. *HID lamps*: Consist of mercury vapor, metal halide, and high- and low-pressure sodium lamps. The low-pressure sodium was the most efficient and has been replaced by LED.

Energy management

The efficiency and management of lighting is becoming a high priority in commissioning new buildings and upgrading existing systems. Indeed, the subject of energy management is expected to become one of the most important considerations within the building regulation documents and have a tremendous impact on the way the construction industry looks at energy. It is apparent that serious measures must now be taken to reduce energy use and waste. This will have an impact on security lighting and the way it is applied. Lighting experts show an increasing urge to work alongside electrical contractors and installers to help them increase their business opportunities by identifying the roles and applications in which energy-efficient lighting should be installed. Electrical contractors are becoming better educated in lighting design that is effective and energy efficient.

Lighting design personnel need to:

- recognize inefficient installations;
- appreciate the environmental, cost, and associated benefits of energy-efficient lighting schemes;
- estimate energy cost savings and calculate the payback period;
- recognize the situations in which expert and specialist knowledge is needed in the design of management systems; and
- think in terms of increasing business trying to preserve the environment.

At certain points of time, it was said that lighting any system brighter was advantageous. However, we are now seeing a trend away from large floodlights illuminating the night sky with a strong white glare, as exterior lighting is becoming much more focused on the minimum lux levels required. We are also seeing a move toward directional beams.

The lighting industry wants to remove itself from a proliferation of public and private external lighting schemes to counter the light pollution problem and becomes more energy and cost conscious in its makeup. There must be a mechanism to tackle the problem of countless floodlights, up lighters, spotlights, decorative installations, and an array of security lighting forms that are badly installed and specified, create light pollution, and use high energy levels.

Lighting pollution is now at the forefront of debates for two main reasons:

1. Light pollution spoils the natural effect of the night skies.
2. The greater the light pollution, the greater is the power consumption.

Unfortunately, a certain degree of light pollution is needed to satisfy safety and security applications. Equally, there is always the desire to have purely decorative lighting installations, so the answer lies in a compromise. Systems must be designed with a degree of thought given to the avoidance of light pollution and energy waste. External lighting must provide minimal light pollution, a safe environment, and an attractive feature. For attractive features, we can see a greater use of fiber optic solutions with color-changing effects and lighting engineered to direct the illumination downward. Bollards or recessed ground luminaries can be set into walkways so there is no spill into the night sky. Intelligently, designed schemes can ensure that lighting is reflected only in a downward direction so that pedestrians are better guided and the lighting has a pleasing effect with little overspill.

Therefore within the lighting industry, there is a need to raise standards in all aspects associated with light and lighting, in particular, when it comes to energy management and light pollution. We need to define and harness the pleasures of lighting but at the same time promote the benefits of well-designed energy-efficient schemes among the public at large. There must also be miniaturization and increased lamp life. Energy management must therefore be a part of security lighting.

Lighting checklist

1. Are all of the perimeters lighted?
2. Is there a strip of light on both sides of fence?
3. Is the illumination sufficient to detect human movement easily at 100 yards?
4. Are lights checked for operation daily prior to darkness?
5. Is extra lighting available at entry points and points of possible intrusion?
6. Are lighting repairs made promptly?
7. Is the power supply for lights easily accessible (for tampering)?
8. Are lighting circuit drawings available to facilitate quick repairs?
9. Are switches and controls
   a. protected?
   b. weatherproof and tamper resistant?
   c. accessible to security personnel?
   d. inaccessible from outside the perimeter barrier?
   e. equipped with centrally located master switch(es)?
10. Is the illumination good for guards on all routes inside the perimeter?
11. Are the materials and equipment in receiving, shipping, and storage areas adequately lighted?
12. Are bodies of water on perimeter adequately lighted?
13. Is an auxiliary source of power available for protective lighting?

Protective lighting checklist

1. Is protective lighting adequate on perimeter?
2. What type of lighting is it?
3. Is the lighting of open areas within the perimeter adequate?
4. Do shadowed areas exist?
5. Are outside storage areas adequately lighted?
6. Are inside areas adequately lighted?
7. Is the guard protected or exposed by the lighting?
8. Are gates and boundaries adequately lighted?
9. Do lights at the gates illuminate the interior of vehicles?
10. Are critical and vulnerable areas well illuminated?
11. Is protective lighting operated manually or automatically?
12. Do cones of light on the perimeter overlap?
13. Are perimeter lights wired in series?
14. Is the lighting at shipping and receiving docks or piers adequate?

15. Is the lighting in the parking lots adequate?
16. Is an auxiliary power source available with backup standby units?
17. Is the interior of buildings adequately lighted?
18. Are top secret and secret activities adequately lighted?
19. Are guards equipped with powerful flashlights?
20. How many more and what type of lights are needed to provide adequate illumination? In what locations?
21. Does security personnel report light outages?
22. How soon are burned-out lights replaced?
23. Are open areas of a campus sufficiently lighted to discourage illegal or criminal acts against pedestrians?
24. Are any areas covered with high-growing shrubs or woods where the light is insufficient?
25. Are the outsides of buildings holding valuable or critical activities or materials lighted?
26. Are interiors of hallways and entrances lighted when buildings are open at night?
27. Are areas surrounding women's dormitories well lighted? Within a college setting?
28. Are campus parking lots lighted sufficiently to discourage tampering with parked cars or other illegal activities?
29. Are the areas where materials of high value are stored well lighted? Safes, libraries, bookstores, food storage areas, and so forth?
30. Lamp life versus efficiency?
31. Lamp CRI?
32. Continuous levels of light at night?
33. Provide specific levels of light for CCTV units? We are in the age of HD cameras and HD television monitors as well as low light cameras, all of which are crime deterrents in some cases.
34. Required light for evening patrols?
35. Complex should have an even and adequate distribution of light?

Lighting levels for visual monitoring

By definition, a foot-candle is a unit of illuminance or light falling into a surface. It stands for the light level on a surface 1 ft from a standard candle. One foot-candle is equal to 1 lm/ft^2.

0.50 fc for perimeter of outer area
0.4 fc for perimeter of restricted area
10.0 fc for vehicular entrances
5.0 fc for pedestrian entrance
0.5–2 fc for roadways
0.2 fc for open years
0.20–5 fc for decks on open piers
10–20 fc for interior sensitive structures

Open parking light levels are a minimum of 0.2 fc in low-level activity areas and 2 fc in high-vehicle activity areas. If there is cash collection, the light level should be a minimum of 5 fc.

- loading docks—15 fc
- loading docks interior—15 fc
- shipping and receiving—5 fc
- security gatehouse—25–30 fc
- security gatehouse interior—30 fc
- for pedestrians or normal CCTV cameras the minimum level of light for
  - detection—0.5 fc
  - recognition—1 fc
  - identification—2 fc
- parking structures—5 fc
- parking areas or open spaces—2 fc
- loading docks—0.20–5 fc
- loading dock parking areas—15–30 fc
- piers and docks—0.20–5 fc

Lighting definitions

Lumens

The quantity or flow of light emitted by a lamp is measured in lumens. For example, a typical household bulb rated at 100 W may output about 1700 lm.

Illuminance is the concentration of light over a particular area and is measured in lux, representing the number of lumens per square meter or foot-candles. One foot-candle is equal to 10.76 lx (often approximated to a ratio of 1:10).

Note: When evaluating the amount of light needed by a particular CCTV camera (or the eye/natural surveillance) to perceive a scene, it is the amount of light shining over the area of the lens iris (camera or eye) or its luminance that is critical.

Reflectance

When we see an object, our eyes are sensing the light reflected from that object. If there is no light reflected from the object, we only see a silhouette in contrast to its background. If the object is illuminated by other than white light, we will see the object in colors that are not true. The color of the surface also impacts reflectance; a light surface, such as a parking lot paved in concrete, will have higher reflectance than a dark surface (a parking lot paved in asphalt or black-top). The measure of reflectance of an object is the ratio of the quantity of light (measured in lumens) falling on it to the light reflected from it, expressed as a percentage.

Color rendition index

The ability of a lamp to faithfully reproduce the colors seen in an object is measured by the CRI. Security personnel need the ability to accurately describe color. It is an important aspect in the apprehension of criminals who are caught on CCTV displays and recordings. CRI is measured on a scale of 1–100. A CRI of 70–80 is considered good, above 80 is considered excellent, and 100% is considered daylight.

A CRI chart should be made to assist in providing context that along with the data collection can provide a visual element as a media in translational science. In many cases, this can assist those who are not familiar with the influence of light on colors a better understanding.

Corrected color temperature

A measure of the warmth or coolness of a light is the corrected color temperature. It has a considerable impact on mood and ambiance of the surroundings.

Lighting in the color temperature range nearing the red end of the spectrum can influence an autonomic response of anxiety. In some instances, changing the color temperature of your exterior lighting toward a white light can alleviate these feelings improving employee satisfaction when working late or coming in early.

Lighting systems

A lighting system consists of a number of components, all of which are important to the effectiveness of a lighting application. A list of the major components and their function is presented next.

- *Lamp (also known as a light bulb).* Manufactured light source that includes the filament or an arc tube, its glass casing, and its electrical connectors. Types of lamps include incandescent and mercury vapor, which describe the type of technologies used to create the light.
- *Luminary (also known as fixture).* Complete lighting unit consisting the lamp, its holder, and the reflectors and diffusers used to distribute and focus the light.
- *Mounting hardware.* Examples are a wall bracket or a light pole used to fix the correct height and location of the luminary.
- *Electrical power.* It operates the lamp, ballasts, and photocells. Some lamp technologies are sensitive to reduced voltage, in particular, the HID family of lamps (metal halide, mercury vapor, and high-pressure sodium).

References

Bowers, D.M., 1995. Let there be light. Secur. Manage. 103–111.
Kunze, D.R., Schiefer, J., 1995. An illuminating look at light. Secur. Manage. 113–116.
National Lighting Bureau, n.d. Lighting for Safety and Security. National Lighting Bureau, Washington, DC. pp. 1–36.
Purpura, P., 1979. Police activity and the full moon. J. Police Sci. Adm. 7 (3), 350.
Smith, M.S., 1996. Crime Prevention Through Environmental Design in Parking Facilities. National Institute of Justice, Washington, DC, pp. 1–4.
Tyska, L.A., Fennelly, L.J., 2000. Physical security. 150 Things You Should Know. Butterworth-Heinemann, Boston, MA.

Further reading

Berube, H., 1994. New notions of night light. Secur. Manage. 29–33.
Fischer, R.J., Halibozek, E., Green, G. (Eds.), 2008. Introduction to Security. eighth ed. Butterworth-Heinemann, Boston, MA.

Websites

National Lighting Bureau. <www.nlb.org>.
Illuminating Engineering Society. <www.iesna.org>.
International Association of Light Management Companies. <www.nalmco.org>.

Appendix 22.A Lighting description

Table 22.A.1 Types of lighting.

Type	CRI	Color of light
Incandescent	100	White Reflects all light
Fluorescent	62	Bluish/white Good color rendition
Mercury vapor	15	Blue/green Fair color rendition When used as a streetlight, there will be a blue label indicating wattage
High-pressure sodium	22	Golden/white Poor color rendition When used as a streetlight, there will be a yellow label indicating wattage
Low-pressure sodium	44	Yellow Very low color rendition
Metal halide	65–90	Bright white Very high color rendition When used as a streetlight, there will be a white label indicating wattage
Halogen/quartz halogen	100	White
LED	95–98	White
Induction	80–100	White

CRI, Color rendition index; *LED*, light emitting diodes.

Table 22.A.2 Operation costs (10 years).

Technology	Wattage	Lamp changes	Energy	Maintenance	Material	Cost of operation
High-pressure sodium	70	3.7	$927	$201	$73	$1201
High-pressure sodium	150	3.7	$1971	$201	$73	$2245
High-pressure sodium	250	3.7	$3154	$201	$73	$3427
High-pressure sodium	400	3.7	$4878	$201	$73	$5151
High-pressure sodium	1000	3.7	$11,563	$201	$224	$11,988

Induction	40	0	$429	$0	$0	$429
Induction	80	0	$858	$0	$0	$858
Induction	100	0	$1072	$0	$0	$1072
Induction	120	0	$1287	$0	$0	$1287
Induction	200	0	$2144	$0	$0	$2144
Metal halide (V)	150	5.8	$1971	$321	$187	$2479
Metal halide (V)	175	8.8	$2263	$482	$278	$3022
Metal halide (V)	250	8.8	$3101	$482	$280	$3863
Metal halide (V)	400	8.8	$4793	$482	$280	$5556
Metal halide (V)	1000	7.3	$11,248	$402	$365	$12,014
Metal halide (H)	150	7.8	$1971	$428	$249	$2648
Metal halide (H)	175	11.7	$2263	$642	$370	$3275
Metal halide (H)	250	11.7	$3101	$642	$374	$4117
Metal halide (H)	400	11.7	$4793	$642	$374	$5810
Metal halide (H)	1000	9.7	$11,248	$535	$487	$12,270
Low-pressure sodium	180	5.5	$2308	$301	$345	$2954
Low-pressure sodium	135	5.5	$1873	$301	$257	$2432
Low-pressure sodium	90	5.5	$1306	$301	$203	$1809
Low-pressure sodium	55	4.9	$838	$268	$161	$1267
Low-pressure sodium	35	4.9	$629	$268	$161	$1057

Based on 24 h of on time, 0.12 kW/h, and 55/h labor charge.
Source: U.S. Energy Technologies, 2007. https://www.nap.edu/read/12091/chapter/10.

Table 22.A.3 Formulas to determine the cost to operate a light source.

Watts × hours = watts hours
Watts hours /1000 = kilowatts
Kilowatts × rate = cost
Information for the formula
Watts: on the bulb or fixture of the light source
Watt hours/1000 = kilowatts
Kilowatts × rate = cost

Source: U.S. Department of Energy, 2009. https://www.eia.gov/outlooks/aeo/nems/overview/index.html.

Protective lighting checklist

1. Is the perimeter of the installation protected by lighting?[1]
2. Does protective lighting provide a means of continuing during the hours of darkness the same degree of protection available during the daylight hours?
3. Are the cones of illumination from lamps directed downward and away from the facility proper and away from guard personnel?
4. Are lights mounted to provide a strip of light both inside and outside the fence?
5. Is perimeter lighting used so that guards remain in comparative darkness?
6. Are lights checked for proper operation prior to darkness?
7. Are repairs to lights and replacement of inoperative lamps affected immediately?
8. Do light beams overlap to provide coverage in case a bulb burns out?
9. Is additional lighting provided at active gates and points of possible intrusion?
10. Are gate guard shacks provided with proper illumination?
11. Are light finishes or stripes used on lower parts of buildings and structures to aid guard observation?
12. Does the facility have a dependable source of power for its lighting system?
13. Does the facility have a dependable auxiliary source of power?
14. Is the protective lighting system independent of the general transit facility lighting or power system?

1. <https://manualzz.com/doc/28293210/physcial-security-survey-checklist>, Oct. 2018.

15. Is the power supply for lights adequately protected?
16. Is there provision for standby or emergency lighting?
17. Is the standby or emergency equipment tested frequently?
18. Is emergency equipment designed to go into operation automatically when needed?
19. Is wiring for protective lighting properly mounted?
20. Is adequate lighting for guard use provided on indoor routes?
21. Are materials and equipment in shipping and storage areas properly arranged so as not to mask security lighting?

Chapter 23

Chain-link fence standards

Chain-Link Fence Manufacturers Institute

Prevention is at the heart of everything Police Scotland does to keep people safe.

Sir Stephen House QPM, Chief Constable.

Introduction

This chapter discusses security fences, including the different types of fences and the standards for security fences. The design features and material specifications are laid out as well as resources for installation and inspection.

Recommendations

Chain-link fencing has been the product of choice for security fencing for over 60 years because of its strength, corrosion resistance, "see-through capabilities," ease of installation, versatility, variety of product selection, and value. A chain-link fence is one of the primary building blocks for a facility's perimeter security system.

The physical security barrier provided by a chain-link fence provides one or more of the following functions:

- gives notice of a legal boundary of the outermost limits of a facility,
- assists in controlling and screening authorized entries into a secured area by deterring entry elsewhere along the boundary,
- supports surveillance, detection, assessment, and other security functions by providing a zone for installing intrusion detection equipment and closed-circuit television (CCTV),
- deters casual intruders from penetrating a secured area by presenting a barrier that requires an overt action to enter,
- demonstrates the intent of an intruder by their overt action of gaining entry,
- causes a delay to obtain access to a facility, increasing the possibility of detection,
- creates a psychological deterrent,
- reduces the number of security guards required and frequency of use for each post,
- optimizes the use of security personnel while enhancing the capabilities for detection and apprehension of unauthorized individuals,
- demonstrates a corporate concern for facility security, and
- provides a cost-effective method of protecting facilities.

Security planning

Chain-link fence enhances the goals of good security planning. In-depth security planning takes into consideration the mission and function, environmental concerns, threats, and the local area of the facility to be secured. This can be translated into an A–B–C–D method that points out the values of chain-link fencing to a security program.

A. *Aids* to security. Chain-link fencing assists in the use of other security equipment, such as the use of intrusion detectors, access controls, cameras, and so forth. Chain-link fences can be employed as aids to protection in an exterior mode or an internal protected property, as a point protection, and for general protection as required.

B. *Barriers* for security. These can be buildings, chain-link fences, walls, temporary checkpoints, and so on.

Handbook of Loss Prevention and Crime Prevention. DOI: https://doi.org/10.1016/B978-0-12-817273-5.00023-5

C. *Controls* support the physical security chain-link fences and barriers, such as an access control system tied into vehicle gates and pedestrian portals, various level identification badges and temporary badges, security escorts, and internal procedures.
D. *Deterrents*, such as a chain-link fence, guards, lighting, signage, and checkpoint control procedures, ensure that intruders will consider it difficult to successfully gain access.

When properly used, the aspects of the A–B–C–D method reinforce and support each other. Thus a chain-link fence is also a deterrent and a barrier, if needed. By combining A–B–C–D, sufficient obstacles are created to prevent an intruder from obtaining information that is being worked on during the day in the controlled access area and then is protected at night, on weekends, and on holidays through the implementation of the security in-depth concept.

More importantly, keep in mind that a chain-link fence is the common denominator of the A–B–C–D system and will reduce overall risk, secure the environment, and reduce security costs if designed and installed properly. However, believing that a fence will eliminate all illegal access is not prudent. A fence system will only delay or reduce intrusion.

To ensure the effectiveness of the facility security fence program, it is recommended that a maintenance program be developed for the proper maintenance of the fence system, gates, gate operators, and related access controls.

Material specifications

Material specifications for chain-link fence are listed in the following:

- Chain-Link Fence Manufacturers Institute Product Manual (CLFMI).
- American Society of Testing Materials (ASTM), volume 01.06.
- Federal Specification RR-F-191 K/GEN, May 14, 1990.
- ASTM F1553, "The Standard Guide for Specifying Chain-Link Fence," provides the appropriate information to develop a specification document.

Framework

The framework for a chain-link fence consists of the line posts, end posts, corner posts, gateposts, and, if required, a top, mid, bottom, or brace rail. The Federal Specification and the CLFMI "Wind Load Guide for the Selection of Line Post Spacing and Size" provide recommended post sizes for the various fence heights. However, the latter document also provides choices of line post types, sizes, and spacings to accommodate selected fence heights and fabric sizes for wind loads at various geographical project locations. The *CLFMI Product Manual*, ASTM F1043, and ASTM F1083, as well as the Federal Specification, list the material specifications for the framework.

Chain-link fabric

The material specifications for chain-link fabric are thoroughly spelled out in the *CLFMI Product Manual*, ASTM, and Federal Specifications. The choice of chain-link fabric will govern the desired security level, and the various fabric-coating choices will govern the corrosion resistance. Light gauge residential chain-link fabric will not be considered in this document. Provided are only those chain-link fabrics that offer a level of security; thus the gauge of wire and mesh size has been narrowed down to the following:

11 ga (0.120 in. diameter)—minimum break strength of 850 lbf
9 ga (0.148 in. diameter)—minimum break strength of 1290 lbf
6 ga (0.192 in. diameter)—minimum break strength of 2170 lbf

Mesh sizes to consider (mesh size is the minimum clear distance between the wires forming the parallel sides of the mesh) are 2-in. mesh, 1-in. mesh, and 3/8-in. mesh. Consider the following regarding mesh size:

- The smaller the mesh size, the more difficult it is to climb or cut.
- The heavier the gauge wire, the more difficult it is to cut.

The various mesh sizes available in the three previously discussed gauges are listed in the order of their penetration resistance/security:

1. Extremely high security: 3/8-in. mesh 11 ga
2. Very high security: 1-in. mesh 9 ga
3. High security: 1-in. mesh 11 ga
4. Greater security: 2-in. mesh 6 ga
5. Normal industrial security: 2-in. mesh 9 ga

Gates

Gates are the only moveable parts of a fence and therefore should be properly constructed with appropriate fittings. Chain-link gate specifications are listed in the *CLFMI Product Manual*, ASTM, and Federal Specifications.

Limiting the size of the opening increases vehicular security and reduces the possibility of one vehicle passing another, and the smaller opening reduces the open–close cycle time. The cantilever slide gate is the most effective for vehicle security, especially one that is electrically operated and tied into an access control system. High-speed cantilever slide gate operators are available for certain applications.

Pedestrian/personnel gates can be constructed using a basic padlock or designed with an electrical or mechanical lock or a keypad/card key system tied into an access control system. Prehung pedestrian gates/portals installed independent of the fence line are available to isolate the gate from fence lines containing sensor systems thus reducing possible false alarms.

Design features and considerations

Some basic design features to consider, which enhance security, are as follows:

- *Height.* The higher the barrier the more difficult and time consuming it is to broach.
- *Eliminating top rail.* Omission of a rail at the top of the fence eliminates a handhold, thus making the fence more difficult to climb. A 7-ga coil spring wire can be installed in place of the top rail.
- *Adding barbwire.* Addition of three or six strands at the top of the fence increases the level of difficulty and time to broach. When using the three-strand 45-degree arm, it is recommended to angle the arm out from the secured area.
- *Bolt or rivet barbwire arms to post.* Barbwire arms are normally held to the post by the top tension wire or top rail. For added security they can be bolted or riveted to the post.
- *Adding barbed tape.* Stainless steel–barbed tape added to the top and in some cases the bottom of the fence greatly increases the difficulty and time to broach.
- *Adding bottom rail.* Addition of a bottom rail that is secured in the center of the two line posts using a 3/8-in. diameter eye hook anchored into a concrete footing basically eliminates the possibility of forcing the mesh up to crawl under the fence. The bottom of the fence, with or without a bottom rail, should be installed not greater than 2 in. above grade.
- *Bury the chain-link fabric.* Burying the fabric 12 in. or more will also eliminate the possibility of forcing the mesh up.
- *Colored chain-link fabric.* One of the security features of a chain-link fence is visibility, allowing one to monitor what is taking place inside or outside of the fence line more efficiently. Color polymer–coated chain-link fabric enhances visibility, especially at night. Complete polymer-coated systems, including coated fabric, fittings, framework, and gates, increase visibility and provide greater corrosion resistance, especially for use in areas adjacent to the seacoast.
- *Double row of security fencing.* It is not uncommon to add an additional line of internal security fencing 10–20 ft. inside the perimeter fence. In many cases, double rows of fencing are used with sensors and detectors or with a perimeter patrol road in the area between the fences.
- *Clear zone.* In wooded or high grassy areas, it is advisable to clear and grub a clear zone on either side of the fence to aid surveillance.
- *Internal security fencing.* Many situations require the need of a separate interior fence to add another level of security for a particular building, piece of equipment, or location.
- *Peen all bolts.* This eliminates the removal of the bolt nut.
- *Addition of a sensor system.* This adds another level of security to the fence system.

- *Addition of lighting*. It increases visibility as well as raises the level of psychological deterrent.
- *Signage*. Installed along the fence line, signs are important to indicate private secured areas (violators may be subject to arrest) and possibly note the presence of alarms and monitoring systems.

Typical design example

We have chosen for our example to list the referenced specifications separately to help identify the various items that need to be specified. The specification writer may use this format or the standard Construction Specifications Institute (CSI) format in developing their document.

In developing specifications for a typical chain-link fence, the design could be described as follows:

*8′0″ high chain-link fence plus 1′0″, three strands of barbwire at top for a total height of 9′0″, consisting of 2 in. mesh 6-gauge chain-link fabric, *_____ o.d. or *_____ "C" line posts spaced a maximum of 10′0″ o.c., 7-gauge coil spring wire at top, secured to the chain-link fabric with 9-gauge hog rings spaced not greater than 12 in., 15/8-in. o.d. bottom rail secured in the center with a 3/8-in. diameter galvanized steel eye hook anchored into a concrete footing, chain-link fabric secured to line post and rail at a maximum of 12 in. o.c. using 9-gauge tie wire.*

**_____ o.d. end and corner posts complete with 15/8-in. o.d. brace rail, 3/8-in. truss assembly, 12-gauge tension bands secured at a maximum of 12-in. o.c., tension bar, necessary, fittings, nuts, and bolts.*

Chain-link fabric shall comply with ASTM ____

** Post and brace rail shall comply with ASTM ____*

** Barbwire shall comply with ASTM ____*

** Fittings, ties, nuts, and bolts shall comply with ASTM ____*

** Coil spring wire shall comply with ASTM ____.**

**Reference is made to ASTM as an example. All chain-link specifications, fabric, posts, fittings gates, and so forth are referenced in ASTM F 1553, Standard Guide for Specifying Chain-Link Fence.*

A typical design/specification for gates would be listed as follows:

*Pedestrian/personnel swing gates shall have a 4′0″ opening by 8′0″ high plus 1′0″ and three strands of barbwire on top. Gate frames shall be fabricated from 2-in. o.d. or 2-in. square members, welded at all corners. Chain-link fabric shall be installed to match the fence line unless otherwise specified. Gateposts shall be *_____ o.d. complete with 15/8-in. o.d. brace rail, 3/8-in. diameter truss assembly, 12-gauge tension bands secured a minimum of 12 in. apart, necessary tension bar, fittings, and nuts and bolts.*

Chain-link fabric shall comply with ASTM ____.

Swing gates shall comply with ASTM ____.

Gateposts size, o.d., shall comply with ASTM ____.

Gateposts shall comply with ASTM ____.

Fittings shall comply with ASTM ____.

*Cantilever slide gates shall be of the opening sizes as indicated on the drawings, having a height of 8′0″ plus 1′0′, and three strands of barbwire. (The construction and design of cantilever slide gates vary; therefore it is best to list the specific specification.) Cantilever slide gates shall be constructed per ASTM F 1184, Class *____. Chain-link fabric shall match the fence line unless otherwise specified. (Cantilever slide gates require 4-in. o.d. gateposts; larger or smaller posts are not recommended.) The 4-in. o.d. gate-posts shall be complete with 15/8-in. o.d. brace rail, 3/8-in. diameter truss assembly, 12-gauge tension bands secured a minimum of 12 in. apart, necessary tension bar, fittings, and nuts and bolts.*

4-in. o.d. gatepost and 15/8-in. o.d brace rail shall comply with ASTM ____.

Fittings shall comply with ASTM ____.

Chain-link fabric shall comply with ASTM ____.

Installation

Installation for the fence line, terminal posts, and gates varies depending on the security level required, site conditions, geographical location, and soil and weather conditions. The best documents to assist you in this process are ASTM F567, "Standard Practice for Installation of Chain-Link Fence" and the CLFMI "Wind Load Guide for the Selection of Line Post Spacing and Size."

Project inspection

Improper material or installation can have a dramatic effect on the required security. It is important to verify that the project materials are in compliance with the contract specifications and that the fence has been installed properly. Procurement or facility managers may want to consider a mandatory requirement of their reviewing material certifications and shop drawings prior to the start of the project. This will ensure that proper products will be installed and that specific installation guidelines have been provided. CLFMI offers a *Field Inspection Guide* document to assist in this process.

Reference is made to various fence specifications; complete information can be obtained by contacting the following:

Chain-Link Manufacturers Institute 10015 Old Columbia Road, Suite B-215, Columbia, MD 21046, United States; Phone: +1 301-596-2583; http://www.chainlinkinfo.org/

Standardization Documents Order Desk Federal Specification RR-191K/GEN Bldg. 4D, Robbins Ave., Philadelphia, PA 19120-5094, United States

ASTM 100 Barr Harbor Drive West, Conshohocken, PA 19428, United States; Phone: +1 610-832-9500; http://www.astm.org/

Construction Specifications Institute 99 Canal Center Plaza, Suite 300, Alexandria, VA 22314, United States; emembcustsrv@csinet.org

In addition to information available from the abovementioned organizations, design and engineering assistance is available through a number of CLFMI member firms. To find these firms, click on "Product/Services Locator" and select "All United States" and "Security Chain-Link Fence Systems" from the product listing. Then click "GO" and the firms who can assist you will be listed (Figs. 23.1–23.5).

FIGURE 23.1

FIGURE 23.2

FIGURE 23.3

FIGURE 23.4

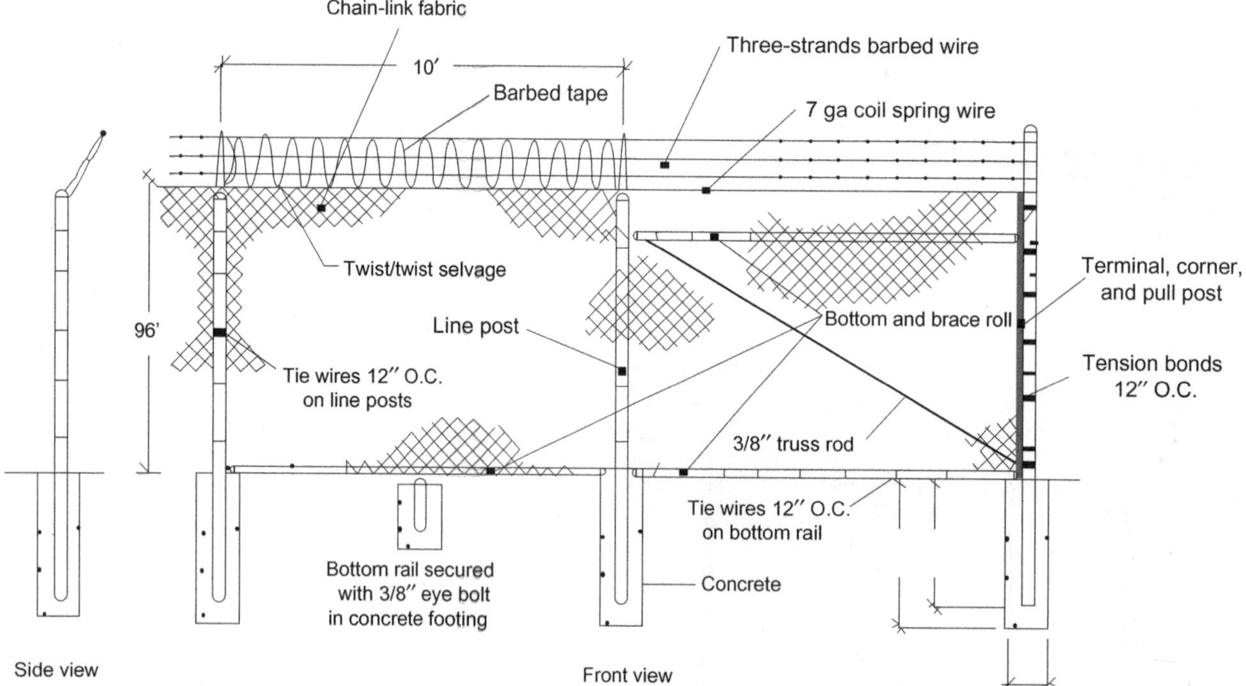

FIGURE 23.5 Typical detail of an 8-ft.-high fence with 1 ft., three-strand barbed wire security.

Conclusion: designing a security fence

When designing a security fence,[1] refer to the CLFMI Product Manual CLF-PM0610, CLFMI Tested and Proven Performance of Security Grade Chain Link Fencing Systems CLF-TP0211, ASTM F1712 "Standard Specification for Steel Chain Link Fencing Materials Used for High Security Applications," ASTM F 2611 "Standard Guide for the Design and Construction of Chain Link Security Fencing," and ASTM F2781 "Standard Practice for Testing Forced Entry, Ballistic, and Low Impact Resistance of Security Fence Systems."

Chain-link fencing has been the product of choice for security fencing for over 60 years because of its strength, corrosion resistance, "see-through capabilities," ease of installation, versatility, variety of product selection, and value. A chain-link fence is one of the primary building blocks for a facility's perimeter security system. The physical security barrier provided by a chain-link fence provides one or more of the following functions:

- Gives notice legal boundary of the outermost limits of a facility.
- Assists in controlling and screening authorized entries into a secured area by deterring entry elsewhere along the boundary.
- Supports surveillance, detection, assessment, and other security functions by providing a zone for installing intrusion detection equipment and CCTV.
- Deters casual intruders from penetrating a secured area by presenting a barrier that requires an overt action to enter.
- Demonstrates the intent of an intruder by their overt action of gaining entry.
- Causes a delay to obtain access to a facility, thereby increasing the possibility of detection.
- Creates a psychological deterrent.
- Reduces the number of security guards required and frequency of use for each post.
- Optimizes the use of security personnel while enhancing the capabilities for detection and apprehension of unauthorized individuals.
- Demonstrates a corporate concern for facility security.
- Provides a cost-effective method of protecting facilities and signage along the fence.

1. https://chainlinkinfo.org/security-fencing-guidelines/, December 14, 2018.

Chapter 24

Bomb threats and the case against immediate evacuation

Brad Spicer
Security Consultant

Introduction

Bomb threats are far more like promises than contracts. They are made to obtain a desired response, which is typically anxiety and confusion. The best response is rarely immediate evacuation; the best response requires an assessment of the situation, a search of the campus, and sound crisis communications.

Understanding the nature of bomb threats and being aware of recent salient events will help improve your ability to assess bomb threats. Imagine an emergency, such as a bomb threat, and place it as an "X" on a time line. Everything after "X" is response and everything before "X" is your opportunity to prevent and prepare for that emergency.

UNCLASSIFIED
ATF
UNITED STATES BOMB DATA CENTER (USBDC)
EXPLOSIVES INCIDENT REPORT (EIR)
2017
The Annual Explosives Incident Report (EIR) reviews bombing and explosives related incidents from information reported to the United States Bomb Data Center (USBDC) through the Bomb Arson Tracking System (BATS).
UNCLASSIFIED

Handbook of Loss Prevention and Crime Prevention. DOI: https://doi.org/10.1016/B978-0-12-817273-5.00024-7

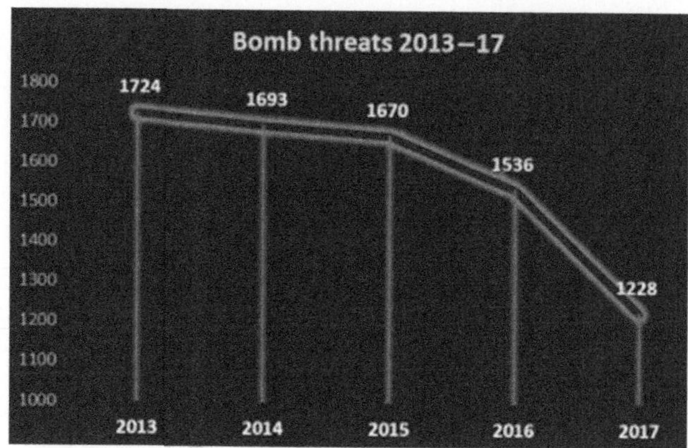

As per the Bureau of American, Tobacco and Firearms (ATF) United States Bomb Data Center Explosive Incident Report for 2017, there were 1228 bomb threats, a decrease from the 1536 threats in 2016. While there were 687 actual explosions that resulted in 58 injuries and 16 deaths, there is no evidence that any of the explosions were preceded by a bomb threat.

Bomb threats are common, bombings are not, and bombings preceded by a bomb threat are exceptionally rare.

Mentality of a bomber

A bomber places a bomb to kill people or destroy a structure. If the goal were to destroy a structure and not kill people, the bomb would be set to go off at a time when the building would not be occupied. If the goal were to kill people, it would be set to go off when the building would be fully occupied. Therefore calling in a bomb threat is counterproductive to either of these goals.

To place a bomb or improvised explosive device (IED), someone must:

1. obtain the knowledge of how to build a bomb,
2. obtain the materials necessary to build the bomb,
3. risk their life to build the bomb, and
4. risk their life and liberty to place the bomb.

To believe a bomb threat, you must believe that a person went through these steps and then at the last minute called to warn you of their intentions. It is certainly a possibility that a bomber would have a change of heart at the last minute and call in a warning. If this were the case, it is likely the bomber would give detailed instructions as to the exact location of the bomb.

While there is little correlation between a bomb threat and an actual bombing or attempted bombing, *no bomb threat should be ignored, and an assessment should be conducted.* When conducting an assessment, you are assessing the situation and facts surrounding the threat, not simply confirming if a threat was made. The goal is not to determine if someone *made* a threat. The goal is to determine if someone (or something) *poses* a threat.

To accomplish this, anxiety must be removed from the analysis. As Gavin de Becker points out in his *New York Times* bestselling "The Gift of Fear," threats are more like a promise than a guarantee. Threats are dispatched to gain a desired response. Threats do not state fact or even intention. If someone in your community wants to plant a bomb inside a facility, it is highly unlikely they will communicate a threat. The reality is that a link between bomb threats and actual bombings rarely exist.

Immediate evacuation upon receipt of a bomb threat might be intuitive, but it is not the best practice as it likely increases danger. Emergency plans (and response) should differentiate between a bomb threat and the discovery of a potential or actual IED. Locating a suspicious object or actual IED immediately removes the "threat" aspect and evacuation protocols that move people away from the device are prudent.

Upon initial receipt of a threat, heightened security measures should be implemented to control access and movement during assessment/investigation. "Heightened security" is operationally similar to a soft lockdown but avoids using the term "lockdown." This is useful because "lockdown" may be associated with an active shooter-type attack and create confusion and increased anxiety. The goal of heightened security is to focus entirely on security. Under heightened security, access to the facility should be prevented and movement inside should be restricted.

Suspicious objects—game changer

The location of a suspicious item changes the incident from a threat to an imminent danger. A suspicious item may be defined as any item (e.g., package, vehicle) identified as potentially containing explosives, an IED, or other hazardous materials, which requires diagnostic skills and specialized equipment of a bomb technician for further evaluation. Suspicious indicators are based upon the prevailing and/or communicated threat, placement and proximity of the item to people and/or valuable assets, and more tangible aspects include, but are not limited to, unexplained wires or electronics, other visible bomb-like components, unusual sounds, vapors, mists, or odors.

Remember, any suspicious device should be treated as an actual IED. What a bomb looks like is limited only to the imagination of the bomber. Leave formal identification to the experts. If a suspicious object is located, continue to search the evacuation route(s) and evacuation rally points—more devices may be present.

Assessment

While it is very rare for a threat to be associated with an actual bomb, no bomb threat should ever be *ignored, and an assessment must be conducted.* When conducting an assessment, remember, you are assessing the situation and facts surrounding the threat, not simply confirming if a threat was made. The goal is not to determine if someone *made* a threat. The goal is to determine if someone *poses* a threat. To accomplish this, anxiety must be removed from the analysis. A threat is more like a promise than a guarantee. Threats are dispatched to gain a desired response. Threats do not state fact or even intention.

When assessing the threat, consider the totality of bomb threats versus actual IED incidents; there is no single deciding factor on whether a bomb threat is legitimate or a hoax. Measure all the facts, their context, and conclude from the whole picture whether the possibility of a "real" threat exists. All threats should be carefully evaluated on an individual basis and called in to local law enforcement regardless of the circumstances.

Search

A search of the campus is a vital element of any assessment. Formal identification must be left to the experts. So, the focus is to identify anything suspicious or possibly dangerous.

A suspicious item is defined as any item (e.g., package, vehicle) potentially containing explosives or other hazardous materials that require specialized evaluation. Suspicious indicators may be based upon the communicated threat, placement, and proximity of the item to people and more obvious aspects include, but are not limited to, unexplained wires or electronics, other visible bomb-like components, unusual sounds, vapors, mists, or odors.

Staff, who are familiar with their work areas, are best suited to identify "suspicious" items. Remember, this search is simply to identify something that might be dangerous, so "Eyes open, hands in pockets" is a good mindset. It is important to educate staff on proper search procedures prior to the receipt of a bomb threat. This will lessen anxiety and improve the assessment process.

If something suspicious is located, the response shifts from a bomb *threat* to a possible explosive device.

The discovery of a suspicious object should not automatically mean the conclusion of a search; more devices may be present, especially outside.

All threats are not equal, and the assessment process will help quantify the threat. If a threat is easily categorized as "low risk," the resources and time spent on the assessment and search can be minimized, whereas a "high risk" or potentially "high risk" threat warrants greater attention.

LOW

☐ **LOW RISK** LACKS REALISM:
A threat that poses a minimum risk to the victim and public safety. Probable motive is to cause disruption.
- ☐ Threat is vague and indirect.
- ☐ Information contained within the threat is consistent, implausible, or lacks detail.
- ☐ Caller is definitely known and has called numerous times.
- ☐ The threat was discovered instead of delivered (e.g., written on a wall).

MEDIUM

☐ **MEDIUM RISK** INCREASED LEVEL OF REALISM:
Threat that could be carried out, although it may not appear entirely realistic.
- ☐ Threat is direct and feasible.
- ☐ Wording in the threat suggests the perpetrator has given some thought on how the act will be carried out.
- ☐ May include indications of a possible place and time.
- ☐ No strong indication the perpetrator has taken preparatory steps, although there may be some indirect reference pointing to that possibility.
- ☐ Indication the perpetrator has details regarding the availability of components needed to construct a bomb.
- ☐ Increase specificity to a threat (e.g. "I know your lunch periods.")

HIGH

☐ **HIGH RISK** INCREASED LEVEL OF REALISM:
- ☐ Threat is direct, specific, and realistic; may include names of possible victims, specific time, location of devices.
- ☐ Perpetrator provides his/her identity.
- ☐ Threat suggests concrete steps have been taken toward carrying out the threat.
- ☐ Perpetrator makes statements indicating they have practiced with a weapon or have had the intended victim(s) under surveillance.

The danger of evacuation

Buildings offer protection in the form of cover and concealment.

Cover is protection from gunfire and explosions (and even chemical exposure).

Concealment prevents attackers from knowing your exact location.

When people are evacuated, this protection is lost. A facility should be evacuated only when it is reasonably believed that people are safer outside. In most bomb threats, the only "evidence" that there is danger inside the facility is the communication from the anonymous criminal who is making the threat.

When a bomb threat is received, most leaders' initial fear is that a bomb is inside. While this is a normal reaction, a bomb inside is the least likely scenario. A bomb threat presents four core scenarios. In order of probability, they are:

1. criminal hoax,
2. bomb/IED outside,
3. diversionary/ambush attack, and
4. bomb/IED inside.

The two main response options are:

1. evacuation and
2. heightened security.

Evacuation is the typical response, but because the actual scenario is unknown, evacuation does not provide the greatest level of safety.

1. *Criminal hoax*

   A criminal hoax is by far the most common bomb threat scenario. While evacuation is likely to result in more lost classroom hours and costs, remaining inside may cause a public relations concern as the public might feel evacuation is safer.

   Likely safest response: Neutral. Since there is no IED, a criminal hoax does not pose immediate danger.

Likely safest response

Evacuation Neutral Heightened security

2. *Bomb/IED outside*

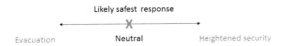

Bombings are very rare. When bombs are present, they are more likely to be placed outside. An IED outside raises two major concerns:

1. It is easier to place a large IED.
2. An IED's blast radius is larger, without the building to contain/compartmentalize the explosion.

A facility with basic access control and situational awareness will likely limit the size of an IED to a backpack, which is certainly dangerous. Outside, a vehicle-borne IED or car bomb is devastating.

Likely safest response: Heightened security.

3. *Diversionary/ambush attack*

A diversionary attack is when an attacker uses a means of deception with the purpose of drawing the target into an area more conducive to attack. While rare, more people have been killed in the United States by diversionary attacks than bombings that were preceded by a bomb threat.

Likely safest response: Heightened security.

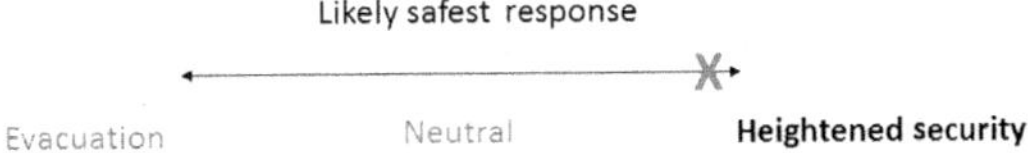

4. Bomb/IED inside

If the people knew, or had reason to believe, there is a device inside the facility, evacuation is the safest response. However, when the presence of a device is unknown, evacuation increases risk if there is an IED outside the facility or there is potential for an ambush-style attack.

Further, while far from optimal, the building will provide protection from the IED blast to the clear majority of people inside. To be clear, if the presence of an IED is known or a suspicious item is located, evacuation is undoubtedly the best response.

Likely safest response: Evacuation.

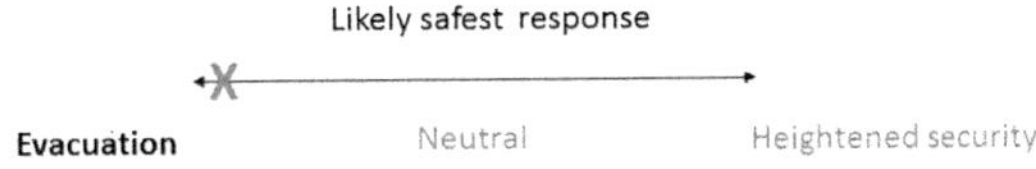

	Likely safest response			
Scenario	**Evacuate**	**Neutral**	**Heightened security**	**Scenario probability**
Criminal hoax		X		Most likely (99% +)
IED outside			X	Second most likely
Ambush			X	Second least likely
IED inside	X			Least likely

IED, Improvised explosive device.

Evacuation is the safest course of action for only one scenario, IED inside, and that scenario is the least likely. This is not to suggest evacuation is not the safest course of action if there is an IED or suspicious object inside; however, when a bomb threat is received, it is unknown which of the four core scenarios is the reality.

When must you evacuate?

When evacuation is warranted or simply preferred due to concerns over public perception, safeguard against secondary attacks (explosive devices or ambush), secondary attack refers to an attack using either a secondary device or diversionary attack or a combination thereof.

Secondary device definition: An explosive device that is placed in an area of evacuation or staging to inflict greater casualties and/or disrupt emergency response.

Diversionary attack definition: A strategy of deception used by an attacker to draw the target into an area more conducive to attack.

One of the most disturbing aspects of a secondary attack is that it preys on the good intentions of personnel, who are attempting to protect students. Nothing is more intuitive than the desire to evacuate students at the sounding of a fire alarm or after receiving a bomb threat. In the event of a fire, or the discovery of a potential IED, those are not only reasonable, but one would be negligent to not enact them. It is the bogus alarm or the baseless bomb threat that should lead officials to consider the possibility of a secondary attack.

When there is no evidence of danger beyond a bomb *threat* or fire *alarm*, consider, *Why does someone want us to evacuate?*

Secondary attacks have been a part of warfare (both conventional and unconventional) for as long as man has engaged in battle. In fact, the single largest loss of life is a school attack: the Bath School disaster in 1927, a school bombing in Michigan, where the killer, Andrew Kehoe, planted explosives in a school and then detonated his truck—targeting emergency responders. As a result, 45 people were killed and another 58 were wounded.

There have been other school attacks that also targeted evacuation as an opportunity to maximize casualties.

Columbine (1997). The original intent was to use IEDs to prompt evacuation into an ambush and vehicle-borne IEDs. When the IEDs failed, the two killers entered the school and carried out a conventional active-shooter attack.

Jonesboro (1998). While IEDs were not used, this attack shows how killers used a fire alarm to force an evacuation to maximize casualties. The 13-year-old killer pulled a fire alarm inside the middle school and joined his 11-year-old accomplice in the woods and shot students and a teacher when they evacuated.

When a facility does have to evacuate, secondary attack countermeasures should be embedded in the emergency plans.

ONGOING COUNTER-MEASURES
- ☐ Security Awareness
- ☐ Enforce visitor check-in policies
- ☐ Properly screen all deliveries
- ☐ Maintain access control

POST-THREAT INTERIOR COUNTER-MEASURES
- ☐ Implement "Heightened Security" procedures to restrict student movement
- ☐ Prevent student access to lockers
- ☐ Search ("eyes open, hands in pockets") for suspicious devices

POST-THREAT EVACUATION COUNTER-MEASURES
- ☐ Request law enforcement of the rally point
- ☐ Prior to evacuation, search exits and paths to rally points
- ☐ Avoid parking lots and prevent access to cars
- ☐ Prevent groups from gathering away from rally point
- ☐ Prevent students from gathering near emergency response vehicles

Proper emergency planning and training will reduce the anxiety associated with bomb threats and enhance response, thereby improving safety. Regardless of whether the facility evacuates, effective crisis communication is critical.

Crisis communications 101: think BLUF

Saving lives is the priority in any emergency. However, an organization's ability to effectively communicate during and after an incident can greatly impact the success of the response as well as the organization's credibility thereafter. Most often, a facility is evacuated because of public perception. Leaders accept that remaining inside does not increase risk but worries the public as they may not understand the rationale behind not immediately evacuating

With regards to emergency management, there are two core communications strategies: risk and crisis. These communication strategies are vital elements of an all-hazards emergency planning efforts.

- *Risk communications*: Proactive messaging to educate and inform your audience about prevention and response procedures before an emergency.
- *Crisis communications:* Postevent messaging designed to improve response and educate stakeholders about the emergency.

Risk communications: compliance and deterrence media

Ultimately security and emergency planning efforts, such as conducting a bomb threat tabletop exercise, should mitigate risks and help reduce staff anxiety. Risk communications should prepare stakeholders and the public by educating them on preparedness efforts and what to do/expect when an emergency happens.

Deterrence media is another value of risk communications. Deterrence media publicizes nonsensitive security and emergency planning efforts to let stakeholders and would-be-bomb-threat-makers know your location, which is not a soft and unprepared target. Security upgrades and staff training are important aspects of preparedness, and publicly releasing general information can have significant deterrent value.

In addition, risk communications improve compliance with emergency response procedures. It is human nature for people to be drawn to the scene of an emergency. This desire increases exponentially if the emergency impacts a loved one. Letting people know that you have a plan before an emergency will increase their confidence in your response during and immediately after the incident.

Crisis communications—just four things

Risk communications occur before the emergency and crisis communications kick in during and after the incident. Within crisis communications, there are two approaches: active and passive.

Active approach: Provide notification and information *before* the community and media may even know about the event.

Passive approach: Wait until the community or media approach you—requesting information.

Depending on the magnitude and public awareness of a specific circumstance, you may respond actively, passively, or use a combination of both approaches.

An active communications strategy is almost always called for after a bomb threat. Here are some general guidelines for when to implement active crisis communications:

- The situation is dangerous or serious, and it affects (or has the potential to affect) many people.
- The situation legally requires disclosure.
- It is imminent that the news media will become aware of the situation and a proactive release of information may minimize the impact. For example, the timing of a news release may contain the situation to a 1-day story versus a 2-day story.

When implementing an active response, remember:

Maximum disclosure, minimum delay

A passive communication strategy is rarely appropriate for an actual bomb threat but could be used if there was a rumor of a bomb threat. Here are some general guidelines for when to implement passive crisis communications:

- The situation is deemed minor.
- Few audiences are affected.
- News media have not been alerted, nor is it likely they will be alerted.
- If news media eventually cover the situation, there will not be negative fallout for failing to alert the media.
- Information available is limited, and speculation may be worse than reality.
- There are no legal requirements regarding disclosure.

Bottom-line up-front

When active communications are required, there are just four things your stakeholders, the public, and the media want to know:

1. *What happened?*
2. *What have you done?*
3. *What are doing next?*
4. *How can people help?*

When and what to disclose

Maximum disclosure and minimum delay are always worth considering, but when and what to release is unique to each incident. In any emergency, but especially with human-based threats, all messages should be coordinated with internal (district, corporate, etc.) and external (law enforcement) release authorities. Releasing sensitive information can jeopardize lives, and disseminating inaccurate information harms credibility and impacts people's confidence in the organization.

When developing messages for an actual emergency, work with your response partners to provide consistent messages that target your audience and stay within your lane. Do not speculate or release unapproved information. Be sure your messages answer the four questions; this will help prevent an information vacuum.

Here is an example of an effective communications strategy to deal with bomb threats:

1. Conduct a tabletop exercise focused on a bomb threat.
2. Invite media to observe the end of the exercise and make the superintendent or other leadership available for interviews.
   a. Key talking points are that you take safety very seriously, and immediate evacuation due to a bomb threat is not always the safest course of action.
3. Send out messages to parents reiterating these messages (risk communications).
   a. Explain things you are doing to make the facility even safer and discourage bomb threats (see something—say something, access control, video, security, staff training, etc.).
   b. Emphasize that the organization has a comprehensive emergency plan.
   c. Tell them how you will notify them of any emergency and explain how they can report any concerns.

When a bomb threat happens (and it will), your crisis communications should refer to previous risk communications messages from after the tabletop exercise and address the four things parents and the media want to know.

1. *What happened?*
   Remember "BLUF." A clear, concise statement that illustrates your organization understands the scope of the incident and taking appropriate actions. Rather than using the term "lockdown," consider using "heightened security."
2. *What have you done?*
   Without jeopardizing operational security, privacy, or ongoing investigations, provide a brief, high-level overview of actions.
3. *What are you doing next?*
   Again, protect operational security and do not divulge too many specifics. For instance, if a facility is to be evacuated, there is no need to publicly divulge where people are being evacuated. Remember, the overarching goal is to communicate you have a plan.
4. *How can people help?*
   The vast majority of people and the media want to help. Create strategies that let them help and prevent them from interfering with response and recovery operations.

At some point, an organization will be impacted by a bomb threat ("X"). Getting before "X" with emergency planning, training, and sound crisis communication will help ensure safety and can turn the media into your ally instead of an adversary.

Further reading

Central Florida Intelligence Exchange (CFIX), 2014. Guidance for Hoax Bomb Threats and Threatening Calls to Schools Nationwide.

Federal Emergency Management Agency (FEMA), 2009. FEMA Course 428 Bomb Damage (Chapter 4).

U.S. Bomb Data Center, 2015. United States Bomb Data Center (USBDC) explosive incidents report. <https://www.atf.gov/file/105076/download>.

U.S. Bomb Data Center, 2015. United States BombData Center (USBDC) explosive incidents report. <https://www.atf.gov/rules-and-regulations/docs/report/2015usbdcexplosiveincidentreportpdf/download>.

U.S. Homeland Security Office for Bombing Prevention, 2012. Bomb Threat Management Student Guide.

Chapter 25

The use of locks in physical crime prevention*

James M. Edgar and William D. McInerney†
Security Consultant

Combining advanced features and compatibility with your home automation system, these door locks allows you to control your home from anywhere.[1]

Smart Homes—Smart Deadbolts

Lock terminology and components

The effectiveness of any locking system depends on a combination of interrelated factors involved in the design, manufacture, installation, and maintenance of the system. A prevention specialist needs to understand the weaknesses and strengths of the various systems, and know how each must be used to achieve maximum benefit from its application. This requires a thorough understanding of the inner workings of the various types of locks. It is not sufficient to know what a good lock is in someone else's opinion. A good lock today may not be as good tomorrow as technology improves and manufacturers alter their designs and production techniques. A lock that is excellent in some applications may be undesirable in others. Knowledge of the basic principles of locking systems will enable a prevention specialist to evaluate any lock and determine its quality and its effectiveness in a particular application.

Key-operated mechanisms

A key-operated mechanical lock uses some sort of arrangement of internal physical barriers (wards and tumblers) that prevent the lock from operating unless they are properly aligned. The key is the device used to align these internal barriers so that the lock may be operated. The lock is ordinarily permanently installed. The key is a separate piece, which is designed to be removed from the lock to prevent unauthorized use.

Three types of key-operated locks will be introduced in this section: disc or wafer tumbler, pin tumbler, and lever.

Tumbler mechanisms

A tumbler mechanism is any lock mechanism having movable, variable elements (the *tumblers*) that depend on the proper key (or keys) to arrange these tumblers into a straight line, permitting the lock to operate. The tumbler, which may be a disc, a lever, or a pin, is the lock barrier element that provides security against improper keys or manipulation. The specific key that operates the mechanism (called the *change key*) has a particular combination of cuts, or bittings, which match the arrangement of the tumblers in the lock. The combination of tumblers usually can be changed

*Permission obtained from National Crime Prevention Institute, School of Justice Administration, University of Louisville.

†. Deceased

1. <https://www.schlage.com/en/home/products/products-connected-devices.html?utm_source = google&utm_medium = paid-search&utm_campaign = Nonbrand-Keyless_Electronic:Broad&utm_term = electronic%20door%20locks&k_clickid = 89dbe0f1-4536-4daa-b46e-50d686c0acec> November 3, 2018.

Handbook of Loss Prevention and Crime Prevention. DOI: https://doi.org/10.1016/B978-0-12-817273-5.00025-9

periodically by inserting a new tumbler arrangement in the lock and cutting a new key to fit this changed combination. This capability provides additional security by protecting against lost or stolen keys.

Tumbler mechanisms and the keys that operate them are produced to specifications that vary with each manufacturer and among the different models produced by each manufacturer. These specifications are known as the *code* of the lock mechanism. The coding for each mechanism provides specifications for both the fixed and variable elements of the lock assembly. Fixed specifications include

- the dimensions of each of the component parts of the lock and the established clearance between each part (e.g., the size and length of the key must match the size and depth of the keyway);
- the spacing of each tumbler position and their relation to each other (Fig. 25.1); and
- the depth intervals or increments in the steps of each cut or bitting (Fig. 25.2).

The relationship between the dimensions of the tumblers and the bitting on the key is shown for a typical pin tumbler mechanism in Fig. 25.3. These codes provide a locksmith with dimensions and specifications to produce a specific key to operate a particular lock or to key additional locks to the combination of a particular key.

The different arrangements of the tumblers permitted in a lock series are its *combinations*. The theoretical or mathematical number of possible combinations available in a specific model or type of lock depends on the number of tumblers used and the number of depth intervals or steps possible for each tumbler. If the lock had only one tumbler, which could be any of 10 lengths, the lock would have a total of 10 combinations. If it had two tumblers, it would have a possible total of 100 (10 × 10) combinations. With three tumblers, 1000 (10 × 10 × 10) combinations are possible. If all five tumblers were used, the lock would have a possible 100,000 combinations. The number of mathematically possible combinations for any lock can be determined by this method.

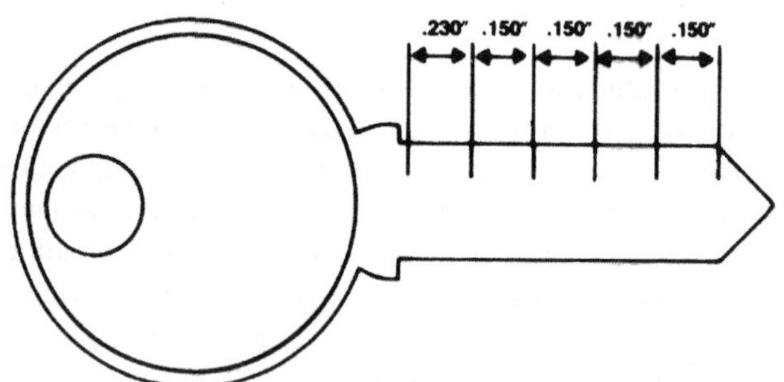

FIGURE 25.1 The spacing or position of each cut on the key is a fixed dimension corresponding to the position of each tumbler in the lock.

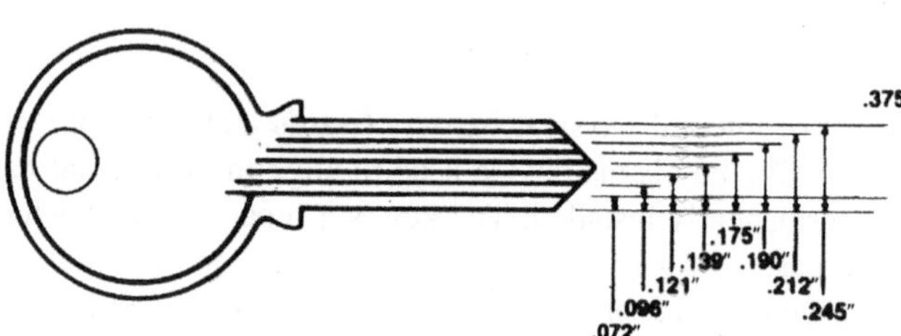

FIGURE 25.2 The depth interval (increment) of the steps of each cut or bitting is a fixed dimension.

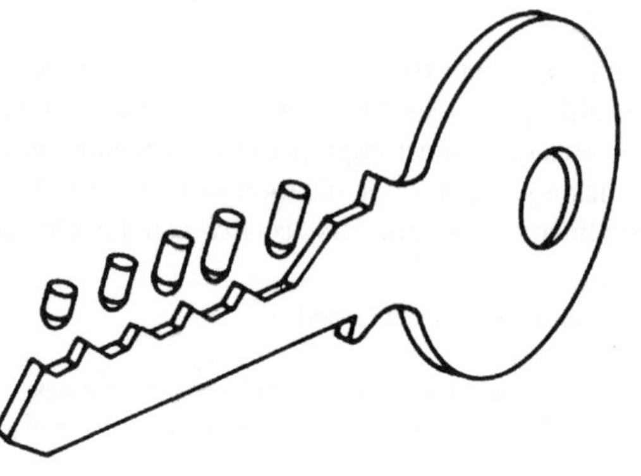

FIGURE 25.3 The depth of each cut corresponds to the length of each tumbler in the lock.

Due to a number of mechanical and design factors, however, not all of these theoretically possible (implied) combinations can actually be used. Some combinations allow the key to be removed from the lock before the tumblers are properly aligned (shedding combinations)—something that should not be possible with a properly combinated tumbler lock. Others, such as equal depth combinations, are avoided by the manufacturers. Some combinations result in a weakened key that is prone to break off in the lock. Others are excluded because the space from one cut in the key erodes the space or positioning of adjacent cuts. The combinations that remain after all of these possibilities have been removed are called *useful combinations*. The useful combinations, which are actually employed in the manufacture of the lock series, are the basis for the *bitting chart* that lists the total combinations used in a particular type of model or lock. When other factors are equal, the more combinations that can actually be used in a lock, the greater the security of the lock. Total useful combinations range from one for certain types of warded locks to millions for a few high-security tumbler key mechanisms.

Disc or wafer tumbler mechanisms

Disc tumbler mechanisms consist of three separate parts: the keys, the cylinder plug, and the cylinder shell (or housing; Fig. 25.4). The plug contains the tumblers, which are usually spring-loaded flat plates that move up and down in slots cut through the diameter of the plug. Variably dimensioned key slots are cut into each tumbler. When no key is inserted or an improper key is used, one or more tumblers will extend through the sides of the plug into the top or bottom locking grooves cut into the cylinder shell, firmly locking the plug to the shell preventing the plug from rotating in the shell to operate the lock. The proper change key has cuts or bittings to match the variations of the tumblers. When inserted, the key aligns all of the tumblers in a straight line at the edge of the cylinder plug (the *shear line*) so that no tumbler extends into the shell, which permits the plug to rotate.

Disc mechanisms generally provide only moderate security with limited key changes or combinations. Depth intervals commonly used are from 0.015 to 0.030 in., which permit not more than four or five depths for each tumbler position. Some models use as many as six tumblers. The more commonly found five-tumbler mechanism, which allows five depth increments for each tumbler position, would have a maximum of 3125 implied combinations. The number of useful combinations would, of course, be considerably fewer for the reasons indicated earlier. Some added security is provided by the common, although not universal, use of warded and paracentric keyways, which help protect against incorrect keys and manipulation. Nevertheless, most of these locks may be manipulated or picked fairly easily by a person with limited skills. In addition, the variations cut into the tumblers can be *sight read* with some practice while the lock is installed. Sight reading involves manipulating the tumblers with a thin wire and noting the relative positions of each tumbler in the

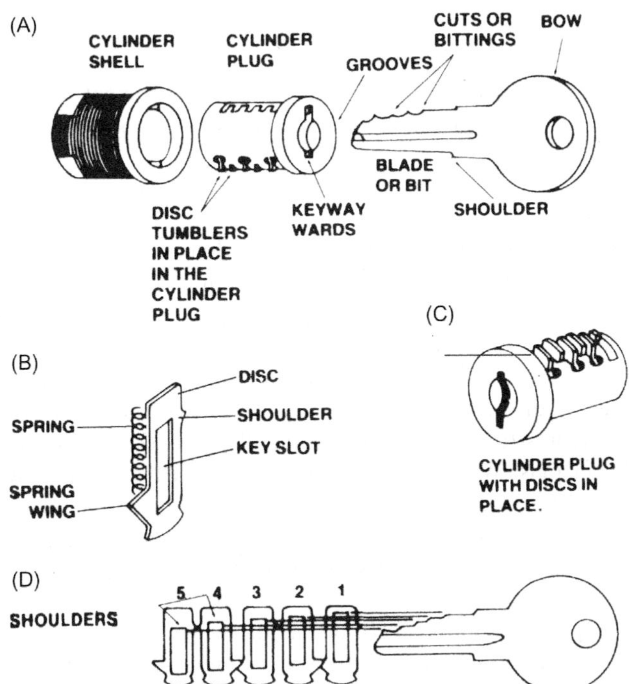

FIGURE 25.4 The key slots in the discs correspond to the cuts, or bittings, cut in the key. Note how each cut in the key will align its corresponding disc in a straight line with the others.

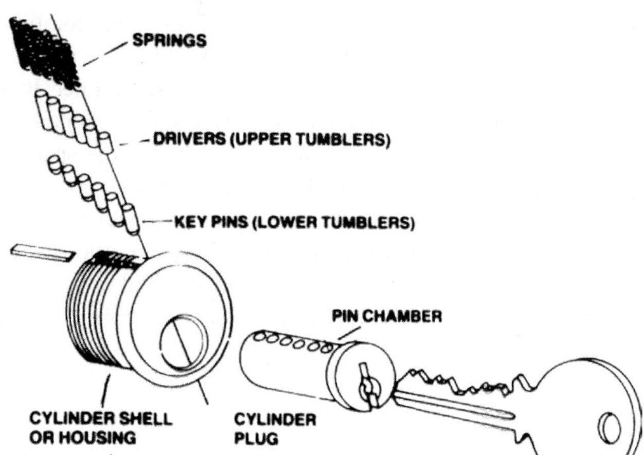

FIGURE 25.5 Basic pin tumbler cylinder lock mechanism.

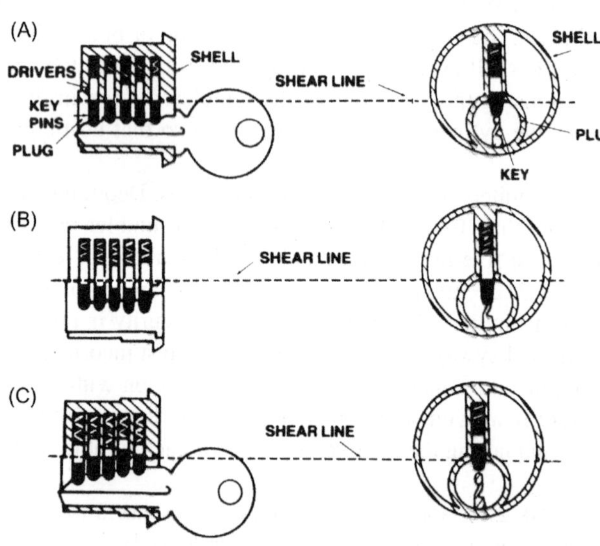

FIGURE 25.6 Operation of a pin tumbler cylinder mechanism: (A) when the correct key is inserted, the bittings in the key align the tops of the lower tumblers (key pins) with the top of the cylinder plug at the shear line. The plug may then be rotated in the shell to operate the lock. (B) When the key is withdrawn, the springs push the upper tumblers (drivers) into the cylinder plug. With the pins in this position, the plug obviously cannot be turned. (C) When an incorrect key is used, the bittings will not match the length of the key pins. The key will allow some of the drivers to extend into the plug, and some of the key pins will be pushed into the shell by high cuts. In either case the plug cannot be rotated. With an improper key, some of the pins may align at the shear line, but only with the proper key will all five align so that the plug can turn.

keyway. Since each lock has only a limited number of possible tumbler increments, the correct arrangement of these increments can be estimated with fair accuracy, permitting a key to be filed or cut on the spot to operate the lock.

Pin tumbler mechanisms

The pin tumbler mechanism is the most common type of key-operated mechanism used in architectural or builders' (door) hardware in the United States. The security afforded by this mechanism ranges from fair in certain inexpensive cylinders with wide tolerances and a minimum of tumblers to excellent with several makes of high-security cylinders, including those that are listed by Underwriters Laboratories (UL) as manipulation- and pick-resistant.

The lock operates very much like disc tumbler mechanisms (see Fig. 25.5). The locking system consists of a key, a cylinder plug, and a cylinder shell or housing. Rather than using discs, the mechanism uses pins as the basis interior barrier. Each lock contains an equal number of upper tumbler pins (drivers) and lower tumbler pins (key pins). The proper key has cuts or bittings to match the length of the lower pins. When it is inserted, the tops of the key pins are aligned flush with the top of the cylinder plug at the shear line. The plug may then rotate to lock or unlock the mechanism. When the key is withdrawn, the drivers are pushed by springs into the cylinder plus, pushing the key pins ahead of them until the key pins are seated at the bottom of the pin chamber. The drivers extending into the plug prevent it from rotating (Fig. 25.6).

If an improper key is inserted, at least one key pin will be pushed into the shell, or one driver will extend into the plug. In either case the pin extending past the shear line binds the plug to the shell. One or more key pins may be aligned at the shear line by an incorrect key, but all will be aligned only when the proper key is used.

Depth intervals commonly used for pin tumbler cylinders vary from 0.0125 to 0.020 in. These intervals allow between 5 and 10 depths for each tumbler position. The number of pins used ranges from three to eight—five or six is the most common number. Maximum useful combinations for most standard pin tumbler cylinders (assuming eight tumbler depth increments) are as follows:

Three pin tumblers approximately	130 combinations
Four pin tumblers approximately	1025 combinations
Five pin tumblers approximately	8200 combinations
Six pin tumblers approximately	65,500 combinations

These estimates assume that the useful combinations amount to not more than 23% of the mathematically possible combinations. Many common pin tumbler locks use fewer than eight increments, so the number of useful combinations for a specific lock may be much lower than the figures given in the table. Master keying will also greatly reduce the number of useful combinations.

Pin tumbler mechanisms vary greatly in their resistance to manipulation. Poorly constructed, inexpensive cylinders with wide tolerances, a minimum number of pins, and poor pin chamber alignment may be manipulated quickly by persons of limited ability. Precision-made cylinders with close tolerances, a maximum number of pins, and accurate pin chamber alignment may resist picking attempts even by experts for a considerable time.

Most pin tumbler lock mechanisms use warded keyways for additional security against incorrect keys and manipulation. The wards projecting into the keyway must correspond to grooves cut into the side of the key, or the key cannot enter the lock. *Paracentric* keyway is when both the wards on one side of the keyway as well as of the other side extend past the centerline of the key (Fig. 25.7). While warded keyways are commonly used on most pin tumbler mechanisms, paracentric keyways are usually restricted to the better locks. They severely hinder the insertion of lockpicks into the mechanisms and the ability of the manipulator to maneuver the pick once it is inserted.

Modifications have been made to the drives in better locks to provide increased security against picking (see Fig. 25.8). The usual modified shapes are the *mushroom* and the *spool*. Both of these shapes have a tendency to bind in the pin chamber when picking is attempted, making it more difficult to maneuver them to the shear line. To be consistently successful in picking pin tumbler cylinders with either type of modified driver, special techniques must be used.

There are a number of variations of the pin tumbler cylinder on the market. One, which is seeing increasingly widespread use, is the *removable core cylinder* (Fig. 25.9). These locks were originally produced by the Best Universal Lock Company, initial patents of which have now expired. Most major architectural hardware manufacturers now have them available in their commercial lock lines. This type of cylinder uses a special key called the *control key* to remove the entire pin tumbler mechanism (called the *core*) from the shell. This makes it possible to quickly replace one core with another having a different

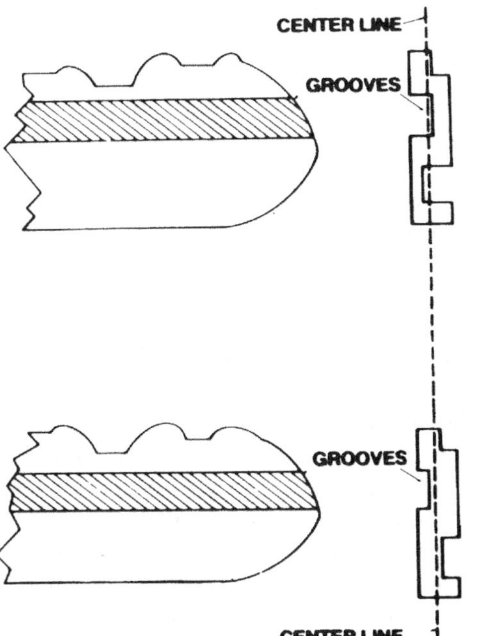

FIGURE 25.7 Milled, warded, and paracentric keys.

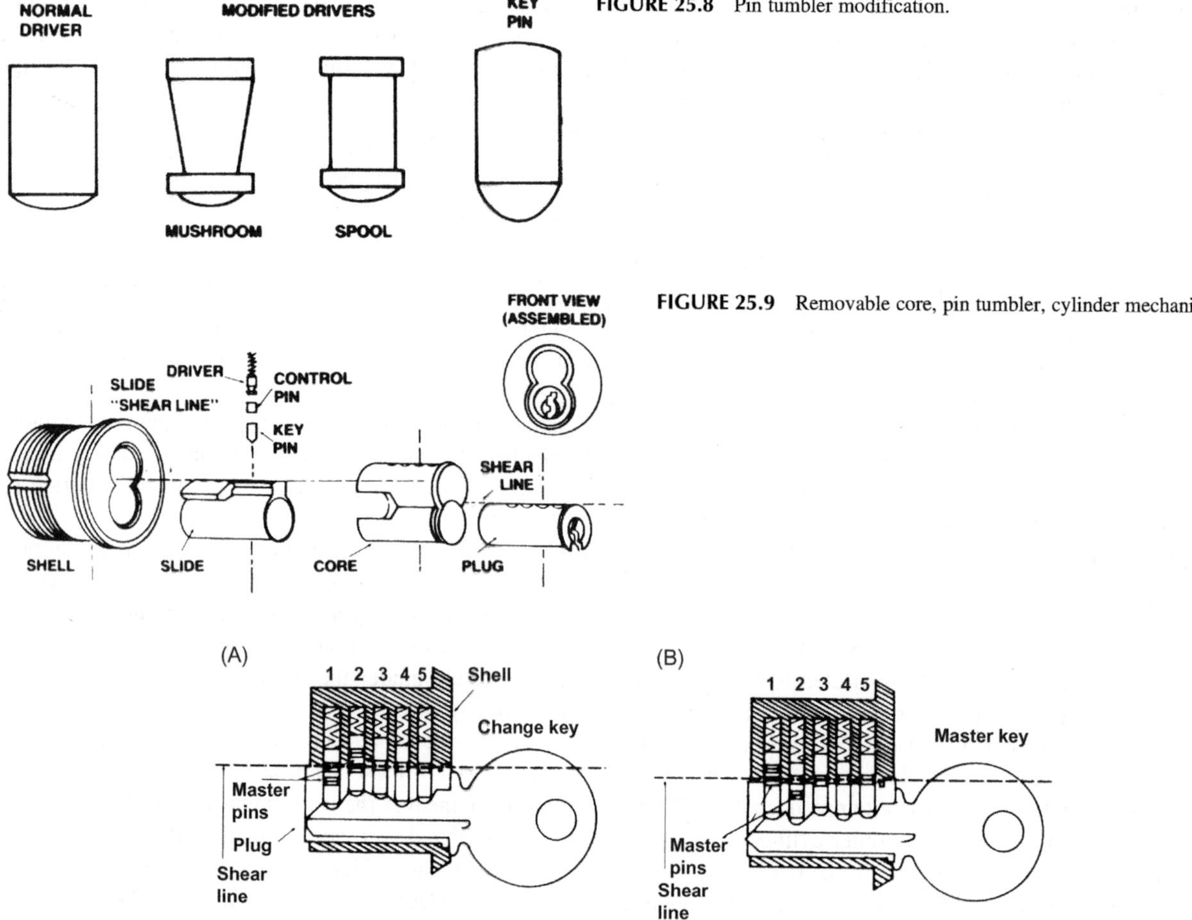

FIGURE 25.8 Pin tumbler modification.

FIGURE 25.9 Removable core, pin tumbler, cylinder mechanism.

FIGURE 25.10 Master-keyed pin tumbler cylinder mechanism. (A) This is a simple master-keyed system using master pins in the first and second tumbler positions. When the change key is inserted, note that the top of the first master pin aligns with the top of the cylinder plug. The remaining positions show the key pins aligned with the top of the plug. This arrangement permits the plug to turn. (B) With the master key inserted, the first position aligns the top of the key pin with the cylinder plug. The master pin is pushed further up the pin cylinder. The second position shows the master pin aligning at the top of the plug. The master pin has dropped further down the pinhole in the plug. The remaining three positions are unchanged. This arrangement also allows the plug to rotate.

combination and requiring a different key to operate. Because of this feature, removable core cylinders are becoming increasingly popular for institutional use and in large commercial enterprises, where locks must be changed often.

Removable core cylinders do not provide more than moderate security. Most systems operate on a common control key, and possession of this key will allow entry through any lock in the system. It is not difficult to have an unauthorized duplicate of the control key made. If this is not possible, any lock, particularly a padlock, of the series may be borrowed and an unauthorized control key made. Once the core is removed from a lock, a screwdriver or other flat tool is all that is necessary to operate the mechanism. In addition, the added control pins increase the number of shear points in each chamber, thus increasing the mechanism's vulnerability to manipulation.

Another variation that has been in widespread use for many years is *master keying*. Almost any pin tumbler cylinder can easily be master-keyed. This involves the insertion of additional tumblers called *master pins* between the drivers and key pins. These master pins enable a second key, the *master key*, to operate the same lock (see Fig. 25.10). In general, an entire series of locks is combinated to be operated by the same master key. There may also be levels of master keys, including submasters, which open a portion, but not all, of a series; master keys that open a larger part; and grand masters that open the entire series. In very involved installations, there may even be a fourth level (great grand master key).

There are a number of security problems with master keys. The most obvious one is that an unauthorized master key will permit access through any lock of the series. Less obvious is the fact that master keying reduces the number of useful combinations that can be employed, since any combination used must not only be compatible with the change key, but with the second, master key. If a submaster is used in the series, the number of combinations is further reduced to those that are compatible with all three keys. If four levels of master keys are used, it should be obvious that the number of useful combinations becomes extremely small. If a large number of locks are involved, the number of locks may exceed the number of available combinations. When this occurs, it may be necessary to use the same combination in several locks, which permits one change key to operate more than one lock (cross keying). This creates an additional security hazard.

One way of increasing the number of usable combinations and decreasing the risk of cross keying is to use a *master sleeve* or ring. This sleeve fits around the plug, providing an additional shear line similar to the slide shear line in a removable core system. Some of the keys can be cut to lift tumblers to sleeve shear line, and some to the plug shear line. This system, however, requires the use of more master pins. Any increase in master pins raises the susceptibility of the lock to manipulation, since the master pins create more than one shear point in each pin chamber, increasing the facility with which the lock can be picked.

Thus while master-keyed and removable core systems are necessary for a number of very practical reasons, you should be aware that they create additional security problems of their own.

The basic pin tumbler mechanism has been extensively modified by a number of manufacturers to improve its security. The common features of high-security pin tumbler cylinder mechanisms are that they are produced with extremely close tolerances and that they provide a very high number of usable combinations. Additional security features include the use of very hard metals in their construction to frustrate attacks by drilling and punching.

Lever-tumbler mechanisms

Although the lever lock operates on the same principles as the pin or disc tumbler mechanism, its appearance is very different. Fig. 25.11 illustrates a typical lever mechanism. Unlike pin or disc tumbler devices, the lever lock does not use a rotating core or plug, and the bolt is usually an integral part of the basic mechanism thrown directly by the key. The only other type of mechanism in which the key directly engages the bolt is the warded mechanism. You will recall that the bolt in pin or disc tumbler systems is usually directly operated by the *cylinder plug*, not the key. The key is used to rotate the plug, but it never comes into direct contact with the bolt.

Despite these somewhat deceptive appearances, the lever lock operates very much like the other tumbler mechanisms. Each *lever* is hinged on one side by the *post*, which is a fixed part of the case. The *leaf springs* attached to the

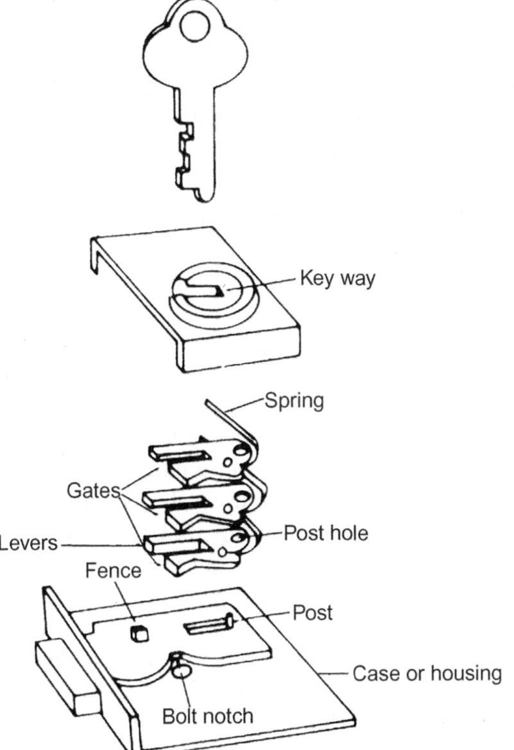

FIGURE 25.11 Lever-tumbler mechanism.

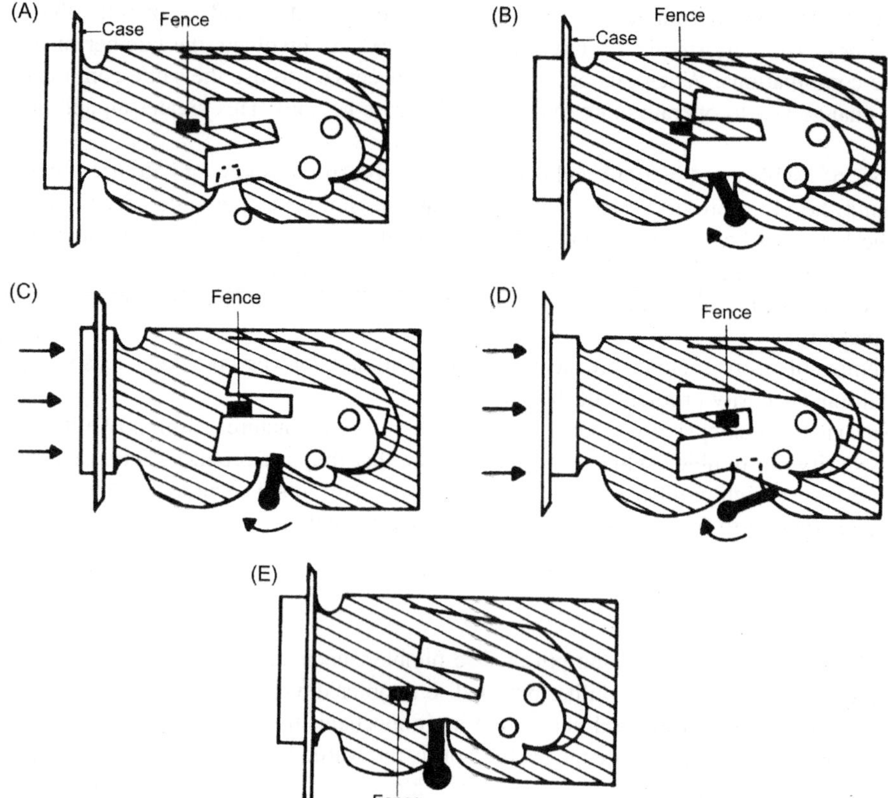

FIGURE 25.12 Operation of a typical lever-tumbler mechanism. (A) The bolt is in the fully extended locked position and the key has been withdrawn from the keyway. In this position the spring forces the lever down toward the bolt notch, trapping the fence against the forward edge (shoulder) of the lever, which prevents the bolt from being forced back. (B) The key has been inserted and the bitting on the key has lifted the lever against the spring tension, aligning the gate with the fence. The bolt can now be moved back into the retracted position. (C) The key has begun to force the bolt back into a retracted position by engaging a shoulder of the bolt notch at the same time it is keeping the lever suspended at the correct height to allow the fence to pass into the gate. (D) The bolt is now fully retracted and the key can be withdrawn. (E) If an improper key is inserted the bitting either will not lift the lever high enough for the fence to pass through the gate or the lever will be raised too high and the fence will be trapped in front of the lower forward shoulder of the lever. From this position the bolt cannot be forced back into the retracted position.

levers hold them down in a position that overlaps the *bolt notch* as shown in Fig. 25.12. In this position the *bolt* is prevented from moving back into a retracted position by its *fence*, which is trapped by the front edges (shoulder) of the levers. When the key is inserted and slightly rotated, the bittings on the key engage the *saddle* of the lever, raising it to a position where the fence aligns with the slot in the lever (called the *gate*). In this position the fence no longer obstructs the movement of the bolt to the rear, and the bolt can be retracted.

The retraction is accomplished by the key engaging the shoulder of the bolt notch. While the bittings of the key are still holding the levers in an aligned position, the key contacts the rear shoulder of the bolt notch, forcing the bolt to retract as the key is rotated. As the bolt is retracted, the fence moves along the gate until the bolt is fully withdrawn. When the key has rotated fully, completely retracting the bolt, it can be withdrawn.

If an improperly cut key is inserted and rotated in the lock, either the levers will not be raised far enough to align all of the gates with the fence, or one or more levers will be raised too high, so that the bottom edge of the lever obstructs the fence (as in Fig. 25.12). In either case the bolt is prevented from being forced to the rear, thus opening the lock.

Fig. 25.13A shows one version of the basic lever. A number of variations are on the market. Some levers are made with projections built into the gate designed to trap the fence in various positions (Fig. 25.13B). The front and rear traps prevent the fence from being forced through the gate when the bolt is in the fully extended or fully retracted position. Fig. 25.13C shows another variation: serrated (sawtooth) front edges. These serrations are designed to bind against the fence when an attempt is made to pick the lock. They are commonly found on high-security lever tumbler mechanisms.

Lever mechanisms provide moderate-to-high security depending on the number of levers used, their configuration, and the degree of care used in the construction of the lock mechanism. Any mechanisms using six or more tumblers can safely be considered a high-security lock. Some mechanisms use a double set of levers, requiring a double-bitted key. The levers are located on both sides of the keyway. This configuration makes the lock very difficult to pick or manipulate.

Lever locks are commonly found in applications where moderate-to-high security is a requirement, including safe deposit boxes, strong boxes, post office boxes, and lockers. The lever mechanisms available in the United States, because of the integrated, short-throw bolt, are not ordinarily used as builders' hardware. But they are commonly used in that application in Europe, and some of these locks have found their way into the United States.

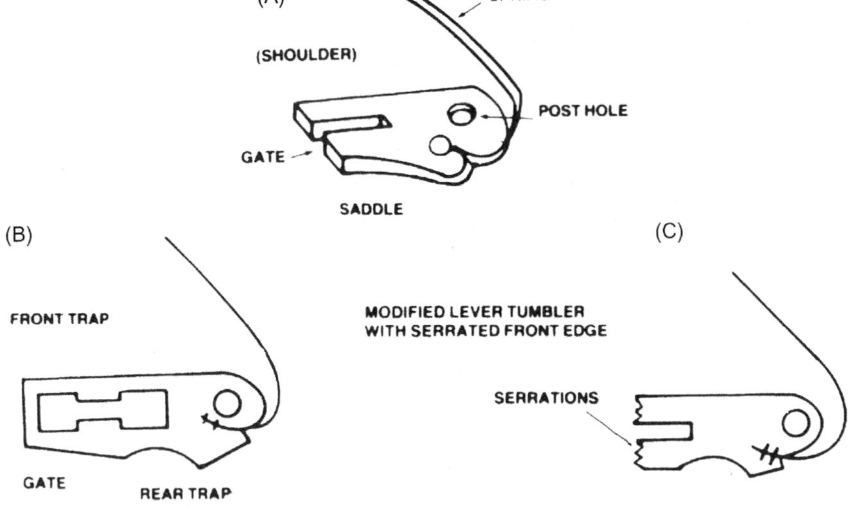

FIGURE 25.13 Lever tumblers. To operate the lock, the key contacts the lever at the saddle, lifting it until the fence is aligned with the gate. The saddles on the various tumblers are milled to different depths to correspond to different cuts on the key.

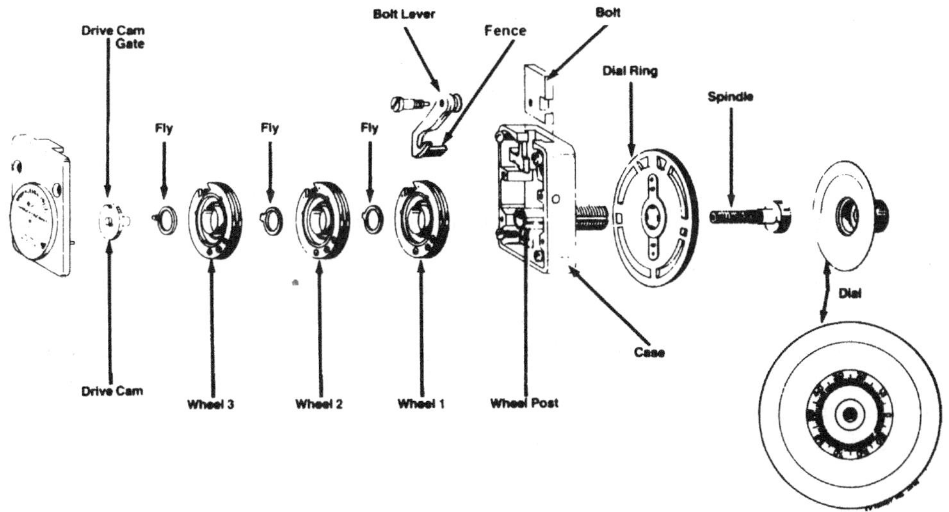

FIGURE 25.14 Three-tumbler combination.

Combination locks

In principle, a combination lock works in much the same way as a lever mechanism. When the tumblers are aligned, the slots in the tumblers permit a fence to retract, which releases the bolt so that the bolt can be opened. The difference is that where the lever mechanism uses a key to align the tumblers, the combination mechanism uses numbers, letters, or other symbols as reference points that enable an operator to align them manually. Fig. 25.14 shows a simplified view of a typical three-tumbler combination lock mechanism. The tumblers are usually called *wheels.* Each wheel has a slot milled into its edge, which is designed to engage the *fence* when the slot has been properly aligned. This slot is called a *gate.* The fence is part of the lever that retracts the bolt. The gates are aligned with the fence by referring to letter, numbers, or other symbols on the dial. The sequence of symbols that permits the lock to operate is its *combination.* A typical combination sequence using numbers is 10–35–75. The fact that three numbers are used in the combination indicates that the lock contains three tumblers. The number of tumblers in a lock always corresponds to the number of symbols used in its combination. Few modern combination locks use more than four tumblers because combinations of five or more symbols are unwieldy and hard to remember. Older models, however, used as many as six.

Both *drive cam* and dial are fixed to the *spindle* so that as the dial is rotated, the drive cam will also rotate in an identical fashion. The drive cam has two functions. It is the means by which motion of the dial is transferred to the wheels, and when all wheels are properly aligned and the fence retracted, it is the mechanism by which the bolt lever is pulled to retract the bolt.

The wheels are not fixed to the spindle but ride on a *wheel post* that fits over the spindle. These wheels are free-floating and will not rotate when the dial is turned unless the *flies* are engaged. The flies are designed to engage pins on the wheels at predetermined points (determined by the combination of that particular lock). When the flies engage these pins, the wheels pick up the rotating motion of the dial. When the flies are not engaged, the wheels will remain in place when the dial is rotated.

To operate a typical three-wheel combination lock, the dial is first turned four times in one direction to allow all of the flies to engage their respective wheels so that as the dial is being turned, all of the wheels are rotating with it. At this point the wheels are said to be *nested*. The object is to disengage each wheel at the spot where its gate will be aligned with the fence. To do this the operator stops the dial when the first number of the combination reaches the index mark on the dial ring. This first stop aligns the gate of wheel 1 with the fence.

The operator then reverses direction to disengage wheel 1, which remains stationary, and rotates the dial three turns to the second number in the combination. When this number is under the index mark, wheel 2 is aligned. Again reversing direction to disengage wheel 2, the operator makes two turns to the last number of the combination. This aligns wheel 3. At this point, all of the gates are aligned with the fence. The operator then reverses direction once again and turns the dial until it stops.

This last operation has two functions. It aligns the gate on the drive cam with the fence, which permits the fence to retract into the space provided by the three gates in the wheels and the fourth gate in the drive cam. The bolt lever is now engaged with the wheels and drive cam. As the operator continues rotating the dial, the drive cam pulls the bolt lever to retract the bolt. When the dial will no longer rotate, the bolt is fully retracted, and the lock is open.

The security afforded by combination mechanisms varies widely. The critical elements are the number of tumblers used in the lock, the number of positions on the tumbler where the gate can be located, and the tolerances in the width of the gate and fence. Wide tolerances allow the fence to enter the gates even when they are not quite completely aligned, so that, although the proper combination may be 10–35–75, the lock may also operate at 11–37–77.

Until the 1940s it was often possible to open many combination locks by using the sound of the movement of the tumblers and feeling the friction of the fence moving over the tumblers as indicators of tumbler position. (Tumblers in combination locks do not click despite Hollywood's contentions to the contrary.) Skilled operators were often able to use sound and feel to determine when each tumbler came into alignment. Modern technology has all but eliminated these possibilities, however, through the introduction of sound baffling devices, nylon tumblers, improved lubricants to eliminate friction, false fences, and cams that suspend the fence over the tumblers so that they do not make contact until after the gates are already aligned (see Fig. 25.14).

Another manipulation technique of recent vintage utilized the fact that the tumbler wheels with gates cut into them are unbalanced: more weight is on the uncut side than on the cut side. By oscillating the dial, these cut and uncut sides could be determined, and the location of the gates estimated. The introduction of counterbalanced tumblers has virtually eliminated this approach to the better mechanisms.

Radiology has also been used to defeat combination locks. A piece of radioactive material placed near the lock can produce ghost images of the tumblers on sensitive plates, showing the location of the gates. Nylon and teflon tumblers and shielding material that are opaque to radiation are used to defeat this technique.

Lock bodies

Most lever-tumbler and warded mechanisms contain an integrated bolt as a part of the mechanism. The key operates directly to throw the bolt, thereby opening and locking the lock. This is not true of pin and disc tumbler locks, which consist of two major components. The cylinder plug, the shell, the tumblers, and springs are contained in an assembly known as the *cylinder*. The other major component is the *lock body*, which consists of the *bolt assembly* and case or housing. The bolt assembly consists of the bolt, a *rollback*, and a *refractor*. This assembly translates the rotating motion of the cylinder plug to the back-and-forth motion that actually operates the bolt. When the cylinder is inserted into the lock body, it is typically connected to the bolt assembly by a *tail piece* or cam. A cylinder can be used in a number of different lock bodies. Here we will be primarily concerned with the types of bodies used on standard residential and light commercial doors. The pin tumbler is the usual mechanism used in these locks, although some manufacturers offer door locks using disc tumbler cylinders (such as the Schlage cylindrical lock).

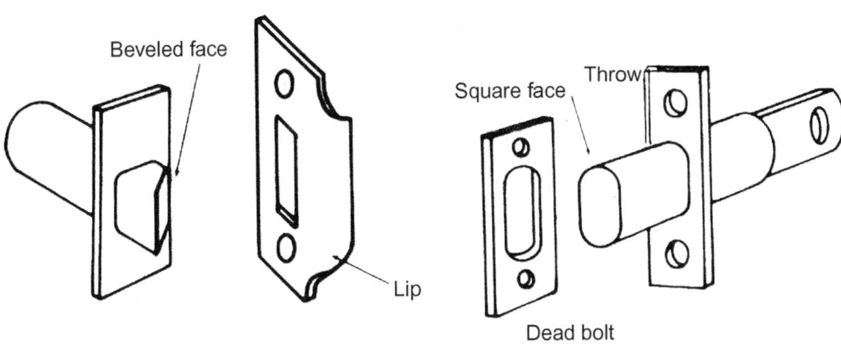

FIGURE 25.15 Basic types of bolts.

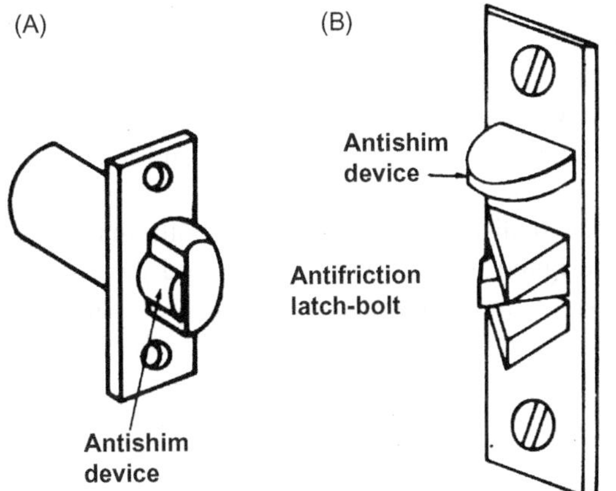

FIGURE 25.16 Modified latch bolts. (A) Latch bolt with antishim device. (B) Antifriction latch bolt with antishim device.

Bolts

There are two types of bolts used for most door applications: the *latch bolt* and the *dead bolt*, which are illustrated in Fig. 25.15. They are easily distinguished from each other. A latch bolt always has a beveled face, while the face on a standard dead bolt is square.

Latch bolt

The latch bolt, which is sometimes simply called a latch, a locking latch (to distinguish it from nonlocking latches), or a spring bolt is always spring-loaded. When the door on which it is mounted is in the process of closing, the latch bolt is designed to automatically retract when its beveled face contacts the lip of the strike. Once the door is fully closed, the latch springs back to extend into the hole of the strike, securing the door.

A latch bolt has the single advantage of convenience. A door equipped with a locking latch will automatically lock when it is closed. No additional effort with a key is required. However, it does not provide very much security.

The throw on a latch bolt is usually 3/8 in. but seldom more than 5/8 in. Because it must be able to retract into the door on contact with the lip of the strike, it is difficult to make the throw much longer. But, because there is always some space between the door and the frame, this means that a latch may project into the strike not more than 1/4 in. (often as little as 1/8 in. on poorly hung doors). Most door jambs can be spread at least 1/2 in. with little effort, permitting an intruder to quickly circumvent the lock.

Another disadvantage of the latch bolt is that it can easily be forced back by any thin shim (such as a plastic credit card or thin knife) inserted between the face plate of the lock and the strike. Antishim devices have been added to the basic latch bolt to defeat this type of attack. They are designed to prevent the latch bolt from being depressed once the door is closed. Fig. 25.16 shows a latch bolt with antishim device. These are often called *deadlocking latches*, a term that is mildly deceptive since these latches do not actually deadlock and are not nearly as resistant to jimmying as deadlocks. Often a thin screwdriver blade can be inserted between the face plate and the strike and pressure applied to break the antishim mechanism and force the latch to retract.

Another type of latch bolt, shown in Fig. 25.16B, is called an *antifriction latch bolt.* The antifriction device is designed to reclosing pressure required to force the latch bolt to retract. This permits a heavier spring to be used in the mechanism. Most modern antifriction latches also incorporate an antishim device. Without it, the antifriction latch is extremely simple to shim.

Dead bolt

The dead bolt is a square-faced solid bolt that is not spring-loaded and must be turned by hand into the locked and unlocked position. When a dead bolt is incorporated into a locking mechanism, the result is usually known as *deadlock.* The throw on a standard dead bolt is also about 1/2 in., which provides only minimal protection against jamb spreading. A *long-throw dead bolt*, however, has a throw of 1 in. or longer. One inch is considered the minimum for adequate protection. Properly installed in a good door using a secure strike, this bolt provides reasonably good protection against efforts to spread or peel the jamb.

The ordinary dead bolt is thrown horizontally. On some narrow-stile doors, such as aluminum-framed glass doors, the space provided for the lock is too narrow to permit a long horizontal throw. The *pivoting dead bolt* is used in this situation to get the needed longer throw (Fig. 25.17A). The pivoting movement of the bolt allows it to project deeply into the frame, at least 1 in., usually more. A minimum of 1 in. is recommended. When used with a reinforced strike, this bolt can provide good protection against efforts to spread or peel the frame.

Increased security against jamb spreading is provided by a number of different types of dead bolts that collectively are known as *interlocking dead bolts.* These are specifically designed to interlock the door and the strike so that the door jamb cannot be spread. The most common of these is the *vertical-throw dead bolt* shown in Fig. 25.17B. This is usually a rim-mounted device. The other two devices shown in Fig. 25.17 (the *expanding dead*

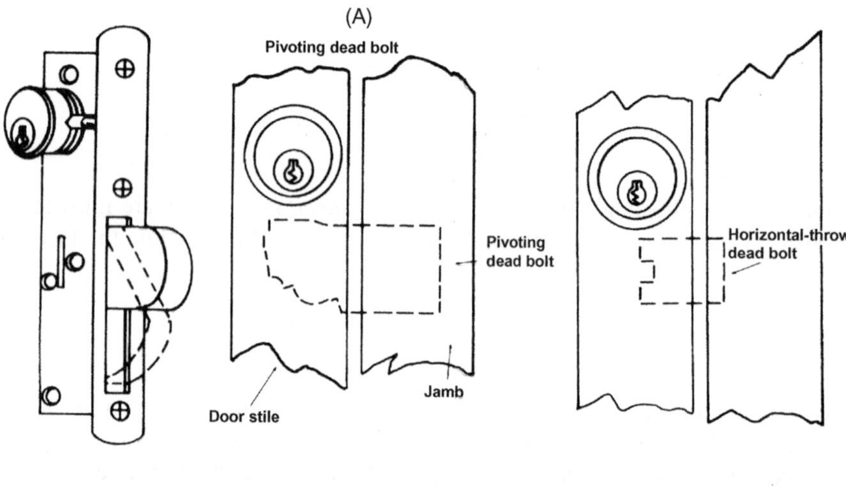

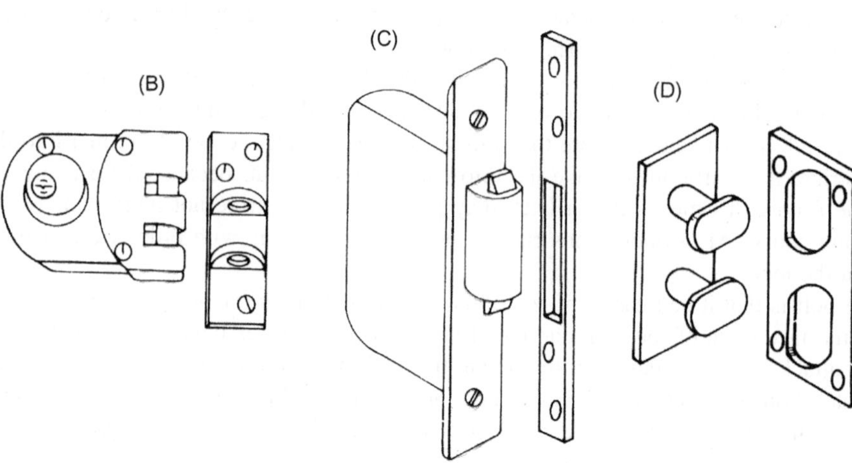

FIGURE 25.17 Modified dead bolts. Note the difference in penetration into the jamb. The deeper penetration afforded by the pivoting bolt increases protection against jamb spreading.

bolt and the *rotating dead bolt*) are meant to be mounted inside the door. These locks require a securely mounted strike or they are rendered ineffective.

Door lock types

Five basic lock types are used on most doors in the United States: mortise, rim-mounted, tubular, cylindrical, and unit. Each of these has a number of advantages and disadvantages from the point of view of the protection offered. Each, however, with the single exception of the cylindrical lockset, can offer sound security when a good lock is properly installed.

Mortise

A few years ago almost all residential and light commercial locks were mortise locks. A mortise lock, or lockset, is installed by hollowing out a portion of the door along the front or leading edge and inserting the mechanism into this cavity. Suitable holes are then drilled into the side of the door in the appropriate spot for the cylinders and door knob spindle (where the door knob is part of the unit, as is usually the case). Fig. 25.18 shows a typical mortise lockset. These mechanisms require a door that is thick enough to be hollowed out without losing a great deal of its strength in the process. One of the major weaknesses of mortise locks is that the cylinder is usually held in the lock with a set screw, which provides very little defense against pulling or twisting the cylinder out of the lock with a suitable tool. Cylinder guard plates can be used to strengthen the lock's resistance to this threat. On some mortise locks the trim plate acts as a cylinder guard.

Rim-mounted

A rim-mounted mechanism is simply a lock that is installed on the surface (rim) of the door (Fig. 25.18). Most are used on the inside surface, since outside installation requires a lock that is reinforced against direct attacks on the case. These are usually supplementary locks installed where the primary lock is not considered enough protection. These may or may not be designed for key operation from the outside. If they are, a cylinder extends through the door to the outside where it can be reached by a key.

Tubular

This lock (sometimes called a bore-in) is installed by drilling a hole through the door to accommodate the cylinder (or cylinders) and a hole drilled from the front edge of the door to the cylinder for the bolt assembly (Fig. 25.18). This type of installation has virtually replaced the mortise lock in most residential and light commercial applications because it can be installed quickly and by persons of limited skill.

Cylindrical lockset

The cylindrical lockset ordinarily uses a locking latch as its sole fastening element (Fig. 25.18). It is installed like the tubular lock by drilling two holes in the door. The cylinders are mounted in the door knobs, rather than in a case or inside the door, which makes them vulnerable to just about any attack (hammering, wrenching, etc.) that can knock or twist the knob off the door. Unfortunately, because it is inexpensive and simple to install, about 85% of all residential locks currently used in new construction in the United States are of this type. It provides virtually no security whatsoever. There is perhaps no harder or faster rule in lock security than the rule that all cylindrical locks should be supplemented by a secure, long-throw dead bolt. Or, better yet, they should be replaced. A number of more secure locks designed to replace the cylindrical lock are now on the market. One of these is illustrated in Fig. 25.18.

Unit locks

A unit lock is installed by making a U-shaped cutout in the front edge of the door and slipping the lock into this cutout. This type of lock usually has the advantage of having no exposed screws or bolts. It is ordinarily used in place of mortise locks where the door is too narrow to mortise without considerable loss of strength. A good unit lock

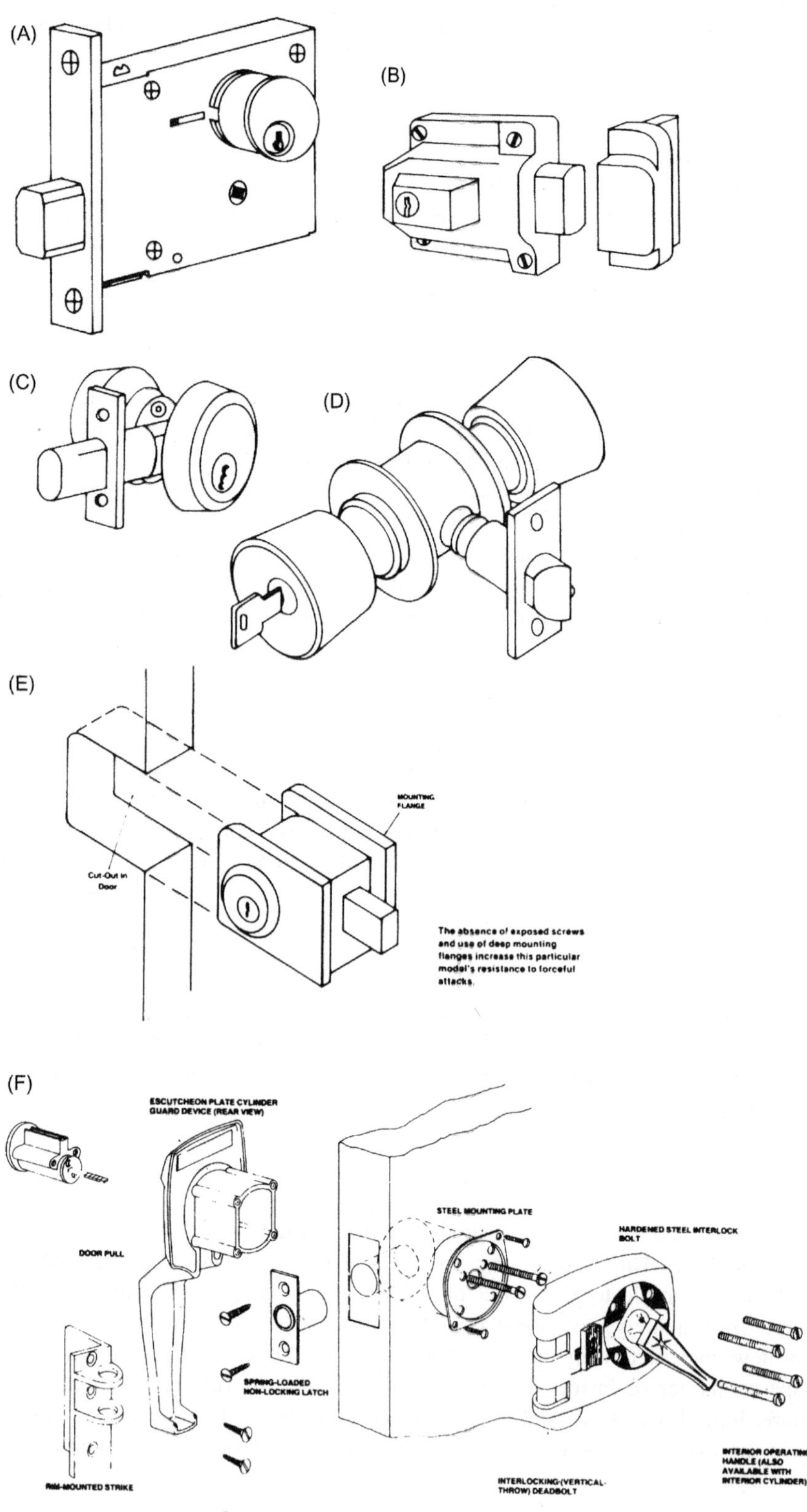

FIGURE 25.18 Lock types. (A) Mortise deadlock, (B) rim deadlock with rim strike, (C) tubular deadlock, (D) cylindrical (lock-in-knob) lockset, (E) unit lock, and (F) ideal Superguard Lock II. Note washers must be used for additional protection against cylinder pulling. These are not supplied with the lock.

properly installed on a solid door provides excellent protection against attempts to remove the cylinder, or to pry or twist the lock off the doors.

Cylinders

Cylinders are mounted in the lock body in a number of ways. Most mortise cylinders are threaded into the lock and secured with a small set screw (Fig. 25.19). Tubular and rim locks use cylinder interlock screws inserted from the back of the lock. Better mechanisms use 1/4 in. or larger diameter hardened steel screws for maximum resistance to pulling and wrenching attacks (Fig. 25.19). Better cylinders incorporate hardened inserts to resist drilling.

Two basic cylinder configurations are available. *Single cylinder* locks use a key-operated cylinder on the outside, and a thumb turn or blank plate on the inside (Fig. 25.20). *Double-cylinder* locks use a key-operated cylinder on both sides of the door (Fig. 25.20). This prevents an intruder from breaking a window near the door, or punching a hole through the door, reaching in, and turning the lock from the inside. The disadvantage of double cylinders is that rapid exit is made difficult since the key must first be located to operate the inside cylinder. If a fire or other emergency makes rapid evacuation necessary, a double-cylinder lock could pose a considerable hazard.

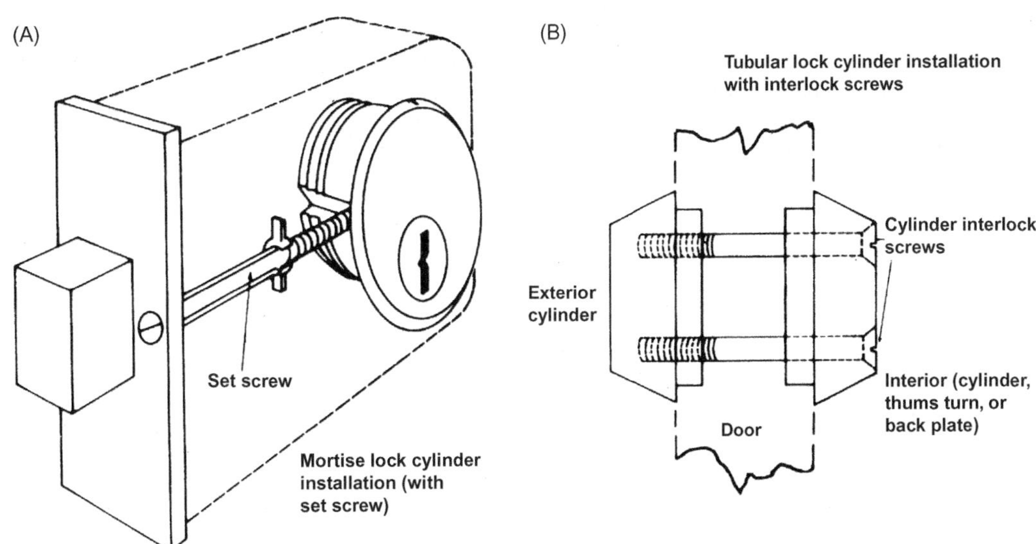

FIGURE 25.19 Mortise lock cylinder installation. (A) With set screw and (B) with interlock screws.

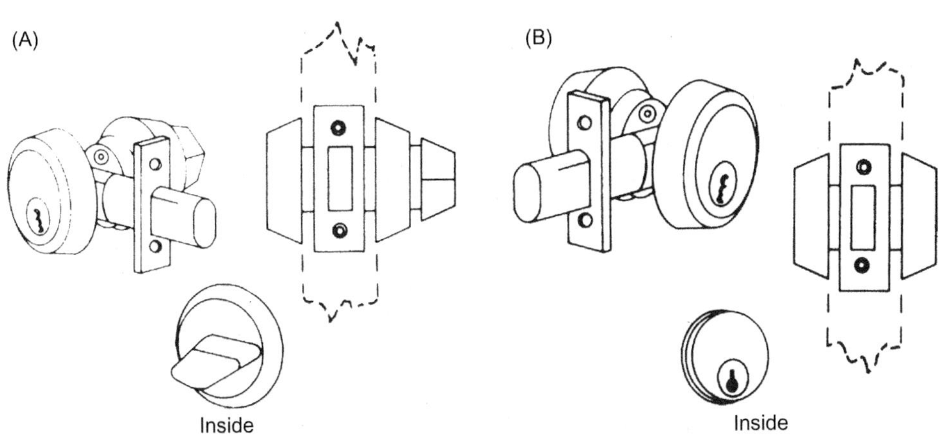

FIGURE 25.20 (A)Single cylinder deadlock with interior thumb turn and (B) double-cylinder deadlock with interior key cylinder.

Padlocks

The distinguishing feature of padlocks is that they use a shackle rather than a bolt as the device that fastens two or more objects together (Fig. 25.21). The shackle is placed through a hasp, which is permanently affixed to the items to be fastened. Three methods are commonly used to secure the shackle inside the lock body. The simplest and least secure method is to press a piece of flat spring steel against an indentation in the shackle. When the key is inserted, it rotates to spread the spring releasing the shackle (Fig. 25.22). This is a locking method commonly found on warded padlocks. It is found more rarely on tumbler-type locks, but it is found occasionally on the less expensive models.

A slightly more secure method uses a locking dog. The dog is spring-loaded and fits into a notch cut into the shackle (Fig. 25.22). The key is used to retract the dog, permitting the shackle to be withdrawn. Both of these spring-loaded mechanisms are vulnerable to attacks that take advantage of the fact that the locking device can be forced back against the spring by a suitable tool. Shimming and rapping are common techniques used to open them. Often a stiff wire can be pushed down the shackle hole to engage and force back the spring or locking dog. Spring-loaded padlocks should not be used where reasonable security is required.

Positive locking techniques do much to reduce the vulnerability of padlocks to these types of attacks. The most common positive locking method uses steel balls inserted between the cylinder and the shackle. In the locked position the ball rests half in a groove in the cylinder, and half in a notch cut into the shackle. In this position the shackle cannot be forced past the steel ball. When the cylinder is turned to the unlocked position, the groove deepens, permitting the ball to retract into the cylinder when pressure is put on the shackle. This releases the shackle and opens the lock. These locks are designed so that the key cannot be removed unless the lock is in the locked position.

Padlocks are vulnerable to attacks at several points. The shackle can be pried out of the lock by a crowbar or jimmy, or it can be sawed or cut by bolt cutters. The casing can be crushed or distorted by hammering. Modifications have been incorporated into better padlocks to reduce their vulnerability to these approaches. Heavy, hardened steel cases and shackles are used to defeat cutting and crushing. Rotating inserts and special hardened materials are used to prevent the sawing of shackles. Toe and heel locking is used to prevent prying (Fig. 25.22).

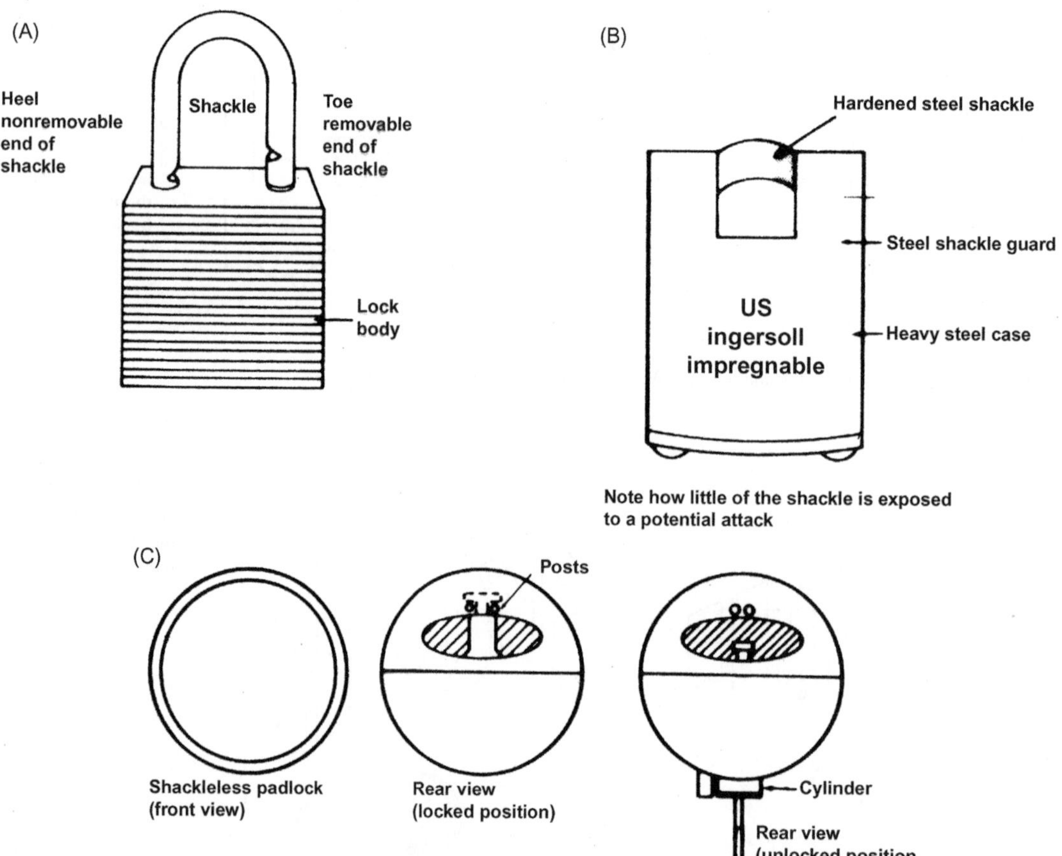

FIGURE 25.21 (A) Warded padlock, (B) high-security padlock, and (C) shackleless padlock.

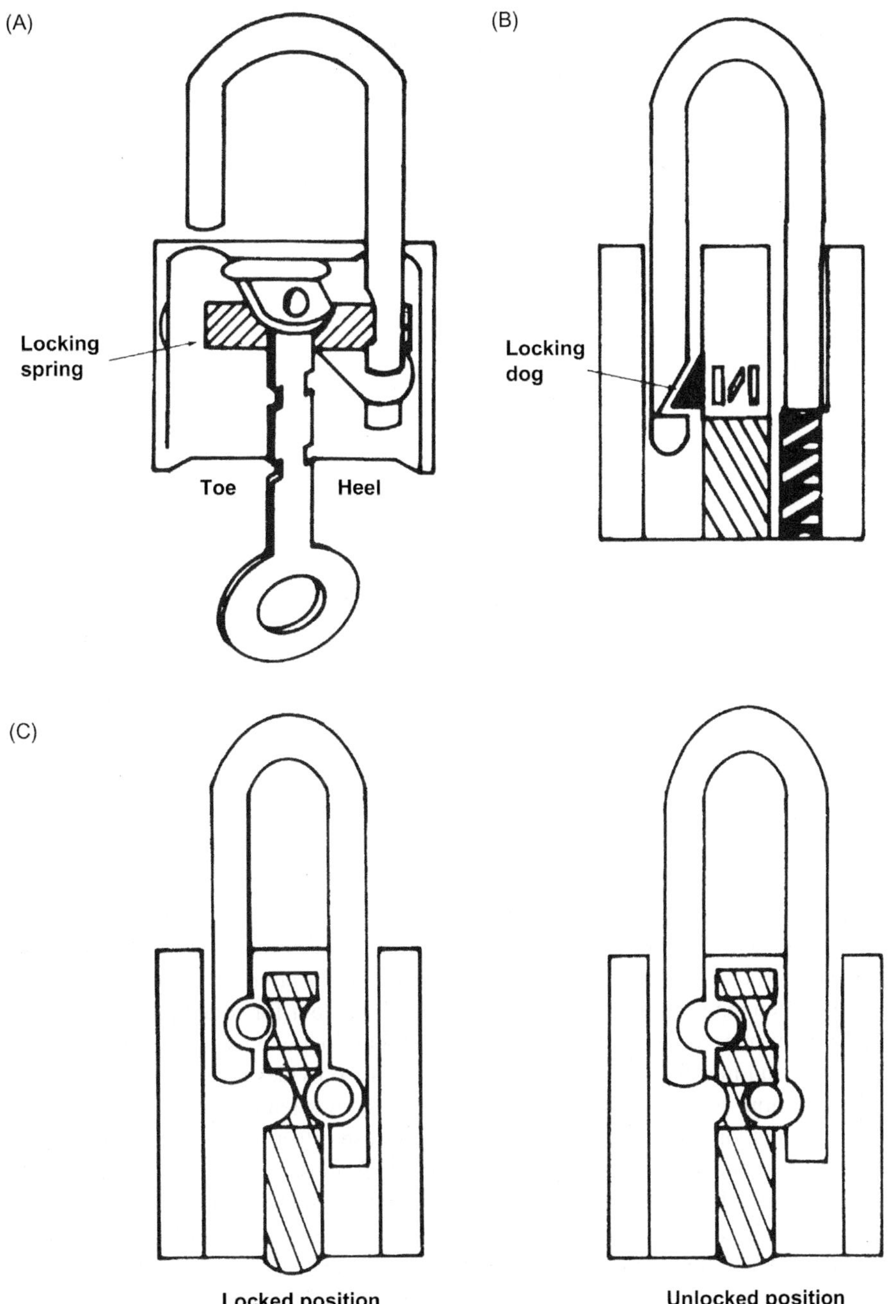

FIGURE 25.22 Three methods of securing the shackle inside the lock body. (A) Warded padlock with locking spring (heel locking), (B) padlock with locking dog (toe locking), and (C) positive locking padlock (heel and toe locking).

High-security padlocks are large and heavy, using hardened metals in the case, and a thick, hardened, and protected shackle. Positive locking methods are always used. As little of the shackle is exposed to attack as possible in the locked position. A typical high-security padlock is shown in Fig. 25.21. In the figure, another padlock, named shackleless, is designed in such a manner that a locking bar, which is contained entirely inside the case, is used in the place of an exposed shackle. This is sometimes called a hasp lock rather than a padlock.

A padlock is, however, no better than the hasp it engages. Hasps offering reasonable security are made of hardened metals. They must be properly mounted on solid materials so that they cannot be pried off. In the locked position, no mounting screw or bolt should be accessible. Padlocks and hasps should always be considered a unit. There is no point in mounting a high-security padlock on an inferior hasp. The hasp and lock should always be about the same quality. Where they are not, the complete device is only as good as its weakest member.

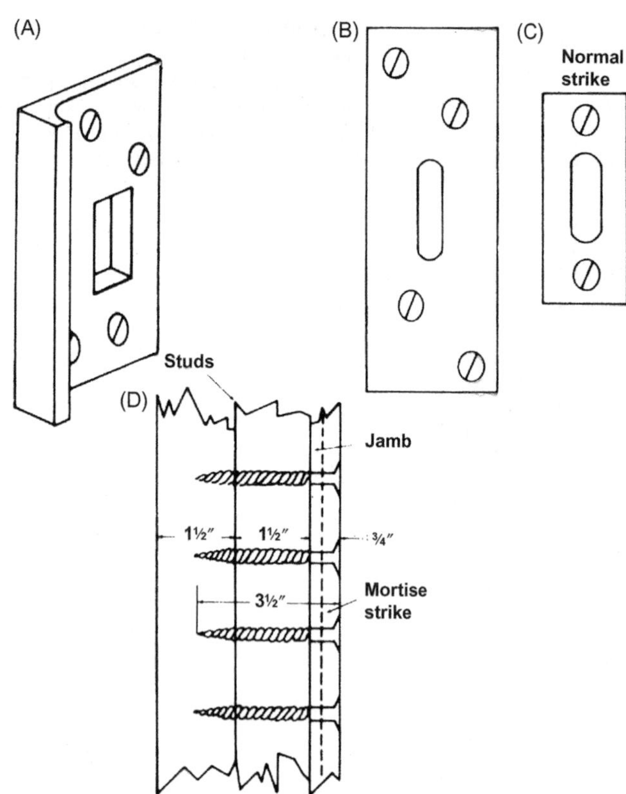

FIGURE 25.23 High-security strikes. (A) Security strike with reinforced lip to prevent jimmying and shimming, (B) security strike for wood frames with offset screws, (C) normal strike, and (D) proper installation of a strike on a wood frame.

Strikes

Strikes are an often overlooked but essential part of a good lock. A dead bolt must engage a solid, correctly installed strike, or its effectiveness is significantly reduced. The ordinary strike for residential use is mounted with two or three short (usually less than 1 in.) wood screws on a soft wooden doorframe. It can be easily pried off with a screwdriver. High-security strikes are wider, longer and often incorporate a lip that wraps around the door for added protection against jimmying and shimming (Fig. 25.23). Three or more offset wood screws at least 3.5 in. long are used to mount the strike. These screws must extend through the jamb and into the studs of the doorframe. This provides added protection against prying attacks. In addition, none of the fastening screws should be in line. In-line screws tend to split soft wood when they are screwed in. Strikes designed for installation on wood frames should always use offset screws as fasteners.

Reinforced steel should be used on metal-framed doors, especially aluminum frames. Aluminum is an extremely soft metal and, unless a reinforced strike is used, the jamb can be peeled away from the strike area exposing the bolt to a number of attacks, or allowing it to clear the jamb thereby freeing the door to open. Bolts should be used to mount strikes in metal frames. If the bolt does not penetrate a substantial steel framing member, then a steel plate should be used to back the bolt (very large steel washers may be an acceptable substitute), which prevents the strike from being pried out of aluminum or thin steel frames.

Attacks and countermeasures

There are two basic methods of attacking locks: surreptitious techniques and force. There are also a number of ways of circumventing a lock by assaulting the objects to which it is fastened. This chapter will be concerned only with techniques used to defeat locks and the measures that can be used to forestall those techniques.

No lock is completely invulnerable to attack. A lock's effectiveness is determined by how long it will resist the best effort of an intruder. An expert can pick an average pin tumbler cylinder in seconds, and no lock can survive strong force applied for a sufficient length of time. The sole object of using any lock at all is to *delay* an intruder. The objective of a good lock is to make entry riskier or more trouble than it is worth. Fortunately, most potential intruders are not experts, thus most moderately secure locks can survive for a reasonable amount of time against common attack techniques.

The proper use of countermeasures will significantly reduce a locking system's vulnerability to breaching by an unauthorized person. However, not all of the countermeasures suggested in the following sections will be appropriate for every application. There is always the necessity of striking a suitable compromise between the expense and inconvenience of a locking system and the value of the items it is designed to protect. Complex and expensive very high-security systems are simply not appropriate for most residential applications. On the other hand a cheap padlock on a warehouse containing valuable merchandise is an open invitation for someone to break in and steal it. The objective should always be to ensure reasonable protection in the circumstances surrounding a particular application. With locks, overprotection is often more harmful than insufficient protection. If the user is faced with a more complex security system than is really necessary, she or he simply will not use it. A great many unlawful entries are still made through *unlocked* doors and windows. The temptation to avoid the inconvenience of constantly locking and unlocking barriers seems to be insurmountable for some people. Contributing to this temptation by insisting on more protection than the user actually needs simply aggravates the problem.

Surreptitious attacks

Four basic surreptitious approaches are used to breach locking devices: illicit keys, circumvention of the internal barriers of the lock, manipulation of the internal barriers, and shimming. The susceptibility of any locking device to these approaches cannot be eliminated but can be minimized through the use of commonsense countermeasures.

Illicit keys

The easiest way of gaining entry through any lock is by using the proper key for that lock. Thousands of keys are lost and stolen every year. A potential intruder who can determine which lock a lost or stolen key fits has a simple and quick means of illicit entry. If an intruder cannot get hold of the owner's key, quite often he or she can make a duplicate. The casual habit of leaving house keys on the key ring when a car is left in a commercial parking lot or for servicing provides a potential intruder with a golden opportunity to duplicate the house keys for later use. One can also find out the owner's address very quickly by examining the repair bill or tracing the automobile license number.

The risk of lost, stolen, or duplicated keys cannot be eliminated entirely, but certain steps can be taken to minimize it.

Maintain reasonable key security

- Under some circumstances, it is almost impossible to avoid leaving at least the ignition key with a parked car, or one to be serviced. But all other keys should be removed.
- When keys are being duplicated, the owner should ensure that no extra duplicates are made.
- Many locks, particularly older locks, have their key code stamped on the front of the case or cylinder. This permits anyone to look up the code in a locksmith's manual and find the proper combination for that lock (or for that combination lock). Codebooks are readily available for most makes of lock, so if the code appears anywhere on the lock where it can be read after the lock is installed and locked, it should be removed by grinding or overstamping. If removal is not possible, the lock or its combination should be changed.
- Managers and owners of commercial enterprises should maintain strict control over master keys and control keys for removable core cylinders. The loss of these keys can compromise the entire system, necessitating an extensive and expensive, system-wide recombination. Too often in large institutions just about everyone can justify a need for a master key. This is nothing more than a demand for convenience that subverts the requirements of good security. The distribution of master keys should be restricted to those who literally cannot function without them.
- Since it is impossible to prevent people from losing keys no matter how careful they are, the next precaution is to *ensure that the lost key cannot be linked to the lock it operates.*
- The owner's name, address, telephone number, or car license number should never appear anywhere on a key ring. This has become common practice to ensure the return of lost keys, but if they fall into the wrong hands, the address provides a quick link between the keys and the locks they fit. The proper protection against lost keys is to always have a duplicate set in a secure place.
- For the same reasons, keys stamped with information that identifies the location of the lock should not be carried around. This used to be a common practice on keys of locker, safety deposit box, and some apartment building. It is no longer as common as it once was, but it still exists. If the keys must be carried, all identifying information should be obliterated, or they should be duplicated on a clean, unmarked key blank.

Recombinate or replace compromised locks

If all these precautions fail and the owner reasonably believes that someone has obtained keys to her or his locks, the combinations of these locks should be changed immediately. Where this is not possible, the locks may have to be replaced. When only a few locks are involved, recombinating cylinders is a fairly quick and inexpensive operation well within the competence of any qualified locksmith.

Another common attack method using a key against which there is less direct protection is the *try-out key*. Try-out key sets are a common locksmith's tool and can be purchased through locksmith supply houses, often by mail. These sets replicate the common variations used in the combination of a particular lock series. In operation, they are inserted into the lock one at a time until one is found that will operate the lock.

Try-out keys are commercially available only for automotive locks. There is nothing, however, to prevent a would-be intruder from building a set for other locks. In areas where one contractor has built extensive residential and commercial developments, most of the buildings will often be fitted with the same lock series. If it is an inexpensive series with a limited number of useful combinations, a homemade try-out key set that replicates the common variations of this particular lock series could be very useful to the potential intruder.

The defense against try-out keys is simply to use a lock with a moderate-to-high number of available combinations. Any lock worth using has at least several thousand useful combinations. No intruder can carry that many try-out keys, so the risk that he or she will have the proper key is minimal.

Circumvention of the internal barriers of the lock

This is a technique used to directly operate the bolt *completely bypassing* the locking mechanism that generally remains in the locked position throughout this operation. A long, thin stiff tool is inserted into the keyway to bypass the internal barriers and reach the bolt assembly. The tool (often a piece of stiff wire) is then used to maneuver the bolt into the retracted, unlocked position. Warded locks are particularly vulnerable to this method (as was indicated earlier), but some tumbler mechanisms with an open passageway from the keyway to the bolt assembly are also susceptible. Some older padlocks and cylindrical mechanisms had an open passageway of this sort. Few of these are manufactured anymore, but some of the older models are still in use. Any lock that has this type of an opening should be replaced with a better device if reasonable security is a requirement.

Manipulation

The term "manipulation" covers a large number of types of attacks. At least 50 discrete techniques of manipulating the mechanism of a lock without the proper key have been identified. Fortunately, however, they all fall rather neatly into four general categories: *picking*, *impressioning*, *decoding*, and *rapping*. Regardless of the specific technique used, its purpose is to maneuver the internal barriers of a tumbler mechanism into a position where they will permit the bolt to be retracted. In a disc or pin tumbler mechanism, this means that the cylinder plug must be freed to rotate; in a lever lock, the levers must be aligned with the fence.

The basic countermeasures against all forms of manipulation are the use of close tolerances in the manufacture of the mechanism and increasing the number of pins, discs, or levers. Close tolerances and a large number of tumblers make manipulation a time-consuming process. A number of specific defenses to the various forms of manipulation have also been developed, which will be presented in some detail in the following sections.

Picking

Lock picking is undoubtedly the best known method of manipulation. It requires skill developed by dedicated practice, the proper tools, time, and often a small dose of good luck. No lock is pickproof, but the high-security locks are so difficult to pick that it takes even an expert a long time to open them. One definition of a high-security mechanism, in fact, is one that cannot be picked by an expert in less than half a minute.

The techniques involved in picking the three basic types of tumbler mechanisms are very similar that an example using the pin tumbler cylinder will serve to illustrate the rest.

All picking techniques depend on the slight clearances that must necessarily exist in a mechanism for it to function. The basic technique requires slight tension to be placed on the part of the mechanism that retracts the bolt (which is the cylinder plug in pin tumbler mechanisms) by a special tension tool designed for that purpose (Fig. 25.24). The result of this tension is shown in Fig. 25.25. The pin chamber in the plug has moved slightly out of alignment with the pin

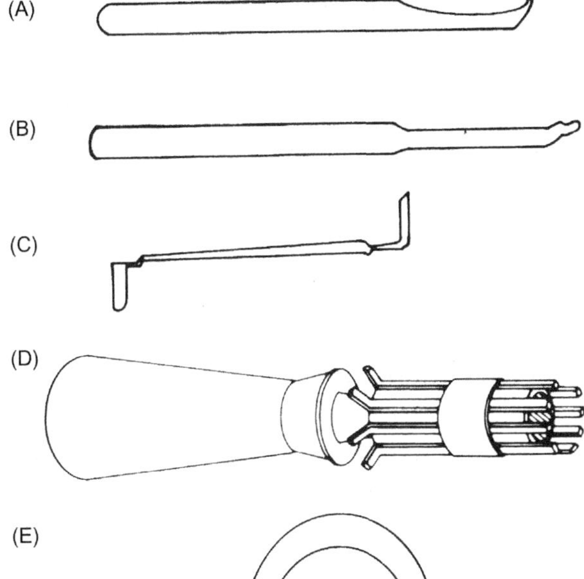

FIGURE 25.24 Lockpicks. (A) Standard pick, (B) rake pick, (C) tension tool, (D) special pick for tubular mechanisms, and (E) pick and tension tool in use.

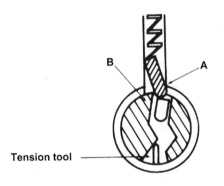

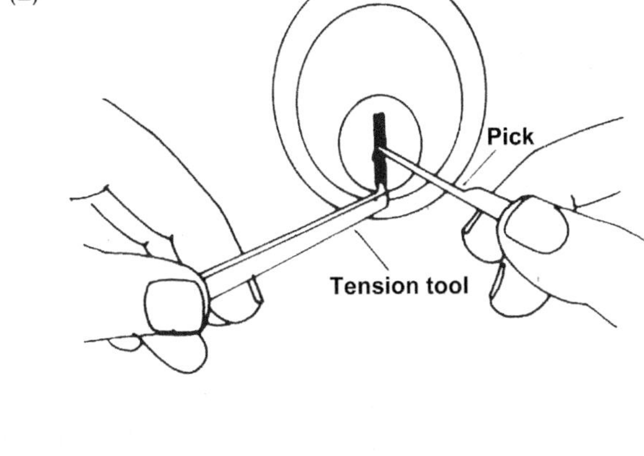

FIGURE 25.25 Illustration of the misalignment caused in a pin tumble cylinder when tension is applied.

chamber in the cylinder shell, creating two *lips* at points A and B. When the key pin is pushed up by the pick, it tends to catch at the shear line because the lip at point A permits it to go no farther. This pushes the driver above the shear line where the lip at point B prevents it from falling down into the cylinder plug once more. As long as tension is maintained, it will stay above the shear line.

This operation is facilitated by the fact that, as shown in Fig. 25.26, the pin chambers in a cylinder plug are seldom in a perfectly straight line. Consequently, the pin closest to the direction of tension will be more tightly bound than the rest of the pins when tension is applied. It can easily be located because it will offer the most resistance to being maneuvered by the pick. Each pin is tested by lifting it with the pick. The pin that is most resistant is picked first. When this pin reaches the shear line, often the cylinder plug will move slightly. The picker receives two important benefits from this very small movement: first it indicates that the pin has indeed been lifted to the shear line, and second, the movement of the cylinder increases the misalignment between the pin chamber in the plug and the one in the shell, making it even less likely that the driver will drop down into the plug (Fig. 25.27). Once this pin has been picked, the

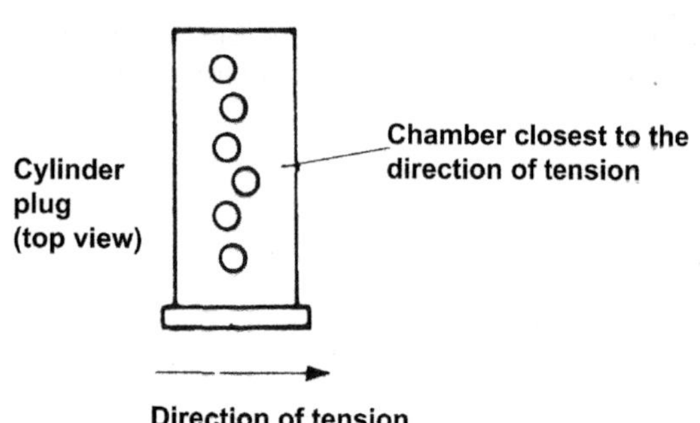

FIGURE 25.26 Pin chamber misalignment. Pin chambers on even the best cylinders are not in a perfectly straight line. The misalignment in this illustration is highly exaggerated for clarity.

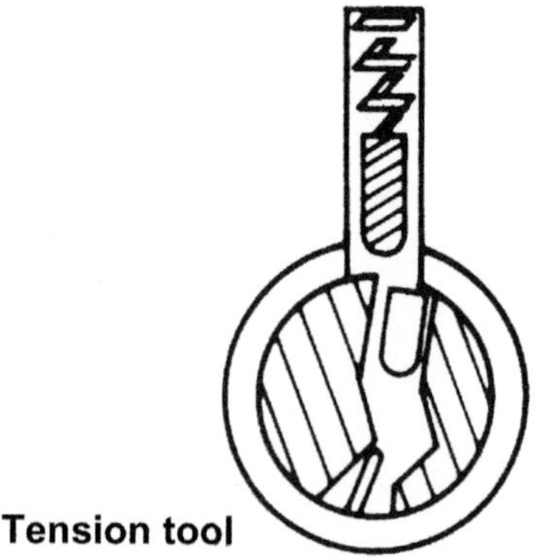

FIGURE 25.27 Increased misalignment occurs as each pin is picked.

next pin nearest the direction of tension will be the most tightly bound. It is located and picked next. The cylinder plug will again move a very small amount. This operation continues until all of the pins are picked above the shear line, and the cylinder plug is free to rotate.

There are endless variations of this basic picking technique. One of the most common is the use of a *rake pick.* When this pick is used, very slight tension is applied to the plug, and then the rake is run along the tumblers lifting them slightly each time until all of them reach the shear line. Raking increases the chance that one or more key pins will inadvertently be pushed up into the cylinder shell, which will not allow the plug to rotate. It is often necessary to release the tension applied to the plug and start over again several times. Nevertheless, it is a very fast technique, and very popular. With luck an expert using a rake can pick an average pin tumbler in a few seconds.

Most of the improvements in lock technology made over the last few thousand years have been devoted to increasing the resistance of locks to picking. The major defense is the use of very close tolerances in the mechanism during manufacture. This makes the forced misalignment between the plug and shell necessary for successful picking more difficult to achieve. The addition of more tumblers is also some protection against picking, since it takes the operator more time to pick all of the tumblers in the mechanism. The Sargent Keso mechanism and the Duo disc tumbler use this basic approach. The 12 pins in the former, and 14 (soon to be 17) discs in the high-security (UL listed) Duo take a reasonably long time to pick successfully. In addition, the unusual configurations of these tumblers make picking even more difficult.

The unusual arrangement of tumblers is also a basic security feature of Ace (tubular) mechanisms. These cannot be picked using ordinary picks, but there are special tools available that facilitate picking this lock. The Ace lock also requires special skills, but these are not too difficult to achieve once basic picking techniques have been mastered.

Modifications of pin design for increased resistance to picking (and other forms of manipulation) are becoming increasingly important as a basic means of precluding this form of attack. As shown in Fig. 25.28, mushroom, spool, and huck pins tend to bind in the pin chamber when tension is applied to the cylinder plug, preventing the key pin from reaching the shear line. The use of these pins does not provide an absolute defense against picking attempts, but a steady hand and a great deal of skill are required to pick them successfully.

Pins that must be rotated provide what is perhaps the maximum protection currently available against picking. Both the Medeco and the new Emhart interlocking mechanisms require pins to be lifted to the shear line *and* rotated to a certain position before the lock will operate. It is very, very difficult to consistently rotate these pins into the correct position. The interlocking pins on the Emhart also make it extremely difficult to pick the key pin to the shear line, since,

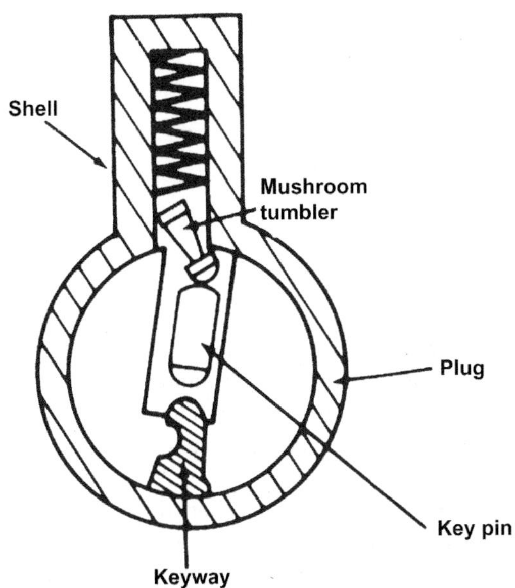

FIGURE 25.28 Mushroom and spool tumblers tend to bind in the pinhole when manipulation is attempted.

when interlocked, the two pins act as if they were one solid pin. The key pin and driver will not split at the shear line unless the pins are first rotated to the correct position.

Fewer such embellishments are possible with discs and levers. Most high-security lever locks, however, do use levers that have a front edge cut in a sawtooth design (serrated). These serrations tend to catch on the fence as it is pushed back to provide pressure on the levers. This often makes it necessary for the operator to release tension and start over again, which increases the time spent picking the lock. The use of two sets of levers with two corresponding fences also increases a lever mechanism's resistance to picking attempts.

Impressioning

Impressioning is a technique used to make a key that will operate the lock. It cannot ordinarily be used against high-security mechanisms, but against the average lock it can be very successful.

To make a key by impressioning, a correct key blank is inserted into the lock. It is then securely gripped by a wrench or pliers (there are also special tools available for this purpose), and a strong rotational tension is applied to the plug. While this tension is applied, the key is moved up and down in the keyway. Since the tumblers are tightly bound in the lock by the tension applied to the plug, they will leave marks on the blank. The longest key pin will leave the strongest impression. The key is then removed, and a slight cut is filed in the blank. The top of the key is smoothed down with a file or abrasive paper, and the key is again inserted to pick up the impression of the next longest pin. As long as the pin leaves an impression, the cut is deepened. When the pin will no longer leave a mark, the cut is at the right depth. When all of the cuts are to the right depth, the key will operate the lock and permit entry.

Certain types of lock mechanisms are more susceptible to impressioning than others. Warded locks are easily defeated by this method since the fixed wards can be made to leave strong impressions, and, as previously stated, the depth of the cut on a warded key is not critical. Lever locks are probably the most immune to this technique, since it is difficult to bind the levers in such a manner that they will leave true impressions on the key blank. The use of serrated levers greatly increases this difficulty.

The average pin and disc tumbler mechanism is vulnerable to this approach, but some of the better high-security mechanisms, because of their unusual keys, are not. The Medeco and Emhart interlocking mechanisms are highly resistant. The correct angles of the slant cuts necessary on these keys cannot be determined by impressioning. The special design of the pins in the BHI Huck-Pin cylinder makes the pins bind almost anywhere in the pinhole except at the shear line. All of the impressions that appear on the key blank are, therefore, likely to be false impressions. So, although this mechanism uses a fairly standard paracentric key, it is still very difficult to defeat by impressioning. Modified spool and mushroom tumblers in any pin tumbler mechanism also tend to increase the difficulty of getting good impression marks.

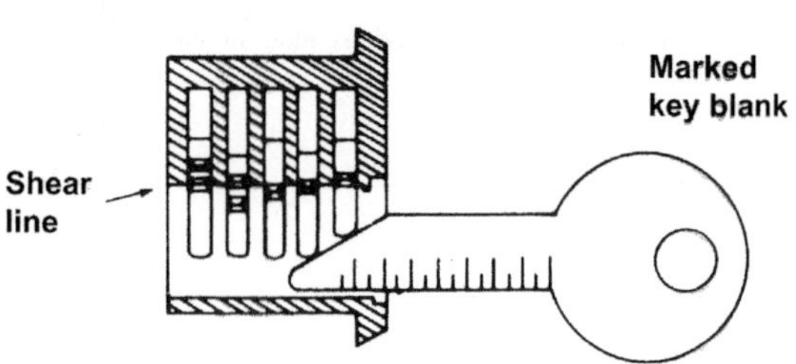

FIGURE 25.29 Decoding using a marked key blank.

Decoding

Another method of making a key for a particular lock is through decoding. It was mentioned earlier that most disc tumbler mechanisms can be sight read fairly easily. Sight reading involves the manipulation of the tumblers with a thin wire while noting their relative positions in the keyway. Since each mechanism has only a limited number of possible tumbler increments, the correct alignment of these increments can be estimated with fair accuracy, permitting a key to be filed or cut on the spot to rotate the lock. This is one method of decoding.

A more common method is to insert a decoding tool or a specially marked key blank for a short distance into the keyway of a pin or disc tumbler mechanism. Using the key, rotational tension is applied to the plug, which causes misalignment between the pin chambers in the plug and shell. The key is then slowly inserted into the keyway until it has forced the first tumbler to the shear line (Fig. 25.29). The length of this first key pin is determined by the distance the blank (or special tool) enters the keyway. The blank is then moved to the second tumbler and so on until the length of all of the tumblers is determined, and a key can be cut.

Pin tumbler cylinders having wide tolerances, which are the mechanisms that are most susceptible to this particular decoding method. Disc tumblers are less so, although most can easily be sight read. (The Duo, however, is very resistant to sight reading.) Lever locks require special equipment to decode.

The special features offered on some high-security pin tumbler systems dramatically increase their resistance to this technique. Some are almost immune. The Ace can be decoded, but it usually requires special tools. The use of mushroom or spool tumblers in almost any mechanism increases its resistance to decoding. And, of course, the close tolerances of any of the better mechanisms are a basic defense against decoding as well as impressioning and picking.

Rapping

This approach relies on the fact that pins in a tumbler mechanism can move freely in the pin chambers. Tension is applied to the plug, resulting in the usual misalignment between the core and shell pin bores. The lock is then struck with a sharp tap just above the tumblers, which causes the pins to jump in their bores. As each key pin reaches its shear line, it pushes the driver before it into the shell where it tends to bind, unable to drop back down into the plug because of the lip caused by the misalignment. Not all of the drivers will be pushed over the shear line by one rap. Several may be required.

Theoretically, almost any lock may be defeated by rapping, but in practice it is a method that is used primarily on padlocks. Since padlocks are not encased in a door, they respond more freely to rapping. Modified, manipulation-resistant pins make rapping very difficult, but not impossible; it is, nevertheless, not a practical approach to high-security padlocks, which use close tolerances and modified pins.

Shimming

Any part of a locking mechanism that relies on spring pressure to hold it in place is vulnerable to shimming unless it is protected. Spring-loaded latch bolts can be shimmed by a thin plastic or metal tool unless they are protected by antishim devices. The locking dogs in padlocks are susceptible to a shim inserted into the shackle hole. The shim acts to force the dog back against the spring pressure releasing the shackle. Padlocks that use heel and toe locking are more difficult to shim, but the safest course to use is a nonsprung, positive locking system that cannot be threatened by shimming.

Forceful attacks

If a potential intruder does not have the skills necessary to decode, impression, or pick a lock, the only course is to find a key or use force against the lock to disable and breach it. Comparatively few intruders have developed manipulative skills, so it is not surprising that the large majority of attacks on locks employ force of one kind or another. Locks can be punched, hammered, wrenched, twisted, burned, pulled, cut, exploded, and pried. Given the right tools and a sufficient amount of time, any lock can be defeated by force. But the nature of forceful attacks entails a number of real disadvantages to an intruder who is trying to gain entry without being discovered in the process. Large and cumbersome tools that are difficult to carry and conceal are often required. This is especially true if one of the better protected locks is being attacked. Second, forceful attacks usually make a considerable amount of noise; especially unusual noise tends to prompt people to investigate. Third, it is always immediately evident to even a casual observer that the lock has been attacked. When surreptitious techniques are used, the lock can be opened without damage and relocked, and no one will be able to tell that an unlawful entry has taken place. This often permits the intruder to thoroughly cover tracks even before an investigation is started.

The object of countermeasures against forceful attacks is to increase these hazards. In general, more force will have to be applied to stronger, better protected locks, requiring larger and more sophisticated tools, taking more time, making more noise, and leaving more evidence that the lock has been defeated.

While it is sometimes possible to wrench, pry, or pull an entire lock out of a door, most attacks are directed at either the bolt or the cylinder. If the bolt can be defeated, the door is open. If the cylinder can be defeated, the bolt can be maneuvered into an unlocked position. The common type of attack will be presented in the next section, along with measures that can be taken to strengthen a lock against them. It bears repeating that no lock is absolutely immune to forceful attacks. The object is to make its defeat more difficult, noisier, and more time-consuming, increasing the chances that an intruder will be detected or simply give up before successfully breaching the lock.

Attacks on bolts

Bolts can be pried, punched, and sawed. The object of these attacks is to disengage the bolt from the strike.

Jimmying and prying

A jimmy is by definition a short prying tool used by burglars. It is a traditional and well-known burglary tool; but other, more lawful, prying tools will work just as well if not better, which include pry bars, crowbars, nail pullers, and large screwdrivers.

The easiest prying attack is against latch bolts with antishim devices. A screwdriver or similar tool with a flat blade is inserted between the strike and latch bolt. Pressure is applied until the antishim mechanism inside the lock breaks. The latch is then easily pushed into the retracted position to open the door. A supplementary long-throw or interlocking dead bolt is the best defense against this attack. Noninterlocking, long-throw dead bolts are theoretically vulnerable to jimmying, but it takes a much larger tool, more time, and the destruction or spreading of part of the door jamb so that the end of the dead bolt can be reached with the prying tool. Even then, a great deal of force is required to push the bolt back into the lock and free the door. These combined disadvantages make direct jimmying attacks against long-throw dead bolts very impractical. They are even more impractical against interlocking dead bolts. If the lock and strike are properly installed, the whole strike would have to be pried loose. This would ordinarily entail the destruction of a considerable portion of the jamb around the strike.

A dead bolt also can be attacked indirectly by prying. An attempt is made to spread the doorframe so that the bolt is no longer engaging the strike (Fig. 25.30). An average man can apply about 600 in.-lb of force using a pry bar 30 in. long. This is usually more than enough to spread a door jamb to clear the normal 72 in. bolt, but a 1 in. (or longer) bolt is more difficult to clear. Interlocking bolts are almost impossible to defeat with this method since they, in effect, anchor the door to the doorframe. To spread the frame the entire strike would have to be pried out. A properly installed security strike is very difficult to remove. Interlocking dead bolts were designed to resist just this type of attack. By and large, they are successful. When properly installed they are, as a practical matter, virtually immune.

Automobile bumper jacks (or similar tools) can also be used to spread a door jamb and release the bolt (Fig. 25.31). Most American jacks are rated at 1 ton. It is probably safe to say that most wooden doorframes will succumb to that much force. Reinforced metal frames are more resistant. Long-throw and interlocking dead bolts provide some protection. They may even provide enough protection in most circumstances, since a jamb can only be spread so far by the jack before it buckles outward releasing the jack. The best defense against jamb spreading, however, is a properly constructed and reinforced doorframe.

Fortunately, this type of attack is fairly rare. An automobile jack is an awkward tool, hard to carry and conceal and requires some time to set up and operate.

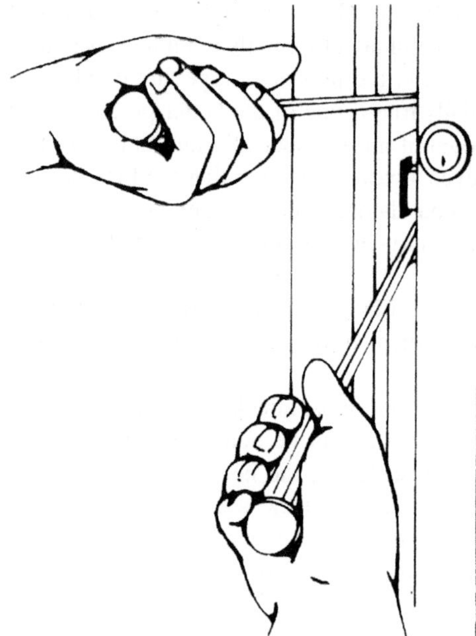

FIGURE 25.30 Jamb spreading by prying with two large screwdrivers.

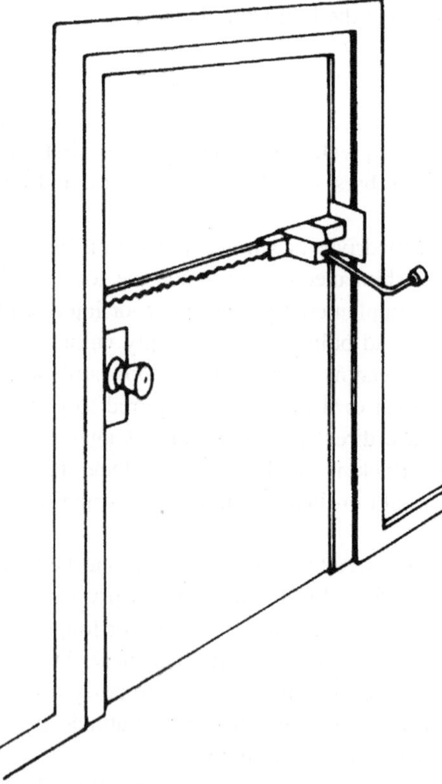

FIGURE 25.31 Use of an automobile bumper jack to spread the doorframe. Standard bumper jacks are rated to 2000 lb. The force of the jack can be applied between the two jambs of a door to spread them and overcome, by deflection, the length of the latch throw.

Punching

The California Crime Technological Research Foundation (CCTRF) identified punching as a possible direct attack on a dead bolt (Fig. 25.32). The attacker would have to punch through the wall and framing members to reach the bolt. It would be fairly easy to miss the bolt on the first few tries, so several attempts may be necessary. In essence, the punch and hammer are used to force the bolt back into the body of the lock, allowing it to clear the strike. CCTRF determined that an average man can apply a force of 125 in.-lb with a 1 lb hammer.

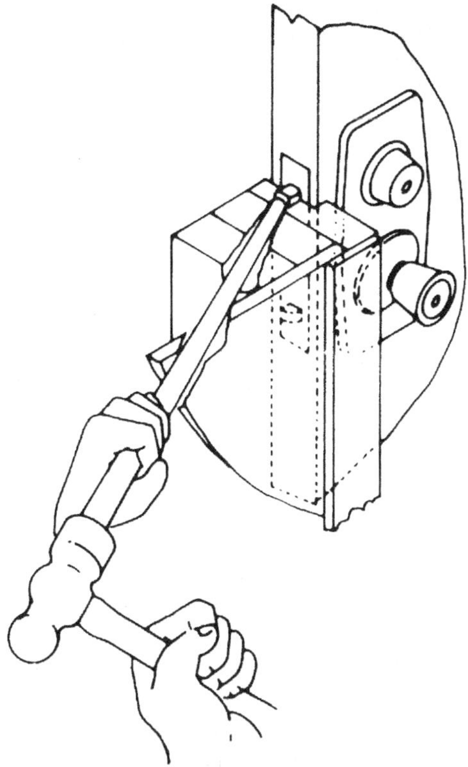

FIGURE 25.32 Forcing the dead bolt with a drift punch and hammer.

Most bolts will probably succumb to a determined punching attack. But it is a noisy approach, and rather hit or miss since it is somewhat difficult to tell if the punch is actually engaging the bolt, and the punch has a tendency to be a serious disadvantage to an intruder, making this an attack of last resort.

Sawing

Bolts can be sawed by inserting a hacksaw or hacksaw blade between the face plate and the strike. (A portion of the jamb will usually be removed or the jamb spread to allow easy access.) Better locks now use hardened bolts or hardened inserts inside the bolt to resist sawing. An even better defense is free-wheeling rollers placed inside the bolt. When the saw reaches these rollers, the sawing action rolls them back and forth but will not cut them. Modified bolts are present in almost all relatively secure locks, and they are virtually immune to sawing attacks.

Peeling

Another way to expose the bolt in metal-framed doors is by peeling. Thin sheet steel and aluminum can be easily peeled. The normal countermeasure against this attack is to use a reinforced strike. Peeling may also be used with prying in an attempt to force the bolt back into the lock.

Attacks on cylinders

Like bolts, cylinders can be pried and punched and also drilled, pulled, wrenched, or twisted. The usual objective of such attacks is to completely remove the cylinder from the lock. Once it has been removed, a tool can be inserted into the lock to quickly retract the bolt.

Cylinder pulling

The tool usually used for cylinder pulling is a slam hammer or dent puller—a common automobile body shop tool ordinarily used to remove dents from car bodies. The hardened self-tapping screw at the end of the puller is screwed into the keyway as far as it will go. The hammer is then slammed back against the handle. More often than not, an

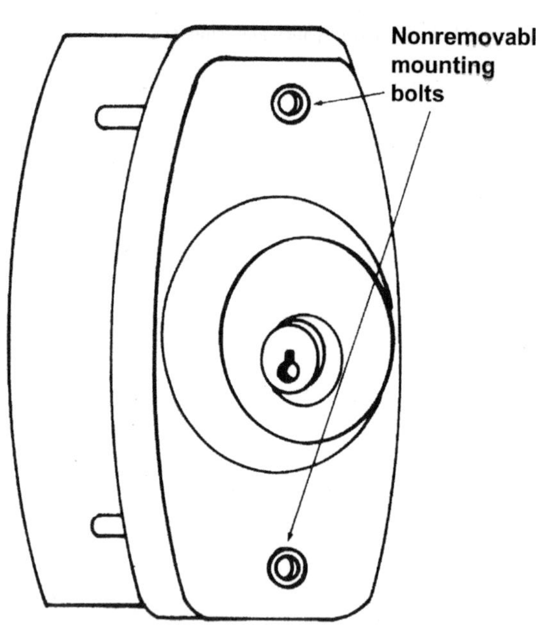

FIGURE 25.33 Bolt-on cylinder guard with back plate. This commercially available plate is of heavy aluminum and is mounted from the inside of the door with hardened steel bolts that enter threaded holes in the guard. It combines good protection with good appearance.

unprotected cylinder will be yanked entirely out of the lock with one or two slams. CCTRF determined that 200 in.-lb of force could be applied to a cylinder by a dent puller using a 2.5 lb hammer having an 8 in. throw.

Many cylinders are vulnerable to this kind of attack because they are poorly anchored in the lock. Mortise cylinders, for example, are ordinarily threaded into the housing and held in place with a small set screw. The threads are usually soft brass or cast iron. A good yank shears both these threads and the set screw.

Most tubular and rim cylinders are held in place by two (or more) bolts inserted from the rear of the lock. This is a much more secure method of retaining the cylinder and one that resists pulling. Retaining bolts of at least 1/4 in. in diameter made of hardened steel are good protection against most pulling attempts.

The threat of pulling can be significantly reduced by the addition of a cylinder guard. Some better lock assemblies are offered with built-in guards. Locks that do not have a built-in guard can be protected with a bolt-on guard. These are bolted over the cylinder using carriage bolts that extend completely through the door (Fig. 25.33). They offer the maximum available resistance to pulling. The cylinder guard, when correctly mounted, cannot be pried off without virtually destroying the entire door.

Cylindrical (lock-in-knob) locksets are extremely vulnerable to pulling. Often the door knob will be pulled off with the cylinder, exposing the entire internal mechanism to manipulation. There is no method of reinforcing a cylindrical lockset against the threat of pulling. The best measure is to replace it or add a good supplementary deadlock with a cylinder guard.

Lug pulling

If the cylinder is protected against pulling, an attacker may turn to the cylinder plug. The plug is much harder to pull, which requires a special tool that looks something like a gear puller. A hardened self-tapping screw is engaged in the keyway and pressure is slowly exerted on the plug until the tumblers snap and the plug can be pulled from the cylinder shell. The bolt mechanism can then be operated by a tool inserted through the shell. The ordinary cylinder guard is no protection against this attack. A special guard is available, however, which is designed to prevent the plug from being pulled (see Fig. 25.34).

Wrenching, twisting, and nipping

Most cylinders project from the surface of the door sufficiently to be gripped by a pipe wrench or pliers. Twisting force is applied to the cylinder by the wrench, which is often sufficient to snap or shear the set screws or bolts that hold the cylinder in the lock. If the cylinder does not project enough for a wrench to be used, a ground-down screwdriver can be inserted in the keyway and twisting force applied to the screwdriver with a wrench. CCTRF found that an 18 in. long

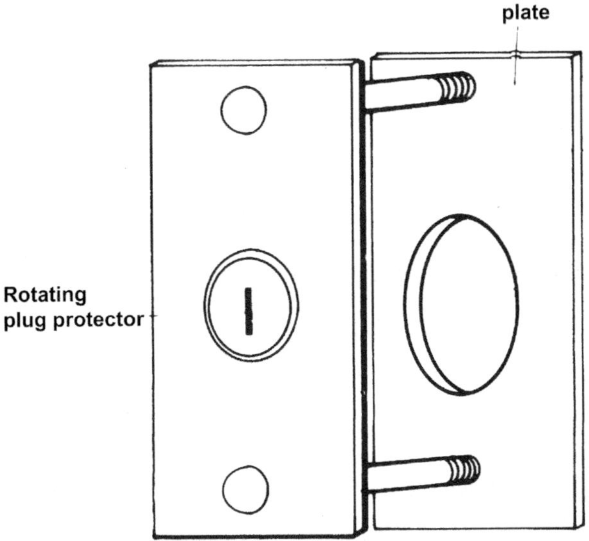

FIGURE 25.34 Cylinder guard with rotating plug protector.

pipe wrench could apply a maximum torque of 3300 in.-lb to a protruding cylinder housing, and a screwdriver turned with a wrench could produce 600 in.-lb.

The proper protection against this threat once again is a cylinder guard. Some of the built-in guards are free-wheeling, which prevents a twisting force from being successfully applied. Those that are not free-wheeling are still made of hardened steel, which does not allow the wrench to get a good bite; but more importantly, it prevents the wrench from reaching the actual cylinder. If a screwdriver and wrench are used, the cylinder might be twisted loose, but it cannot be pulled out. Although the lock might be damaged, it will not be defeated.

Bolt nippers also can be used to remove protruding cylinders by prying and pulling. Cylinder guards also forestall this type of attack.

Cylindrical locksets are very susceptible to wrenching, twisting, and nipping attacks. Some of the better cylindrical devices have free-wheeling door knobs that provide some protection against wrenching and twisting. Some incorporate breakaway knobs, which do not expose the internal mechanism of the lock when the knob is twisted off. Nevertheless, combinations of twisting, pulling, and hammering attacks usually quickly defeat these devices. The best remedy is to replace cylindrical mechanisms or supplement them with guarded deadlocks.

Drilling

Cylinder plugs can be drilled out using a fairly large drill bit, but the most common drilling attack is centered on the shear line between the plug and shell (Fig. 25.35). A smaller bit is used to drill through the pins, creating a new shear line and releasing the plug, which can then be rotated using a screwdriver or key blank in the keyway. Most of the better locks incorporate hardened inserts to frustrate drilling. Any lock receiving UL approval incorporates these features. Hardened materials do not prevent drilling, but drilling through tempered steel is a long and slow process, which greatly increases the chances of detection.

BHI's Huck-Pin cylinder has an added protection against drilling. When most cylinders are drilled at the shear line, the drivers will fall out of the shell into the plug, releasing the plug to rotate. BHI's drivers are flanged, which prevents them from falling out, so they still effectively lock the mechanism after it is drilled. This does not prevent the entire cylinder from being drilled out, but this is an even longer and slower process than drilling along the shear line.

Punching

Rim-mounted deadlocks are particularly vulnerable to punching. These are ordinarily mounted on the back of a door with wood screws. But, since most of the currently available doors are made with particle board cores under a thin veneer overlay, screws are seldom able to take much pressure. Several good blows with a hammer and punch on the face of the cylinder will often drive it through the door, pulling the screws out, so the entire lock body is dislodged.

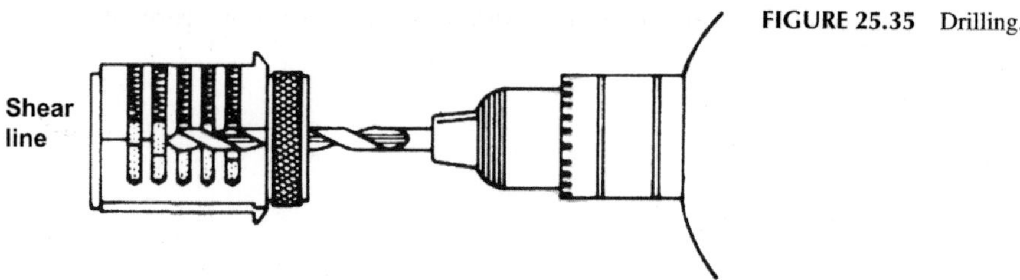

FIGURE 25.35 Drilling.

Correctly mounting the lock using bolts that extend through the door and engage an escutcheon plate (or even large washers) on the front side generally frustrates punching attacks.

Cylindrical locksets are vulnerable to combination punching and hammering attacks. The knob is first broken off, then the spindle is punched through the lock, exposing the latch bolt assembly to manipulation.

Hammering

Hammering, as well as pulling, wrenching, and twisting, is a quick and very effective way to disable cylindrical locksets. It is not as effective against cylinders, particularly those that are protected by cylinder guards. Ordinarily the knob on a cylindrical mechanism can be quickly broken off by one or two strong blows. There is no direct defense against this type of attack. Again, the only viable solution is a supplementary guarded deadlock, or replacement of the cylindrical lockset with a more secure lock.

Locks and the systems approach to security

Locks are an essential part of most security systems. They are, however, only one part. The effectiveness of a lock cannot be considered apart from the effectiveness of the entire system. A lock is no better than the door it is on, or the frame in which the door is mounted. The strongest lock available on a substandard door does not prevent the door from being defeated, even though the lock cannot be.

The degree of protection required from any security system reflects the value of the items to be protected. Most residences require only a modest degree of security—sufficient to thwart the casual or opportunistic intruder. Jewelry stores, banks, and other establishments, which must keep valuable items on the premises, attract a more determined attacker. The degree of protection for these places must, therefore, necessarily be greater. But whatever the degree of protection required, the actual protection offered by any system is no greater than the vulnerability of its weakest member. A good lock on a poor door does not provide more protection than the strength of the door. A good lock on a solid door in a substandard wall is as vulnerable as the wall is weak.

The locks employed in any protection system must complement the system. If a moderate degree of security is required (as in a residential application), a good cylinder properly installed in a secure lock body must be correctly mounted on a good, solid door. The door must be correctly hung, using good hardware, on a properly constructed doorframe that must be strongly braced and secured to the wall. The wall must be at least as strong as the door system installed in it. If the lock, the door, the frame, or the wall is significantly weaker than the rest of the system, it is the point most likely to be successfully attacked.

A good lock is essential to a good security system. It is often the point at which an intruder will focus an attack. But good locks are not synonymous with good security. Always examine the system as a whole.

Appendix 25.A Key control[2]

Eugene D. Finneran

Before an effective key control system can be established, every key to every lock that is being used in the protection of the facility and property must be accounted for. Chances are good that it will not even be possible to account for the most critical keys or to be certain that they have not been copied or compromised. If this is the case, there is but one alternative—rekey the entire facility.

2. Originally from Finneran, E.D., 1981. Security Supervision: A Handbook for Supervisors and Managers. Butterworths, Stoneham, MA.

Once an effective locking system has been installed, positive control of all keys must be gained and maintained. This can be accomplished only if an effective key record is kept. When not issued or used, keys must be adequately secured. A good, effective key control system is simple to initiate, particularly if it is established in conjunction with the installation of new locking devices. Some of the methods used to gain and maintain effective key control are outlined:

1. *Key cabinet.* A well-constructed cabinet will have to be procured. The cabinet will have to be of sufficient size to hold the original key to every lock in the system. It should also be capable of holding any additional keys that are in use in the facility but are not a part of the security locking system. The cabinet should be installed in such a manner so as to be difficult, if not impossible, to remove from the property. It should be secured at all times when the person designated to control the keys is not actually issuing or replacing a key. The key to the key cabinet must receive special handling, and when not in use it should be maintained in a locked compartment inside a combination-type safe.
2. *Key record.* Some administrative means must be set up to record key code numbers and indicate to whom keys to specific locks have been issued. This record may take the form of a ledger book or a card file.
3. *Key blanks.* Blanks used to cut keys for issue to authorized personnel must be distinctively marked for identification to ensure that no employees have cut their own keys. Blanks will be kept within a combination-type safe and issued only to the person authorized to cut keys and then only in the amount that has been authorized by the person responsible for key control. Such authorization should always be in writing, and records should be maintained on each issue, which will be matched with the returned key. Keys damaged in the cutting process must be returned for accountability.
4. *Inventories.* Periodic inventories will have to be made of all key blanks, original keys, and all duplicate keys in the hands of the employees to whom they have been issued. This cannot be permitted to take the form of a phone call to an employee, supervisor, or executive asking if they still have their key. It must be a personal inspection of each key made by the person who has been assigned responsibility for key control.
5. *Audits.* In addition to the periodic inventory, an unannounced audit should be made of all key control records and procedures by a member of management. During the course of these audits a joint inventory of all keys should be conducted.
6. *Daily report.* A daily report should be made to the person responsible for key control from the personnel department, indicating all persons who have left or will be leaving the employ of the company in the near future. A check should be made, upon receipt of this report, to determine whether the person named has been issued a key to any lock in the system. In the event a key has been issued, steps should be initiated to ensure that the key is recovered.

Security force personnel will normally be issued master keys, when such a system is in effect, or they will be issued a ring of keys permitting them to enter any part of the guarded facility. Keys issued to the security force should never be permitted to leave the facility. They should be passed from shift to shift and must be receipted for each time they change hands. The supervisor must ensure that all security personnel understand the importance of not permitting keys to be compromised.

A lost master key compromises the entire system and results in a breakdown of the security screen. Such compromise will necessitate the rekeying of the entire complex, sometimes at a cost of thousands of dollars.

If rekeying becomes necessary, it can most economically be accomplished by installing new locking devices in the most critical points of the locking system and moving the locks removed from these points to less sensitive areas. Of course, it will be necessary to eventually replace all of the locks in the system, but by using the procedure just described the cost can be spread over several budgeting periods.

New standard set for exit devices, locks, and alarms (Security Beat, 2002)

The Builders' Hardware Manufacturer's Association (BHMA) has announced a new American National Standard for exit locks and exit alarms for the safety and security of building occupants.

Developed by BHMA, the new standard was recently approved by the American National Standards Institute (ANSI).

In effect, the new standard recognizes the increased importance of locks, alarms, and other devices that control egress from a building. The standard establishes general requirements as well as operational tests and finish tests for these products. In addition, it gives descriptions and type numbers of exit locks and exit alarms.

Revisions include increased performance requirements with respect to the recommended tests and a slam test not part of the earlier standards has been added. Testing of products in accordance with this standard allows for certification to the ANSI/BHMA standard to be established by third-party testing laboratories.

For more information, or to purchase copies of the ANSI/BHMA A156.29 Standard, please visit http://www.buildershardware.com.

Reference

Security Beat, February 19, 2002. [weekly newsletter by publisher of Access Control and Security Systems] 2, no. 7.

Appendix 25.B Key control and lock security checklist[3]

John E. Hunter

1. Has a key control officer been appointed?
2. Are locks and keys to all buildings and entrances supervised and controlled by the key control officer?
3. Does the key control officer have overall authority and responsibility for issuance and replacement of locks and keys?
4. What is the basis for the issuance of keys, especially master keys?
5. Are keys issued only to authorized personnel? Who determines who is authorized? Is the authorization in writing?
6. Are keys issued to other than installation personnel? If so, on what basis? Is it out of necessity or merely for convenience?
7. Are keys not in use secured in a locked, fireproof cabinet? Are these keys tagged and accounted for?
8. Is the cabinet for duplicate keys regarded as an area of high security?
9. Is the key or combination to this cabinet maintained under appropriate security or secrecy? If the combination is recorded, is it secured?
10. Are the key locker and record files in order and current?
11. Are issued keys cross-referenced?
12. Are current records maintained indicate the following:
    - a. Buildings and/or entrances for which keys are issued?
    - b. Number and identification of keys issued?
    - c. Location and number of duplicate keys?
    - d. Issue and turn in of key?
    - e. Location of locks and keys held in reserve?
13. Is an audit ever made, asking holders to actually produce keys, to ensure that they have not been loaned or lost?
14. Who is responsible for ascertaining the possession of key?
15. Is a current key control directive in effect?
16. Are inventories and inspections conducted by the key control officer to ensure compliance with directives? How often?
17. Are keys turned in during vacation periods?
18. Are keys turned in when employees resign, are transferred, or are fired?
19. Is the removal of keys from the premises prohibited when they are not needed elsewhere?
20. Are locks and combinations changed immediately upon loss or theft of keys or transfer or resignation of employees?
21. Are locks changed or rotated within the installation at least annually regardless of transfers or known violations of key security?
22. Are current records kept of combinations to safes and the dates when these combinations are changed? Are these records adequately protected?
23. Has a system been set up to provide submasters to supervisors and officials on a need basis with facilities divided into different zones or areas?
24. If master keys are used, are they devoid of marking identifying them as master keys?
25. Are master keys controlled more closely than change keys?

3. Prepared by Hunter, J.E. U.S. National Park Service.

26. Must all requests for reproduction or duplication of keys be approved by the key control officer?
27. Are key holders ever allowed to duplicate keys? If so, under what circumstances?
28. Where the manufacturer's serial number on combination locks and padlocks might be visible to unauthorized persons? Has this number been recorded and then obliterated?
29. Are locks on inactive gates and storage facilities under seal? Are seals checked regularly by supervisory or key control personnel?
30. Are measures in effect to prevent the unauthorized removal of locks on open cabinets, gates, or buildings?
31. Are losses or thefts of keys and padlocks promptly reported by personnel and promptly investigated by key control personnel?
32. If the building was recently constructed, did the contractor retain keys during the period when construction was being completed? Were locks changed since that time? Did the contractor relinquish all keys after the building was completed?
33. If removable core locks are in use, are unused cores and core change keys given maximum security against theft, loss, or inspection?
34. Are combination lock, key, and key control records safeguarded separately (i.e., in a separate safe or file) from keys, locks, cores, and other such hardware?
35. Are all locks of a type that offer adequate protection for the purpose for which they are used?

Appendix 25.C Terms and definitions for door and window security[4]

access control a method of providing security by restricting the movement of persons into or within a protected area.

accessible window (1) residential—any window located within 3.7 m (12 ft.) of grade or a building projection. (2) Commercial—any window located within 4.6 m (18 ft.) of grade or within 3 m (10 ft.) of any fire escape or other structure accessible from public or semipublic areas.

accordion gate see *sliding metal gate.*

ace lock a type of pin tumbler lock in which the pins are installed in a circle around the axis of the cylinder and move perpendicularly to the face of the cylinder. The shear line of the driver and bottom tumblers is a plane parallel to the face of the cylinder. This type of lock is operated with a push key.

active door (or leaf) the leaf of a double door that must be opened first. It is used in normal pedestrian traffic. This leaf is usually the one in which a lock is installed.

anchor a device used to secure a buildings part or component to adjoining construction or to a supporting member. See also *floor anchor, jamb anchor,* and *stud anchor.*

antifriction latch a latch bolt that incorporates any device that reduces the closing friction between the latch and the strike.

applied trim a separately applied molding used as the finishing face trim of a frame.

apron the flat member of a window trim placed against the wall immediately beneath the windowsill.

architectural hardware see *finish builders' hardware.*

areaway an open subsurface space adjacent to a building that is used to admit light or to provide a means of access to the building.

armored front a plate or plates secured to the lock front of a mortised lock by machine screws in order to provide protection against tampering with the cylinder set screws. Also called *armored face plate.*

astragal a member fixed to, or a projection of, an edge of a door or window to cover the joint between the meeting of stiles; usually fixed to one of a pair of swinging doors to provide a seal against the passage of weather, light, noise, or smoke.

auxiliary lock a lock installed on a door or window to supplement a previously installed primary lock. Also called a *secondary lock.* It can be a mortised, bored, or rim lock.

back plate a metal plate on the inside of a door that is used to clamp a pin or disc tumbler rim lock cylinder to the door by means of retaining screws. The tail piece of the cylinder extends through a hole in the back plate.

backset, flush bolt the distance from the vertical centerline of the lock edge of a door to the centerline of the bolt.

backset, hinge on a door the distance from the stop face to the edge of the hinge cutout. On a frame the distance from the stop to the edge of the hinge cutout.

backset, lock the horizontal distance from the vertical centerline of the face plate to the center of the lock cylinder keyway or knob spindle.

backset, strike the distance from the door stop to the edge of the strike cutout.

baffle see *guard plate.*

balanced door a door equipped with double-pivoted hardware designed to cause a semicounterbalanced swing action when it is opened.

barrel key a key with a bit projecting from a round, hollow key shank that fits on a post in the lock.

4. Reprinted courtesy United States Department of Commerce, National Bureau of Standards.

barricade bolt a massive metal bar that engages large strikes on both sides of a door. Barricade bolts are available with locking devices, and are completely removed from the door when not in use.

bead see *glazing bead.*

bevel (of a door) the angle of the lock edge of the door in relation to its face. The standard bevel is 0.32 cm in 5.1 cm (1/8″ in 2″).

bevel (of a latch bolt) a term used to indicate the direction in which a latch bolt is inclined: regular bevel for doors opening in, reverse bevel for doors opening out.

bevel (of lock front) the angle of a lock front when not at a right angle to the lock case, allowing the front to be applied flush with the edge of a beveled door.

bicentric pin tumbler cylinder a cylinder having two cores and two sets of pins, each having different combinations. This cylinder requires two separate keys, used simultaneously, to operate it. The cam or tail piece is gear operated.

bit a blade projecting from a key shank that engages with and actuates the bolt or level tumblers of a lock.

bit key a key with a bit projecting from a round shank. Similar to the barrel key but with a solid rather than hollow shank.

bitting see *cut.*

blank an uncut key or an unfinished key as it comes from the manufacturer, before any cuts have been made on it.

blind stop a rectangular molding, located between the outside trim and outside sashes, used in the assembly of a window frame. Serves as a stop for storm, screen, or combination windows and to resist air infiltration.

bolt that part of a lock which, when actuated, is projected (or "thrown") from the lock into a retaining member, such as a strike plate, to prevent a door or window from moving or opening. See also *dead bolt, flush bolt,* and *latch.*

bolt attack a category of burglary attack in which force, with or without the aid of tools, is directed against the bolt in an attempt to disengage it from the strike or to break it.

bolt projection (bolt throw) the distance from the edge of the door, at the bolt centerline, to the furthest point on the bolt in the projected position.

bored lock (or latch) a lock or latch, the parts of which are intended for installation in holes bored in a door. See also *key-in-knob lock.*

bottom pin one of a number of pin tumblers that determines the combination of a pin tumbler cylinder and is directly contacted by the key. These are varied in length and usually tapered at one end, enabling them to fit into the "V" cuts made in a key. When the proper key is inserted, the bottom pins level off at the cylinder core shear line, allowing the core to turn and actuate the lock.

bottom rail the horizontal rail at the bottom of a door or window connecting the vertical edge members (stiles).

box strike a strike plate that has a metal box or housing to fully enclose the projected bolt and/or latch.

breakaway strike see *electric strike.*

buck see *rough buck.*

builders' hardware all hardware used in building construction, but particularly that used on or in connection with doors, windows, cabinets, and other moving members.

bumping a method of opening a pin tumbler lock by means of vibration produced by a wooden or rubber mallet.

burglar-resistant glazing any glazing that is more difficult to break through than the common window or plate glass, designed to resist burglary attacks of the hit-and-run type.

butt hinge a type of hinge that has matching rectangular leaves and multiple bearing contacts, and is designed to be mounted in mortises in the door edge and in the frame.

buttress lock a lock that secures a door by wedging a bar between the door and the floor. Some incorporate a movable steel rod, which fits into metal receiving slots on the door and in the floor. Also called *police bolt/brace.*

cabinet jamb a doorframe in three or more pieces, usually shipped knocked down for field assembly over a rough buck.

cam the part of a lock or cylinder that rotates to actuate the bolt or latch as the key is turned. The cam may also act as the bolt.

cam, lazy a cam that moves less than the rotation of the cylinder core.

cam lock see *crescent sash lock.*

cane bolt a heavy cane-shaped bolt with the top bent at right angles; used on the bottom of doors.

case the housing in which a lock mechanism is mounted and enclosed.

casement hinge a hinge for swinging a casement window.

casement window a type of window that is hinged on the vertical edge.

casing molding of various widths and thicknesses used to trim door and window openings at the jambs.

center-hung door a door hung on center pivots.

center rail the horizontal rail in a door, usually located at lock height to separate the upper and lower panels of a recessed panel type door.

chain bolt a vertical spring-loaded bolt mounted at the top of door. It is manually actuated by a chain.

chain door interviewer an auxiliary locking device that allows a door to be opened slightly but restrains it from being fully opened. It consists of chain with one end attached to the door jamb and the other attached to a keyed metal piece that slides in a slotted metal plate attached to the door. Some chain door interviewers incorporate a keyed lock operated from the inside.

change key a key that will operate only one lock or a group of keyed-alike locks, as distinguished from a master key. See also *keyed-alike cylinders* and *master key system.*

changes the number of possible key changes or combination changes to a lock cylinder.

checkrails the meeting rails of double-hung windows. They are usually beveled and thick enough to fill the space between the top and bottom sash due to the parting stop in the window frame.

clearance a space intentionally provided between components to facilitate operation or installation, to ensure proper separation, to accommodate dimensional variations, or for other reasons. See also *door clearance*.

clevis a metal link used to attach a chain to a padlock.

code an arrangement of numbers or letters used to specify a combination for the bitting of a key or the pins of a cylinder core.

combination (1) the sequence and depth of cuts on a key. (2) The sequence of numbers to which a combination lock is set.

combination doors or windows storm doors or windows permanently installed over the primary doors or windows. They provide insulation and summer ventilation and often have self-storing or removable glass and screen inserts.

common entry door (of a multiple dwelling) any door in a multiple dwelling that provides access between the semipublic, interior areas of the building, and the out-of-door areas surrounding the building.

communicating frame a double-rabbeted frame with both rabbets prepared for single-swing doors that open in opposite directions. Doors may be of the same or opposite hand.

component a subassembly that is combined with other components to make an entire system. Door assembly components include the door, lock hinges, jamb/strike, and jamb/wall.

composite door a door constructed of a solid-core material with facing and edges of different materials.

connecting bar a flat metal bar attached to the core of a cylinder lock to operate the bolt mechanism.

construction master keying a keying system used to allow the use of a single key for all locks during the construction of large housing projects. In one such system, the cylinder cores of all locks contain an insert that permits the use of a special master key. When the dwelling unit is completed, the insert is removed and the lock then accepts its own change key and no longer accepts the construction master key.

continuous hinge a hinge designed to be the same length as the edge of the moving part to which it is applied. Also called a *piano hinge.*

coordinator a mechanism that controls the order of closing of a pair of swing doors and used with overlapping astragals and certain panic hardware that require that one door close ahead of the other.

core see *cylinder core.*

crash bar the crossbar or level of a panic exit device that serves as push bar to actuate the lock. See also *panic hardware*.

cremone bolt a surface-mounted device that locks a door or sash into the frame at both the top and bottom when a knob or lever is turned.

crescent sash lock a simple cam-shaped latch that does not require a key for its operation; usually used to secure double-hung windows. Also called a *cam lock.*

cut an indentation made in a key to make it fit a pin tumbler of a lock. Any notch made in a key is known as a cut, whether it is square, round, or V-shaped. Also called *bitting.*

cylinder the cylindrical subassembly of a lock, including the cylinder housing, the cylinder core, the tumbler mechanism, and the keyway.

cylinder collar see *cylinder guard ring.*

cylinder core (or plug) the central part of a cylinder, containing the keyway, which is rotated to operate the lock bolt.

cylinder guard ring a hardened metal ring, surrounding the exposed portion of a lock cylinder, which protects the cylinder from being wrenched, turned, pried, cut, or pulled with attack tools.

cylinder housing the external case of a lock cylinder. Also called the *cylinder shell.*

cylinder lock a lock in which the locking mechanism is controlled by a cylinder. A double-cylinder lock has a cylinder on both the interior and exterior of the door.

cylinder, mortise type a lock cylinder that has a threaded housing which screws directly into the lock case, with a cam or other mechanism engaging the locking mechanism.

cylinder, removable core a cylinder, the core of which may be removed by the use of a special key.

cylinder, rim type a lock cylinder that is held in place by tension against its rim, applied by screws from the interior face of the door.

cylinder ring see *cylinder guard ring.*

cylinder screw a set screw that holds a mortise cylinder in place and prevents it from being turned after installation.

cylindrical lock (or latch) see *bored lock.*

dead bolt a lock bolt that does not have an automatic spring action and a beveled end as opposed to a latch bolt, which does. The bolt must be actuated to a projected position by a key or thumb turn and when projected is locked against return by end pressure.

deadlatch a spring-actuated latch bolt with a beveled end and incorporating a feature that automatically locks the projected latch bolt against return by end pressure.

deadlock a lock equipped with a dead bolt.

deadlocking latch bolt see *deadlatch.*

disc tumbler a spring-loaded, flat plate that slides in a slot that runs through the diameter of the cylinder. Inserting the proper key lines up the disc tumblers with the lock's shear line and enables the core to be turned.

dogging device a mechanism that fastens the crossbar of a panic exit device in the fully depressed position, and retains the latch bolt or bolts in the retracted position to permit free operation of the door from either side.

dogging key a key-type wrench used to lock down, in the open position, the crossbar of a panic exit device.

door assembly a unit composed of parts or components that make up a closure for a passageway through a wall. It consists of the door, hinges, locking device or devices, operational contacts (such as handles, knobs, and push plates), miscellaneous hardware and closure, the frame including the head and jambs, the anchorage devices to the surrounding wall, and the surrounding wall.

door bolt a rod or bar manually operated without a key attached to a door to provide a means of securing it.

door check/closer a device used to control the closing of a door by means of a spring and hydraulic or air pressure or by electrical means.

door clearance the space between a door and its frame or the finished floor or threshold, or between the two doors of a double door. See also *clearance.*

doorframe an assembly of members surrounding and supporting a door or doors, and perhaps also one or more transom lights and/or sidelights. See also *integral frame.*

door jambs the two vertical components of a doorframe called the hinge jamb and the lock jamb.

door light see *light.*

door opening the size of a doorway, measured from jamb to jamb and from floor line or sill to head of frame. The opening size is usually the nominal door size, and is equal to the actual door size plus clearances and threshold height.

door stop the projections along the top and sides of a doorframe against which a one-way swinging door closes. See also *rabbeted jamb.*

double-acting door a swinging door equipped with hardware that permits it to open in either direction.

double-bitted key a key having cuts on two sides.

double-cylinder lock see *cylinder lock.*

double door a pair of doors mounted together in a single opening. See also *active door* and *inactive door.*

double egress frame a doorframe prepared to receive two single-acting doors swinging in opposite directions; both doors are the same hand.

double glazing two thicknesses of glass, separated by an air space and framed in an opening, designed to reduce heat transfer or sound transmission. In factory-made double glazing units, referred to as insulating glass, the air space between the glass sheets is desiccated and sealed airtight.

double-hung window a type of window, composed of upper and lower sashes that slide vertically.

double-throw bolt a bolt that can be projected beyond its first position, into a second, or fully extended one.

double-throw lock a lock incorporating a double-throw bolt.

driver pin one of the pin tumblers in a pin tumbler cylinder lock, usually flat on both ends, which are in line with and push against the flat ends of the bottom pins. They are projected by individual coil springs into the cylinder core until they are forced from the core by the bottom pins when the proper key is inserted into the keyway.

drop ring a ring handle attached to the spindle that operates a lock or latch. The ring is pivoted to remain in a dropped position when not in use.

dry glazing a method of securing glass in a frame by use of a performed resilient gasket.

drywall frame a knocked down (KD) doorframe for installation in a wall constructed with studs and gypsum board or other drywall facing material after the wall is erected.

dummy cylinder a mock cylinder without an operating mechanism, used for appearance only.

dummy trim trim only, without lock; usually used on the inactive door in a double door.

Dutch door a door consisting of two separate leaves, one above the other, which may be operated either independently or together. The lower leaf usually has a service shelf.

Dutch door bolt a device for locking together the upper and lower leaves of a Dutch door.

dwelling unit entry door any door giving access to a private dwelling unit.

electric strike an electrically operated device that replaces a conventional strike plate and allows a door to be opened by using electric switches at remote locations.

escutcheon plate a surface-mounted cover plate, protective or ornamental, containing openings for any or all of the controlling members of a lock such as the knob, handle, cylinder, or keyhole.

exit device see *panic hardware.*

expanded metal an open mesh formed by slitting and drawing a metal sheet. It is made in various patterns and metal thicknesses with a flat or an irregular surface.

exterior private area the ground area outside a single family house, or a ground floor apartment in the case of a multiple dwelling, which is fenced off by a real barrier and is available for the use of one family and is accessible only from the interior of that family's unit.

exterior public area the ground area outside a multiple dwelling, which is not defined as being associated with the building or building entry in any real or symbolic fashion.

exterior semiprivate area the ground area outside a multiple dwelling, which is fenced off by a real barrier, and is accessible only from the private or semiprivate zones within the building.

exterior semipublic area the ground area outside a single family house or multiple dwelling, which is accessible from public zones, but is defined as belonging to the house or building by symbolic barriers only.

Face (of a lock) see *face plate.*

face glazing a method of glazing in which the glass is set in an L-shaped or rabbeted frame. The glazing compound is finished off in the form of a triangular bead, and no lose stops are employed.

face plate the part of a mortise lock through which the bolt protrudes and by which the lock is fastened to the door.

fast pin hinge a hinge in which the pin is fastened permanently in place.

fatigue structural failure of a material caused by repeated or fluctuating application of stresses, none of which is individually sufficient to cause failure.

fence a metal pin that extends from the bolt of a lever lock and prevents retraction of the bolt unless it is aligned with the gates of the lever tumblers.

fidelity loss a property loss resulting from a theft in which the thief leaves no evidence of entry.

filler plate a metal plate used to fill unwanted mortise cutouts in a door or frame.

finish builders' hardware hardware that has a finished appearance as well as a functional purpose and may be considered part of the decorative treatment of a room or building. Also called *finish hardware* and *builders' finish hardware*.

fire stair any enclosed stairway that is part of a fire-resistant exitway.

fire stair door a door forming part of the fire-resistant fire stair enclosure and providing access from common corridors to fire stair landings within an exitway.

floor anchor a metal device attached to the wall side of a jamb at its base to secure the frame to the floor.

floor clearance the width of the space between the bottom of a door and the rough or finished floor or threshold.

flush bolt a door bolt designed that, when installed, the operating handle is flush with the face or edge of the door. Usually installed at the top and bottom of the inactive door of a double door.

flush door a smooth-surface door having faces that are plain and conceal its rails and stiles or other structure.

foot bolt a type of bolt applied at the bottom of a door and arranged for foot operation. In general, the bolt head is held up by a spring when the door is unbolted.

forced entry an unauthorized entry accomplished by the use of force upon the physical components of the premises.

frame the component that forms the opening of and provides support for a door, windows, skylight, or hatchway. See also *doorframe*.

frame gasket resilient material in strip form attached to frame stops to provide tight closure of a door or window.

front (of a lock) see *face plate*.

gate a notch in the end of a lever tumbler, which when aligned with the fence of the lock bolt allows the bolt to be withdrawn from the strike.

general circulation stair an interior stairway in a building without elevators that provides access to upper floors.

glass door a door made from thick glass, usually heat tempered, with no structural metal stiles.

glass stop see *glazing bead*.

glazing any transparent or translucent material used in windows or doors to admit light.

glazing bead a strip of trim or a sealant such as calking or glazing compound, which is placed around the perimeter of a pane of glass or other glazing to secure it to a frame.

glazing compound a soft, dough-like material used for filling and sealing the spaces between a pane of glass and its surrounding frame and/or stops.

grand master key a key designed to operate all locks under several master keys in a system.

grating, bar type an open grip assembly of metal bars in which the bearing bars, running in one direction, are spaced by rigid attachment to crossbars running perpendicular to them or by bent connecting bars extending between them.

grout mortar of such consistency that it will just flow into the joints and cavities of masonry work and fill them solid.

grouted frame a frame in which all voids between it and the surrounding wall are completely filled with the cement or plaster used in the wall construction.

guard bar a series of two or more crossbars, generally fastened to a common back plate, to protect the glass or screen in a door.

guard plate a piece of metal attached to a doorframe, door edge, or over the lock cylinder for the purpose of reinforcing the locking system against burglary attacks.

hand (of a door) the opening direction of the door. A right-handed door is hinged on the right and swings inward when viewed from the outside. A left-handed door is hinged on the left and swings inward when viewed from the outside. If either of these doors swings outward, it is referred to as a right-hand reverse door or a left-hand reverse door, respectively.

handle any grip-type door pull. See also *lever handle*.

hasp a fastening device consisting of a hinged plate with a slot in it that fits over a fixed D-shaped ring, or eye.

hatchway an opening in a ceiling, roof, or floor of a building, which is large enough to allow human access.

head top horizontal member of a door or window frame.

head stiffener a heavy-gauge metal angle or channel section placed inside, and attached to, the head of a wide doorframe to maintain its alignment; not a load-carrying member.

heel of a padlock that end of the shackle on a padlock that is not removable from the case.

hinge a device generally consisting of two metal plates having loops formed along one edge of each to engage and rotate about a common pivot rod or "pin" and used to suspend a swinging door or window in its frame.

hinge backset the distance from the edge of a hinge to the stop at the side of a door or window.

hinge edge or hinge stile the vertical edge or stile of a door or window to which hinges or pivots are attached.

hinge reinforcement a metal plate attached to a door or frame to receive a hinge.

hold-back feature a mechanism on a latch that serves to hold the latch bolt in the retracted position.

hollow core door a door constructed so that the space (core) between the two facing sheets is not completely filled. Various spacing and reinforcing material are used to separate the facing sheets; some interior hollow core doors have nothing except perimeter stiles and rails separating the facing sheets.

hollow metal hollow items such as doors, frames, partitions, and enclosures that are usually fabricated from cold-formed metal sheet, usually carbon steel.

horizontal sliding window a type of window composed of two sections, one or both of which slide horizontally past the other.

impression system a technique to produce keys for certain types of locks without taking the lock apart.
inactive door (or leaf) the leaf of a double door that is bolted when closed; the strike plate is attached to this leaf to receive the latch and bolt of the active leaf.
integral frame a metal doorframe in which the jambs and head have stops, trim, and backbends all formed from one piece of material.
integral lock (or latch) see *preassembled lock.*
interior common-circulation area an area within a multiple dwelling that is outside the private zones of individual units and is used in common by all residents and the maintenance staff of the building.
interior private area the interior of a single family house; the interior of an apartment in a multiple dwelling; or the interior of a separate unit within commercial, public, or institutional building.
interior public area an interior common-circulation area or common resident-use room within a multiple dwelling to which access is unrestricted.
interior semipublic area an interior common-circulation area or common resident-use room within a multiple dwelling to which access is possible only with a key or on the approval of a resident via an intercom, buzzer-reply system.
invisible hinge a hinge so constructed that no parts are exposed when the door is closed.
jalousie window see *louvered window.*
jamb the exposed vertical member of either side of a door or window opening. See also *door jambs.*
jamb anchor a metal device inserted in or attached to the wall side of a jamb to secure the frame to the wall. A masonry jamb anchor secures a jamb to a masonry wall.
jamb depth the width of the jamb, measured perpendicular to the door or wall face at the edge of the opening.
jamb extension the section of a jamb that extends below the level of the flush floor for attachment to the rough door.
jamb peeling a technique used in forced entry to deform or remove portions of the jamb to disengage the bolt from the strike. See *jimmying.*
jamb/strike component of a door assembly that receives and holds the extended lock bolt. The strike and jamb are considered a unit.
jamb/wall that component of a door assembly to which a door is attached and secured by means of the hinges. The wall and jamb are considered a unit.
jimmying a technique used in forced entry to pry the jamb away from the lock edge of the door a sufficient distance to disengage the bolt from the strike.
jimmy-pin a sturdy projecting screw, which is installed in the hinge edge of a door near a hinge, fits into a hole in the door jamb, and prevents removal of the door if the hinge pins are removed.
keeper see *strike.*
key an implement used to actuate a lock or latch or both into the locked or unlocked position.
key changes the different combinations that are available or that can be used in a specific cylinder.
keyed-alike cylinders cylinders designed to be operated by the same key. (Not to be confused with master-keyed cylinders.)
keyed-different cylinders cylinders requiring different keys for their operation.
keyhole the opening in a lock designed to receive the key.
key-in-knob lock a lock with the key cylinder and the other lock mechanism, such as a push or turn button, contained in the knobs.
key plate a plate or escutcheon having only a keyhole.
keyway the longitudinal cut in the cylinder core with an opening or space with millings in the sides identical to those on the proper key, thus allowing the key to enter the full distance of the blade. See also *warded lock.*
knifing see *loiding.*
knob an ornamental or functional round handle on a door; may be designed to actuate a lock or latch.
knob latch a securing device with a spring bolt operated by a knob only.
knob shank the projecting stem of a knob into which the spindle is fastened.
knocked down (KD) disassembled; designed for assembly at the point of use.
knuckle the enlarged part of a hinge into which the pin is inserted.
laminate a product made by bonding together two or more layers of material.
laminated glass a type of glass fabricated from two layers of glass with a transparent bonding layer between them. Also called *safety glass.*
laminated padlock a padlock, the body of which consists of a number of flat plates, all or most of which are of the same contour, superimposed and riveted or brazed together. Holes in the plates provide spaces for the lock mechanism and the ends of the shackle.
latch (or latch bolt) a beveled, spring-actuated bolt, which may or may not include a deadlocking feature.
leading edge see *lock edge.*
leaf, door an individual door, used singly or in multiples.
leaf hinge the most common type of hinge, characterized by two flat metal plates or leaves, which pivots about a metal hinge pin. A leaf hinge can be surface mounted or installed in a mortise. See also *butt hinge* and *surface hinge.*
lever handle a bar-like grip that is rotated in a vertical plane about a horizontal axis at one of its ends; designed to operate a latch.
lever lock a key-operated lock that incorporates one or more lever tumblers, which must be raised to a specific level so that the fence of the bolt is aligned with the gate of the tumbler in order to withdraw the bolt. Lever locks are commonly used in storage lockers and safety deposit boxes.

lever tumbler a flat metal arm, pivoted on one end with a gate in the opposite end. The top edge is spring-loaded. The bitting of the key rotates against the bottom edge, raising the lever tumbler to align the gate with the bolt fence. Both the position of the gate and the curvature of the bottom edge of the lever tumbler can be varied to establish the key code.

light a space in a window or door for a single pane of glazing. Also, a pane of glass or other glazing materials.

lintel a horizontal structural member that supports the load over an opening such as a door or window.

lip (of a strike) the curved projecting part of a strike plate that guides the spring bolt to the latch point.

lobby that portion of the interior common area of a building that is reached from an entry door and provides access to the general circulation areas, elevators, and fire stairs and from these to other areas of the building.

lock a fastener that secures a door or window assembly against unauthorized entry. A door lock is usually key-operated and includes the keyed device (cylinder or combination), bolt, strike plate, knobs or levers, and trim items. A window lock is usually hand-operated rather than key-operated.

lock clip a flexible metal part attached to the inside of a door face to position a mortise lock.

lock edge the vertical edge or stile of a door in which a lock may be installed. Also called the *leading edge*, the *lock stile*, and *strike edge*.

lock edge door (or lock seam door) a door that has its face sheets secured in place by an exposed mechanical interlock seam on each of its two vertical edges. See also *lock seam*.

lock face plate see *face plate*.

locking dog (of a padlock) the part of a padlock mechanism that engages the shackle and holds it in the locked position.

lock-in-knob. see *key-in-knob lock*.

lockpick a tool or instrument, other than the specifically designed key, made for the purpose of manipulating a lock into a locked or unlocked condition.

lock rail the horizontal member of a door intended to receive the lock case.

lock reinforcement a reinforcing plate attached inside of the lock stile of a door to receive a lock.

lock seam a joint in sheet metal work, formed by doubly folding the edges of adjoining sheets in such a manner that they interlock.

lock set see *lock*.

lock stile see *lock edge*.

loiding a burglary attack method in which a thin, flat, and flexible object such as a stiff piece of plastic is inserted between the strike and the latch bolt to depress the latch bolt and release it from the strike. The loiding of windows is accomplished by inserting a thin stiff object between the meeting rails or stiles to move the latch to the open position, or by inserting a thin stiff wire through openings between the stile or rail and the frame to manipulate the sash operator of pivoting windows. Derived from the word "celluloid." Also called *knifing* and *slip-knifing*.

loose joint hinge a hinge with two knuckles. The pin is fastened permanently to one and the other contains the pinhole. The two parts of the hinge can be disengaged by lifting.

loose pin hinge a hinge with a removable pin that permits the two leaves of the hinge to be separated.

louver an opening with a series of horizontal slats arranged to permit ventilation but to exclude rain, sunlight, or vision.

louvered window a type of window in which the glazing consists of parallel, horizontal, movable glass slats. Also called a *jalousie window*.

main entry door the most important common entry door in a building, which provides access to the building's lobby.

maison keying a specialized keying system, used in apartment houses and other large complexes, which enables all individual unit keys to operate common-use locks such as main entry and laundry room.

masonry stone, brick, concrete, hollow tiles, concrete blocks, or other similar materials, bonded together with mortar to form a wall, pier, buttress, or similar member.

master disc tumbler a disc tumbler that will operate with a master key in addition to its own change key.

master key system a method of keying locks that allows a single key to operate multiple locks, each of which will also operate with an individual change key. Several levels of master keying are possible: a single master key is one which will operate all locks of a group of locks with individual change keys, a grand master key will operate all locks of two or more master key systems, and a great grand master key will operate all locks of two or more grand master key systems. Master key systems are used primarily with pin and disc tumbler locks and, to a limited extent, with lever or warded locks.

master pin a segmented pin used to enable a pin tumbler to be operated by more than one key cut.

meeting stile the vertical edge member of a door or horizontal sliding window, in a pair of doors or windows, which meets with adjacent edge member when closed. See also *checkrails*.

metal-mesh grille a grille of expanded metal or welded metal wires permanently installed across a window or other opening in order to prevent entry through the opening.

mill finish the original surface finish produced on a metal mill product by cold rolling, extruding, or drawing.

millwork in general, all building components made of finished wood and manufactured in millwork plants and planing mills. It includes such items as inside and outside doors, window and doorframes, cabinets, porch-work, mantels, panelwork, stairways, moldings, and interior trim. It normally does not include flooring, ceiling, or siding.

molding a wood strip used for decorative purposes.

mono lock see *preassembled lock*.

mortise a rectangular cavity made to receive a lock or other hardware; also, the act of making such a cavity.

mortise bolt a bolt designed to be installed in a mortise rather than on the surface. The bolt is operated by a knob, lever, or equivalent.

mortise cylinder see *cylinder*.

mortise lock a lock designed for installation in a mortise, as distinguished from a bored lock and a rim lock.

mullion (1) a movable or fixed center post used on double door openings, usually for locking purposes. (2) A vertical or horizontal bar or divider in a frame between windows, doors, or other openings.

multiple dwelling a building or portion of a building designed or used for occupancy by three or more tenants or families living independently of each other (includes hotels and motels).

muntin a small member that divides the glass or openings of sash or doors.

mushroom tumbler a type of tumbler used in pin tumbler locks to add security against picking. The diameter of the driver pin behind the end in contact with the bottom pin is reduced, so that the mushroom head will catch the edge of the cylinder body at the shear line when it is at a slight to its cavity. See also *spool tumbler*.

night latch an auxiliary lock with a spring latch bolt that functions independently of the regular lock of the door.

nonremovable hinge pin a type of hinge pin that has been constructed or modified to make its removal from the hinge difficult or impossible.

offset pivot (or hinge) a pin-and-socket hardware device with a single bearing contact, by means of which a door is suspended in its frame and allowed to swing about an axis, which normally is located about 1.9 cm (3/4″) out from the door face.

one-way screw a screw specifically designed to resist being removed, once installed. See also *tamper-resistant hardware*.

opening size see *door opening*.

operator (of a window sash) the mechanism, including a crank handle and gear box, attached to an operating arm or arms for the purpose of opening and closing a window. Usually found on casement and awning type windows.

overhead door a door that is stored overhead when in the open position.

padlock a detachable and portable lock with a hinged or sliding shackle or bolt, normally used with a hasp and eye or staple system.

panel door a door fabricated from one or more panels surrounded by and held in position by rails and stiles.

panic bar see *crash bar*.

panic hardware an exterior locking mechanism that is always operable from inside the building by pressure on a crash bar or lever.

patio-type sliding door a sliding door that is essentially a single, large transparent panel in a frame (a type commonly used to give access to patios or yards of private dwellings); "single" doors have one fixed and one movable panel; "double" doors have two movable panels.

peeling see *jamb peeling*.

picking see *lockpick*.

pin (of a hinge) the metal rod that serves as the axis of a hinge, thereby allowing the hinge (and attached door or window) to rotate between the open and closed positions.

pin tumbler one of the essential, distinguishing components of a pin tumbler lock cylinder, more precisely called a *bottom pin, master pin*, or *driver pin*. The pin tumblers, used in varying lengths and arrangements, determine the combination of the cylinder. See also *bottom pin, driver pin*, and *master pin*.

pin tumbler lock cylinder a lock cylinder employing metal pins (tumblers) to prevent the rotation of the core until the correct key is inserted into the keyway. Small coil compression springs hold the pins in the locked position until the key is inserted.

pivoted door a door hung on pivots rather than hinges.

pivoted window a window that opens by pivoting about a horizontal or vertical axis.

plug retainer the part often fixed to the rear of the core in a lock cylinder to retain or hold the core firmly in the cylinder.

preassembled lock a lock that has all the parts assembled into a unit at the factory and, when installed in a rectangular section cutout of the door at the lock edge, requires little or no assembly. Also called *integral* lock, *mono* lock, and *unit* lock.

pressed padlock a padlock, the outer case of which is pressed into shape from sheet metal and then riveted together.

pressure-locked grating a grating in which the crossbars are mechanically locked to the bearing bars at their intersections by deforming or swaging the metal.

privacy lock a lock, usually for an interior door, secured by a button, thumb turn, etc., and not designed for key operation.

projection see *bolt projection*.

push key a key that operates the Ace type of lock.

quadrant see *Dutch door bolt*.

rabbet a cut, slot, or groove made on the edge or surface of a board to receive the end or edge of another piece of wood made to fit it.

rabbeted jamb a door jamb in which the projection portion of the jamb that forms the door stop is part of the same piece as the rest of the jamb or securely set into a deep groove in the jamb.

rail a horizontal framing member of a door or window sash that extends the full width between the sites.

removable mullion a mullion separating two adjacent door openings that is required for the normal operation of the doors but is designed to permit its temporary removal.

restricted keyway a special keyway and key blank for high-security locks, with a configuration that is not freely available and must be specifically requested from the manufacturer.

reversible local a lock that may be used for either hand of a door.

rim cylinder a pin or disc tumbler cylinder used with a rim lock.

rim hardware hardware designed to be installed on the surface of a door or window.
rim latch a latch installed on the surface of a door.
rim lock a lock designed to be mounted on the surface of a door.
rose the part of a lock that functions as an ornament or bearing surface for a knob and is normally placed against the surface of the door.
rotary interlocking dead bolt lock a type of rim lock in which the extended dead bolt is rotated to engage with the strike.
rough buck a subframe, usually made of wood or steel, which is set in a wall opening and to which the frame is attached.
rough opening the wall opening into which a frame is to be installed. Usually, the rough opening is measured inside the rough buck.
sash a frame containing one or more lights.
sash fast a fastener attached to the meeting rails of a window.
sash lock a sash fast with a locking device controlled by a key.
screwless knob a knob attached to a spindle by means of a special wrench, as distinguished from the more commonly used side-screw knob.
screwless rose a rose with a concealed method of attachment.
seamless door a door having no visible seams on its faces or edges.
secondary lock see *auxiliary lock.*
security glass (or glazing) see *burglar-resistant glazing.*
setback see *backset.*
shackle the hinged or sliding part of a padlock that does the fastening.
shear line the joint between the shell and the core of a lock cylinder; the line at which the pins or discs of a lock cylinder must be aligned in order to permit rotation of the core.
sheathing the structural exterior covering, usually wood boards or plywood, used over the framing studs and rafters of a structure.
shell a lock cylinder, exclusive of the core. Also called *housing.*
shutter a movable screen or cover used to protect an opening, especially a window.
side light a fixed light located adjacent to a door within the same frame assembly.
signal sash fastener a sash-fastening device designed to lock windows that are beyond reach from the floor. It has a ring for a sash pole hook. When locked, the ring lever is down; when the ring lever is up, it signals by its upright position that the window is unlocked.
sill the lower horizontal member of a door or window opening.
single-acting door a door mounted to swing to only one side of the plane of its frame.
skylight a glazed opening located in the roof of a building.
slide bolt a simple lock that is operated directly by hand without using a key, a turnpiece, or other actuating mechanism. Slide bolts can normally only be operated from the inside.
sliding door any door that slides open sideways.
sliding metal gate an assembly of metal bars that is jointed so it can be moved to and locked in position across a window or other opening in order to prevent unauthorized entry through the opening.
slip-knifing see *loiding.*
solid-core door a door constructed so that the space (core) between the two facing sheets is completely filled with wood blocks or other rigid material.
spindle the shaft that fits into the shank of a door knob or handle. Also serves as its axis of rotation.
split astragal a two-piece astragal, one piece of which is surface mounted on each door of a double door and is provided with a means of adjustment to mate with the other piece and provide a seal. See also *astragal.*
spool tumbler a type of tumbler used in pin tumbler locks to add security against picking. Operates on the same principle as the mushroom tumbler.
spring bolt see *latch.*
spring bolt with antiloiding device see *deadlatch.*
stile one of the vertical edge members of a paneled door or window sash.
stool a flat molding fitted over the windowsill between the jambs and contacting the bottom rail of the lower sash.
stop (of a door or window frame) the projecting part of a door or window frame against which a swinging door or window closes, or in which a sliding door or window moves.
stop (of a lock) a button or other device that serves to lock and unlock a latch bolt against actuation by the outside knob or thumb piece. Another type holds the bolt retracted.
stop side that face of a door that contacts the door stop.
store front sash an assembly of light metal members forming a continuous frame for a fixed glass store front.
storm sash, window, or door an extra window or door, usually placed on the outside of an existing one as additional protection against cold or hot weather.
strap hinge a surface hinge of which one or both leaves are of considerable length.
strike a metal plate attached to or mortised into a door jamb to receive and hold a projected latch bolt and/or dead bolt in order to secure the door to the jamb.
strike, box see *box strike.*

strike, dustproof a strike placed in the threshold or sill of an opening or in the floor that receives a flush bolt and is equipped with a spring-loaded follower to cover the recess and keep out dirt.
strike, interlocking a strike that receives and holds a vertical, rotary, or hook dead bolt.
strike plate see *strike.*
strike reinforcement a metal plate attached to a door or frame to receive a strike.
strike, roller a strike for latch bolts with a roller mounted on the lip to reduce friction.
stud a slender wood or metal post used as a supporting element in a wall or partition.
stud anchor a device used to secure a stud to the floor.
subbuck (or subframe) see *rough buck.*
surface hinge a hinge having both leaves attached to the surface and thus fully visible.
swing see *hand.*
swinging bolt a bolt that is hinged to a lock front and is projected and retracted with a swinging rather than a sliding action. Also called *hinged* or *pivot bolt.*
tail piece the unit on the core of a cylinder lock that actuates the bolt or latch.
tamper-resistant hardware builders' hardware with screws or nut-and-bolt connections that are hidden or cannot be removed with conventional tools.
template a precise detailed pattern used as a guide in the mortising, drilling, etc., of a door or frame to receive hardware.
template hardware hardware manufactured within template tolerances.
tension wrench an instrument used in picking a lock. It is used to apply torsion to the cylinder core.
three-point lock a locking device required on "A-label" fire double doors to lock the active door at three points—the normal position plus top and bottom.
threshold a wood or metal plate forming the bottom of a doorway.
throw see *bolt projection.*
thumb piece (of a door handle) the small pivoted part above the grip of a door handle, which is pressed by the thumb to operate a latch bolt.
thumb turn a unit that is gripped between the thumb and forefinger and turned to project or retract a bolt.
tolerance the permissible deviation from a nominal or specified dimension or value.
transom an opening window immediately above a door.
transom bar the horizontal frame member that separates the door opening from the transom.
transom catch a latch bolt fastener on a transom that has a ring by which the latch bolt is retracted.
transom chain a short chain used to limit the opening of a transom; usually provided with a plate at each end for attachment.
transom lift a device attached to a doorframe and transom by means of which the transom may be opened or closed.
trim hardware see *finish builders' hardware.*
try-out keys a set of keys including many commonly used bittings. They are used one at a time in an attempt to unlock a door.
tumbler a movable obstruction in a lock that must be adjusted to a particular position, as by a key, before the bolt can be thrown.
turn piece see *thumb turn.*
unit lock see *preassembled lock.*
vertical bolt lock a lock with two dead bolts that move vertically into two circular receivers in the strike portion of the lock attached to the door jamb.
vision panel a fixed transparent panel of glazing material set into an otherwise opaque wall, partition, or door; a nonopening window. See also *light.*
ward an obstruction that prevents the wrong key from entering or turning in a lock.
warded lock a lock containing internal obstacles that block the entrance or rotation of all but the correct key.
weather-stripping narrow or jamb-width sections of flexible material that prevent the passage of air and moisture around windows and doors. Compression weather-stripping also acts as frictional counterbalance in double-hung windows.
wet glazing the sealing of glass or other transparent material in a frame by the use of a glazing compound or sealant.
window frame see *frame.*
window guard a strong metal grid-like assembly that can be installed on a window or other opening; types of window guards include metal bars, metal-mesh grilles, and sliding metal gates.
wire glass glass manufactured with a layer of wire mesh approximately in the center of the sheet.

Chapter 26

Security officers in the 21st century

Lawrence J. Fennelly
Security Consultant

Security officer skills and needs are changing due to updated technology and integrated services. End users need a different caliber of security officer who handle more technology- and security management-oriented tasks instead of simply basic patrol, observe and report functions. This provides value to end users' business units that many don't consider – but which all appreciate once they come to fruition.

Ed Finkel, Contributing Editor; Security Magazine, December 2018.

Introduction

Security Magazine in December 2018 had a special report on page 20 on robotic technology. In the report, they said and projected a "Growth at a compound rate of 20 percent over the next five years . . . by 2023."

The report went on to say that "Robots are not to replace humans."

Dr. Travis Deyle, CEO of Cobalt Robotics, estimates that less than 500 robots have been deployed worldwide for use in physical security positions. In addition, we have the use of outdoor drones and outdoor robots that will be deployed. But with this technology, will come training to partner with the respective technology.

Highlights of some of their features:

- *360-degree video* that provides complete awareness and feeds to a security operations center,
- *thermal imaging* for identifying fires and gauging proper environmental temperature settings,
- *license plate recognition* that is an example of a computational task that may include data collection in a large parking facility, and
- *intercom and broadcast capability* that can be programmed to relay messages or alert security personnel to immediately dispatch law enforcement.

Robots performing duties that were previously the work of security officers are examples of the new technology available in the security industry.

For many years now the use of K9 dogs partnered with a security officer has been used in location successfully. These dogs have worked out well in reducing disturbances and searching for suspicious persons, but they have proven to be a successful deterrent.

The point is we are seeing a change in the profession and positive results in crime stats. Tom Conley, president of the Conley Group recently said, "Too many organization, haven't yet crossed the bridge towards a modern security force." So if we assume that the profession is changing, over the next 5 years, should not we get ready for the change and demands of the job, through progressive training of our security officers and their supervisors.

We put together "100 things security officers need to know" as well as "100 things supervisors need to know" for just this purpose, to help you *cross that bridge to modern security force management.*

Handbook of Loss Prevention and Crime Prevention. DOI: https://doi.org/10.1016/B978-0-12-817273-5.00026-0

Workplace injuries

Potential causes of workplace injuries[1] and death range from fatigue (due to inadequate ergonomics or overexertion); substance abuse; slips, trips, and falls; to natural and man-made disasters, including workplace violence. If a major emergency occurs or you get hurt on the job, everyone pays the price—in downtime, lost productivity, low morale, and economic impacts. But when we work together to create a safer place to work, we are all more productive and satisfied with our jobs and business operations are better prepared to recover. For the purposes of this post, we will focus on workplace safety before, during, and after disasters.

Security officers, who strive to help maintain safe and secure workplaces, schools, shopping malls, and communities, deserve heartfelt appreciation. Hardworking, highly trained men and women, security officers are counted among our country's first responders. These individuals deter crime, lead evacuations, provide information, work closely with local law enforcement, and are constantly vigilant in their efforts to keep us safe.

Body cameras for law enforcement and the private sector

Body cameras have quickly become a hot-item issue for both law enforcement and security officers in the private sector.[2] There is certainly a chance for increased liability with the use of body cameras among private security officers, but in the long run, it may be a boon to insurers, security guard companies, and the people they protect.[3]

Legal issues with audio recording

Some states require only one person (i.e., person wearing the recording device), whereas others require two people to know that a conversation is being recorded. Visual recording and audio recording legal requirements do not always align.

Training

Training is required so that officers and security will know where and when they can legally record a person. Privacy and the "expectation of privacy" must be understood by those wearing body video technologies.

Department

Officers and security officer who use video technology are more likely to act appropriately and maintain their composure.

Program goals/program components

Video surveillance technology, already in use by law enforcement in the form of CCTV, has been adapted to be worn by frontline police officers in order to assist in the gathering of evidence and to record police encounters with the public. This involves equipping an officer with an audiovisual-recording apparatus (i.e., a body-worn camera), which is small enough to be worn by police officers without encumbering them in the conduct of regular police work, and developing a system to store and review the data gathered by the device. Advances in the field of miniaturization have led to the development of small yet robust devices that can be worn on the chest, collar, or shoulder or mounted on glasses or a helmet. These cameras operate as mobile CCTV units and record police activity and encounters while officers are out in the field.

There are a number of reasons for police to use body-worn cameras. One is to help in the gathering of evidence and accurate reporting of events. Another objective is to encourage mutual accountability during difficult police–citizen encounters. The objective of having police use body-worn cameras is to reduce the number of use-of-force incidents and reduce the number of complaints from the community by monitoring all police–citizen encounters.

1. Allied Universal Fire, Life Safety Training Systems, December 2018. <https://rjwestmore.com/2018/09/3313/national-security-officer-appreciation-week/#more-3313Allied>.

2. Fennelly, L.J., Perry, M. (Eds.), 2017. Physical Security, 150 Things You Should Know. Elsevier, p. 162 and 163.

3. Brownyard, T., 2015. <http://www.securitymagazine.com/authors/1806-tory-brownyard>.

One jurisdiction that has adopted the use of body-worn cameras is Rialto, California. The Rialto Police Department serves a population of approximately 100,000 residents and employs 115 sworn police officers and 42 nonsworn staff. The devices used in Rialto are small enough to fit into the officers' shirt pockets; they also provide high-definition color video and audio, are water resistant, and have a battery life greater than 12 hours. Police are instructed to use these cameras for every police interaction with the public, except in cases of sexual assault of a minor or when dealing with police informants. The devices are visible to the citizens who are interacting with the officers. All the data are automatically uploaded, collated, and inventoried in a web-based, video-management system at the end of each shift.[4]

100 Things security officers need to know

1. Know your scope of responsibility.[5]
2. Study your post orders.
3. Pay attention to all training programs.
4. Understand there is an art to service to be prepared to provide good service to your community.
5. Your daily reports can either make your shine or . . .
6. In your report, do not misspell any words or make scratches.
7. Reports have a purpose that you must understand.
8. Wearing a sharp uniform that makes a professional appearance.
9. A secret to reduce overtime is to have several floaters available.
10. Are all cameras and intercoms/exterior phones working?
11. Are all fire extinguishers full?
12. Lights—which ones are burnt out and which ones on in daytime?
13. The value of reports is to report defects and vulnerabilities.
14. Develop professional telephone skills.
15. Be professional—100% of the time.
16. Social media has no place in the workplace.
17. Neither do movies, iPads, or porn on the computer.
18. If you are working from 8:00 a.m. to 4:00 p.m., be there at 7:30 a.m. to allow for emergency delays, such as bad traffic.
19. Read 16 and 17 again. Why? Because it is reason for termination.
20. CPTED standards for crime prevention through environmental design and the first generation of CPTED have seven concepts and strategies.
21. Change your routine, knowing that bad actors may be watching and planning their attack.
22. Be unapologetic about questioning strangers and visitors about their intentions, what they are carrying, etc.
23. Use your intuition. If something does not feel right, pursue.
24. Note unusual things in your daily report—someone else may be connecting dots.
25. Pace yourself during the shift and make sure you are always hydrated and have a clear, engaged mind.
26. Do not let your guard down at shift change, a very vulnerable time.
27. While on duty, do not drink alcohol, take illegal drugs or prescription drugs that could impair your job performance.
28. Be a good "team" member.
29. Have good personal hygiene.
30. Be polite—say "please," and "thank you" to clients, customers, coworkers, visitors, contractors, and vendors.
31. Keep your hair and fingernails clean.
32. Do not falsify reports—your reports may be verified by video surveillance.
33. Be truthful.
34. Use proper patrol techniques while performing walking or vehicle rounds.
35. Stay informed about "issues" or potential problems in your area.
36. Remember that much of your job is customer service and your actions reflect on the client—positively or negatively.

4. https://www.crimesolutions.gov/ProgramDetails.aspx?ID=499
5. Prepared by Lawrence J. Fennelly, CPOI, CSSI, Marianna Perry, CPP, CPOI, John O'Rourke and Dr. Jennifer Hestermann November 2018.

37. Write reports legibly. Do not use “white-out” or erasers. Instead draw a single line through errors and make the correction.
38. Write legibly.
39. Do not forget that your reports may be used in a civil or criminal proceeding and you may be called to testify.
40. Study emergency procedures and know what to do for an active assailant, inclement weather, civil unrest, etc.
41. Do not carry a weapon while on duty unless you are trained and you are assigned as an “armed” officer.
42. Protect the client’s assets.
43. Take care of your issued equipment.
44. Check equipment at the beginning of every shift to ensure it is operational.
45. Report damaged or inoperable equipment as soon as possible.
46. Do not sleep while on duty.
47. Be alert and aware of your surroundings.
48. While on duty, cell phones are to be used for emergencies or for business communication.
49. Do not use curse words on the phone, PA, or intercom.
50. Use appropriate radio protocol.
51. Answer the phone promptly and politely.
52. Perform duties safely.
53. Perform your job duties with integrity.
54. Be dependable.
55. Use good judgment.
56. When you are on duty, “check” your judgments at the door.
57. Be a good listener.
58. Be a problem solver and help find solutions.
59. Work your assigned schedule.
60. Practice your interpersonal skills.
61. Be efficient, while on patrol observe employees’ work habits and conduct to prevent employees’ misbehavior and mitigate workplace injuries, while on patrol look for workplace hazards to prevent accidents, that is, wet floors.
62. Communicate clearly and comprehensively.
63. Have a positive attitude.
64. Have the initiative to perform your job duties without “around the clock” supervision.
65. Have an aptitude for self-motivating and motivate others.
66. Accept responsibility when you make mistakes.
67. Be willing to learn new things.
68. Know the difference between decisiveness and recklessness.
69. Have the ability to work well under pressure.
70. Be open-minded to new tasks or job responsibilities.
71. Have the ability to establish rapport with those you come into contact with.
72. When you are introduced to someone, stand up, make eye contact, and shake hands.
73. Learn to be a good listener.
74. Report accidents and injuries as soon as possible.
75. Practice good housekeeping, disposing of trash properly, and keep your post area clean.
76. Learn to assess different environments and identify hazards.
77. Practice situational awareness.
78. Do not stand at a stationary post with your hands in your pants or jacket pockets.
79. Do not chew gun while on duty. Learn healthy ways to deal with stress.
80. Do not wear too much cologne or have a bad body odor. No one should smell you before they see you.
81. Report hazards (i.e., nonoperational lighting or broken locks) as soon as possible.
82. If you work or patrol in a hazardous environment, use the appropriate PPE for the job (hearing protection, eye protection, etc.).
83. Be helpful when assisting individuals with disabilities.
84. Work well with first responders when there is an incident.
85. Pay attention during training classes and have the willingness to learn new skills.
86. Lift heavy items safely by using your legs and not your back.
87. Be careful when patrolling on wet or slick surfaces.

88. Be fair, objective, and honest.
89. Utilize your authority or power carefully—personal versus position.
90. Be aware of your nonverbal or paraverbal communication.
91. Be able to adapt to change.
92. Do not disclose confidential or proprietary information.
93. Do not post anything about clients or details about security procedures on social media.
94. Do not steal or pilfer from the client or your employer.
95. Be systematically unsystematic in your patrol, daily routines, and response.
96. Study your work environment to understand what is "ordinary" so you can immediately identify the "inordinary."
97. If you observe the "inordinary," do not dismiss it. Inquire about it. Do not move on until you are certain that there is not a security concern, that is, unknown person walking around. Do not assume he is with someone, ask and verify.
98. During patrol pay attention to where the AED and first aid kits are located.
99. When the opportunity avails itself, run "what if" scenarios through you mind to help prepare you for a quick response, that is, what if there is a fire in the lounge, where is the fire extinguisher? What if someone fell and needed oxygen, where is the oxygen?
100. Understand body language to identify when an employee is nervous, angry, or acting bizarre. Do not ignore a person's personality changes, even if slight. Report your concerns to your supervisor, that is, remember the "ordinary" versus the "inordinary."

Supervisory oversight

This may be the most important of all the procedures as it is the supervisor who will ensure all policies and procedures are followed.[6] As such, detailed procedures for supervisory oversight must be outlined. These procedures should include random inspections of officers and locations being protected. Video reviews must be conducted to ensure that suspicious activity is not taking place or being missed by security officers. Most protected facilities and grounds have cameras, supervisors should take advantage of this and inspect the video for officer behavior and patrolling techniques. Moreover, guard tour patrol system technology should be utilized to ensure officers are alert and attending to their assigned duties. This technology captures a digital record of the officer's location and points checked. Reports can be generated from this technology to audit the officer's activity and efficiency while working. These reports can help supervisors identify problematic patterns that may create vulnerability in the layers of security. This type of oversight will produce an effective and alert security guard staff.

Without continuous oversight, officers are likely to be less effective and become part of the security problem. Without this necessary management tool, officers oftentimes develop relationships within the work environment and start to become permissive to minor infractions to policy. Moreover, officers might take advantage of the lack of oversight and not patrol as effectively as when they know their activities are being monitored.

Just as it is incumbent for management to put in place the policies and procedures necessary to deliver an effective security patrol program, it is equally important for a security officer to put things in place for their patrol duties. Preparation for security patrol is much more than just reporting to work 5 minutes early and beginning your shift. Officers must mentally prepare for patrol if they want to be effective in their duties. Too often, this is not the case, which illustrates the need for security oversight.

What is a supervisor?

What does it mean to be a supervisor? First, supervisors may be called on to handle numerous conflicts. Second, they will be required to meet management's or their client's expectations in the daily routine of operational activities. The supervisor is the backbone of the organization. His or her scope of responsibility is rather unique:

- The person who represents higher authority.
- The person who assesses situations and conditions to make on-the-spot judgments without favor, prejudice, or fear.
- The person who is a responder to any and all situations.
- The person who must galvanize the efforts of many to attain stated goals.

6. O'Rourke, J., 2019. Patrol principles. In: Davies, S., Fennelly, L.J. (Eds.), The Protection Officers Security Handbook. Elsevier Publishers.

- The person who must assign tasks and ensure compliance and constant quality performance.
- The person who is accountable and, therefore, first in line to shoulder reaction, both good and bad.
- Finally, the person who must make a decision for management based on his or her professional development. The supervisor is the backbone of the organization. His or her scope of responsibility is rather unique.

100 Things the security supervisors need to know

1. *The first part of a security audit should be to ensure proper employee conduct in the work environment and to identify problematic and/or suspicious behavior.* The second phase of the audit is to check to see if the systems are operating correctly.[7]
2. Managers should regularly, at least monthly, check all physical security devices and need to properly manage that they are in good operating condition. Consider having an audit logs for key management, fire extinguisher checks, AED unit functionality, emergency light checks, and all alarm systems and network video operations.
3. Network video/security surveillance systems (CCTV) used for employee surveillance, especially when it concerns employee performance, are contentious. In many geographic locations, CCTV in the workplace is closely regulated or controlled by either legislation or union contracts. Perhaps either removing or amending the statement is in order.

   This is now a *very* international certification, and any references within the resource should be internationally generic and definitely must account for laws and regulations that may exist outside of the United States. Certainly not to specify or isolate every law or rule, but cautionary statements made to make the reader aware of laws that may exist outside of the United States candidates need to be aware of.
4. Is every light working properly and no lights are *on* during the daytime?
5. Does total number of employees line up with the total number of access badges issued?
6. Are all fire extinguishers accounted for and checked regularly as well as trained in basic fire suppression techniques using facility fire extinguishers?
7. Are all exterior intercoms or phones working?
8. Are keys properly secured and turned in upon termination?
9. Is exterior lighting cost effective?
10. Is signage on or about the property adequate?
11. The physical security of cyber systems is an important component of cyber security and cyber hygiene.
12. Do not overrely on electronic security systems and technology solutions. Remember to balance electronic, mechanical, and human tools for risk mitigation. Recognize the value of effective training, policies, business practices, and people as part of your overall risk management strategy.
13. Recognize that "IT security" is *not* the same thing as "security IT." Protecting IT assets is very different than using IT assets to support an organization's security systems/program. Keep the distinction clear in your mind and when you communicate with people.
14. Always ensure that your security program/assets protection strategy is aligned with the strategic goals of the organization you support ... and make it very apparent that your goals are aligned. Whether your organization is a business, a government agency, a nonprofit, or another type of entity—this is critical.
15. The school SRO's and K-12 school practitioner: emergency operations planning, tabletop and functional exercises, hazard, risk, vulnerability assessment, athletics and after-school activities, safety and security, parent/student reunification, life safety, and security and communications systems are all issues you need to be aware of and on top of.
16. Post orders, training material, and security manuals when issued should be signed for and documented.
17. All supervisors should be properly trained for the job, in order to properly discharge their duties effectively and according to policy.
18. The secret of obtaining great security personnel is the proper conducting of the interview, with prepared questions to ask the candidate.
19. Unity of command means that the security officer is under the direct control of his immediate supervisor.
20. Span of control is when a supervisor can effectively control only a limited number of people, which is normally 12 employees or under.

7. Prepared by Lawrence J. Fennelly, CPOI, CSSI, Marianna Perry, CPP, CPOI, John O'Rourke and Dr. Jennifer Hestermann, November 2018.

21. Discipline, can be complicated depending on the issue. However confer with your supervisor if unsure of the course of action to take.
22. Emergency management of any incident *begins* beforehand awareness of the facilities are key.
23. Span of control under the National Incident Management System (NIMS) is a key component of any security and response organization.
24. Security officers *are* first responders and training needs to reflect it.
25. The officers *must* be trained and properly educated in all phases of the facilities emergency management *culture* and operations.
26. Preplanning must be an integral part of any officers on boarding process.
27. What we expect our protection officers are to do in the first moments of an emergency are critical to the best outcomes.
28. The effective implementation of an emergency management plan requires that all the involved ones have proper training and are given exercises to ensure the visibility of existing plans.[8]
29. The secret of success in many organizations is to hire and retain the right people.[9] Reliable preemployment screening is at the core of successful operations management. This is particularly the case for protection programs. Security personnel are selected in much the same way as other workers in an organization; however, higher standards for determining applicants' previous legal, moral, and ethical behavior guide employment decisions.
30. Security officers should be familiar with and train with police, fire, and EMS responders.
31. Reducing and mitigating risk is a primary responsibility of security officers.
32. Training and exercises conducted beforehand will impact the outcome of any event.
33. No checkbox training, focus on competency.
34. Security offices will benefit from completion of NIMS 700 and 100 training.
35. Security officers should be trained in GHS and NFPA 704 systems.
36. Security officers are primary eyes in ensuring housekeeping is maintained.
37. Security officers should be trained in how to respond to white powder, hazmat releases, as well fire, EMS, etc.
38. Security officers should be informed anytime a sprinkler or alarm system is OOS.
39. Fire behavior should be a curriculum topic in security officer training.
40. Security managers should realize their officers will be first on the scene of any incident. This means they need to have a level of all hazards training for the first 10 + minutes. Old saying in fire service is the first 5 minutes influences the next 5 hours. Step up initially and be prepared for a very long day. Security officers are professional and should be considered as such.
41. Managers should periodically conduct drills and tabletop exercises for security personnel to ensure proper delivery of procedures is known and followed.
42. I think that the biggest thing that needs to be said is that IT and physical security are intrinsically connected, they are *not* separate disciplines. One cannot have one without the other. In today's world, there is no IT security without physical security and there is no physical security without IT security. Organizations will continue to be unacceptably vulnerable until they approach security as one risk reduction discipline.
43. Security problems can only ever be resolved by developing a cohesive culture, focused on the overall welfare of everyone. Until everyone in a culture virtually shares the same general cultural values and goals (the overall welfare of everyone), and it becomes culturally unacceptable to do harm to others, terrorism and crime will be a significant problem to the detriment of everyone. Terrorism and crime thrive in an environment of "I deserve, so I will take from others ... or kill others who do not agree with my beliefs." A homogeneous culture virtually eliminates this.
44. Due to the increasingly complex global environment that many organizations operate in today, engaging in proactive crisis planning with relevant stakeholders is critical. This requires top leadership commitment and support at every step of the process to be successful. In essence, top leadership is the catalyst for success in this important arena.
45. Emerging technologies, including robots, drones, and software that analyzes video footage for anomalies, could allow companies to expand surveillance without having to adopt intrusive inspections, experts said.[10] (Police officers are seen at YouTube headquarters following an active shooter situation in San Bruno, California, United States, April 3, 2018. REUTERS/Elijah Nouvelage.)

8. Maras, M.-H., Shapiro, L.R., 2018. Security Management. p. 70.
9. McCrie, R., 2016. Security Operation Management. Elsevier Pub., p. 116.
10. REUTERS News. Technology News April 4, 2018, 9:12 PM, 8 days ago.

46. Obtain officer input for any policy and procedure implemented or significant changes to existing policies and procedures.
47. Conduct a comprehensive background investigation on all security officers prior to hiring and on a regular basis after employment.
48. Provide a means of confidential employee communication to security management via an anonymous "hotline."
49. Any security patrol scheme should be conducted in varied and unpredictable manner. Occasionally repatrolling the area immediately after the initial patrol is an effective method to avoid predictability and keep a potential criminal from discerning a routine patrol pattern.
50. Review with and practice with the security staff the policies and procedures related to demonstrations and mass-gathering events that may impact your organization. Stress the importance of perimeter patrol and restraint.
51. Instill in the security staff that civil and/or criminal liability can arise from negligent performance of their duties and responsibilities. This applies to both the organization and the security staff.
52. Remind the security staff that protection of life takes precedence over protection of property in all cases. This is the top priority.
53. Develop a security awareness and crime prevention program and travel advisory program for the organization's personnel traveling abroad.
54. Develop data-driven security metrics to demonstrate the effectiveness of the security program to top management.
55. Apply a business case approach when promoting new security projects to top management, utilizing the return on investment and total cost of ownership concepts.
56. Push security out beyond the workplace by using concentric rings of security to identify and address threats well before they get to your front door.
57. Fight over reliance on security technology and keep humans involved in the process for a holistic view of your vulnerabilities and the threat.
58. Do not assume that serious insider threats are not in your organization; know which employees are struggling and the danger they may bring to the workplace.
59. Create a culture of safe reporting so employees will come forward with security concerns without fear of reprisal.
60. Do not assume that security rules are followed; have good policy and procedures, but also regularly assess compliance.
61. Build your crisis leadership skill set before bad things happen; practice how you and your staff will handle an emergency.
62. Focus your time and energy on preparing for crisis, not predicting or calculating whether or not it will happen.
63. Craft the messages you will put on social media and give to the press in the event of a crisis in your organizations.
64. In this unpredictable security landscape, your mitigation and response plans must be fluid and based on emerging threats.
65. People want to feel safe and will make their own assessment about whether to use your facilities or services; robust security will pull them in, not push them away!
66. Managers should have and/or develop an incident management system (IMS). *An IMS provides the data required to effectively manage current or potential problems, issues, investigations, and planning for effective physical protection systems.*
67. All incidents should be investigated by either a security officer or manger. The findings of the investigation should be documented and logged into the IMS. All hazards or problematic behavior should be immediately reported to the security manager or director.
68. Managers should have a notification system, which clearly identifies who should be notified in case of an emergency, incident occurring, or any other noteworthy occurrence.
69. Managers should ensure their security officers have a patrol log to memorize patrol activities and observations during patrol.
70. Managers should ensure policies and procedures for all employees are clearly written and defined to ensure proper enforcement of these rules by security.
71. Managers should tailor their security applications to fit the environment they are protecting. Not all applications work in certain environments.
72. Managers should be well read and versed on managerial concepts and leadership.

73. Managers should lead by example; how managers expect their subordinates to act and comport themselves, they should do the same.
74. It is important that managers document the progress of their subordinates. Many managers fail to accurately document an employee's performance. Too often, they only document the negative and not the positive.
75. Communications
    a. Names and cell phone contact info for immediate executive leadership, vice president (VP)-operations, VP-human resources or on call representative, corporate counsel, and corporate communications team.
    b. The security manager (SM) should know the address, with cross streets and landmarks, for every facility under supervision or where business occurs, in the event an emergency call to 911/first responders is necessary.
    c. The SM should be capable of using all communications platforms and trained to perform basic service or diagnostics on equipment to trouble shoot in case of crisis (when there is no time to call the help desk or the help desk is out of service).
    d. Names and contact info for fire and law enforcement and emergency response leaders with jurisdiction over the facility.
    e. Names and contact info for all building systems contractors, including plumbing, HVAC, fire systems, overhead doors and access control equipment, and city water service/sewer service issues.
    f. Names and contact info for all vehicle and transportation equipment maintenance providers in case of an accident, breakdown, or service need.
    g. Connections with a good professional organization (IFPO, ASIS) for networking, mentoring, and advice on problem solving.
    h. A good SM should know how to communicate effectively with officers, public, executives, laborers, and all levels of constituents.
    i. A good SM should have curiosity about current events locally, regionally, and globally, and the SM should be reading or checking the news for updated information on events locally relevant.
    j. A good SM must know how to inspire, manage, reward, develop, support, and discipline employees within the company culture's expectations and within the law.
76. Training
    a. Use-of-force policy and training credentials for all officers.
    b. Emergency medical training, such as AED, CPR, and Stop the Bleed, and to have a certified instructor or program to immediately train new hires and update staff.
    c. Laws of self-defense, such as protection of life versus protection of private property.
    d. Verbal Judo, de-escalation, conflict resolution, and management of aggressive behavior.
    e. Formal observational training, surveillance, and counter surveillance training.
    f. Physically fit and healthy as an example to others.
    g. Trained in use of all specialized security surveillance systems, access control, alarms, and monitoring equipment used by the SMs department.
    h. Basic ability to communicate in second languages that might be expected in the SMs duties. This may also include access and knowledge on who to contact for interpreter services.
    i. What is the incident command system that will be used when fire/EMS/police arrive for a significant event.
    j. All training needs to be documented and saved in the officers files.
77. Do you understand the difference between ERM (enterprise risk management) and ESRM (enterprise security risk management)? Both are built on risk practices and risk principles, but ESRM is narrowly focused on security risks. "ESRM is a security program management approach that links security activities to an enterprise's mission and business goals through risk management methods. The security leader's role in ESRM is to manage risks of harm to enterprise assets in partnership with the business leaders whose assets are exposed to those risks. ESRM involves educating business leaders on the realistic impacts of identified risks, presenting potential strategies to mitigate those impacts, then enacting the option chosen by the business in line with accepted levels of business risk tolerance." (Petruzzi, 2017)
78. Do you understand the difference between integration and unification?
79. Do you have a seat at the C-Suite table? Security directors should be at the C-Suite table to participate in planning and key decision-making. "C-Suite gets its name from the titles of top senior executives, which tend to start with the letter C, for chief, as in chief executive officer (CEO), chief financial officer (CFO), chief operating officer (COO), and chief information officer (CIO). Also called "C-level executives." (Investopedia, 2018)

80. Are you involved in business continuity planning?
81. Are you aware of alternative revenue sources to fund security initiatives, such as grant writing?
82. Do you know how to construct a formal RFP?
83. Do you know how to write a formal after action report?
84. Do you know how to conduct or plan exercises—tabletop, functional, and full-scale?
85. Do you know how to complete an HRV analysis?
86. Do you have controls in place to meet all (local, county, state, and federal) requirements?
87. Do you have an audit schedule (controls) in place for specific areas?

    Do you understand NIMS and are you organized around an incident command structure for emergency response? NIMS provides a comprehensive, national approach to incident management.

    "ICS is a widely applicable management system designed to enable effective, efficient incident management by integrating a combination of facilities, equipment, personnel, procedures, and communications operating within a common organizational structure. ICS is a fundamental form of management established in a standard format, with the purpose of enabling incident managers to identify the key concerns associated with the incident—often under urgent conditions—without sacrificing attention to any component of the command system. It represents organizational 'best practices' and, as an element of the Command and Management Component of NIMS, has become the standard for emergency management across the country." (Homeland Security, 2018)
88. An EOP is an emergency operations plan. The security director is a key stakeholder and should be familiar with the organization's plan. The security director should be an important part of the incident command system and on the incident command team to manage emergencies, which always include security components
89. Do you have an EOP and do you know the essential elements of a plan?
90. Does your EOP have action plans for special events, third-party rentals, etc.?
91. Does your third-party rental include security standards and costs?
92. Are you familiar with how to use and monitor social media? The security director represents the "boots on the ground" perspective and provides valuable insight in determining the selection of many life safety, security and communication systems. He/she should be a part of the process, not just an end user. Once the systems are selected, the security director and his/her team should be trained in the use of these systems. Communications systems are foundation to managing an incident, especially one that is time-sensitive and/or presents a threat so redundancy in communication tools is critical. Beyond landlines, radios, and e-mail notifications, other communication tools may include the public address system, mass notification systems, and social media.
93. Do you have a plan for parent/student reunification?
94. Are you a decision maker in the selection and life safety, security and communication systems (fire, access control, phone, PA, mass notification, etc.)?
95. Are you involved in formulating a crisis communications plan? Have you reached out to local media to establish a working relationship?
96. Does your place of business employ CPTED concepts and principles?
97. Has your staff been trained in de-escalation and other mental health protocols?
98. Has your staff been trained in CPR/AED/First Aid/Stop the Bleed?
99. Are you a mentor or are you being mentored? Are you current with HR policies and procedures (interviewing, hiring, firing, harassment, etc.)? The HR director and security director should work hand in hand from the initial stages of interviewing a prospective employee (background checks) to the release of an employee and many practices in between. Some examples include drug testing, investigations (theft), clearances (access control), threat assessments (protective orders), employee conduct (harassment), cybersecurity policies (lack of adherence to company policies), and many others.
100. Have you reached out to your local first responders to establish a working relationship and to invite them to become familiar with your facility?
101. Have all agencies' radios been tested on the property and confirmed to be working with no dead spots?
102. *Linda A. Hill* is a professor at the Harvard Business School, and has been now for several years. She wrote the book which is titled "Being the Boss." The book is broken down into three sections:
    a. Part one: Manage Yourself
    b. Part two: Manage Your Network
    c. Part three: Manage Your Team

Emerging trends

We found that it was possible to do more than 100 items but it was decided to cut it off at a hundred, which tells us you have a lot to learn as you go through the advances of your career. Our suggestion is to buy several security books and start reading and learning about various concepts and strategies as well as text on physical security.

Appendix 1 Saving a life, it is in your hands

Michael J. Fagel and Greg Benson

First aid training for everyone can save lives. The Protection officers must learn how to render lifesaving immediate first aid measures in a crisis.

The rules of engagement have changed, and, we Must train AND Educate our protection officers for an increasingly important role in today's era of mass casualty incidents. Training for "Stopping the Bleeding" is a critical first step in this effort.

There are numerous campaigns about stopping the immediate bleeding before trained technical EMT's responders arrive. During an emergent crisis, the victims need our help and, sadly may not survive without it.

Just look at this sobering event: TSA Officer Gerardo Hernandez bled to death, while waiting 33 minutes to be wheeled into an ambulance. Reports indicate that Paramedics were kept away from the scene by law enforcement due to the scene being unsafe or "hot" (November 2013).

It is our role to be prepared and have the necessary lifesaving equipment at our fingertips. When I was in uniform, I carried a small pack commonly called an IPOK (Individual Patrol Officer Kit) along with 2 CAT tourniquets.

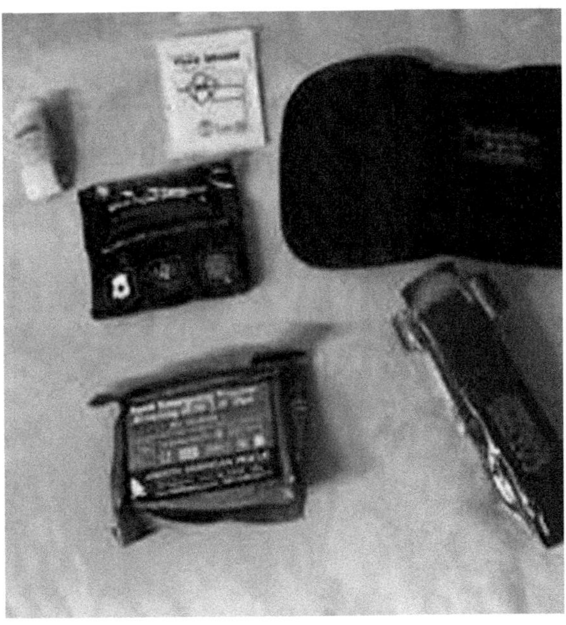

IPOK KIT (Photo by Mike Fagel) (Available from numerous vendors)

I had 3 devices I could apply to myself or have one to throw to another individual to apply. I have trained hundreds of public safety personnel in this life saving skill set you can carry with you at all times. You can learn how to utilize these critical tools by partaking in a "Stop the Bleed" campaign training, your local Trauma Hospital team, or Fire-Rescue-EMS may be able to assist you.

It is not "someone else's job, it's YOUR job to learn this lifesaving skill. The life you save may be your own. As an instructor for several of the coalitions listed below:

1. Add these critical lifesaving skills to your tool belt, at work, at home, everywhere you go.
2. Be prepared.
3. Safety is in YOUR hands.

Get the facts

How much do you know about tourniquets?

Think you know all there is to know about tourniquets? Take this quick quiz and see just how much you know. Be sure to challenge your friends' knowledge while you are at it, and share this quiz on social media.

First,[11] Apply pressure! Remember, pressure stops the bleeding. Here is how it works, Just apply continuous pressure until bleeding stops. Q. How Long? A. There is no definite amount of time. Use your hands to apply a firm but steady amount of pressure until the bleed stops. As a rule you should hold pressure for at least 5 minutes before looking at the wound. If the bleeding does not stop, call 911 and continuing applying pressure until medical help arrives.

If you can, try to ensure the injured person is on a firm surface. That way, when you apply force to the bleeding, you are pressing into something. Using? If you have gauze available, use that. If not, use whatever we you have available, such as a shirt, newspaper or your hand.

Then continue applying pressure until medical help arrives.

Finally

So far approximately 275 city of Victorville, CA, employees have been trained in Stop the Bleed. Community groups are next. Our goal is 1000 by the year end (2018).

Websites to get added information:
www.Aurorasafety.com
https://www.dhs.gov/stopthebleed
http://stopthebleedingcoalition.org/
https://www.dhs.gov/stb-learn-how-stop-bleed
https://www.bleedingcontrol.org/
https://www.nsc.org/safety-training/first-aid/courses/emergency-medical-response

11. https://www.bleedingcontrol.org/

Chapter 27

Information technology systems infrastructure*

Thomas Norman
Security Consultant

Critical thinking is to thinking as economics is to money management. Critical thinking applies a scientific process to the act of thinking that helps result in far superior conclusions and helps the thinker to support his/her conclusions with rational and defend-able arguments . . .

Critical thinking helps assure that personal weaknesses, prejudices, or personal agendas are not forwarded as part of the conclusions . . .

Critical thinking is important because it enables one to think about a problem more completely and to consider many factors that may not be intuitively apparent.[1]

Thomas Norman.

Introduction

This may be one of the most important sections in the book. The designer who does not thoroughly understand Transport Control Protocol/Internet Protocol (TCP/IP) is at a severe disadvantage in design, in construction management, and in system commissioning. The designer is at the mercy of installers and physics, both of which can harm him or her. Not understanding TCP/IP is like not being able to read or write. This is not a comprehensive tome on TCP/IP. I suggest that the reader may buy several other books on the subject. This description is intended for the novice designer.

Basics of Transport Control Protocol/Internet Protocol and signal communications

TCP/IP is the basic protocol of digital systems. From the understanding of that protocol, all knowledge about digital systems flows.

How Transport Control Protocol/Internet Protocol works

The purpose of TCP/IP is to guide information from one place to another on a digital network. In the beginning, when computers were owned only by the government, military, universities, and really big business (banks and insurance companies), computers were not networked. Universities and the military held discussions on how to network their machines. The first network, called ARPANET, was developed in 1969 using Network Control Protocol, an early predecessor to TCP/IP. Although this permitted limited communications, several problems were evident, mainly that computers could only talk to other computers of the same manufacturer using the same operating system and software. This was not good, since the whole idea was to allow communication, not to limit it. After several iterations, TCP/IP evolved. I will not go into the entire long story; you can look that up on Google under "TCP/IP history." TCP/IP is really two separate protocols. TCP is the Transport Control Protocol, and IP is the Internet Protocol. TCP was

---

*Originally from Norman, T., 2007. Integrated Security Systems Design. Butterworth-Heinemann, Boston, MA. Updated by the editor, Elsevier, 2011.

1. Norman, T.L. *Risk Analysis and Security Countermeasure Selection*, second ed. CRC Press, p. 71.

Handbook of Loss Prevention and Crime Prevention. DOI: https://doi.org/10.1016/B978-0-12-817273-5.00027-2

developed in 1974 by Kahn and Cerf and was introduced in 1977 for cross-network connections. TCP was faster, easier to use, and less expensive to implement. It also ensured that lost packets would be recovered, providing quality of service to network communications. In 1978 IP was added to handle routing of messages in a more reliable fashion. TCP communications were encapsulated within IP packets to ensure that they were routed correctly. On the receiving end the TCP packets were unpacked from their IP capsules. Experts quickly realized that TCP/IP could be used virtually for any communication medium, including wire, radio, fiber, and laser, as well as other means. By 1983, ARPANET was totally converted to TCP/IP, and it became known as the Internet.

TCP/IP operates on Open Systems Interconnection levels 3 (IP) and 4 (TCP)

One of the basic functions of networking involves the process of layering communications. Like making a sandwich, one cannot begin by spreading mayonnaise on one's hand. You have to put it on bread. Then you add the meat, lettuce, pickles, and so forth, and finally a last layer of bread. Network communications are like that. To send a packet of video, audio, or data, one must build up a series of layers. At the other end, those layers are taken off until the packet is ready for viewing or listening. There are seven layers to the Open Systems Interconnection (OSI) reference model. Each layer adds a protocol. Dick Lewis (Lewis Technology, www.lewistech.com/rlewis/Resources/JamesBondOSI2.aspx) uses an example of James Bond to describe how the seven layers work (Fig. 27.1). The following is his description:

James Bond meets Number One on the seventh floor of the spy headquarters building. Number One gives Bond a secret message that must get through to the U.S. embassy across town.

Bond proceeds to the sixth floor, where the message is translated into an intermediary language, encrypted, and miniaturized.

Bond takes the elevator to the fifth floor, where security checks the message to be sure it is all there and puts some checkpoints in the message so his counterpart at the U.S. end can be sure he's got the whole message.

On the fourth floor, the message is analyzed to see if it can be combined with some other small messages that need to go to the U.S. end. Also, if the message was very large it might be broken into several small packages so other spies can take it and have it reassembled on the other end.

The third-floor personnel check the address on the message and determine who the addressee is and advise Bond of the fastest route to the embassy.

On the second floor, the message is put into a special courier pouch (packet). It contains the message, the sender, and destination ID. It also warns the recipient if other pieces are still coming.

Bond proceeds to the first floor, where Q has prepared the Aston Martin for the trip to the embassy.

Bond departs for the U.S. embassy with the secret packet in hand. On the other end, the process is reversed. Bond proceeds from floor to floor, where the message is decoded.

Seven layers of the OSI model

Layer no.	Layer	Functions	Methods	Transmit	Receive
7	Application	Communication partners identified, quality of service identified, user authentication, data syntax	E-mail, network software, telnet, FTP	⇩	⇧
6	Presentation	Encryption	Encryption software	⇩	⇧
5	Session	Establishes and terminates network sessions between devices and software requests	CPU process	⇩	⇧
4	Transport	Error recovery and flow control	CPU process	⇩	⇧
3	Network	Switching and routing, network addressing, error handling, congestion control, and packet sequencing	Switcher, router	⇩	⇧
2	Data link	data packets encoded/decoded into bits	Media access control (MAC) and logical link control (LLC)	⇩	⇧
1	Physical	Electrical, light, or radio bit stream	Cables, cards, Ethernet, RS-232, ATM, 802.11a/b/g	⇩	⇧

FIGURE 27.1 OSI layers. *OSI*, Open Systems Interconnection.

The U.S. ambassador is very grateful the message got through safely.

"Bond, please tell Number One I'll be glad to meet him for dinner tonight."

The important point to understand is that in any network, today, each packet is encapsulated (enclosed) seven times and, when received, is decapsulated seven times. Each encapsulation involves checking and packaging to make the trip a sure and safe one for the data. Each decapsulation reverses that process:

- Data begins its trip at layer 7, the application layer, which includes software programs, Microsoft Word, and so forth.
- It is passed down to layer 6, the presentation layer, which adds data compression, encryption, and other similar manipulations of the data.
- It is then passed down to layer 5, the session layer, which provides a mechanism for managing the dialog between the two computers, including starting and stopping the communications and what to do if there is a crash.
- From there, it goes to layer 4, the transport layer (TCP), which ensures reliable communications between the machines. The packet changes from data to segments in the TCP layer.
- Down to layer 3, the network layer (IP), where error control and routing functions are described. The segments are combined or broken up into defined-sized packets at the IP layer. Routers are layer 3 devices.
- Down to layer 2, the data link layer, where functional and procedural means to transfer data between network entities and detection and correction of errors that could occur on the lowest layer take place. It is on this layer that the addressing of exact physical machines, each with their own media access control (MAC) address, is found. Each digital device attached to any network has its own unique MAC address, allowing sure identification that the device is authorized for connection to the communication or network. Network switches are layer 2 devices.
- Finally, down to layer 1, the physical layer that includes cable, voltages, hubs, repeaters, and connectors.

Transport Control Protocol/User Datagram Protocol/Real-Time Protocol

One of the major advantages of TCP/IP is that it is able to fix bad communications. It does this by keeping track of packet lists for a given communication. Andrew G. Blank, author of *TCP/IP Foundations*,[2] uses a wonderful illustration of a children's soccer team at a pizza parlor with an attached game arcade:

> *Let's say that I take my son's soccer team to an arcade and restaurant for a team party. I have the whole team outside the arcade. My task is to get the team to the other side of the arcade, to my wife who is waiting for them in the restaurant. In this analogy, the team represents the complete file on one host, and each child represents a data packet. One of my goals is to lose as few of the kids as possible.*
>
> *While we are standing outside, it is easy to put the team in order; all the children are wearing numbered jerseys. I tell the kids that we will meet on the other side of the arcade in a restaurant for pizza and that they should all move as fast as possible through the arcade and to the restaurant.*
>
> *After I open the door and say "Go," the kids enter one at a time. Entering the arcade one at a time represents the fragmenting and sending of the file. Just as each of the kids has a numbered jersey, each packet has a number so that the receiving host can put the data back together.*
>
> *Now picture a dozen 6-year-olds moving through the arcade. Some of the children will take a short route; others will take a long route. Possibly, they'll all take the same route, though it is much more likely that they will all take different routes. Some will get hung up at certain spots, but others will move through faster. My wife is in the restaurant waiting to receive the team. As they start arriving at the restaurant, she can reassemble the children (packets) in the correct order because they all have a number on their backs. If any are missing, she will wait just a bit for the stragglers and then send back a message that she is missing part of the team (file).*
>
> *After I receive a message that she is missing a child (a packet), I can resend the missing part. I do not need to resend the entire team (all the packets), just the missing child (packet or packets).*

2. This book is no longer available, but references to it still exist on a number of Internet Web pages, most notably on www.wikipedia.com under the search string "OSI model."

Please note, however, that I would not go look for the lost child; I would just put the same numbered jersey on a clone of the lost child and send him into the arcade to find the restaurant.

TCP is designed to reconstruct lost packets so that an entire communication is intact. This is very important for files, such as employee records, word processing files, and spreadsheets, where a missing packet can cause the whole file to be unreadable.

User datagram protocol

For video and audio, another protocol is required. TCP can cause problems with audio and video files, because its attempt to resend lost packets results in portions of the communication occurring out of place and therefore in the wrong sequence, making the video or audio communication intelligible. The human eye and ear are very good about rebuilding lost portions of communications. Imagine a restaurant in which you are overhearing a conversation at an adjacent table. You may not be able to hear the entire conversation—not every word because of the noise from others talking—but you can still follow what is being said.

Instead, what we need is a protocol that will send the data without error correction and without attempting to resend lost packets. That protocol is the User Datagram Protocol (UDP). UDP is called a connectionless protocol, because it does not attempt to fix bad packets. It simply sends them out and hopes they arrive. The transmitting device has no way of knowing whether they do or not.

UDP and its partner, Real-Time Protocol (RTP), work together to ensure that a constant stream of data (hence the term "streaming data") is supplied for a receiving program to view or hear. RTP is used for audio and video. Typically, RTP runs on top of the UDP protocol.

As an industry default, all network data are called TCP/IP data, whether it is TCP/UDP or RTP. It is kind of like calling any tissue Kleenex or any copier a Xerox machine. It is not accurate; it is just that everyone does it.

Another important set of protocols that security designers will need to know about are unicast and multicast protocols. These are discussed in detail later in this chapter.

Transport Control Protocol/Internet Protocol address schemes

Each network device has a network card, which connects that device to the network. The network interface card (NIC) has a MAC address and a TCP/IP address to identify itself to the network. The MAC address is hardware assigned at the factory when the device is manufactured. It can never be changed. The TCP/IP address is assignable, and it defines where in the network hierarchy the device is located. TCP/IP addresses are used to ensure that communication errors do not occur and that the address represents the logical location on the network where the device resides. TCP/IP addresses are like postal addresses, which identify where a house is on what street, in what neighborhood, in what city, in what state, and in what country. MAC addresses are like the name of the person who resides in the house. The MAC address will change if one replaces a computer with another, but the TCP/IP address can stay the same on the network for the user of the computer so that all messages to that user, worldwide, do not need a new MAC address in order to reach him or her.

There are two versions of TCP/IP addresses, which are known as IP version 4 (IPv4) and IP version 6 (IPv6). IPv4 was the original version under which the whole Internet worked until it was determined that the number of available addresses would soon run out. So a larger array of numbers was defined, called IPv6. IPv6 can accommodate a very large (virtually infinite) number of connected devices.

In IPv4, addresses are broken down into what is called decimal notation for the convenience of the user. Remember, each address is actually a series of binary data (ones and zeros), but they are grouped together in a fashion that is much easier to understand. Four groups are combined together, separated by decimals. Each group (byte) can be a number from 0 to 255 (a total of 256 numbers). This is an 8-bit value. A typical address can be from 0.0.0.0 to 255.255.255.255. IPv4 provides for in excess of 4 billion unique addresses. IPv6 replaces the 8-bit value with a 12-bit value (0.0.0.0 to 4095.4095.4095.4095). The IPv6 address range can be represented by a 3 with 39 zeros after it. It is a large number. IPv4 is still adequate for today's networks, but IPv6 is coming.

Briefly, the first one or two bytes of data, depending on the class of the network, generally will indicate the number of the network. The third byte indicates the number of the subnet and the fourth byte indicates the host (device) number on the network. The host cannot be either 0 or 255. An address of all zeros is not used, because when a machine is booted, which does not have a hardware address assigned to it, it provides 0.0.0.0 as it addresses until it receives its assignment. This would occur for machines that are remote booted (started up) or for those that boot dynamically using the Dynamic Host Configuration Protocol (DHCP). The part of the IP address that defines the network is called the network ID, and the latter part of the IP address is called the host ID.

Regarding the use of automatic or manual device addressing, we recommend manual addressing for security systems. DHCP incurs the possibility of security breaches that are not present with static addressing.

Networking devices

Security system digital networks are composed of five main types of network devices.

Edge devices

Edge devices include digital video cameras, digital intercoms, and codecs. These are the devices that, for the most part, initiate the signals that the rest of the system processes. One exception to this is that codecs can also be used to decode digital signals and turn them back into analog signals for viewing of digital video signals or listening to digital audio signals. The most common use of the decoding codec is for security intercoms, where an analog intercom module is a must in order to hear and speak from the console.

Communications media

Digital signals are communicated along cable or wirelessly. The most common type of wired infrastructure is an Ethernet cabling scheme. Although other types exist (ring topology, etc.), none are prevalent. Ethernet is a wired scheme that allows many devices to compete for attention on the network. It is designed to handle collisions that occur when two or more devices want to talk simultaneously.

Devices contend for attention and are granted permission to speak when all other devices listen. Contention can slow a network, reducing its throughput. A network can be segmented by switches and routers to reduce contention and regain efficiency.

Ethernet is defined under IEEE[3] Standard 802.3. Ethernet classes vary by speed, with the slowest being 10Base-T (10 Mbps). Fast Ethernet is called 100Base-T and operates at 100 Mbps. Gigabit or 1000Base-T operates at 1 Gbps. Wiring distances depend on wire type and speed. Ethernet is wired using unshielded twisted pair four-pair wiring on RJ-45 connectors. Category 5 (Cat5) or Category 5 Enhanced (Cat5E) wiring is used for 10Base-T, 100Base-T, and 1000Base-T (up to 328 ft). Category 6 (Cat6) wire is useful for 1000Base-T runs up to 328 ft. For 1000Base-T connections, all four pairs are used, whereas for 100Base-T connections, only two pairs of wires are used.[4]

Cat5, Cat5E, and Cat6 cables use four pairs, where the colors are as follows:

- Pair 1—white/blue
- Pair 2—white/orange
- Pair 3—white/green
- Pair 4—white/brown

The second most common type of wired infrastructure is fiber optic. These come in two types: single mode and multimode. When told that the difference between the two is the number of signals they can carry, newbies often think that the single mode will carry one and the multimode will carry more. In fact, just the opposite is true.

Single-mode fiber is based on a laser, whereas multimode may use either a laser or a light-emitting diode (LED) for a signal source (Fig. 27.2). Multimode fiber is typically plastic, whereas single-mode fiber is made of glass. Multimode fiber has a large cross-sectional area relative to the wavelength of the light transmitted through it, typically either 50 or 62.5 μm (micron) fiber diameter compared to 1.3 μm for 1300 nm modulated light frequency. Accordingly, multimode bounces the light off the inside of the fiber (Fig. 27.3). As the light bounces off the walls of the fiber, it takes many different paths to the other end, which can result in multiple signals at the other end. The result is a softening or rounding of the square digital signal. Over distance the signal becomes more difficult to read at the receiver—thus the limited distance of multimode fiber.

3. The Institute of Electrical and Electronics Engineers (IEEE) is the world's leading professional association for the advancement of technology.
4. Hewlett-Packard, 2000. 1000Base-T Gigabit Ethernet Tutorial. Hewlett-Packard. Available from <http://www.docs.hp.com/en/784/copper_final.pdf>.

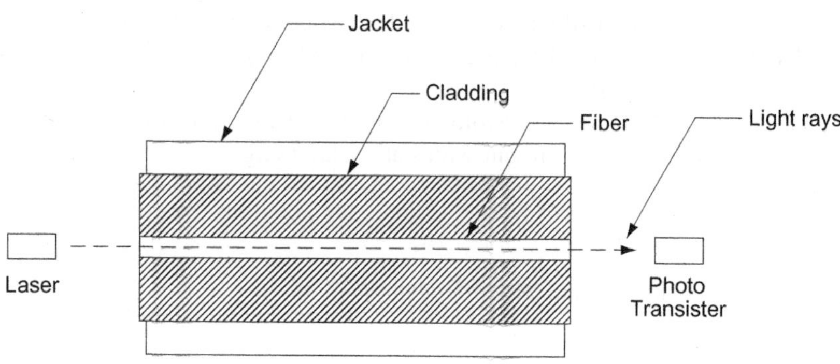

FIGURE 27.2 Single-mode fiber.

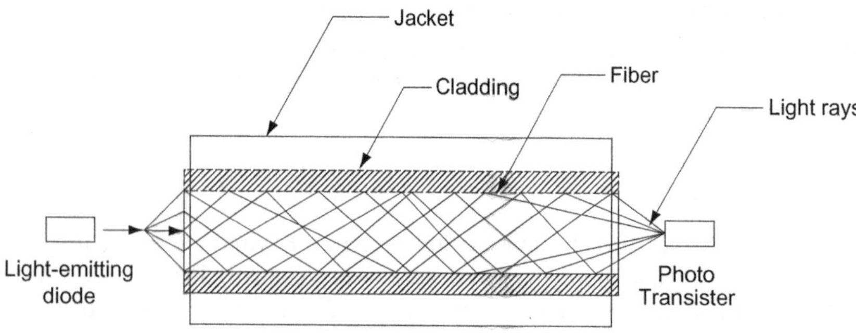

FIGURE 27.3 Multimode fiber.

Distance is also a factor of bandwidth. You can use multimode at longer distances with less speed. Fast Ethernet (100 Mbps) can travel farther than gigabit Ethernet (1000 Mbps). Check the manufacturer's specification sheets both for the fiber and the transceivers you intend to use for exact limits based on speed.

Single-mode fiber is made of glass, and it pipes the laser directly down the middle of the glass tube like a waveguide.[5] This is because single-mode fiber has a small cross-sectional area (8 or 9 μm) relative to the frequency of the light transmitted through it (1.3 μm at 1300 nm). The laser can carry multiple signals on its carrier.

The most commonly used frequencies are 1550, 1310, and 850 nm. The 1550 and 1310 nm frequencies are very common to single-mode fiber, and 850 nm is most commonly used in multimode fiber. The 1310 and 1550 nm frequencies are exclusively transmitted using lasers, and the 850 nm frequency is exclusively transmitted using LEDs. By using multiple frequencies (1310 and 1550 nm), it is possible to transmit and receive bidirectionally over a single fiber. Although this is not a common practice, some transceivers can accommodate two frequencies on a single fiber, especially with single-mode fiber. Typically, 1300 nm is used to send and 1550 nm is used to receive at one end and vice versa at the other end. More commonly, bidirectional communication is accommodated by using two separate fibers on the same frequency. No standard has been developed for multiple frequencies on a single fiber on multimode cable, but at least one security fiber optic company has developed a fiber optic media converter that can both transmit and receive on a single multimode fiber using two separate frequencies.[6]

Manufacturers have long since surpassed the IEEE 802.3z standard in terms of the distances served. Multimode fiber distances are typically limited to 1640 ft for fast Ethernet connections. Gigabit speeds are commonly limited to 1000 ft. Single-mode fiber distance limitations vary and can commonly be 43–62 mi with economical equipment;[7] much farther

5. A waveguide is a structure that guides very high frequency radio waves (radar, microwave, etc.) down a tube from a transmitter to an antenna or from a receiving antenna to a receiver. Above normal radio frequencies, conventional wires are useless for carrying the signal because of the "skin effect." The skin effect is an effect of physics that results in radio waves traveling increasingly closer to the outside of a conductor as the frequency rises, eventually losing connection with the conductor altogether. Above that frequency, a waveguide must be used to contain the transmission because normal wiring is unusable. The low-frequency cut-off of a waveguide is half of the wavelength of the frequency being passed. In general, waveguides are useful above 1 GHz.

6. American Fibertek 47-LX series 1000Base-LX Ethernet Fiber Optic Media Converter uses a single multimode fiber and transmits and receives on two frequencies (1310 and 1550 nm). This company also makes a 100Base-LX converter "45-LX series." Both units use a laser to transmit and receive on a single multimode fiber. This company also makes LED two-fiber single-mode and multimode solutions, as do many other firms.

7. Cisco Gigabit Interface Converter 1000Base-ZX GBIC media converter using premium single-mode fiber or dispersion shifted single-mode fiber.

distances are possible (up to 500 mi) with more sophisticated media converters.[8] With commonly available equipment, it is possible to achieve distances of up to 93 mi with single-mode or multimode at 100Base-T speeds and 75 mi at 1000Base-T speeds.[9]

Lastly, single-mode transceivers and fiber are more costly than their comparable multimode equivalents. The cost delta can be vast. Use multimode for shorter distances (e.g., on a campus) or where cost is a factor. However, the cost delta can sometimes be worth it if there is available single-mode fiber in the ground on a campus and the only cost to mount up the system is that of the transceivers.

Gigabit switches and routers are usually supplied with single- or multimode fiber ports. This is the preferred connectivity method over the use of separate transceivers.

TCP/IP signals can also be communicated via radio, microwave, or laser. The most common type of radio communication network is in the 802.11 band. This band is available in two major categories: backhaul or client service. The backhaul type is delivered by 802.11a, whereas client services are often provided by 802.11b/g/i. 802.11a makes available 10 channels, and with the correct antennas one can use all the 10 channels in the same airspace. 802.11b/g/i are very similar but differ by the bandwidth provided and the level of security implemented. 802.11b provides 11 Mbps maximum, whereas 802.11g/i provide 54 Mbps. It is possible to find 802.11g devices that provide 108 Mbps. These are full-duplex devices that use a separate transmitter and receiver to double the bandwidth. This function is very common in 802.11a, which also provides 54 Mbps per available channel. 802.11b/g/i have 13 available channels, but cross-traffic is a problem. Do not plan to use more than six channels in a single airspace.

Network infrastructure devices

Network infrastructure devices comprise those devices that facilitate the movement of data along the communications media. Digital cameras and codecs connect to a digital switch in order to get on the network.

Hubs

The most basic type of network device is a hub. A hub is simply a device with Ethernet connectors, which connects all devices together in parallel with no processing. A few hubs have power supplies and provide LEDs to indicate port activity, but do not confuse this with active electronics. Hubs are dumb. Hubs have no ability to control the collisions that naturally occur in Ethernet environments, so when too many devices are connected together on a hub, the network throughput suffers due to delays caused by the collisions. It is inadvisable to use a hub for all but the simplest networks (less than eight devices). Hubs, which offer no security services, are OSI level 1 devices and connect devices.

Switches

A switch is a smart hub. Unlike a hub that presents each signal to all connected devices, a switch is able to read the TCP/IP packet header and direct the signal to the appropriate port(s). Switches are OSI level 2 devices and control where data may go.

Routers

Routers are one step up from switches. In addition to directing the traffic of individual ports, they can in fact make decisions about data that is presented to them and can decide if that data belongs on that section of the network. Routers can create subnets of the greater network. This allows functions and devices to be segmented into logical groups. Subnets reduce the overall amount of network traffic, making the network operate more efficiently. Subnets can be used to separate different sites, campuses, and buildings and are sometimes even used to separate edge devices from client workstations. Routers control what data may go.

8. Goleniewski, L., 2001. Telecommunication Essentials: The Complete Global Source for Communications Fundamentals, Data Networking and the Internet, and Next Generation Networks. Addison-Wesley, Reading, PA.

9. For example, FibroLAN TX/FX H.COM 10/100 provides 100Base-T speeds up to 93 mi (150 km) over single mode or multimode. Their GSM1000 and GSM1010 provide gigabit speeds up to 75 mi (120 km) over single mode or multimode. Prices vary from a few hundred to a few thousand dollars, depending on the range required and the required.

Firewalls

Firewalls are used with routers to deny inappropriate data traffic from another network. Firewalls can be configured in either hardware or software. Security systems that are connected to any other network should be connected through a firewall. Otherwise, a security system is not secure and, thus, the facility will not be secure. Firewalls deny malicious data.

Intrusion detection systems

Intrusion detection systems (IDSs) can also be either hardware or software devices. They continuously monitor the traffic into and out of the network to detect any unauthorized attempt to gain access to the network. The IDS will warn the network administrator of the attempt and provide insight into how the attack attempt was executed in order to adjust the firewall to limit future attempts using that method. IDSs warn the system administrator about attempts to probe the network or insert malicious data.

Servers

Servers process and store data for use by workstations. For security systems, there are several possible types of servers. These may be combined on a single machine or may be distributed across several physical servers.

Directory service server

The directory service is an index for all workstations to use to find the data for which they are searching. It tells them where to find the correct camera, intercom, or archive stream. Additional functions may include Internet information services (IISs), domain name service (DNS), and other network management services.

Archive service

The archive server stores data for future reference.

Program service

The program service allows programs to reside on the server rather than on the workstation. This is not recommended because the few dollars saved result in a slower system.

FTP or HTTP service

This is very useful for remote monitoring and retrieval of data from a remote site to a central monitoring station, for example, or for a manager to "look in" on a site.

E-mail service

Servers can send or manage e-mail.

Broadcast service

Servers can broadcast alerts or alarms to pagers, cell phones, loudspeakers, printers, and so forth.

Workstations

Workstations provide a human interface to the network. Workstations can be single purpose or multiuse, serving other types of programs and other networks. For large sites, it is often best to use single-purpose machines on a dedicated network. Workstations can support many video monitors in order to display digital video, alarm/access control, intercom, report and analysis software, browser, and so forth. We often design systems that have up to six monitors per workstation. It is also possible to operate more than one workstation with a single keyboard and mouse in order to support more functions than a single workstation can handle. This is often necessary for systems that do not prioritize intercom audio over video.

Printers

Printers can be connected to a workstation or directly to the network, where they can serve multiple workstations.

Mass storage

Digital video systems can store a lot of data—much more data than any other type of system. It is not unusual for us to design systems with many terabytes of video storage. This amount of storage cannot be contained in a single server or workstation. There are two ways of extending the storage: network-attached storage (NAS) and storage area networks (SANs). The names are so similar that they can be confusing, but the differences are extensive.

NAS units include a processor and many disk or tape drives (or a combination of both). They are typically configured to "look" like a disk drive to the system, and they connect directly to the network, just like a server or a workstation. This means that a large volume of data traffic is on the network to feed the NAS.

A SAN is on its own network in order to separate the vast amount of traffic it generates away from the common network. This is a good idea, even for small systems. SANs can be created easily by adding a second NIC to the archive server and connecting the SAN to that NIC.

Network architecture

Simple networks

The simplest networks connect two devices together on a cable (Fig. 27.4). Basic networks connect several devices together on a single switch. This creates a local area network (LAN) (Fig. 27.5). From there, tree architecture is common. There may be a single workstation/server (one computer serving both purposes) that is connected through one or more switches to a number of cameras, intercoms, codecs, access control panels, and so forth (Fig. 27.6).

Advanced network architecture

Backhaul networks

Beyond simple tree architecture, as network size grows, it is common to create a backhaul network and a client network. This can be achieved in its simplest form with gigabit switches. A simple gigabit switch is equipped with a number of fast Ethernet (100 Mbps) ports to connect edge devices, such as cameras, codecs, intercoms, or access control panels, and a backhaul connection that supports gigabit (100 Mbps) speeds.

The result looks like an organization chart in which the server/workstation is at the top on the gigabit backhaul network and the edge devices (clients) are on the 100 Mbps ports of the switches (Fig. 27.7).

Subnets

A subnet is basically virtual LAN (VLAN) that is a logical subset of the overall LAN.

Subnets are used for several reasons, the most common of which are to limit network bandwidth to manageable levels or to minimize traffic that is not appropriate for certain devices, such as segregating buildings on a campus.

Subnets to limit network traffic As network bandwidth increases, it can task the switches to a point at which they begin to drop packets. I recommend that you do not pipe more than 45% of the rated bandwidth of any device, because

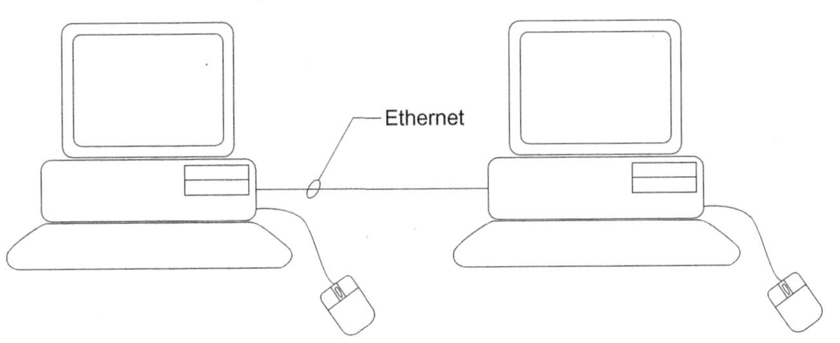

FIGURE 27.4 Simple network.

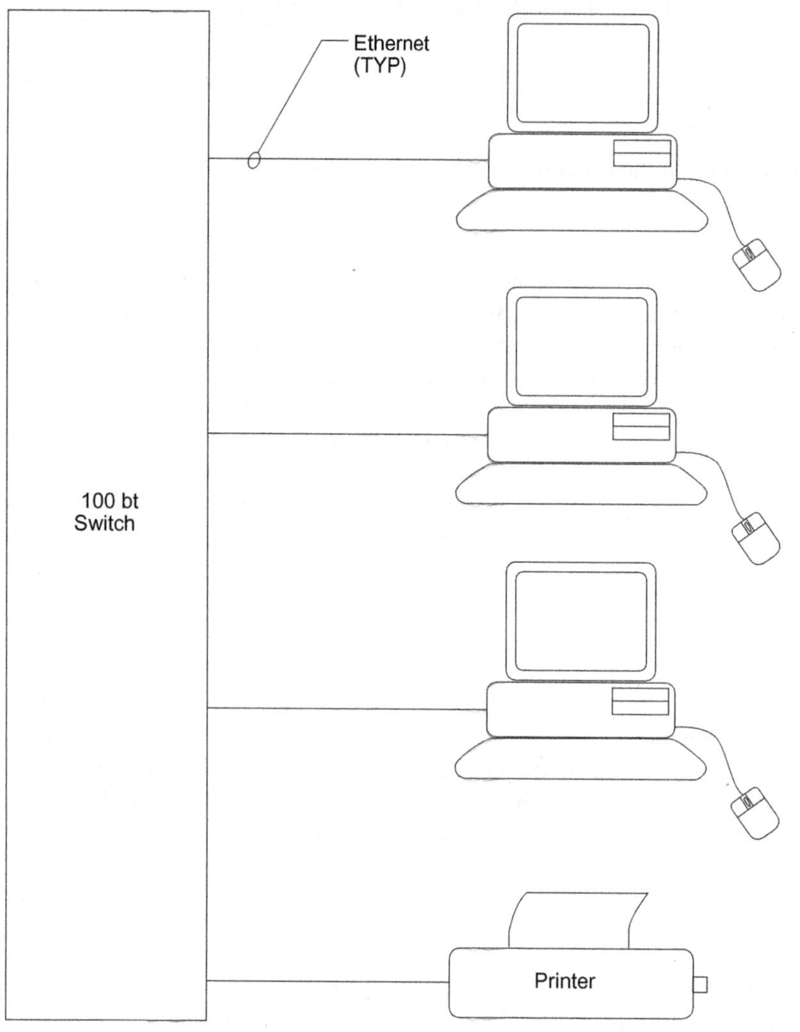

FIGURE 27.5 Switch-connected network.

FIGURE 27.6 Simple tree network.

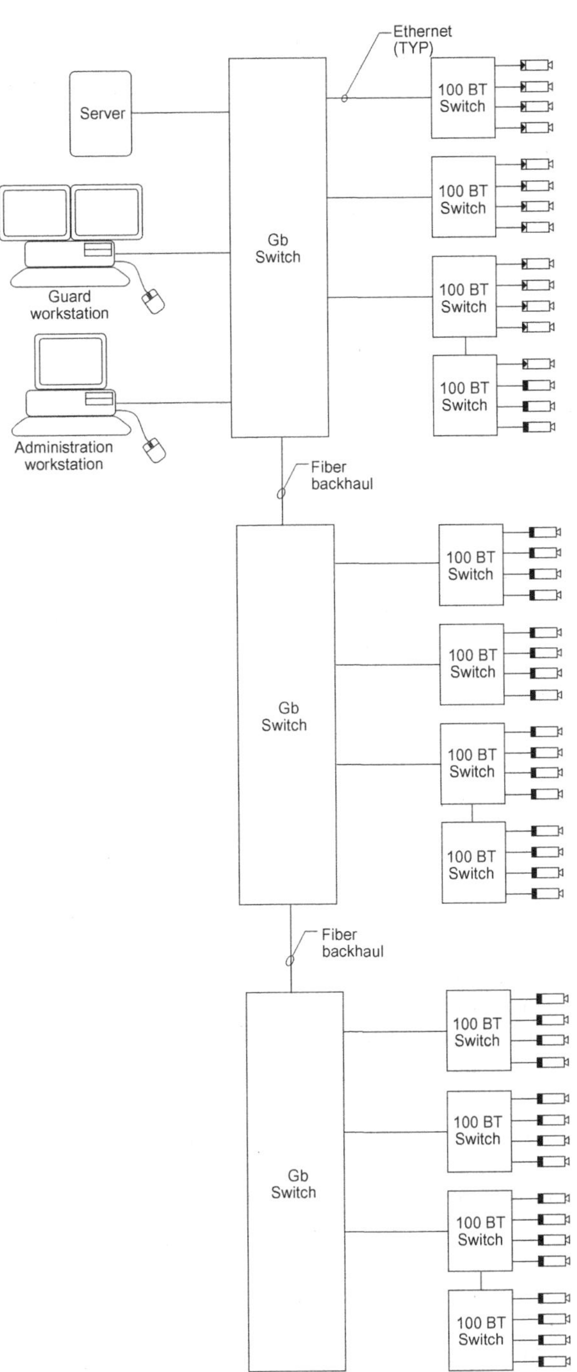

FIGURE 27.7 Backhaul network.

the rated bandwidths are based on normal network traffic and not on streaming data, such as video. Stay under 45% and you will not usually experience problems. A VLAN is created by joining two or more networks by routers.

Typically, routers are placed on the backhaul network, and they in turn may have their own backhaul networks that serve many edge devices. Architected thus, no single subnet will have too much traffic on it (Fig. 27.8).

Subnets to segregate network traffic When a security system serves many buildings on a campus, it is not useful to have the traffic of one building on the network of others. So, each building can be joined to the main backhaul network through a router such that its traffic is limited only to data that are relevant to that building alone (Fig. 27.9).

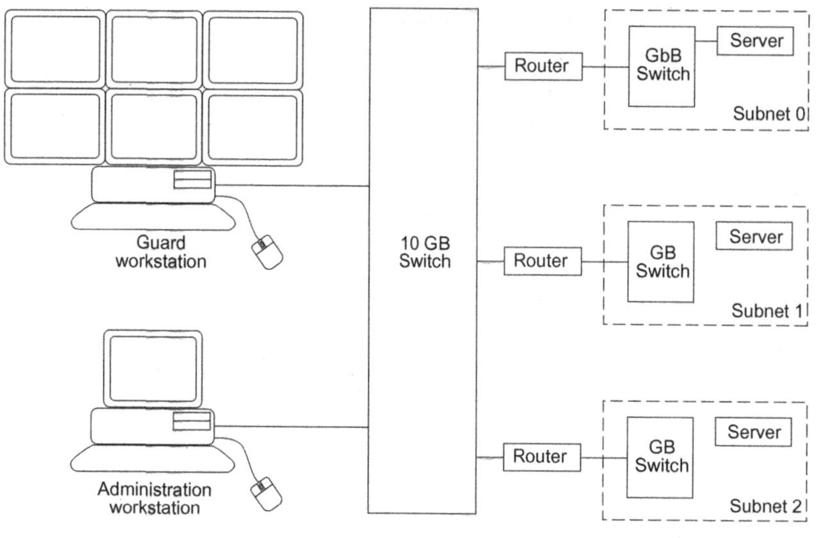

FIGURE 27.8 Subnet for limiting network traffic.

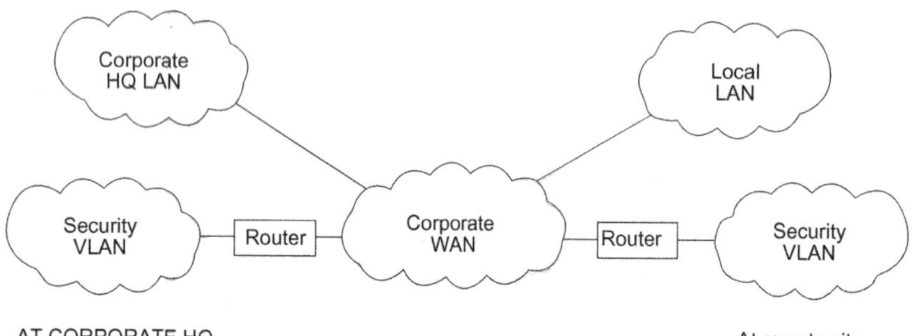

FIGURE 27.9 Subnet to segregate network traffic.

The security system could be placed on the larger organization's network as a subnet. Subnets can be integrated onto a larger network in a way that would seem by their physical connections to be blending the two networks, whereas in fact they operate as completely segregated networks, totally isolated from each other by routers and firewalls. Be advised that enterprise security systems using large amounts of digital video can tax the bandwidth of virtually any organization's business network architecture to the breaking point.

It is often advisable to physically segregate the networks. In addition, when the security system is placed on the organization's network, significant additional effort is required to secure the security system network from the organization's network, which will never likely be as secure as the security system network, notwithstanding the assertions of the organization's information technology department (Fig. 27.10).

Virtual local area networks

VLANs are global subnets. Like a subnet, a VLAN segregates a data channel for a specific purpose or group. Unlike a subnet, which is a hierarchical daughter of a physical LAN, a VLAN can coexist across the mother LAN as a VLAN though there were two separate sets of hardware infrastructure. It does this by operating on a dedicated port to which only the VLAN has privileges. Therefore, cameras, intercoms, and access control system controllers can be plugged into the same managed switch with workstations and printers of the organization's business LAN, and when the security devices' ports are dedicated to a security VLAN, those devices will not be apparent or accessible to the users or the LAN. This is one of the best methods for sharing networks between security and business units.

Network configurations

A network is composed of a series of TCP/IP devices connected together. There are a variety of ways to do this, and each way has its own advantages and limitations.

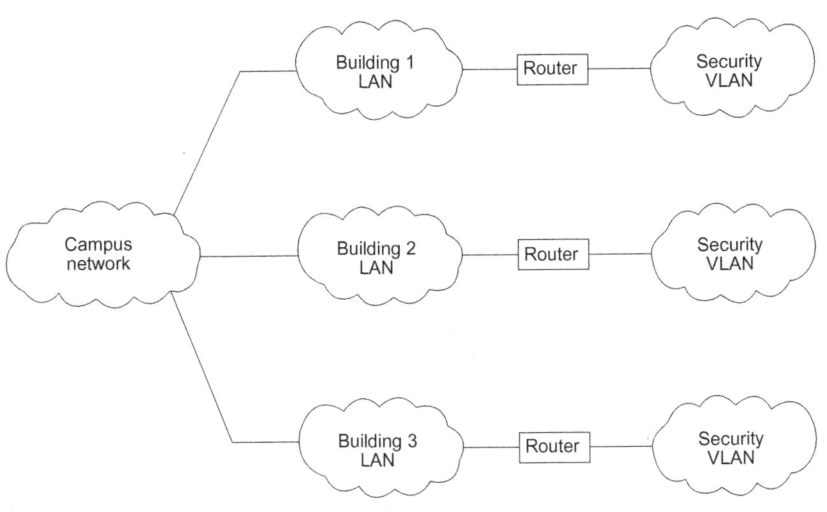

FIGURE 27.10 Subnet used to blend networks.

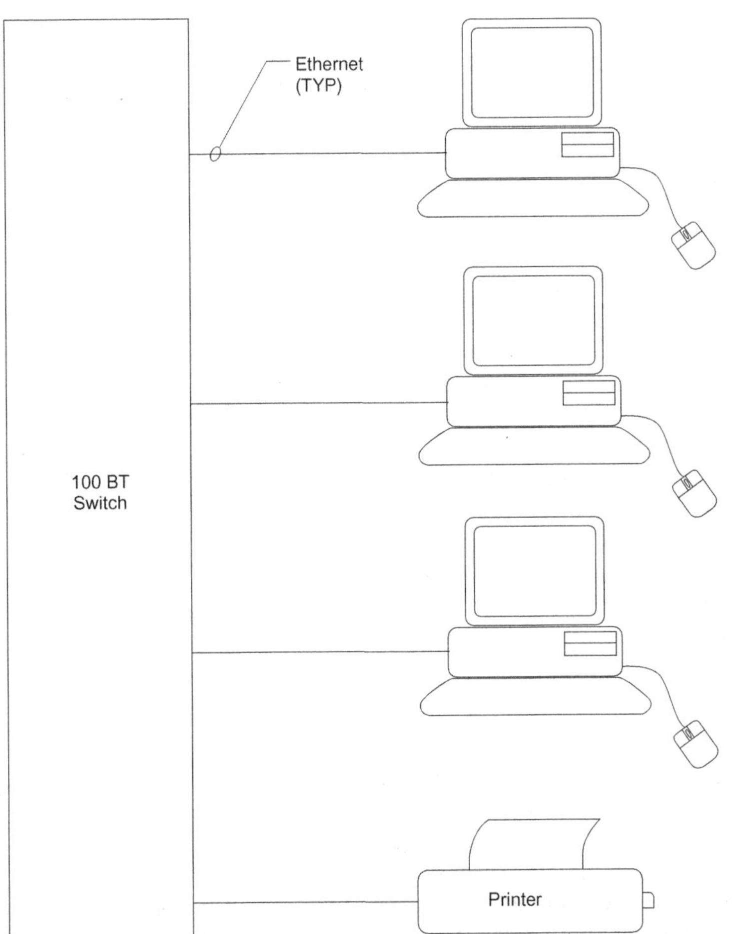

FIGURE 27.11 Peer-to-peer network.

Peer-to-peer

The most basic network is a stand-alone peer-to-peer network. Peer-to-peer networks are created by connecting each device together through a hub or switch. Each computer, codec, or access control panel is equal in the eyes of the switch. This is adequate for very small networks (Fig. 27.11).

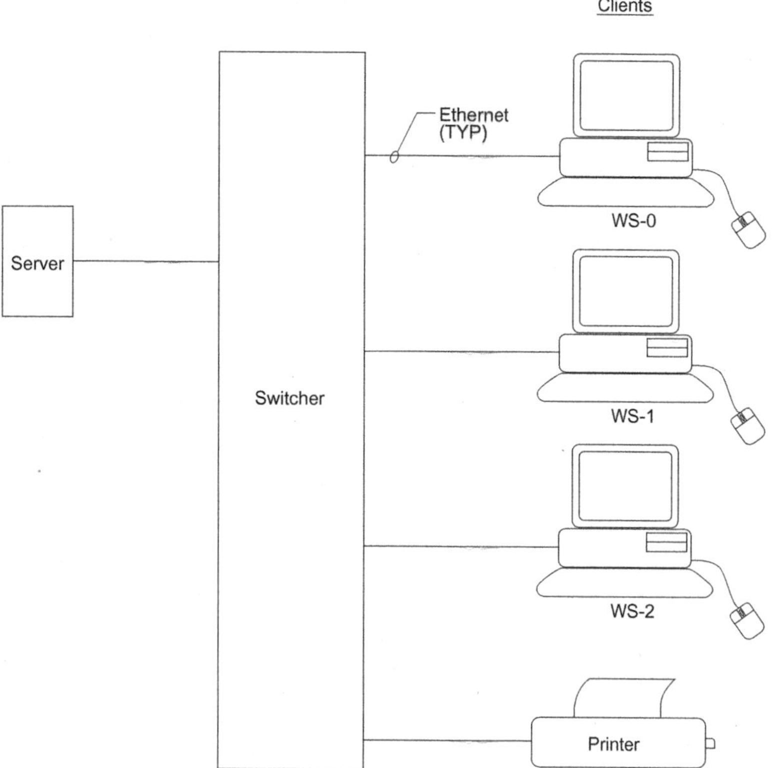

FIGURE 27.12 Client/server network.

Client/server configuration

As network sizes expand, a client/server configuration is preferred. Major processing is performed in one or more servers, and the human interface is accommodated with client devices or workstations (Fig. 27.12). Cameras, intercoms, access control readers, locks, door position switches, request-to-exit devices, alarm-triggering devices, and so forth are all human interface devices, as are guard and lobby workstations, intercom master stations, and so forth.

Typically, the human interface devices are connected to processing devices that interface to the network via TCP/IP connection, usually Ethernet. These may include codecs and alarm/access control panels.

On larger networks, it is common to use multiple servers. Commonly, there will be multiple archive servers.

It is also common to use a second set of servers as a backup to the primary servers in the case of a disaster that disables the primary servers. This allows for remote access to the data up to the second of the disaster in order to analyze the event and to provide a business continuity record of all network data.

Creating network efficiencies

One of the major advantages of enterprise security systems is the opportunity for remote monitoring of distant buildings. This often requires blending the security system network with the organization's business network.

The most common requirement is to monitor remote sites. It is not necessary to send all of the data from the monitored site to the site doing the monitoring. The monitoring center only needs to see the data it wants to look at. When you are watching a sports broadcast on TV on channel 11, you do not usually care much about the opera playing on channel 4. Likewise, it is advisable to attach the remote monitoring center only to those data that are relevant at the moment. You do not need to send the video of all the cameras all the time. Using this method, great efficiencies can be gained. Overall network bandwidth can be limited only to the cameras being monitored. I use cameras as an example here because they consume the most bandwidth.

There are two very efficient ways to remotely monitor over a business network: browser and virtual private network (VPN). A browser connection is quick, easy, and does not consume any bandwidth when it is not sending data. It consumes only what it displays. One can configure simple monitoring centers with browser connections to the remotely monitored sites. When one wants to see the site, one makes the connection; otherwise, the connection is closed.

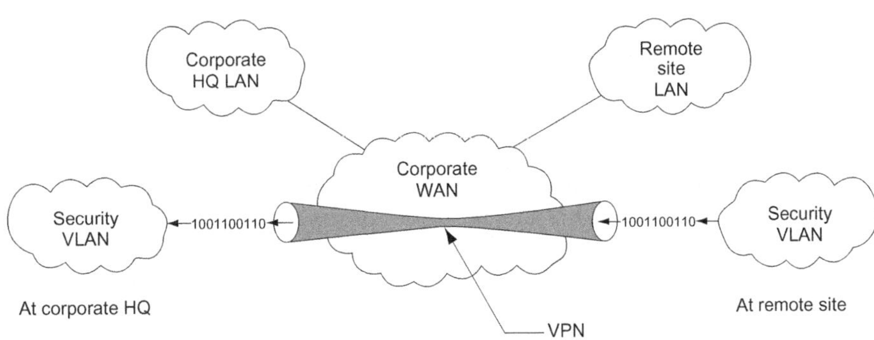

FIGURE 27.13 Virtual private network.

However, browser connections consume data even when minimized, whether or not the data is sent to the screen. This will consume both network bandwidth and workstation processing power. So it is advisable to close browsers when not being viewed. Alarms can be sent on a separate data link to alarm monitoring software that is always open. These consume virtually no bandwidth, so they can stay open at all times. Browsers should be run under https rather than http (https is a higher security environment), and secure socket layer encryption is often advisable to ensure the security of the system being monitored. Even so, browsers are not as secure as VPNs. Browser connections can be hacked.

A VPN can open and close like a browser, but it has vast advantages in terms of network security. A VPN is a tunnel between the server being monitored and the server that is requesting its data. That tunnel is firewalled and encrypted. It is as good as gold for security. It takes extremely high skill levels to hack a VPN. The disadvantage of VPNs is that they utilize a fixed bandwidth. When a VPN connection is open, that amount of bandwidth is in use regardless of the number of cameras being monitored.

That bandwidth is no longer available for the business network connection to that site (Fig. 27.13).

Digital video

Cameras and codecs

Digital video cameras are available in two types: digital or analog cameras with digital codec converters. Digital cameras are an emerging trend. The predominance of cameras available is still analog, and to use them in a digital video system one must add a codec.

Digital cameras do not provide a baseband video output (PAL or NTSC). They are equipped with either a USB or Ethernet connection. They issue digital images directly.

A codec is a device that converts analog to digital. There are a variety of codec types, in the following categories:

- *Number of channels*: Single-channel codecs support only one camera. Multiple-channel codecs support multiple cameras. Single-channel codecs are the best choice when the wiring infrastructure is predominantly digital, and multiple-channel codecs are a good choice when most of the wiring is analog. Multiple-channel codecs facilitate wiring a number of cameras to a single point where perhaps an analog video switch used to be, its space now being occupied by codecs.
- *Number of video data streams*: Many codecs output only one data stream per camera. Some support two, which is better. Each data stream can typically be configured to adjust the frame rate and resolution. With two data streams, you can adjust one for live viewing and the second for archiving. You might adjust the live viewing data stream at, for example, 15 fps and at medium resolution and the second stream at 4 fps and high resolution. In general, it is desirable for archiving retrievals to display higher resolution than for live viewing, since you are looking for detail rather than just a transient image.
- *Audio/no audio*: Some codecs support an audio channel and some do not. The audio channel will be its own separate data stream, usually under the same TCP/IP address.
- *Input and output contacts*: Many codecs also provide one or more dry-contact inputs and outputs. These are useful to control nearby devices or to cause some activation in the system. For example, it could be used to unlock a door or to cause an alert if a door opens.
- *Compression schemes*: Different codecs use different compression schemes, which are discussed later.

A basic digital image, such as a BMP (bitmap), is composed of a large number of picture elements called pixels, with each pixel having its own data attributes. These images take a lot of data space. It is common for a single BMP image to require several megabits of data. These large files are not useful for network transmission, because they use too much network bandwidth. The images can be compressed (made into smaller packets) literally by throwing away useless data.

There are two major types of digital video compression schemes: Joint Photographic Experts Group (JPEG) and Moving Pictures Experts Group (MPEG). JPEG is a scheme that results in a series of fixed images, strung together like a movie. MPEG is a similar group that from its inception created compression algorithms specifically meant for moving pictures.

- MPEG-1 was the earliest format and produced video CDs and MP3 audio.
- MPEG-2 is the standard on which digital television set-top boxes and DVDs are based. This is very high-quality video.
- MPEG-3 (MP3) is an audio codec.
- MPEG-4 is the standard for multimedia for the fixed and mobile web.
- MPEG-7 and MPEG-21 also exist but are for future projects.

Digital video security codecs and cameras are typically MJPEG (a series of JPEG images strung together as a stream of data) or MPEG-4.

BMP images are resolution dependent; that is, there is one piece of data for each separate pixel.

JPEG compression basically replicates similar data rather than storing it. For example, if there was a picture of a flag, the red portion might only be stored in a single pixel, but there will be a note to replicate the red pixel everywhere it existed in its original BMP file. This can achieve very high compression compared to BMP files.

MPEG compression takes this process one step further. For a sequence of images the first one is stored as a JPEG image, and each subsequent image stores only the differences between itself and the previous image. The first frame is called an "I-frame," and subsequent frames are called "P-frames." When too much updating is occurring, the process stores a new I-frame and starts the process all over again. The MPEG protocol results in very efficient file compression.

Advantages and disadvantages

Each JPEG image is a new fresh image. This is very useful where the frame rate must be very low, such as on an offshore oil platform with a very low bandwidth satellite uplink or where only a dial-up modem connection is available for network connectivity. I used JPEG on an offshore platform with only a 64 kb/s satellite connection available. MPEG is most useful where there is adequate data bandwidth available for a fast-moving image but where it is desirable to conserve network resources for future growth and for network stability.

Digital resolution

Digital image resolution is the bugaboo of digital video. You can never have enough resolution. However, high resolution comes at a high price in network bandwidth usage and in hard disk storage space. There is always a tradeoff between resolution and bandwidth/storage space. Thankfully, the cost of storage keeps dropping (I think we will soon see terabyte hard drives blister-packed for 99 cents), but I think that network bandwidth will always be a problem.

JPEG resolution is measured in pixels per inch. Proper resolution is required for good viewing. Ideally, you should be displaying 1 pixel of video image onto each pixel on the video monitor. If you display a JPEG image at a greater size on paper or screen than its native resolution, you will see a very fuzzy image (Fig. 27.14). Common file sizes are from 120 × 160 to 720 × 480. Larger sizes are available with even higher resolution.

MPEG resolution is measured in common intermediate format (CIF). In NTSC, CIF provides 352 × 240 pixel. In PAL, it provides 352 × 288 pixel. The lowest resolution MPEG image is a quarter CIF (QCIF) at 176 × 120 pixel, followed by CIF, 2CIF (704 × 240, NTSC), and (704 × 288, PAL), and finally 4CIF (704 × 480, NTSC) and (704 × 576, PAL). 16CIF will soon be available with very high resolution (1408 × 1152 for both formats), and there is also an amazingly low resolution SQCIF (128 × 96, NTSC). Most digital codecs provide CIF, 2CIF, and sometimes 4CIF resolutions (Fig. 27.15).

FIGURE 27.14 Fuzzy JPG image.

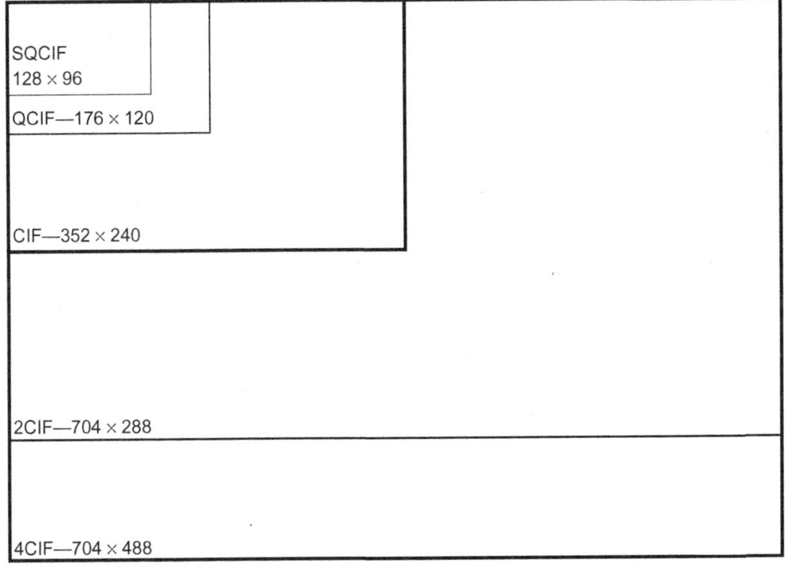

FIGURE 27.15 MPEG resolutions. *MPEG*, Moving Pictures Experts Group.

Frame rates

In order to see moving images, they have to move. Frame rate is the rate at which one frame of video is replaced by another. The speed at which this occurs is measured in frames per second. Some unique applications result in very slow frame rates of seconds per frame.

The human eye can visualize real-time motion as low as 12 or 13 fps. A minimum frame rate of 15 fps is recommended for real-time images. Many users prefer 30 fps because that is what is displayed on analog video. However, that frame rate is not required unless objects are moving rapidly.

Like resolution, frame rates affect both bandwidth and storage capacity in direct proportion to the frames per second.

Display issues

Display parity

Display parity is one of the problems that the security industry has not dealt with yet. This is achieved when the number of pixels sent to a screen is exactly the same as the number of pixels on the screen.

If one is displaying nine cameras in a window on a 20 in. LCD high-resolution screen, one might have only 160 × 120 pixel available on the screen for each image. Why would one want to send a 4CIF image (704 × 480) to that number of pixels? Why indeed? What happens to all those extra pixels? They are wasted, thrown away. The problem is that they are thrown away on the screen. They occupy tons (if that is a measure of screen processing) of central processing unit (CPU) and video card processing power before it gets thrown away on the LCD monitor.

No problem you say? Who cares? You do, if you are smart. Here is the problem. A 4CIF image generates 337,920 pixel. Each individual pixel requires a great deal of CPU processing power and many more graphics processing units (GPUs). Both CPUs and GPUs are consumed for each pixel. The original supercomputer, the Cray-1 developed at Los Alamos National Laboratory in 1976, was capable of 80 Mflops of processing power (flops is a unit of CPU or video card processing effort; it is an abbreviation of floating point operations per second). Although there is not a direct correlation between flops and pixel processing (there are approximately 40 variables involved in the calculation, making a calculation essentially meaningless), you can rely on the fact that it takes a lot of processing power to process video to the screen or to archive. At 30 fps, the computer is processing 10,137,600 pixel (10.1 megapixel) for each image at 30 fps. Remember, we were displaying nine images that calculate to 91.2 megapixel per second, which is just for the video. You are also running the video application, and on larger systems you are also processing audio for the intercom, alarm/access control, and perhaps other data. One can easily exceed 100 megapixel being processed per screen on one's desktop. For 16 images, at 30 fps at 4CIF, the number exceeds 160 megapixel being processed in real time, and that is just on one screen. That will crash virtually any workstation regardless of processing power. High-resolution times and high frame rate times many images can easily equal a computer crash. In addition, pixels thrown away on the screen present a rough look to the images. Without a doubt, display parity results in the best appearance.

The ideal process here is to have software in the server that disposes of unneeded pixels before they are sent to the workstation. This approach of prerendering the video image has many advantages in quality of display and network throughput. However, to date, no software vendor that we know of is even thinking about this problem.

So what has a designer to do? Well, there are only three variables available to manage this problem: image resolution, frame rate, and processing power.

First, there is little need to display images at 4CIF or greater unless one is displaying at full screen. It is better to send live images to the screen at 2CIF because the extra pixels will just be thrown away and no good will be served by the extra resolution that is consuming unneeded network bandwidth and processing power.

Second, archived images do not usually need to be displayed at 15 or 30 fps. Use a slower speed and higher resolution for archived video. When one calls up archived video, one is usually interested in seeing as much detail in the image as possible. Use higher resolution and lower frame rate. There are a few applications in which this is not appropriate, such as for casino environments, where fast-moving hands hold the secret to cheating.

Finally, I usually design systems with lots of processing power, typically dual Xeon computers as workstations. Dual-core processors better that. Expected advances will put teraflops of graphics processing power at hand.

Storage issues

As with display, storage consumes lots of data and processing power. Unless there is a compelling reason otherwise, it is best to store data at a slower frame rate than for live viewing. This not only saves disk and tape space but also helps ensure growth capacity.

Managing data systems throughput

Network throughput management requires math, sometimes lots of math, but it is a good investment. I do not recommend running any network or network segment beyond 45% of its rated capacity. If there is a segment that has a capacity of 100 Mbps, keep traffic to 45 Mbps. If it is a gigabit backhaul segment, keep the traffic to 450 Mbps. If you have to exceed 450 Mbps, it is better to use multiple gigabit communications paths or a 10 GB path. Your client will not likely understand, but he or she will not sue you either.

There are two ways of managing network throughput: more capacity and network segmentation. The cost/benefit is usually in favor of network segmentation.

By segmenting the network into subnets or VLANs, one can manage the traffic to manageable levels. All traffic does not have to be everywhere. By recording video remotely rather than centrally, traffic is diminished. If a backup is needed, or if there is a concern about the loss of data in remote storage, centralized recording is possible at far greater cost in network traffic and infrastructure cost. An alternative is "neighborhood" archiving, where a few sites are gathered together for storage, limiting traffic on the enterprise network.

System architecture

Servers

Servers provide the guidance and direction for the entire system and store its activities and history. A server can operate several applications simultaneously, and a server equipped with a dual-core CPU can also prioritize those services, ensuring that, for example, intercom calls always go through. Servers provide several basic services.

Directory service

The directory service provides the routing information to locate cameras, intercoms, and archived video on demand. It also maintains the necessary information for all system devices to communicate effectively.

Directory services can be local or global. In an enterprise-integrated security system the directory service may be both, with a global directory service centrally controlled, and local servers may maintain their own subordinate automatic fail-over directory services in the case of loss of communications with the global directory server.

Enterprise-integrated security systems also typically use an automatic fail-over server that runs parallel to the main server but in another location, ready to take over its activities immediately upon a failure of the main server.

Archiving data

The server will typically archive alarm/access control, video, and intercom activity, indexing it by date and time and often correlating video and voice data to alarm and security events so that the operator has immediate access to appropriate video and voice as he or she views alarm activity. Enterprise systems also typically use an automatic fail-over archive server.

Remote access services

Web access

A VPN helps ensure data integrity for off-site Web service connections. Remote access from within the domain is often accommodated by use of a VLAN.

E-mail and pager notification service

The server software may support e-mail and pager notification. These will require exchange server or similar software or a dial-up or Web connection for a pager.

Hardware configurations

Central processing units

In general, it is appropriate to specify the fastest or nearly fastest CPU available for the server with significant cache memory and a very fast front side buss.

Memory

More is better. At least 2 GB of RAM should be considered in 2007 era terms. As this book ages, more memory should be considered. Fill the thing to capacity. You will not regret it, and memory is almost cheaper than candy bars.

Disk storage

Operating systems and programs

All system servers should be equipped with multiple disks, including two mirrored automatic fail-over drives for operating systems and programs, complete with current configurations. These should be kept up-to-date so if one fails, the other takes over immediately. This is also less expensive than a full hot redundant off-site fail-over server and should be done even when a redundant server is used.

Additional disk slots should be dedicated to data archive up to the server's capacity. Disks are so inexpensive that it is almost always appropriate to specify the largest disks available. RAID-5 should be considered and configured to 500 GB segments for rapid searching of archived data.

Where additional disk capacity is necessary, external storage capacity should be considered. There are two methods of external storage.

Tape or disk

External storage is available in both tape and disk. It is generally recommended to use both. Disks can store up to a given time depth. Beyond that you can store endlessly on tape. For very large storage requirements a tape carousel automatically handles the process of keeping fresh tapes loaded and used tapes stored and ready for use. The carousel can be expanded to store as much or as little as is appropriate based on network archive usage and the length of time storage is desired.

Network-attached storage

NAS is external storage that is attached directly to the server switch. This is the least expensive option, but it has a negative effect on network throughput. Accordingly, I do not recommend NAS.

Storage area network

A SAN is a separate network on the backside of the server that is dedicated only to moving storage data between servers and the external storage media. There is a perception that SANs are unnecessarily expensive, but this does not have to be the case. A SAN can be created simply by placing an additional NIC in the server and porting archive data out the back to the external storage. A SAN switch handles the task, where multiple servers or multiple external storage units are required. SANs make the best use of the primary data network over which live data are flowing. They place virtually no additional burden on the live data network, conserving its spare capacity for system growth. SANs are always recommended for external storage, even if there is only one server and one external storage unit.

Workstations

A workstation is a computer used by a person who operates the system. There are a variety of basic workstation types.

Security-monitoring (command) workstations

Security command workstations are used in security command centers, typically in enterprise security systems. A security command center typically includes two or more security command workstations and may include an array of large-screen video monitors to support the joint viewing of images by operators at several consoles. These workstations typically include alarm/access control/digital videos and security intercoms as well as report-writing programs.

Guard or lobby-desk workstations

A guard or lobby-desk workstation is a single computer dedicated to supporting a guard's desk duties in a lobby. These may include alarm/access control, digital video, and intercom.

Administrative workstations

An administrative work station supports the management of an integrated security system, including system configuration, database management, and reports.

Photo ID workstations

Photo ID workstations are used to create identification badges for use with the access control system. A photo ID workstation typically includes a camera, backdrop, light source, sitting chair, digital camera, and workstation and may include a posing monitor to help the subject pose to his or her satisfaction. On larger systems, there may be several photo ID workstations in a single area.

Access-verification workstations

On high-security installations, an access-verification workstation may be used in conjunction with a mantrap and card reader to ensure that the person passing into a secure area is indeed who he or she claims to be and that his or her credential is valid for the secure area. The access-verification workstation displays a photo of the cardholder each time a card is presented. This allows a guard at the workstation to verify that the face is that of the valid cardholder.

Edge devices

Edge devices include cameras, intercoms, card readers, alarm detection devices, electrified door locks, and request-to-exit detectors. These are the devices that interface with the user. On a typical integrated security system the edge device connects with a data controller or codec, which converts its native signal (audio/video, dry contact, or data) to a uniform TCP/IP standard. Thus controllers and codecs are also edge devices. The edge devices typically connect to the system through a data switch.

Infrastructure devices

Between edge devices and servers/workstations is the digital infrastructure, which connects the system together and manages its communication rules.

Switches

Digital switches are the connection points for almost all system devices. A digital switch is a device that not only provides a connection point but also can manage how each device communicates with the system. A digital switch is like a mail carrier on a mail route, which ensures that each house gets the mail that is addressed to it for the neighborhood it serves.

Switches can segregate communications between devices and manage the priority and limit the bandwidth of the data of different devices. Switches generally have a number of RJ-45 eight-conductor modular jacks (typically 8–48) and can cascade communications in a ring or tree architecture. The switch must be specified to support the amount of data that is expected to go into its edge ports and out of its infrastructure ports. It is wise not to exceed more than 45% of the rated capacity of any switch for all signals combined, under the worst case conditions. Switches are OSI layer 2 devices, but better switches can also perform OSI layer 3 management functions. These are commonly called "managed" switches. Switches should be able to support IGMP querying and IGMP snooping in order to support video multicast. Ample memory is recommended (at least 100 kB per port), and the switch should be able to support VLAN operation. If the switch may need to become part of a trunk within a VLAN, then it should also be able to support 802.1Q protocol. For outdoor operation a robust environmental tolerance is needed. The switch should be able to operate from well below freezing (−10°F/−23°C) to high temperatures (160°F/71°C is ideal). These are commonly called "hardened" switches. Redundant power supplies are also recommended.

Routers

Routers manage data traffic at a more global level and are OSI level 3 devices. An edge router is like a local post office that routes mail from one locale to another, where it will be handed off to the neighborhood postal worker (the switch). A router that manages traffic for an entire organization to the Internet is called a core router.

Routers are capable of segregating traffic into subnets and VLANs, creating logical separations of data and making communications within the network much more efficient and secure.

Firewalls

A network firewall is a computing device that is designed to prevent communications from and to some devices in support of an organization's network security policy.

Wireless nodes

Wireless nodes are radio-frequency transceivers that support network communications. Often, they also incorporate network switches, and sometimes they can incorporate routers and even firewalls. They also commonly encrypt data placed on the wireless link.

Network communications speeds

There are four common speeds of network communications:

- 10Base-T: 10 Mbps
- 100Base-T: 100 Mbps
- 1000Base-T: 1 Gbps
- 10000Base-T: 10 Gbps

Cabling

Network cabling can be wired or fiber optic. Fiber optic cabling types include single mode and multimode.

Wired cabling

Cat5E and Cat6 cables are used for network cabling. Both have a native distance limit of 300 ft. Cat5E and Cat6 cables can support 10Base-T, 100Base-T, and 1000Base-T connections, with distance decreasing as the speed increases.

Fiber optic

Fiber optic cabling can support faster speeds, longer distances, and simultaneous communications. Unlike wired cable, fiber only supports a single communication on a single frequency at one time.

Multimode

Multimode fiber uses inexpensive LEDs operating at 850 or 1500 nm to transmit data. Multimode fiber is made of inexpensive plastic. In multimode fiber the light propagates through the fiber core, bouncing off its edges (thus multimode). Multimode fiber can support only one communication at a time on each frequency. Typically, two fibers are used together, one to transmit and one to receive.

Single mode

Single-mode fiber uses more expensive lasers and optical glass. Single-mode communication is right down the center of the glass fiber, never bouncing (thus single mode). Single-mode fiber can stand higher power and thus yields longer distances.

Scaling designs

Systems can be scaled by creating subnets, which can segregate the system based on function or location. This approach allows the master system to have oversight and observation of the activities of all of its subsystems while not allowing the subsystems to see or affect each other.

Interfacing to other enterprise information technology systems

Enterprise local area network or wide area network

The fundamental interface of the integrated security system is to the organization's enterprise LAN or wide area network (WAN). The recommended interface is to configure the enterprise security system as a VLAN on the enterprise LAN/WAN.

Remote monitoring from inside the enterprise LAN can be accomplished by placing the monitoring computer on the VLAN. If the monitoring computer is used on the business network, it should be equipped with two NICs to better segregate the VLAN from the LAN.

Remote monitoring over the Internet should be accomplished by the use of a VPN.

Process-control networks

Integrated security systems are classified as process-control networks. A process-control network differs from a business network in that it is a closed network, dedicated to a special purpose, and is segregated from the business network. The integrated security system may integrate with other types of process-control networks, including building automation systems (BASs), elevators, telephony systems, fire-alarm systems, parking management systems, and vending systems.

Building automation systems

BASs include controls for HVAC, lighting, signage and irrigation control, and the control of other building systems. BASs may interface to the integrated security system via RS-232 or TCP/IP. The common interface language is ASCII delimited files, although sometimes database integration is possible.

Elevators/lifts

There is often good reason to integrate security systems with the elevator system of a building. This interface permits the control of who goes to what floor, on which elevator, and at what time. In addition, it is common to place video cameras and intercoms within elevators.

There are two basic types of elevators: traction and hydraulic. Traction elevators are used in high-rise buildings and hydraulic elevators are commonly used in low-rise buildings and parking structures.

Access control interfaces

There are two common types of elevator access control interfaces: floor-by-floor control and hall call control. Hall call control simply enables or disables the hall call pushbuttons in the elevator lobby. Floor-by-floor control allows control over the selection of individual floors in each car for each cardholder. Floor-by-floor control components include a card reader in the elevator and an access control system controller that enables or disables each floor select button based on the authorizations for the individual card presented to the reader in the car.

More sophisticated floor-by-floor access control systems provide an indication of which floors the card can select by turning off the button lights to floor select buttons for which the cardholder is not valid and may also keep a record of which floor was actually selected. Today, those functions are handled in the programming of the elevator controller. For older elevators, as was done in the past, those functions can be accomplished with elegant relay logic programming.

Elevator control mechanisms affect the design of the elevator access control system. There are three common types: automated, relay, and on-the-car control. These are covered in detail elsewhere in this book.

Video cameras can be interfaced up the hoistway by using coax, ribbon cable, laser, or radio-frequency methods.

Intercoms can be the direct ring-down type or dedicated intercom type. They must ring to a location that will always be answered and must never be unmanned, even for a few minutes.

Private automatic branch exchange interfaces

Private automatic branch exchange (PABX) systems facilitate the connection of a number of analog or digital station sets to a central switch. The PABX switch will accommodate a number of central office telephone lines (from a couple to hundreds) and a number of telephone station sets (from six to thousands). The PABX switch routes incoming calls to the correct extension and routes outgoing calls to an available central office line.

Additional features of PABX switches may include direct inward dialing so that certain extensions can be dialed directly from the outside without going through the switch, an automated attendant, call waiting, voice mail, and many other unique features. Internal intercom functions are usually standard.

Station sets may be simple or complicated. Simple station sets may look like a home phone, whereas more complicated sets may display time/date and incoming caller ID. The set also may have many speed-dial buttons and may also show the line status of frequently called internal numbers. An operator's station set may display the status of every extension in the system by a field of lamps and select buttons or in software.

PABX systems are normally controlled by a dedicated computer located in the main telephone closet. They are capable of doing sophisticated interfaces to other systems, including security systems.

The security designer can use the PABX system as a security intercom system by utilizing door stations in lieu of standard station sets (depending on the manufacturer and model of the PABX system).

For almost every installation, it is important for the security console to be equipped with a direct central office telephone that is not routed through the PABX switch. This serves as an emergency communication link in the case of total power or equipment failure.

Voice over Internet Protocol systems

PABX switch systems are rapidly being replaced by Voice over IP (VoIP) systems. VoIP systems do not rely on central office telephone lines for their connection to the telephone company. Rather, they utilize the Internet for that connection.

The telephone station sets may be either conventional station sets with a VoIP converter or network devices.

VoIP phone systems are extremely flexible, since all of their functions operate in software. However, they suffer from two major potential problems relating to the security of the organization they serve. VoIP systems are subject to Internet outages, which are much more common than central office line outages that operate on battery power from the central office. With central office lines, if electrical power fails, it is likely that the telephone lines will still work. This is not the case with VoIP phones. In addition, VoIP phone systems are subject to intrusion by skilled hackers, making communications on a VoIP phone extremely unsecure.

VoIP phones are natural for integration with other systems, although those interfaces have yet to be developed by the industry.

VoIP systems should easily accommodate integration with IP-based security intercoms and with pagers. Digital two-way radios are also a natural point of integration. I expect to see such integration before the first revision of this book.

Fire-alarm systems

Fire-alarm systems are among the oldest of process-control networks used in commercial buildings. These typically have their own proprietary infrastructure that may be unique to the manufacturer. However, they often interface to other systems by means of RS-232 serial data streams or TCP/IP Ethernet. Typically, the interface is an ASCII delimited data stream that identifies the change of state of a fire-alarm zone. Occasionally, a designer may see access to a database that displays real-time status of all points in the system.

Public address systems

Public address systems can be configured with an analog or a digital infrastructure. The interface to a public address system will always be a one-way audio signal from the security system to the public address system for paging purposes.

Typically, the interface between the systems includes an audio signal and a zone selection, plus a push-to-talk momentary trigger. The interface may be analog or digital. Typically, analog interfaces are used on smaller public address systems, and larger systems may receive an analog or a digital interface for the audio stream.

Analog interfaces employ a microphone or line-level input to the paging system and one or more dry-contact inputs to select one or more zones. Often, it is possible to select groups of zones or an "All Call" selection, in which all zones will be paged.

Digital interfaces employ a digitized audio feed and a data string that performs the zone selection. On larger systems, both analog and digital, multiple public address amplifiers may be used to support different areas of a building or different buildings on a campus. In such cases the zone selections employ a hierarchical zone selection, in which one string may select the building, another selects the amplifier, and still another selects the zone on the amplifier.

We have also used the alarm/access control system to perform zone selections, controlling a single audio buss. This is an effective way to make a simple public address system operate like a very expensive one.

Parking-control systems

Parking-control systems perform a number of functions:

- Allow vehicles into a parking structure (car park) or parking lot
- Direct cars within a parking structure to one area or another
- Meter the number of cars in the structure
- Display up/down count signage of available spaces to drivers of cars entering
- Produce tickets for cash transactions
- Read the tickets and facilitate cash transactions for parking

- Use buried vehicle-sensing loops to verify the presence of a car at a card reader or in the path of a barrier gate, or to notify the gate that it can close after a car has passed through
- Access control systems interface with parking systems to facilitate the entry of cars to the parking area
- Access control readers may simply provide a dry-contact closure to notify the gate to open

The parking system may also feedback a dry-contact signal that causes the card reader to refuse to read cars if the parking area is full. Access control card readers may be of short range (6 in.) or long range (3 ft), or they may be overhead vehicle tag readers that do not require the driver to roll down the window.

The access control system may also be integrated with the parking monthly cash control system such that the card is enabled or disabled based on the payment of a monthly fee. The card readers may also permit special privileged parking for handicapped, expectant mothers, high-rent tenants, high-level executives, and so forth.

Vending access management systems

Vending access management systems are a variation of access control systems that are interfaced with a product vending system to provide product in kind for a prepayment or a charge account. In effect, the access control system is used like a credit or debit card.

Vending systems may include fuel management and vending machines, or the card may be used at a school bookstore and so forth. This requires a database interface between the access control system and the vending system such that the vending system has daily status on the validity of the card and it keeps a running database of credits and debits.

More protocol factors

Both wired and wireless digital security systems use unicast and multicast protocols to communicate. Unicast protocols, commonly TCP/IP, are meant to communicate a signal from one device to another. They ensure that the communication occurs by verifying the receipt of every packet of data. Unicast protocol is commonly used for pure data, such as alarm and access control data. Most networks are inherently based on TCP/IP protocol.

Multicast protocols, such as UDP/IP and RTP/IP, are used to broadcast data to any number of receiving devices. Unlike unicast TCP data, if a packet is not received, there is no mechanism or attempt to verify that and resend the packet. Multicast is widely used for video and audio data.

Do not confuse multicast protocol with multipath. Multipath is the phenomenon caused by radio-frequency reflections, and multicast is the distribution of a single digital signal to more than one destination using a single signal to which each receiving device signs up on a subscription.

Multicast can both reduce and increase network traffic, depending on how the network is configured. Multicast can reduce network traffic because there is no attempt to resend data. It is sent only once. Especially for radio frequency and satellite systems, where latency (circuit delays) can be a factor, the receiving computer can make many requests for unreceived packets. This has the effect of increasing data traffic for no good purpose, because the video frame or audio signal cannot be received in time to be useful, since it has already been displayed or heard.

However, because multicast transmits to any device that will listen, it is important to configure the network to adapt to multicast protocol so that devices that do not need to process the data will not hear it. Otherwise, many devices are kept busy trying to process data that are of no use to them. On security systems, some devices have a capability of only 10Base-T (10 Mbps). Their input can be swamped by the signals of only a few video cameras, rendering them incapable of communicating. The effect is similar to a denial-of-service attack on a Web site, where it is flooded with unwanted traffic, bringing it down.

It is important to understand that multicast was designed for an entirely different application than to support distributed video cameras. It was designed to support a single source transmitting data to many destination devices. In video systems, there are many sources (cameras and intercoms) transmitting to a few destination devices (servers and workstations). This difference can have unintended consequences for the uninitiated. For example, in conventional multicast environments, the "edge" switches (those at the outermost devices) do not have to be managed switches. However, in distributed digital video systems, the outermost switches should be managed, because when multicast touches a device that cannot handle multicast protocol, that device broadcasts a return message for each packet it sees, often bringing down the entire network. When managed edge switches are used, however, each individual port can be set up with IGMP snooping to prevent multicast signals from getting to unicast devices (e.g., alarm/access control system panels).

Multicast anomalies

In addition, be advised that multicast traffic can have unanticipated side effects even on systems that are properly configured for it. For example, adding a set of mirrored backup archive servers to a security system requires the system to operate in multicast mode, since both the primary and the backup servers are receiving the data of all digital cameras at all times. On a typically configured digital video system, this can result in directing 200 Mbps of data traffic across the backhaul network to the backup servers. It is a little known fact that multicast data traffic can have an adverse effect on intercom codecs. I was once confronted with an enterprise security system that exhibited audio distortion in its intercoms when the backup servers were turned on. The additional data traffic was enough to cause the intercom talk codecs to distort the audio only when the archive servers were turned on (changing the system from unicast to multicast for all video signals). By reducing the volume setting of the talk intercoms, the "clipping" of audio signals was eliminated. This condition is especially obvious where audio converters are used to convert two-wire intercoms to four-wire for use with conventional audio codecs, because the two-/four-wire converter also inserts an additional volume control in series in the circuit.

Multicast is a very "user surly" environment. It is especially not friendly to radio traffic and should not be used on such by the unsophisticated designer. Many configuration settings are required to operate multicast on a wireless mesh network to ensure that the radios do not retransmit the multicast traffic endlessly, thus flooding the mesh with unnecessary traffic.

It is ideal to configure the digital video network into two distinct VLANs, where VLAN1 is the camera-to-server network and VLAN2 is the server-to-workstation network. Run VLAN1 (the cameras) in unicast and VLAN2 (clients) in multicast. Configure IGMP querying on a primary and backup core switch, and configure all switches to support IGMP snooping to ensure that no unicast devices retransmit multicast signals. IGMP querying asks which switch ports want to sign up for multicast signals, and IGMP snooping sends those signals only to those ports. Utilize managed switches to ensure IGMP conformance.

Summary

Understanding information technology infrastructure is the basis for a successful integrated security system design. The reader should carefully read and understand this chapter in order to succeed as a designer.

The TCP/IP suite of protocols is the basis for information technology network systems. This chapter provides a detailed description of how TCP/IP works. The designer will not achieve success without a comprehensive understanding of TCP/IP.

TCP/IP operates on levels 3 and 4 of the OSI networking model. Data are encapsulated from the application program through the seven layers down to the network wire, sent across the network, and then decapsulated backup the seven layers to the application on the other end.

TCP protocol is able to fix bad communications. Other protocols in the TCP/IP family include UDP and RTP, which do not fix bad communications but are better suited for streaming data, such as video and audio.

TCP/IP is also an addressing scheme. Each network-connected device is assigned a TCP/IP address that identifies its location on the network. Addresses can be assigned automatically or manually.

Common wiring schemes include Ethernet and fiber optic cables. Ethernet is available on Cat5, Cat5E, and Cat6 cable at speeds of 10, 100, and 1000 Mbps or 10Base-T, 100Base-T, or 1000Base-T (gigabit Ethernet). Fiber optic runs can be on either single-mode or multimode fiber. Single-mode fiber can carry more data farther. Multimode cable and transducers are less expensive. Gigabit switches are often available with fiber connectors to link switches together over long distances, and RJ-45 connectors are used for short runs of Ethernet cables to local devices.

Edge devices include IP video cameras, IP intercoms, and codecs. Network infrastructure and wiring is connected using hubs, switches, routers, and firewalls. Hubs are rarely used today, because they simply connect wires together and do nothing to handle network contention. Switches handle the connection of local devices. Routers control where network communications can go. Firewalls exclude unauthorized devices from gaining access to the network. IDSs monitor the network firewall to detect any attempt to intrude into the network.

Integrated security system network computers include servers and workstations. Servers can include directory service servers (Windows directory service), IISs, DNS, and other network management services. Other services may include archiving, application program service, ftp, http, e-mail, and broadcast services. Workstations provide the interface between users and the network. Printers and mass storage systems round out the network-attached devices. Mass storage systems include NAS and SANs.

Network architecture includes simple networks, LANs, and WANs. Advanced network architecture includes back-haul networks, subnets, and VLANs. Network connection types include peer-to-peer and client/server configurations. Systems can be monitored remotely and safely using browser (http) or VPNs. Digital cameras can link directly to the network, whereas analog video cameras require a codec interface.

Typical video compression schemes include MJPEG, MPEG-2, and MPEG-4. MJPEG is a stream of individual images strung together to show movement, whereas MPEG schemes display a single image and then update subsequent frames only with the changes in the image.

Workstation types include security-monitoring centers, guard or lobby-desk workstations, administrative workstations, photo ID workstations, and access-verification workstations.

Integrated security systems can interface to many other types of systems, including process-control networks, BASs, elevators, PABXs, VoIP systems, fire-alarm systems, public address systems, parking-control systems, and vending systems.

Multicast protocol is sometimes used in digital video systems, but it is fraught with many nuances requiring special skills and knowledge. I recommend a thorough understanding before implementing multicast protocol.

Chapter 28

Internal theft controls*

Robert Fischer†, Edward L. Halibozek and Gion Green†
Security Consultant

Introduction

It is sad but true that *virtually* every company suffers losses from internal theft—and these losses can be enormous. Early in this new century, even the large corporate giants, such as Enron and WorldCom, were affected by internal corruption that reached the highest levels of the organization. *Security* reports that, in the retail business alone, 1 in every 27 employees is apprehended for theft from their employer. Internal theft in the retail business outstrips the loss from shoplifting approximately 7.9 times. Loss prevention consultants reported the significance of the employee-theft problem. Their study, based on the confessions of 345 employee thieves, documents a combined shrinkage of over $1 million over a 4-year period. The study notes that employee theft is not seasonal, and accessibility rather than need triggers the desire to steal. The report notes, however, that 51% of the thieves over 41 years of age reported that they stole to satisfy financial needs. Younger employees tend to steal gadgets, while older thieves take money.

The significance of employee theft is pointed out in a 2007 University of Florida and National Retail Federation report. Dr. Richard Hollinger, the report's lead author, reported that $19.5 billion was lost to retailers thanks to thieving employees.

What is honesty?

Before considering the issue of dishonest employees, it is helpful to understand the concept of honesty, which is difficult to define. Webster says that honesty is "fairness and straightforwardness of conduct, speech, etc.; integrity; truthfulness; freedom; freedom from fraud." In simple terms, honesty is respect for others and their property. The concept, however, is relative. According to Charles Carson, "Security must be based on a controlled degree of relative honesty" since no one fulfills the ideal of total honesty. Carson explores relative honesty by asking the following questions:

1. If an error is made in your favor in computing the price of something you buy, do you report it?
2. If a cashier gives you too much change, do you return it?
3. If you found a purse containing money and the owner's identification, would you return the money to the owner if the amount was $1/$10/$100/$1000?

Honesty is a controllable variable, and how much control is necessary depends on the degree of honesty of each individual. The individual's honesty can be evaluated by assessing the degree of two types of honesty: moral and conditioned. Moral honesty is a feeling of responsibility and respect that develops during an individual's formative years; this type of honesty is subconscious. Conditioned honesty results from fearing the consequences of being caught; it is a product of reasoning. If an honest act is made without a conscious decision, it is because of moral honesty, but if the act is based on the conscious consideration of consequences, the act results from conditioned honesty.

Honesty is a controllable variable, and how much control is necessary depends on the degree of honesty of each individual.

*Originally from Fischer, R., Halibozek, E.L., Green, G., 2008. Introduction to Security. Butterworth-Heinemann, Boston, MA. Updated by the editor, Elsevier, 2011.

† Deceased

Handbook of Loss Prevention and Crime Prevention. DOI: https://doi.org/10.1016/B978-0-12-817273-5.00028-4

It is vital to understand these principles because the role of security is to hire employees who have good moral honesty and condition employees to greater honesty. The major concern is that the job should not tempt an employee into dishonesty.

Unfortunately there is no sure way to recognize potentially dishonest employees. Proper screening procedures can eliminate applicants with unsavory pasts or those who seem unstable and therefore possibly untrustworthy. There are even tests that purport to measure an applicant's honesty index. But tests and employee screening can only indicate potential difficulties. They can screen out the most obvious risks but can never truly vouch for the performance of any prospective employee under circumstances of new employment or under changes that may come about in life apart from the job.

The need to carefully screen employees has continued to increase. In today's market, there are many individuals who have been called the "I deserve it!" generation. According to a study by the Josephson Institute for the Advanced Study of Ethics, "cheating, stealing and lying by high school students have continued their alarming, decade-long upward spiral." The institute, which conducts nonpartisan ethics programs for the Internal Revenue Service, the Pentagon, and several major media organizations and educators, states that their findings show "evidence that a willingness to cheat has become the norm and that parents, teachers, coaches and even religious education have not been able to stem the tide." To support the research the institute notes that, in 2002, 37% of the high school youth reported that they would be willing to lie to get a good job, compared to 28% in 2000 and 25% in 1992. Seventy-four percent of high school students reported they cheated on tests during 2002 compared to 61% in 1992. The good news is that the 2006 results reported a decline of those who reported cheating on a test to 60%. The 2006 study found that young people believe that ethics and character are important but are cynical about whether they can be ethical and succeed.

The dishonest employee

Since there is no fail-safe technique for recognizing the potentially dishonest employee on sight, it is important to try to gain some insight into the reasons why employees may steal. If some rule of thumb can be developed that will help to identify the patterns of the potential thief, it would provide some warning for an alert manager.

There is no simple answer to the question of why heretofore-honest people suddenly start to steal from their employers. The mental and emotional processes that lead to this are complex, and motivation may come from any number of sources.

Some employees steal because of resentment over real or imagined injustice that they blame on management indifference or malevolence. Some feel that they must maintain status and steal to augment their incomes because of financial problems. Some may steal simply to tide themselves over in a genuine emergency. They rationalize the theft by assuring themselves that they will return the money after the current problem is solved. Some simply want to indulge themselves, and many, strangely enough, steal to help others, or employees may steal because no one cares, because no one is looking, or because absent or inadequate theft controls eliminate the fear of being caught. Still others may steal simply for excitement.

The theft triangle

A simplified answer to the question of why employees steal is the theft triangle. According to this concept, theft—much like fire—occurs when three elements are present: (1) motive, (2) desire, and (3) opportunity.

In simple terms, motive is a reason to steal. Motives might be the resentment of an employee who feels underpaid or the vengefulness of an employee who has been passed over for promotion. Desire builds on motive by imagining the satisfaction or gratification that would come from a potential action. "Taking a stereo system would make me feel good, because I always wanted a good stereo system." Opportunity is the absence of barriers that prevent someone from taking an item. Desire and motive are beyond the scope of the loss prevention manager; opportunity, however, is the responsibility of security.

A high percentage of employee thefts begin with opportunities that are regularly presented to them. If security systems are lax or supervision is indifferent, the temptation to steal items that are improperly secured or unaccountable may be too much to resist by any but the most resolute employee.

Many experts agree that the fear of discovery is the most important deterrent to internal theft. When the potential for discovery is eliminated, theft is bound to follow. Threats of dismissal or prosecution of any employee found stealing are never as effective as the belief that any theft will be discovered by management supervision.

Danger signs

The root causes of theft are many and varied, but certain signs can indicate that a hazard exists. The conspicuous consumer presents perhaps the most easily identified risk. Employees who habitually or suddenly acquire expensive cars or clothes and who generally seem to live beyond their means should be watched. Such persons are visibly extravagant and appear indifferent to the value of money. Even though such employees may not be stealing to support expensive tastes, they are likely to run into financial difficulties through reckless spending. Employees may then be tempted to look beyond their salary checks for ways to support an extravagant lifestyle.

Poor hiring decisions are at the root of many management problems.

Employees who show a pattern of financial irresponsibility are also a potential risk. Many people are incapable of handling their money. They may do their job with great skill and efficiency, but they are in constant difficulty in their private lives. These people are usually not compulsive spenders, and they do not always have expensive tastes. (They probably live quite modestly since they have never been able to manage their affairs effectively enough to live otherwise.) They are simply people unable to come to grips with their own economic realities. Garnishments or inquiries by creditors may identify such employees. If there seems a reason to make one, a credit check might reveal the tangled state of affairs.

Employees caught in a genuine financial squeeze are also possible problems. If they have been hit with financial demands from illnesses in the family or possibly heavy tax liens, they may find the pressures too great to bear. If such a situation comes to the attention of management, counseling is in order. Many companies maintain funds designated to make low-interest loans in such cases. Alternatively, some arrangement might be worked out through a credit union. In any event, employees in such extremities need help fast. They should get that help both as a humane response to the needs and as a means of protecting company assets.

In addition to these general categories, specific danger signals should be noted:

- gambling on or off premises
- excessive drinking or signs of other drug use
- obvious extravagance
- persistent borrowing
- requests for advances
- bouncing personal checks or postdated checks

What employees steal

The employee thief will take anything that may be useful or has resale value. The thief can get at the company funds in many ways, directly or indirectly, through collusion with vendors and outside thieves or hijackers, fake invoices, receipting for goods never received, falsifying inventories, payroll padding, false certification of overtime, padded expense accounts, computer-record manipulation, overcharging, undercharging, or simply by gaining access to a cash box.

This is only a sample of the kinds of attacks that can be made on company assets using the systems set up for the operation of the business. The greatest losses can occur in these areas, since they are frequently based on a systematic looting of the goods and services in which the company deals and the attendant operational cash flow.

Significant losses do occur, however, in other, sometimes unexpected, areas. Furnishings frequently disappear. In some firms with indifferent traffic control procedures, this kind of theft can be a very real problem. Desks, chairs, computers and other office equipment, paintings, and rugs—all can be carried away by the enterprising employee thief.

Office supplies can be another problem if they are not properly supervised. Beyond the anticipated attrition in pencils, paper clips, note pads, and rubber bands, sometimes these materials are often stolen in case lots. Many firms that buy their supplies at discount are in fact receiving stolen property. The market in stolen office supplies is a brisk one and becoming more so as the prices for this merchandise soar.

The office equipment market is another active one, and the inside thief is quick to respond to its needs. Computers always bring a good price, as well as calculators and equipment used to support computers.

Personal property is also vulnerable. Office thieves do not make fine distinctions between company property and that of their fellow workers. The company has a very real stake in this kind of theft since personal tragedy and decline in morale follow in its wake.

Although security personnel cannot assume responsibility for losses of this nature since they are not in a position to know about the property involved or to control its handling (and they should so inform all employees), they should make every effort to apprise all employees of the threat. They should further note from time to time the degree of carelessness the staff displays in handling of personal property and send out reminders of the potential dangers of loss.

Methods of theft

A 2007 report by Gaston and associates pointed out that the American Management Association believes that 20% of business failures were the results of employee dishonesty.

Therefore the need to examine the shapes that dishonesty frequently takes is very real. There is no way to describe every kind of theft, but some examples may serve to give an idea of the dimensions of the problem:

1. payroll and personnel employees collaborating to falsify records by the use of nonexistent employees or retaining terminated employees on the payroll;
2. padding overtime reports and kicking back part of the extra unearned pay to the authorizing supervisor;
3. pocketing unclaimed wages;
4. Splitting increased payroll that has been raised on signed, blank checks for use in the authorized signer's absence;
5. maintenance personnel and contract service people in collusion to steal and sell office equipment;
6. receiving clerks and truck drivers in collusion on falsification of merchandise count (extra unaccounted merchandise is fenced);
7. purchasing agents in collusion with vendors to falsify purchase and payment documents (the purchasing agent issues authorization for payment on goods never shipped after forging receipts of shipment);
8. purchasing agent in collusion with vendor to pay inflated price;
9. mailroom and supply personnel packing and mailing merchandise to themselves for resale;
10. accounts payable personnel paying fictitious bills to an account set up for his or her own use;
11. taking incoming cash without crediting the customer's account;
12. paying creditors twice and pocketing the second check;
13. appropriating checks made out to cash;
14. raising the amount on checks after voucher approval or raising the amount on vouchers after their approval;
15. pocketing small amounts from incoming payments and applying later payments on other accounts to cover shortages;
16. removal of equipment or merchandise with the trash;
17. invoicing goods below regular price and getting a kickback from the purchaser;
18. manipulation of accounting software packages to credit personal accounts with electronic account overages;
19. issuing (and cashing) checks on returned merchandise not actually returned;
20. forging checks, destroying them when they are returned with the statement from the bank, and changing cash account records accordingly; and
21. appropriating credit cards, electronic bank accounts, and other electronic data.

The contagion of theft

Theft of any kind is a contagious disorder. Petty, relatively innocent pilferage by a few spreads through the facility. As more people participate, others follow, until even the most rigid break down and join in. Pilferage becomes acceptable, even respectable. It gains general social acceptance reinforced by almost total peer participation. Few people make independent ethical judgments under such circumstances. In this microcosm the act of petty pilferage is no longer viewed as unacceptable conduct. It has become not a permissible sin but a right.

The docks of New York City were an example of this progression. Forgetting for the moment the depredations of organized crime and the climate of dishonesty that characterized that operation for so many years, even longshoremen not involved in organized theft had worked out a system all their own. For all of the many cases of whisky unloaded, for example, one case went to the men. Little or no attempt was made to conceal this. It was a tradition, a right. When efforts were made to curtail the practice, labor difficulties arose. It soon became evident that certain pilferage would have to be accepted as an unwritten part of the union contract under the existing circumstances.

This is not a unique situation. The progression from limited pilferage through its acceptance as normal conduct to the status of an unwritten right has been repeated time and again. The problem is, it does not stop there. Ultimately, pilferage becomes serious theft, then the real trouble starts. Even before pilferage expands into larger operations, it presents a difficult problem to any business. Even when the amount of goods taken by any one individual is small, the aggregate can represent a significant expense. With the rising costs of materials, manufacture, administration, and distribution, there is simply no room for added, avoidable expenses in today's competitive markets. The business that can operate most efficiently and offer high-quality goods at the lowest prices because of the efficiency of its operation has a huge advantage in the marketplace. When so many companies are fighting for their economic life, there is simply no room for waste—and pilferage is just that.

Moral obligation to control theft

When we consider that internal theft accounts for at least twice the loss from external theft (i.e., from burglars and armed robbers combined), we must be impressed with the scope of the problem facing today's businesspeople. Businesses have a financial obligation to stockholders to earn a profit on their investments. Fortunately, steps can be taken to control internal theft. Setting up a program of education and control that is vigorously administered and supervised can cut losses to relatively insignificant amounts.

It is also important to observe that management has a moral obligation to its employees to protect their integrity by taking every possible step to avoid presenting open opportunities for pilferage and theft that would tempt even the most honest people.

This is not to suggest that each company should assume a paternal role toward its employees and undertake their responsibilities for them. It is to suggest strongly that the company should keep its house sufficiently in order to avoid enticing employees from acts that could result in great personal tragedy as well as in damage to the company.

Program for internal security

As for all security problems, the first requirement before setting up protective systems for internal security is to survey every area in the company to determine the extent and nature of the risks. If such a survey is conducted energetically and exhaustively and its recommendations for action are acted on intelligently, significant losses from internal theft will be a matter of history.

Need for management support

Once concerns have been identified, it is especially important that the strong support of top management be secured. To implement needed security controls, certain operational procedures may have to be changed. This requires cooperation at every level, and cooperation is sometimes hard to get in situations where department managers feel their authority has been diminished in areas within their spheres of responsibility.

The problem is compounded when those changes determined to be necessary cut across departmental lines and even, to some degree, alter intradepartmental relationships. Affecting systems under such circumstances requires the greatest tact, sales ability, and executive ability. Failing that, it may be necessary to fall back on the ultimate authority vested in the security operation by top management. Any hesitation or equivocation on the part of either management or security at this point could damage the program before it has been initiated.

Without sound procedures and tight inventory controls, it may be difficult to determine what the problem is and who is responsible.

This does not, of course, mean that management must give security carte blanche. Reasonable and legitimate disagreements inevitably arise. It does mean that proposed security programs based on broadly stated policy must be given the highest possible priority. In those cases where conflict of procedures exists, some compromise may be necessary, but the integrity of the security program as a whole must be preserved intact.

Communicating the program

The next step is to communicate necessary details of the program to all employees. Many aspects of the system may be proprietary or on a need-to-know basis, but since part of it will involve procedures engaged in by most or all of company personnel, they need to know those details to comply. This can be handled by an ongoing education program or by a series of meetings explaining the need for security and the damaging effects of internal theft to jobs, benefits, profit sharing, and the future of the company. Such meetings can additionally notify all employees that management is taking action against criminal acts of all kinds at every level and that dishonesty will not be tolerated.

Such a forceful statement of position in this matter can be very beneficial. Most employees are honest who disapprove of those who are criminally inclined. They are apprehensive and uncomfortable in a criminal environment, especially if it is widespread. The longer the company condones such conduct, the more they lose respect for it, and a vicious cycle begins. As they lose respect, they lose a sense of purpose. Their work suffers, morale declines, and at best, effectiveness is seriously diminished. At worst, they reluctantly join the thieves. A clear, uncompromising policy of theft prevention is usually welcomed with visible relief.

Continuing supervision

Once a system is installed, it must be constantly supervised if it is to become and remain effective. Left to their own devices, employees soon find shortcuts, and security controls are abandoned in the process. Old employees must be reminded regularly of what is expected of them, and new employees must be adequately indoctrinated in the system they are expected to follow.

A continuing program of education is necessary if expected results are to be achieved. With a high turnover within the white-collar workforce, it can be expected that the office force, which handles key paperwork, is replaced at a fairly consistent rate. This means that the company has a regular influx of new people who must be trained in the procedures to be followed and the reasons for these procedures.

Program changes

In some situations, reasonable controls create duplication of effort, cross-checking, and additional paperwork. Since each time such additional effort is required there is an added expense, procedural innovations requiring it must be avoided wherever possible, but most control systems aim for increased efficiency. Often this is the key to their effectiveness.

Many operational procedures, for a variety of reasons, fall into ponderous routines involving too many people and excessive paper shuffling. This may increase the possibility of fraud, forgery, or falsification of documents. When the same operational result can be achieved by streamlining the system and incorporating adequate security control, it should be done immediately.

Virtually every system can be improved and should be evaluated constantly with an eye for such improvement, but these changes should never be undertaken arbitrarily. Procedures must be changed only after the changes have been considered in the light of their operational and security impacts, and such considerations should further be undertaken in the light of their effect on the total system.

No changes should be permitted by unilateral employee action. Management should make random spot checks to determine if the system is being followed exactly. Internal auditors or security personnel should make regular checks on the control systems.

Violations

Violations should be dealt with immediately. Management indifference to security procedures is a signal that they are not important, and where work-saving methods can be found to circumvent such procedures, they will be. As soon as any procedural untidiness appears and is allowed to continue, the deterioration of the system begins.

It is good to note that, while efforts to circumvent the system are frequently the result of the ignorance or laziness of the offender, a significant number of such instances are the result of employees probing for ways to subvert the controls to divert company assets for their own use.

Procedural controls

Auditing assets

Periodic personal audits by outside auditors are essential to any well-run security program. Such an examination will discover theft only after the fact, but it will presumably discover any regular scheme of embezzlement in time to prevent serious damage. If these audits, which are normally conducted once a year, were augmented by one or more surprise audits, even the most reckless criminal would hesitate to try to set up even a short-term scheme of theft.

These audits normally cover an examination of inventory schedules, prices, footings, and extensions. They should also verify current company assets by sampling physical inventory, accounts receivable, accounts payable (including payroll), deposits, plant, and outstanding liabilities through an ongoing financial audit. In all these cases a spot check beyond the books can help establish the existence of legitimate assets and liabilities, not empty entries created by a clever embezzler.

Cash

Any business handling relatively few cash payments in and out is fortunate indeed. Such a business can avoid much of the difficulty in this security-sensitive area, since cash handling is certainly the operation most vulnerable and the most sought after by larcenous staff members.

Cash by mail

If cash is received by mail—a practice almost unheard of in most businesses—its receipt and a responsible, bonded supervisor or supervisors must undertake handling. This administrator should be responsible for no other cash handling or bookkeeping functions and should personally see to it that all cash received is recorded by listing the amount, the payer, and other pertinent information as established procedures have indicated. There is clearly a danger here at the very outset. If cash is diverted before it is entered into the accounting system, there is no record of its existence. Until it is channeled into company ledgers in some way and begins its life as a company asset, there is no guarantee that it will not serve some more private interests. This requires supervision of the supervisor. In a firm doing a large catalog business that receives large amounts of cash in spite of pleas for checks, credit card purchases, or money orders, it has sometimes been felt that the operation should be conducted in a special room reserved for the purpose.

Daily receipts

All cash-accounting entries must be checked against cash on hand at the end of each day. Spot checks on an irregular basis should be conducted.

Cash receipts should be deposited in the bank, and each day's receipts should be balanced with the daily deposit. Petty cash as needed should be reimbursed by check.

All bank deposits should be accompanied by three deposit slips: one is receipted by the bank and returned by the cashier to the person making the deposit, the second should be mailed to the office accounting department, and the third is the bank's copy.

Bank statements

Bank statements should be received and reconciled by someone who is not authorized to deposit or withdraw funds or to make a final accounting of receipts or disbursements. When bank statements are reconciled, canceled checks should be checked against vouchers for any possible alterations and for proper endorsement by the payee. Any irregularities in the endorsements should be promptly investigated. If the statement seems out of order by way of erasure or possible alteration, the bank should be asked to submit a new statement to the reconciling official's special personal attention.

Petty cash

A petty cash fund set aside for that purpose only should be established. The amount to be carried in such a fund is based on past experience. These funds must never be commingled with other funds of any kind and should be drawn from the bank by check only. They should never be drawn from cash receipts. No disbursements of any kind should be made from petty cash without an authorized voucher signed by the employee receiving the cash and countersigned by an authorized employee. No voucher should be cashed which shows signs of erasure or alteration. All such vouchers should be drawn up in ink or typed. In cases of typographical error, new vouchers should be prepared rather than correcting the error. If there is any reason for using a voucher on which an erasure or correction has been made, the authorizing official should initial the change or place of erasure. Receipts substantiating the voucher should accompany it and should, wherever possible, be stapled or otherwise attached to it.

The petty cash fund should be brought up to the specified amount required by a check to the amount of its depletion. The vouchers on which disbursements were made should always be verified by an employee other than the one in charge of the fund. All vouchers submitted and paid should be canceled to avoid reuse.

Petty cash should be balanced occasionally by management, at which time vouchers should be examined for irregularities.

Separation of responsibility

The principle of separation of responsibility and authority in matters concerning the company's finances is of prime importance in management. This situation must always be sought out in the survey of every department. It is not always easy to locate. Sometimes even the employee who has such power is unaware of the dual role. But the security specialist must be knowledgeable about its existence and suggest an immediate change or correction in such operational procedures whenever they appear.

An employee who is in the position of both ordering and receiving merchandise or a cashier who authorizes and disburses expenditures are examples of this double-ended function in operation. All situations of this nature are potentially damaging and should be eliminated. Such procedures are manifestly unfair to company and employee alike. They are unfair to the company because of the loss that they might incur; they are unfair to the employee because of the temptation and ready opportunity they present. Good business practice demands that such invitations to embezzlement be studiously avoided.

It is equally important that cash handling be separated from the record-keeping function. Cashiers who become their own auditors and bookkeepers have a free rein with that part of company funds. The chances are that cashiers will not steal, but they could and might. They might also make mathematical mistakes unless someone else double-checks the arithmetic.

In some smaller companies, this division of function is not always practical. In such concerns, it is common for the bookkeeper to act also as cashier. If this is the case, a system of countersignatures, approvals, and management audits should be set up to help divide the responsibility of handling company funds from that of accounting for them.

Access to records

Many papers, documents, and records are proprietary or at least available to only a limited number of people who need such papers in order to function. All other persons are deemed off limits. They have no apparent need for the information. Such records should be secured under lock and key or through access control in the case of electronically stored data and, depending on their value or reconstructability, in a fire-resistant container.

Forms

Certain company forms are often extremely valuable to the inside as well as the outside thief. They should be secured and accounted for at all times. They should be sequentially numbered and recorded regularly so that any loss can be detected at a glance.

Blank checks, order forms, payment authorizations, vouchers, receipt forms, and all papers that authorize or verify transactions are prime targets for thieves and should therefore be accounted for.

Since many effective operational systems are used to order, ship, or receive goods as well as to authorize payments, from petty cash to regular debt discharge, no one security system to protect against illegal manipulation within such systems applies universally. It can be said, however, that, since every business has some means of authorizing transactions of goods or money, the means by which such authorizations are made must be considered in the security program. Security of such means must be considered an important element in any company's defense against theft.

Generally speaking, all forms should be prenumbered and, wherever possible, used in numerical order. Any voided or damaged forms should be filed and recorded, and forms reported lost must be accounted for and explained. All such numbered forms of every kind should be inventoried and accounted for periodically.

In cases where purchase orders are issued in blocks to various people who need such authority, such issuance must be recorded and disposition of their use should be audited regularly. In such cases, it is customary for one copy of the numbered purchase order to be sent to the vendor, who uses that number in all further dealings on that particular order; another copy is sent to accounting for payment authorization and accrual if necessary; and one copy is retained by the issuing authority. Each block issued should be used sequentially, although since some areas may have more purchasing activity than others, purchasing order copies as they are forwarded to accounting may not be in overall sequence.

Computer records or electronic mail and funds transfer or fax

The computer is the most powerful tool for record-keeping, research and development, funds transfer, electronic mail, and management within most companies today. It is essential that the computer and its support equipment and records be adequately password protected from the internal thief. In addition to the computer the transfer of information via fax has become an everyday occurrence.

Purchasing

Centralized responsibility

Where purchasing is centralized in a department, controls always are more effective. Localizing responsibility as well as authority reduces the opportunity for fraud accordingly. This is not always possible or practical, but in areas where purchasing is permitted by departments needing certain materials and supplies, there can be confusion occasioned by somewhat different purchasing procedures. Cases have been reported of different departments paying different prices for the same goods and services, thus bidding up the price the company is paying. Centralization of purchasing overcomes this problem. The use of computers and networking has allowed for centralized control with decentralized operations.

Purchasing should not, however, be involved in any aspect of accounts payable or the receipt of merchandise other than as an information ally.

Competitive bids

Competitive bids should be sought wherever possible. This, however, raises an interesting point that must be dealt with as a matter of company policy. Seeking competitive bids is always good practice, both to get a view of the market and to provide alternatives in the ordering of goods and materials, but it does not follow that the lowest bidder is always the vendor with whom to do business.

Such a bidder may lack adequate experience in providing the services bid for or may have a reputation of supplying goods of questionable quality, even though they may meet the technical standard prescribed in the order. A firm may also underbid the competition in a desperate effort to get the business, then find it cannot deliver materials at that price, no matter what it has agreed to in its contract. To function wisely and exercise good judgment in its area of expertise, purchasing must be permitted some flexibility in its selection of vendors. This means that the low bidder is not always the one who wins the contract.

Since competitive bidding provides some security control in reducing favoritism, collusion, and kickbacks between the purchasing agent and the vendor, these controls would appear to be weakened or compromised in situations where the purchasing department is permitted to select the vendor on considerations other than cost. This can be true to some degree, but this is a situation in which business or operational needs may be in some conflict with tight security standards and in which security should revise its position to accommodate the larger demands of efficiency and ultimate economy. After all, cheap is not necessarily economical.

Controls in this case could be applied by requiring that, in all cases where the lowest bid was not accepted, a brief explanation in outline form be attached to the file along with all bids submitted. Periodic audits of such files could establish if any pattern of fraud seems likely. Investigation of the analysis or assumptions made by purchasing in assigning contracts might be indicated in some situations to check the validity of the stated reasoning in the matter.

Other controls

Copies of orders containing the amount of merchandise purchased should not be sent to receiving clerks. These clerks should simply state the quantity actually received with no preconception of the amount accepted. Payment should be authorized only for the amount actually received.

Vendor invoices and receipts supporting such vouchers should be canceled to avoid the possibility of their resubmission in collusion with the vendor.

Purchasing should be audited periodically, and documents should be examined for any irregularities.

Payroll

It is important that the payroll be prepared by persons not involved in its distribution. This is consistent with the effort to separate the various elements of a particular function into its components, then distribute the responsibility for those parts to two or more persons or departments.

Every effort should be made to distribute the payroll in the form of checks rather than cash, and such checks should have a different color from those used in any other aspect of the business. They should also be drawn on an account set aside exclusively for payroll. It is important that this account be maintained in an orderly fashion. Avoid using current cash receipts for payroll.

Personnel records

Initial payroll information should be prepared from personnel records, which in turn have come from personnel as each employee is hired. Such records should contain basic data, such as name, address, attached W-2 form, title, salary, and any other information that the payroll department may need. The record should be countersigned by a responsible executive verifying the accuracy of the information forwarded.

This same procedure should be followed when an employee terminates employment with the company. All such notifications should be consolidated into a master payroll list, which should be checked frequently to make sure that payroll's list corresponds to the current personnel employment records.

Unclaimed payroll checks

Unclaimed paychecks should be returned to the treasurer or controller after a reasonable period of time for redeposit in the payroll account. Certainly such cases should be investigated to determine why the checks were returned or why they were issued in the first place. All checks so returned should be canceled to prevent any reuse and filed for reference. Since payrolls reflect straight time, overtime, and other payments, such payments should be supported by time sheets authorized by supervisors or department heads. Time sheets of this nature should be verified periodically to prevent overtime padding and kickbacks. Time cards should be marked to prevent reuse.

Payroll audits

The payroll should be audited periodically by external auditors for any irregularities, especially if there has been an abnormal increase in personnel or net labor costs.

To further guard against the fraudulent introduction of names into the payroll, distribution of paychecks should periodically be undertaken by the internal auditor, the treasurer, or some other responsible official. In large companies, this can be done on a percentage basis, providing at least a spot check of the validity of the rolls.

Accounts payable

As in the case of purchasing, accounts payable should be centralized to handle all disbursements on adequate verification of receipt and proper authorization for payment.

These disbursements should always be by checks that are consecutively numbered and used in consecutive order. Checks that are damaged, incorrectly drawn, or, for any reason, unusable must be marked as canceled and filed for audit. All checks issued for payment should be accompanied by appropriate supporting data, including payment authorizations, before they are signed by the signing authority. It is advisable to draw the checks on a check-writing machine that uses permanent ink and is as identifiable to an expert as handwriting or a particular typewriter. Checks should be printed on safety paper that shows almost any attempted alteration.

Here, as in order departments, periodic audits must be conducted to examine the records for any sign of nonexistent vendors, irregularities in receipts or payment authorizations, forgeries, frauds, or nonbusiness-like procedures that could lead to embezzlement.

General merchandise

Merchandise is always subject to pilferage, particularly when it is in a transfer stage, such as being shipped or received. The dangers of loss at these stages are increased in operations where controls over inventory are lax or improperly supervised.

Separation of functions

To control sensitive aspects of any operation involving the handling of merchandise, it is desirable to separate three functions: receiving, warehousing, and shipping. These functions should be the responsibility of three different areas.

Movement of merchandise from one mode to another should be accompanied by appropriate documents that clearly establish the responsibility for special amounts of merchandise passing from one sphere of authority to another.

Receipt for a shipment places responsibility for a correct count and the security of the shipment on the receiving dock. This responsibility remains there until it is transferred and receives a proper receipt from the warehouse supervisor. The warehouse supervisor must verify and store the shipment that is then the warehouse supervisor's responsibility until it is called for (e.g., by the sales department) or directed to be shipped by an authorized document. The warehouse supervisor ensures that the goods are assembled and passed along as ordered and receives a receipt for those goods when they are delivered.

In this process, responsibility is fixed from point to point. Various departments or functions take on and are relieved of responsibility by use of receipts. In this way a perpetual inventory is maintained as well as a record of responsibility for the merchandise.

Requisitions must be numbered to avoid the destruction of records or the introduction of unauthorized transfers into the system. In addition, merchandise stock numbers should accompany all of that merchandise's movement to describe the goods and thus aid in maintaining perpetual inventory records.

In small firms where this separation of duties is impractical and receiving, shipping, and warehousing are combined in one person, the perpetual inventory is essential for security, but it must be maintained by someone other than the person actually handling the merchandise. The shipper–receiver–warehouse–person should not have access to these inventory records at any time.

Inventories

Inventories are always an important aspect of merchandise control, no matter what operations are in effect. Such inventories must be conducted by someone other than the person in charge of that particular stock. In the case of department stores, for purposes of inventory, personnel should be moved to a department other than their regularly assigned one.

In firms where a perpetual inventory record is kept, physical counts on a selective basis can be undertaken monthly or even weekly. In this procedure a limited number of certain items randomly selected can be counted and the count is compared with current inventory record cards. Any discrepancy can be traced back in an attempt to determine the cause of the loss.

Physical security

It is important to remember that personnel charged with the responsibility for goods, materials, and merchandise must be provided the means of properly discharging that responsibility. Warehouses and other storage space must be equipped with adequate physical protection to secure the goods stored within. Authorizations to enter such storage areas must be strictly limited, and the responsible employees must have means to further restrict access in situations where they feel that the security of goods is endangered.

Receiving clerks must have adequate facilities for storage or supervision of goods until they can be passed on for storage or other use. Shipping clerks must also have the ability to secure goods in dock areas until they are received and loaded by truckers. Without the proper means of securing merchandise during every phase of its handling, assigned personnel cannot be held responsible for merchandise intended for their control, and the entire system breaks down. Unreasonable demands, such as requiring shipping clerks to handle the movement of merchandise in such a way that they are required to leave unprotected goods on the dock while filling out the rest of the order, lead to the very reasonable refusal of personnel to assume responsibility for such merchandise. When responsibility cannot be fixed, theft can result.

The mailroom

The mailroom can be a rich field for a company thief. Not only can it be used to mail company property to an ally or to a prearranged address, but also it deals in stamps—and stamps are money. Any office with a heavy mailing operation must conduct regular audits of the mailroom.

Some firms have taken the view that the mailroom represents such a small exposure that close supervision is unnecessary. Yet, the head of the mailroom in a fair-sized eastern firm got away with over $100,000 in less than 3 years through manipulation of the postal meter. Only a firm that can afford to lose $100,000 in less than 3 years should think of its mailroom as inconsequential in its security plan. In addition, recent events related to bioterrorism make mailroom security an even greater responsibility.

Trash removal

Trash removal presents many problems. Employees have hidden office equipment or merchandise in trash cans, then picked up the loot far from the premises in cooperation with the driver of the trash-collecting vehicle. Some firms have a problem when they put trash on the loading dock to facilitate pickup. Trash collectors made their calls during the day and often pick up unattended merchandise along with the trash. On-premises trash compaction is one way to end the use of trash containers as a safe and convenient vehicle for removing loot from the premises.

Every firm has areas vulnerable to attack. What and where they are can be determined only by thorough surveys and regular reevaluation of the entire operation. There are no shortcuts. The important thing is to locate the areas of risk and set up procedures to reduce or eliminate them.

When controls fail

On occasions when a company is so beset by internal theft that problems seem to have gotten totally out of hand, it is often difficult to localize the problem sufficiently to set up specific countermeasures in those areas affected. The company seems simply to "come up short."

Management is at a loss to identify the weak link in its security, much less to identify how theft is accomplished after security has been compromised.

Undercover investigation

In such cases, many firms similarly at a loss in every sense of the word have found it advisable to engage the services of a security firm that can provide undercover agents to infiltrate the organization and observe the operation from within.

Such agents may be asked to get into the organization on their own initiative. The fewer people who know of the agents' presence, the greater is the protection and the more likely they are to succeed in investigations. It is also true that, when large-scale thefts take place over a period of time, almost anyone in the company could be involved. Even one or more top executives could be involved in serious operations of this kind. Therefore secrecy is of great importance. Since several agents may be used in a single investigation and they may be required to find employment in the company at various levels, they must have, or very convincingly seem to have, proper qualifications for the level of employment they are seeking. Over- or underqualification in pursuit of a specific area of employment can be a problem, so they must plan their entry carefully. Several agents may have to apply for the same job before one is accepted.

Having gotten into the firm's employ, agents must work alone. They must conduct the investigation and make reports with the greatest discretion to avoid discovery. But they are in the best possible position to get to the center of the problem, and such agents have been successful in a number of cases of internal theft in the past.

These investigators are not inexpensive, but they earn their fee many times over in breaking up a clever ring of thieves. It is important to remember, however, that such agents are trained professionals. Most of them have had years of experience in undercover work of this type. Under no circumstances should a manager think of saving money by using employees or well-meaning amateurs for this work. Such a practice could be dangerous to the inexperienced investigator and would almost certainly warn the thieves, who would simply withdraw from their illegal operation temporarily until things had cooled down after which they could return to the business of theft.

Prosecution

Every firm has been faced with the problem of establishing policy regarding the disposal of a case involving proven or admitted employee theft. They are faced with three alternatives: to prosecute, discharge, or retain the thief as an employee. The policy that is established is always difficult to develop because there is no ready answer. There are many proponents of each alternative as the solution to problems of internal theft.

However difficult it may be, every firm must establish a policy governing matters of this kind. And the decision about that policy must be reached with a view to the greatest benefits to the employees, the company, and society as a whole. An enlightened management would also consider the position of the as-yet-to-be-discovered thief in establishing such policy.

Discharging the thief

Most firms have found that discharge of the offender is the simplest solution. Experts estimate that most of those employees discovered stealing are simply dismissed. Most of those are carried in the company records as having been discharged for "inefficiency" or "failure to perform duties adequately."

This policy is defended on many grounds, but the most common are as follows:

1. Discharge is a severe punishment, and the offender will learn from the punishment.
2. Prosecution is expensive.
3. Prosecution would create an unfavorable public relations atmosphere for the company.
4. Reinstating the offender in the company—no matter what conditions are placed on the reinstatement—appears to condone theft.
5. If the offender is prosecuted and found not guilty, the company is open to civil action for false arrest, slander, libel, defamation of character, and other damages.

There is some validity in all of these views, but each one bears some scrutiny.

As to learning (and presumably reforming), as a result of discharge, experience does not bear out this contention. A security organization found that 80% of the known employee thieves they questioned with polygraph substantiation admitted to thefts from previous employers. Now, it might well be argued that, since they had not been caught and discharged as a result of these prior thefts, the proposition that discharge can be therapeutic still holds or at least has not been refuted. That may be true, and it should be considered.

Prosecution is unquestionably expensive. Personnel called as witnesses may spend days appearing in court. Additional funds may be expended investigating and establishing a case against the accused. Legal fees may be involved. But, can a company afford to appear so indifferent to significant theft that it refuses to take strong action when it occurs?

As to public relations, many experienced managers have found that they have not suffered any decline in esteem. On the contrary, in cases where they have taken strong, positive action, they have been applauded by employees and public alike. This is not always the case, but apparently a positive reaction is usually the result of vigorous prosecution in the wake of substantial theft.

Reinstatement is sometimes justified by the circumstances. There is always, of course, a real danger of adverse reaction by the employees, but if reinstatement is to a position not vulnerable to theft, the message may get across. This is a most delicate matter that can be determined only on the scene.

As far as civil action is concerned, that possibility must be discussed with counsel. In any event, it is to be hoped that no responsible businessperson would decide to prosecute unless the case was a very strong one.

Borderline cases

Even beyond the difficulty of arriving at a satisfactory policy governing the disposition of cases involving employee theft, some cases are particularly hard to adjudicate. Most of these involve the pilferer, the long-time employee, or the obviously upright employee in financial difficulty, who steals out of desperation. In each case the offender freely admits guilt and pleads being overcome by temptation. What should be done in such cases? Many companies continue to employ such employees, provided they make restitution. They are often grateful, and they continue to be effective in their jobs.

In the last analysis, individual managers must determine the policy in these matters. Only they can determine the mix of toughness and compassion that guides the application of policy throughout.

It is hoped that every manager will decide to avoid the decision by making employee theft so difficult and so unthinkable that it will never occur. That goal may never be reached, but it is a goal to strive for.

Consider the following actual case study, then decide how you would answer the questions posed at the end.

Case study

J. Jones, a sales representative traveling a territory in his own car, receives a travel allowance of 45 cents a mile from his company to pay all car expenses. The vehicle is also used as a second family car when he is at home. He considers the 45 cents a mile figure too low considering the price of gas.

Jones reclaims this and other travel expenses in a monthly expense account. In this account, he is required to list only a total of miles driven each day and a total of miles for the month. He always claims total miles each month, business and personal, by making a small daily increase in mileage driven on company business. Around Christmas time, his personal expenses are higher and his company car travel is less. His practice then is to add extra miles arbitrarily to his expense account for November and December.

The company pays expense accounts each month without auditing them. External auditors select a few sales reps each year for expense account audit. The sales reps know this because any errors located in this random audit are reported to them, and the errors, plus or minus, are corrected.

Jones arbitrarily increased the total monthly expense by $200. He knew he could keep this if his expense accounts were not chosen for the audit that year. If caught in an audit, he knows it would simply be attributed to an error in addition on his part.

Jones's total increase of reported expenses over actual expenses this year was about 5%. He has no unusual expenses of a nonrecurring nature.

Summary

The issue of internal theft is probably the single most important issue for a loss prevention manager. More companies fail as a result of employee theft than from another security or loss prevention vulnerability. Understanding the nature of theft provides a basis for its control. The simple most effective measure in reducing employee problems is a thorough background check.

Further reading

Zalud, B., 2002. 2002 Industry Forecast Study Security Yin-Yang: Terror Push, Recession Drag. Security.

Security, 1990. Weak Awareness Secures Sky-High Theft Figures. Security, p. 13.

Gramnis, K., 2018. Retail Losses Hit $41.6 Billion Last Year, According to the National Retail Security Survey. National Retail Federation. <www.nrf.com>.

Chapter 29

Multiresidential security

Norman R. Bottom[†]

The role of security is related to the prevention of unauthorized entry, circulation, and exit of personnel and vehicles; perimeter fences and entrance areas; protective lighting and alarm systems; passes, badges, and identification systems; and the prevention and detection of crime.

Louis A. Tyska, CPP

Introduction

The deterioration of America's cities favors multiresidential, controlled environments. It was reported that one out of eight Americans lived in communities governed by community associations. The three basic types of community associations are condominiums, homeowners associations, and cooperatives. Although the single-family home, with all its advantages, taps a deep root, almost all people have some experience in multiresidential housing.

Security is often a key marketing strategy for apartments and condominiums in today's crime and fear-ridden society. Newspapers, TV, radio, flyers, and brochures are commonly used as well as social media outlets. Many announcements use security terms. Among those are "access control," "24-security," and "state-of-the-art security." One Texas condominium used the term "superb security" in a radio spot.

Marketing (including pitches by sales agents) sometimes stretches reality. Applicants or prospective buyers may be told that a police officer lives on the premises. The implication is that the officer is there to provide some tenant/owner protection. It may not be the case. A guardhouse may be prominent, but it may never be staffed. The sales agent may point out a marked police car parked on the premises. The officer may be asleep or off the premises.

Tenants and owners often feel a "false sense of security" when they hear security terms or see a gate house or police car. They may let down their guard. Other phrases that could mislead are "Luxury" and "Ideal for the Woman Professional." It seems reasonable to assume that luxury facilities should have luxury-level security. An ideal site for the woman professional should recognize her security needs. For example, rapists prey on condominiums and apartments. They know many female owners and tenants live alone.

Criminal activity

The same criminal activity that affects residents of condominiums and apartments affects residents of mobile home parks. Such locations are planned communities that provide a space to park the mobile home, a limited amount of "yard," and some common recreational and utility areas (such as laundry facilities). Parks may cater to specific populations, such as the elderly, retired persons, or winter visitors. Access control and resident and visitor control are common challenges. If tenants are absent much of the year, burglary is a special problem. Adequate lighting, antitrespass signs, speed bumps, and low speed limits are a priority. Neighborhood watch is especially important, considering the ease of illegal entry into mobile homes. After-dark patrol, in a golf cart, is useful.

Many living facilities are multiuse. Some have a few retail shops and a few have shopping centers, and most have recreational facilities. These include club houses, restaurants, golf courses, swimming pools, lakes, tennis courts,

†. Deceased

Handbook of Loss Prevention and Crime Prevention. DOI: https://doi.org/10.1016/B978-0-12-817273-5.00029-6

jogging paths, and more. There is an inherent conflict in the access control needs of purely residential properties and those retail establishments that welcome strangers.

Poor maintenance environment

Poor maintenance may increase risk. Ladders left out have been used by criminals to break into apartments and condominiums. Furniture discards, allowed to accumulate, have been used as "steps" by burglars who placed such items under a window. Failure to crop vegetation around windows provides cover and concealment for the burglar's illegal entry. Failure to replace burned-out lights provides concealment for criminals.

Reduction of security by apartment or condominium management is like playing with a loaded gun. It is dangerous and foolish unless there is evidence that the reduction is justified or an equivalent substitution has been made. Professional and technical grounds for the reduction of personnel, procedures, and hardware may be hard to find. Cutting solely for the sake of cost reduction is slim justification.

Apartments

Many states have apartment associations that provide security-related information. For example, the Texas Apartment Association (TAA) has long been advising its membership (apartment owner/operators) of tenant security needs. TAA created "Security Guidelines for Residents" (Form 87-M) to be attached to tenant leases. It provides 30 crime prevention tips.

TAA also created a "red book," which has an extensive section on security with useful security recommendations: educate tenants, check exterior lighting weekly, keep vacant units locked, install dead bolts and peepholes and strengthen striker plates, protect master keys, and screen employees.

TAA offered its members a sample lease (Apartment Lease Contract) with security provisions as early as 1982. Tenants are supposed to initial paragraphs. One such paragraph attempts to deny any owner/operator's liability for crimes against tenants, their persons, and/or property. More recently (1991), the lease also alerts tenants to their "security rights" under Section 92.151, and following sections, of the Texas Property Code. This code allows tenants to request repairs to locks and additional door locking devices and peepholes. The owner must comply with tenant requests.

Failure to warn tenants of criminal activity is considered negligence in many jurisdictions. TAA provides a sample form for notifying Texas tenants of crime. This form calls for identification of the type of crime, such as rape, murder, robbery, or burglary. But, instead of identifying the crime site, on or off the premises, a TAA sample crime notice form (1989) uses the phrase "in the immediate area of the apartment[s]." This notice concludes, "Please remember that your security is the responsibility of yourself [sic] and the local law enforcement agencies."

Texas plaintiff attorneys do not appear convinced, however, that TAA has eroded owner/operator's liability by these forms.

Similar lease provisions are being used in other states. For example, a lease, used in Arizona, says, "*Guarded Gates.* Regardless of whether the complex has a guarded entrance, Residents acknowledge and agree that Management does not provide any type of security for the deterrence or prevention of crime and that Tenants are responsible for their own safety."

Condominiums

Condominium associations seem to breed the most disagreeable persons on the earth. A small percentage of owners are childish, beyond reason, mean, vindictive, dictatorial, and arrogant. Sometimes, the association officers have such traits. Condominium management companies often provide indifferent service, and there is frequent management turnover at many locations. These facts make the provision of security at a condominium challenging, to say the least.

For many years it was deemed impossible for an owner to sue the condominium association for failure to provide reasonable security. It was reasoned that the owner, a member of the association, could not sue himself or herself. All that has changed. Recent security verdicts in favor of owners and against their associations made it urgent to provide reasonable security at condominiums.

The Community Associations Institute (CAI) is the major organization serving the condominium community. Located at 1423 Powhatan Street, Suite 7, Arlington, VA 22314, CAI has local chapters; produces a magazine, newsletters, and reports; holds educational seminars; and conducts annual meetings. Probably nothing causes more hostility in condominium projects than parking regulations. Parking spaces are assigned by unit. There are often few visitor spaces.

Illegal parking is a special problem for condominiums adjacent to a public beach. Florida governs the right to tow in Florida Statute 715.07. Proper signs must be posted to create a "tow-away zone" in order to make a tow legal. There is an exception. If an officer of the condominium, or an employee of the association, gives personal notice to the owner of an illegally parked vehicle, it can be towed legally.

Identification cards (IDs) are often issued by condominium associations, which also may issue numbered bracelets to be worn or carried in the common recreational area. Fences, walls, and gates cannot keep all trespassers out. IDs are a good way to identify the resident and discover the trespasser. Resident IDs complement window stickers that authorize the entry, and parking, of authorized vehicles.

Levels of security

Broadly considered, three lines of possible defense should be considered in any multiresidential security program. The first is represented by all sides of the perimeter, including entrances. One side, or several, may border on developed property, undeveloped property, woods, water, or roadways. Special hazards of two, three, or four different types of property, located on various sides, may have to be taken into account.

Common areas, including roadways, parking lots, marinas, lawns, and walkways, and recreational areas form the second area of possible defense that requires some types of security. The third area is represented by building and unit entrances, as well as balconies and windows. The unit door and associated locking devices, as well as any unit windows and their locks, usually represents the last line of defense to the tenant/owner.

There is a wide variety of security provided in multiresidential properties. Door and window locks may be almost worthless or true high-security items. Landscaping may be trimmed, to allow good natural surveillance. Vegetation may be allowed to grow and spread for aesthetic value, giving good cover and concealment for a criminal. Residents may cooperate with access control security measures or be careless in loaning keys and access cards and prop open lobby doors for convenience.

Management may exercise care about who it accepts or strives only for full occupancy. Some take government money to house individuals with various social (and criminal) problems. Management may claim that security problems are minor, centering on noise, pets, children, and parking. Criminal intrusion is taken more seriously at other locations.

Multiresidential security may be as simple as some outside lighting and some sort of door lock. It may involve special auto stickers or providing identification to a gate guard or being identified by a guard at the building entrance. Foyers and elevators may be accessible to all or require a key, punching in code numbers, or an access control card. There may be a private police/security and fire department. Security may be on patrol day and night. A resident may patrol on a golf car in the evenings or a security car may roll through several times a day. Several guards or the so-called courtesy officers (off-duty police residents) may be available on call.

A computerized cable TV security system is available in some locations. Smoke and heat and passive infrared detectors or a laser-beam intruder detection system may be standard equipment in every unit. A central computer may contain information on residents and approved visitors and a complete medical history of every resident. More and more management people are looking very close at Crime Prevention Through Environmental Design (CPTED) concepts and strategies.

Personnel

Courtesy officers

Courtesy officer is a strange term for security personnel that originated in Texas. It appears to define off-duty police, themselves tenants of apartment complexes, who agree to perform certain duties in exchange for pay or rent reduction. Courtesy officer duties often have little or nothing to do with tenant protection. Courtesy officers are normally expected to enforce apartment rules and protect the owner/operator's property. They often patrol in police uniforms and have take-home police cars. Other tenants frequently assume the officers are there to protect them and their own property.

The following items are in a sample courtesy officer agreement:

1. To respond to problems such as emergencies, solicitors, lock outs, and so forth.
2. To patrol the grounds while off duty several times each day and night, sometimes on foot and sometimes in a vehicle. To patrol while on duty if possible.
3. To check outside lighting weekly.
4. To complete a report for each call for service.

5. To lock up the pool area and laundry at 11:00 p.m., to check recreational buildings and office doors after hours, and to reopen the laundry and pool at 8:00 a.m.
6. To monitor all parking areas, checking for expired licenses, abandoned vehicles, vehicles on blocks, and so forth.
7. To enforce policies that forbid car washing, car repair, double parking, violations of pool rules, and so forth.
8. To accompany office personnel serving eviction and/or warning notices.
9. To arrange for a substitute when on vacation.

Drive-through security patrol

Some contract guard companies offer daily drive-through patrol service for apartment sites. Uniformed officers, sometimes armed, patrol in marked vehicles. The fee for such intermittent service is less than it would cost for an officer to remain on-site during a 12- or 24-hour shift. A property may be visited once or often in the specified 12 or 24 hours. Other properties may contract for additional duties and visits at specific hours. Additional, optional, duties for the drive-through patrol officer include responding to lock outs, requests for tenant escort, property walk-throughs, and responding to suspicious activity and reports of crime.

Some guard companies require their drive-through patrol officers to respond to commercial alarms. Alarm responses, escorts, or reports of suspicious activity usually have higher priority than drive-through patrol. Traffic and weather problems often interfere with the officer's ability to complete the daily drive-through schedule. For example, lightning storms frequently cause multiple false alarms. Officers may start patrol with a backlog of reported alarms to which they must respond before beginning the drive-through schedule. Another problem is too many scheduled "hits" (property visits) on a particular route. This makes it impossible to complete scheduled duties during the shift, even if alarm response, optional duties, and weather do not hinder the officer.

Drive-through patrol supervision is often sketchy during evening hours. The clients usually do not have the ability to check on the frequency or completeness of patrol activity. Guard companies often use supervisors to fill in for no-show officers. Some drive-through report forms, left with the client, specify the officer's arrival time(s) but not the departure time(s). The time spent on-site remains unknown.

Job task analysis

The selection of security personnel is made easier by the job task analysis (JTA). Ideally, the JTA is accomplished before interviewing, testing, or hiring contract or proprietary security or off-duty police personnel. It can, however, be done when security personnel are on the job. The JTA offers an additional benefit. It represents clear evidence that a reasonable effort has been made to provide well-selected, well-trained, and well-equipped personnel.

There are three steps to the JTA. The job task inventory comes first, which is a comprehensive list (inventory) of all duties expected to be accomplished, shift by shift. Time to complete each duty and the expected frequency of the duty should be calculated as well. Second, those duties believed critical must be closely tied into selection and training. Third, an evaluation process must occur periodically. Evaluation determines how closely actual work performance correlates to owner/operator's expectations.

Let us presume, for the sake of illustration, that a property previously employed some types of security personnel or is currently doing so. To complete the first step (job task inventory), all abovementioned of security responsibilities and duties should be culled from internal documents. The same is true for promotional material used to solicit tenants or buyers whether used in print, radio, or TV media. Internal statements on security often can be located in policy documents, bulletins, operating manuals, newsletters, and so on. Contract guard manual, in-house security manuals, postorders, and special orders, as well as daily logs and incident reports, should be analyzed for duties performed and their regularity. Lack of detail usually means more discretion for the officers; often, it is too much discretion.

Serving security personnel should be asked to fill out a job task inventory that describes what they do and when. Management should assign an employee to spend a shift or two with the officers to better understand how time is actually spent on the different shifts. Two scales can be used to evaluate security tasks.

The *significance scale* rates importance and frequency. Each task should be rated separately:

1. always critical, frequent need (daily, hourly, etc.);
2. always critical, occasional need (weekly, seasonal, etc.);
3. important, frequent need;
4. important, occasional need;

5. useful, frequent need;
6. useful, occasional need; and
7. no longer a need.

A second scale relates to *ease of accomplishment* and *the need for training*. Each task should be rated separately:

1. full competence necessary prior to hiring;
2. full competence necessary prior to unsupervised work;
3. to be acquired on the job, within 2 months;
4. to be acquired on the job, within 2 weeks;
5. to be acquired on the job, within 2 days;
6. little or no training required; and
7. not currently a required duty.

Few apartments and condominium associations have any systematic and professional evaluation process directed toward security personnel. Lacking foresight, most hire a security company based solely on a low bid. Here are some telling examples of failure to evaluate from documents discovered after serious crimes:

- Contract guard logs, kept at the guard shack at a Texas condominium, stated that no evening patrols were performed for 2 weeks because the flashlight had no batteries.
- Two South Florida condominium associations shared the cost for an off-duty police patrol using a police car. Officers completed a voucher at the end of each shift showing hours and mileage. Reported mileage varied from 12 to 65 miles per night. The reasonable average was 12 miles. Where were the officers on the 65 mile nights?
- A north Florida apartment decided to solve its security needs by offering several police officers rent-free units. No instructions were given. Availability and performance were not issues. One of the officers was actually living off the premises with a lady friend.

Involving owners and tenants

Police resources seemed particularly stretched in the late 1990s. It is incumbent on all citizens to report problems and be the "eyes and ears" for police.

Trained crime prevention specialists are available in many cities. They provide free physical surveys; can supply information on prior crime in the immediate, adjoining, and adjacent areas; put on antirape seminars; organize block and neighborhood watch groups; help owners mark their property; teach how not to give off "victim" signals; and so forth.

In some cases, citizens armed with citizen band (CB) radios are organized to patrol their territory, looking for suspicious persons, vehicles, and circumstances.

Sun City Center is a Florida retirement community that uses such volunteers. Money is raised annually for a mostly volunteer security force. Contributions support patrol vehicles, radios, office staff, and liability insurance. Sun City Center began this security effort in 1982. Two persons per vehicle patrol 10 miles of property, for an average of 3 hours, until relieved. The volunteers also provide courtesy transportation, perform a house watch for residents away, check community buildings after hours, and respond to various calls. They carry no weapons and contact the local sheriff's department when necessary.

In addition to the local police crime prevention officer, various organizations are willing to assist apartment and condominium dwellers to reduce crime vulnerability. For example, the American Association of Retired Persons (AARP) provides volunteer consultants and prints useful literature. For more information about these services, write AARP Criminal Justice Services, Code GS, 1909 K Street, NW, Washington, DC 20049.

Staff personnel

Most multiresidential facilities have employees in the office, in the grounds, or in the shop. Care should be taken in hiring and retaining each person. Part-time workers need the same attention. In one northern Virginia case, for example, a young man, who lived with his parents in their condominium, was paid for part-time maintenance. No attempt had been made by the management company to look into his background before he was hired. He later raped an owner, gaining access using keys kept by management for emergencies. After the incident, it was discovered that he had previously served federal prison time for felony convictions involving drugs.

All regular employees should be required to wear an official ID (picture type) while on duty. Nonoffice staff members should wear a distinctive uniform. Contract maintenance or landscaping personnel should be issued a temporary identification while on the premises. Each temporary worker should surrender some identification (such as a driver's license). It should be held in the office until the temporary identification is returned.

Emergency first-responder training is available from the Red Cross and many other sources. All security personnel should be qualified in dealing with medical emergencies where immediate action is critical. During office hours, at least one staff member on duty should be qualified to provide cardiopulmonary resuscitation (CPR) and know how to deal with bleeding and shock. Some residential facilities have the luxury of nurses or doctors on the premises.

Tenants/owners may include medical personnel and emergency medical technicians; a list of such persons should be kept handy but not given out. In many areas, there is rapid response by medical and rescue personnel. In a disaster situation the usual rapid response may not take place. Medical and safety equipment kept on-site might well include several good first aid kits, placed in strategic locations; a portable oxygen unit; a wheelchair; a stretcher or two; and a pool hook and torpedo buoy. It is wise to consult a physician about appropriate supplies considering the resident population.

Tenant screening

Managers and associations do not want problem tenants who fail to pay their rent or create security problems. A number of service companies are willing to check on applicants for a fee. Subscribers are urged to provide regular information on "tenant performance" and any lease violations. Reports may show evictions or skips (left while owing rent). Gang activity, drug selling, and prostitution are not limited to public housing sites. Condominiums and apartment projects frequently find they are infested with criminal residents. Some care in approving applications can go a long way to reducing these in-house problems.

Many screening services retrieve information on an applicant in numerous states, using information provided by their subscribers and local court records. (The applicant's name, driver's license, and/or social security number must be provided to the service company.) For an additional fee, services provide a criminal or credit check.

Physical security and hardware

There are many choices in perimeter fencing. The best fencing for security is a see-through type, such as chain-link fencing. Aesthetic values and security needs often conflict in this area. Walls and fences should enclose the perimeter, allowing limited vehicular access. They provide a psychological effect, establishing a sense of territoriality. They will not stop a determined intruder. Vehicular access can be controlled by gate attendants or some types of gate with a locking system. Pedestrian gates are often controlled by code locks, access control cards, or keys. The most common vehicle control gates used in residential communities are barrier arm, metal slide, metal swing, and pop-up gates.

The barrier arm cycles the fastest but is the least secure. The wooden gate arm is easily broken. Pedestrians are not hindered. The metal slide gate looks secure but cycles slowly (about 2 ft/s). This gate requires more maintenance and does not stop the tailgater. Metal swing gates are slightly faster but are the most expensive and prone to damage. Pop-up gates are often used in underground garages. They cycle fairly fast.

Some entryways combine two systems: metal gates and barrier arm gates. The metal gate keeps out the pedestrian trespasser; the barrier arm gate allows only one car at a time to enter. Alternatively, the barrier arm is used only during the day and the combination of gates is used after dark.

Vehicular gates are often open in the daytime, due to numerous deliveries and the presence of employees, such as landscape or maintenance workers, to keep an eye on incoming traffic. Vehicular gates are usually secured after dark. They may or may not be guarded. Pedestrian gates are usually controlled 24 hours. Maintenance problems often cause gates to recycle slowly or be left open. Tailgating, one car following another before the gate closes, is a persistent problem due to the slowness of gate operation. In some jurisdictions, fire and police personnel are provided entry codes, or a lock box near the gate provides a means of entry.

Doors and locks in multiresidential units are mostly similar to what is found on single-family homes. Key-in-knob locks represent no challenge to the burglar. Dead bolt locks and peepholes are considered essential for outer doors. Night chains, sometimes called *courtesy chains*, do not provide intruder protection. Duress or panic alarms may be an amenity, although there is usually a price tag. An alarm device can be used to signal for medical, fire, or police response. Condominium owners often pay for intrusion detection systems. Alarm devices (bells and sirens) may be local, heard only at the intrusion site, or connected to a central alarm facility that contacts the authorities on receipt of an alarm signal.

Many apartment projects have done away with master key systems, finding they are too difficult to secure in the absence of careful record keeping in a well-designed system. A master key system operates by the addition of extra pins in one or more lock cylinders. The more master pins in a given lock, the more it is vulnerable to picking and cross-keying. In a poor system, many keys open more than one unit. The loss, or misuse, of a master key destroys the security of every unit. The loss of a master key requires all units on that system to be rekeyed at once.

The issuance of staff master keys often leaves much to be desired. There may be too many, records are poor, and for no good reason, the master keys are routinely carried off the premises.

An adequate key control system requires an overall plan and the proper selection of locks and key blanks, blind key codes, and comprehensive records. Locks should be changed or rekeyed when a new party moves in or if a door key is lost. Records of key changes or lock swaps, from one door to another, must be accurate and up to date. Key machines and blanks and key lockers require close control. If management requires an extra key to open units in an emergency, keys should be kept in a sealed packet or special onetime plastic key box. This way a key cannot be removed without clear evidence of the action.

Sliding glass doors must be equipped with auxiliary locks. It is best to install sheet metal screws in upper tracks to reduce play and the opportunity for a burglar to lift the window out of the frame. An inside pin or bar should be installed to keep the door shut. Windows are also vulnerable. A burglar may make a small hole and release the latch. It is best to use auxiliary locks on all windows. Various auxiliary locks, pins, and bars are available in hardware and specialty stores. Most apartment tenants can request to have management install auxiliary door and window locks; however, the cost often must be borne by the tenant. Condominium owners must pay all costs. The majority of multiresidential locking systems are mechanical. Mechanical devices need maintenance. This may require lubrication, latch adjustment, or a replacement. Maintenance seldom takes place until a complaint is made. It is wiser to have regular inspection and maintenance.

Visitor intercom systems may be audio (voice only) or audio and video. Audio systems have long been available. An electric door strike allows the resident to remotely release the door. A person wishing access to an audio-equipped building may push one, or more, unit buttons; someone usually releases the door. There is usually a postal-lock feature, allowing mail carriers to enter the building without having to signal a resident.

A video intercom system, including a telephone for verbal communication, allows the resident to see who requests entry and to speak with that person. The camera is connected via cable to each resident's TV and set on a certain channel. Closed-circuit TV (CCTV) is frequently used in residential buildings and parking facilities. For effective threat recognition and response, someone must be watching a CCTV monitor. Often that person has other duties that interfere with observation. Newer (chip) CCTV digital cameras maintain their quality far longer than tube cameras. Monitors must be changed when resolution suffers. New construction and vegetation or loss of light can interfere with CCTV surveillance.

Grills, security screens, and bars

First-floor locations are most vulnerable to illegal entry, especially if on the perimeter of the property or near woods or undeveloped land. One physical security measure, much used in South Florida, is the window and door security bar, grate, or screen. Condominium associations may not allow exterior use. Such devices, however, can be mounted on the interior. In apartment settings, they may be permitted if the tenant pays for materials and labor. Local fire codes may forbid installation or specify what kinds are acceptable. The threat of fire, and possible inability of residents to exit through such a protected opening, must be considered.

In the case of large parking lots and garages, especially underground garages, there is a need for emergency call buttons that announce a problem at a monitored location. Many facilities couple the alarm with network video systems (CCTV) or a microphone to allow vision or two-way communication.

Lighting is critical to security in any residential environment. All common areas, all parking areas, and all perimeters should be well lit. Some locations employ incandescent lighting in globes on low (6 ft) poles. This is sometimes called *romantic lighting*. Adequate lighting is best achieved by using modern, cost-effective high-intensity discharge lighting. The latest trend is with LED lights because they are energy efficient and are best mounted on tall poles for full benefit. Wall packs, or building mounted, may be an acceptable substitute if light beams reach far enough. Fluorescent lighting is often found in older garages. It loses intensity and does not respond well to cold weather.

Existing lighting can sometimes be improved. For example, wattage can be increased or clear bulbs and globes can replace frosted ones. In parking structures, walls and ceilings can be painted white. It may be possible to move some fixtures to provide better coverage. In any case, it is necessary to measure lighting against the local code and standards of the Illuminating Engineering Society of North America. Adequate lighting must provide ample light. It must be uniform so that shadows do not allow easy trespass and loitering. Lighting should overlap so that the loss of one fixture does not create a large dark area. (See chapter on security lighting.)

Speed bumps—traffic calming

Speed bumps are often used to discourage drive-through trespass and speeding. The best design discourages speeding but minimizes vehicle damage. It is not necessary to use narrow, steep bumps. Those with a gradual slope and at least one foot width (at the top) work well. Local codes may set forth speed bump standards. Notice of their presence should be posted at each vehicular entrance. Speed bumps should be painted, or striped, in yellow or international orange, for safety. Openings for bicycles are recommended.

If contract or in-house guards are hired to patrol the property, they need certain equipment. A uniform is essential, as is a large metal flashlight if there is night patrol. They should be furnished with pens, notebooks, log forms, and incident reports. Some type of two-way communication is vital. It may be a radio or cellular telephone. Unless the property is very small, vehicular transportation is needed. Often a golf cart allows patrol where a normal vehicle cannot go. Weapons are carried by off-duty police. A residential location using guards can specify whether or not they are allowed to carry weapons. An employer must carefully consider the advantages and disadvantages of allowing security guards to carry handguns. Truly dangerous situations are best handled by trained police, on or off duty.

Procedures

Active tenants/owners can be the best resource for crime prevention. To tap this resource, there are many advantages to forming security committees in all multiresidential housing. A standing security committee should be part of each tenant's association. Every condominium association also should create a standing security committee. The security committee can monitor and evaluate security hardware, personnel, and procedures with a view to eliminating loopholes for criminal activity.

Resident complaints about crime can be funneled to this committee. The committee can investigate claims of guard services and equipment suppliers and recommend a security budget. A member of the security committee can serve as liaison to the local police and fire department. Periodic resident attitude surveys on crime and security are another useful committee function. The committee can design a disaster plan and coordinate installation and maintenance of fire suppression and detection equipment. Setting up a "buddy system" for checking on single elderly residents is another good committee task.

If a security procedure, such as an escort service, is available to residents, they must be made aware of how it works. This includes knowing who to contact, knowing how long it may take for an escort to be provided, and what hours it is available. An escort service is a good idea if there is a late-operating laundry facility. It is also a good idea during hours of darkness.

Newsletters are an excellent way to disseminate crime prevention information to the apartment tenant and condominium dweller. Many may be unable to attend meetings. Others will neglect bulletin boards.

Visitor identification procedures, such as a guest register form, are useful in discouraging criminal intrusion. If coupled with the visitor's driver's license number or vehicle tag, the results are even better. The same is true for service employees who must enter apartments or office areas to do work. Delivery personnel, unless known, should be identified, too.

Security personnel, including off-duty police, need written instructions that can be easily accessed. These instructions typically include a security manual with policy statements and guidelines, such as dress standards, equipment, reporting, radio procedures, and so forth. Separate postorders cover the dos and don'ts of a particular assignment, when certain tasks are to be done, and list emergency telephone contacts. Numbers should include police; fire; locksmiths; AAA and other emergency automobile services; 24-hour elevator repair; the power and gas companies; emergency medical technician (EMT) and hospital services; 24 hour plumbers, electricians, and air-conditioning services; managers on call; maintenance on call; and so on.

Postorders should also contain information on the location of vital controls (such as time clocks, water valves, and electric switches), the emergency procedures manual, and emergency equipment (such as fire and medical). Special orders often are issued to convey new and temporary instructions. Written instructions are an important criterion for evaluating the performance of security personnel.

All security personnel should be instructed to report problems such as light outages, suspicious events and persons and vehicles, trespassers, criminal activity, and hazardous conditions of every sort. These items should be addressed the next day, if possible. A visual record of crime, updated daily, should be kept. The ideal method is to place a plastic overlay over a large map board, using colored dots to represent various types of activity. Successive plastic overlays, added yearly or more often, show concentrations of past problems.

The elderly

Many elderly persons live in apartments and condominiums in North America. They often live alone or with other elderly citizens. As the North American population becomes older (the so-called graying of America), this population group will have more security needs. The elderly, as a group, have special health problems. For example, they are less able to fight or flee in emergency situations. Hearing loss, especially in elderly men, tends to be significant. Limited vision or hearing increases vulnerability.

The operation of access control equipment or fire suppression equipment (such as extinguishers) may create problems for the elderly. They may require more escort services and special parking consideration. Home deliveries may increase traffic and access control problems. One benefit to security is their attitude; they usually welcome security and do not resent the presence of security devices or personnel.

Some congregate in living locations, such as nursing homes and continuing care or retirement communities, which provide daily living needs to residents, including nursing and medical care. An ongoing problem in such locations is the wandering patient. A common method for dealing with this hazard is equipping the resident with a special bracelet that causes an alarm at exits equipped with sensing devices (monitors). Emergency buttons or pull cords in bedrooms or bathrooms may trigger buzzer and light signals. Visitors represent a special problem in continuing care facilities. It is necessary to identify visitors and escort them to the guest/patient. The family of the guest/patient may employ an aide or companion. Such a facility should make an effort to check the background of such a person as well as staff. The press has reported notorious incidents of employees who committed sexual assaults or theft in such settings.

Fires are a real hazard when tenants may be unable to walk or need help in movement. There is a need for sprinkler systems, fire doors, extinguishers, smoke detectors, alarm-pull stations, fire wardens, and staff training. If there is a kitchen and cafeteria, they should have a fire suppression system that releases dry chemicals over the cooking area when a certain temperature is reached. Most local codes require adequate fire control systems. Storage locker rooms require inspection to reduce fire hazards. Pharmacies, if present, need high-grade locks and alarms. Certain employees should be certified in CPR.

Some special areas of vulnerability

Day care

Day-care centers are more in use than ever. You can find them at hospitals, businesses, government facilities, and at some multiresidential facilities. At day-care centers, access control is critical as well as panic buttons in staff areas. No one should be able to walk into the facility without prior approval. Due to "parental kidnaping" problems, it is essential that children be released only to approved persons, no matter what excuse or story is offered. Fire suppression is also a high priority.

Elevators and elevator lobbies

Apartments and condominium buildings often have elevators. Elevator lobbies should be in plain view and not screened by vegetation. Elevators and lobbies should be well lit, day and night. Mirrors should be placed in each elevator so that a user can see if anyone suspicious is already in the elevator. Alarm buttons connected to the resident manager's unit and an outside central station are necessary, as is a telephone. Some consideration should be given to limiting elevator service at late hours.

Laundry room

Laundry room rapes are a special problem in apartment settings. Too often laundry rooms are located in remote settings and lack access control. Laundry room locks should require a tenant key. The door should be equipped with a window.

A panic button or telephone should be available. Interior lighting should be wired to stay on permanently during the hours of operation. If the location is difficult to protect, hours should be limited.

Lakes, rivers, streams, canals, and pools

Many residential communities have swimming facilities. Others have access to navigable streams. Some have man-made lakes for boating enthusiasts. In certain parts of the country, drainage canals run through or on the perimeter of the property. All outdoor water amenities are a hazard to those who choose to use them and especially children who might wander off and fall into them.

Local ordinances usually require that pools be fenced. Many residential facilities fence pools but provide no lifeguards. Lakes, rivers, and streams are usually open and not protected by a fence. All residents must be warned about water dangers. In the case of units adjacent to water, it is prudent to install a fence, at least around the back of such units.

Disasters

Every area is subject to some types of natural disaster. For example, the hurricane season causes much concern in Florida and the southeast. A hurricane is an intense low-pressure system, a giant whirlwind that rotates counterclockwise (in the Northern Hemisphere) and reaches winds that exceed 74 mph. Some hurricanes exceed 150 mph and cause storm surges of 15 ft and higher. Hurricane Andrew, which struck South Florida on August 24, 1992, created immense property damage. Much more loss of life would have occurred if the community had not been long aware that a hurricane was overdue. Still, many were unprepared.

National Fire Prevention Association

All multiresidential locations face the threat of a fire disaster. The National Fire Prevention Association and the local fire department can provide helpful information. Expensive litigation and negative publicity, following a serious criminal incident, is another disaster threat. Local trial lawyers, and security consultants who provide expert testimony, can assist in preparing documentation that becomes vital in a lawsuit after a serious criminal incident.

Some areas face lightning problems or heavy winter storms and associated problems. In other areas, it may be tornadoes or earthquakes. Structural failure can take place anywhere. A written disaster plan must be prepared for each disaster conceived to be well within the realm of possibility. The plan must be tested before a disaster takes place. Almost every county has personnel assigned to disaster preparedness. Federal and state guidelines are useful as a baseline. CAI produced a useful document in this regard called GAP Report 14, Disaster Management for Community Associations.

The makeup of the resident population should already be known (to plan for crime prevention and deterrence). The elderly, and those without transportation, will need help with evacuation, if necessary. If elevators are vital and power fails, an evacuation team will be needed. The staff may not be able to get to work if local roads are damaged or their own homes and families need help. Telephone failure makes cellular telephones important. Power failures incapacitate computers and make it impossible to recharge cellular batteries. An ordinary generator can be used to recharge batteries but cannot be used to operate computers. The possible inability to access computer databases mandates that all disaster-related plans and materials must be in hard copy and regularly updated.

If units are vacant, it may be necessary to enter them to shut off utilities. Keys and alarm codes may not be available without adequate planning. Residents or management may have outdoor furniture, lawn equipment, and potted plants that could become missiles in a high wind. Someone must be assigned to move these items to a specified storage area. In the case of high-rise properties, practice evacuation should take place. This practice is most critical when residents are elderly or not mobile.

Residents should be encouraged to keep disaster supplies. These include flashlights and batteries, a battery-operated radio, bottled beverages including water, canned food, a camping or propane stove, a water purification kit or pump, first aid supplies, extra medicine, and so forth. Extra oil and gasoline for a generator or motor vehicle can be an excellent idea. All units should have smoke detectors. Fire extinguishers should be abundant. Many jurisdictions require electrically wired smoke detectors in new structures. Florida adopted a statewide Fire Safety Code (101), which directs that all buildings be converted to that standard.

Legislation

Local ordinances, building codes, and state laws must be consulted in the design of a security program in a residential setting. For example, Florida Statute 83.51 requires landlords to provide locks and keys to doors and windows and to maintain the areas in a reasonably safe condition, including taking measures to secure against foreseeable criminal conduct. The South Florida Building Code gives specifics on locks and windows and doors. Dade County, Florida, adopted much of the language of the South Florida Building Code on physical security matters.

Another political subdivision, Euclid, Ohio, began regulating aspects of apartment security in 1973. Chapter 763.10, Security Guards at Apartments, requires that apartments with more than one building and more than 400 dwelling units provide "at least one private policeman or security guard to patrol the buildings and private parking lot at all hours of each day." Properties with less than 400 U may be required to provide security if the director of public safety so orders. Properties with more than 700 U must have at least two guards between 8 p.m. and 4 a.m.

Basic steps to remember in multiresidential security

1. Physical security survey (including measurement of lighting)
2. Tenant attitude survey on security and crime
3. Recognition of vulnerable populations and places (such as women living alone and laundry rooms)
4. Analysis of area and on-site crime types and patterns
5. Analysis of tenant/owner's complaints about crime and security
6. Honest reporting of crime problems and what security is provided tenants/owners
7. Honest reporting of crime and changes in provided security to tenants/owners
8. Design of a written security program, including use of personnel, physical (hardware), and procedures—perimeter and interior control
9. Scheduled regular evaluation of crime risks and the state of provided security (including all fences, gates, lights, unit door, and window hardware, effectiveness of patrol)
10. Timely change (improvement) to security to reduce risk
11. Good local police liaison, including timely gathering of police reports for crime on the property and frequent drive-through patrol
12. Daily evaluation of security/courtesy logs and reports

Chapter 30

Twenty-one ideas for a safer and more secure school

Jason Thomas Destein
Security Consultant

Before an effective strategy can be developed, it is important to identify and understand risk factors involved. It is essential to give high priority to local factors, for example a survey of crime in the immediate area, should be carried out.[1]

Ian Colquhoun

Introduction

Few issues have captivated the attention of our society as school crime and violence. School-based violence, on K-12 campuses, is a serious concern for parents and educators. School-based violence as outlined by the Center for Disease Controls is "Youth violence is the intentional use of physical force or power to threaten or harm others by young people ages 10–24. It typically involves young people hurting other peers who are unrelated to them and who they may or may not know well. Youth violence can take different forms. Examples include fights, bullying, threats with weapons, and gang-related violence. A young person can be involved with youth violence as a victim, offender, or witness" (Center for Disease Control, 2018).

To counter these instances of violence and deviance, school systems have deployed a myriad of strategies to reduce the potential of risk on campuses. Among these programs are advanced video surveillance platforms, faster lockdown capabilities, enhanced training programs and other technologies to help improve response times. All of these programs are designed to provide for a safer and more secure facility, but are we falling into the trap of relying too heavily on these technologies? And are we further falling into the trap of the same technologies being the only solution to every problem schools face?

Just because a school has cameras, locks, incident reporting systems, threat assessments teams, resource officers, and other initiatives, it does not mean that is safe. Maybe it is safer with these measures than without, but these measures do not create safety. These measures are largely responsive in nature meaning the only time they are called upon is when an adverse act is taking place. Yes, there is some deterrent value to some of these items, but it is important to keep in mind that school safety is not something you can just purchase, rather it is something you have to create.

What is a safe school

What, then, is a "safe" school? Keeping in mind there are no guarantees against victimization on campus, schools that place safety and security at the forefront of the administrative agenda are more likely to have taken steps to mitigate risk on campus. Some characteristics of a safe school are observed in the following cases:

- Students and faculty are not preoccupied with issues pertaining to personal safety.
- There is a strong partnership between schools and public service agencies to reduce crime and deviance and promote safety.

1. Design Out Crime, by Ian Colquhoun, Elsevier, 2004, p. 301.

Handbook of Loss Prevention and Crime Prevention. DOI: https://doi.org/10.1016/B978-0-12-817273-5.00030-2

- Members of the school community demonstrate a sense of ownership in their physical environment.
- There is support from the administration to allow faculty and site administrators to engage in new approaches to the prevention of crime and deviance.
- A commitment to reducing the risk of personal and property victimization is demonstrated through the annual training of personnel in crime and deviance prevention.
- Decision-making is based on actionable intelligence rather than raw information.

The British Home Office and the National Crime Prevention Institute of the University of Louisville define *crime prevention* as the anticipation, recognition, and appraisal of a crime risk and the initiation of some action to remove or reduce it. This is an excellent description of the philosophy behind crime prevention, and it is a workable definition of a *risk assessment* or a *safety/security survey*. However, when addressing the problems of unsafe schools, acts disruptive to education may include behavior not characterized as criminal but delinquent.

Tailoring a definition of *crime prevention* to support the reduction of crime and delinquency in schools requires a broader approach. Therefore a definition of *school crime prevention* should focus on the initiation of any action that improves the quality of life for a school and the community in which it resides. Educators and members of the public service community must caution against viewing the problems associated with school safety as driven by forces at work only on the campus.

The following is a list of recommendations, in no particular order for parents, teachers, administrators, and law enforcement in reducing the risk of victimization on school campuses. While it is by no means all-inclusive, the implementation of these strategies can promote the commitment of schools and communities in maintaining learning environments where students can learn, and faculty can teach without the debilitating fear of some form of violence.

Emphasize prevention during teacher training

The primary role of a teacher is to educate. However, in light of recent concerns over school violence, teachers and administrators must be familiar with concepts such as character education, security, conflict management, threat identification, and identifying other warning signs of potential violence. Periodic and cursory in-service training concerning these issues give educators only a basic awareness of these problems. Education curricula on the collegiate level should incorporate theoretical and applied considerations of how to reduce the risk of victimization on campuses. While curricula in higher education are important, it does not address those who are in the classroom today who have not had that more focused training. Therefore schools should consider other outside trainings that focus on these and other issues, by bringing in outside experts to work with school personnel, schools can deliver this critical training to better prepare their staffs. Focused expertise on violence prevention, violence awareness, preincident indicators identification, and body language identification are all highly important areas for teachers and other school personnel to familiarize themselves with.

Maintain a sense of pride in school grounds and the surrounding neighborhood

In keeping with Wilson and Kelling's "broken windows" thesis, run-down and unkept property is an invitation for victimization and increases the likelihood of a breakdown of community social controls. Trash and graffiti should be removed as soon as possible. Cosmetic improvements such as paint and landscaping demonstrate that members of the school community care about their environment and will not tolerate vandalism and wanton destruction. Poorly maintained grounds reinforce the perception that attention to detail is overlooked, therefore those with ill intent feel their actions can go largely unnoticed until it is too late. Conversely, well-maintained properties create the perception that the facility is cared for and attended too regularly, thus those with ill intent are forced to consider other locations for their actions.

Conduct periodic risk assessments or security surveys and audits

To address the risk of victimization on campuses, educators and law enforcement must be aware of where the greatest risk is. Thorough security surveys can illustrate current security threats and future concerns. This is a crucial action and can yield valuable information that, if harnessed correctly, can provide some of the most important actionable intelligence. Actionable intelligence is what will allow you to begin creating the safe and secure school environment we all strive for and will help to foster the proper learning climate.

Clearly state rules and regulations

For students to behave as expected, they must be made aware of the institution's code of conduct. In addition, parents should also receive a copy of the code of conduct to avoid possible confusion. It is also important for parents and guardians of students to understand the established rules and regulations and to help the school reinforce these practices.

Develop an incident mapping system

Closely correlated with crime and deviance analysis, incident mapping details where unwanted events occur. The significance of this for administrators is to determine where to place personnel to deter deviance and crime. Once likely perpetrators are forced to change from familiar environments to alien ones, the likelihood of success decreases. Those with ill intent go to locations where they feel most comfortable. By using an Incident Mapping System, you can track and identify patterns, and as a result of this effort, you can identify those locations where unwanted actions occur. From there you can place school resource officers, teachers or perhaps parent volunteers in areas where unwanted actions occur. This Incident Mapping System does not have to be complex, and it can be created with basic computing software such as Microsoft Excel.

Utilize parent volunteers as monitors and student aides

This is an inexpensive means of deterrence. It incorporates parents as partners in prevention. Students may be less likely to misbehave when they are watched by someone they see on a regular basis. As mentioned earlier, parent volunteers can be used in those areas that seem to produce unwanted activities such as stairwells, in front of restrooms, or other obscure areas in the buildings that students may try to advance their unwanted behaviors on others.

Institute after-school programs

With most families dependent on the income of both parents, there has been an increase in the number of latchkey children who are unsupervised between the times school lets out and the parents or guardians arrive home. The investment by school systems in programs that keep children occupied in positive activities during this time frame reduces the likelihood of deviance. This is another area where parent volunteers may be able to step in and spend an hour or so on social skills development, proper use of social media, or any other topic that may have a benefit in your community. These can be low cost if done correctly, and the benefits could be far reaching, but you have to be willing to try something new.

Security considerations should be incorporated from the "ground up"

A frequent complaint of security professionals is that crime prevention concerns are not addressed during the initial planning and construction of new facilities. The design of schools should take into consideration concepts of natural surveillance and target hardening before and during construction. This commitment to security makes the tasks of faculty, administrators, and law enforcement easier during the years to come.

Establish in-class communication between teachers and administration

Once the classroom door is closed and class begins, monitoring students becomes left primarily to the teacher. In the event of a crisis, it is necessary for teachers to be able to request assistance. Intercoms, cellular phones, and two-way radios are among the devices that can be utilized to maintain contact with administration or security. This is surprisingly often overlooked, although budget restrictions can influence what technologies are obtained, this is an area that should be given priority.

Implement an intelligence-based threat assessment team

Having a threat assessment team can be a great way to intervene before a crisis occurs, but how you establish that team is critical and can set the tone for how successful that team will be. A threat assessment team will only be successful if they have the ability to collect incident-based information, build trend models on the threats, and then create "actionable intelligence reports" that allow for that proper intervention to occur. Too many times threat assessment teams work with partial information and often have to react rather than take proactive measures. Having partial information will only lead to partial resolutions, and that will not further the overall safety of the school or students. So, when establishing this team it is critical that the team is focused on gather intelligence that allows for proper interventions.

Value the contributions of custodial personnel, bus drivers, and facility management

One of the most valuable, but often overlooked, assets regarding school crime prevention is custodians. I have heard them describing themselves as "invisible" people. They go about their business in the midst of students and staff and routinely observe the behaviors of others. I have had administrators scoff at this notion, because they contended that people untrained in educational administration have little expertise and advice to offer. This irresponsible and dangerous notion fails to appreciate the wealth of common sense and experience these people often have. Seldom does anyone associated with an organization have any better understanding of the physical structure than custodians and maintenance personnel.

Train personnel in graffiti interpretation

Gangs in and out of school pose genuine risks to the safety of communities plagued by them. A chief indicator of gang activity is graffiti. However, there is considerable confusion as to what constitutes vandalism, tagging, and graffiti. Very simply stated, vandalism is usually considered the wanton destruction of property, generally by teenagers and adolescents. "Tagging" is perpetrated by "crews" utilizing a wide color scheme to construct what they consider art. Gang graffiti generally serves as territorial markers. However, this eclectic collection of words, symbols, characters, and so forth is often mistaken for vandalism or tagging. Campus personnel should be trained in the basic characteristics of traditional gang graffiti. While it should be common practice to remove graffiti as soon as possible, photographs should be taken of the scene to share with local law enforcement.

It is not about "doing something," it is about doing the right thing

In talking with principals, vice principals, and other school administrators, I have often found a certain reticence to implement crime prevention and security procedures. Schools want to act in a proactive manner but sometime have a hard time understanding what that looks like or how to accomplish this. Considering the seriousness of providing a safe environment for students and staff, their reluctance is understood. Just because school safety and security is expensive, it does not mean you cannot obtain your goals. There are dozens of ways to reduce risk in your school the proper way without breaking the budget. Small efforts can go a long way, but it may take some out of the box thinking and creativity, but it can be done. Do not deploy countermeasures just to say you did something, if there is no strategy or if the strategy is vague and meaningless, then you could be creating more harm than good. Small efforts with purpose are more valuable and meaningful than expensive efforts with no purpose.

Foster students' beliefs they are connected to the school

Students that view their campus as more than just a place to be endured are less likely to mistreat facilities. Efforts should be made to incorporate students in activities during and after school that they enjoy. Particular emphasis should be made to include those students that may feel marginalized. Traditionally, extracurricular programs have targeted those students who are talented in athletics, music, and drama. However, this does not take into consideration those who lack the ability or interest to fully enjoy these. This should be considered when addressing budgetary allocations for extracurricular support.

Exercise caution when using student monitors

Students should be consulted when planning for safe school designs. They are the primary group to be protected from victimization. Their knowledge and concerns are invaluable in addressing risk. However, their use in crime and deviance prevention should be limited. While fewer schools are using students as hall monitors and in other types of patrol capacities, all schools should abstain from their use in this manner. Students picked for this responsibility might have their own agendas and not report a friend for a violation. Students also might not recognize a violation. It is almost certain they will not be familiar with the entire criminal code of the municipality in which the school resides. Another concern is the fear of retaliation from a student who has been reported. Revenge is easier to plot and carry out against a fellow student than a member of the staff.

The "Combustible Engine" model of school communities

Drawing analogies to a community as diverse as what generally populates a school campus is challenging. However, one model that can demonstrate the variety of people that study and work in a school is that of a car engine. Each piece works in concert with the other to move the automobile from point A to point B. Although it is necessary for each part to work with the others to achieve the desired result, each retains its own identity and responsibility. A school works in much the same way. All personnel from students to staff to parents should have a vested interest in ensuring the system works to provide the best education possible. To ensure the smooth operation of a school, each player should be aware of the part others play in obtaining that result. People are different. Everyone comes from a slightly or notably different background. All those who work and study on a campus should be made aware of these differences. An increased awareness of cultural variations among people can reduce the friction that may result when applied to a school "engine."

Create a crisis management plan

While everyone hopes that his or her child's school is safe and secure, it is a sound policy that plans should be made in the event of human-made or natural disaster. These plans should address education, preparedness, administration, and eventual resolution. Support agencies from within the school's community should be identified and consulted when instituting preparedness plans. While crises, by their nature, are fluid and unpredictable, plans should be as unambiguous as possible to speed response times.

Train personnel in conflict resolution

When signs of interpersonal or group conflict occur, it is essential that the situation be calmed before it can escalate. Educators and support staff should be trained in conflict resolution techniques that focus on calming participants and fostering communication. Initially, the cause behind the problem is not the issue to address immediately. Upset students should be calmly persuaded to leave the area. After a "cooling-off" period, they should be encouraged to talk through the issues that angered them and discover ways to address conflict without resorting to violence.

Implement character education curricula

Monitoring student behavior to dissuade deviance is the key to creating a safe school environment. However, mere monitoring of students on school grounds does little to encourage compliance with community values while not on campus. Students who are not taught the basic values appreciated by society may have little chance to learn them, especially if they live in a toxic home environment. Values such as honesty, integrity, respect for others, and loyalty form the foundation of a person's character and encourage citizenship. These moral and ethical principles should be taught to students early in their academic career and reinforced whenever possible.

Establish "communities within schools"

As students mature and move out of elementary school to middle school, a significant change in instruction is that they move from class to class throughout the school day rather than stay in the same room with all instruction delivered by one teacher. In addition to being introduced to new teachers, students are exposed to students outside of the core group they know from elementary school. Programs that promote smaller groups of students familiar with each other foster greater peer support and flexibility in instructional techniques.

Dealing with the problem

No child should ever be in fear of going to school. Schools must develop a zero-tolerance program against verbal bullying, cyber bullying, and any other forms of harassment or hate or intolerance that develops. Communities are calling for greater penalties to stop bullying as well as student training programs.

Young students today are texting all day long, even in school. Cyber bullying starts by sending out messages about another student. Then it continues, soon 20, then 30, then 50 kids get the same nasty message. They are all laughing at the student. The student starts to cry, and everyone is still laughing. Many have committed suicide as a result of this harassment because they cannot take it anymore. Children should not ever be in fear of going to school. They should be happy in school, not depressed or threatened. In December of 2018 a 9-year-old girl named McKenzie Adams of Tuscaloosa, Alabama, hung herself after being bullied by a group for having friends who were white.

Too often schools overlook the root cause of violence and think that by installing certain technologies or adding more locks to doors, those the problems will go away. I think we wish it would be that easy. School security and safety is not easy, but if we continue to overlook the problem or put the so-called solution in place before we truly identify the root problem, we will continue to see stories about further acts of violence or suicide. Advancements in technology are great and can help schools increase security, but they do not get to the root causation of a problem, if we are going to make any improvements to the overall school safety and security environment or improve the learning climate, then we must think differently, start new conversations, and resolve the true challenges before they escalate out of control.

To a degree the school environment mirrors that of the cities and towns in which they reside. Any symptoms the community suffers from will also be reflected in its schools.

A major challenge we must overcome in addressing the issue of school safety is recognizing that "canned" programs cannot be depended on to address all security concerns for any facility, especially schools. To address the individuality of schools and the students and faculty that learn and work there, programs to increase the safety of personnel must be tailored to address site-specific safety and security concerns.

Reference

Center for Disease Control, 2018. Preventing Youth Violence, "What Is Youth Violence". Retrieved from: <https://www.cdc.gov/violenceprevention/pdf/yv-factsheet508.pdf>.

Further reading

Lab, S.P., 2010. Crime Prevention, Approaches, Practices & Evaluations, seventh ed Anderson Publishing, Southington, CT.

Chapter 31

Crime and crime prevention

Bronson S. Bias
Retired, Protective Services for Nova University, Fort Lauderdale, FL, United States

---

Crime Prevention is a pattern of attitudes and behaviors directed at reducing the threat of crime and enhancing the sense of safety and security.

National Crime Prevention Council

Introduction

An effective crime-prevention program on a college or university campus is a community-based concept. The demographics of the occupants of the campus are evaluated by the crime-prevention administrator for the institution in the same manner as with any community.

The central theme of the campus crime-prevention program is awareness and self-protection. The self-protection philosophy includes the full utilization of the campus law enforcement and security administration elements to encourage and enable this self-protection concept. Programs dealing with awareness are ongoing.

The primary objective of the campus crime-prevention program is to educate the campus occupants in how to protect themselves from harm and crime. The campus law enforcement and security department(s) are a tool—albeit a major one—in the self-protection concept. The campus protective service (law enforcement or security) provides the basis for and the support of the crime-prevention program.

Communication

Effective communication is critical in providing campus crime prevention. The most important communication element for any campus law enforcement or security department is the telephone. Of course, on some campuses, this includes emergency "ring-down" telephones that call campus public safety immediately. The basic COMM-LINE numbers to contact the campus protective department should be advertised clearly and frequently. There should be no doubt to anyone on the campus, even the casual visitor, about the method for contacting help. This can be accomplished through advertising the protective department's services. It is important to display the emergency telephone contact number in a prominent space within any such advertisement.

Without basic communication lines, most crime-prevention programs, dependent on communicating with the protective service, fail. Campus occupants lose faith in campus protection quickly due to a less than reasonable response by protectors and caregivers.

Key elements in a campus crime-prevention program

The basic campus crime-prevention program consists of the following key elements:

1. *Research.* Study campus risks, with emphasis on personal safety. This includes evaluating the risks and assigning evaluative priorities for addressing the risks.
2. *Schedule of implementation.* Plan and schedule the crime-prevention program implementation.
3. *Formal program to train the trainers.* Train crime-prevention specialists in field protective services (law enforcement and security) and clerical and support staff in the creation of an awareness program.

Handbook of Loss Prevention and Crime Prevention. DOI: https://doi.org/10.1016/B978-0-12-817273-5.00031-4

4. *Theme*. Create a flyer, brochure, or booklet with detailed information on crime-prevention techniques. Themes can be tailored to the institution's identity, such as "Spartan Watch." Generic program material, such as "Officer McGruff, Take a Bite Outta Crime," can also be used.
   a. *Advertise*: Judiciously "paper" the campus with these informative publications. Prominently display the emergency telephone contact number for the protective department.
   b. *Alert decals*: Develop adhesive stickers for building doors and exterior windows using an identical or related crime-prevention theme with contact telephone numbers.
   c. *Telephone alert decals*: Utilize smaller decal stickers with the emergency telephone contact number for the protective department. Place, or have campus occupants place, these decals on the front base of each private and public telephone on campus. Everyone on campus will see the protective department's name, logo, and telephone number several times a day. Product identity is assured.
5. *Security surveys*. Provide and promote security surveys to departments, centers, offices, and individuals. Use the security survey to "sell" the campus occupants a crime-prevention lecture, seminar, or meeting.
6. *Lectures*. Provide basic and comprehensive crime-prevention lectures at orientations and residential hall meetings.
7. *Reassessment*. Reassess the effectiveness of the crime-prevention program at least once per year. The effectiveness of a successful crime-prevention program is not necessarily measured in the number of surveys, lectures, and personal contacts completed. Other measurements are significant, such as crime statistics, crime event reduction in specific areas, protective department image, and departmental morale.

Commitment

It is imperative that all members of the core protective service department be a part of the crime-prevention program. Each, in his or her own way, contributes to the success of the overall program. To some degree—some greater, some lesser—everyone in the protective department must be aware of the philosophy and concepts of campus crime prevention and, more importantly, endorse and promote the crime-prevention program.

Effective crime prevention cannot be successful if the campus protective department has some of its own members working against the system.

Cycle of activity

Campus crime prevention involves a cycle of activity. This cycle includes planning, preparation, prevention, and reevaluation and reassessment.

Planning

It is desirable and most effective to begin prevention programs by systemizing them during the planning phase of a facility or a function. Specific knowledge can be applied to supply the optimum schedule of environmental [Crime Prevention Through Environmental Design (CPTED)], barrier, spatial, lighting, locking device, and procedural security applications.

However, in reality, the vast majority of crime-prevention applications follow construction. There is great value in evaluating a facility or a function as it is in place and working. The actual operation of the functional facility can be evaluated to determine true concerns and issues. Within reason, upgraded physical, procedural, and personnel security measures can be applied. Knowledge in the process should be recorded and applied to future projects.

Preparation

Adequate funding and allocation of crime-prevention programs and personnel is essential to the success of an effective program.

All protective department personnel should be provided with basic crime-prevention philosophy and concepts. Also, the simple techniques of crime prevention should be conveyed to these personnel so that they may not only utilize them to protect themselves but have a better understanding of the role of the crime-prevention practitioners.

Persons assigned to the prime responsibility of crime-prevention program delivery should be exposed to formal instructional training whenever possible to build their own personal knowledge of the facts and concepts of the program. The better formalized crime-prevention training programs certify the courses by conducting examinations. Currently, independent certification is available for a crime-prevention practitioner after specific courses of study.

One of the most effective learning methods is networking with other campus protective service departments. Each of the contributing agencies can share its own experiences, techniques, and tactics.

Prevention

The prevention phase involves the delivery of crime-prevention services: awareness, advertising, evaluations, lectures, and training. Prevention also includes conducting basic, progressive, and advanced security surveys on campus to determine the security risks of the facility or property.

Although the campus as a whole fits under the crime-prevention umbrella, to be more effective, the crime-prevention practitioner should evaluate the parts of the campus as individual entities. Security surveys should be conducted by facility, by department, and by function. The assembled data can then be measured in more manageable amounts. This closer evaluation reveals the needs and application of the crime-prevention services more clearly.

Only rarely does a crime-prevention practitioner have large groups of campus occupants to instruct. Usually, the contacts are more informal and more personal. Crime-prevention practitioners must be ready at any time to give advice and instruction to others, including members of their own department.

Not surprisingly, the most opportune time to provide or schedule a security survey or lecture is during the reporting and investigative phase of a crime on campus. Campus crime victims are usually more apt to welcome crime-prevention advice and departmental help during this critical period. This makes it imperative that an on-scene investigation be conducted after a crime, no matter how long it has gone unreported. Follow-up on crimes occurring on campus demonstrates to campus occupants that the protective department is concerned. This personal contact can pave the way for initial or improved relationships regarding crime prevention.

Reevaluation and reassessment

Crime prevention in a college or university campus is an ongoing activity. Primarily, because of size, a campus community provides a closer relationship between the occupants and the protective service dedicated to law enforcement and crime prevention. This favorable index allows the crime-prevention professional better opportunity to revisit security survey and lecture sites for assessment of crime-prevention progress. The crime-prevention authority can determine which programs are effective and which are not. Crime-prevention techniques, methods, and ideas that work can be fostered. Those that are less than successful can be altered, eliminated, or replaced to provide updated productive crime prevention.

If successful, municipal and county crime-prevention units are exposed to massive demands for program implementation. This further stretches the resources of the crime-prevention unit of the local law enforcement agency. The demand also reduces the opportunity for the agency to revisit previous crime-prevention survey and lecture sites.

In contrast the crime-prevention practitioner at a college or university usually has daily exposure to persons or departments under consideration. This improves basic communication and fosters the ability to reassess the effectiveness of programs.

It is not unusual for a campus crime-prevention practitioner to evaluate a facility or function through formal surveys more than once in a year. Ongoing crime-prevention training and lectures are supplied as a matter of course. Updated crime-prevention evaluation data obtained through survey methods should continue to be the basis for ongoing crime avoidance instruction.

Specific programs

The most important crime-prevention programs are those that directly affect the prevention of crimes of violence against persons: murder, rape, assault (including aggravated), robbery, carjacking, threats and intimidation, gang-related violence, and stalking.

Lesser crimes, such as auto theft, auto break-ins, bike theft, books and book-bag theft, residence hall room theft, purse theft, office-related item theft, locker room theft, common theft, fraud, information (usually computer related) theft, telephone use theft, shoplifting, vandalism (including graffiti), and "quality-of-life" crimes also, are important. Quality-of-life crimes include drunkenness and drug abuse; disorderly and noisy conduct; minor harassment; offensive acts, words, or deeds; and panhandling, loitering, and vagrancy.

Prevention of crime on campus employs a variety of methods. These methods are organized into three categories: physical, procedural, and personnel methods.

Physical methods

Physical methods include proper and useful campus lighting, effective (reasonable and acceptable) barriers, high-quality locking and security devices, closed-circuit television (CCTV) systems, electronic alert, alarm and access control systems.

Procedural methods

Procedural methods include effective campus rules and regulations; use of facility requirements; security and safety signs; and crime-prevention information, including surveys, awareness, and training.

Personnel methods

Personnel methods include campus law enforcement and security personnel, collateral law enforcement personnel (when the local law enforcement agency has the primary jurisdiction), parking control personnel, students assigned to security duties, facility and residence hall monitors, and any person who takes an active role in reporting and discouraging criminal acts.

The protection of a campus involves the employment of tactics and techniques of physical, procedural, and personnel in a variety of methods. Sometimes, a crime-prevention function is both physical and procedural, such as Operation Identification, Neighborhood Watch, which involves engraving a personalized identification on an item, such as a television. The act of engraving the owner's driver's license or social security number on the television is physical in nature. However, the use of the awareness of this crime-prevention action is actually a procedural method, because it is a sign to warn opportunistic thieves.

The effectiveness of a campus crime-prevention program depends on the application of all these methods of prevention.

The Campus Security Act of 1990

Disclosure law

The Campus Security Act of 1990—revised in 1998, 2000, and 2010, is a disclosure law and a motivational tool. The law requires colleges and universities to publicize significant crime incident statistics, notifications, and procedures. This crime incident awareness, as crime-prevention practitioners know, helps to prevent crime by alerting potential victims to crime risks. Also, this awareness allows everyone on a school campus an opportunity to plan for crime prevention.

The statistical categories of the Campus Security Act, revised 2010, are as follows:

1. The institution must report certain statistics concerning the occurrence of crime on or near the campus during the last three years.
2. The institution must also report certain information and/or statistics regarding: the number of arrests and/or administrative acts for liquor law violations, drug abuse violations, and weapons violations, as well as missing student response, burglary crime reports, hate crime reports, fire incident reports, and emergency response procedures and resources.
3. Potential exists for further revisions to the Campus Crime Act, including: transportation safety guidelines, weapon (firearms and other) on campus policies and procedures, methicillin-resistant Staphylococcus aureus (MRSA) and infectious disease response procedures, and stalking and threat response and statistical reporting.

Most campus administrators are aware of the criminal statistics portion of the Campus Security Act of 2000. Schools must report seven other categories regarding their campus law enforcement and security elements and significant crime-prevention issues:

1. a statement of current policies regarding procedures for students to report crime and emergencies;
2. a statement of current policies concerning security and access to campus facilities;
3. a statement of current policies concerning campus law enforcement;
4. a description of programs designed to inform students and employees about campus security;
5. a description of programs designed to inform students and employees about the prevention of crimes;

6. a statement of policy concerning the monitoring and recording through local police agencies of criminal activities at off-campus student organizations recognized by the institution;
7. a statement of policy regarding the possession, use, and sale of alcoholic beverages; the enforcement of underage drinking laws; the possession and the use of illegal drugs; and the enforcement of federal and state drug laws.

This information must be made available to new students and employees on request.

It is obvious to any crime-prevention practitioner that these policies and programs identify the elements of a campus crime-prevention program. This new campus crime disclosure act brought these policies, programs, and protective systems into close focus by campus administrators who scrambled to ensure compliance with the law.

Impact of the Campus Security Act

The impact of the Campus Security Act of 2000, on campus crime prevention, has been significant. Many institutions were committed to sound campus crime-prevention programs prior to the enactment of this law. However, the majority of schools had not even considered publishing crime incident statistics or notifying students, faculty, and employees of criminal acts taking place on the campus. That all changed on September 1, 1992, when the original federal law, the Campus Security Act, came into effect. Educational institutions energized their security planners to develop law enforcement, security, and protective services policies to comply with the law.

Communication

The Campus Security Act of 2000 is primarily a law-mandating communication. The act does not order campuses to create, institute, and develop these crime responses and crime-prevention systems and programs. This law only mandates that they "disclose" or report on the systems and programs.

Compliance creates programs

To comply with the Campus Security Act of 2000, schools enlisted their protective service management to create or enhance the crime information delivery system for students and staff. Some protective professionals created their "new" campus crime-prevention programs using standard crime-prevention information and techniques.

To their delight, most campus crime-prevention officers found that suddenly they had easier access to a multitude of information delivery services on campus to spread crime risk awareness and crime-prevention information. These notification programs include the following:

- crime prevention and protective services booklets and handout materials
- campus newspapers
- bulletin board notices
- video production presentations at cafeterias, in dormitories, and in gathering locations on campus
- crime-prevention lectures, workshops, and seminars
- speaking engagement and awareness programs
- instructive classes for residential life and student life management and staff
- "instant" bulletins on campus regarding special crime risks
- other innovative and creative methods for dispersing crime-prevention information and teaching techniques; for example, dissemination of information on programmable FAX machines

Crime-prevention representatives on campuses increased their networking with other educational institution's campus protective departments. The exchange of crime-prevention methods, techniques, and activities reached an all-time high in the campus crime-protection industry. Many new and innovative crime-prevention methods were developed and shared by law enforcement and security personnel.

Positive results of the act

The results of the impact of the Campus Security Act of 2000 are still being measured. However, it is obvious that the effectiveness of campus crime prevention has been enhanced immensely. Also, the outlook is excellent for even more campus crime-prevention program action and interaction in the future. In this way the Campus Security Act of 2000 is an unqualified success.

Neighborhood Watch on the college campus

A Neighborhood Watch is, generally speaking, not a program geared for the college community. However, the principles of the program can be applied. The objectives are

- to request individual cooperation and look out for one another's property,
- to report suspicious persons,
- to report crime regardless of the amount stolen, and
- to increase the community's awareness through educational programs on how to reduce crime.

Information, notification, and emergency communication

Incidences of individual and mass casualty events on campuses have increased emphasis communication—especially emergency communication. Evolving electronic technology in safety and security communication has enhanced the ability of institutions to inform, warn, and direct persons regarding their personal and group safety measures. Emergency communication on campus includes: a university police and/or security central communications operations center; electronic message boards in classrooms, residential halls, lobbies, common areas, and walkways; emergency intercoms and telephones, some with CCTV interaction campus sirens and loudspeakers; broadcast e-mails; telephone and desktop alerts; Internet and satellite communications methods; police, public safety, and staff posted at locations on campus, including the perimeter; and university homepages and switchboard telephone and intermate hotlines.

Thefts in the library

A recent survey among several colleges throughout the country showed that the biggest problem among officials was the theft of wallets while studying at the college library. This is attributed to negligence on the part of the victim. Frequently, the victim reports that he or she left a coat, backpack, or purse containing money on an unoccupied table while going to locate a book. On returning, belongings are found in disarray and the wallet or money is missing. One answer to this problem is to give out a flyer to everyone who enters the library advising of the crime problem.

Bicycle theft prevention

A recent crime-analysis study revealed that bikes with poor quality locks are stolen most frequently. To combat this crime problem, two flyers can be distributed.

The first flyer alerts the owners to the problem and urges the owner of the bike to obtain a better quality lock. It also highlights the following crime-prevention tips on the security of bicycles:

1. Locks are worthless if not used properly.
2. When not in use, lock the bike to an immovable object, such as a bike rack.
3. Lock the bike through both wheels and around the frame, and then secure it to an immovable object.
4. Bikes locked outside should be left in a well-lighted and frequently traveled area.
5. Bikes brought inside should be locked in the dormitory room or area of high activity.

The second flyer urges students to register their bicycles. If bikes are registered, there is a good chance they will be returned if stolen.

Administration office security programs

According to a survey conducted on five college campuses, the most common items stolen are wallets, cash and credit cards, calculators, petty cash, and computers.

Wallets are generally taken because of carelessness—left in an unsecured and unoccupied area. At times the theft of a wallet goes beyond that of just cash, when credit cards and checks, which were inside the wallet, are used. Defensive measures for this type of larceny are to conduct meetings informing students and staff of the problem and seek their support, in addition to conducting a security survey.

The theft of office equipment generally can be prevented by bolting down typewriters, calculators, and the like and utilizing the operation identification program, which is geared to deterring such thefts.

Petty cash thefts for the past year should be analyzed as to why and how such thefts occurred. Members of the crime-prevention unit should meet with members of the controller's office where the crime-prevention security tips can be passed on to those handling petty cash. These tips should include the following:

1. Do not maintain a petty cash fund in an amount larger than necessary. Most departments have found that a fund in the $25–$50 range is adequate.
2. Keep the fund in a properly secured place. Avoid desk drawers or cabinets, which have locks that are easily opened by a common key.
3. As a matter of policy, the person designated on the controller's records as the petty cash fund custodian should be the only person with access to the fund.
4. In no instance should the responsibility for a petty cash fund be given to a part-time employee or anyone hired on a contractual basis.

Operation Identification

Operation Identification started in 1963 in Monterey Park, California, as a burglary prevention program. Probably, it is the most frequently discussed crime-prevention program in the country. A unique identifier is placed on items to be used to link recovered property to a specific crime or criminal. The deterrent effects of Operation Identification rely upon the burglar's assumed belief that Operation Identification items marked properly increase the risk of apprehension and lower the economic gain.

Intrusion alarms

Intrusion alarms are necessary equipment for proper security. Unfortunately, the installation of such a system is accompanied by numerous false alarms. Basically, there are five causes of false alarms:

1. faulty installation of equipment
2. equipment failure
3. telephone line malfunction
4. subscriber's error (human problem)
5. natural acts, such as rain, high winds, or electrical storms

On a national scale, more than 90% of all false alarms are caused by these factors. Again on a national scale, more than 50% of all false alarms are caused by the subscriber's error. Such simple matters as neglecting to properly secure doors or windows alarmed with magnetic contacts and permitting personnel to enter alarmed areas by an alarm key are a couple of common errors on the subscriber's part.

Again, let us look closer at the five causes of false alarms:

1. *Faulty installation of equipment:*
   a. incapable installer or installer's helpers
   b. installation does not meet the requirements of Underwriters Laboratories' (UL) standards
   c. wrong equipment designed for intended job
2. *Equipment failure: dead batteries*
   a. breakdown in control panel, wires, relays or shunt-key cylinder
   b. poorly designed equipment that has no UL listing
3. *Telephone line malfunction:*
   a. telephone company causing an open circuit in the lines
   b. telephone company repairman working in the general area of alarmed site
4. *Subscriber's error:*
   a. complex not properly secured and alarm turned on
   b. operation of alarm never properly stated to subscriber by alarm company
5. *Natural acts:*
   a. electrical storms and blackouts
   b. heavy rain, winds, and floods affecting alarmed area or telephone wires

What can be done to reduce false alarms? The existing alarm system can be modified. All control panels installed on campus should be of the finest quality, as listed by the UL.

Then, look carefully at other features: a locked panel to prevent unauthorized entry and possible tampering with the alarm, an entrance/exit delay feature that allows the subscriber 30 seconds to enter or leave before the panel registers an intrusion, and the hookup of an audible horn. This feature allows the subscriber, if leaving the property and failing to observe the meter on the control panel, 30 seconds before the audible horn goes off and an additional 30 seconds for the subscriber to shut off the alarm before the signal is sent to the police station.

On all construction or renovation projects, standards should be developed with the planning office regarding the installation of alarms.

The intrusion alarm, then, should be installed by an UL-listed alarm vendor; however, if the general contractor has the responsibility for such installation, then options are to use a union or nonunion UL-listed alarm vendor or to use the campus's own electricians.

If it is decided to use the latter, the system must be inspected by a UL-listed alarm vendor before being tied into the police board. In this way, it is certain the products and installation are done correctly.

In addition, it is helpful to educate users of the alarm system in the proper method of handling it to reduce the rate of false alarms.

CPTED Landscape Security

An important element of CPTED that defines semi-private and private space within a complex is your landscape design. It is recommend that the height of bushes be no higher than 3 feet. We have recently read that FEMA recommends the height of bushes to be 18 inches. And that tree branches are between 7 and 8 feet *off the ground as a means for Natural Surveillance and Safety. You want to be able to detect intruders and not allow them a hiding spot. Your landscape if properly laid out can also be a deterrent and prevent criminal opportunity. Landscape furniture should be vandal-resistant and if benches are installed, they need to be designed so that individuals can't be sleeping on them. Also, take under consideration, exterior lighting, video surveillance, vegetation, maintenance, barriers, the entrance & exit of your property, signage and the surface structure.

Conclusion

We realize the many problems with active shooter and executive protection and coverage for special events, which have developed over the years, but we still have to address crime issues.

Except for random crime that occurs spontaneously, most crimes can be deterred, avoided, prevented, or thwarted. To deal with campus crime the educational institution's law enforcement or security agency must be able to adapt to increasingly difficult and different security risk challenges. The protective force must have an ongoing, progressive campus crime-prevention program in place. The department must be able to continually develop meaningful programs.

There are no perfect formulas for the application and implementation of a campus crime-prevention program. There are systematized methods of identifying crime risks, measuring these risks, and identifying remedial solutions for planning and assessing priorities for the delivery of reasonable methods of crime prevention.

Virtually every educational institution has committed to campus crime prevention in some form or another. Campus crime prevention is really a grassroots program. The most effective crime-prevention programs succeed in enlightening campus occupants and enlisting them in using reasonable means to prevent criminal acts.

Security Magazines

Security on Campus. Available from: <securityoncampus.org>.
International Association of Campus Law Enforcement. Available from: <iaclea.org>.
America Society for Industrial Security. Available from: <asisonline.org>.
International Association of Chiefs of Police. Available from: <theiacp.org>.
Campus Safety Magazine. Available from: <campussafetymagazine.com>.

*8 feet clearance is also recommended by ASIS Physical Security Principle Book, 2015, p. 214.

Chapter 32

Domestic violence, take a stand against violence

Inge Sebyan Black
Security Consultant

When I began writing about domestic violence in 1996, I referred to my chapter as, The Crime of the Nineties.

Inge Sebyan Black, 1996.

Introduction

Someone you know, your friend, your sister, mother, daughter, or wife has been a victim or will be a victim of violence. According to Partnership Against Domestic Violence, every 9 seconds, another woman in the United States has been beaten.[1] It is estimated that 13 million women are victims of physical assault by their intimate partner, and 1 in 5 murder victims in the United States was killed by their partner.

National Domestic Violence Statistics shows that one in four women and one in seven men will experience domestic violence sometime in their lifetime.[2] One in 10 women in the United States will be raped by an intimate partner in her lifetime.[3] Over half of all men and women in the United States will experience psychological abuse by their intimate partner during their lifetime.

Domestic violence continues to be a serious social threat and *it is everybody's business*, because it does not just affect victims at their homes, it can also affect us at our schools and the workplace. Closing our eyes to this tragedy would further threaten our culture. This chapter is written with the hopes of sharing some insight on this subject as it is today. Although our society is working to dispel the view that domestic violence is a "private family matter," I still hear family members of victims comment that police should never be called because it is a personal family matter, but it really is matter of public awareness and public safety. It also creates a substantial financial burden on society in general. If we cannot get control of domestic violence, what kind of future ramifications would this have?

When I began writing about domestic violence in 1996, I referred to my chapter as, "The Crime of the Nineties," because it was not until some high-profile cases, such as murder of Nicole Brown Simpson, that domestic violence was publicly discussed and in the headlines of the front pages. It had previously been a subject only talked about behind closed doors. Twenty-three years later, however, the statistics continue to be both overwhelming and disturbing. Domestic violence continues to be a threat to our society and is a national problem. We need to educate society, make more resources available, and have more viable options for survivors. We know that the best indicator of future behavior is past behavior; therefore, it is essential that we find ways to actively report and monitor offenders.

Everyone can make a difference by educating themselves and others and by speaking up to stop this violence. Each of us plays a role in stopping the cycle of violence. Your role will ultimately determine the future for the victims and their loved ones, even if you are a friend or relative of the violator, your silence only enables them. You can also call on your public officials to support lifesaving domestic violence services and hold the perpetrator accountable. It is up to all of us because until the victim comes to terms with the dynamics of their abusive

1. Domestic Shelters.org.
2. CDC, 2017.
3. CDC, 2010.

Handbook of Loss Prevention and Crime Prevention. DOI: https://doi.org/10.1016/B978-0-12-817273-5.00032-6

relationship or well into recovery, they do not recognize the signs that they and the ones close to them need help. No matter how many people tell victims to do something, they do not take action until *they* are ready. It is better to tell the victim that he/she is a good person and that he/she can make a good life without any mental or physical abuse from anyone. Promoting self-esteem and independence are critically important for victims. It may take 1 incident or 20 separate incidents. It may be after 1 month or 20 years. Everyone's ability to tolerate abuse is different, and there are many forms of abuse. Verbal abuse may be tolerated for years, whereas other forms may not be tolerable for long. From experience, I understand how frustrating it is for the loved ones of the victim because it seems like the victim is the only one who does not see the abuse. Loved ones see the escalation growing and the danger increasing and yet, somehow, the victim continues to protect their perpetrator. Wanting to help may often push the victim further into isolation or denial. Therefore coming to terms with what actions are necessary is critical for your safety and theirs. Understanding the reasons why victims stay in denial, such as financial destruction, family breakup, emotional damage, embarrassment, fear of failure, and fear for their life, are important in helping the victim make the decision to leave. Couples counseling is not the answer in an intimate violent abusive relationship. *The only way to end the violence is to end the relationship.*

What is domestic violence?

The description of "intimate partner violence" is those acts that are inflicted by either a current or former intimate spouse, dating partner or sexual partner and includes actual or threats of physical violence or sexual violence, emotional or psychological abuse, stalking, and financial abuse among other forms of abuse.[4]

The legal definition of battering varies from state to state; according to the law in various states, it can be described as physical, sexual, and psychological abuses that may include one or all of the following: physical harm, bodily harm, assault (such as hitting, kicking, slapping, pushing, stabbing, or the infliction of fear of imminent physical harm), sexual abuse, manipulation, threats, emotional abuse, harassment, intimidation, isolation, using children, using male privilege, ridiculed, minimizing and blaming, economic coercion, and a variety of behaviors used to maintain fear, intimidation, and power. It can be referred to as a pattern of coercive, controlling behavior that can lead to physical abuse, emotional or psychological abuse, sexual abuse, or financial abuse. The National Coalition Against Domestic Violence defines battering "as more than simply a measure of physical behavior, it is a pattern of behavior, with the effect of establishing power and control over their partners." Power and control are the common denominators in domestic violence. Understanding the abuse patterns that are commonly seen will help us help the victims. Domestic violence is a pervasive, life-threatening crime that affects millions of individuals across the United States. Although domestic violence is most commonly known as violence by an intimate partner, it also includes abuse from another family member. Some states, such as Minnesota, have broadened the scope of domestic violence by including roommates, brothers, aunts, uncles, and essentially anyone that lives together. This makes it easier for law enforcement to make an arrest on a domestic charge. Often one person is charged, or at least forced to leave the residence.

This chapter will not cover all the reasons, all the different victims, or all the answers. My hope is to ultimately address the need to educate the public, police, probation officers, justice system, judges, and employers. Domestic violence is a threat to our culture both socially and economically speaking. The economic impact is serious when we take into account: the children left behind, the psychological damage done, the prenatal injuries and death, the increased homelessness among women and children, costs related to education, relation to addiction, the cost incurred by the legal and law enforcement community, and the higher health-care costs. It is also important to note that workplace violence can occur when a domestic situation enters the workplace. This is discussed further in Chapter 33, Workplace violence: 2020 and beyond. With this chapter, I also hope to stimulate further in-depth studies and discussion into the nature and prevention of violence. I challenge everyone that witnesses abuse in any form, to report or tell someone that can help. What will our future response be? Will we ultimately be able to truly account for all the victims and change the thought behind the behavior? Will we be able to understand a lesbian, gay, grandparent, and man when they tell us of their fear and need our help? I certainly hope so.

Who are the victims?

Domestic violence is not discriminatory and occurs between people of any social class, any race, religion, sexual orientation, and all age-groups. Other victims besides the immediate ones are family, children, parents, grandparents, employers, coworkers, and friends. The extent of their suffering, which is endured behind closed doors, is kept private.

4. SafeHorizon, 2019. Domestic Violence.

Studies are somewhat inconclusive because victims in higher income groups and status sometimes have resources to deal with domestic violence privately. There are also cultural and religious factors that tend to deal with these issues privately. There are also many victims who feel that reporting such a crime would only cause them more personal harm. There are many other reasons for not reporting domestic violence, but a few include embarrassment, economics, legal ramifications (loss of job or professional licenses), threats toward the children, and religious beliefs. Aside from all these barriers, reports show that victims of battering are disproportionately women. Although men are also victims, each year, almost 1 million women, reported being victimized by intimates (spouse, ex-spouse, boyfriend, or girlfriend) in comparison to 160,000 men. Since nonreporting is high, some of the statistics are not accurate. These statistics state that urban women and younger women are at higher risk. Domestic violence is also associated with unemployment and cultures. The severity and frequency of abuse can increase with a bad economy. With a weak economy, there are also fewer options for the survivor to seek safety or escape. Victims may also have a more difficult time finding a job in order to become financially independent of their abuser.

No one should ever have to endure either the physical or emotional suffering that comes from domestic abuse. While everyone would agree, the victim suffers the most, there are often many other victims such as family members, friends, and coworkers. The police, courts, and governments are also burdened with the cost of domestic violence.

The fact that 50% of the women killed in this country are killed by their intimate partner is, to say the least, alarming. The FBI estimates that there is a less than 10% arrest rate for abusers, and most men charged with assaulting their partners end up without consequences. One organization working to end the violence is The National Network to End Domestic Violence (NNEDV). The NNEDV addresses complex causes and the far-reaching consequences of domestic violence.[5] It has created a social, political, and economic environment in which violence against women no longer exists. Their primary membership includes the 56 statewide and territorial coalitions against domestic and sexual violence. NNEDV provides training, resources and assistance to the coalitions, victim advocates, judges, law enforcement personnel, prosecutors, governmental agencies, and corporations. The organization advances public awareness of domestic violence issues and advocates for federal legislation and funding for victims and holds perpetrators accountable. NNEDV uses social media for action alerts and updates on almost every social media sites such as Facebook, Instagram, Twitter, Google+ , Snapchat, Spotify, YouTube, LinkedIn, and Pinterest. They have movie night conversation guides, coloring pages to download, movie ideas, online book clubs, empowerment playlists, and more advocacy programs. These are all ways for the public to learn about domestic violence and how everyone can make a difference in survivors' lives.

Why do abusers abuse?

This is the subject of intense debate. In the previous edition of this book, I looked at the history of men assuming ownership of their wives. Control and power are part of that ownership. Professionals agree that this problem is so complex that there is no single theory. Some feel that the gender analysis of power, back to the patriarchal organization of society, is the root of the problem. Critics claim that traits in the individual, such as growing up abused, personality disorders, or early traumatic life experiences, are symptomatic to underlying emotional problems, therefore, causing an individual to act out behaviors that we know to be unacceptable. Jealousy and insecurity can also be factors where the violator feels inadequate or inferior to the victim and is trying to bring them down to their level. Others feel that changes in our society, such as the equal rights movement, may have created hostility and rage acted out in their behavior toward others. Certainly, our family system has changed, but if you look carefully at the victims and perpetrators, I think you would agree that power and control are underlying factors and key to a majority of battering situations. Maybe it would be safe to say that there can certainly be more than one factor that contributes to someone hurting someone they are intimate with.

What we do know

We do know women of color, older women, women with a language barrier, disabled women, and lesbians often have no access to linguistically and culturally appropriate services. We also know that violence knows no gender. Men endure violence with almost nonexistent shelters and resources. We know violence breeds violence and we must consciously accept our own responsibility toward ending the cycle. We know that our attitude must be one of acceptance. We need to take the lessons we have learned, coupled with all the new recommendations. Starting with our children,

5. NNEDV.org

we must teach respect, patience, and values. *It is up to us to change the cycle of violence.* Society today is indoctrinated daily into violence on TV, movies, and the Internet. Even the news is more concerned with sensationalism and violent stories than good family interest stories. The real thing that must change is the way we treat each other.

Leaving, the most dangerous time

We know why victims return to or remain with their abuser. In fact, a victim's risk of getting killed greatly increases when they are in the process of leaving or have just left. On average, three women die at the hands of a current or former intimate partner every day. According to experts, leaving such a relationship puts women in a potentially life-threatening danger.

"Research has shown the risk of domestic homicide becomes the highest during the period of separation and the intensity of domestic violence escalates when the abused person decides to leave the relationship." stated by Betty Jo Barrett, an intimate partner violence researcher and an associate professor in the women's and gender studies program at the University of Windsor.[6] The power and control the perpetrator seeks may escalate his violence, forcing the victim to return to her abuser or remain in place.

Law enforcement response

Law enforcement plays a key role in domestic abuse because the police responding to a domestic abuse call may be the victim's first contact with a law enforcement agency. The way the domestic call is handled will impact how the victim views the system regarding seriousness on the part of the police and whether the victim receives adequate support at the time that is most critical and potentially life-threatening. Law enforcement has historically been apprehensive about responding to domestic abuse calls for many reasons, they know that the situation can be volatile for both them and the abuser's victim. Another reason that police can be apprehensive is the frustration oftentimes the victim turns on the police, after they arrive, siding with the spouse out of fear, guilt, and/or embarrassment. The victim may then become reluctant to file charges. Although state laws vary, in Minnesota, whether the victim wants to have anyone arrested or not, the police can make the decision to arrest if there is evidence of assault. In some states, it is mandatory to arrest if there is any sign of injury. This takes the decision out of the victim's hands.

Police find themselves struggling with their own conflicting attitudes on private family matters. They must learn to separate their values and opinions. Training plays a key role in law enforcement learning objectivity. Their role should be to protect all parties, without judging, but it is unrealistic to think that the officer will not make a judgment based on what someone might have said or what they see. Although there have been many changes in police policies and procedures, officers are still faced with an ambiguous situation. Several years ago, a government-funded study examined spousal abuse and determined that the police, when responding to misdemeanor abuse cases, would opt for one of three courses of action: some abusers would be arrested; others would be removed from the home in order that all parties could cool off; and the third group was simply counseled. Among the group arrested, 19% had subsequent spousal abuse arrests within a 6-month period. Of those who were spared arrest, 35%, almost double, committed spousal abuse within a 6-month period. The effect of the arrest (at least short term) seems adequately demonstrated. Also, only 2.2% of all those arrested were convicted. In some cities, such as Duluth, Minnesota, a first-time offender may receive 30 days in jail and be put on probation pending completion of a 26-week batterer's program. If he/she misses classes, he/she will usually be sent to jail.

No one would argue with the fact that a police officer's job is not marriage counseling or family therapy, and we are not suggesting that they try to act as mediators. We do, however, suggest they be trained specifically on family violence and how to diffuse potentially explosive situations. Having some knowledge on family dynamics can make a difference in what to say and how to say it. Not surprisingly, many officers come from homes involving domestic abuse or are involved in an abusive situation themselves as a victim or an assaulter. How departments hire their officers regarding age, experience, and how they train and communicate their philosophy toward domestic incidents may determine an officer's response. Officers must be able to stay neutral, keep their bias out of the situation, remain calm, be fair, assist the victim to a safe place, protect all parties, and be a good listener. This may seem like a lot; however, there is a legal precedent requiring the judicial system to protect victims. Law enforcement, as well as the courts, must learn new ways to combat this violence. If several individuals are involved in a domestic dispute, what determines who is arrested? If both show injuries, should it be both or neither since arresting one based on an officer's opinion or statements may

6. Lauren, P., Dec. 8, 2016. Toronto/Domestic Violence. CBC News.

cause the wrong person to be charged, thus causing further victimization. Clearly the police are making their decisions based on interviews, statements, and evidence, which is their judgment call based on their values, beliefs, and experience. Law enforcement must learn from cases such as *Thurman v. City of Torrington*, where Tracey Thurman continually called the police, and the police ignored her calls and plea for help. Subsequently, on June 10, 1983, Tracey's husband stabbed her repeatedly around the chest, neck, and throat. Twenty-five minutes later, the police officer arrived but did not arrest the husband. Not until he came at her again, while on a stretcher, was he arrested and taken into custody. Since 1983 many police agencies have revised their policy on handling domestic abuse calls. Those agencies understand what the "equal protection" of the Fourteenth Amendment means and realize they must assume a portion of the responsibility to remain neutral and take appropriate measures to ensure everyone's safety. Law enforcement and the courts, as well as social agencies, are and will be held accountable, if they fail to protect.

Law enforcement officers are better trained today to deal with the complex and dangerous conditions of domestic abuse. Increasingly, the job of a police officer is not about enforcing or not to enforce but is about resolving bad situations. This can only be accomplished with cooperation with other agencies within the community. The police must establish a clear protocol when local officers are friends of the local batterers. This may require handing this situation over to a different officer. Currently there is domestic violence training for national organizations, including the National Sheriff's Association. Because of the correlation between the perpetrators need for power and control, law enforcement officers represent the authority to take away their freedom, therefore the possibility of the offender murdering the police officers when responding to a domestic violence call.[7] More information about domestic violence training for officers is available on the National Sheriff's Association website.

Law enforcement policies differ from city to city, it is helpful for survivors to understand how police are trained to domestic violence situations. Every call should be treated as a high priority call as it may be life-threatening. Because of the serious nature of domestic violence calls, many police departments continue to respond even if the victim cancels the request to respond or is the victim hangs up on a 911 call. Another common policy is for two officers to respond. This will make the call more manageable while being able to separate the abuser and the victim and checking arrest warrants and prior history of both. Having two officers also helps determine if there are firearms on the premises thus removing them. Collecting evidence, such as obtaining statements, taking picture, all priorities, will be easier with two officers. Many departments now encourage the officer to assist in developing a safety plan.

A 3-year statewide study found that inconsistent response is the major obstacle toward ending domestic violence. While statewide victim advocates praise the overall approach to domestic violence, they acknowledge that there are shortfalls. There are often differences, sometimes subtle and others glaring, between what a victim can expect from one community to the next. Many agencies have a *mandatory arrest policy*. There is much debate over mandatory arrests, including the arrest leading to an escalation in violence and the arrest allowing the victim to have time to consult with advocates. We must maintain consistency on a "must arrest" statute. It is important to send a message of hope and justice for all victims. It is the role of the police to enforce the ruling of a judge and protect the victim.

Options for protection

Whether it is a restraining order or an order for protection, depending on the state, for our purpose, we will call this protection an "order for protection" or "order."

To obtain an order, you can go to the clerk's office in the county courthouse or superior or probate court during normal business hours. You can obtain an order against a spouse, former spouse, a household member, a blood relative, minor child, parent of a minor child, or someone you have had a substantial dating relationship with. You can get protection whether you currently live with the abuser. It will be necessary to write a statement explaining the events leading up to this course of action. There is no cost and you do not need an attorney. The process of getting an order has been made easier, with more assistance and programs in place. Cultures that were not educated about what constituted abuse and what options were available now have formed shelters and assistance. If the violence occurs after available hours, an emergency order may be obtained through your local police department.

Several different requests can be made regarding an order:

- *No abuse order*: The abuser is ordered not to hurt you, not to attempt to hurt you, and not to threaten you.
- *Vacate order*: The abuser is ordered to move out of and stay away from your home, surrender keys, and stay away from your place of work.

7. Domestic Shelters.org.

- *No contact order*: The abuser is ordered to not contact you in person or by telephone, mail, or any other way.
- *Temporary custody/support order*: This gives you, the victim, temporary custody of your children and the abuser is ordered to pay reasonable support.
- *Money compensation order*: The abuser may be ordered to repay you for expenses incurred as a result of the abuse, such as medical expenses or lost wages.
- *A confiscation order:* The abuser is ordered to surrender any weapons, such as guns, even if he has a license to carry a weapon.

After the judge hears your story, a temporary order will be issued; this order is usually good for 10 days. The police are then responsible for serving the order to your abuser. Only after he is served is the order valid. It is necessary to inform the court of all the places the abuser may always be and to keep your copy of the order on you.

After the 10 days, you must return to the court to petition for a 1-year order. The judge will then ask your abuser to tell his side of the story and will then decide on the extension at that time. If the abuser does not show up in court, the court feels the abuser has admitted his guilt, and will extend the order. Keep in mind state laws may vary slightly; we have tried to give a sample of how this works. In no way have we spelled out the exact system as it pertains to every jurisdiction. A restraining order/order for protection is a civil document. Only after the order is violated or criminal charges are sought can a person be arrested. Police are mandated to arrest the abuser when an active order has been violated. Any changes to an order can be obtained by returning to court. If you are employed, you should also advise security and/or your supervisor that such an order exists and is active.

The main reason victims seek help through the court system is to end the abuse. When the abuser is someone the victim is emotionally attached to, the issue of being safe in their home is often mixed with feeling of guilt, love, embarrassment, and fear. There are many feelings and pressures these victims have. Recognizing the pressures placed on the victim, the prosecuting attorney can help remove some of them by using the court system to place controls on your abuser. These vary from state to state and from county to county; however, the general idea applies in different specific terms:

- The prosecuting attorney can sign the complaint. Therefore it is the state, and not the victim, who is filing charges. This makes the victim a witness rather than a plaintiff. If the victim is being pressured into dropping charges, they simply say they have no power to do so, and since the victim did not file the charges, they cannot tell the prosecutor how to do his job.
- The prosecuting attorney can subpoena the victim as a witness for the state. This will shield the victim from pressure not to appear since they are now required by law to go to court.
- The prosecuting attorney can demand a court trial within 60 days (or in some states 30 days). This can relieve the victim of uncertainty about when the court date will be.
- If the victim suspects further violence while charges are pending, the attorney can refer them to the Clerk of Family Court, or an advocate could help file a protection order. The court could also exclude the abuser from the place of residence.

Through the process of the system, there is a trial to determine whether the abuser violated the law. This decision can be made by a judge alone, or by a jury. Next, there is sentencing, which is a legal proceeding in which the judge orders the abuser be punished for the crime. The court has many options for punishment: imposing a fine of money, time in jail, probation with conditions (which often includes counseling), unsupervised probation, or no punishment.

Government involvement

The only true way to achieve our goal is to have all government agencies involved in making a difference. One great example is when the Minnesota State Legislature passed legislation in 1992 directing the Higher Education Coordinating Board to survey recent college graduates in the state and evaluate the adequacy of the professional education they had received about violence and abuse.

A task force of higher education and licensing board representatives reviewed the survey results as well as an inventory of current courses on violence and abuse. I was lucky enough to participate in the outreach meeting and focus groups. Ultimately their recommendation to the state legislature was to establish a Higher Education Center against Violence and Abuse. The legislature recognized the critical role of professional education in preparing graduates to be part of the state's strategy to reduce violence, abuse, and harassment by taking the task force's recommendations. The Minnesota Higher Education Center against Violence and Abuse works in cooperation with organizations statewide to develop higher education programs that prepare professionals to provide safety and services to victims of violence, holds perpetrators accountable for their actions, and addresses the root causes of violence. The center also serves as a resource for all Minnesota higher education institutions and selected professional licensing agencies. This task force evaluates professionals within four professional areas: law, education, health services, and human services. The focus is on training and licensing of teachers, school administrators, guidance counselors, law enforcement officers, lawyers, physicians, nurses, psychologists, and social workers. They also assess and recommend changes in current programs. In addition to their focus on training, the center has developed an electronic clearinghouse of information that can assist faculty and staff in developing higher education curricula on violence and abuse. This state effort demonstrates what can be accomplished when government agencies take a lead role in stopping the violence.

Legislation and funding to establish the Higher Education Center against Violence and Abuse was part of the 1993 Omnibus Crime Bill. A grant was awarded to the School of Social Work, in the College of Human Ecology, at the University of Minnesota to establish the center.

Conclusion

This chapter does not begin to touch on the effects of domestic violence or the factors involved, nor does it give all the options or answers to steps taken by the judicial system. Instead it is sending the message that the problem is not a private family matter, but everybody's problem. Society is beginning to respond to the psychological needs of all parties involved, such as the abuser, abused, and the children. Public awareness, education, and understanding are essential. We can do more as a community to ensure the safety of victims when they leave. It will be a long journey before people accept responsibility for their behavior toward others and realize what acceptable behavior is and what aggressive, violent, destructive, and illegal behavior is. Does the current legislation in place really protect victims of domestic violence? We are not there yet as we have a long way to go.

The real change will come when the Federal Government enacts legislation to protect the victim and punish the perpetrator.

The Violence Against Women Act 2000 was reauthorized, after President Bush signed it into law in 2006, with a few improvements, additions, and funding increases. One of the major components of the legislation with funding authorization was the Services and Training for Officers and Prosecutors grant of $925 million to states distributed among police, prosecutors, courts, and state and local victims' services agencies for the purpose of enhancing law enforcement activities. Funds were also given to shelter services, civil legal assistance, transitional housing, dating violence programs, and grants for disabled and older women among other funding initiatives.

The change we need to support is consistency in education on domestic violence. There are excellent curricula developed for children in kindergarten through high school, but there is no consistency on how young people are educated about this. Education is critical in the prevention and eventual elimination of domestic violence. The New York State Office developed their "Model Domestic Violence Policy for Counties" for their schools. This is an example of what all states can do to preserve our society.

When we talk about domestic violence, it is not about men versus women or women versus men; it is about control over respect.

Men are also victims of domestic abuse. In a 2001 US study, it was revealed that 85% of the victims were female with a male batterer. The other 15% includes intimate partner violence in gay and lesbian relationships and men who were battered by a female partner.

Further readings

Bachman, R., Salzman, L., 2000. Violence Against Women: Estimates From the Redesigned Survey 1. U.S. Bureau of Justice Statistics, Washington, DC.

Hobbes, Meredith, October 29, 2010. Domestic Violence is a Workplace Issue, Say Law Firms. http://www.ncdsv.org/publications_workplace.html.

National Network to End Domestic Violence (NNDEV), 2010. Domestic Violence Counts 2009: A 24-Hour Census of Domestic Violence Shelters and Services. NNDEV, Washington, DC.

Oakland County Coordinating Council Against Domestic Violence. Bloomfield Hills, MI. https://www.michigan.gov/mdhhs/0,5885,7-339-71548_7261—,00.html.

Chapter 33

Workplace violence: 2020 and beyond

Inge Sebyan Black
Security Consultant

Introduction

On any given day, another incident of workplace violence will be news headline, where an employee has used violence or deadly force at their work site. Workplace violence is increasing at an alarming rate, yet until it happens, many companies remain uncommitted to putting adequate policies and procedures in place for their employees, visitors, and contractors.

We are way past the time to act. Throughout this paper, we will examine the responsibilities of company leadership and their management, as well as their employees. Employees have the right to expect a safe and secure work environment, no matter what occupation they work. The effect of workplace violence affects us all. According to the National Institute for Occupational Safety and Health, workplace violence falls into four categories: criminal intent, customer/client, worker against worker, and personal relationships.[1] The statistics for violence-related deaths and injuries are occurring in all occupations. We will also address external factors such as domestic violence and active shooter incidents, both likely to be carried out at the workplace.

A safe and secure workplace

OSHA (Occupational Safety and Health Administration) issued a Directive on Workplace Violence on September 8, 2011.[2] This directive outlines enforcement procedures for OSHA field officers to help them investigate employers for alleged workplace violence. OSHA's general duty clause requires employers to maintain a workplace that is free from recognized hazards that cause or are likely to cause death or serious physical harm. OSHA can cite and fine employers for failing to provide workers with adequate safeguards against workplace violence after an investigation. This directive does not require OSHA to respond to each complaint or incident related to workplace violence but it does help provide guidance for field officers to help determine whether an investigation should be pursued and if a citation is appropriate. This Directive is an initiative on OSHA's part to examine the issues surrounding workplace violence. Although OSHA issued guidelines for preventing workplace violence for health-care and social service workers in the past, in 2016, OSHA published "Guidelines for Preventing Workplace Violence for Healthcare and Social Service Workers." In 2009 OSHA published "Recommendations for Workplace Violence Prevention Programs in Late-Nite Retail Establishments"[3] and in 2010, they issued a FACT Sheet for tax drivers. Due to the heightened interest in the subject of workplace violence, OSHA is actively fining and citing employers, on the basis, that death or physical harm was likely to result from hazards which the employer knew or should have known about. OSHA believes that a well-written and implemented workplace violence prevention program, combined with controls and training can reduce the incidence of workplace violence.[4]

The consequences of violence in the workplace have had devastating effects on businesses, both financially and in lost lives. Employers have a legal and moral obligation, along with the responsibility, to provide a safe and secure work environment. Every day thousands of employees are subjected to workplace violence in one form or another.

1. https://wwwn.cdc.gov/wpvhc
2. OSHA Guidelines for Preventing Workplace Violence
3. https://www.osha.gov/pls/publications/publication.athruz?pType = Industry&pID = 231
4. https://www.osha.gov/SLTC/workplaceviolence/

Handbook of Loss Prevention and Crime Prevention. DOI: https://doi.org/10.1016/B978-0-12-817273-5.00033-8

Workplace violence includes any use of physical force against or by a worker that causes or could cause physical injury, threatening behavior, harassment, veiled threats and intimidation. It also includes anger-related incidents, rape, arson, property damage, vandalism, and theft. Incidences can occur at off-site business-related functions such as conferences, trade shows, social events, or meetings, but we refer to it as workplace violence because it takes place at work. The US Bureau of Labor Statistics reported that assaults and violent acts, including homicides, accounted for 18% of the overall fatal work injuries in 2010.[5] The Bureau of Labor Statistics' Census of Fatal Occupational Injuries reported, "16,890 workers in the private industry experienced trauma from nonfatal workplace violence in 2016."[6] These incidents resulted in lost days from work.

When talking about the legal responsibility or duty of employers to safeguard employees, customers, and others from preventable harm, we also need to keep in mind the employer's obligation to respect employee rights and appropriate management of these investigations. Having recognized the possibility of workplace violence is the first step in planning and mitigating such an event when it occurs.

Finland provides the only European example of a large-scale, systematic study of workplace violence.[7] This study was conducted over three time frames, all indicating alarming increase in workplace incidents. Even more evident than the increase in frequency were the severity of the incidents and the expanded array of businesses that had an incident. While it would be an understatement to say the costs are staggering, there are other impacts, such as deaths, injuries, loss of productivity, and psychological ramifications.

Because few countries have comprehensive national information relative to violence in the workplace, it is hard to estimate the extent of this serious problem. Many countries only collect information on fatal incidents rather than collecting workplace violence statistics into a separate category. According to studies done in Europe,[8] some evidence of the nature and quality of client contact is changing, leading to higher violence risks. Violence was clearly related to specific characteristics of workers and their work environment; however, these variables could not explain the increased levels of violence.

The United Kingdom has conducted research indicating that millions of Britons have experienced physical aggression in the workplace, with millions more subjected to intimidation, humiliation, and rudeness.[9] Cardiff and Plymouth, through a joint study, found that employment policies fail to deal with hostile treatment in the workplace. This research revealed that those workers in the health and social work, education and public administration and defense were most at risk for attacks by outsiders, while workers in the private sector were more likely to be assaulted by their coworkers.

Workplace violence should be considered a serious threat at businesses in every country. Security professionals throughout the world have taken on the task of educating and training businesses and their counterparts on how to address and prevent violence in their workplace. Every company *must have a well-defined* program in place. Only a workplace violence policy that is fully endorsed by management, approved legally, and one that lets their employees know that their safety is a priority, will be embraced. While many public and private businesses/agencies may have clear policies, polices alone are not enough. We must do more to train our leaders to recognize warning signs, how and when to report behavior, how to de-escalate if necessary, to minimize loss and mitigate the event when it occurs. If risk factors are identified and appropriate action is taken to mitigate the incident, the incident might be prevented or the impact minimized. Businesses can mitigate this risk through training, planning, and preparation.

The risk of workplace violence

Workplace violence is a *risk*, and the possibility of an incident is a realistic concern for employers. Through risk-based programs, such as risk analysis, risk assessments, and threat risk assessments, a risk assessment specific to workplace violence is recommended. A workplace violence risk assessment provides indicators such as vulnerability of specific threats, the likelihood of an event, and the impact of specific threats. The risk assessment will recommend mitigating options to minimize your risk. Adopting procedures for conducting individual risk assessments, if a threat or incident occurs, assists in mitigating a possible incident. A threat team, if in place, can then make decisions based on the risk assessment, further mitigating an occurrence. Both risk assessments and creating a threat team are discussed throughout this chapter when we identify what is needed to minimize the risks associated with workplace violence.

5. US Bureau of Labor Statistics, US Department of Labor, 2012.
6. https://www.jdsupra.com/legalnews/workplace-violence-and-shootings-in-the-75940/
7. https://www.tandfonline.com/doi/abs/10.1080/02678379508256886?journalCode = twst20
8. https://www.tandfonline.com/doi/full/10.1080/1359432X.2012.690557?src = recsys
9. https://www.theguardian.com/money/2011/nov/02/uk-workers-violence-workplace

To ensure success in the delivery of a solid workplace violence prevention program, it must be part of the strategic management initiative and have the full commitment of Senior Management. Every organization must have a workplace violence prevention plan that is developed specifically for them, as every work environment will have unique vulnerabilities and potential threats.

The risk of workplace violence has many variables, both internally and externally. External variables may include domestic violence, stalking, and other forms of unknown, aggressive behavior that enters the workplace. It is impossible to understand all the psychological and physical factors that might push an individual into committing a violent or aggressive act. For this reason, workplace violence is a very complex issue, requiring us to look at all aspects of the risk/threat spectrum and be prepared to respond to any type of violence whether it is an active shooter, suicidal employee or domestic partner. Every person reacts differently to stress, making it impossible to determine which one of the two, three, or more stressors might lead a particular person to commit a violent act.

Conducting a workplace violence risk assessment, specifically identifying the risks associated with workplace violence, aids in evaluating the controls currently in place against controls that are recommended to be in place. Having a security risk assessment is an extremely important process in identifying security concerns and risks. A workplace violence needs assessment will go beyond reviewing general vulnerability to assessing the possibility of violence from internal and external sources. We want to identify threats that might pertain to a particular industry type or organization, relationships that exist between a perpetrator and an organization, or relationships that may exist between a perpetrator and a current or former employee. It is important to consider the following factors:

- Are employees working alone, at a remote location or at night?
- Do employees handle cash or other valuable assets?
- Do employees work with the general public?
- Is the workplace in a high-crime area?
- Is your business targeted for terrorism, animal or human rights?
- Is this workplace known for high stress, threatening behavior?
- What physical security is currently in place? ID badges, access control, CCTV, and lighting.

These are a few of the factors that should be considered when doing a violence needs assessment but there are many more. Again, each workplace environment will have unique factors to consider.

Workplace violence prevention plan

The success and driving force behind your workplace violence prevention program will depend on the commitment of senior management. This will allow that proper resources are allocated for the development of a workplace violence prevention plan and execution of the plan. Commitment of senior management will also drive the effectiveness of incident management, physical security design, training, and other factors leading to success of this program. This plan must be established as the organization's top priority. Your plan should be a living and breathing document, evaluated and updated often. The plan should clearly identify the representatives that are responsible for implementing and maintaining the plan and then holding them accountable. Development of a workplace violence prevention team should include employees, which allows them to feel invested in this program. Since employees can often be the first to communicate signals of potential violent behavior, they should play a role in developing the workplace violence prevention plan. Having the employees buy-in to your plan increases the likelihood of acceptance.

Threat assessment team

Workplace violence is a complex problem that requires a multidisciplinary approach and needs to include a variety of stakeholders/business partners that can effectively establish a prevention plan, an intervention plan, and a threat management team. This team should include a representative from security, legal, human resources, mental health, and employee assistance program (EAP). If you have a union environment, a union representative should be considered. In high-risk work environments, such as health-care and social services, unions have played a key role in developing and implementing successful workplace violence programs.[10] These various leaders help draw on the different parts of the

10. ASIS/SHRM WVPI.1-2011.

management structure, with different perspectives and areas of knowledge. It would also be helpful to include a member of your local law enforcement. Remember to identify the personnel who will carry the primary responsibility for preventing and responding to incidents of violence. You want to provide them with necessary resources, policies, procedures, and guidelines, to assist them with a coordinated response. Training, including tabletop exercises, will better prepare the threat assessment team, while opening the lines of communication. It is necessary that the team has the authority and guidelines before an incident occurs. Threat assessment teams sometimes include an individual from the local police department or local emergency management office.

Planning includes the steps:

- Contract for an impartial, complete risk assessment and specific violence assessment. This should be designed to evaluate risks from both within and outside the company.
- Prepare and publish a written workplace violence policy developed by management, with designated employee representatives. Incorporate multidisciplines to research and write this policy. Use clear examples of acceptable behavior. Use firm, clear and concise language.
- Institute and communicate a firm harassment and zero tolerance policy.
- Communicate your organizations view on workplace violence, harassment.
- Involve all employees.
- Set up standards and compliance for all third party contractors.
- Implement an incident reporting system.
- Conduct training for new hires.
- Conduct annual for all employees to reenforce policies.
- Train the receptionist with additional training in the areas of detection and facial recognition.
- Train front line supervisors and management on indicators, de-escalation and reporting.
- Train all management in nonviolent conflict resolution.
- Develop partnerships with local police and emergency departments as well as mutual aid agreement with another business.
- Conduct tabletop exercises.
- Monitor and adjust training as needed based on statistics of success and intervention.
- Outline and communicate the investigation process and investigate every incident.
- Offer a confidential EAP allowing employees to seek help and provide support services for victims of violence.
- Have evacuation plans, sheltering in place and specific safe zone off site.
- Maintain copies of company diagrams and property off site.

Supervisors and managers need specialized training in identification, reporting, ways of diffusing aggressive behavior, conflict resolution, employee relations, personal security measures, and communication skills. These are not inclusive.

Workplace violence prevention policy

The workplace policy must be written, using firm, clear, and concise language. It should be clearly communicated, both at new hire orientation as well as ongoing one, that there is a "zero tolerance with regards to threats and violence." The policy should emphasize the employer's commitment in providing a safe and secure workplace environment along with a clear definition of unacceptable behavior. The policy should state the code of conduct, prohibiting all threats, violent behavior, and other behavior that might be interpreted as intent to cause physical harm.

After you have written this policy and communicated it, it will be important to require prompt reporting of suspected violations along with enforcement of the policy. The policy should also include the following:

- All reports to management are confidential and treated with discretion.
- All reports will be promptly investigated.
- Every witness and complainant will be treated fairly and impartially while investigated.
- Include members of the investigation staff and their qualifications.
- Identify how information about potential risks of violence will be communicated to all employees if necessary.
- Define how investigations are void from conflicts of interest, that is, not investigated by their respective supervisor.
- HR should communicate problematic employees to security.
- Offer an EAP program to all employees.

- The commitment for nonretaliation by an employee making any report in good faith.
- State any applicable regulatory requirements.
- Indication of discipline for policy violation.

Train to identify warning signs

As security professionals, we know that some employees may have a higher risk of behavior issues or tendencies. Training and experience are the keys to understanding what behaviors might lead to violence. In many cases, attacks are perpetrated by individuals who display some of the following characteristics; however, every attacker has different psychological characteristics, so it is important to be aware of behavioral clues that cause someone to act out.

- Prior history of violence: involvement in previous incidents of violence, verbal abuse, antisocial activities, and disruptive behavior.
- Domestic situations: an employee caught in a domestic dispute or family turmoil may impact the work place.
- Suspicious behavior and indicators.
- Mental disorders: mood swings, depression, bizarre statements, paranoid behavior, overly aggressive, and unstable behavior.
- Life-changing events: whether the employee has suddenly lost a family member, a pet, extreme medical changes, divorce, or other major life changes.
- Financial stresses such as bankruptcies, mortgage arrears, or heavy debt load.
- Obsession with another employee: may be romantic or not.
- Chemical dependence: drugs or alcohol abuse.
- Increased interest in weapons: ownership of guns or gun collection, other offensive weapons. They want to talk about guns often.
- Disgruntled employee: an employee feels the company no longer cares about them or other employees creating a sense of mistrust, recently laid off or terminated.

Education and training

Make training a priority, decide what training is relevant and for whom. Consider periodic updates, based on changes in policies, physical elements, legal considerations, and/or risk factors. Training for employees should include acceptable behavior, understanding what workplace violence is, identification of early warning signs of workplace violence, and whom and how to report it.

It is important to communicate individual responsibility, sending a message that every employee has a role to play in maintaining a safe and secure work environment. The employees need to understand policies for access control, piggybacking and reporting red flags. They also need to understand how important it is to notify HR of potential domestic issues. Statistics show that when a perpetrator kills, on average, three to five innocent bystanders are also killed.

Training for supervisors and managers should include all of the training employees receive along with training in

- the issues of workplace violence
- their role in identification of violence
- ways of de-escalating or diffusing violent behavior
- recognize behavioral clues
- conflict resolution
- communication skills
- personal security options
- EAP program
- various cycles of anger and managing anger
- crisis management
- high-risk terminations
- security procedures
- emergency procedures relative to a violent incident

Proactive initiatives for a safer workplace

A recap to safeguarding your workplace from violence requires that you incorporate a variety of procedures as the following:

- Hiring practices that incorporate comprehensive background checks on new hires. In addition, consider conducting random or annual background checks on your current workforce.
- Establish vetting procedures for contractors and compliance audits.
- Incorporate a zero tolerance policy and acceptable behavior standards.
- Establish reporting mechanisms to report problem behavior through anonymous ways, that is, employee tip-line and have ensure an immediate and useful response.
- Foster a work environment that supports the reporting of misconduct and also prohibits retaliation to those who report the conduct.
- Investigate all incidents and properly document.
- Implement procedures for investigations of misconduct, ensuring they are viewed as fair.
- Implement specific workplace violence training for new hires, annual training for current employees, and specialized training for management.
- Conduct a risk assessment with a workplace violence assessment.
- Utilize your threat team and your plan.
- Incorporate a fully integrated facility security program, utilizing structural barriers, ID badges, access control, lighting, key control, locks, documentation, communications, CCTV, and environmental design.
- Utilizing the security system adequately.
- Review your termination practices, having a plan for high-risk terminations.
- Liaison with local law enforcement, medical staff, hospitals, and fire department.
- Develop an emergency plan including evacuation procedures and disaster recovery plans and update both frequently. Partner with business continuity.
- Develop partnerships with other like businesses for alternate work location.
- Evaluate and update your workplace violence policies and plans as necessary.

This list is not inclusive, and each individual business will have specific needs beyond what I have suggested.

Everyone plays a role in preventing violence through observation, communication, and reporting. No organization can afford to ignore signs of workplace violence as lives are lost daily due to such tragedies. Being proactive through initiatives, planning, exercising, and mitigating will make the difference of how many lives are lost when an incident occurs.

Chapter 34

Glass and windows

Lawrence J. Fennelly and Marianna A. Perry
Security Consultant

Introduction

The purposes of windows, aside from esthetics, are to let sunlight in, allow visibility, and provide ventilation. When you research the types of windows and glass available you start to see terms such as *weather ability*, *durability*, *thermal performance*, *triple-insulating glass*, *thermal barriers*, and *solar windows*. Every day another building is going "green," such as by diffusing light that enters a building, which cuts down on cooling costs, and the technology goes on and on from there.

"Healthy" buildings using current and innovative technology are contributing to healthier people, through the use of proper cleaning chemicals and green cleaning. All of this creates a better environment and reduced energy costs.

Types of glass

There are five main types of glass: laminated, sheet, tempered, bullet-resistant, and float.

Laminated glass. This is a type of safety glass that contains polyvinyl butyral or a similar substance and therefore holds together when shattered. It comes in high-performance laminated glass for structurally efficient glazing.

Sheet glass. This is least expensive and most vulnerable to breakage, with a thickness of typically 3–4 mm.

Float glass/annealed glass. It has the quality of plate glass combined with the lower production cost associated with sheet glass manufacturing and is virtually distortion and defect free.

Tempered glass. Tempered glass is the most widely used commercial glass and is often required by law. It is stronger than residential glass by four to six times and is also designed to shatter in small harmless pieces when broken, as opposed to residential glass which breaks into large sharp pieces. Laminated glass consists of a piece of thick plastic glued between two panes of glass. This increases protection in the event of a natural or man-made disaster by making the window stronger and causing broken glass to stick to the plastic center rather than shatter outwardly.[1]

Bullet-resistant glass. It is constructed using a strong, transparent material such as polycarbonate thermoplastic or by using layers of laminated glass. The polycarbonate layer is often sandwiched between layers of regular glass, and since the glass is harder than the plastic, the bullet is flattened and prevents penetration. It can be designed for both bullet and blast resistance. It will let light in and keep out trouble.

Glass and security

Take, for example, a police department recommends to a company that for tighter security a glass wall and counter need to be added to create a barrier between the general public and the receptionist. In addition, a glass door is also installed that works off an access control, and if a visitor needs access, he or she would be escorted inside by a personnel member. Some people might not like this inconvenience, but it is the trade-off for security.

1. https://itstillworks.com/types-windows-commercial-buildings-7516851.html

Handbook of Loss Prevention and Crime Prevention. DOI: https://doi.org/10.1016/B978-0-12-817273-5.00034-X

Glazing

Glazing refers to the number of glass panes that make up the window. There are single, double, triple, and higher glazes. The greater the number of window panes, the more heat and noise insulation there will be. Manufacturers also produce multiple pane glazings that use a combination of glass and plastic. These windows may be less expensive and easier to install than all-glass windows.[2]

The following are factors to be considered for the selection of the type and size of a window:

- energy efficiency and quality of unit
- amount of sunlight, ventilation, and visibility
- material and desired finish:
- wood
- metal, aluminum, and stainless steel
- finish color and "green" products

Window hardware should have durability, function, and lock fitting. Consider the following:

- type of glazing available for effectiveness of weather stripping and wind pressure, explosion blasts, and fire
- the size and shape to prevent access, and the cost to replace if vandalized
- the use of grills or bars inside or outside
- there are three types of glass:
  - plate glass
  - sheet glass
  - float glass

Window glass types:

- float glass
- annealed glass
- heat-strengthened glass
- fully tempered glass
- heat-soaked tempered glass
- laminated glass
- wire glass
- insulated glass unit
- low-emissivity glass

Tinted glass

Tinted glass is made by altering the chemical formulation of the glass with special inorganic additives. The color is durable and does not change over time. Its color and density change with the thickness of the glass. Coatings can also be applied after manufacture. Every change in color or combination of different glass types affects *visible transmittance*, *solar heat gain coefficient*, *reflectivity*, and other properties. Glass manufacturers list these properties for every color, thickness, and assembly of glass type they produce.

Tinted glazings are specially formulated to maximize their absorption across some or all of the solar spectrum and are often referred to as heat-absorbing. All of the absorbed solar energy is initially transformed into heat within the glass, thus raising the glass temperature. Depending upon climatic conditions, up to 50% of the heat absorbed in a single pane of tinted glass may then be transferred to the inside via radiation and convection.

Tinted glazing is more common in commercial windows than in residential windows. In retrofit situations, when windows are not being replaced, tinted plastic film may be applied to the inside surface of the glazing. The applied tinted films provide some reduction in solar gain compared to clear glass but are not as effective as spectrally selective films or reflective glue-on films and are not as durable as tinted glass.[3]

2. https://itstillworks.com/types-windows-commercial-buildings-7516851.html
3. https://www.commercialwindows.org/tints.php

In addition, the following are other considerations to keep in mind:

- Whether to use tempered glass, laminated glass, wired glass, bullet-resistant glass, and plastic glazing (e.g., polycarbonate or acrylic).
- Visibility requirements.
- The thickness; by altering thickness and composition, such as adding layers of glass or polycarbonate, security glass laminates can be customized to meet your requirements for specific risks/threats.
- The solution to security problems are to identify risk factors through assessment, use laminated glass with a thicker vinyl interior layer, and use compression operating window frames, awnings, and casements.
- Float glass can be broken with an average rock and toughened glass will shatter when it breaks.
- A crowbar can break or destroy standard window frames.
- Standard laminated glass (6.38 mm thick) can be broken with several blows from a hammer (see footnote 1).
- Energy savings.
- Hardware, such as glass door hinges, locks, sliding glass door systems, and clamp supports, are available online or at any hardware store.
- Sliding glass doors should be installed so as to prevent the lifting and removal of the glass door from the frame from the exterior of the building.
- Fixed panel glass door (nonsliding) should be installed so that the securing hardware cannot be removed or circumvented from the exterior of the building.
- Each sliding panel should have a secondary locking or securing device in addition to the original lock built into the panel. The secondary device should consist of:
  - Charlie bar–type device, secondary locking device;
  - track lock, wooden or metal dowel; and
  - inside removable pins or locks securing the panel to the frame.
- All "glass" used in exterior sliding doors and fixed glass panels should be made of laminated safety glass or polycarbonate sheeting. Plexiglas or single-strength glass will not qualify.
- Doors should open on the inside track, not the outside track.

The following are factors to consider when selecting the type and size of windows:

1. requirements for light, ventilation, and view;
2. material and desired finish—wood, metal, aluminum, steel, and stainless steel;
3. window hardware—durability, function;
4. types of glazing: sheet, plate, or float;
5. effectiveness of weather stripping;
6. appearance, unit size, and proportion;
7. method of opening (hinge or slider), choice of line of hinges;
8. security lock fittings;
9. accessible louver windows;
10. ground floor—recommend lower windows, large fixed glazing, and high windows, small openings;
11. size and shape to prevent access;
12. size because of cost due to vandalism;
13. use of bars or grills on inside;
14. glass:
    - a. double-glazing deterrent
    - b. types of glass:
        - i. acrylic glass, also known as Plexiglas or polycarbonate
        - ii. tempered glass and laminated glass
        - iii. wired glass and bullet-resistant glass
        - iv. mirrors and transparent mirrors
        - v. electrically conductive glass
        - xvi. rough or patterned glass
    - c. vision requirements;
    - d. thickness;
    - e. secured fixing to frame;

f. laminated barrier glass—uses;
g. use of plastic against vandalism;
h. fixed, obscure glazing for dwelling house garages; and
i. shutters, grilles, and louvers for sun control and visual barriers as well as security barriers.

Various types of windows are discussed in the following sections:

Replacement windows

Have a cracked or shattered window?[4] Fix it with a replacement window to seamlessly match the existing windows in your home.

Sliding windows

Sliding windows slide open horizontally, saving space while offering a clean, modern design.

Storm windows

Storm windows provide extra protection from inclement weather while adding energy-saving and noise-reducing insulation.

Double-hung windows

Double-hung windows have upper and lower sashes that move, allowing for extra airflow and easier maintenance.

Single-hung windows

Single-hung windows are more cost-effective than double-hung windows as they contain a fixed upper sash that does not open.

Basement windows

From sliders and casement windows to fixed or awning windows, give your basement some natural light with a window in any style.

Bay windows

Add extra dimension and maximum views to a living room, bedroom, or kitchen with a stylish bay window.

Vinyl

Vinyl windows are built to resist heat transfer and condensation. Their durable build requires minimal upkeep with no painting necessary. Add extra dimension and maximum views to a living room, bedroom, or kitchen with a stylish bay window.

Wood-framed

Genuine wood-framed windows offer superior insulation from heat, cold, and sound. If cared for properly, wood windows can last a lifetime.

Aluminum

Aluminum windows are practical and stylish, offering low maintenance and durability paired with a slim, narrow profile.

Window ironmongery

- security window locks built-in during manufacture
- security window locks fitted after manufacture

---

4. www.lowes.com/c/Windows-Windows-doors?cm_mmc = search_bing-_-Millwork-_-Nb_mlw_135_millwork%20Windows_bmm-_-%2Bwindow&k_clickID = bi_303224108_1308418876439436_81776213627116_kwd81776205031854:loc190_c_101262&msclkid = 1e276e2a19bd130fb349326822a7cecf

- transom window locks
- locking casement stays
- remote-controlled flexible locks

Double-hung wood

1. All locking devices to be secured with 3/4-in. full-threader screws.
2. All window latches must have a key lock or a manual (nonspring-loaded or flip-type) window latch. When a nonkey-locked latch is used, a secondary securing device must be installed. Such secondary securing devices may consist of
   a. each window drilled with holes at two intersecting points of inner and outer windows and appropriate-sized dowels inserted in the holes. Dowels should be cut to provide minimum grasp from inside the window.
   b. a metal sash security hardware device of an approved type may be installed in lieu of doweling.
   Note: Doweling is less costly and of a higher security value than more expensive hardware.
3. Follow balanced design principle. The glass falls first approach; that is, the walls are stronger than the anchors, the anchors are stronger than the frame, and the frame is stronger than the glazing.

Windows require protection when they

- are less than 18 ft from ground level,
- are less than 14 ft from trees, and
- have openings larger than 96 in.^{2}

Bullet-resistant materials, bullet-resistant glazing for a secure workplace

Total Security Solutions offers a full line of bullet-resistant glass in acrylic, polycarbonate, and glass-clad polycarbonate. These products are available at UL protection levels 1–8, providing protection against guns ranging from a 9 mm to a 12 gauge. These bullet-resistant products are typically used in banks, credit unions, gas stations, and convenience stores, but they are appropriate for any business with cash on hand that wants to provide their employees with a secure work environment.

In addition to providing bullet-resistant products to glaziers and mill shops, Total Security Solutions provides custom milling and installation of secure barrier systems. Typical materials used in construction or sold directly include

- interior/exterior transaction windows,
- bulletproof doors,
- ballistic counters,
- package passers,
- bullet-resistant barriers and framing, and
- bullet-resistant transparencies and fiberglass.

Bullet-resistant fiberglass wall panels

These are used to provide bullet-resistant protection to the walls of corporate executive offices, boardrooms, conference rooms, lobbies, reception area counters, customer service counters, and safe rooms. This bullet-resistant fiberglass can be installed by the manufacturer or even by a general contractor. Once installed, this product will never be seen but will provide high-quality ballistic protection and peace of mind for years and years to come.

Bullet-resistant doors

Along with protection for the walls and lobbies of offices, there are a wide variety of bullet-resistant doors to meet different needs, for example, solid executive-style veneered doors to match existing doors but with bullet-resistant protection. Again, this is invisible bullet-resistant protection; hence, nobody will know it is there. In addition, there are also full-vision clear doors, half-vision clear doors, plastic laminated no-vision doors, and bullet-resistant steel doors. All of these doors are prehung, so any contractor can install them within minutes.

Bullet-resistant windows

Bullet-resistant windows can be custom built for the needs of each individual client. Office windows can be replaced with bullet-resistant windows ranging from levels 1–5, or existing windows can be left in place and a second bullet-resistant window can be added behind the existing window in such a way that it will be virtually invisible to the general public.

Bullet-resistant executive office products

The following can be used for offices, boardrooms, and conference rooms:

- high-quality executive-style bullet-resistant doors
- bullet-resistant wall armor to line all the walls of an office
- bullet-resistant custom-made windows to protect all existing window locations
- high-security electronic mag-locks to lock doors in the event of an attack

Bullet-resistant transaction or reception area

- Bullet-resistant transaction window systems.
- Package exchange units.
- Bullet-resistant reception door with electric strike.
- Bullet-resistant fiberglass for reception counter die wall.
- Stainless steel deal trays for small transactions.

Residential high-level security for corporate executives

- Provide bullet-resistant protection at point of entry (garage, front doors, front windows, etc.).
- Build safe room including walls, doors, windows, high-security locksets.
- Convert closet into a high-level safe room.
- Convert master bedroom into a high-level safe room (add invisible bullet-resistant protection to all walls, doors, and windows). Finally, be advised that there are standards that apply to these installations and products.

Window film

Window film is not bulletproof, and there is *no* film product out there that is. Window film can be resistant to small arms and shotguns, however. Lumar window film products have a bomb blast proof film product.

Window film comes in four categories:

1. *Security or safety film.* The benefits are an outer pane of glass may break but the inner will stay intact. It is used to protect retail, commercial, and residential buildings and other types of window structures from the damages of flying glass due to earthquakes, windstorms, attacks, vandalism, theft, and accidents.
2. *Decorative film.* This makes glass surfaces clear and visible, enhances safety in public spaces, and allows you to customize your space with a corporate logo.
3. *Antigraffiti window film.* This is a protective film that helps prevent scribbling or other defacing a base surface. The film is easy to peel off and replace, eliminating graffiti and the cost to replace glass.
4. *Solar film.* This has many benefits, such as it reflects and absorbs heat and light, and it increases energy efficiency, reduces HVAC cost, protects furniture and carpets and provides greater temperature stability.

Further reading

Stegbor, 2011. Security data sheet, V1. Available from: <www.stegbor.com>.

Additional web resources

International Window Film Association. <www.iwfa.com>.
Extreme Window Solutions. <www.extremewindowsolutions.com>.
Ace Security Laminates. <www.acelaminate.com>.
Total Security. <www.securityfilm.biz/index.htm>.
Pacific Bulletproof. <www.pacificbulletproof.com>.

Chapter 35

Fire alarm systems

Lawrence J. Fennelly
Security Consultant

Security and fire protection should go hand in hand, prepare a checklist so it can point out your fire vulnerabilities and concerns.

Inspector William Fennelly, Boston Fire Department, 1979

Fire alarm systems

Of all the alarm systems,[1] it is most critical for security officers to understand the basic operation and interaction of fire alarm systems. Fire alarm systems are regulated by building and fire alarm codes adopted by the municipality in which the facility resides. Because different municipalities may adopt different codes, how a system operates or is installed at one location might be quite different at another location. As fire alarm systems are so essential for the safety of the employees and the well-being of the facility, it is critical to have a thorough working knowledge of the operation of the system and the security officer's role in its successful use. It is also very important to understand the proper operation of the system and expectations of the fire department.

Fire alarm systems typically have a main control panel with a display. If necessary, additional displays can be installed in other areas. Larger systems may incorporate a graphical display of the facility and locations of the various sensors therein. Where the alarm must be monitored off site, a communicator is installed to allow the fire alarm to send alerts to an alarm company central station or, in some rare cases, to the fire department.

Like intrusion alarm systems, fire alarms can be connected with a number of devices on a zone. Newer, larger fire alarm systems (and intrusion alarm systems as well) utilize a multiplex loop, where all of the devices are connected on the same loop, with each device having its own unique identifier or address. This type of system is known as a multiplex or addressable system. The largest fire alarm systems integrate dozens or hundreds of control panels across several facilities, with a dedicated main computer in the company command center for monitoring (Fig. 35.1).

The fire alarm annunciator

A fire alarm system[2,3] has a number of devices working together to detect and warn people through visual and audio appliances when smoke, fire, carbon monoxide, or other emergencies are present. These alarms may be activated automatically from smoke detectors and heat detectors or may also be activated via manual fire alarm activation devices such as manual call points or pull stations. Alarms can be either motorized bells or wall mountable sounders or horns. They can also be speaker strobes, which sound an alarm, followed by a voice evacuation message, which warns people inside the building not to use the elevators. Fire alarm sounders can be set to certain frequencies and different tones including low, medium, and high, depending on the country and manufacturer of the device. Most fire alarm systems in Europe sound like a siren with alternating frequencies. Fire alarm electronic devices are known as horns in the United

1. Ellis, J., 2019. Alarm systems fundamentals. In: Davies, S., Fennelly, L.J. (Eds.), The Protection Officers Handbook, Elsevier Publishers. Updated.
2. A Summary of the BS 5839-1:2013. <https://en.wikipedia.org/wiki/Fire_alarm_system> (18.01.19.).
3. *Safelincs.* www.bing.com/search?q=fire+alarm+system&qs=LS&pq=fire+alarm&sk=LS1&sc=8–10&cvid=0A8753282DB24EA18E16EDFAB02FDF6B&FORM=QBRE&sp=2&ghc=1 (retrieved 18.01.19.).

Handbook of Loss Prevention and Crime Prevention. DOI: https://doi.org/10.1016/B978-0-12-817273-5.00035-1

FIGURE 35.1 A fire alarm notification appliance that is used in the United States and Canada.

States and Canada and can be either continuous or set to different codes such as Code 3. Fire alarm warning devices can also be set to different volume levels. Fire alarm systems in the United Kingdom are tested at a weekly basis in compliance with the BS-fire 2013 regulations.

Fire alarm sensors

The ability of fire to devastate lives and property should never be underestimated. Fire alarm sensors seek to prevent significant damage by detecting fires in their earliest stages, allowing protection officers and fire officials ample time to respond. Fire alarm sensors include the following (J. Russell, personal communication, July 8, 2009):

- *Heat detectors*. These measure changes in a room's ambient temperature. They are programed to a certain baseline temperature and when the room's temperature exceeds the baseline, a fire alarm is triggered.
- *Photoelectric smoke detectors*. This type of detector contains an electric eye, generating a beam of infrared (IR) light within its housing. When smoke enters the detector, it refracts that IR light, and an alarm is triggered in response.
- *Ionization detectors*. These devices contain a tiny amount of radioactive material, which creates radiation in an ionization chamber. Any smoke that enters will absorb some of the radiation and change the electrical charge within the chamber, prompting the device to send an alarm signal to the monitoring station.

Smoke and fire smart alarm

The Universal Security Instruments MI3050SB 2-in-1 Smoke and Fire Smart Alarm[4] provides 10 years of continuous protection against deadly threats in the home. New patented Universal Smoke Sensing Technology provides the benefits of both photoelectric and ionization alarms in one device to protect against fast flaming and slow smoldering fires. Perfect for new or replacement installations, this maintenance-free alarm is suitable for houses, apartments, and mobile homes in every room. The sealed battery (included) will never have to be replaced throughout the life of the alarm, giving you a decade of peace of mind even in the event of a power outage. Permanent power also saves money from battery replacements (up to $38.00 over the 10-year life of the alarm), eliminates annoying low battery chirps, and helps the environment by reducing environmental waste from disposed batteries.

4. www.beeslighting.com/usi-smoke-alarm/p/MI3050SB?gdffi=171595469a5046ef921081cd6627148c&gdfms=F17EAB0D21BF4B258F2F81040ACB84DB&keyword=%7Bbkeyword%7D&creative=%7Bbcreative%7D&msclkid=5e1804777f241052c39558355c697dc9

- 2-in-1 smoke and fire smart alarm provides 10 years of continuous protection against fast flaming and slow smoldering fires.
- Sealed battery (included) will never have to be replaced throughout the life of the alarm.
- Features microprocessor intelligence to virtually eliminate nuisance alarms.
- Quick activation battery pull tab makes the alarm easy to install while the deactivation key makes the batteries safe for disposal.
- Comes with a 10-year limited warranty.

Heat detector

A residential heat detector

A *heat detector*[5] is a fire alarm device designed to respond when the convected thermal energy of a fire increases the temperature of a heat sensitive element. The thermal mass and conductivity of the element regulate the rate flow of heat into the element. All heat detectors have this thermal lag. Heat detectors have two main classifications of operation, "rate-of-rise" and "fixed temperature." The heat detector is used to help in the reduction of damaged property. It is triggered when temperature increases.

NFPA 72

As per NFPA 72, 18.4.2 (2010 Edition) Temporal Code 3 is the standard audible notification in a modern system. It consists of a repeated 3-pulse cycle (0.5 s on 0.5 s off, 0.5 s on 0.5 s off, and 0.5 s on 1.5 s off). Voice evacuation is the second most common audible in a modern system. Legacy systems, typically found in older schools and building, have used continuous tones alongside other audible schema.

Air sampling detectors. These are often used to protect rooms filled with sensitive equipment, such as computer servers. They continuously take in air from the room and analyze the air samples for smoke or combustion particles. If a positive result is received, the detector generates an alarm and, in many cases, immediately causes a fire suppressant to be discharged within the room.

Beam detectors. These utilize an electric eye, which extends a beam of IR light across an entire room, rather than within the housing of a photoelectric detector. They are most often used in rooms with very high ceilings, where it would be impractical to install and maintain a smaller detector. Again, the beam of light will be refracted by smoke in the room and an alarm will be triggered.

Flame detectors. These are able to spot actual flames rather than sense smoke or combustion particles. They typically incorporate ultraviolet light sensors, IR light sensors, or visible light sensors.

Pull stations. These switches are strategically placed throughout a protected facility, and when a person observes fire or smoke, he or she is encouraged to manually pull the nearest switch, triggering a fire alarm and speeding evacuation of the area. Unfortunately, pull stations are easily abused. To activate a pull station in order to cause a false public alarm is a criminal offense in most jurisdictions; therefore protection officers responding to such alarms should be prepared to enforce their organization's relevant policy or involve local law enforcement as appropriate.

Building automation sensors

Building automation sensors are typically used to measure and adjust the heating, ventilation, air-conditioning, lighting, and other environmental conditions in a protected facility. They include the following.

Gas detectors. There are several different types of gas detectors, each of which will measure the levels of a particular type of gas in the air (such as natural gas, carbon monoxide, carbon dioxide, and radon). If the gas levels exceed a preset tolerance, an alarm is generated.

Level indicators. These are often applied to tanks that hold liquids or gases that are critical to a facility's operation. When the amount of liquid or gas in the tanks drops below a preprogramed level, a notification can be sent to the central monitoring station or to personnel who will refill the tanks (J. Russell, personal communication, July 8, 2009).

5. https://en.wikipedia.org/wiki/Fire_alarm_system

Temperature sensors. As the name suggests, these measure the ambient temperature in a room. They are often utilized in rooms where scientific experiments are being conducted, and the temperature must be kept extremely hot, extremely cold, or within a specific range. If the temperature falls out of the preset range, an alarm is triggered.

Power failure sensors. These are integrated with the electrical system of a facility. When a power failure occurs, a notification alarm can be sent to the central monitoring station. At the same time, devices, such as backup generators and emergency lights, can be automatically activated.

Integrated sensors. Some of the same devices used to detect intruders—magnetic door switches and motion sensors, for example—can be integrated with lighting systems. In this way, lights can be programed to turn on automatically when a staff member enters a darkened room.

Smoke Detectors

Smoke detectors[6] come in many shapes and sizes as well as perform different functions as noted in the following.

Heat detector: A heat detector is a fire alarm device designed to respond when the convected thermal energy of a fire increases the temperature of a heat sensitive element.

Smoke detector: A fire alarm system, while household smoke detectors, also known as smoke alarms, generally issue a local audible or visual alarm from the detector itself.

Flame detector: (IR) array flame detectors (0.7−1.1 μm), also known as visual flame detectors, employ flame recognition technology to confirm fire by analyzing near thermographic camera (redirect from thermal scope) development of detectors was mainly focused on the use of thermometer and bolometers until the World War I. A significant step in the development of detectors occurred.

Carbon monoxide detector: Smoke/CO detectors are also sold. Smoke detectors warn of smoldering or flaming fires by detecting the smoke they generate, whereas CO detectors detect.

Fire alarm system: It may be activated automatically from smoke detectors, and heat detectors or may also be activated via manual fire alarm activation devices such as manual.

Fire damper, the ducts: When a rise in temperature occurs, the fire damper closes, usually activated by a thermal element which melts at temperatures higher than ambient. Thermal imaging camera that has five components: an optic system, detector, amplifier, signal processing, and display. Fire-service specific thermal imaging cameras incorporate these crystal detector frequencies he used these detectors did not function as rectifying semiconductor diodes like later crystal detectors, but as a thermal detector called a bolometer.

Flame ionization detector: Flame ionization detectors are used very widely in gas chromatography because of a number of advantages. Cost: Flame ionization detectors are relatively.

Photodetector (redirect from optical detectors): Microbolometer is a specific type of bolometer used as a detector in a thermal camera. Cryogenic detectors are sufficiently sensitive to measure the energy of nonionizing radiation (section thermal radiation) single particle to ionize. A familiar example of thermal ionization is the flame ionization of a common fire, and the browning reactions in common food items.

Pyrometer: In thermal contact with the object most other thermometers (e.g., thermocouples and resistance temperature detectors) are placed in thermal contact. Transvaro (redirect from Engerek thermal optics) equipment and system design and production. Night vision devices, thermal cameras, mine detectors, periscopes, binocular and telescopes, velocity radars, Message 1830: Leopoldo Nobili made the first thermopile IR detector. 1840: John Herschel produced the first thermal image, called a thermogram. 1860: Gustav Kirchhoff Lead selenide (section Methods to manufacture PbSe IR detectors) crystalline solid material. It is used for manufacture of IR detectors for thermal imaging, operating at wavelengths between 1.5 and 5.2 μm.

IR thermometer design essentially consists of a lens to focus the IR thermal radiation on to a detector, which converts the radiant power to an electrical signal

Fire station: A fire station (also called a fire house, fire hall, firemen's hall, or engine house) is a structure or other area for storing firefighting apparatus.

6. https://en.wikipedia.org/w/index.php?search=Thermal+Fire+Detectors&title=Special%3ASearch&go=Go

Fire safety issues

What should employers do to protect workers from fire hazards?[7] Employers should train workers about fire hazards in the workplace and about what to do in a fire emergency. If you want your workers to evacuate, you should train them on how to escape. you expect your workers to use firefighting equipment, you should give them appropriate equipment and train them to use the equipment safely (see Title 29 of the Code of Federal Regulations Part 1910 Subparts E and L; and Part 1926 Subparts C and F).

What does OSHA require for emergency fire exits? Every workplace must have enough exits suitably located to enable everyone to get out of the facility quickly. Considerations include the type of structure, the number of persons exposed, the fire protection available, the type of industry involved, and the height and type of construction of the building or structure. In addition, fire doors must not be blocked or locked when employees are inside. Delayed opening of fire doors, however, is permitted when an approved alarm system is integrated into the fire door design. Exit routes from buildings must be free of obstructions and properly marked with exit signs. See 29 CFR Part 1910.36 for details about all requirements.

Does OSHA require employers have to provide portable fire extinguishers? No. The local fire code authority has jurisdiction will provide guidance to comply with local fire safety codes. If you are required to have portable fire extinguishers, you must establish an educational program to familiarize your workers with the general principles of fire extinguisher use. If you expect your workers to use portable fire extinguishers, you must provide hands-on training in using this equipment. For details, see 29 CFR Part 1910 and any local adopted codes.

When required, employers must develop emergency action plans that:

- describe the routes for workers to use and procedures to follow;
- account for all evacuated employees;
- remain available for employee review;
- include procedures for evacuating disabled employees;
- address evacuation of employees who stay behind to shut down critical plant equipment;
- include preferred means of alerting employees to a fire emergency;
- provide for an employee alarm system throughout the workplace;
- require an alarm system that includes voice communication or sound signals such as bells, whistles, or horns;
- make the evacuation signal known to employees;
- ensure emergency training;
- require employer review of the plan with new employees and with all employees whenever the plan is changed;
- all fire prevention and evacuation plans must be available for employee review;
- include housekeeping procedures for storage and cleanup of flammable materials and flammable waste;
- address handling and packaging of flammable waste (recycling of flammable waste such as paper is encouraged);
- cover procedures for controlling workplace ignition sources such as smoking, welding, and burning, if applicable;
- provide for proper cleaning and maintenance of heat producing equipment such as burners, heat exchangers, boilers, ovens, stoves, and fryers and require storage of flammables away from this equipment, if applicable;
- inform workers of the potential fire hazards of their jobs and plan procedures; and
- require safety plan review with all new employees and during the on boarding process.

Review the plan, with all employees whenever the plan is updated or changed.

What are the rules for fixed extinguishing systems? Fixed extinguishing systems throughout the workplace are among the most reliable firefighting tools. These systems detect fires, sound an alarm, and send water to the fire and heat. To meet OSHA, standards employers who have these systems must:

- substitute (temporarily) a fire watch of trained employees to respond to fire emergencies when a fire suppression system is out of service;
- ensure that the watch is included in the fire prevention plan and the emergency action plan;
- post signs for systems that use agents (e.g., carbon dioxide, Halon 1211) posing a serious health hazard, if applicable; and
- for a comprehensive list of compliance requirements of OSHA standards or regulations, refer to Title 29 of the Code of Federal Regulations. The voice phone is (202) 693–1999. See also OSHA's website at www.osha.gov.

7. Fennelly, L.J., Perry, M., 2018. 150 Things You Should Know About Security, second ed. Elsevier.

Workplace fire safety

Pursuant to the OSHA, a fire prevention plan must be[8]:

1. in writing;
2. kept in the workplace;
3. made available to employees for review;
4. an employer with 10 or fewer employees may communicate the plan orally to employees;
5. a list of all major fire hazards, proper handling and storage procedures for hazardous materials, potential ignition sources and their control, and the type of fire protection equipment necessary to control each major hazard;
6. procedures to control accumulations of flammable and combustible waste materials;
7. procedures for regular maintenance of safeguards installed on heat producing equipment to prevent the accidental ignition of combustible materials;
8. the name or job title of employees (many times security officers) responsible for maintaining equipment to prevent or control sources of ignition or fires; and
9. the name or job title of employees responsible for the control of fuel source hazards.

An employer must inform employees upon initial assignment to a job of the fire hazards to which they may be exposed. An employer must also review with each employee those parts of the fire prevention plan necessary for self-protection.[9]

The NFPA Fire Prevention Week is intended to focus on the importance of fire safety in the home, in schools, and at work, but workplace fire safety is also addressed by OSHA. The principal focus is on saving lives and preventing injuries due to fire.[10]

When workplace inspections are conducted, employers are checked for compliance with OSHA standards for fire safety as well as the NFPA 101: Life Safety Code, which is the most widely used source for strategies to protect people based on building construction, protection, and occupancy with features that minimize the effects of fire and related hazards. It is the only document that covers life safety in both new and existing structures.[11]

Employers must provide proper exits, firefighting equipment, emergency plans, and employee training to prevent fire deaths and injuries in the workplace.

Building fire exits

1. Each workplace building must have at least two means of escape remote from each other to be used in a fire emergency.[12]
2. Fire doors must not be blocked or locked to prevent emergency use when employees are within the building. Delayed opening of fire doors is permitted when an approved alarm system is integrated into the fire door design.
3. Exit routes from buildings must be clear and free of obstructions and properly marked with signs designating exits from the building.

Administrative and planning phase

1. Are copies of all locally enforced codes maintained on-site for reference?[13]
2. Does the facility meet the requirements of the locally enforced building code?
3. Does the facility meet the requirements of the locally enforced fire prevention code?
4. Does the facility meet the requirements of the locally enforced life safety code?
5. Does the facility have a written and appropriately distributed fire prevention and response plan? Is this plan known to all employees? Is training provided to those with defined responsibilities? Is all training documented and securely filed? Is the plan reviewed annually, updated as required, and redistributed?

---

8. Fennelly, L.J., Perry, M., 2018. 150 Things You Should Know About Security, second ed. Elsevier.

9. Fire prevention plan requirements. Retrieved from: <https://www.osha.gov/SLTC/etools/evacuation/fire.html> (14.12.18.).

10. Fire prevention week. Retrieved from: <http://www.nfpa.org/public-education/campaigns/fire-prevention-week>.

11. Codes and standards. Retrieved from: <http://www.nfpa.org/codes-and-standards/all-codes-and-standards/list-of-codes-and-standards?mode=code&code=101>.

12. Emergency plans. Retrieved from: <https://www.osha.gov/SLTC/etools/evacuation/fire.html>.

13. Stroberger, M.A., 2012. Appendix 3.B Physical security survey. In: Handbook of Loss Prevention and Crime Prevention, sixth ed.

6. Does the facility maintain a fire brigade? Is the fire brigade training documented and securely filed? Is the fire brigade training conducted in conjunction with the local fire department? Is the fire brigade composed of persons, or positions, that are present or represented at all times?
7. Are all inspection reports retained for a reasonable number of years, as defined by local codes, insurance requirements, or industry standards? Are inspection reports filed in a secure location?
8. Are all employees trained in basic fire prevention concepts and fire event response procedures? Is the content of this training consistent and reasonably inclusive? Is this training documented and securely filed? Is annual refresher training conducted? Is annual refresher training documented and securely filed?

General physical inspection phase

1. Are all fire exit routes clearly marked? Are all exit routes unobstructed at all times? Are all exit routes and egress hardware items in compliance with the Americans with Disabilities Act requirements?
2. Are all fire doors and egress hardware items in proper working order?
3. Are service areas secured against unauthorized entry when not in use?
4. Are all areas free of loose or disorganized combustible items (such as rags or empty boxes)?
5. Are all storage areas well organized to allow ease of access in emergency situations?
6. Are flammable or combustible items properly stored to protect against accidental ignition?
7. Are flammable or combustible items properly stored to protect against unauthorized usage or tampering?
8. Are all fire lanes clearly marked? Are fire lanes maintained in an unobstructed condition at all times?
9. Are master keys available at all times for fire department use?
10. Are all electrical panels accessible at all times? Are all panels clearly marked to facilitate emergency power disconnection?
11. Are gas line shutoff valves accessible at all times?
12. Are all gas-operated pieces of equipment inspected for wear and damage with reasonable frequency? Are inspections documented and filed in a secure location?
13. Are all heat-generating devices (such as boilers, furnaces, and dryers) provided with a reasonable clear zone, based on levels of heat output, where storage of any kind is prohibited?
14. Are all ducts inspected regularly and cleaned as required?
15. Is the use of extension cords discouraged in all areas?
16. Are all electrical cords and electrically operated items inspected for wear or damage with reasonable frequency? Are such inspections documented?
17. Are designated smoking areas clearly defined and at a proper minimum safe distance from any common or identified ignition threats? Are appropriate ash and cigarette receptacles available for use in these areas?

High-quality fire extinguishers

Whether you need a new extinguisher, an inspection, or testing, we can replace parts for extinguishers from any manufacturer.[14] You will have a peace of mind knowing that you, your family, and your property are protected.

Pressurized water models

They are appropriate for use on Class A fires only. These must never be used on electrical or flammable liquid fires.

Carbon dioxide

These extinguishers contain pressurized liquid carbon dioxide, which turns to a gas when expelled. These models are rated for use on Class B and C fires but can be used on a Class A fire. Carbon dioxide does not leave a residue.

14. http://www.gorhamfire.com/quincy-ma-fire-extinguishers.htm

Dry chemical extinguishers

Sodium bicarbonate

This is a dry chemical, suitable for fighting Class B and C fires, which is preferred over other dry chemical extinguishers for fighting grease fires. Where provided, always use the extinguishing system first. This also shuts off the heat to the appliance.

Potassium bicarbonate

Potassium bicarbonate, urea-base potassium bicarbonate, and potassium chloride—dry chemicals that are more effective and use less agent than sodium bicarbonate on the same fire.

Foam (or AFFF and FFFP) extinguishers

These coat the surface of a burning flammable liquid with a chemical foam. When using a foam extinguisher, blanket the entire surface of the liquid to exclude the air.

Classifying fire extinguishers

Class A. This includes ordinary combustible materials, such as wood, cloth, paper, rubber, and many plastics. They burn with an ember and leave an ash. They extinguish by cooling the fuel to a temperature that is below the ignition temperature. Water and other extinguishing agents are effective.

Class B. It includes flammable liquids (burn at room temperature) and combustible liquids (require heat to ignite). Petroleum greases, tars, oils, oil-based paints, solvents, lacquers, alcohols, and flammable gases are some examples. They are high fire hazard; water may not extinguish. They extinguish by creating a barrier between the fuel and the oxygen, such as layer of foam.

Class C. This includes fuels that would be A or B except that they involve energized electrical equipment. They require special techniques and agents to extinguish, most commonly carbon dioxide or dry chemical agents. Use of water is very dangerous because water conducts electricity.

Class D. This includes combustible metals, such as magnesium, titanium, zirconium, sodium, lithium, and potassium. Most cars contain numerous such metals. Because of extremely high flame temperatures, water can break down into hydrogen and oxygen, enhancing burning or exploding. They extinguish with special powders based on sodium chloride or other salts and also clean dry sand.

Class K. This includes fires in cooking appliances that involve combustible cooking media (vegetable or animal oils and fats).

1. During an emergency, the actual shutdown of equipment should be assigned to people familiar with the process.
2. Plan ahead! If a fire breaks out in your home or office, you may have only a few minutes to get out safely once the smoke alarm sounds. Everyone needs to know what to do and where to go if there is a fire.

Conclusion

An old friend of mine said once, "Why are you putting fire information in a security book?" In the event of fire where I'm working, I responsible, both before and after the fire. I have to secure the building after the fire 24 × 7. This will require overtime and a cost to management, so why not be proactive and monitor the fire equipment like you would an intrusion alarm system. Four things to keep in mind: (1) job safety analysis, (2) hazard identification, (3) fire accident investigation and root cause analysis, and (4) effective corrective action.

Chapter 36

Safes, vaults, and accessories*

Russell Kolins
Security Consultant

The effectiveness of any locking system depends on a combination of interrelated factors involved in the design, manufacture, installation, and maintenance of the system. A prevention specialist needs to understand the weaknesses and strengths of the various systems, and know how each must be used to achieve maximum benefit from its application. This requires a thorough understanding of the inner workings of the various types of locking devices.

James M. Edgar, CPP and William D. McInerney, 1982

Choose the right container

A safe or vault ideally should occupy the innermost ring of concentric *protective rings* around a secured premise. Other security equipment (fences, gates, vehicle barriers, doors, and access controls) selected for the outer protective rings is usually specifically designed for its function, but the security vault at center often is not.

The value and physical nature of a vault container's contents should dictate the type of container and degree of protection sought; but people tend to categorize all combination-locked security containers as "safes" because of one common denominator—combination locks. This is a mistake.

There are fire-resistant safes, burglary-resistant chests, safes for EDP media, and insulated filing cabinets. Each can be combination locked, but to regard any combination-locked container as a safe is to disregard the fact that different types and levels of protection exist. Such disregard invites losses.

High-value items stored in a fire-resistant safe or insulated filing cabinet are vulnerable to burglary—the average insulated container can quickly be forced open with a few simple, accessible hand tools. Similarly, important documents stored in a burglary chest are much more secure from burglars than in an insulated container but are also more likely to be incinerated in a fire.

Underwriters Laboratories (UL) systematically tests the fire- and burglary-resistant qualities of representative security containers submitted by their manufacturers (see Appendix 36.A). Makers of those containers that meet specific test requirements may affix a UL-rating label to their products. The presence of a UL label signifies that a comparable unit of the same design successfully passed systematic tests performed by UL for resistance to burglary or fire. The label denotes the type and severity of test conditions.

Possibly the best protection are those safes that bears UL labeling for both fire and burglary protection. Such containers are simply burglary chests housed inside insulated containers. Similar protection can be obtained by buying a burglary chest and a fire safe separately, then placing the burglary-resistant chest inside the fire safe, thus establishing separate storage areas for documents and high-value items.

Since UL ratings are recognized by the American insurance industry as reliable rating standards for security containers, comprehensive insurance policies often specify or otherwise require minimum UL security container ratings. Reduced mercantile insurance rates may be applicable if a selected security container has the recommended minimum rating.

Whether or not a security container provides fire or burglary protection, its inherent security can be increased with special-function locks. Very often, the purchaser of a fire safe or money chest is not told of all the optional equipment available with the security container being considered. Salespeople often prefer not to risk confusing their clients with

*Originally compiled by Kenneth Dunckel and Gion Green, updated January 2019.

Handbook of Loss Prevention and Crime Prevention. DOI: https://doi.org/10.1016/B978-0-12-817273-5.00036-3

too many options. Optional equipment boosts the sale price and thus can jeopardize a sale. People who buy security containers should nevertheless be aware of what is available and decide for themselves. If unwisely chosen, the security container can cause new operational and logistical problems, which could be solved by the use of special-function equipment.

For instance, the presence of a quality burglary-resistant chest on the premises of a cash-handling business means that a bank deposit does not necessarily have to be made daily, even if daily deposits are supposed to be the usual procedure. An attitude of "nothing to worry about—just put in the safe overnight" can easily develop. But an after-hours visit by a dishonest employee with the combination can double the loss potential. So, too, can a properly timed holdup. The situations that can be prevented or alleviated by wisely chosen security equipment are numerous, and safe buyers should be aware of them. The following sections describe a few such possibilities and the security equipment that is presently available for prevention.

Underwriters Laboratories–rated combination locks

A good quality combination lock is a basic need. On well-made containers, the most common combination locks are those certified in accordance with UL standards (UL 768). Combination locks are classified as Group 1, 1R, 2M, or 2 classification. A lock bearing a UL label has met or exceeded detailed criteria for quality, security, and durability.

The UL testing procedure for combination locks involves ascertaining that the lock can be set to various combinations and operated within specified tolerances.

Other sections of UL 768 describe tests for mechanical strength, impact resistance, manufacturing tolerance, product endurance, and operability after prolonged exposure to adverse conditions. The testing for UL Group 1 (manipulation-resistant) and Group 1R (manipulation and resistant) labels includes all tests performed on Group 2–rated locks plus the requirement that the lock tested must, by virtue of its design and construction, resist skilled surreptitious attempts to learn the combination numbers by manipulation, the use of instruments, or radioactive isotopes (Group 1R test only) for 20 worker-hours of networking time. Group 2M locks have 2 working hours of resistance to expert or professional manipulation.[1]

In most instances a Group 2 combination lock provides adequate security. Although many legitimate safe and vault technicians are trained in combination lock manipulation techniques, criminals with the skill and knowledge necessary to surreptitiously open a Group 2 lock by manipulation are few in number. Most safe burglars use forceful methods. High-security installations, however, such as jewelry safes or containers protecting extremely sensitive or classified information, should be outfitted with manipulation-resistant Group 1 locks to block every possible avenue of criminal approach.

Defense contractors who deal with classified information are required to protect such information in security containers that meet certain government specifications. One such specification, MIL-L-15596, defines the type of combination lock that is acceptable. This specification covers much the same territory as the UL standard regarding Group 1 and 1R manipulation- and radiation-resistant locks.

Relocking devices

A relocking device, or relocker, is an auxiliary bolt or bolt-blocking mechanism for which there is no control from outside the container. Relockers protect security containers against torch, drill, and punching attacks. The relocker is an especially important feature on burglary-resistant units, because these containers are designed to protect items of high dollar value and are therefore more attractive to skilled burglars. Relockers are important enough in preserving a container's security to warrant a separate standard for rating them, UL 140.

Known in bygone days as *dynamite triggers*, relockers can be simple in design; often they are no more than spring-driven bolts held in a cocked (loaded) position until activated by a burglar's attack. With normal usage of a relock-equipped container, the relocker's presence is undetectable to the user. When activated, the relocker blocks the retraction of the door bolts, combination bolt, or both, even if the correct combination for the lock is known.

Relocking devices are often held cocked by a piece of metal attached by screws to the combination lock's back cover. When thus situated, relockers protect against spindle or dial punching, the most common (and in earlier times one of the most effective) forms of forceful burglary attack.

1. Group 2M listed under classifications.

In a typical punching attack the burglar first knocks the dial off the safe to expose the end of the spindle, a threaded shaft that connects the numbered safe dial to the combination lock's wheels. The spindle end is then punched inward with a hand sledge and drift punch. When the spindle is driven inward in this manner, one or more of the lock's wheels are slammed against or even through the back cover of the lock. A punching attack may completely dislodge all the wheels (or tumblers) in the lock.

Most currently manufactured combination lock back covers are purposely designed to be dislodged by a punching attack. Because the relock checking device is fastened to the lock cover or located very near it, dislodging the cover also dislodges the relock check. A spring (or in some cases gravity) then takes over, moving the relock to its triggered position.

After spindle punching the burglar can insert tools through the spindle hole and fish the combination bolt to a retracted position. If not for relockers the safe door could be opened. A triggered relocker, however, is not easily located or easily released from outside the container. Containers incorporating some form of relocking device now outnumber older, nonrelock-equipped containers; an unsuccessful punching attempt on a recently built container signifies a lack of knowledge and skill.

Although makers of fire-resistant containers are not required to include a relocking device in the container design, many do so to thwart the type of punching attack just described. Safe makers realize that, because the cost per cubic inch of space in a fire-resistant container is appreciably less than that of a burglary-resistant container of the same size, many clients store high-value items in fire-resistant containers instead of burglary chests, even after being advised not to.

Thermal relocking devices hinder skilled burglars who use cutting torches or other burning tools. A thermal relock activates when the part of the mechanism that holds the relock cocked (usually a fusible link made from a metal with an extremely low melting point) heats to its melting point, at which time a spring can activate a bolt-blocking mechanism. A thermal relock is not necessarily part of the combination lock but is usually nearby, because torching burglars tend to burn in an area fairly close to the combination lock.

Current Group 1, 1R, and 2 combination locks have simple but effective built-in relocking devices designed to be activated by spindle-punching attacks. Some also incorporate thermal protection. Many safe makers, however, do not rely totally on the protection provided by these built-in relockers, preferring to include relockers of their own design, situated outside the combination lock.

Some safe makers use a sophisticated type of relocking device that simultaneously guards against punching, drilling, and burning attacks. A *nerve plate* of tempered glass is mounted between the combination lock and the inner surface of the container door. Taut wires or cords are strung from one or more spring-driven relocking devices and fastened to the glass. The placement of such nerve plates ensures that most unskilled and semiskilled burglary attacks will severely shock and thus shatter the glass nerve plate. Similarly, a skilled operator who attempts to drill into the lock case and manipulate the combination wheels will encounter the nerve plate before penetrating the lock. Any attempt to penetrate further will shatter the glass and release the tension on the wires that hold the relocks cocked.

Glass nerve plates have been popular with foreign safe makers for some time. They are an extremely efficient way to hinder even highly skilled burglars. Some makers of high-security units string the relock wires around a series of posts before attaching them to the nerve plate in front of the combination lock. Relockers and the wires can be placed randomly within a production run of like models, defeating those burglars armed with blueprints made by taking exact measurements from a comparable model.

UL tests and certifies relocking devices under the standard UL 140. Safe makers whose relocking devices are successfully tested under the conditions described in UL 140 are entitled to affix labels to that effect on their containers.

Locking dials

Locking combination dials are used to ensure that no one person has control of a security container's contents. Companies whose employees handle large amounts of cash or other valuables use locking dials to satisfy dual custody requirements. Typically, one person is assigned the key that unlocks the dial, and another is assigned the combination. A locked dial will not turn to allow the combination to be dialed until the keyholder unlocks it. The keyholder can lock or unlock the dial but cannot open the container without the combination.

A typical application of dual custody is for a supermarket safe. Usually, notice is posted to the effect that two people are required to open the safe; the store manager has only the combination, and the armored car guard has the dial key. When this procedure is used, such arrangements deter or complicate holdups.

When used according to strictly observed procedures, locking dials also help reduce the opportunity for a lone dishonest person to abuse a position of trust and can help protect innocent persons from unwarranted suspicion when mysterious losses are noted.

Lockable handles

Lockable bolt control handles perform much the same function as lockable dials. A locking handle allows the combination to be dialed, but the bolt control handle does not retract the door bolts until it is unlocked. Again, this arrangement allows dual custody of the container's contents.

Users of walk-in vaults often leave the combination dialed and the door bolts retracted during business hours. Holdup gangs have used this fact to their advantage by herding their victims into the vault and then simply turning the bolt handle and spinning the combination dial to lock them in to ensure a clean getaway. When installed on the door of a walk-in vault, locking bolt control handles helps to prevent this tactic, because the door bolts can be immobilized during the business day.

Time locks

Time locks are considered standard equipment on bank vault doors but may also be used on any security container whose door has enough usable surface area to permit installation. A time lock ensures that, once closed and locked, the safe or vault door remains so for a predetermined amount of time. Time locks were hailed by 19th century bankers as devices that would discourage the kidnapping of bank officials and their family members to force disclosure of vault combinations. Before time locks, this was a common tactic of holdup and burglary gangs who did not balk at committing brutal crimes to learn vault combinations.

The most common time locks are mechanical windup mechanisms; their internal design and operation is quite similar to that of ordinary timepieces, but their mainsprings perform additional duties besides powering the clockworks.

When a mechanical time lock is wound, a shutter in its case closes. Usually, a rod or projection extends from the door bolts; when the bolts move, the rod moves. During bolt retraction (i.e., opening the safe door), this rod would normally enter the time lock case via the shutter hole, but the closed shutter blocks the rod's passage, which translates to a door bolt blockage. As the time lock's movements wind down, the mainspring's energy is harnessed to open the shutter. The shutter reopens fully when the first movement has wound down.

A typical time lock relies on at least two, but as many as three or four, separate windup movements in a single case. It can be used on safes as well as vaults. The presence of at least two movements gives reasonable assurance that a single movement's failure does not cause a lockout; the more movements used, the more the chance for lockout is reduced. Only one movement must wind down for the container to open.

Time-delay combination locks

No lock can prevent an armed robber from forcing another person to disclose a combination. This type of robbery is often committed against restaurant or store employees in the hours before or after closing. Such crimes often net rich hauls for criminals and can easily involve injury to the victims.

The robbers gain entry to the premises by various methods: by capturing an employee while entering or exiting, by using a seemingly legitimate pretext, or sometimes by breaking into the premises and lying in wait for the holder of the safe combination. Once identified, that person is forced to open the safe.

Time-delay combination locks, also known as *delayed action timers*, are one solution to the problem, because such locks can foil or deter robberies. A time-delay lock is a combination lock with one or more timer movements attached. The action of dialing the safe combination winds a timer. The operator must wait for a predetermined period after dialing before the delay mechanism permits the combination lock bolt to retract. Delay times range from as a few as 3 minutes to as many as 45 minutes and in some cases are changeable.

The most sophisticated time-delay combination locks boast alarm compatibility. A store manager ordered by a robber to open the safe can discreetly dial a special combination and activate a holdup alarm. Alarm-compatible time-delay combination locks give police a better chance of arriving in time to make an arrest.

Time-delay locks reduce both robbery losses and the incidence of robbery. Businesses using time-delay locks usually postconspicuous notices to this effect, causing prospective robbers to take their business elsewhere. Robbers rely on speed of execution—even the hint of a delay reduces a target's appeal.

Alarmed combination locks

Alarmed combination locks incorporate microswitches capable of shunting alarms and signaling unauthorized opening attempts or openings made under duress.

Perhaps the most generally useful are the switches designed to send *duress* alarm signals. They are designed to discreetly send an alarm signal when a special duress combination is dialed. Like the regularly used combination, the duress combination also opens the safe so that a robber does not realize an alarm is being sent.

The typical robber orders the victim not to set off an alarm, and things can get ugly if the robber suspects otherwise. Because the alarm is set off by a seemingly innocent dialing procedure performed in accord with the robber's demands, combination locks with duress or ambush features could be categorized as compliance alarms.

Tamper switches help protect combination-locked containers during those hours when no persons, not even authorized combination holders, are allowed access to the contents. The dial is set at a predetermined number and sometimes locked in place, and then the alarm protection is turned on. Any attempt to dial the combination while the protection is on causes an alarm.

Another switch arrangement can be used to monitor the status of the container or as an alarm shunt. This switch is placed in such a way that, when the combination lock bolt is retracted to the open position, the switch is actuated. This lets remote monitors track the container's openings and closings. A shunt switch allows the burglary alarm circuit to remain active 24 hours a day while still allowing combination holders access to the contents.

Vision-restricting and shielded dials

Standard combination dials are known as *front-reading*, meaning that their numbers are visible from a horizontal line of sight. It is possible for prying eyes to see the numbers that are dialed when a front-reading dial is used, which of course makes the safe's protection ineffective. If a combination must be dialed while persons not authorized to know the numbers are nearby, a front-reading dial is best replaced with a vision-restricting, or *spyproof*, dial.

Various types of vision-restricting dials are available, and each safe lock manufacturer has its own version. One of the most common is the top-reading dial, whose numbers are etched into an outer rim perpendicular to the safe door. To effectively see the combination numbers, the dialer must stand squarely in front of the dial and look down at the numbers while dialing. A raised flange guards the sides of the dial from view; only a small portion of the dial's numbered area can be seen at any given time.

Other vision-restricting designs incorporate covered dials with louvered windows or tinted and polarized lenses at the index area. Covering the entire dial except the turning knob shields the dial face from finger marks. People who dial safe combinations tend to place one finger on the dial face as a brake. This leaves smudges on the safe dial at fairly regular distances from the actual combination numbers, thus making it possible to learn a safe's combination by composing test combinations as suggested by the smudges' locations.

Combination changing

A positive aspect of combination locks is user changeability. Although many companies leave this task to service vendors as a matter of policy, some have policies dictating that company personnel do the changing to absolutely ensure exclusive knowledge of combination numbers. New safes, chests, and insulated files, if combination locked, usually come with detailed instructions for changing and special change keys.

Safe dealers often remove the changing instructions and changing keys before delivery, and with good reason. The customer's first suspicion might be that the safe dealer would much rather profit from future service calls to change combinations than let the clients do it themselves. This is partly true, but there is a valid reason for withholding changing tools and instructions.

Safe buyers who have changing instructions and try to change keys often fall victim to a common syndrome. They attempt combination changes before having fully read or understood the instructions and thus cause a lockout.

The client calls the dealer for help and, because the lockout is attributable to error rather than a defective product, is charged for the work. Not wishing to pay a service fee, the client does not admit the error, claiming instead that the unit is defective and that the work should be covered by warranty. The dealer's representative knows better: combination-changing errors are glaringly obvious to a technically experienced person. The dealer's subsequent refusal to write the work off as a warranty job incurs the client's wrath and creates bad will.

Combination changing is a relatively simple task, but mistakes can be costly in terms of both lost time and dollars. Safes are unforgiving—a lockout resulting from a combination-changing error may dictate that the container be forced open. Lockouts can be avoided by exercising a high degree of care when working with the combination lock components and always trying new combinations several times with the safe door open. This is probably the most important yet most ignored part of combination changing.

Safe burglaries

At a time in the not-so-distant past, gangs of skilled safe burglars operated in America; pickings were easy and plentiful. In today's world, where the need for instant gratification often supersedes reason, fewer criminals spend the time necessary to learn safe burglary skills and properly plan and execute safe burglaries. Contemporary criminals tend to prefer crimes that require much less time or technical skill; a fast exchange of drugs and money in a motel parking lot can easily net more than a weekend of work with a cutting torch.

Highly skilled, knowledgeable safecrackers are by no means extinct in America, but there are a lot fewer of them today. The remaining safecrackers with sufficient skill to breach a well-built jeweler's chest or bank vault do not need to work as often as other thieves; consequently, their exploits do not get the continual press coverage that more prolific criminals receive.

The burglar most likely to visit a business or residential premises is fairly average in terms of technical skill. Such individuals work fast and often. While very good at defeating or circumventing door and window locks, this type of burglar is usually stumped when confronted by even a thin-walled insulated safe—quite often his or her best effort will be an unsuccessful attempt at prying or dial punching, after which the container may be locked more securely than before. In addition to technical ignorance, the would-be safecracker usually suffers from a faint heart and would rather leave than invest much time in the effort.

Some burglars, however, inhabit a middle ground with respect to skill. They have learned to recognize and prepare for those situations in which they have a fair chance of getting into some of the safes they may encounter. These individuals find enough opportunities and enjoy enough success within the parameters of their limited skills that they usually do not make the effort to become more technically proficient. They pose a real threat, because part of their expertise is in the exploitation of human error and complacency, failings to which even users of high-security containers are subject.

The only defense against the semiskilled opportunistic safe burglar is knowledge, awareness, and strict adherence to proper security procedures. The following are some of the ways these individuals gain access to safe contents and suggestions for defeating them.

Hidden combinations

Many people, fearful of forgetting the safe combination, write down the numbers and dialing sequences and hide them somewhere near the safe or in a wallet or address book. Smart burglars know more places to look for combination numbers than the average person can dream of and systematically search for and discover them, no matter how well hidden the safe user may think they are. Combination numbers can be memorized, a fact that makes combination locks more secure than the majority of key-operated mechanisms. Writing out the combination is a real help for burglars and can complicate police investigations. Safe users who write down combinations often do so in violation of company security policies. Therefore they are reluctant to admit it, forcing investigators to guess at the facts. Prevention is simple: memorize the numbers.

Using birthdays, phone numbers, addresses, and the like

Such numbers are appealing because they are already committed to the user's memory, but smart burglars have been known to take the time to do some research on their victims, learning the same numbers and composing test combinations with them. Similarly, many safe users tend to select combination numbers ending in 5 or 0, such as 10-20-50 or 25-35-15, because such numbers are more clearly marked on the safe dial. Doing so greatly limits the combination possibilities. A safe combination should ideally be a random set of numbers with no special significance to the user.

Failing to fully scramble the combination when locking

This is especially common in cases where the safe is outfitted with a locking dial. For daytime convenience the combination numbers are left dialed, then the bolt is left extended and the dial locked with the key. The safe door can be opened by merely turning the dial key and moving the dial just a few numbers' worth of travel, rather than having to redial completely. Safe users mistakenly think the dial lock and combination lock afford equal protection, but they do not. The combination lock is protected inside the safe door while the dial lock is exposed on the outside. Safes without locking dials can also be locked but not fully scrambled and thus afford opportunities for patient thieves to walk the dial a number at a time in hope of finding the last number of the combination. Whenever a safe is closed, it is a good practice to turn the dial at least four full revolutions before considering it locked.

Smart burglars confronted with a locking dial can sometimes make a big score by merely clamping a heavy pair of pliers on the dial and twisting, because people who hate to dial safe combinations can easily slip into the habit of using the dial lock for nighttime locking as well as daytime convenience. Daytime robbers have also been known to give the same treatment to safes secured only by locking dials during business hours. Simply stated, the dial lock protects the dial, and the combination lock protects the safe.

Punching

The majority of burglary-resistant safes are protected in some way against punching; relocking devices and punch-resistant spindles are the most popular methods. Many insulated safes built in the last 20–30 years also feature relocking devices. Punching is generally a sign of technical ignorance. The safe dial is pried or knocked off and a punch or lineup tool is used in conjunction with a hand sledge to drive the spindle inward. The intent is to knock the lock components completely out of position so they no longer block the retraction of the door bolts. In safes not equipped with relocking devices or other protective measures, punching is usually effective. The best defense against punching attacks is to buy a safe equipped with a UL-listed relocking device.

While protection against burglary is not an absolute necessity in a fire-resistant container, many makers of such containers realize that safe users often treat their products as if they were burglary-resistant chests and store high-value items in them. With this in mind the safe makers usually include relocking protection of some sort, if only by being certain to use a combination lock with built-in relock protection.

Peeling

Insulated containers can often be peeled open in much the same way as a sardine can. Often the burglar will pound with a sledge near one of the door's corners in an effort to buckle it inward, thus permitting the insertion of wedging and prying tools. The door is then peeled back by virtue of sheer force until the contents can be removed. In another type of peeling attack, a chisel separates the outer metal skin from the door. This outer skin of older fire safes was in many cases merely spot-welded in several locations along the door's edge. When the initial separation has been achieved, a larger chisel (fire axes and heavy prying tools have been used) continues the process of breaking the remaining spot welds all the way down the door's edge, until the outer skin can be bent or peeled out of the way. The intent in such attacks is to dig or chop through the door insulation and inner skin, eventually exposing the combination lock or door bolts and overcome them with heavy tools and brute force. More recently made insulated containers have seam-welded door skins to make this type of attack extremely difficult, if not unfeasible. Although fire safes can be peeled by both semiskilled and skilled criminals, the neatness and efficiency of the work gives an indication of the criminal's skill and experience. A sturdily built money or jewelry chest cannot be peeled.

Ripping or chopping

These forms of attack are most often successful when carried out against insulated containers. The burglar may be unskilled, semiskilled, or professional. Heavy metal-cutting tools cut a hole in the container's door, side, or bottom. When the hole is made, the burglar simply reaches in and removes the contents. Defeating the peelers and rippers of the world requires only that the safe purchased be a burglary chest rather than an insulated container. If both fire and burglary protection are necessary, a burglary-resistant container can be installed inside an insulated container.

Carting off

Also known by burglary investigators as a *kidnap* or *pack-off*, this is the simplest but perhaps the nerviest safe defeat. If the container can be moved and transported easily enough, the burglar or burglars simply steal the entire container and open it at their leisure in a secure location. The majority of existing insulated containers are wheeled, making this task even easier than it should be. Often a bolt-down kit is available, which enables the safe owner to attach the safe to the floor of the premises and hinder burglars who might try stealing it. At the very least the wheels of a fire safe should be removed after delivery. To protect a smaller burglary-resistant chest, install it inside a box or metal jacket bolted or anchored to the floor and filled with concrete. The concrete jacket adds appreciably to the weight of the unit and severely complicates its unauthorized removal as well as side attacks by skilled and semiskilled safecrackers.

Skilled attacks

The skilled safecracker is relatively rare in America, but a few are in business. Their skills and specialties vary, and they have a wide variety of easily available equipment to choose from: high-speed drills, low-rpm/high-torque drills, core drills, Carborundum cutters, saber saws, cutting torches, oxy-arc lances, burning bars, and explosives. The only way to defeat safe burglars who work with such effective gear is to ensure that the actual attack is time-consuming and fraught with the danger of discovery or capture. The less appealing the target, the more likely the professional is to seek easier pickings.

If there is genuine concern about the possibility of a skilled attack, the first and most obvious thing to do is to buy a burglary-resistant container with a rating equal to or exceeding the recommendation of a knowledgeable insurance agent. Today, safes are designed to put up a staunch fight against even the well-equipped, highly skilled professional safecrackers of the world. A reliable intrusion detection system is necessary; it should protect both the perimeter of the premises and the safe. If the safe is to be used commercially, a security policy should be established and rigorously adhered to. A security policy should define and expressly prohibit breaches of security such as those described earlier (i.e., writing down combination numbers or leaving the combination partially dialed): all such actions should be expressly forbidden.

Overcoming safe-opening problems

Safe users often experience difficulty when trying to open a safe. The combination just does not seem to catch when it is dialed. This problem, on the surface, is an operational inconvenience, but there are security implications as well.

Safe users often learn to live with balky safes and combination locks: the money for repair and adjustment just is not in the budget, or they may wonder if the difficulty is entirely the safe's fault. Many people hesitate to make an issue of a dialing problem for fear of exhibiting ignorance or inability to perform what, on the surface, is a simple rote task. Consequently, they accept that they must dial and redial to open the safe each day, breathe a sigh of relief when the combination finally takes, then do something that may constitute a breach of their employers' security policy. Rather than opening the safe, removing what is needed, closing the door, throwing the door bolts, and rescrambling the combination, the irritated safe user leaves the combination dialed to avoid the added irritation of the dial—redial routine several more times during the business day.

This usually works nicely until the day when everybody goes out for lunch and forgets that a turn of the door handle is all that is necessary to open the safe door. A lunchtime office prowler finds it hard to resist trying the safe handle and is rewarded for this small expenditure of energy. The scenario varies but is generally the same: people who use safes and combination locks often adapt to the inconveniences caused by malfunctioning locks, improper dialing procedures, or maintenance-starved mechanisms by shortchanging their own security procedures.

Another all-too-possible situation, the robbery, presents more grave considerations. The same person who must routinely make several tries at opening the safe is ordered by armed robbers to open the safe immediately, then the criminals interpret fumbling as a delaying tactic and react violently.

These are only a few reasons why it is in the best interest of all concerned to have a properly maintained security container and well-trained users of that container. The following information helps safe users open those balky safes with fewer tries. But, these guidelines should not be interpreted as another set of adaptive measures to forestall necessary maintenance.

- When dialing a safe combination, stand squarely in front of the safe and look directly at the numbers. Viewing them from an angle causes improper dial settings.
- Align the dial numbers exactly with the index mark at the top of the dial.

- Follow the safe maker's dialing instructions exactly. If the safe used has no factory-supplied dialing instructions, contact the factory or a local safe dealer for some. Usually, they will be supplied at no charge.
- Do not spin the dial—this accelerates wear and can cause breakage.

When the safe does not open after thc combination has been correctly dialed, a few dialing techniques usually get results. The first is to add one number to each of the combination numbers and dial as if this were the actual combination. For example, if the combination numbers are 20-60-10, try 21-61-41 using the same dialing procedure as usual.

If adding 1 to each of the combination numbers does not help, subtract 1 from each of the actual combination numbers. For example, with an actual combination of 20-60-40, the next combination to try would be 19-59-39. One of these two procedures works surprisingly often.

If neither of these procedures is successful, the next procedure is to progressively add 1 to each setting and dial the other numbers as usual, again using the normal dialing procedure. For example, if the correct combination is 20-60-40, the progression would be to dial 21-60-40, 20-61-40, then 20-60-41. If this procedure is unsuccessful, the next procedure is to progressively subtract from each combination setting. For example, if the original combination is 20-60-40, dial 19-60-40, 20-59-40, and 20-60-39.

These procedures overcome lock wear and dialing errors—users may habitually and unconsciously misalign combination numbers at the dialing index mark. Interpret the success of any of these procedures as a signal that the mechanism needs inspection and service. It is a mistake to simply continue using the safe without correcting the condition that required using a set of numbers other than those actually set. If the condition that necessitated these dialing procedures was caused by a need for service or adjustment, a future lockout is a strong possibility if service is not obtained.

Appendix 36.A Rating files, safes, and vaults

Gion Green

The final line of defense at any facility is at the high-security storage areas where papers, records, plans or cashable instruments, precious metals, or other especially valuable assets are protected.[2] These security containers will be of a size and quantity that the nature of the business dictates.

The choice of the proper security container for specific applications is influenced largely by the value and the vulnerability of the items to be stored in them. Irreplaceable papers or original documents may not have any intrinsic or marketable value, so they may not be a likely target for a thief; but since they do have great value to the owners, they must be protected against fire. On the other hand, uncut precious stones, or even recorded negotiable papers that can be replaced, may not be in danger from fire, but they would surely be attractive to a thief; therefore they must be protected.

In protecting property, it is essential to recognize that, generally speaking, protective containers are designed to secure against burglary *or* fire. Each type of equipment has a specialized function, and each type provides only minimal protection against the other risk. There are containers designed with a burglary-resistant chest within a fire-resistant container, which are useful in many instances; but these, too, must be evaluated in terms of the mission.

Whatever the equipment, the staff must be educated and reminded of the different roles played by the two types of container. It is all too common for company personnel to assume that the fire-resistant safe is also burglary-resistant, and vice versa.

Files

Burglary-resistant files are secure against most surreptitious attacks. On the other hand, they can be pried open in less than half an hour if the burglar is permitted to work undisturbed and is not concerned with the noise created in the operation. Such files are suitable for nonnegotiable papers or even proprietary information, since these items are normally only targeted by surreptitious assault.

Filing cabinets, with a fire rating of 1 hour, and further fitted with a combination lock, would probably be suitable for all uses but the storage of government classified documents.

2. From Fischer, R.J., Green, G., 1998. Introduction to Security, sixth ed. Butterworth-Heinemann, Boston, MA.

Safes

Safes are expensive, but if they are selected wisely they can be one of the most important investments in security. Safes are not simply safes. They are each designed to perform a particular job to a particular level of protection. To use fire-resistant safes for the storage of valuables—an all too common practice—is to invite disaster. At the same time, it would be equally careless to use a burglary-resistant safe for the storage of valuable papers or records, because if a fire were to occur, the contents of such a safe would be reduced to ashes.

Ratings

Safes are rated to describe the degree of protection they afford. Naturally, the more protection provided, the more expensive the safe will be. In selecting the best one for the requirements of the facility, an estimate of the *maximum* exposure of valuables or irreplaceable records will have to be examined along with a realistic appraisal of their vulnerability. Only then can a reasonable permissible capital outlay for their protection be achieved.

Fire-resistant containers are classified according to the maximum internal temperature permitted after exposure to heat for varying periods (Table 36.A.1). A record safe rated 350-4 (formerly designated "A") can withstand exterior temperatures building to 2000°F for 4 hours without permitting the interior temperature to rise above 350°F.

UL tests that result in the various classifications are conducted to simulate a major fire with its gradual buildup of heat to 2000°F and where the safe might fall several stories through the fire damaged building. In addition, an explosion test simulates a cold safe dropping into a fire that has already reached 2000°F.

The actual procedure for the 350-4 rating involves the safe staying 4 hours in a furnace that reaches 2000°F. The furnace is turned off after 4 hours, but the safe remains inside until it is cool. The interior temperature must remain below 350°F during the heating and cooling-out period. This interior temperature is determined by sensors sealed inside the safe in six specified locations to provide a continuous record of the temperatures during the test. Papers are also placed in the safe to simulate records. The explosion impact test is conducted with another safe of the same model that is placed for 30 minutes in a furnace preheated to 2000°F. If no explosion occurs, the furnace is set at 1550°F and increased to 1700°F over a half-hour period. After this hour in the explosion test, the safe is removed and dropped 30 ft onto rubble. The safe is then returned to the furnace and reheated for 1 hour at 1700°F. The furnace and safe are allowed to cool; the papers inside must be legible and uncharred.

350-2 record safes protect against exposure up to 1850°F for 2 hours. The explosion/impact tests are conducted at slightly less time and heat. 350-1 gives 1 hour of protection up to 1700°F and a slightly less vigorous explosion/impact test. Computer media storage classifications are for containers that do not allow the internal temperature to go above 150°F. Insulated vault door classifications are much the same as for safes except that they are not subject to the explosion/impact test.

TABLE 36.A.1 Fire-resistant containers: Underwriters Laboratories record safe.

Class	Resistance to attack	Attack time	Description
Fire			
350°	Not tested	N/A	For paper and document storage
150°	Not tested	N/A	For storage of magnetic computer tapes and photographic film
125°	Not tested	N/A	For storage of flexible disks
Burglary			
TL-15	Door and body	15 min	Resists against entry by common mechanical and electrical tools
		30 min	Door and *entire body* must resist attack with tools and torches listed above plus electric impact hammers and oxy-fuel gas cutting or welding torches
TXTL-60	Tool, torch, and explosive resistant	60 min	Weight: at least 1000 lb. Door and entire safe body must resist attack with tools and torches listed above plus 8 oz of nitroglycerine or equal

UL testing for burglary resistance in safes does not include the use of diamond core drills, thermic lance, or other devices yet to be developed by the safecracker.

In some businesses a combination consisting of a fire-resistant safe with a burglary-resistant safe welded inside may serve as a double protection for different assets, but in no event must the purposes of these two kinds of safes be confused if there is one of each on the premises. Most record safes have combination locks, relocking devices, and hardened steel lock plates to provide a measure of burglar resistance, but it must be reemphasized that record safes are designed to protect documents and other similar flammables against destruction by fire. They provide only slight deterrence to the attack of even unskilled burglars. Similarly, burglar resistance is powerless to protect the contents in a fire of any significance.

Chapter 37

Corporate policy and procedures

Lawrence J. Fennelly and Mark Beaudry
Security Consultant

One rule of thumb that deserves mention concerns the number of staff required to cover a single post around the clock, providing coverage for three 8 hour shifts. The number is not three, but four and a half or five persons, to allow for days off, vacation, sick time, training, and other administrative tasks. The design of the property is a factor to be considered.

H.Skip Bryant.

Introduction

Employee manual

The policy and procedure manual(s) and employee handbooks are essential to the consistent, productive, and efficient administration of any business. This is especially true in the lodging industry, where there are many diverse services offered, numerous departments with different goals and responsibilities, and a myriad of problems that could arise.

It is therefore recommended that in addition to a company-wide policy and procedure manual, each hotel should have its own facility manual. Chances are that the company-wide manual covers policies and procedures that are general for the entire company, which may sometimes include vital, yet fundamental practices and procedures for each department within a hotel. This type of manual is usually referred to only as a guideline, which allows the individual facility to develop its own manuals and handbook based on their geographic location. Most lodging facilities will also have a detailed manual for each department with an emphasis on its operational departments.

Security department manual

In the event that there is a corporate-generated "security manual" that should be used as an outline for the facility security manual. A separate manual specifically for the security department is an indispensable tool for assuring that all security personnel have been given the same information regarding the purpose, functions, and procedures carried out by the department. The security department manuals typically consist of a series of policies and procedures, directives, and references to information that may be critical or at least helpful, to security personnel.

Manuals should be designed for quick reference whenever a need arises and they should also be readily accessible. Little is accomplished when a well-written and well-designed security manual is locked up in the security manager's office after regular business hours. Ideally, every officer is given their own copy of the manual, and all manuals are updated as it becomes necessary, generally on an annual basis.

The contents of a manual should have three basic categories:

1. General Information
2. Department Policies
3. Emergency Procedures

The General Information section could include a description of the department's mission, organizational chart, dress code, and job descriptions for security personnel. Department Polices are written statements that indicate the objective of the policy and any relevant procedures that the officer is expected to follow. Finally, the Emergency Procedures

Handbook of Loss Prevention and Crime Prevention. DOI: https://doi.org/10.1016/B978-0-12-817273-5.00037-5

section would include detailed information on the steps to be taken by security and other hotel personnel during an emergency. For example, an emergency procedure for a fire would state the responsibilities of security staff and indicate the roles expected of other nonsecurity personnel.

Example format: Fire Emergency Assignment for Security Dispatcher.

Upon noting the single-point alarm indicator activation, call the following personnel separately on the radio in the following order and wait for acknowledgment before going on:

- Unit 1—Security supervisor
- Unit 6—Front desk assistant manager
- Unit 7—Watch engineer

Manuals are, however, meant to be used as a guideline for expected behavior during a given situation. No one has yet to write a policy, procedure, or directive that covers every situation that could arise, as well as a definitive procedure to prevent a situation.

Constructing policy and procedures

Policies and procedures for every aspect of the security operation need to be developed. By using a generic outline format, you can fill in the pertinent information as you develop your manual. This ensures that there is a set way to deal with specific tasks and situations as outlined in the following sections.

Patrolling

Routine patrols

Check all employee areas, including locker rooms, and service areas to include the kitchens. Check all bars, restaurants, and function rooms. It is important to utilize a checkpoint in all of these areas.

Lobby patrols

Maintain a visible presence in the lobby checking all doorways, escalators, retail shops, and so forth.

Basic patrols

Check all guest room floors for suspicious persons, vandals, and misguided individuals. Check all fire exits, fire exit signs, lights, pipes, guest room doors, peepholes, and so forth to ensure a safe and secure environment. Again, utilize checkpoints to your advantage to ensure that officers are checking areas and documenting their stops.

Not all hotel employees have access to or are even aware of the existence of the security department's operation manual. Every hotel should, however, have a general company-wide policy and procedure manual that includes a variety of essential documents. As stated at the beginning of this section, the fundamental policies and procedures of each department need to be covered in the company-wide manual.

This is especially true in the area of security. Many people think security policies only involve how to patrol the premises or the methods employed when conducting an investigation. However, there are many areas that fall under the realm of security, and all employees of the hotel need to be aware of the appropriate steps to be taken in all situations that are likely to arise. Such situations may include

- dealing with employee theft,
- implementing emergency fire evacuation procedures,
- actions to take/avoid during strikes or collective bargaining negotiations,
- sexual harassment involving employees,
- lost and found,
- dignitary protection,
- escorting terminated employees,
- providing first aid and CPR and Stop the Bleed program,
- key management and access control,
- confidentiality procedures,
- safety deposit box procedures for cash handling,
- suicide, and
- alcohol-related incidences.

By including the essential steps to take in certain situations in the company-wide manual, it can be assured that proper policies will be followed, and employees throughout the hotel will act in a similar and consistent manner.

Report writing

The hotel security department is an integral part of a business; therefore the security manager should think and act like a business manager. This includes generating various types of reports that disclose and describe the issue, problems, and concerns encountered by the security department. Many security managers spend too much time trying to assimilate with law enforcement and lose sight of the fact that their departments are a vital component of the hotel. By producing reports as simply and clearly as possible, the security department will

- have an accurate record of the number and types of incidents it deals with, it may determine trends that may exists, and it also establishes a record for the department;
- learn how to most efficiently allocate manpower;
- determine areas of weaknesses and potential security violations; and
- ascertain which policies and procedures need modification and be able to identify new areas of concern for which there may not have been policy.

The importance of accurate report writing—legal implications

The security manager must ensure that all essential parts of any incident report are taken by all security personnel and that they are the facts. Names, descriptions of individuals, vehicles, buildings, surroundings, and correct dates, and times are critical when attempting to reconstruct on paper what actually took place. Often a report is not written until after an event has occurred, and people who can provide answers may no longer be available for questioning. Every security person should always carry a pen and small pocket notebook in order to document key facts as they occur. Names, titles, and descriptions can often be noted quickly—even during an emergency.

This information can prove to be critical months later. Author Ralph Brislin offers the following helpful hints to remember when you are reconstructing the incident from your notes in preparation for writing a report in his book *Effective Report Writing for Security Personnel*:

1. Write what happened in chronological order. What happened first, and then what happened next, and next . . ..
2. Be sure to include all names, positions, titles, and department numbers of all employees.
3. Include names, addresses and, if possible, telephone numbers of all nonemployees who witnessed or were involved in the incident.
4. Explain in plain, simple English what happened. If you mention a building by its name or number, give its location as well. Remember, many people who read this report are not as familiar with directions and location as you are.
5. When you begin to write your report, constantly refer to your notes. Do not include your opinion or comments and do not editorialize. You can give your opinion or comments about the incident in person to your supervisor.
6. Do not discard your notes. Keep them until your superior advises you to discard them.
7. Write your report before you leave work. Leaving the job before your report is written gives an unfavorable impression of your security department.

Utilization of the six questions who, what, where, when, why, and how are necessary to complete any report. All reports, log books (including front desk or managers log book), and all checklists have the potential to become legal documents. Therefore it is critical that information is recorded completely and accurately. In criminal prosecution cases against the hotel, defense counsel has absolute access to all such reports. In civil actions, insurance claims require the production of all relevant reports to defend a claim. Any type of report generated by the hotel pertinent to a claim will be considered a relevant report. Also, when a lawsuit is commenced, the discovery process will require the production of all documents, including reports, memos, notes, and so forth. Company attorneys' work products and investigations done at the attorney's request are not necessarily available. The accuracy of the reports is paramount when considering the potential legal problems wrong information could pose, as well as the unprofessional image it tends to bestow upon the department, and ultimately the entire hotel.

First, false information may lead to defamation and libel suits. Such additional charges only complicate the original suit and increase the amount of time and money spent on the matter. Further, the torts of libel and defamation are avoidable with the accurate and factual recording of information. Second, the professional image of the security department, and in turn of the hotel, is affected by the quality of the reports produced. Sloppy and erroneous reports reflect sloppy and apathetic employees. Professionalism means that reports are prepared prudently. It also means that reports are not merely filed away after they are generated. Professionalism dictates that reports are analyzed for content, distribution to appropriate personnel, and examined for benefits and concerns they may offer to the department. Internally, it is the senior management that reads most reports. Externally, however, attorneys and insurance company representatives read the security department's reports.

Record retention

Depending on your state and legal advisors recommendations, a general time period should be set forth for retaining various types of records. Listed below are a few examples:

- Incident reports—Should be maintained for a period of 5 years or based on your statutory laws.
- Records relating to pending litigation—Until final settlement and released by legal advisor.
- Records involving minors—Maintain until a minor reaches the age of majority.
- Record of General Liability claim—Maintain until final settlement and released by legal advisor, could be 1–6 years after actual settlement.

Conclusion

Every security manager who assumes a position in the lodging industry also assumes that the hotel has a security department manual. Unfortunately, this is not the case, and some managers have to step into a position and start from scratch. Technically, if a department has been operating without a security manual, the hard part is not writing the manual, it is implementing it. Why hotels are *not* willing to share security manuals is beyond me. Security managers need guidance just like other managers and who better to get a manual from than another security manager. Even if a security manager has a fairly decent manual, you can always learn something from someone else's operation. It is unjust if hotels from the same chain do *not* accept this method. Finally, every 5 years all policies should be reviewed and updated.

Chapter 38

The importance of CPR/AED and first aid training for security officers and SROs

Marianna A. Perry
Security Consultant

The first step any security officer should take when responding to a medical emergency is to call 911.

Marianna Perry 2010

Until recently, the majority of security officer positions did not require much security industry knowledge or lifesaving skills, and there was a lack of industry training standards.

With that in mind, approximately 610,000 people die of heart disease in the United States every year—that is, one in every four deaths—and heart disease is the leading cause of death for both men and women.[1] About 47% of all sudden cardiac deaths occur outside a hospital.[2]

These statistics must be recognized as important arguments for required industry training for security officers in first aid, CPR (cardiopulmonary resuscitation), and AED (automated external defibrillator) operation since many times security officers are the first responders on the scene.

An article written in 2014 for The Center for Investigative Reporting stated that lobbying by the security industry and big businesses has derailed attempts to require rigorous training standards for armed security officers across the country, most of whom face fewer state training requirements than a manicurist in a California nail salon. For example, in California, an armed security officer must have received 14 hours of gun training, six of them on a shooting range, in addition to 40 hours of instruction. Manicurists in the Golden State must complete 400 hours of training.

When security officers do get training, their experiences vary from state to state and company to company. Some spend a few hours watching a video or a few days in a classroom or on a shooting range. In some states, security officers are required to put themselves through basic training by attending a school, then receive more training from a company once they are hired. Other security officers simply complete their training on the job.

Introduction

In the past decade, industry organizations, including the National Association of Security Companies, helped pave the way for regulations in many states, but they faced resistance from some security officer company operators, restaurant owners, and retailers, who argued that training requirements would give an unfair advantage to larger companies that can more easily absorb costs.

In the 1990s, federal lawmakers introduced more than a dozen bills related to national training standards and background checks. But the efforts were criticized as toothless or interfering with states' rights. Due to a lack of support from most of the industries and lawmakers, the efforts failed. The article further reported that there are no federal training standards, leaving a hodgepodge of state-by-state rules or no rules at all.[3]

1. Heart Disease in the United States. From: <https://www.cdc.gov/heartdisease/facts.htm> (Retrieved on 20.01.19.).
2. CDC, 2002. State specific mortality from sudden cardiac death: United States, 1999. MMWR 51 (6), 123–126.
3. Walter, S., December 2014. Why Legislative Efforts to Improve Security Guard Training Keep Failing. The Center for Investigative Reporting, Revealnews.org.

Handbook of Loss Prevention and Crime Prevention. DOI: https://doi.org/10.1016/B978-0-12-817273-5.00038-7

In early 2001, the Commission on Guidelines was established by ASIS International (ASIS) in response to a concerted need for guidelines regarding security issues in the United States. As the preeminent organization for security professionals worldwide, ASIS has an important role to play in helping the private sector secure its business and critical infrastructure whether from national disaster, accidents, or planned actions, such as terrorist attacks and vandalism.

The ASIS Guidelines outline the framework for effectively selecting private security officers. Training criteria are the proposed training requirements considered essential for each regulating body and subsequent propriety or contract security agency to consider in the training of their private security officers. The Private Security Officer Selection and Training Guidelines, training criteria, and training topics include the recommendations that consideration should be given to emergency response procedures for critical incident response to national disasters, accidents, human-caused events, and life safety awareness that includes safety hazards and blood-borne pathogens, etc.[4]

Industry standard training for security officers includes company rules and regulations, their own general duties, public relations, customer service, terrorism awareness, criminal law, search and seizure, report writing, fire prevention and suppression, etc., along with CPR/AED and first aid.

Part of a security officer's training is to be observant or practice situational awareness. A well-trained and experienced security officer is constantly aware of the people who are in their immediate vicinity as well as activities that taking place around them.[5]

Situational awareness is not only used to alert a security officer to potential security issues but can also be an important skill to possess during medical emergencies. If there is a disturbance or emergency situation and someone's life is in danger, a security officer is often the first to arrive on the scene. Well-trained security officers who are confident in the skills and abilities learned through training are incredible resources for their workplaces as well as their communities.

Security needs are growing as technology advances

With the growth of the internet, the need for security in the area of surveillance has increased. There are a number of emerging concerns, such as cyber threats, that need to be addressed in order to remain efficient and secure. The assets that governments and companies need protected are no longer just physical objects. Keeping knowledge and information safe is more important than ever.

Security degree programs are on the rise

Whether it is cyber, criminal justice, or information technology, the degree programs associated with security are on the rise. Colleges that offer degrees in this field know the impact of industry training. In addition, these programs, upon the completion of degree requirements, will help get the attention of employers.

The security industry requires particular skills

Among security companies, decision-making, oral communication, critical thinking, maximizing others' performance, and persuasive influencing are the competencies that will be required for tomorrow's security professionals. ASIS International found that there are 22 areas that security industry professionals need in order to be successful, but the lack of cohesion across various industry sectors and standards at educational institutions will be the biggest challenge for private and public sector stakeholders.[6]

It is not only technology that is making an impact on the security industry. The security officers of today not only need to be tech savvy and be able to respond in high-pressure situations, but they also must be prepared for a variety of emergencies.

As security officers assume a greater level of responsibility a higher level of training is necessary. When there is an emergency, it does not matter whether it is a medical situation, a natural disaster, workplace violence incident, or a workplace safety issue; there is a first responder that can make the difference between life and death—the one who is well trained.

4. ASIS GDL PSO 09 2004 Advancing Security Worldwide. Private Security Officer Selection and Training Guideline.

5. Knowing What is Going on Around You (Situational Awareness). From: <http://www.hse.gov.uk/construction/lwit/assets/downloads/situational-awareness.pdf> (retrieved 19.01.19.).

6. Hirepurpose. 5 Things You Need to Know About the Security Industry. <http://www.taskandpurpose> (18.08.18.).

There are a variety of jobs in the industry

ASIS International did a study that reveals that jobs in the security industry are extremely diverse. Companies across the world need security specialists to deal with computer and network security, liability insurance, access control, workplace violence, parking lot and garage security, terrorism, and violent crime.[7]

Most commonly, when we think about individuals who are trained for life-threatening situations, we think police officers, fire fighters and emergency medical staff (EMS), but in many cases, there is someone on the scene prior to the arrival of law enforcement, fire fighters, and EMS personnel, and this is the security officer. Security officers work in many different environments, such as in schools, banks, retail stores, and in the workplace and may come into contact with thousands of people each day.

What may make the difference between life and death is whether or not these security officers are well trained and ready to provide emergency assistance on many levels.[8]

Cardiopulmonary resuscitation/automated external defibrillator

The first step any security officer should take when responding to a medical emergency is to call 911, and while he/she is waiting for EMS to arrive with advanced medical training, the security professional could be performing lifesaving CPR or giving first aid and/or other industry standard lifesaving techniques. In certain situations the security officer may be the only individual on-site who knows how to perform CPR and how to operate an AED. It is critical, especially in a cardiac emergency that someone acts quickly and makes the decision to help save lives.

There are also ethical, legal, and cultural factors to consider that may influence decisions about when to provide CPR for someone experiencing a cardiac incident, this is when it becomes critical for security officers to have the proper industry training.

There are sometimes early warning signs that may alert others when someone is experiencing a cardiac emergency:

- chest pain or discomfort
- upper body pain or discomfort in the arms, back, neck, jaw, or upper stomach
- shortness of breath
- nausea, lightheadedness, or cold sweats

In many of these situations the person experiencing a cardiac emergency does not react to their symptoms and seek medical care, so the cardiac emergency does not occur in a hospital setting. This is evident since almost half of cardiac deaths occur outside the hospital. An observant security officer may recognize this behavior and be prepared to intervene—by calling 911 and then performing CPR. Without quick intervention, many times from a security officer performing lifesaving CPR and defibrillation, death from sudden cardiac arrest is certain.

Chain of survival

The Cardiac Chain of Survival[9] was developed in 1990 by the American Heart Association and has become the standard of care for cardiac victims. When there is a cardiac emergency, first responders are encouraged to follow the four-step sequence below:

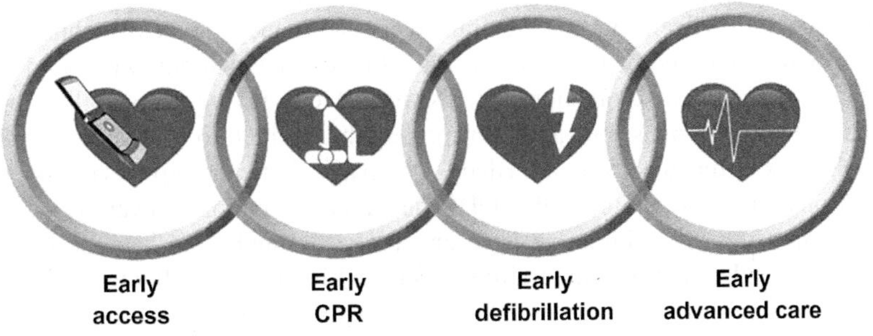

7. Hirepurpose. 5 Things You Need to Know About the Security Industry. <http://www.taskandpurpose> (18.08.18.).

8. How Life Safety Training Turns Security Officers into First Responders. From: <https://www.securitymagazine.com/articles/84845-how-life-safety-training-turns-security-officers-into-first-responders> (Retrieved on 18.01.19.).

9. Chain of Survival. From: <https://www.aedbrands.com/resource-center/choose/chain-of-survival/> (retrieved 25.01.19.).

The first step, *early access* is recognizing that there is a cardiac emergency and calling 911. It is important to call 911 right away so that an advanced support life support team can respond quickly.

The warning signs of sudden cardiac arrest are

- loss of consciousness,
- no pulse,
- unresponsiveness, and
- not breathing.

The second step, *early CPR* is providing CPR (compressions and breaths) to keep oxygenated blood flowing through the body's most vital organs—the heart and brain. Early CPR increases the sudden cardiac victim's chances of survival, but CPR alone cannot save their life. If the first responder has not been trained in CPR, they may be able to receive assistance from the 911 operator. Many dispatchers are trained to coach callers through the basic steps of CPR, but it is important to remember that CPR must be started immediately.

Early defibrillation, the third step is the only way to stop sudden cardiac arrest because when sudden cardiac arrest occurs, the heart must be restarted by an electrical shock. Outside the hospital environment, the only way to restart the heart is by using an AED. When the electrodes from an AED are placed on the victim's chest, electricity flows from the electrodes through the chest to the heart. Time is critical because for each minute that defibrillation is delayed, the victim's chance of survival decreases from 7% to 10%.

The fourth step, *early advanced care* is given by paramedics and other trained medical personnel on the scene when the victim is being transported to the hospital. Advanced care is needed to help maintain a normal heart rhythm after successful defibrillation.

First aid

To complement to CPR/AED training, first aid training will help nonmedical professionals, such as security officers to provide emergency care before professional first responders, such as EMS arrive. Topics covered in first aid training include:

- asthma emergencies;
- anaphylaxis;
- burns;
- choking;
- diabetic emergencies;
- external bleeding;
- environmental emergencies;
- poisoning;
- neck, head, and spinal injuries;
- stroke; and
- seizure.[10]

Medical emergency: Protection officers in a large high-rise building were called to the scene of a collapsed individual. Upon arrival the protection officers, who were trained as emergency medical technicians, checked the scene to ensure that it was safe to enter and then began to assess the situation. The patient was found to have stopped breathing and had no pulse. Utilizing an AED, the protection officers were able to revive and stabilize the patient until emergency medical services personnel arrived on scene and transported the patient to a nearby hospital. The Department of Homeland Security (DHS) has initiated a "Stop the Bleed" campaign that can help to save lives.[11]

In addition to traditional first aid training, the DHS developed a national awareness campaign called, *Stop the Bleed*.[12] The goal of the *Stop the Bleed* initiative is to encourage bystanders to become trained to help in a bleeding emergency until medical responders arrive. This training is critical in an active shooter situation, a terrorist attack or in other incidents involving mass casualties. *Stop the Bleed* is an excellent training program for security officers, and it can be incorporated into existing training curricula.

10. What is First Aid? From: <https://www.redcross.org/take-a-class/first-aid/performing-first-aid/what-is-first-aid> (retrieved 18.01.19.).
11. https://www.dhs.gov/stopthebleed
12. Stop the Bleed. From: <https://stopthebleed.usuhs.edu/> (retrieved 19.01.19.).

It does not matter whether it is a security breach, a safety issue, or a medical emergency, the public relies on security officers to be able to handle any of these situations and those who employ security officers have a moral and ethical responsibility to ensure that they are providing well-trained first responders. Security is a proactive discipline, and having security officers who are trained in CPR/AED and first aid is a part of being proactive by being prepared to respond—regardless of the emergency situation. Well-trained security officers are able to provide the best value to their employers as well as the people they protect—especially in the most critical, life and death situations.

Chapter 39

Identity theft

Lawrence J. Fennelly and Marianna A. Perry
Security Consultant

Identity theft is the deliberate use of someone else's identity, usually as a method to gain a financial advantage or obtain credit and other benefits in the other person's name, and perhaps to the other person's disadvantage or loss. The person whose identity has been assumed may suffer adverse consequences, especially if they are held responsible for the perpetrator's actions.

Wikipedia 2019

Introduction

Identity (ID) theft is a crime in which a thief steals your personal information, such as your name, your social security number (SSN) or your credit card information to commit fraud. The ID thief can use your information for fraudulent purchases or to fraudulently apply for credit, file taxes, or get medical services. These crimes can damage your credit status and cost you time and money to restore your good name. You may not know that you are the victim of ID theft until you experience a financial consequence (mystery bills, credit collections, and denied loans) from actions that the thief has taken with your stolen ID.[1]

Steps you can take to protect yourself[2]:

- *Be aware of camera phones*—If you are paying at a register or at a restaurant, watch for people fidgeting with their phones. They could be trying to take a picture of your card.
- *Keep an eye on your credit card*—Whenever you hand your card to a waitress, clerk or cashier, pay attention to where it goes and for how long. Card skimming or copying your credit card information may be occurring.
- *Shop with a slim wallet*—Remove everything except one credit card and your driver's license from your wallet. Carrying multiple credit cards increases your risk of ID theft.
- *Be alert for pickpockets*—Tuck your purse under your arm, keep your wallet in your front pocket and do not put your purse or wallet down where someone else may grab it.
- *If you are shopping online*—If you pay by credit or charge card online, your transaction will be protected by the Fair Credit Billing Act.[3] Under this law, you can dispute charges under certain circumstances and temporarily withhold payment while the creditor investigates them. In the event that someone uses your credit card without your permission, your liability, generally, is limited to the first $50 in charges. Never shop online using a public Wi-Fi network and shop on secure sites with a URL that begins with "https" instead "http."
- *If you are making large purchases or electronics purchases*—Most credit cards offer their own warranty protection for your purchases just for using a credit card for the transaction. Some of those warranties go beyond what is offered by the manufacturer and offer you extra coverage, which is really useful for electronics, appliances, or other large purchases.
- *If you are traveling*—If you're away from home, use your credit card for purchases because debit cards do not offer you the same protections. Also, only carry the cards which are necessary.

1. https://www.usa.gov/identity-theft
2. www.creditcards.com
3. https://www.ftc.gov/enforcement/rules/rulemaking-regulatory-reform-proceedings/fair-credit-billing-act

Handbook of Loss Prevention and Crime Prevention. DOI: https://doi.org/10.1016/B978-0-12-817273-5.00039-9

Steps you can take to protect yourself from ID theft:

- Do not carry your social security card in your wallet or write your number on your checks. Only give out your SSN when absolutely necessary.
- Do not respond to unsolicited requests for personal information (your name, birth date, SSN, or bank account number) by phone, mail, or online.
- Watch out for "shoulder surfers." Shield the keypad when typing your passwords on computers and at ATMs.
- Collect mail promptly. Ask the post office to put your mail on hold when you are away from home.
- Pay attention to your billing cycles. If bills or financial statements are late, contact the sender.
- Review your receipts. Ask for carbon copies and incorrect charge slips as well. Promptly compare receipts with account statements. Watch for unauthorized transactions.
- Shred receipts, credit offers, account statements, and expired cards to prevent "dumpster divers" from getting your personal information.
- Store personal information in a safe place at home and at work.
- Install firewalls and virus-detection software on your home computer.
- Create complex passwords that ID thieves cannot guess easily. Change your passwords if a company that you do business with has a breach of its databases
- Order your credit report once a year and review to be certain that it does not include accounts that you have not opened. Check it more frequently if you suspect someone has gained access to your account information.

Identity theft

ID theft[4] happens when someone steals your personal information to commit fraud.

The ID thief may use your information to fraudulently apply for credit, file taxes, or get medical services. These acts can damage your credit status and cost you time and money to restore your good name.

You may not know that you are the victim of ID theft immediately. You could be a victim if you receive

- bills for items you did not buy,
- debt collection calls for accounts you did not open, and
- denials for loan applications.

Children and seniors are both vulnerable to ID theft. Child ID theft may go undetected for many years. Victims may not know until they are adults, applying for their own loans. Seniors are vulnerable because they share their personal information often with doctors and caregivers. The number of people and offices that access their information put them at risk.

Types of identity theft

There are several common types of ID theft that can affect you:

- Tax ID theft—Someone uses your SSN to falsely file tax returns with the Internal Revenue Services (IRS) or your state.
- Medical ID theft—Someone steals your Medicare ID or health insurance member number. Thieves use this information to get medical services or send fake bills to your health insurer.
- Social ID theft—Someone uses your name and photos to create a fake account on social media.

Take steps to avoid being a victim of ID theft. Secure your internet connections, use security features, and review bills. Read more about how you can prevent ID theft.

Prevent identity theft

Take steps to protect yourself from ID theft:

- Secure your SSN. Don't carry your social security card in your wallet. Only give out your SSN when absolutely necessary.
- Do not share personal information (birth date, SSN, or bank account number) just because someone asks for it.

4. https://www.usa.gov/identity-theft

- Collect mail every day. Place a hold on your mail when you are away from home for several days.
- Pay attention to your billing cycles. If bills or financial statements are late, contact the sender.
- Use the security features on your mobile phone.
- Update sharing and firewall settings when you are on a public Wi-Fi network. Use a virtual private network, if you use public Wi-Fi.
- Review your credit card and bank account statements. Compare receipts with account statements. Watch for unauthorized transactions.
- Shred receipts, credit offers, account statements, and expired credit cards to prevent "dumpster divers" from getting your personal information.
- Store personal information in a safe place.
- Install firewalls and virus-detection software on your home computer.
- Create complex passwords that ID thieves cannot guess. Change your passwords if a company that you do business with has a breach of its databases
- Review your credit reports once a year. Be certain that they do not include accounts that you have not opened. You can order it for free from Annualcreditreport.com.
- Freeze your credit files with Equifax, Experian, Innovis, TransUnion, and the National Consumer Telecommunications and Utilities Exchange, for free. Credit freezes prevent someone from applying for and getting approval for credit account or utility services in your name.

Report identity theft

Report ID theft to the Federal Trade Commission (FTC) online at IdentityTheft.gov or by phone at 1-877-438-4338.

If you report ID theft online, you will receive an ID theft report and a recovery plan. Create an account on the website to update your recovery plan, track your progress, and receive prefilled form letters to send to creditors. If you decide not to create an account, you need to print or save your ID theft report and recovery plan. Without an account, you will not be able to access them on the website in the future. Download the FTC's publication (PDF, Download Adobe Reader) for detailed tips, checklists, and sample letters.

You can also report ID theft to the FTC by phone at 1-877-438-4338. The FTC will collect the details of your situation, but will not give you an ID theft report or recovery plan. You may also choose to report your ID theft to your local police station. It could be necessary if

- you know the ID thief,
- the thief used your name in any interaction with the police, and
- a creditor or another company affected by the ID theft requires you to provide a police report.

Report specific types of identity theft

You may also report specific types of ID theft to other federal agencies.

- Medical ID theft—Contact your health insurance company's fraud department or Medicare's fraud office.
- Tax identity theft—Report this type of ID theft to the Internal Revenue Service and your state's Department of Taxation or Revenue.

Report identity theft to other organizations

You can also report the theft to other organizations, such as follows:

- Credit-reporting agencies—Contact one of the three major credit-reporting agencies to place fraud alerts or freeze on your accounts. With a freeze in place, no one can apply for credit with your name or SSN. Also get copies of your credit reports, to be sure that no one has already tried to get unauthorized credit accounts with your personal information. Confirm that the credit-reporting agency will alert the other two credit-reporting agencies.
- National Long-Term Care Ombudsman Resource Center—Report cases of ID theft that resulted from a stay in a nursing home or long-term care facility.
- Financial institutions—Contact the fraud department at your bank, credit card issuers, and any other places where you have accounts.

- Retailers and other companies—Report the crime to companies where the ID thief opened credit accounts or even applied for jobs.
- State consumer protection offices or attorney general—Your state may offer resources to help you contact creditors, dispute errors, and other helpful resources.

You may need to get new personal records or identification cards if you are the victim of ID theft. Learn how to replace your vital identification documents after ID theft.

Tax identity theft

Tax-related ID theft occurs when someone uses your SSN to get a tax refund or a job. You may not be aware of the problem until you e-file your tax return and find out that another return has already been filed using your SSN. If the IRS suspects tax ID theft, they will send a 5071C letter to the address on the federal tax return. Keep in mind, the IRS will never start contact with you by sending an email, text, or social media message that asks for personal or financial information. Watch out for IRS imposter scams, when someone contacts you saying they work for the IRS.

Report tax identity theft

If you suspect you have become a victim of tax ID theft—or the IRS sends you a letter or notice indicating a problem—take these steps:

- File a report with the FTC at IdentityTheft.gov. You can also call the FTC Identity Theft Hotline at 1-877-438-4338 or TTY 1-866-653-4261.
- Contact one of the three major credit bureaus to place a fraud alert on your credit records:
  - Equifax: 1-888-766-0008
  - Experian: 1-888-397-3742
  - TransUnion: 1-800-680-7289
- Contact your financial institutions and close any accounts opened without your permission or that show unusual activity.
- Respond immediately to any IRS notice and call the number provided. If instructed, go to the IRS Identity Verification Service.
- Complete IRS Form 14039, Identity Theft Affidavit (PDF, Download Adobe Reader); print, then mail or fax according to instructions.
- Continue to pay your taxes and file your tax return, even if you must do so by paper.
- Check with your state tax agency to see what steps to take at the state level.

How to protect yourself

Follow these steps to prevent tax ID theft:

Dos

File your income taxes early in the season, before a thief can file taxes in your name. Also, Keep an eye out for any IRS letter or notice that states:

- More than one tax return was filed using your SSN.
- You owe additional tax, you have had a tax refund offset, or you have had collection actions taken against you for a year you did not file a tax return.
- IRS records indicate you received wages from an employer unknown to you.

Don'ts

Do not reply to or click on any links in suspicious email, texts, and social media messages. Make sure to report anything suspicious to the IRS.

Medical identity theft

Medical ID theft can occur when someone steals your personal identification number to obtain medical care, buy medication, access your medical records, or submit fake claims to your insurer or Medicare in your name.

Report medical identity theft

If you believe you have been a victim of medical ID theft, call the FTC at 1-877-438-4338 (TTY: 1-866-653-4261) and your health insurance company's fraud department. You can report the theft through IdentityTheft.gov to share with the FTC and with law enforcement. Also get copies of your medical records and work with your doctor's office and insurance company to correct them.

If you suspect that you have been the victim of Medicare fraud, contact the US Department of Health and Human Services' Inspector General at 1-800-447-8477.

Prevent medical identity theft

Take these steps to prevent medical ID theft:

- Guard your social security, medicare, and health-insurance identification numbers. Only give your number to your physician or other approved health-care providers.
- Review your explanation of benefits or Medicare Summary Notice to make sure that the claims match the services you received. Report questionable charges to your health-insurance provider or Medicare.
- Request and carefully review a copy of your medical records for inaccuracies and conditions that you do not have.

Identity theft

Tips to protect your identity

- Never carry your social security card in your wallet. This is considered the gateway to your ID. Leave it locked away at home or in a safe deposit box until you need it to conduct business.
- Check other cards that you normally carry in your wallet, as some of them may contain your SSN, too. Examples are your Medicare card, insurance cards, or even driver's licenses.
- Put as little information as you can on your checks. Never put your SSN and use a post office box instead of a physical address if possible.
- Mailing bills from a United States Post Office location or box is safer than putting them out for the mailman at home. ID thieves cruise neighborhoods looking for outgoing mail, knowing they are likely to find outgoing bill payments containing account numbers and other personal information.
- Do not have your new checks mailed to your home. Send them to your bank, instead. ID thieves think that they have hit the jackpot when they find a box of checks in a mailbox.
- Keeping charge receipts in your car is asking for trouble. ID thieves would much rather have your personal account information than your car stereo.
- Photocopy both sides of all credit cards and keep this information in a safe place. If you lose your wallet, you will have the account numbers and phone numbers at your fingertips.
- Protect yourself against loss by removing any card from your wallet that you do not use on a daily basis. This way, if you have a theft, you will not have to notify as many entities.
- Report lost or stolen cards the moment you realize you are not in possession of the card. This will limit your liability.
- Secure personal information in your home, especially if you have roommates, employ outside help, or are having service work done in your home.
- Ask about information security procedures at your place of work. Find out who has access to your personal information and verify that your records are kept in a secure location. Ask about the disposal procedures for those records as well.
- Never provide personal information over the phone unless you initiated the call. Remember, ID thieves are skilled professional liars, trained to sound legitimate and sincere.

- Shred everything. Do not assume that simply because you put an item in the trash, no one will see it. That person you see dumpster diving could very well be an ID thief. Unless you want them to have your private information, shred, shred, shred.
- Consider a credit monitoring service. Such services watch your credit bureau activity, and alert you if someone tries to open an account in your name, attempt to change the mailing address for statements, and other such activities that could signal ID theft.
- Credit reports can be obtained free of charge from each of the three major credit bureaus every 12 months by going to www.annualcreditreport.com. Staggering your requests among bureaus allows you to keep an eye on activity year-round.
- Never click on links sent in unsolicited emails; instead, type in a web address you know. Use firewalls, antispyware, and antivirus software to protect your home computer; keep them up-to-date. Visit *OnGuardOnline.gov* for more information.
- Do not use an obvious password like your birth date, your mother's maiden name, or the last four digits of your SSN.

Source: National Foundation for Credit Counseling.
If you are a victim of ID theft:

- Contact the three major credit-reporting bureaus and request a fraud alert be placed on your credit file.
- Consider placing a security freeze on your credit file.
- Order a credit report from each bureau and examine it carefully for fraud.
- Continue to check your reports periodically to make sure no new reports are fileds.
- Contact all creditors, starting with the accounts that have been tampered with or opened fraudulently. Close those accounts, even activity has occurred.
- When establishing new accounts, select new PIN numbers and passwords.
- File a police report, as you may need this documentation to prove the theft. Order copies of the police report to have on hand and submit to creditors.
- File a complaint with the FTC online at www.ftccomplaintassistant.gov, or through their Identity Theft Hotline at (877) 438-4338.

Source: Federal Trade Commission, 2008.

Federal government resources

Federal Trade Commission (FTC)
www.ftc.gov/idtheft
Department of the Treasury
Identity Theft Resource Page
http://www.identitytheft.gov
Identity Theft and Your Tax Records—http://www.irs.gov/privacy/article/0,id = 186436,00.html
US Secret Service (USSS)
Criminal Investigators—http://www.secretservice.gov/criminal.shtml
Department of Justice (DOJ)
Identity Theft and Fraud
http://www.justice.gov/criminal/fraud/websites/idtheft.html
Social Security Administration
Identity Theft and Your SSN
http://www.ssa.gov/pubs/10064.html
Social Security: Your Number and Card
http://www.ssa.gov/pubs/10002.html
US Postal Inspection Service
ID theft: Safeguarding Your Personal Information—http://www.usps.com/cpim/ftp/pubs/pub280/welcome.htm
Consumer and Professional Organizations
International Association of Chiefs of Police: ID Safety
http://www.theiacp.org/idsafety

Privacy Rights Clearinghouse: Identity Theft Resources
http://www.privacyrights.org/identity-theft-data-breaches
Call for Action / Identity Theft
http://www.callforaction.org/?cat = 10

Credit bureaus

Equifax
http://www.equifax.com
1-800-525-6285
Experian
http://www.experian.com
1-888-397-3742
TransUnion
http://www.transunion.com
1-800-680-7289

Chapter 40

Doors and door locks

Lawrence J. Fennelly
Security Consultant

Understand the process of security and the importance of security system integration.

Marianna Perry, MA, CPP, 2010.

Introduction

Some key point to remember, specific locks go to specific doors, plus remember to conform with state laws, and the NFPA (National Fire Protection Association). Finally always buy a quality locking device for your specific door.

What kind of door locks do building codes require?

Although many people assume their local building codes require a minimum level of quality and security for the door locks installed on their homes, most building codes do not even require a lock on exterior doors, let alone a minimum level of quality. Most contractors select the locks based on price and quality.

Advantages to keyless locks

- Convenience.
- Can leave an audit trail of who enters or exits.
- Can be used as a timekeeping device for employees.
- No cost for replacing lost or stolen keys.
- No keys to return from terminated employees.
- Access to a building or an area can be immediately turned off.

Residential door locks

Use Grade 1 (ANSI designation) deadbolt type locks on:

- exterior doors;
- doors between attached garages and living spaces; and
- garage man doors (even if the garage is not attached to the house).

What kind of door locks do building codes require?

Although many people assume their local building codes require a minimum level of quality and security for the door locks installed on their homes, most building codes do not even require a lock on exterior doors, let alone a minimum level of quality.

Most contractors select the locks based on price.

A burglar can enter the home through a door using several methods[1]:

1. doorhardware-onestop.com/html/picking_right_lock_for_home.htm

Handbook of Loss Prevention and Crime Prevention. DOI: https://doi.org/10.1016/B978-0-12-817273-5.00040-5

- The door can be left unlocked.
- Doors can be kicked in.
- Door locks can be picked.
- Door locks can be hammered until they fall off.
- Doors can be pried open.
- Doorframes can be spread apart with a spreader bar.
- Door locks can be "drilled out" using a power drill.
- Locks can be pried off with pipe wrenches or pliers.
- Panes of glass in or beside doors can be broken so the intruder can reach in and unlock the lock.
- Sometimes thieves obtain a copy of the house key from an acquaintance.

How to protect your home from intruders:

1. *Install locks with deadbolts.*
   In residential construction there are basically two types of bolts used on exterior doors: latch bolts and deadbolts. Some locks combine the two bolts into one.
2. *Install locks with an ANSI Grade 1 classification.*
   There is a grading system that measures the security and durability of door locks. The American National Standards Institute (ANSI) has standards, developed and maintained by The Builders Hardware Manufacturers Association Inc., that comparatively measure the security and durability performance of door locks. Not all Grade 1 locks are equal. Different types of door locks are tested differently under ANSI standards. But the grade designation system is the same.
3. *Install locks with key control.*
   Key control is simply controlling who has copies of keys to your home. Many door keys can be copied at a local hardware or retail store. However, many manufacturers now offer locks using keys that cannot be copied except by certain locksmiths or only by the manufacturer themselves.

Strike plates

The strike plate's attachment to the doorframe is usually the weakest point in the entire door/doorframe/lock system. High-security strike plates are available. They sometimes come with a heavy gauge metal reinforcing plate that mounts under the cosmetic strike plate and come with 3″ long screws that secure the strike to the wall framing, not just to the doorframe jamb. The screw holes that are staggered so the screws do not penetrate into the same grain of wood. The concept of screwing into different wood grains in the doorframe and wall framing is to make it more difficult to split the wood doorframe or wall framing when the door is impacted. This feature should be considered at every exterior door and at those doors coming from attached garages.

Important features in door locks—*install a door lock with a deadbolt type bolt*[a]
Every door lock has a bolt that extends from the lock into the strike, which is mounted into or on the doorframe
The type of bolt has a great effect on the lock's strength. In residential construction, there are basically two types of bolts used on exterior doors: latch bolts and deadbolts. Some locks combine the two bolts into one
The latch bolt is a spring-loaded, bevel-shaped bolt. The spring keeps the latch bolt extended. It will retract by turning the door knob or lever handle. When the door is fully closed, the spring-loaded bolt extends into the strike plate about 1/4″ to 1/2″

[a]doorhardware-onestop.com/html/picking_right_lock_for_home.htm

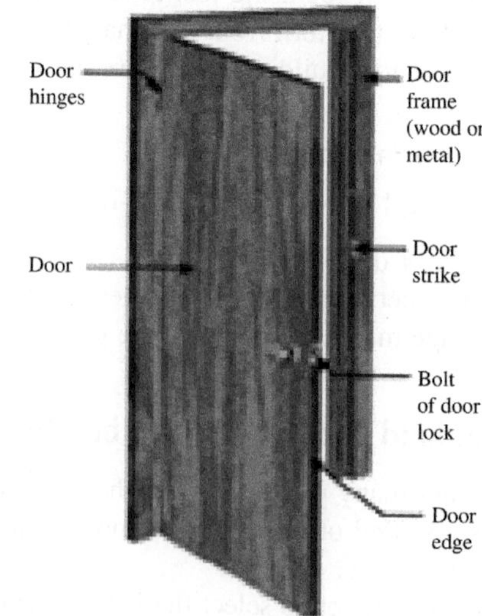

Locks

1″ Minimum throw on deadbolt—The throw of the deadbolt is the length that the deadbolt extends out of the door edge. A minimum throw of 1″ is recommended. Longer throws makes it more difficult to gain entry by spreading the doorframe.

Saw-resistant bolts—Some deadbolts come with internal antisaw pins. The pins spin freely inside the bolt. If someone tries to break in by sawing off the deadbolt, the pin will make this difficult because it spins back and forth with every movement of the saw blade.

Captured key deadbolt—Burglars can gain entry through a locked door by breaking the glass in the door light or sidelight, reaching in, and simply unlocking the door. Many homeowners, in an effort to prevent this, install double cylinder deadbolt locks with keyholes on both sides of the door. Do not let double cylinder deadbolts create a fire safety danger to your family. In the case of a fire when the family needs to get out of the house quickly, you do not want to be wasting time looking for the key to unlock the door. Most building codes do not allow this type of lock on doors that are used to exit the house for this very reason. To solve this conflict between family safety and security, one manufacturer has developed a deadbolt lock with a feature called a captured key. On the interior side of the door the deadbolt lock has a thumb turn that can be removed from the lock, leaving a keyhole. The idea is that when no one is home, there is no need for the thumb turn. The last person to leave removes the thumb turn and creates a double cylinder deadbolt condition.

Captured key thumb turn—The thumb turn cannot be removed without having a key to the lock. Therefore small children cannot remove the thumb turn from the lock. Also, the thumb turn can actually be used as a house key. It is important that whenever anyone is in the home that the thumb turn is left in the lock at all times.

Hardened cased steel and beveled casings—On a typical deadbolt lock the outside housing of the lock is called the "casing" or "case." Many lock manufacturers make their casings out of hardened steel, and many make the casing beveled. The hardened cased steel makes the casing more resilient against blows from a hammer. Beveling the casing makes it very difficult to get pliers or pipe wrenches to stay on the lock when trying to twist it loose.

Antidrill feature—Some intruders know how to drill out a lock. Some manufacturers combat this by installing hardened steel chips within the lock housing. When the drill bit hits these steel chips, it tears up the drill bit.

Three types of doors

Hollow Core—It is made from thin sheets of wood veneer glued over a wood frame with a cardboard insert.
Solid wood/solid wood core—It is made from solid wood or wood veneer that is glued over a solid wood door.
Metal—It is made from either galvanized zintec or a thin, metal sheet of steel that glued over a solid wood door.

How to secure doors that have glass panels

1. Install a clear, unbreakable polycarbonate panel over the glass on the inside of the door or use the pane to replace the existing glass. Fasten the panel securely on the inside of the door.
2. Install grated wire mesh, a wrought iron grille, or decorative wire grate over the glass. Make sure there is no access through the grate.
3. Install a clear antipenetration film over the glass.

If there is glass in a door and it is unsecured, it should be 40″ or more from the lock.

Problem doors

Sliding patio doors—Place locking mechanism that vertically secures the top and the bottom of the door to the track. These locks can be key-operated or hand-tightened. A wooden dowel place in the track to block the door from being opened can be defeated.

Sliding patio doors should have antilift devices and locks fitted to the top and bottom to stop them being removed from outside, unless they already have a multilocking system. Get specialist advice. If you are getting new or replacement patio doors, ask the system supplier for their high-security specification.

Patio doors present several security problems:

- The glass panels of many doors can be lifted out of their tracks and removed.
- The locking mechanism can easily be pried open and provides little security.
- The fixed panel is sometimes held in place by brackets with screws exposed to the exterior.

To stop the door from being lifted out of its frame the "jimmy plates" or screws should be mounted at the top of the track to reduce any vertical play in the door.

A "Charlie Bar" folds down horizontally and blocks movement of the sliding portion of the door. This type of locking device has the advantage of high visibility which may deter a potential intruder and is also easy to install.

A metal rod, a cut down hockey stick to a length of wooden doweling fitted snugly along the bottom of the door track, is an easy do-it-yourself method of preventing a patio door from being forced open.

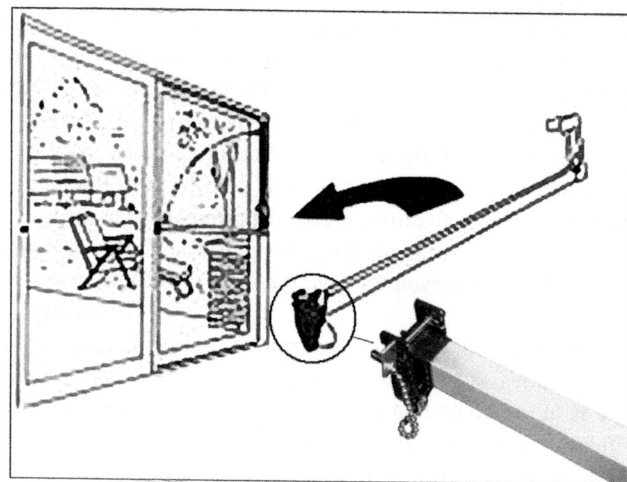

Auxiliary bolts, which operate with or without a key, can be installed at the top or bottom of patio door tracks. There are various types of patio door locks available with various secondary locks as well.

Pet doors—Convenient, but may be an easy point of entry for a burglar.

Garage doors—If you use an automatic door opener, change the code from the factory setting. When you go on vacations, disable the opener and place a padlock through the track.

Storm door—Offer minimal security protection. One cannot rely on for security unless they are reinforced with steel and deadbolt lock.

French or double doors—The first area of concern with double doors is to ensure that one door is braced to reduce the inward give of the doors. This leaves only one door active. You can make wooden doors stronger by fitting a steel strip and plates to the doorframe and around the lock. Fit bolts to the top and bottom of French doors.

- If the doors have glass panes then install long slide bolts at the top and bottom of the door that you are bracing.
- On the active door, install a jimmy proof deadbolt with a double cylinder. This lock not only secures the active door but also bolts the two doors snugly together.

Doors and doorframes

Make sure the doors and frames are strong and in good condition. Wooden doors should be solid and at least 44 mm (1.75″) thick. Fit deadlocks to all outside doors, including French doors. While all the exterior doors should have an equal resistance to forced entrance, the front door is the most important one to make secure.

It is the most obvious, usually the easiest to get to, and is the first one tried by a burglar. The quality of the door is equally as important as the lock installed. Steel doors or solid core wooden doors provide satisfactory resistance against forced entry. Any hollow core door should be replaced or at least reinforced by adding exterior grade plywood on the outside of the door.

A hollow core door is filled with corrugated cardboard and is easily broken through. The panel edge is the weak point in a stile, and rail door and should be reinforced with exterior grade plywood. A stile and rail door has stiles and rails as part of the face of the door; the remainder is composed of inset glass or wooden panels, which can easily be forced.

Exposed hinges

If the door opens outward, you must make sure that your exposed hinges are secured. If exposed hinge pins can be removed, an intruder can gain entry by swinging the door on the lock after prying open the single hinge.

- Ensure that your door is equipped with nonremovable hinge pins.
- Drill a matching hole in each hinge leaf or remove a matching screw from each. In one hole, insert a screw that is 1/2″ longer than the hole is deep. Cut off the screw head with a hacksaw so that when the door closes, the headless screws will fit into the hole on the opposite leaf and hold the door to the frame even with the hinge pins removed.
- Prevent the removal of the hinge pins by drilling a small hole into the hinge and inserting a small steel pin or screw to hold the pin.

Door viewers

Door viewers should have a field-of-view of 180 degrees. All exterior doors should have a door viewer unless there is a window for seeing who is outside the door before it is opened.

Crime Reduction Canada.

Exterior doors in commercial or business applications

- Should be numbered on the interior and exterior so they can be easily identified in the event of an emergency. Use clockwork numbering.
- Should have signage indicating whether the door is to be used for emergency exit, employee entrance, authorized personnel only, or directing all visitors to enter through a specific door. People accessing the building need to be directed to the appropriate door.

References: 1. Appendix X4 of ASTM F476-84 (Reapproved 1991) Standard Test Methods for Security of Swinging Door Assemblies; American Society for Testing and Materials/State Farm.

2. How to pick the right door lock for your home: doorhardware-onestop.com/html/picking_right_lock_for_home.htm

1 Appendix X4 of ASTM F476-84 (Reapproved 1991) Standard Test Methods for Security of Swinging Door Assemblies; American Society for Testing and Materials State Farm believes the information contained in the Disaster Survival House is reliable and accurate.

3. How To. . .Door Levers. . .Baldwin. . .Deadbolts. . .Amherst. . .Hinges
Expert Security Tips—Commercial Doors, Locks & Security
https://goldylocksinc.com/.../commercial/expert-security-tips

Source: 1Appendix X4 of ASTM F476-84 (Reapproved 1991) Standard Test Methods for Security of Swinging Door Assemblies; American Society for Testing and Materials. State Farm believes the information contained in the Learning Center is reliable and accurate.

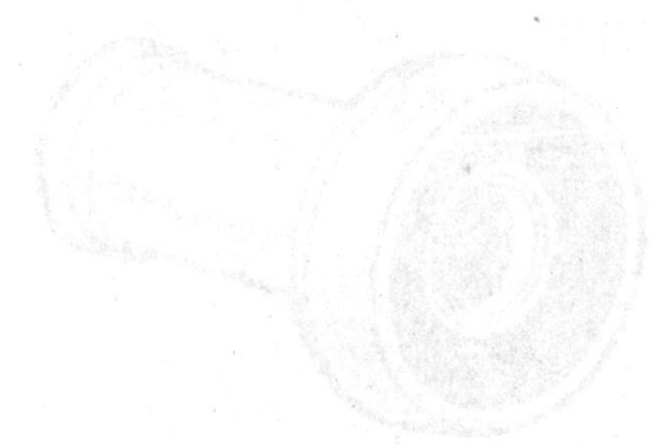

Chapter 41

Protective barriers and deterrents

Lawrence J. Fennelly
Security Consultant

Risk can not always be eliminated. Properly, however, it can usually be managed.

Risk Assessment Guidelines, General Security, ASIS International, 2003

Introduction

Protective barriers are used to define the physical limits of an installation, activity, or area. Barriers restrict, channel, or impede access and are fully integrated to form a continuous obstacle around the installation. They are designed to deter the worst case threat. The barriers should be focused on providing assets with an acceptable level of protection against a threat.

Overview

Protective barriers form the perimeter of controlled, limited, and exclusion areas. Utility areas (such as water sources, transformer banks, commercial power and fuel connections, heating and power plants, or air-conditioning units) may require these barriers for safety standards. Protective barriers consist of two major categories: natural and structural.

- Natural protective carriers are mountains and deserts, cliffs and ditches, water obstacles, or other terrain features that are difficult to traverse.
- Structural protective barriers are man-made devices (such as fences, walls, floors, roofs, grills, bars, roadblocks, signs, or other construction) used to restrict, channel, or impede access.

Barriers offer important benefits to a physical-security posture. They create a psychological deterrent for anyone thinking of unauthorized entry. They may delay or even prevent passage through them. This is especially true of barriers against forced entry and vehicles. Barriers have a direct impact on the number of security posts needed and on the frequency of use for each post.

Barriers cannot be designed for all situations. Considerations for protective structural barriers include the following:

- weighing the cost of completely enclosing large tracts of land with significant structural barriers against the threat and the cost of alternate security precautions (such as patrols, ground sensors, electronic surveillance, and airborne sensors) and
- sizing a restricted area based on the degree of compartmentalization required and the area's complexity

As a rule, size should be kept to a minimum consistent with operational efficiency. A restricted area's size may be driven by the likelihood of an aggressor's use of certain tactics. For example, protecting assets from a vehicle bomb often calls for a substantial explosives standoff distance. In these cases, mitigating the vehicle bomb would often be more important than minimizing the restricted area to the extent necessary for operational efficiency.

Protective barriers should be established for

- controlling vehicular and pedestrian traffic flow,
- providing entry control points where ID can be checked,
- precluding visual compromise by unauthorized individuals,
- delaying forced entry, and
- protecting individual assets.

Handbook of Loss Prevention and Crime Prevention. DOI: https://doi.org/10.1016/B978-0-12-817273-5.00041-7

If a secured area requires a limited or exclusion area on a temporary or infrequent basis, it may not be possible to use physical structural barriers. A temporary limited or exclusion area may be established where the lack of proper physical barriers is compensated for by additional security posts, patrols, and other security measures during the period of restriction. Temporary barriers (including temporary fences, coiled concertina wire, and vehicles) may be used. Barriers are not the only restrictive element, and they may not always be necessary. They may not be ideal when working with limited or exclusion areas or when integrated with other controls.

Because barriers can be compromised through breaching (cutting a hole through a fence) or by nature (berms eroded by the wind and rain), they should be inspected and maintained at least weekly. Guard-force personnel should look for deliberate breaches, holes in and under barriers, sand dunes building up against barriers, and the proper functioning of locks.

Perimeter entrances

Active perimeter entrances should be designated so that security forces maintain full control without an unnecessary delay in traffic. This is accomplished by having sufficient entrances to accommodate the peak flow of pedestrian and vehicular traffic and having adequate lighting for rapid and efficient inspection. When gates are not operational during nonduty hours, they should be securely locked, illuminated during hours of darkness, and inspected periodically by a roving patrol. Additionally, warning signs should be used to warn drivers when gates are closed. Doors and windows on buildings that form a part of the perimeter should be locked, lighted, and inspected.

Entry-control stations

Entry-control stations[1] should be provided at main perimeter entrances where security personnel are present. Considerations for construction and use should be based on the information outlined in USACE STD 872-90 series.

Entry-control stations should be located as close as practical to the perimeter entrance to permit personnel inside the station to maintain constant surveillance over the entrance and its approaches. Additional considerations at entry-control stations include

- Establishing a holding area for unauthorized vehicles or those to be inspected further. A turnaround area should be provided to keep from impeding other traffic.
- Establishing control measures such as displaying a decal on the window or having a specially marked vehicle.

Entry-control stations that are manned 24 hours each day should have interior and exterior lighting, interior heating (where appropriate), and a sufficient glassed area to afford adequate observation for personnel inside. Where appropriate, entry-control stations should be designed for optimum personnel ID and movement control. Each station should also include a telephone, a radio, and badge racks (if required).

Signs should be erected to assist in controlling authorized entry, to deter unauthorized entry, and to preclude accidental entry. Signs should be plainly displayed and be legible from any approach to the perimeter from a reasonable distance. The size and coloring of a sign, its letters, and the interval of posting must be appropriate to each situation.

Clear zone

Clear zones should be kept clear of weeds, rubbish, or other material capable of offering concealment or assistance to an intruder attempting to breach the barrier. A clear zone of 20 ft or more should exist between the perimeter barrier and exterior structures, parking areas, and natural or man-made features. When possible, a clear zone of 50 ft or more should exist between the perimeter barrier and structures within the protected area, except when a building's wall constitutes part of the perimeter barrier. Ammunition supply points (ASPs) will have clear zones 12 ft outside of the ASP and 30 ft inside, and the vegetation will not exceed 8 in. (4 in. for high-threat and highly controlled areas). Refer to AR 190-11 and DOD 0-2000.12-H, Appendix EE, for further information (Fig. 41.1).

Entry-control stations should be hardened against attacks according to the type of threat. The methods of hardening may include

- reinforced concrete or masonry;
- steel plating;

1. https://www.globalsecurity.org/military/library/policy/army/fm/3-19-30/ch4.htm.

FIGURE 41.1 Photo Marianna Perry, CPP, reflects Bollard protecting the side of a building.

- bullet-resistant glass;
- sandbags, two layers in depth; and
- commercially fabricated, bullet-resistant building components or assemblies.

Internal barriers

Have you ever watched a trespasser come into a building? He walks slowly, he looks around, and his eyes go right and left. He is 8 ft into your lobby and sees the turnstile and realizes he has been denied access. So he proceeds to the security desk with a simple question of employment.

Barriers are psychological deterrents allowing unauthorized access. Turnstiles and access control are physical barriers that control entry points and complement your security program and your security officers.

Functions of structural and/or natural barriers are as follows:

1. *Define* protection area boundaries.
2. *Delay*—slow traffic or access. Consider speed bumps.
3. *Direct* access to garages, parking lots, and building entrances.
4. *Deny* unauthorized access and allow only authorized visitors.

Designing security and layout of site

Designing security into a new or renovated complex can begin with the exterior or interior. Since we are discussing protective barriers in this chapter, let us assume we started the layout discussion on the outside.

Your main lines of defense are your perimeter barriers or the outer edge to your property line. The second line of defense is the exterior of the building, which includes the roof and roof access and walls, doors, and windows. Remember to eliminate all but essential doors and windows. If this is not done in early stages, they will have to be alarmed and set up as emerging exits. Also included should be adequate lighting (cost-effective) that meets standard and supports exterior closed-circuit TV (CCTV). The third line of defense is the interior. It is important to reduce access points by using access control and have specific areas zoned for access control and added security.

Passive structural barriers

1. Jersey barriers
2. Large boulders or rocks
3. Large round cement stones
4. Road blocks or closed roads
5. Fences
6. Gates
7. Bollards at entrances

Active structural barriers

1. Hydraulic bollards
2. Motor-operated lift-arm gates
3. Pop-up wedges
4. All geared to control traffic for entrances and exits

Barrier planning

When planning a perimeter barrier, the following should be taken into account:

- Walls are usually more expensive than fences, observation enclosures, and a Network Video System (CCTV), and exterior cost-effective lighting. Opaque fences may provide a cheaper alternative.
- Fences and walls provide only limited delay against intruders; the least secure types can only delay a skilled intruder for a few seconds. A perimeter barrier intended to provide substantial protection against intruders should therefore combine a fence or wall with security lighting, an intruder detection system, a network video system (CCTV), and a security guard forces.
- The perimeter should be as short as possible and illuminated.
- The perimeter should run in straight lines between corner posts to facilitate surveillance.
- Drains or culverts giving access beneath the perimeter barrier should be protected.
- The ground on both sides of the perimeter barrier should be cleared to deny cover to an intruder.
- Emergency gates may be required to prove safe evacuation routes.
- A sterile zone protected by a double fence may be required for certain types of intruder-detection sensors.
- A security guard force should support the perimeter security system.
- Exterior emergency phones connected to security officer's desk.
- Barriers are deterrents. They come in a variety of acceptable sizes and shapes.

Fence standards

The perimeter should have a fence or wall that meets the requirements of local planning and licensing authorities while remaining an effective deterrent against intruders. As a guide, any fence less than 7 ft high is unlikely to do more than demarcate a boundary.

Generally, the basic perimeter fence should have concrete fence posts with three strands of barbwire at the top. The barbwire should be at a 45 degree angle pointing upward and outward. The foot tall chain-link fences should be embedded in a concrete curb in the ground that slants away on both sides from the fence to shed water and be burned deep enough to prevent burrowing.

Where local factors require an enhanced level of security, antiintruder fencing is recommended to a height of 7 ft with razor or barbwire at the top. The base of the fence should be embedded as previously described.

Where the value of the protected side is particularly high and there is known risk (such as terrorist attack), consideration should be given to augmenting the selected fence with security lighting, Network Video System (CCTV), an intruder detection system, and a security guard force.

Types of security fences

The following fences are available for security use and are listed in ascending order of their effectiveness against intrusion:

- Industrial security chain-link fence.
- Standard antiintruder chain-link fence.
- Standard steel palisade fence, security pattern standard expanded metal (Expamet) security fence.
- High-security steel palisade fence.
- Power fencing. This is similar to cattle fencing in which it will give an electric shock to anything touching it. This type of fencing is generally safe to use around hydrocarbon sites, but the manufacturer's advice should be sought on its exact deployment. Power fencing sends an alarm when touched, thus making it a barrier with intruder detection. It is also good to use above walls in high-risk areas on domestic properties.

- Palisade fences are more expensive than chain-link fences but have better potential upgrading to increase effectiveness against intruders and for the addition of fence-mounted intrusion detection sensors. Galvanized palisade fences have a much longer life than chain-link fences, Expamet, or weld-mesh fences. The high-security fences are significantly more effective against intruders than the other fences.

Deterrents

By definition—"Serving to Deter Relating to deterrence"[2]

Category A

- security surveillance system used to prevent crime in private and public locations
- CPTED principles and concepts
- defensible space principles and concepts
- situational crime prevention principles and concepts
- lighting that meets standards and design by increased visibility
- biometrics and access control to specific areas
- CPTED design
- CPTED landscape principles
- signage or visible security signs
- padlocks and door locks and peepholes
- intrusion alarms and signage of alarm
- security surveillance systems (CCTV)
- security awareness programs
- planters and thorny bushes, and barbwire on top of fences
- bollards or barricades closing down streets.
- barking dog, inside or outside
- vehicle in driveway
- area traffic and escape route available
- policy and procedures
- training programs
- metal detectors

Category B

- Security officers armed and unarmed in private function, that is, hotel door man, bus drivers, tickets sellers or ticket takers, conductors.
- Police officers in uniform and armed security who may deduce that a crime is about to be committed and deter the incident in their presence.
- Security officer patrolling the parking lots of hotels, hospitals and retail locations, protecting corporate assets and customer protection.
- Guardian angels patrolling streets, neighborhoods, and subways.
- People in the area

Crime displacement theory by target hardening and soft target moving to another *location*.
Category C
Guard shacks if occupied are a deterrent.
CPTED strategies

1. natural access control
2. natural surveillance
3. territorial reinforcement (Crowe 1999)
4. environmental maintenance and image

Defensible space—This concept was developed in the public housing environment. It is similar to CPTED strategies (Crowe 1999).

2. Fennelly, L.J., Perry, M., 2017. Physical Security—150 Things You Should Know, second ed. Butterworth-Heinemann, Boston, MA, p. 103.

Environmental security differs from CPTED in which it uses a broader range of crime control strategies including social management, social media, target hardening activity support, and low enforcement.

CPTED landscape principles:

1. For natural surveillance but back bushes to a height of 3 ft.
2. Cut back the tree branches to 8 ft from the ground.
3. Chain-link fence height 8 ft plus three strands of barbed wire.
4. Height of a stone wall—8 ft.
5. A least 10 ft of clear space both sides of the fence and wall.[3]

Situation crime prevention incorporates other crime prevention and law enforcement strategies in an effort to focus on place-specific crime problems.

Results and objectives:

- reduce violent crime
- reduce property crime
- displacement of crime
- eliminate the threats and risk
- reduce the likelihood of more incidents
- eliminate vulnerabilities and protect assets.
- padlocks (case harden) and door locks and peepholes
- intrusion Alarms System and Signage of Alarm
- security surveillance systems, a network video system (CCTV)
- security awareness programs
- planters and thorny bushes, and barbwire on top of fences
- bollards or barricades closing down streets.
- barking dog, inside or outside
- vehicle in driveway
- area traffic and escape route available
- policy and Procedures

  Risk Management is defined[4] as the process by which an entity identifies its potential losses and then decides what is the best way to manage these potential losses.
- Risk: Exposure to possible loss (i.e., fire, natural disasters, product obsolescence, shrinkage, and work stoppages).
- Security managers are primarily interested in crime, shrinkage, accidents, and crises.
- Risk managers generally are more focused on fire and safety issues.
- Pure risk: Risk in which there are no potential benefits to be derived (i.e., earthquake and flood)
- Dynamic risk: Risk that can produce gain or profit (i.e., theft and embezzlement)
- Possible maximum loss: Maximum loss sustained if a target is *totally destroyed.*
- Probable maximum loss: Amount of loss a target is *likely to sustain.*

Conclusion

Keep in mind that structural barriers physically and psychologically deter and discourage the undetermined, delay the determined, and channel the traffic flow through entrances. Fences and walls provide only limited delay against intruders; the least secure types can only delay a skilled intruder for a few seconds. A perimeter barrier intended to provide substantial protection against intruders should, therefore, combine a fence or wall with security lighting, an intruder detection system, a Network Video System (CCTV), and a security guard forces.

Further reading

FM 3-19.30 Field Manual Department of Army, Protective Barriers, Chapter 4, Section 4-1. March 1, 1979 and 2001.

Fennelly, L.J., Perry, M., 2017. Physical Security—150 Things You Should Know., second ed. Butterworth-Heinemann, Boston, MA.

Fennelly, L.J., 2017. Effective Physical Security, fifth ed. Butterworth-Heinemann, Boston, MA.

3. Broder, J.F., 2006. CPP Risk Analysis and the Security Survey, third edition. Elsevier.
4. Broder, J.F., 2006. CPP Risk Analysis and the Security Survey, third edition. Elsevier.

Chapter 42

Planning, management, and evaluation*

Charles M. Girard†

Effective crime prevention communications make people feel both responsible and competent in respect of a given issue.[1]

Introduction

Every law enforcement and corporate security official uses the tools of planning, management, and evaluation. For example, a patrol officer plans how to cover a beat, makes rounds or manages activities, and evaluates how he or she did at the end of the day. An officer plans what to do and how to do it before taking any action. Unfortunately, this same approach is not consistently applied in police agencies and security operations as a whole. In fact, although a certain degree of planning is usually conducted by all prevention organizations, the major emphasis has traditionally been on the management and evaluation of an officer's work; every sergeant knows to manage a police force in such a way that the commander will conclude that he or she is doing a good job.

The major purpose of the discussion that follows is to provide crime prevention and security personnel information about planning, management, and evaluation so that they can take advantage of these tools in performing their jobs.

The concepts defined

Planning

One of the most effective tools available to a crime-prevention unit is planning. Police and security authorities across the country have come to recognize the importance of this tool as a critical factor on which the ultimate effectiveness of operations depends. Although total agreement does not exist as to the most effective planning method, there is general agreement that planning should be regarded as an indispensable function. Unfortunately, although a certain degree of planning is carried out in all police and security operations, neither the substance nor level of intensity of the process has been sufficiently systematized to realize its full potential.

One possible reason for the limited application of planning as a management tool within such organizations is the false jargon that frequently surrounds the concept. As a means of avoiding this pitfall, therefore, *planning* for the purposes of this discussion is defined as

> *An activity concerned with proposals for the future, the evaluation of alternative proposals, and the methods to achieve such proposals.*

It must be further noted that a good plan is considered the one that, within the bounds of reason, best suits the situation.

Defined in this sense, planning is rational and adaptive thought is applied to the future and to matters over which crime prevention and security officers have a certain degree of control. Further, by using this definition, planning is placed in a framework of organizational reality so that it can be used as a tool to assist in program implementation.

*Originally from Girard, G. Understanding crime prevention. Boston, MA: Butterworth-Heinemann; 2001. Updated by the editor, Elsevier, 2019.

†Deceased

1. https://www.cardiff.ac.uk/crime-security-research-institute/publications/research-briefings/behavioural-crime-prevention-using-nudges,-tugs-and-teachable-moments-in-crime-prevention-communications

Handbook of Loss Prevention and Crime Prevention. DOI: https://doi.org/10.1016/B978-0-12-817273-5.00042-9

Management

This somewhat hackneyed term is generally construed to mean planning, organizing, and controlling the work of oneself or others. There are, of course, a variety of approaches to management. One type has been termed the *art of muddling through* and is sometimes referred to as *seat-of-the-pants* management. An example of this type of management is the crime-prevention officer who comes into the office in the morning with no plan of action other than to respond to whoever or whatever makes the loudest noise first, whether that is a demand from the chief's office, a request to make a security survey, or a request from a police administration student to respond to a lengthy questionnaire on the *modus operandi* of the crime-prevention bureau.

Another approach to management is more systematic in nature and has been termed *management by objectives and results.* Through this technique an organization's intended results are defined in advance and the program steps required to achieve such results are clearly outlined.

In reality, neither type of management approach is practiced consistently by any one individual or organization. Further, it is unrealistic to suggest that the day-to-day pressures of crime-prevention and security programs can be put aside to accommodate a truly systematic and inflexible approach that calls for all actions to be based on well-thought-out strategies. Nonetheless, crime prevention and security units can be expected to draw from the *management by objectives* approach to improve the implementation of their programs and to design and execute their activities within a framework responsive to local and corporate needs.

Evaluation

Police and security administrators have long felt a need to determine the effectiveness of operating activities. Each year, as fewer dollars become available, combined with increasing public outcries for more and better services and corporate demand for decreased shrinkage and loss, the desire to weed out programs that are deadwood continues to grow. To assist police officials to assess project effectiveness and develop information that can be used in the competition for dollars, the National Advisory Commission on Law Enforcement Standards and Goals, in its report, "A National Strategy to Reduce Crime," urged that evaluation be made an integral part of all projects. The commission further pointed out that the use of this concept would identify what works and what does not in dealing with crime problems.

Unfortunately, although the guidelines, mandates, and directives as to how evaluation should be instituted and operated have been set forth at the highest levels of government and organization, implementation at the grassroots levels has been inconsistent and, in many cases, ineffective. As a result, evaluation has often been looked at from a negative standpoint and serves as an audit of program activities, rather than a positive tool to improve and refocus ongoing project efforts. The discussion that follows emphasizes the latter perspective and couples evaluation with the planning and management approaches discussed previously. As such, the definition used to describe *evaluation* is

The process of determining the value of the amount of success in achieving predetermined goals and objectives.

Planning, management, and evaluation—associates in a dynamic process

As pointed out earlier, planning can serve as the basis on which program directions are identified. If this is done, programs can subsequently be managed and evaluated in relation to stated targets. Fig. 42.1 illustrates the component parts of the planning, management, and evaluation process.

In embarking on this process, initial activities should focus on examining the situation for which solutions are being sought to determine the most appropriate strategies to deal with identified problems. When alternative program approaches are examined or tried and objectives set, with the least feasible or workable discarded, the evaluation process is in effect. Notably, nothing is wrong with altering a plan after evaluating its utility. In fact, that is the purpose of the entire process. When this approach is utilized, measurement strategies and monitoring approaches can be designed to consider whether a project or approach is having the desired effect on the targeted problem.

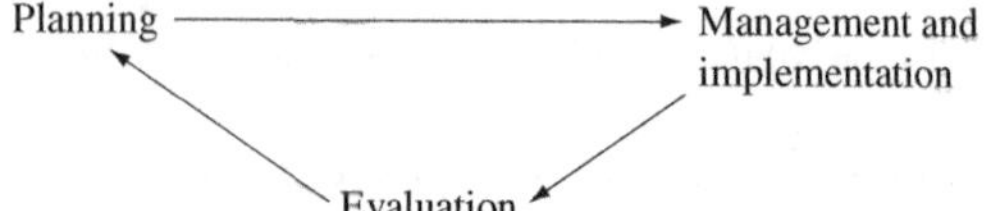

FIGURE 42.1 The planning and evaluation cycle.

It is important to remember that management, planning, and evaluation do not provide rules that dictate action or guarantee positive results. Their main purpose is to provide a sound base for decision making and program implementation. Intuition and experience are not enough to decide what course to follow. Moreover, planning, management, and evaluation within a security or crime-prevention operation can be used to

- clarify purposes,
- organize relevant information,
- generate alternatives,
- offer early information on important positive and negative aspects of programs so that appropriate action can be taken,
- provide direction and purpose to the security or crime-prevention unit, and
- ensure that the unit's overall efforts are less crisis oriented.

Statistical information: the backbone for design of a prevention program

Various types of data are used for similar as well as different purposes in the design, management, and evaluation of a crime-prevention program. For example, crime statistics are essential to the design of a program, provide an ongoing perspective as to program accomplishments during a specified period, and are key indicators to judge the overall success of the program. Demographic data, however, are most valuable in the design and evaluation phases of the project.

Fortunately, all data required need not be collected at the same time or at an identical level of detail. That is, the process of data collection and maintenance should parallel the overall implementation of a crime-prevention or security program. For example, at the outset of the project, it will be necessary to gather as much crime data and demographic information as is reasonably accessible. Efforts to maintain such data over the project, however, fluctuate; that is, as work is undertaken, crime statistics have to be monitored, but demographic data no longer need be gathered and analyzed.

Moreover, the following discussion provides insights as to such subjects regarding data:

- When to collect the information and why
- What information should be aggregated
- Where such data are generally available
- Time periods for which the information should be organized
- How to organize and maintain information to facilitate its use

To assist in the preparation and maintenance of the information, the discussion is organized in much the same manner as program implementation takes place. Program design is the first topic of consideration. The elements of program management and evaluation are then discussed.

Two specific types of data are critical to the design of security and crime-prevention programs: crime statistics and demographic data.

Crime statistics

Detailed information that pinpoints the types and locations of the crime problems of a jurisdiction or organization is the key to the design of a prevention program. The following focuses on such statistics. Because burglary is becoming a crime of epidemic proportion in this country, the outline of data elements relates directly to that crime. In those instances where a jurisdiction or organization is also interested in robbery, shoplifting, and the like, similar types of data about those crime types have to be pulled together for program design purposes.

When to collect data and why

Crime statistics must be gathered as a first step in the design of a prevention program. In addition, they have to be maintained throughout the program. In fact, they should be maintained on a daily basis and summarized monthly.

This information serves as a baseline for designing, managing, and evaluating the program. In addition, these data provide useful detail for inclusion in speeches, news stories, briefing memorandums, and so on.

What data to gather

The following data elements should be considered essential in the design of a burglary prevention program. The degree to which a particular organization can gather such data, of course, depends on the nature of existing records systems. The essential elements include the following:

- *Location of occurrence.* Beats, districts, census tracts, and the exact location of crimes being analyzed should be gathered. This information is valuable in identifying program target areas.
- *Date of occurrence.* The day, month, and year of incidents, or reporting dates if exact dates are not known, should be analyzed. These dates indicate whether particular crimes are related to seasonal patterns, weekly community habits, and so forth; for example, shoplifting increases during the Christmas holidays, and on weekends, large numbers of people might get out of town in some sites or plant operations might close down, thus enhancing burglar opportunities. This information is useful in formulating strategies to deal with the crime.
- *Time of occurrence.* The exact time of occurrence, when known (or morning, afternoon, evening, when a range of time is given) should be analyzed. This information is helpful to the prevention unit in terms of making personnel allocation plans.
- *Category of premises.* Information concerning whether residences, businesses, or other structural categories are being victimized should be aggregated. These data should further be broken down by the specific types of premise: single family, apartment, jewelry store, variety store, office complex, warehouse, and so on. This information is helpful in the design of public information, patrol, and target-hardening strategies.
- *How entry was made.* Record what was done to get inside the facility. This might include whether force was used, a door or window had been left open and was utilized, a lock or alarm system was defeated to gain entry, and so forth. These data are valuable to the formulation of public information and target-hardening strategies.
- *Type of property taken.* Information on the types of items taken, such as money, sound equipment, or office equipment, should be developed. Keep such accountings general in nature. This information is helpful in the design of target-hardening strategies; for example, it might be used to indicate what items need to be marked through the operation-identification program.
- *Property identification.* Record whether property taken was identified with special markings, such as driver's license number. In addition, note whether operation identification or alarm and security warning devices (stickers) were prominently displayed at various building entrances. This is valuable in terms of designing a program as well as evaluating its impact.
- *Dollar amount taken.* Record the total reported dollar loss of all items taken. These data can be used to help analyze the impact of the program; for example, dollar value loss before and after the implementation of a program.
- *Property damage resulting from entry.* Note the dollar losses in property damage resulting from the crime. This information can be utilized to evaluate the impact of the program; for example, dollar loss through property damage before and after the implementation of a program.
- *How the incident was reported.* Gather data on who detected and reported the crime, such as a neighbor, employee, police, alarm, or victim. This is useful in designing a program: Crime-prevention programs are theoretically designed to increase citizen and employee participation and reporting/baseline statistics have to be developed to see if this actually happens.

In addition to the preceding data elements, other items may be useful in the design, monitoring, and evaluation of a program. However, they should be considered optional. They may, nonetheless, be gathered if time is available, if the reporting systems used by the organization include the items, if information is available through a computer/data-processing system, and so on. As such, each unit has to consider its own situation to determine whether the following items should be gathered. Such items include the following:

- *Point of entry.* Record where entry was made, such as door, window, or air vent.
- *Occupancy status.* Record whether premises were occupied when the reported crime occurred.
- *Instrument used to gain entry.* Data on the kind of tool or instrument used, such as screwdriver, pry bar, or saw should be gathered.
- *Street and exterior lights.* In the case of crimes occurring at night, note the existence of street and exterior lights.
- *Point of entry lighting.* For nighttime crimes, record the existence of lights at point of entry.
- *Visibility at points of entry.* Record whether the point of entry was visible to patrolling units.
- *Alarm systems.* Record whether the alarm was activated, defeated, and so forth.
- *When detected.* Record whether the crime was detected while in progress, on the day of occurrence, next day, and so forth.

Where data can be found

A police prevention unit should not gather and tabulate raw data, except in specific short-term instances. Available resources simply do not allow for such an approach. Therefore the unit must rely on others to provide information. The police divisions, depicted in Fig. 42.2, are among the more common suppliers of information that can be used by a prevention unit. Unfortunately, this might not be the case in private security operations. So, private sector security units may also have to gather and tabulate raw data to ensure the effectiveness of their program planning and design process.

The nature of the reports that may be provided by such divisions and are important to the development of a comprehensive crime database are presented in Table 42.1.

Notably, the information to be extracted from such reports is not prepared primarily for analysis purposes. That is, the information is an accounting of each agency's activity or is designed to aid in the apprehension and prosecution of violations. Nonetheless, it is necessary to make the best of what exists. To help with this task a few comments as to the most relevant records to use in pulling together the preceding data elements follow:

- *Initial crime reports (offense report).* The basic written record that should be employed in gathering data is the offense report. This report contains a great deal of information valuable to a prevention unit. For example, data concerning location, victim, suspect, evidence, witness, *modus operandi*, and so forth, are included in such reports.
- *Follow-up or supplemental reports.* These reports are usually narrative in nature and add information to that collected during the initial investigation. Reports may come from patrol, detective, or special units. Such reports often consist of different categories and information, including changes in the crime classification, case disposition, and evidence information, from that which appeared in the initial crime report. They may also provide the crime-prevention unit with data elements missing from the initial crime report.

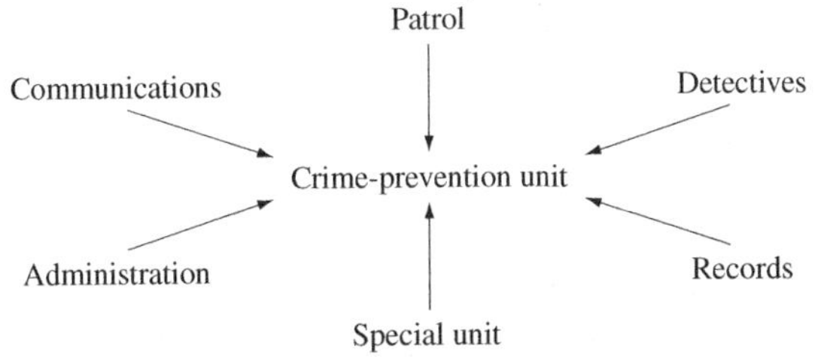

FIGURE 42.2 Crime-prevention unit information sources within a traditional police agency.

TABLE 42.1 Example source reports by division.

Division	Reports supplied
Communications	Complaint-dispatch report NCIC/state crime data Teletype reports and requests
Patrol	Initial crime report Follow-up crime report Crime against person report Crime against property report Stolen vehicle reports
Special Units	Any of the patrol or detective reports Special crime reports Crime intelligence reports
Records	Statistical data Special crime data
Administration	Statistical data Special crime data

- *Complaint-dispatch reports and operational logs*. In some instances, these reports are useful. Their utility, however, varies with the nature of the report form. For example, if a program is conceived to focus on bicycle theft and this item is accounted for on such reports, it will be necessary to review these documents at the outset of the project. In addition, they would have to be monitored throughout the project period unless a special arrangement is made. Moreover, the review of these documents should depend on the time and resources available and the specific nature of a program.

Time period to be considered

As noted, it is unlikely that data of this nature are readily available for any particular period. In fact, it is an unusual circumstance if this occurs in any agency. Hence, prevention staff members have to develop such information in relation to time periods meaningful to the design, management, and evaluation phases of the program. At a minimum, such data should be developed for the 1-year period preceding the calendar year during which the project is to be undertaken. If time permits, a 2-year breakdown should be developed.

How to organize data

A variety of indicators or data elements can be employed to gain an understanding of crime within a community or corporation. Analyzing this information and developing conclusions relative to specific prevention programs is a more complicated matter. One acceptable method for breaking data into meaningful units for review and program design is geographical analysis. The basis of such an analysis is a graphic presentation of crime patterns within a community, for example, census tracts and beats or corporate complex. Notably, prior to deciding what subarea breakdown to use, it would be advisable to determine how the demographic (census) data in the community are maintained. The crime information should be maintained in relation to the geographic and socioeconomic databases available.

The collection of crime data on this basis is important for a number of reasons:

1. It illustrates what the community's crime profile looks like.
2. The data allow for contrasts to be made among various subsections of the community to identify the severity of the crime throughout the jurisdiction.
3. Subarea analysis points out the exact nature of the particular problem in each area; for example, burglary of apartments versus burglary of single-family residences may be a problem in a residential area.
4. Aggregating data in this manner helps determine whether a concentrated (narrow and focused) or general (broad and multifaceted) program should be implemented.

Demographic data

Every prevention officer has a basic understanding of the nature of that particular community or organization and its physical, socioeconomic, and demographic characteristics. The nature and use of related data may, however, be a mystery. Some of the more significant data elements relating to the socioeconomic conditions of a community follow. A brief explanation of how each type of information might be used to develop a burglary prevention program is also presented.

When to collect data and why

Demographic information must be gathered at the outset of a project. Additional information of this nature need not be aggregated after the overall prevention program is designed.

This information is used in the design of the overall prevention program from a number of perspectives. On the one hand, it is valuable to the development of the public information strategies to be designed for use in particular areas of the community. On the other hand, the data, when analyzed in conjunction with crime statistics, are useful in targeting program approaches within the community. As such, these factors relate to the impact the crime-prevention program will have on the community:

- *Population for city and selected subdivisions by sex and age*. This information can be used to help identify portions of the community with groups of potential offenders (e.g., young men).
- *Median education levels for city and selected subareas*. This information can provide a perspective on how sophisticated the techniques or materials to be used to describe or promote a program need to be understood by potential users.

- *Non–English speaking persons by native language for city and selected subareas.* This information can be used to help prepare public education materials if such items accompany the projects to be undertaken.
- *Median rental costs for city and selected subareas.* This information provides insight as to the type of security improvements that might be suggested in such units.

Where data can be found

Census data are not traditionally maintained by law-enforcement agencies or private corporations. In some instances, however, various divisions in these organizations may have gathered such information to develop a financial or marketing plan, design a personnel allocation plan, and so forth. Therefore efforts should be made to check with the chief administrator's office, planning and research division, and the marketing division.

If such information is not available in the detail needed, prevention staff members must go to other departments within the city government or outside the local government structure. For example, information concerning the physical, social, economic, and demographic environment of the community is available from the following agencies: city, county, or regional planning departments; libraries; school districts; colleges and universities; chambers of commerce; and civic organizations.

Time period to be considered

Data of this nature are available through the US Census Department on the basis of 10-year intervals, that is, 1990–2000 or 2000–10. For prevention program design, it will be advisable to get only the data for the 10 years preceding the most current date, such as 2010–20. In addition, these various departments and agencies may have prepared special studies regarding such topics since the conduct of the national census.

How to organize data

Information of the type noted is generally maintained in terms of geographic subsections of communities. The key point to remember when gathering such data is that areas selected for census data analysis should be identical to those for which crime data were gathered. (As suggested earlier, every effort should be made to develop crime data on a geographical basis to avoid problems in data comparison.)

Efficiency analysis: measuring activity

Three types of data are important if prevention programs are to be monitored and evaluated. The first is efficiency analysis data. Measures of efficiency are used to judge and document the amount of prevention program activity that takes place in relation to stated goals, objectives, and strategies. As such, this measure represents an assessment of energy, regardless of impact.

When to collect data and why

Data regarding program activity should be gathered from the outset of a prevention effort. In addition, such information should be carefully maintained throughout the program on a daily basis. It should be summarized monthly.

This information answers such questions as, What did the prevention unit do? and to a lesser extent, How well was the work performed? As such, it is valuable in managing and evaluating the program and reporting program results to various officials within and outside the organization.

What data to gather

The exact nature of the data elements to be gathered and maintained depends on the thrust and focus of particular prevention programs. A few examples of data elements that reflect activity include the numbers of

- crime-prevention brochures distributed and time spent;
- security surveys conducted and time spent;
- generalized speeches given, number in attendance, and time spent;

- special presentations made, number in attendance, and time spent (neighborhood security, commercial, rape, and the like, and broken down by type);
- crime-prevention in-service training sessions held, number of officers or employees involved, and time spent;
- crime patterns identified through the analysis of data and time spent; and
- special projects conducted that focus on the achievement of program goals and objectives, including number participating and time spent.

How to organize and maintain data

The organization and maintenance of the information will be largely a matter of personal preference among prevention organizations. The following approaches, which focus on ensuring that the data are readily accessible and, therefore, *useable*, might be considered:

- *Time reports* can be constructed to include information regarding time spent conducting security surveys, time spent preparing public speeches, time spent training employees, and so on.
- *Tally sheets, activity logs, or card files* can be used to document the number of each type of a specific activity (e.g., 18 security surveys, 4 speeches, and 5 special presentations were conducted during November). Notably, other pertinent information, such as how many people attended, should be included in the record.

An additional means to organize and maintain data for ease of retrieval might also be considered. For illustrative purposes a hypothetical prevention unit consisting of three officers is used. Because of this limited personnel, it becomes crucial to utilize an easily maintainable analysis system in relation to the various projects being implemented. One of these projects might focus on the conduct of security surveys to reduce burglary. The analysis form in Fig. 42.3 may be used to summarize information the unit can develop to identify where burglaries are occurring, the time of occurrence, and method of entry. The tabulation sheet can also be used to indicate when a survey is offered to a particular resident, whether it was accepted, and if a repeat burglary occurred at that address or location.

As is evident from a review of this form, the primary indexing technique is the street number/name reference. Through this form, even a small unit can pinpoint where surveys are needed and whether additional violations have occurred at sites where such surveys have been provided. Thus it can determine the success of this approach.

During the daily review of offense reports a prevention analyst can examine the initial crime reports, indexed by street name, to log new offenses and determine if repeat burglaries have occurred where surveys have been offered and either turned down or carried through. If a burglary has occurred where a survey was turned down, the victim can be recontacted for a survey. If the crime occurs where a survey was completed, the victim can also be recontacted to be offered additional advice provided in the security analysis. If, after a predetermined period (i.e., 1 year), no report burglaries have occurred at survey sites, conclusions may be drawn about the target-hardening values of this crime-prevention approach.

Effectiveness analysis: measuring program impact

The second type of measure concerns program effectiveness. This measure is used to evaluate the impact of program activities on an identified problem. Indicators used should be end oriented and relate to what is to be ultimately achieved as defined by program goals, objectives, and strategies, not the *way* in which things are to be achieved. As such, these measures assess the result of an effort rather than the effort itself.

Street number or name	Initial report	Date of burglary	Time of burglary	Method of entry			Survey offered	Action performed	Repeat burglary
				Open	Locked	Force			

FIGURE 42.3 Illustrative residential burglary analysis form.

When to collect data and why

The development and maintenance of impact statistics should be undertaken at two specific times. First, as part of the program design phase, a variety of crime statistics are documented that, in fact, serve as impact or effectiveness indicators—burglary rate, value of property stolen, and so on. Thus a good portion of the work begins at the outset of any project. Monitoring the crime statistics selected as impact indicators in relation to program goals and objectives, of course, has to be continued on a systematic basis throughout the project, preferably daily, and summarized monthly.

Second, due to the nature of the goals and objectives of a prevention program, new impact statistics might have to be developed. For example, if calls for service in a particular area where a neighborhood awareness strategy is to be used provide one type of effectiveness indicator, the unit has a twofold responsibility. On the one hand, staff members must go back at least one calendar year prior to beginning the project and documenting the number of calls for service. On the other hand, as soon as the neighborhood program kicked off, they would have to begin monitoring and recording the calls for service in the area to draw some conclusion regarding the work performed; for example, whether the calls increased as a result of program implementation.

In short the degree to which additional data collection is required to evaluate the program impact depends on two factors: the scope of the crime statistics data gathered and the unique nature of the program or need to select specific indicators due to program goals, objectives, and strategies.

Impact data has a number of uses throughout the implementation of the program:

- indicating program results,
- satisfying various reporting requirements,
- strengthening the public information program by documenting actual results, and
- providing staff members an understanding of what their efforts actually produced.

What data to gather

The exact nature of the data elements to be gathered and maintained depends on the thrust and focus of particular prevention programs as defined in program goals, objectives, and strategies. A few examples of data elements that reflect effectiveness follow. Remember, however, that the nature of a particular program may require factors other than those presented.

- an absolute reduction or alteration in the incidence of particular crimes prevention programs are designed to affect (burglary, shoplifting, etc.),
- an increase in the number of thwarted burglary attempts (resulting from the use of improved security hardware, posted signs, or sticker information about the existence of an alarm),
- reduced victimization among persons participating in various crime-prevention activities (e.g., property marketing programs, implementation of security survey recommendations, and neighborhood watch programs),
- an increase in the return of stolen property among persons participating in property marking programs,
- a decrease in the dollar value of property lost due to selected crimes (e.g., burglary, stolen credit cards, and bad checks), and
- an increase in the calls for service in areas where concentrated citizen awareness efforts have been initiated.

How to organize and maintain data

Generally, the organization of these data parallels that of the crime statistics, which is geographical in nature. Numerous methods may be used to maintain the data. The one selected should be a matter of personal preference. That is, it should be understood by all those involved with its use, it should be easy to maintain, and it should provide adequate detail with a minimum amount of effort. A number of appropriate methods are outlined already with regard to activity data—tally sheets, logs, special forms. In addition, a unit may wish to use these methods to keep track of the program's impact:

- *Mapping analysis techniques*. This approach uses a variety of maps, including pin maps, dot maps, or other means of depicting the actual geographic location of a particular criminal event. For example, a pin map displaying the actual location of day or night residential burglaries over a given period of time could be useful in designing and monitoring crime-prevention efforts.

- *Graphic analysis methods*. Rather than employing maps of a particular jurisdiction, comparisons based on statistical analysis of crimes may be presented on various types of graphs. For example, a bar graph representing percentage figures for a particular crime category, such as residential burglary, for different beats, districts, or census tracts within a given period of time provides a visual representation of reported crime by geographic area.

Regardless of the method employed, it is important that it be easy to use, understand, and maintain. Methods that do not meet these requirements should be abandoned in favor of aids that are more functional. Remember, the goal is to implement crime-prevention programs; do not get too involved in the preparation and maintenance of evaluation aids or they will become nuisances instead of tools.

Attitudinal analysis: gathering opinions on the program impact

The third type of evaluation indicators is opinion measures. These are measures of whether the unit is actually satisfying client/public expectations. In other words, they measure whether the program is doing the right thing according to those receiving services. This type of evaluation is based on the attitude of those who received services from or participated in a prevention program.

When to collect data and why

Such information should be collected during two specific time periods. Some attitude information should be gathered immediately following a crime-prevention unit's actions; for example, presentation of a speech or special program. In addition, the unit should collect this type of data after the public has been exposed to the program over time; for example, after radio spots or specialized information programs have been used for at least 3 months.

This information is useful for at least two reasons: first, the information can be used by the unit to help judge whether its activities are meeting client needs. As such, the measures serve as a management tool. Second, findings of this nature serve as objective testimonials from the community on the impact of the program. Such findings can, thus, provide valuable input to the public information program as well as the evaluation element of a crime-prevention project.

What data to gather

The exact nature of the data to gather depends on the particular elements of the crime-prevention analyzed. A few examples of data that can be used as indicators of program effectiveness follow. Remember, however, specific factors have to be decided on when evaluating each unique program goal, objective, and strategy. Some examples of questions that produce effectiveness indicators from persons who have received direct crime-prevention services from unit personnel (i.e., have received security surveys and utilized Operation ID hardware) follow:

1. Has crime prevention actually reduced crime in your neighborhood or corporate facility?
2. Has crime prevention reduced the fear of crime or victimization?
3. Has crime prevention changed the image and acceptance of the police or security unit?
4. Has crime prevention changed your attitude as the role of the citizen or employee in terms of protecting yourselves (as opposed to the police or security unit being the exclusive protectors of persons and property)?
5. Were the services provided or points covered by prevention staff what was needed?
6. Have the recommendations or suggestions provided by prevention staff been implemented? If not, why so?

A number of questions that could be raised with persons not having direct involvement in a program (e.g., other than that which they might have picked up from the local newspaper, radio, and television presentations) and used as effectiveness indicators are as follows:

1. Are you aware of the city's crime-prevention program?
2. Do you think crime prevention can have any effect on the incidence or fear of victimization?
3. How would you explain what crime prevention is?

How to organize and maintain data

The methods for organizing this data should be based on the procedures used to gather the information. That is, because a prevention unit, in most cases, develops this information in-house, it should design data-gathering tools and develop methods that lend themselves to easy organization and maintenance.

One tool that can be used is the questionnaire. Care should be taken, however, to contract questionnaires so that most, if not all, answers are of a yes or no nature. This tool can be used, for example, following speaking engagements or as the basis of a telephone survey. If the questionnaire is constructed as suggested, the answers to all inquiries can be summarized and maintained on one original form.

A strategy to facilitate implementation of the evaluation

Geographic targeting

In terms of how to evaluate crime-prevention efforts, as noted earlier, program goals, objectives, and strategies provide the baseline for analysis. In addition, however, evaluation research methodologies can be employed to systematically judge program accomplishments and, thereby, provide valuable management information. Although a variety of such techniques are available, it is unlikely that a prevention unit has the time or budget to employ the more sophisticated designs. One approach that can realistically be employed is the *quasiexperimental* design.

This design requires that two sectors of a community be involved. Briefly, conditions in each of the sectors selected should be documented before crime-prevention efforts are undertaken. One of the areas should be exposed to the prevention program. After such exposure the conditions the program was intended to affect should be measured in both areas. If data indicate that conditions were altered as hoped for in the area exposed to the prevention activities and no significant alterations were experienced in the sector where nothing was done, it can be concluded that the crime-prevention efforts had a positive effect on the identified program.

To further illustrate this process an example of how a quasiexperimental design might be structured is presented. Obviously, it may be difficult to reach even the level of detail illustrated in the example; yet as the example shows, evaluation can be reduced to a straightforward and uncomplicated process. In addition, it can be used as an integral part of the ongoing implementation process to ensure that a unit has the best chance of getting its job done; that is, a small unit can more systematically perform its work in a limited area than in a jurisdiction as a whole. Importantly, these data elements serve as the basis for the design and implementation of this evaluation approach.

To illustrate how such a design might actually be used a hypothetical example focusing on burglary is structured. For the example, assume that the following steps in the planning/evaluation process have been taken:

1. Burglary was selected as a target crime after analysis of community or organization crime problems.
2. A crime-prevention database was developed and organized so burglary data could be isolated and analyzed in relation to various sectors of the community.
3. Specific goals, objectives, and strategies with regard to efficiency and effectiveness in the conduct of the burglary prevention program were detailed.
4. The security survey was one strategy chosen to deal with the problem.

To implement this approach a number of specific steps would have to be taken. Each step is summarized next:

1. *Site selection*. The first step to be taken in implementing this technique would be to select two noncontiguous areas (census tracts, beats, etc.) that have similar burglary rates and trends. In addition, the areas selected should have similar socioeconomic and demographic characteristics (i.e., population groupings, and income). Fig. 42.4 illustrates

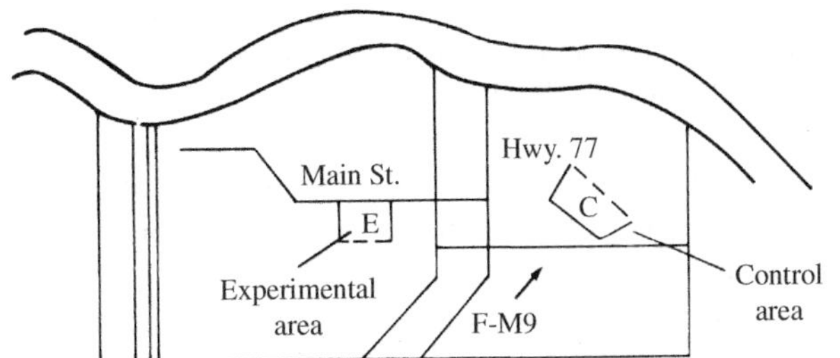

FIGURE 42.4 Geographic targeting of crime-prevention efforts.

how such areas might appear on a map of any city. When considering the use of this approach, the following points with regard to site selection should be kept in mind:

a. The implementation of any new program is bound to surface unforeseen problems.
b. If initiated in a high-crime area, the program might be discontinued prematurely because of its lack of immediate success in mitigating the problem.
c. If initiated in a low-incidence area, the kinks and bugs can be worked out at relative leisure while consideration is given to further the implementation of the program in a high-crime area.

2. *Program implementation.* Following the selection of the two areas, the crime-prevention unit should focus its efforts in only one area; for example, the security survey program should be conducted in one area and nothing should be done in the other section of the community (the control area).
3. *Program monitoring and evaluation.* As the program is implemented, crime statistics should be monitored. Further, after a predetermined time period, local attitudes and other indicators should be checked. If the indicators change in a positive sense in the experimental area and do not change markedly in the control area, it could be concluded that the survey program was successful in achieving the desired objective. Obviously, this also indicates that the unit has achieved what it set out to accomplish.

When to report evaluation results

How frequently a prevention unit should prepare formalized statements on its internal efficiency, and external effectiveness depends on a variety of factors, such as implementation pressures, reporting requirements, and the need for information to support the program with the press, management, and so forth. In any case, unit activities should be monitored and data maintained to document efficiency and effectiveness on an ongoing basis and summarized and reported at least quarterly, yearly, and when the project is terminated.

Care should be exercised in deciding what intervals to select for analysis in relation to the progress achieved. For example, during the first months of a program, materials, hardware, and so forth that will play an important role in implementation might not be available. Therefore it would be inappropriate to evaluate the effectiveness or results of the program until the unit is totally geared up for operation.

This may require that a critical look at the external impact of a program be set aside for as long as 6 months so that appropriate data can be gathered. Evaluation of the efficiency of the unit in terms of implementation of various methods should be instituted in the first month of the program and continue throughout the project period.

How to report monitoring and evaluation findings

As pointed out earlier, the organization and maintenance of the information and data used in the monitoring and evaluation of programs will be largely a matter of personal preference among prevention organizations.

To aid prevention personnel in this process, the form titled Detailed Information Concerning Program Implementation and Evaluation (Fig. 42.5) is very useful. A copy of the form should be maintained for each program strategy used in implementing goals and objectives. The form should be used as a daily log sheet to report activity, and the information can later be summarized at monthly and quarterly intervals.

Data to gather

The following data elements should be considered essential in the design of a program. The degree to which a particular agency can gather such data, of course, depends on the nature of available research. The essential elements include the following:

- *Population of the city and selected subdivisions.* The total population of the city and designated subareas, such as neighborhoods, census tracts, planning areas, or beat areas, should be noted. This information is useful in calculating crime rates per population area.
- *Median value of houses or household income.* Document the housing values or income levels for the total city and subareas. This information can be used as an estimate of property values and affluence to provide, for example, guidelines for magnitude and type of security improvements that are economically feasible.
- *Housing units by type for the city and designated subareas.* Determine the total number of housing units by type (such as single family or multifamily) for both the city and designated geographic subareas. These data serve as a base to compare crime statistics. They also are useful in the design of the prevention approach.

Detailed information concerning
Program implementation and evaluation

GOAL: as stated in program plan
OBJECTIVE: as stated in program plan
STRATEGY: as stated in program plan

1. Activity accomplishments
   a. Planned this quarter
   b. Undertaken this quarter

Activities accomplished (i.e., 100 security surveys)	Time spent in activity (i.e., 24 h)

   c. Problems encountered

2. Activity Accomplishments for Next Quarter

3. Effectiveness Accomplishments
   a. Effectiveness findings (decreases in crime rates; increased calls for service, etc.)
   b. Attitudinal findings (letters from citizens, responses to questionnaires, commendations from employees, etc.)

4. Revisions Planned–Explain

A separate form should be used for each strategy used to accomplish an objective.

FIGURE 42.5 Evaluation outline. A separate form should be used for each strategy taken to accomplish the objective.

- *Number of commercial establishments by type*. Document the number and type of commercial establishments in the city. It would be desirable to be able to block out the geographic location of principal commercial concentrations in the city by type. This can be used to focus program activities and determine opportunity levels for criminal activity.

  In addition to these data elements, other information may also be useful for designing and implementing a program.

Chapter 43

Proprietary information*

John J. Fay
Security Consultant

Proprietary information is sensitive information that is owned by a company and which gives the company certain competitive advantages. Proprietary information assets are critical to the success of many, perhaps most businesses.[1]

Introduction

Proprietary information is information owned by a company or entrusted to it that has not been disclosed publicly and has value. Information is considered proprietary when the following conditions take place:

- It is not readily accessible to others.
- It was created by the owner through the expenditure of considerable resources.
- The owner actively protects the information from disclosure.

Very critical forms of proprietary information are intellectual properties. Most countries recognize and grant varying degrees of protection to four intellectual property rights: patents, trademarks, copyrights, and trade secrets.

Patents

These are grants issued by a national government conferring the right to exclude others from making, using, or selling the invention within that country. Patents may be given for new products or processes. Violations of patent rights are known as infringement or piracy.

Trademarks

These are words, names, symbols, devices, or combinations thereof used by manufacturers or merchants to differentiate their goods and distinguish them from products that are manufactured or sold by others. Counterfeiting and infringement constitute violations of trademark rights.

Copyrights

These are protections given by a national government to creators of original literary, dramatic, musical, and certain other intellectual works. The owner of a copyright has the exclusive right to reproduce the copyrighted work, prepare derivative works based upon it. Distribute copies, and perform or display it publicly. Copyright violations are also known as infringement and piracy.

Trade secrets

These can be formulas, patterns, compilations, programs, devices, methods, techniques, and processes that derive economic value from not being generally known and not ascertainable except by illegal means. A trade secret

*Originally from Fay, J.J., 2007. Encyclopedia of Security Management. Boston, MA, Butterworth-Heinemann. Updated by the editor, Elsevier, 2019.
1. uslegal.com/p/proprietary-information

Handbook of Loss Prevention and Crime Prevention. DOI: https://doi.org/10.1016/B978-0-12-817273-5.00043-0

violation in the vocabulary of the law is a misappropriation resulting from improper acquisition of disclosure. The key elements in a trade secret are the owner's maintenance of confidentiality, limited distribution, and the absence of a patent.

The Paris Convention is the primary treaty for the protection of trademarks, patents, trade names, utility models, and industrial designs. Established in 1883, the convention is the oldest of the international bodies concerned with the protection of intellectual properties. It is based on reciprocity, that is, it grants the same protections to member states as those granted to its own nationals and provides equal access for foreigners to local courts to pursue infringement remedies.

Data protection

Data are a valuable corporate asset. Consider these examples:

- In the minerals extraction industry, finding ores depends on data. It is no exaggeration to say that before a single shovel is placed into the ground, hundreds of millions of dollars will have been spent collecting and interpreting seismic and other scientific data.
- Hotels routinely build patron-oriented information databases that enable them to provide personalized service.
- Retailers collect data to help their managers monitor the flow of products moving from manufacturing plants to warehouses, stores, and ultimately purchasers. The process makes sure that sellable items are on the shelves in the right stores, at the right time, and in the right quantities.
- Transportation firms routinely track movement of packages, even to the extent of allowing customers to access the information.
- Manufacturers have refined data-dependent "just-in-time" techniques to ensure that source materials reach the beginning of the production line not a day sooner or later than required and that the final products leave the plant already sold.

Industrial espionage

Industrial espionage by definition is the theft of information by legal or illegal means.

Bugging

Bugging by illegal means is the interception of communication without the consent of the parties involved.

Encryption

Encryption requires two phones/cell phones/fax machines to be encrypted in order to properly transmit and receive unintercepted calls.

Proprietary information

The term "proprietary information" can be used to describe a broad range of things that the owner considers confidential. It is any type of data that the owner wishes to restrict who know about it or its contents. Proprietary information is another way of saying something is a trade secret.[2]

Today's successful organizations are very competent at collecting and making good use of data. Only a few, however, are fully competent in protecting their data assets, which are growing in value and volume. In some circles, information moves from owner to owner, similar to the way money moves in financial markets. Three dynamics seem to be at play: knowledge has become an economic resource, information technology is expanding, and the number of people familiar with information technology is growing by leaps and bounds.

Knowledge is emerging as an economic resource. Production in the United States is moving away from a dependence on capital, natural resources, and blue-collar labor. One hundred years ago, the nation's wealth derived from oil, coal, minerals, ores, and farmlands. Today's wealth derives from the creation and use of knowledge, and the raw materials that create knowledge are in the form of data.

2. www.swensonlawfirm.com/what-constitutes-proprietary-information/

A second dynamic is information technology. New computer hardware and software come online every day in dazzling arrays. All functions and subfunctions of business are addressed in the information technology marketplace. The Internet, company intranets, and multicompany extranets open doors wide for the collection and dissemination of huge volumes of information. Critical data, such as client lists and strategic plans, are moved around the globe in the blink of an eye by e-mail, fax, and cellular phone.

A third dynamic is the increasing ability of the average employee to work competently and comfortably with data. Add to this a very large and rapidly growing new employee class called information workers. In some companies the entire workforce consists of people who work only with data.

Data protection is a challenge not easily met. For example, how does an organization balance the need to use data and the need to protect it from harmful disclosure? The clash between use and protection is problematic. An operations manager will consider data an essential resource to be fully exploited, therefore requiring it to be assessable at all times. He/she will say, "If data can't be used, our bottom line suffers." The manager is right; the value of the data is directly related to its use.

Chief security officer

The chief security officer (CSO) may agree with the operations manager but feel compelled to point out: "If our data is damaged, lost or compromised, the company may fail." The CSO's concern appears valid in light of at least one study. An insurance company found that 40% of companies that experienced major data loss as the result of disaster (e.g., fire, flood, hurricane, and terrorist action) never resumed business operations, and a third of the companies that initially recovered went out of business within 2 years.

The CSO can enhance data protection by following commonsense suggestions:

- Stay on top of the issue.
- Keep pace with data-related technology, not necessarily at the detail level, but certainly at a level that permits a clear understanding of the risks.
- Look for countermeasures that take advantage of new techniques and leading edge technology.
- Maintain a frank and ongoing dialog with data managers about risk avoidance, and do not be preachy or harp on a shortcoming unless you have a solution in mind.
- Spread the word among supervisory employees that data protection is their responsibility.

Chapter 44

Ten risk factors

Lawrence J. Fennelly and Marianna A. Perry
Security Consultant

Part 1: How secure is your security operation?

Introduction

A former surgical resident impersonated[1] a physician and gained access to restricted areas to observe surgical procedures and participate in patient rounds at Brigham and Women's Hospital in Boston, MA. Cheryl Wang, who was previously dismissed from a residency program in New York City, wandered into operating rooms in official Brigham scrubs and was thought to have obtained from a previous visit. Although Brigham staff is required to scan their identification badges to enter operation rooms, Wang slipped into the surgical suites by walking in behind other employees who were holding the door open for each other. Following the security breach, the hospital says it has strengthened its policy for allowing observers into its operating rooms. Physicians now are required to verify that a doctor-in-training is in good standing with his or her educational institution. The hospital also plans to educate staff about the dangers of "tailgating," or letting people follow staff into restricted areas without scanning an ID card. Electronic card access and security surveillance cameras are considered security best practices, but hospital security experts are considering other safeguards, including turnstiles, security officers, and biometric systems.

We have always felt that if someone looked professional, greeted others, and gave the impression that they "fit in," they could gain access practically anywhere. We frequently get to test our theory because some organizations want penetration testing conducted to determine whether or not their access control policies and procedures are effective. We were doing such an exercise at a country club in California at 3:00 p.m. on a Sunday afternoon. As we drove up to the guardhouse, the security officer on duty waved as he let us in. Another time while doing an assessment at a school, the facilities manager took us to the third floor of the administration building, pointed to different offices, and said, "This is the president's area, the VP's office is over there, the controller is there and my office is at the other end. This is a secure area, so you don't have to worry about this part of the building." When we came back later that night, we took the elevator to the second floor, walked down the hall to the freight elevator, and pushed the third floor button. We were not really surprised when the elevator door opened and we were in the "secure area." We went into the facility manager's unlocked office and left a note on his desk. *So, how secure is your security operation?*

Access control

Two security practitioner talking about access control as follows:

So Joe, "when I took over I had 1532 people who had access to our building and I go to the head of personnel and ask as of today how many people work in this complex"? He replied "about 992." Joe said he had the same thing only nationally it was worse than you could imagine. An active badge is as bad as poor key control, the employees leaves the company, delete his badge.

1. The intruder in the Brigham OR—how did she get there? Retrieved on February 8, 2017 from: <https://www.bostonglobe.com/metro/2017/02/04/dressed-scrubs-she-roamed-hospital-but-she-wasn-supposed-there/3OkuPYs4PklE3MGdeLirhM/story.html>.

Handbook of Loss Prevention and Crime Prevention. DOI: https://doi.org/10.1016/B978-0-12-817273-5.00044-2

Part 2: Identity theft

Introduction

Identity (ID) theft is a crime where a thief steals your personal information, such as your name, your social security number (SSN), or your credit card information to commit fraud. The ID thief can use your information for fraudulent purchases or to fraudulently apply for credit, file taxes, or get medical services. These crimes can damage your credit status and cost you time and money to restore your good name. You may not know that you are the victim of ID theft until you experience a financial consequence (mystery bills, credit collections, and denied loans) from actions that the thief has taken with your stolen ID.[2]

Seven steps you can take to protect yourself

1. *Be aware of camera phones*—If you are paying at a register or at a restaurant, watch for people fidgeting with their phones. They could be trying to take a picture of your card.[3]
2. *Keep an eye on your credit card*—Whenever you hand your card to a waitress, clerk, or cashier, pay attention to where it goes and for how long. Card skimming or copying your credit card information may be occurring.
3. *Shop with a slim wallet*—Remove everything except one credit card and your driver's license from your wallet. Carrying multiple credit cards increases your risk of ID theft.
4. *Be alert for pickpockets*—Tuck your purse under your arm, keep your wallet in your front pocket, and do not put your purse or wallet down where someone else may grab it.
5. *If you are shopping online*—If you pay by credit or charge card online, your transaction will be protected by the Fair Credit Billing Act.[4] Under this law, you can dispute charges under certain circumstances and temporarily withhold payment while the creditor investigates them. In the event that someone uses your credit card without your permission, your liability generally is limited to the first $50 in charges. Never shop online using a public Wi-Fi network, and shop on secure sites with a URL that begins with "https" instead "http."
6. *If you are making large purchases or electronics purchases*—Most credit cards offer their own warranty protection for your purchases just for using a credit card for the transaction. Some of those warranties go beyond what is offered by the manufacturer and offer you extra coverage, which is really useful for electronics, appliances, or other large purchases.
7. *If you are traveling*—If you are away from home, use your credit card for purchases because debit cards do not offer you the same protections. Also, don't carry more cards than necessary.

Eleven steps you can take to protect yourself from identity theft

1. Don't carry your social security card in your wallet or write your number on your checks. Only give out your SSN when absolutely necessary.
2. Don't respond to unsolicited requests for personal information (your name, birthdate, SSN, or bank account number) by phone, mail, or online.
3. Watch out for "shoulder surfers." Shield the keypad when typing your passwords on computers and at ATMs.
4. Collect mail promptly. Ask the post office to put your mail on hold when you are away from home.
5. Pay attention to your billing cycles. If bills or financial statements are late, contact the sender.
6. Review your receipts. Ask for carbon copies and incorrect charge slips as well. Promptly compare receipts with account statements. Watch for unauthorized transactions.
7. Shred receipts, credit offers, account statements, and expired cards, to prevent "dumpster divers" from getting your personal information.
8. Store personal information in a safe place at home and at work.
9. Install firewalls and virus-detection software on your home computer.
10. Create complex passwords that ID thieves cannot guess easily. Change your passwords if a company that you do business with has a breach of its databases.
11. Order your credit report once a year and review to be certain that it does not include accounts that you have not opened. Check it more frequently if you suspect someone has gained access to your account information.

2. https://www.usa.gov/identity-theft.

3. www.creditcards.com.

4. https://www.ftc.gov/enforcement/rules/rulemaking-regulatory-reform-proceedings/fair-credit-billing-act.

How to report identity theft

If you are a victim of ID theft, report it immediately. The Federal Trade Commission (FTC)[5] and your local police department are critical in filing the complaint. Once you file the ID theft with the FTC, you will have an ID theft affidavit. Print and take this with you to file a report with the local police department. These two documents together are your ID theft report. Your ID theft report will be very important as you resolve the problem with creditors, banks, and any other companies where fraudulent accounts were set up in your name.

In addition to government agencies, you should also report the theft to other organizations, such as

Credit reporting agencies—Contact the three major credit reporting agencies to place fraud alerts or freezes on your accounts so that no one can apply for credit with your name or SSN. Also get copies of your credit reports, to be sure that no one has already tried to get unauthorized credit accounts with your personal information.

- Equifax: 1-888-766-0008
- Experian: 1-888-397-3742
- TransUnion: 1-800-680-7289

Financial institutions—Contact the fraud department at your bank, credit card issuers and any other places where you have accounts. You may need your ID theft reports from the police and FTC in order to report the fraud.

Retailers and other companies—You will also need to report the fraud to companies where the ID thief created accounts, opened credit accounts, or even applied for jobs in order to clear your name.

State consumer protection offices or attorney general—Your state may offer resources to help you contact creditors, dispute errors and other helpful resources.

The FTC offers a publication, *Taking Charge—What to Do If Your Identity Is Stolen* that shares detailed tips, checklists, along with sample letters.[6]

Part 3: Need a new year's resolution? How about changing your passwords?

Everyone online is potentially at risk for cybercrime. In fact, you are probably more likely to have your e-mail account hacked than your home broken into

Online crime is a serious threat in our Internet-connected culture.[7] There are approximately *1.5 million cyberattacks annually*, and online crime is a real threat to anyone who uses the Internet. This means there are *more than 4000 cyberattacks every day, 170 attacks every hour, or nearly three attacks every minute!*[8]

With all of these online attacks, why do people continue to use the 25 worst passwords listed below?[9]

1. 123456
2. Password
3. 12345678
4. Qwerty
5. 12345
6. 123456789
7. Football
8. 1234
9. 1234567
10. Baseball
11. Welcome

5. https://www.ftc.gov.
6. https://www.consumer.ftc.gov/articles/pdf-0009-taking-charge.pdf.
7. These cybercrime statistics will make you think twice about your password: where is the CSI cyber team when you need them? Retrieved December 28, 2016 from: <http://www.cbs.com/shows/csi-cyber/news/1003888/these-cybercrime-statistics-will-make-you-think-twice-about-your-password-where-s-the-csi-cyber-team-when-you-need-them-/>.
8. These cybercrime statistics will make you think twice about your password: where is the CSI cyber team when you need them? Retrieved December 28, 2016 from: <http://www.cbs.com/shows/csi-cyber/news/1003888/these-cybercrime-statistics-will-make-you-think-twice-about-your-password-where-s-the-csi-cyber-team-when-you-need-them-/> (retrieved 28.12.16.).
9. These are the Worst Passwords That You Still Keep Using. Retrieved December 28, 2016 from: <http://fortune.com/2016/01/20/passwords-worst-123456/>.

12. 1234567890
13. abc123
14. 111111
15. 1qaz2wsx
16. Dragon
17. Master
18. Monkey
19. Letmein
20. Login
21. Princess
22. Qwertyuiop
23. Solo
24. passw0rd
25. starwars

If you are using one of the passwords on this list, take the time to change it *right now*!

According to traditional advice, a strong password[10]:

- *Has 12 characters, minimum*: You need to choose a password that is long enough. There is no minimum password length everyone agrees on, but you should generally go for passwords that are a minimum of 12–14 characters in length. A longer password would be even better.
- *Includes numbers, symbols, capital letters, and lowercase letters*: Use a mix of different types of characters to make the password harder to crack.
- *Is not a dictionary word or combination of dictionary words*: Stay away from obvious dictionary words and combinations of dictionary words. Any word on its own is bad. Any combination of a few words, especially if they are obvious, is also bad. For example, "house" is a terrible password. "Red house" is also very bad.
- *Does not rely on obvious substitutions*: Do not use common substitutions, either—for example, "H0use" is not strong just because you have replaced an o with a 0. That is just obvious.

In addition to the traditional advice listed previously, you can also create a passphrase, which is a password that involves multiple random words. The randomness of the word choice and length of the passphrase makes it strong. For example, "cat in the hat" would not be a good combination because it is such a common phrase and the words make sense together. A passphrase such as "correct horse battery staple" or "seashell glaring molasses invisible" is random. The words do not make sense together and are not in grammatically correct order.[11]

It is difficult to remember all of your passwords without duplicating any. Consider using a password manager, and the only password that you will have to remember is your strong master password.

Should you be worried about the cyberattacks on businesses and government agencies? The answer is, "YES!" These big organizations have information on all of us!

IBM estimates that *businesses are attacked an average of 16,856 times a year*. That is *46 attacks every business has to deal with every day—or nearly 2 attacks an hour*. The majority of these attacks do not actually get past an organization's defenses, but *an average of 1.7 per week are successful*.[12]

Why is cybercrime so prevalent—and so hard to fight? Laws on cybercrimes vary throughout the world, and the overwhelming majority of cybercrimes cross national borders. This can make solving cybercrimes a problem that has to be investigated through international collaboration and can make it difficult for law enforcement to locate and prosecute cybercriminals.[13]

---

10. How to Create a Strong Password (and Remember It). Retrieved December 28, 2016 from: <http://www.howtogeek.com/195430/how-to-create-a-strong-password-and-remember-it/>.

11. How to Create a Strong Password (and Remember It). Retrieved December 28, 2016 from: <http://www.howtogeek.com/195430/how-to-create-a-strong-password-and-remember-it/>.

12. These Cybercrime Statistics Will Make You Think Twice About Your Password: Where's the CSI Cyber Team When You Need Them? Retrieved December 28, 2016 from: <http://www.cbs.com/shows/csi-cyber/news/1003888/these-cybercrime-statistics-will-make-you-think-twice-about-your-password-where-s-the-csi-cyber-team-when-you-need-them-/>.

13. These Cybercrime Statistics Will Make You Think Twice About Your Password: Where's the CSI Cyber Team When You Need Them? Retrieved December 28, 2016 from: <http://www.cbs.com/shows/csi-cyber/news/1003888/these-cybercrime-statistics-will-make-you-think-twice-about-your-password-where-s-the-csi-cyber-team-when-you-need-them-/>.

Part 4: Displacement of crime or diffusion of crime

The research evidence regarding displacement as a result of focused policing interventions in contrast suggests overall that threats of displacement are much overstated. Indeed, studies to-date have been more likely to identify a "diffusion of crime control benefits" around targeted areas than evidence of displacement. That is, in a number of studies an unanticipated crime decline has been found in untargeted areas surrounding intervention sites.[14]

Over the years, we have read a lot of material from many criminologists, but we find we disagree with many of them when it comes to Displacement of Crime. Ask a practitioner of someone in law enforcement if Crime Displacement works and they will tell you, "Yes It Does." Plus it does not just move around the corner; in many cases, it totally disappears and goes away. What about the victims, and what about the increase of the fear of crime. If an apprehension cannot be made then by all means, displacement and diffusion of the hot spots is in order.

Be proactive not reactive!

Part 5: Solutions to the problems of bullying, cyberbullying, teasing, hazing, and harassing behavior

Introduction

Bullying is often a difficult and upsetting topic to talk about.[15] Our advice to parents of bullying victims is to document everything. When talking with your child, be a good listener and be alert for changes in your child's behavior or personality. If you find that your child is the victim of a bully at school, first schedule a meeting with the principal and your child's teacher. If you do not get results, send letters to the state department of education, the school superintendent, the principal, the teachers, and to your attorney, so everyone is aware of the bullying behavior that your child is experiencing and that you expect something to be done about it.

Check at your child's school to ensure that teachers are good role models, and that they are trained to recognize and deal with this problem. Consider enrolling your child in martial arts, not just for confidence and building self-esteem but also for self-defense. Talk to your child about the problem of bullying. Be aware that bullying may escalate into physical violence against your child—if it has not already. Call other parents at your child's school and organize them, so the group can approach the school officials in a united front. Obtain legal advice and file a civil suit against the school, the bully, the bully's parents, and anyone who knew the bullying was taking place and failed to take action.

Consider contacting the local media for help, but first make sure that it will not make the situation worse for your child. Ask your attorney to attend Parent Teachers Association (PTA) meetings to ensure better results from the school. Above all, know your rights! Don't you, as a parent, become the bullying victim of the school or the bully's parents. *Bullying behavior must not be tolerated, and the action taken must be swift and consistent in every case.*

When discussing the problem of bullying, some people say, "Just implement a zero-tolerance policy," but it is not that simple. Many schools are now implementing a "Student Bill of Rights," moving away from zero-tolerance and moving toward evaluating each bullying infraction based on the circumstances and the merit of the evidence presented. BUT, bullying is also in the workplace and not just in schools.

It is all about creating a culture of inclusion, respect and safety for all children, employees, and this requires the support of school staff, teachers, students, parents and community, and management members by educating them about the problem.

---

14. https://www.scribd.com/document/111422217/Weisburd-Et-Al-2010-The-Police-Foundation-Displacement-and-Diffusion-Study September 2010. The Police Foundation Displacement and Diffusion Study. By David Weisburd, Laura A. Wyckoff, Justin Ready, John E. Eck, Josh Hinkle, and Frank Gajewsk.
15. ASIS School Safety & Security Council, Copyright 2014, Lawrence J. Fennelly & Marianna Perry, CPP.

Part 6: Reinventing security performance

Introduction

Some time ago, we wrote that security assessments *should* be conducted at least annually, whenever changes are made to buildings or property and also at times of crisis. We have seen terrorist attacks in Paris; London; Belgium; San Bernardo, CA; Orlando, FL; and Brussels—just to name a few. Because of these attacks, we have also seen threat levels as well as security awareness increase in these areas.

So, what have you done recently to increase security awareness and your level of security?

An assessment? More training? Did you request that additional doors be secured or additional cameras be installed? During these times of crisis, it is our recommendation that you also increase your level of protection. As *national* threat levels go up, so should your *local* threat awareness.

Many times, it is only during a time of crisis that security components get updated, and additional security measures often get approved. Conducting annual assessments or monthly security reviews and improving security at your site will fuel overall security performance.

Consider thinking outside the box when it comes to improving the many aspects of security. Think about new ways to demonstrate the value and return on investment (ROI) for security budget increases. *Consider* logic models to evaluate your existing security program, know what works (and sometimes more importantly, what does not work) and be sure to implement industry best practices. *Consider* upgrading the components in your video surveillance system using thermal imaging or facial recognition cameras, switching to energy-efficient LED lighting, or installing solar panels to provide energy for exterior lighting fixtures and cameras.

At times, ALL security programs need a shot in the arm or a wake-up call!

For example, improve visible security coverage by varying the route and patrol schedules of your security officers, set up a schedule to test alarm sensors to ensure they are working properly, schedule random audits of your security cameras to make certain they are recording, review your landscape maintenance program, and develop a schedule to routinely test *all* components in your security program for operation-ability. All of your security components must be fully operational to provide you with the best protection possible.

Be proactive and not reactive!

Part 7: Controlling physical deterioration and disorder

Introduction

Physical deterioration, wear and tear, and large-scale accumulations of graffiti and trash routinely occur in many older, urban neighborhoods. If people or agencies do not do anything for a significant period of time about such deterioration or accumulations, residents and businesses in the neighborhood feel increasingly vulnerable.

Feeling more concerned for their personal safety, residents and businesses will begin to participate less in the maintenance and order of public places. They are less likely to stop teens or adults who are "messing around," "being rowdy," or "hassling people." Sensing fewer "eyes on the street", delinquent preteens and teens in the neighborhood become emboldened and harass or vandalize more frequently. Increasingly convinced they can get away with it, delinquents commit more minor crimes, and youths become increasingly disorderly.

Residents, sensing that some local youths are becoming increasingly troublesome, withdraw further from the public spaces in the neighborhood and become more concerned about protecting their own person and property.[16]

At this point, potential offenders from outside the neighborhood sense the area is vulnerable. They are drawn to the neighborhood because crimes committed there are less likely to be detected and responded to. The neighborhood crime rate increases dramatically.

Six points to the broken window theory[17] as follows:

1. Increase in unrepaired physical deterioration.
2. Increased concern for personal safety among residents and property owner.
3. Decreased participation in maintaining order on the street.

---

16. CPTED Security. Retrieved on May 14, 2017 from: <http://cptedsecurity.com/cpteddesignguidelines.htm>.
17. Physical Environment and Crime. NIJ, May, 1996.

4. Increased delinquency, rowdiness, vandalism, and disorderly behavior among locals.
5. Further increase in deterioration; further withdrawal from the streets by residents and other locals.
6. Potential offenders from outside the neighborhood, attracted by vulnerability, move into area.

Crime Prevention Through Environmental Design (CPTED) and the "broken window theory" suggest that one "broken window" or nuisance, if allowed to exist, will lead to others and ultimately to the decline of an entire neighborhood. Neglected and poorly maintained properties are breeding grounds for criminal activity. Formal CPTED-based maintenance plans will help preserve property values and make the neighborhood a safer place.

Reducing opportunities for crimes perpetrated by employees can indeed bring substantial net reductions in crime and eventually results in healthy profit margins. Situational crime prevention introduces discrete managerial and environmental changes in order to reduce the opportunity for crime to occur in business organization. It is a proactive measure that seeks to forestall the occurrence of crime rather than to wait for detection and sanctioning of offenders. Therefore it evolves around the crime settings rather than upon those committing criminal acts.

Part 8: The importance of security policies and procedures

Introduction

Security policies and procedures should protect the people, property, and information of an organization.[18] Security procedures should be tied to specific security policies of the organization. It is crucial that security policies and procedures be effectively communicated to all staff members who will then be expected to perform accordingly.

Policies

Security policies establish strategic security objectives and priorities for the organization, identify the representatives within the organization that are primarily responsible for physical security, and determine responsibilities and expectations for managers, employees, and others in the organization. Security policies are general statements of the way an organization performs business functions. Security policies are generally reviewed, approved, and issued at the executive level of an organization and emphasize the commitment of management to ensuring workplace security and show due diligence to address security vulnerabilities to help keep the workplace safe. Management commitment increases the probability of employee compliance with the policy. Once established, security policies tend to remain in place for an extended period of time. They should be aligned with the overall business objectives of the organization. An organization may increase liability if it ignores the policy, applies it inconsistently, or becomes complacent in its enforcement. A concerted effort to address security issues on a policy level shows due diligence and that management was aware of such issues and attempted to address them.

Security policies should address the following and include general issues, people, property, and information:

General assets

- Organization's general objectives in security matters
- Accountability of top management in security matters
- General responsibilities of line management
- General responsibilities of all staff
- Specific responsibilities relating to the development of subsidiary policies
- Reporting, auditing and review arrangements

People

- Workplace violence and active shooter/active assailant
- Emergency evacuation and shelter/defend-in-place
- Use (tailgating, piggybacking, sharing of credentials, access hours, levels of access, credential tampering, replacement, number of attempts allowed) and display of access control badges/access control cards
- Challenging of individuals not displaying an access control badge/access control card
- Workplace access control management

18. Fennelly, L.J. Handbook of Loss Prevention and Crime Prevention, fifth ed. Boston, MA, Elsevier Publishers, 2012.

- Prohibited items and substances
- Searches of purses, backpacks, and briefcases
- Security awareness education
- Escorting staff and visitors

Property

- Safeguarding employer property
- Acceptable personal use of employer assets
- Limitations on who can direct security staff
- Investigations
- Property control, marking, and disposal
- Key control and accountability
- Incoming goods and materials
- Vehicle access control
- Occupational safety and health
- Environment (light pollution, etc.)

Information and reputation

- Disclosure and protection of proprietary information
- Information handling, including marking, storage, transmission, disposal, and destruction
- Declassification schedule, process, or expiration of protection

Procedures

Security procedures are implementation instructions for personnel to comply with security policies. Procedures change more often than policies to meet the changing needs of the organization, and a policy may remain in place for a long period of time, but the procedures implemented to carry out the policy may change without management involvement. Security procedures are detailed implementation instructions for staff to carry out security policies. Procedures are often presented as forms or as lists of steps to be taken. Organizations should develop procedures that address people, property, and information. Each procedure should ultimately connect to a policy.

Security procedures should address the following and include people, property, and information:

People

- Responding to a threat of workplace violence
- Activating the crisis management team after an executive kidnaping
- Facility or operation-specific checklist for evacuating an area in the event of an emergency
- Employee access control badging/access control cards, including varying levels of access permission and lost access control badges/access control cards
- Identifying and managing suspicious packages
- Protection of employees working alone
- Visitor management
- Accommodation of disabled or physically impaired individuals

Property

- Marking of facility property
- Securing of valuable property
- Removal of property from the facility
- Key issuance and management
- Security officer duties (post orders)
- Security incident reporting

Information

- Marking, storage, transmission, disposal and destruction of confidential documents.
- Management of confidential meetings
- Technical surveillance countermeasures (*bug sweeps*)

Many times, organizations mistakenly think that technology is the answer to all of their security needs. In order to have an effective security program, it is important to have the right mix of enforced security policies and procedures, security technology, and people with security awareness.

Part 9: AMBER Alerts

Introduction

The AMBER Alert[19] Program[20] is a voluntary partnership between law-enforcement agencies, broadcasters, transportation agencies, and the wireless industry to activate an urgent bulletin in the most serious child-abduction cases. The goal of an AMBER Alert is to utilize the resources of the entire community to assist in the search for and the safe recovery of the child. The US Department of Justice coordinates the AMBER Alert program.

AMBER Alerts are broadcast through radio, television, road signs, and all available technology referred to as the AMBER Alert Secondary Distribution program. These broadcasts let law enforcement use the eyes and ears of the public to help quickly locate an abducted child.

The AMBER Alert Program was named in honor of 9-year-old Amber Hagerman who was abducted while riding her bicycle in Arlington, Texas, and was later found murdered. The program is active in all 50 states, the District of Columbia, Puerto Rico, and the US Virgin Islands. To see a map of all AMBER Alert plans, visit the following:

When signing up for AMBER Alerts, you will receive geographically targeted information to help identify an abducted child, a suspected abductor or a vehicle suspected to be involved in an abduction. You can sign up at www.missingkids.com/AmberSignUp.

As of January 1, 2013, AMBER Alerts will now be automatically sent through the Wireless Emergency Alerts (WEA) program to millions of cell phone users. If you have a WEA-enabled phone, you are automatically enrolled for the three alerts: President, imminent threat, and AMBER Alerts. The addition of AMBER Alerts to this notification system is a result.

Part 10: Design against crime

In the book titled Design Against Crime, by Barry Poyner, he describes an eight-step program set out by the British Home Office, Research Unit, which was

1. target hardening,
2. target removal,
3. removing the means to crime,
4. reducing the payoff,
5. formal surveillance,
6. natural surveillance,
7. surveillance by employees, and
8. environmental management.

Emerging Trends in 2019

Security operation, must improve and advance in the 21st century, we are seeing the use of robots by companies now. The advancement of this technology going forward will make the robot more useful. I love biometrics, once I had a very security area that needed high security, that is, only 12 people were allowed into this space, so I had installed an Iris scanner. Twelve people only were scanned and allowed to enter the space.

19. http://www.missingkids.org/AMBER.

20. http://www.missingkids.com/en_US/documents/AmberMap.pdf.

The problems of ID theft are not going away, and we all have to be very careful of the many scams that are out there. The rule of thumb is it sounds good, really good it is probably a scam. I had a friend, his daughter saw online that she could bid $15.00 for an Apple iPad, and she did and she won. Filled out the paperwork and gave her credit card information, and the three numbers on the back of the card. You can guess the rest.

Passwords, the biggest pain we all have, passwords for America on Line (AOL), Yahoo, banks, accounts, government websites, etc. How can we remember all the required passwords we have. Use the same number, NO, not good.

Read the paper again, and try to follow the instruction on passwords.

Displacement of Crime works, I have been successful several times and not only stop crime but prevented from occurring again. Criminologist will say show me the data. What we did was not for an experiment it was real.

Bullying, not going away even with zero-tolerance policies. Such cruelty, which has forced children to kill themselves. I have written article on this, and tougher rules need to implemented.

Controlling physical deterioration and disorder, an argument against improvements is the cost is too high, well budget for improvements next year if you have too. Let me address just common trash, debis, coffee cups, newspapers, etc. Someone needs to pick this stuff up daily followed by a campaign to keep the complex clean. Maybe more trash buckets are needed. Read closely to next section of the paper on broken windows theory.

What is a master plan?

A master plan is a document that delineates the philosophies, strategies, goals, programs, and processes. It is used to guide the organizations development and direction in these areas in a manner consistent with the town's overall business plan for this site. It also provides a detailed outline of the risks and the mitigation plans for them in a way that creates a 5-year business plan.

There is a formula used for such a program: security plan, physical security, formulation of partnerships, an ongoing process to foster change, participation, accountability and transparency, promoted through awareness and training, adhere to best practices, and standards and regulations.

By developing a good (positive) and sustainable culture becomes an ongoing process that will deliver a ROI for the entire community. The way things are done needs to be changed because they are not and have not been working.

Enterprise Security Risk Management

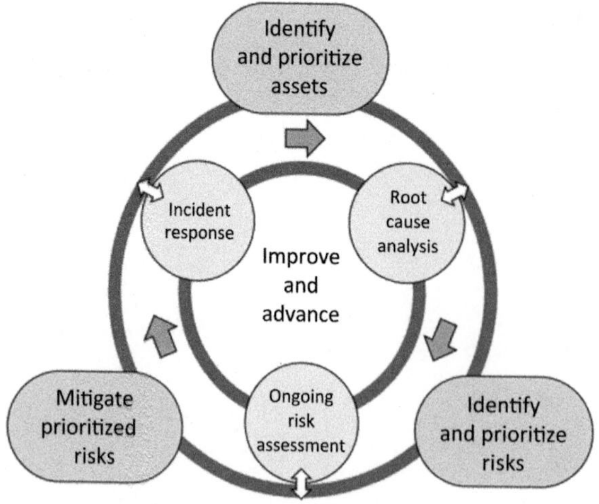

ESRM defined by our security partner as Enterprise Security Risk Management (ESRM) is a strategic security program management approach that ties an organizations security practices to its mission and goals using globally established and accepted risk management principles.

ESRM recognizes that security responsibilities are shared by both security and business leadership, but that all final security decision-making is the responsibility of the business leaders. The role of the security leader in ESRM is to manage security vulnerabilities to enterprise assets in a risk decision-making partnership with the organization leaders in charge of those assets.[21]

Keywords

Alarms, association, blog, cameras, case study, CCTV, commercial, conference, data breach, distributor, distributors, domes, door entry, education, event, event security, exhibition, government, Greenwich university, health, health and safety, interview, intruder, its security, lens, locks, news, police, press release, security, security consultant, security news, security system, transport, video door entry.

Finally we wish to add that the concept of discussing Emerging Trends is important to you to be aware of the various aspects of our future.

21. ASIS website, April 29, 2019.

Index

Note: Page numbers followed by "*f*" and "*t*" refer to figures and tables, respectively.

G

H

I

O

P

Q

R